Pretty Guardian Sailor Moon 4

Naoko Takeuchi

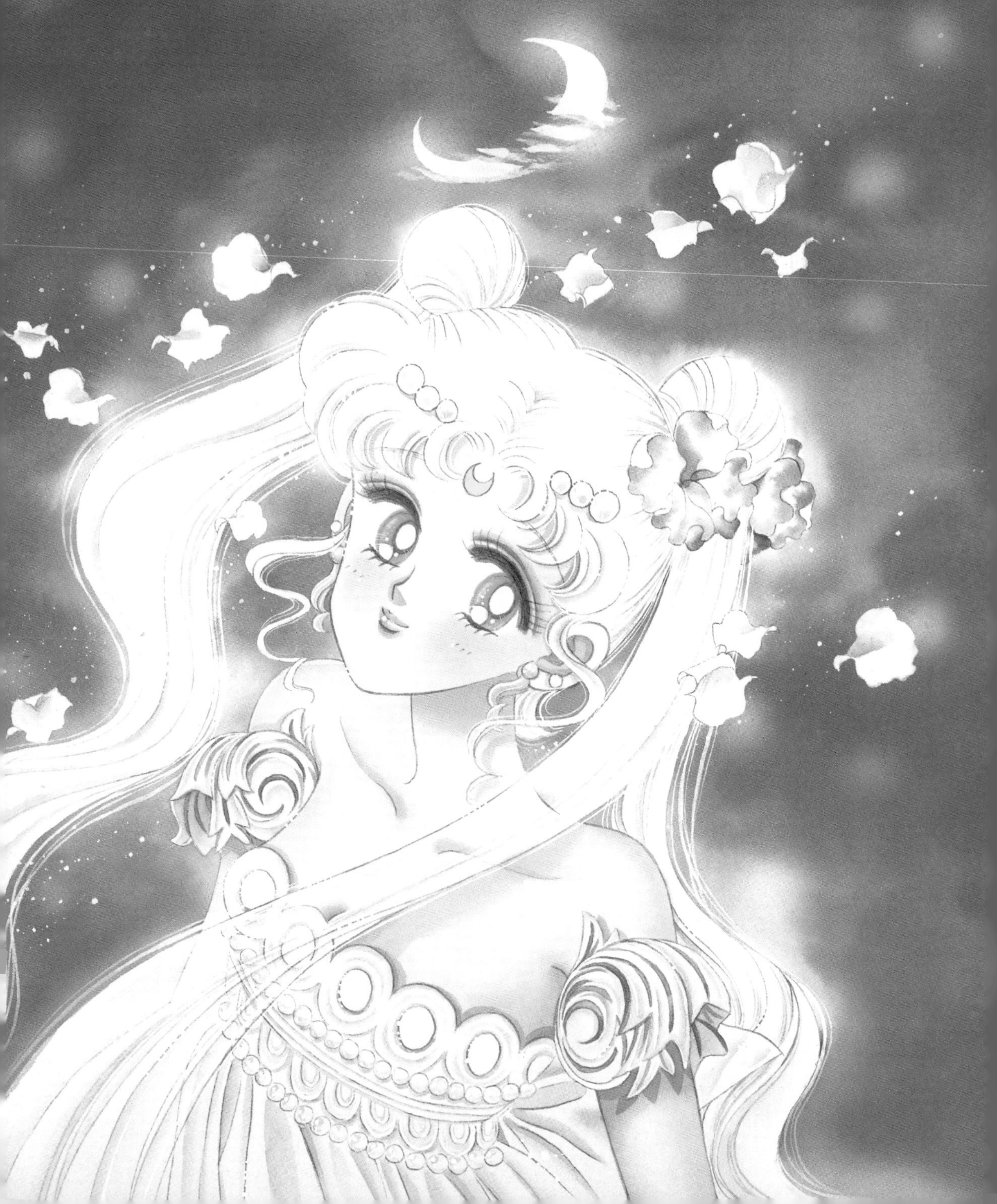

CONTENTS

Act.22 Hidden Agenda: Nemesis … 3

Act.23 Puppet Master: Wiseman … 51

Act.24 Attack: Black Lady … 97

Act.25 Confrontation: Death Phantom … 141

Act.26 Rebirth: Never-Ending … 191

Chibi Usa's Picture Diary, Chapter 1:
Beware of the Transfer Student! … 251

Casablanca Memory … 277

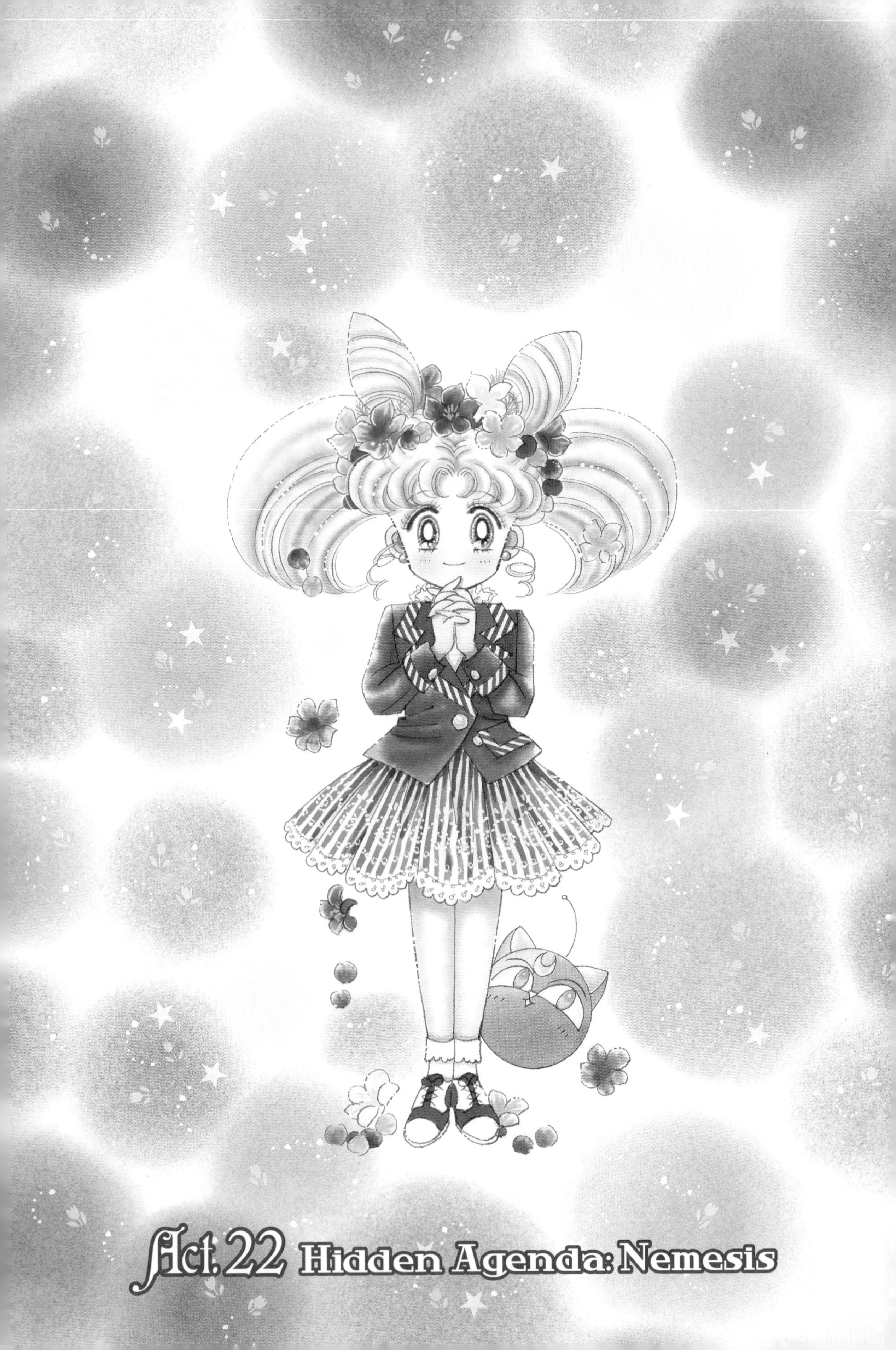

Act. 22 Hidden Agenda: Nemesis

Pretty Guardian

Sailor Moon

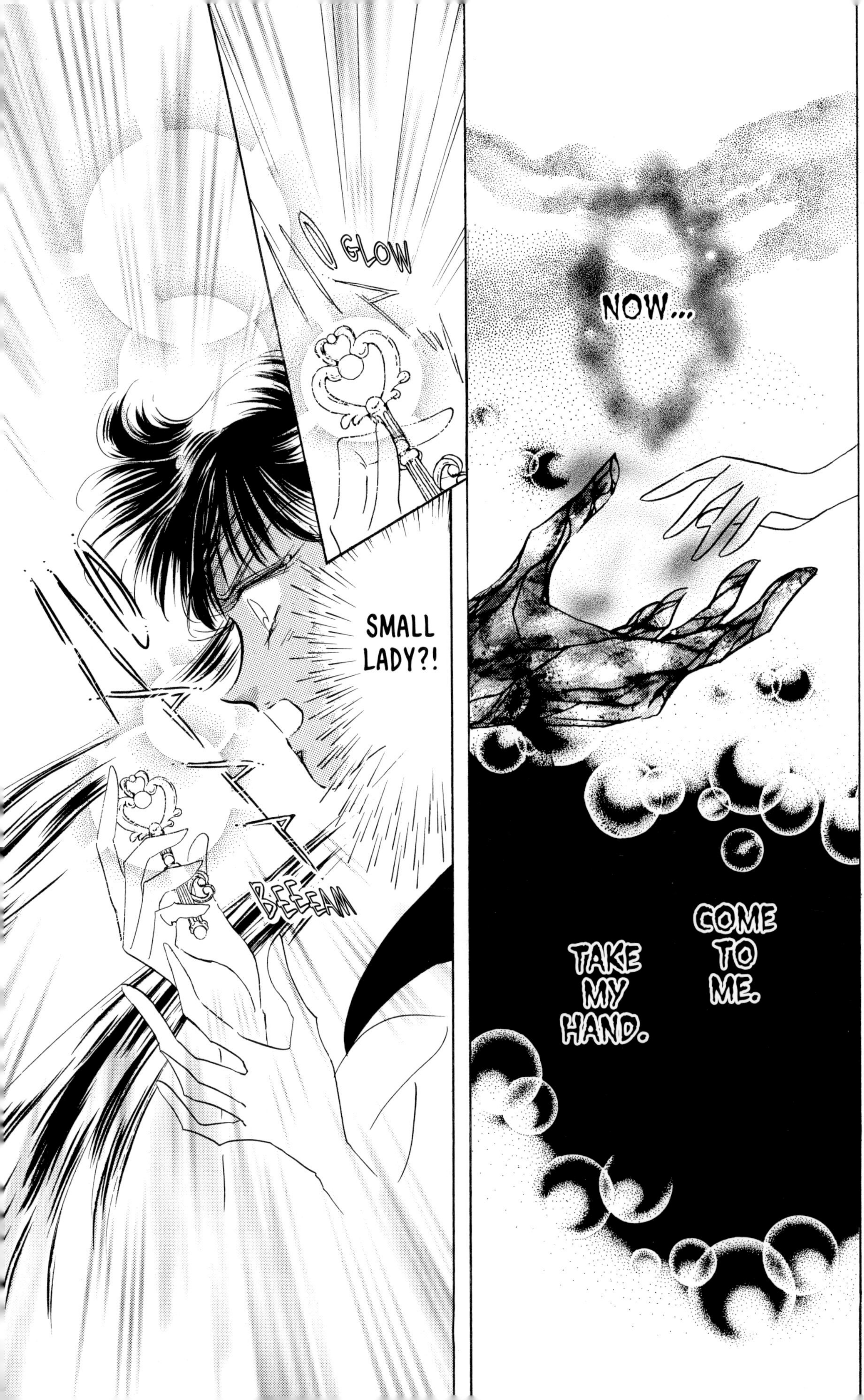
NOW...
COME TO ME.
TAKE MY HAND.
GLOW
SMALL LADY?!
BEEEAM

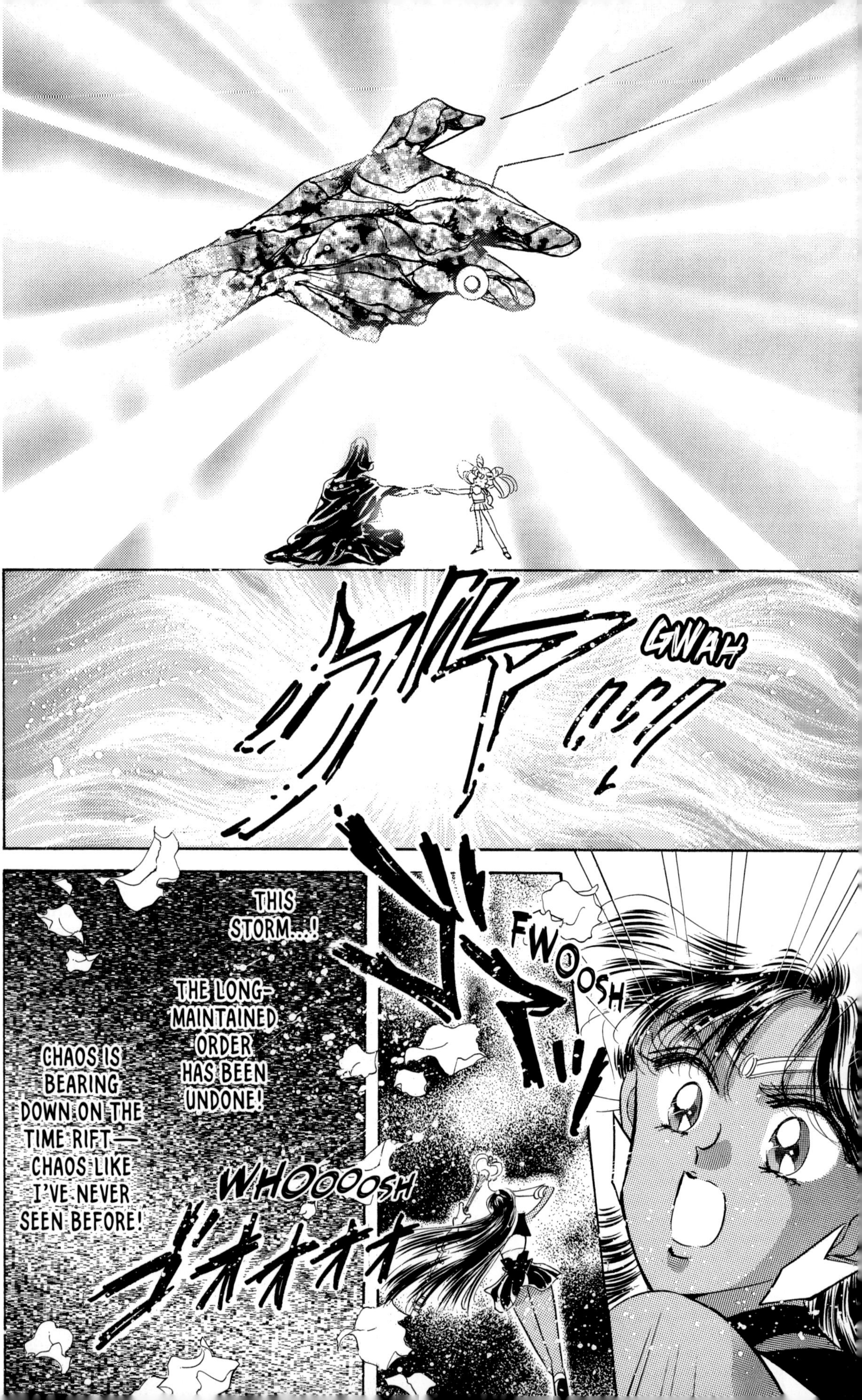
GWAH
FWOOSH
THIS STORM...!
THE LONG-MAINTAINED ORDER HAS BEEN UNDONE!
WHOOOOOSH
CHAOS IS BEARING DOWN ON THE TIME RIFT—CHAOS LIKE I'VE NEVER SEEN BEFORE!

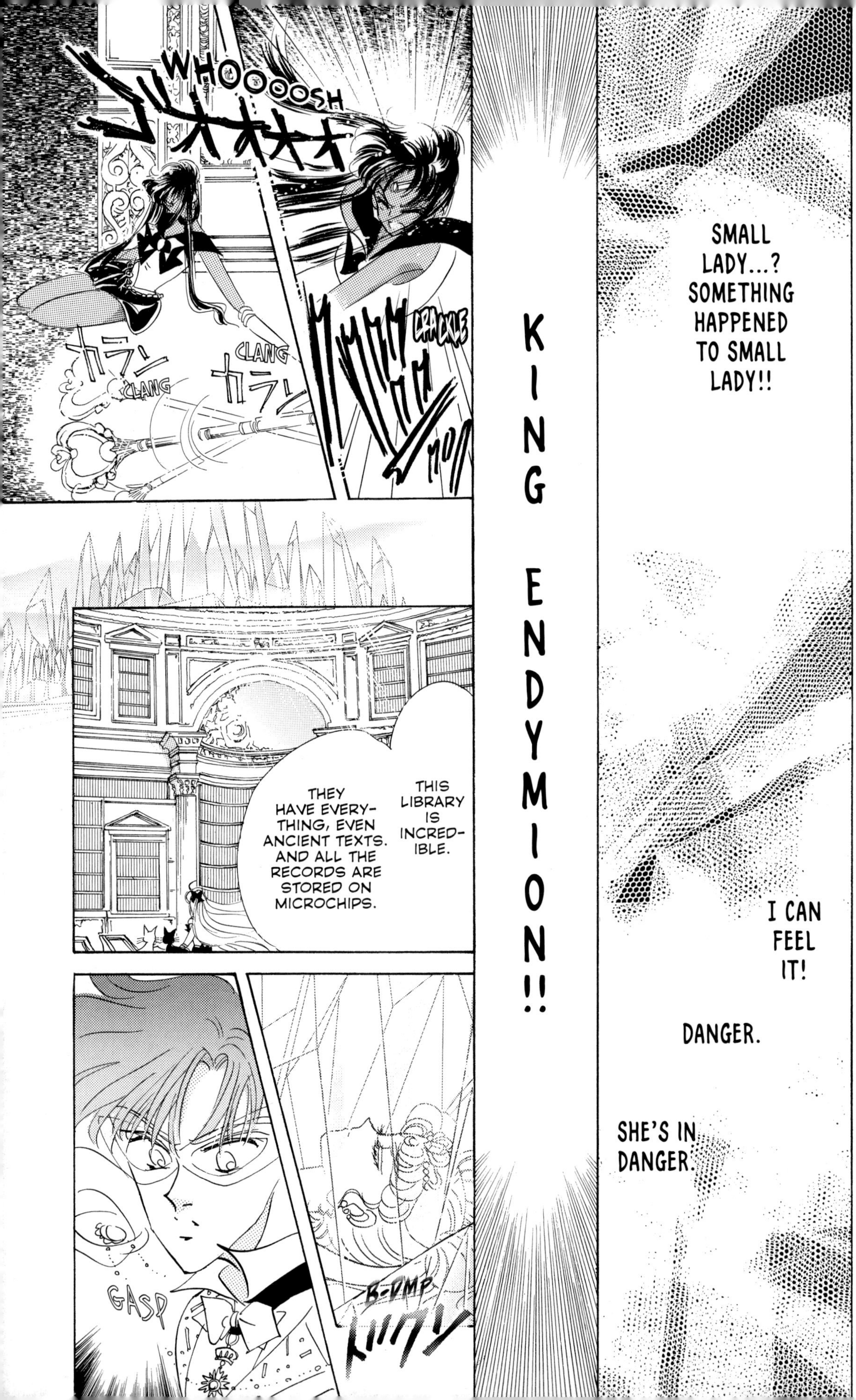
SMALL LADY...? SOMETHING HAPPENED TO SMALL LADY!!
I CAN FEEL IT!
DANGER.
SHE'S IN DANGER.
KING ENDYMION!!
WHOOOOSH
CRACKLE
CLANG
CLANG
THIS LIBRARY IS INCREDIBLE.
THEY HAVE EVERYTHING, EVEN ANCIENT TEXTS. AND ALL THE RECORDS ARE STORED ON MICROCHIPS.
B-DMP
GASP

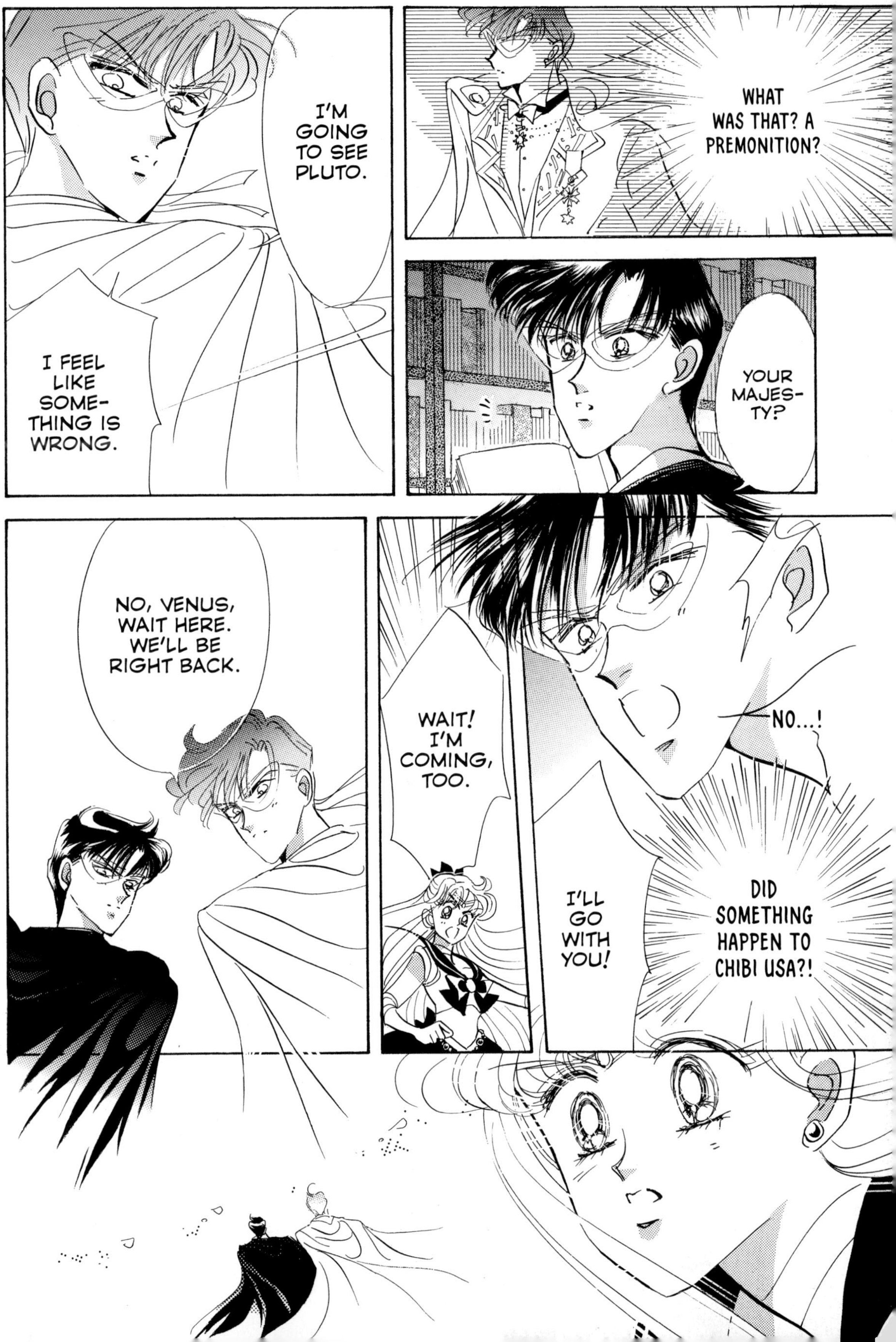
WHAT WAS THAT? A PREMONITION?
YOUR MAJESTY?
I'M GOING TO SEE PLUTO.
I FEEL LIKE SOMETHING IS WRONG.
NO...!
DID SOMETHING HAPPEN TO CHIBI USA?!
I'LL GO WITH YOU!
WAIT! I'M COMING, TOO.
NO, VENUS, WAIT HERE. WE'LL BE RIGHT BACK.

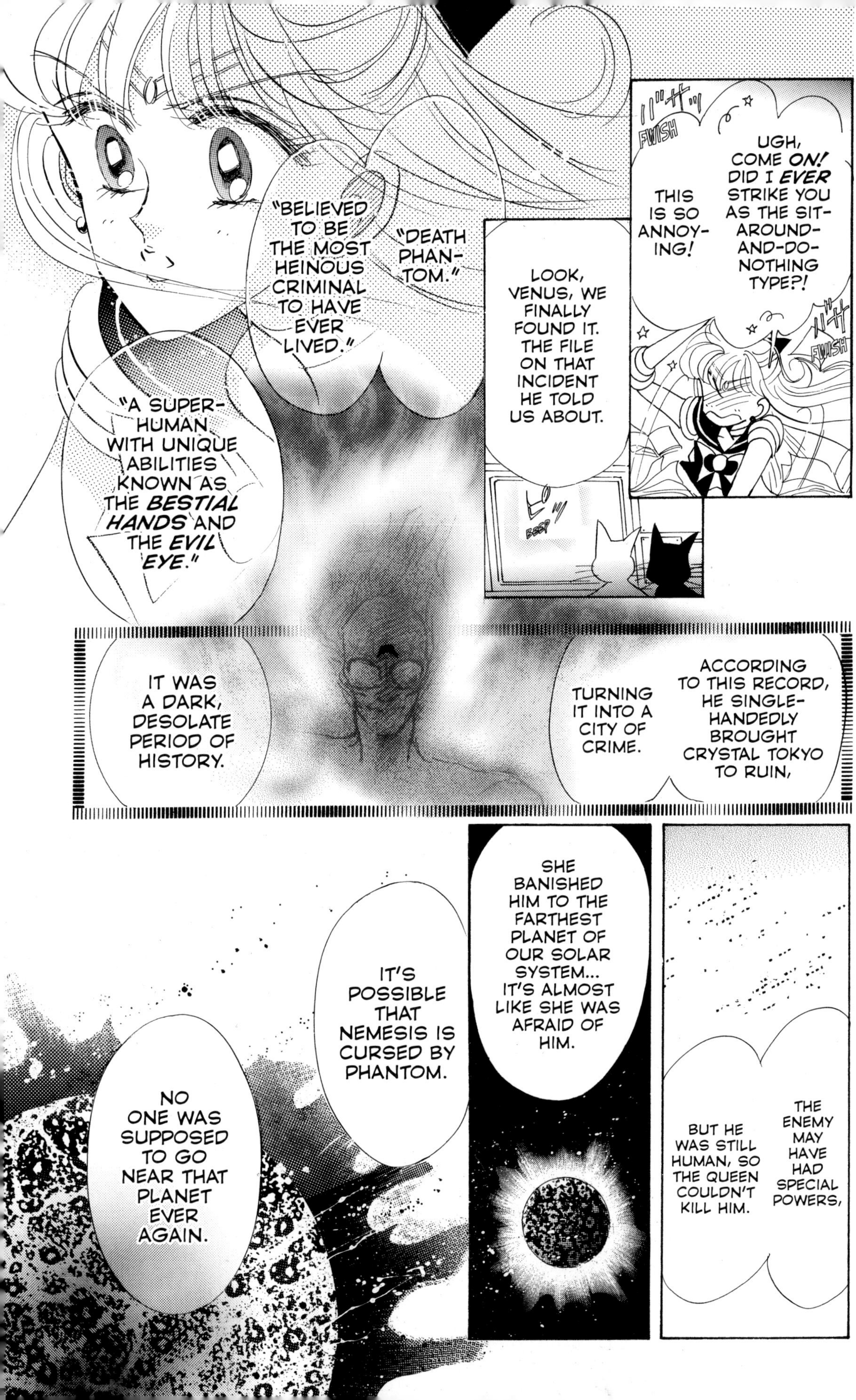
FWISH
UGH, COME ON! DID I EVER STRIKE YOU AS THE SIT-AROUND-AND-DO-NOTHING TYPE?!
THIS IS SO ANNOYING!
FWISH
LOOK, VENUS, WE FINALLY FOUND IT. THE FILE ON THAT INCIDENT HE TOLD US ABOUT.
BEEP
"DEATH PHANTOM."
"BELIEVED TO BE THE MOST HEINOUS CRIMINAL TO HAVE EVER LIVED."
"A SUPER-HUMAN WITH UNIQUE ABILITIES KNOWN AS THE BESTIAL HANDS AND THE EVIL EYE."
ACCORDING TO THIS RECORD, HE SINGLE-HANDEDLY BROUGHT CRYSTAL TOKYO TO RUIN,
TURNING IT INTO A CITY OF CRIME.
IT WAS A DARK, DESOLATE PERIOD OF HISTORY.
THE ENEMY MAY HAVE HAD SPECIAL POWERS,
BUT HE WAS STILL HUMAN, SO THE QUEEN COULDN'T KILL HIM.
SHE BANISHED HIM TO THE FARTHEST PLANET OF OUR SOLAR SYSTEM... IT'S ALMOST LIKE SHE WAS AFRAID OF HIM.
IT'S POSSIBLE THAT NEMESIS IS CURSED BY PHANTOM.
NO ONE WAS SUPPOSED TO GO NEAR THAT PLANET EVER AGAIN.

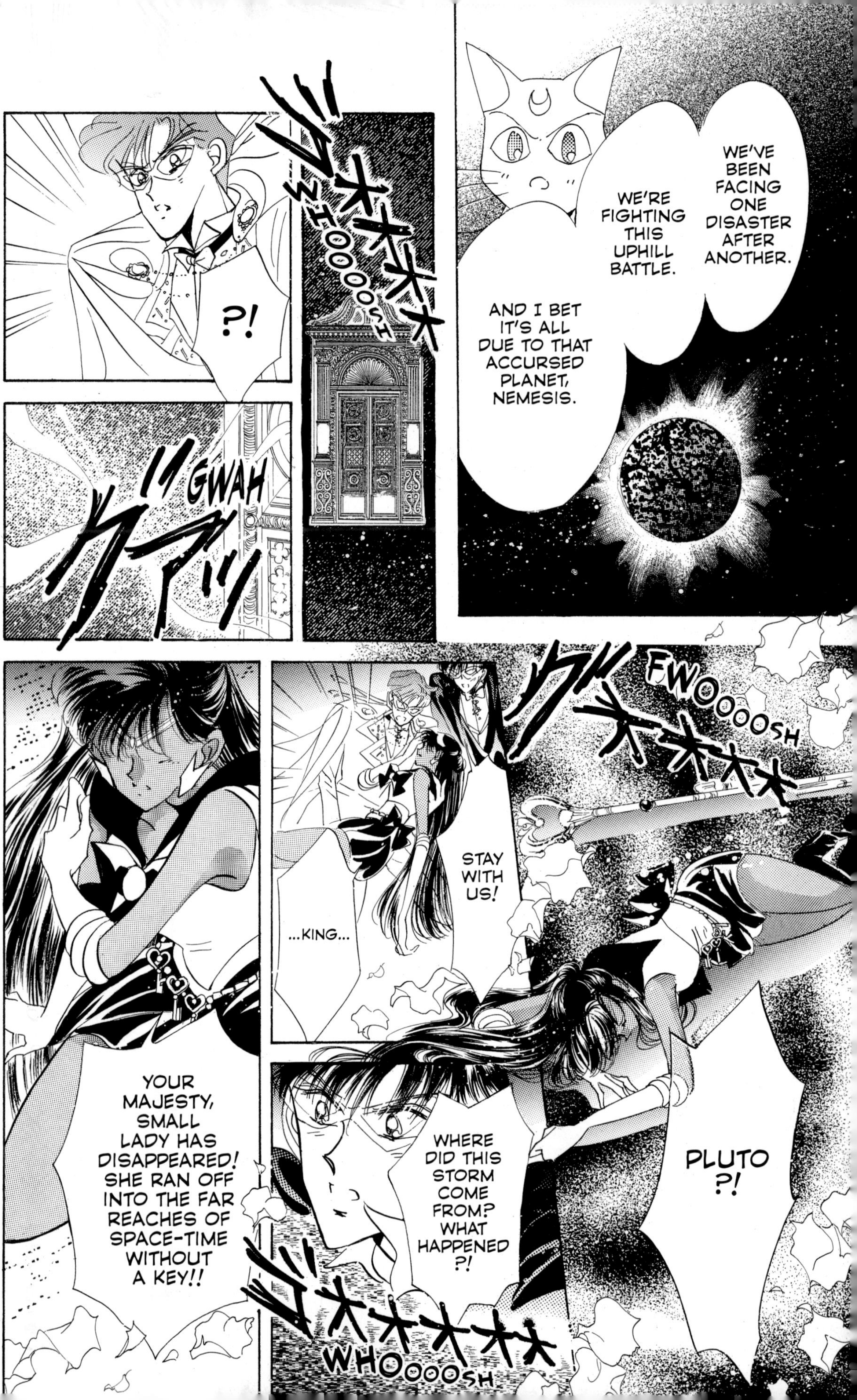
WE'VE BEEN FACING ONE DISASTER AFTER ANOTHER.
WE'RE FIGHTING THIS UPHILL BATTLE.
AND I BET IT'S ALL DUE TO THAT ACCURSED PLANET, NEMESIS.
WHOOOOOSH
?!
GWAH
FWOOOOOSH
PLUTO ?!
STAY WITH US!
...KING...
WHERE DID THIS STORM COME FROM? WHAT HAPPENED ?!
WHOOOOSH
YOUR MAJESTY, SMALL LADY HAS DISAPPEARED! SHE RAN OFF INTO THE FAR REACHES OF SPACE-TIME WITHOUT A KEY!!

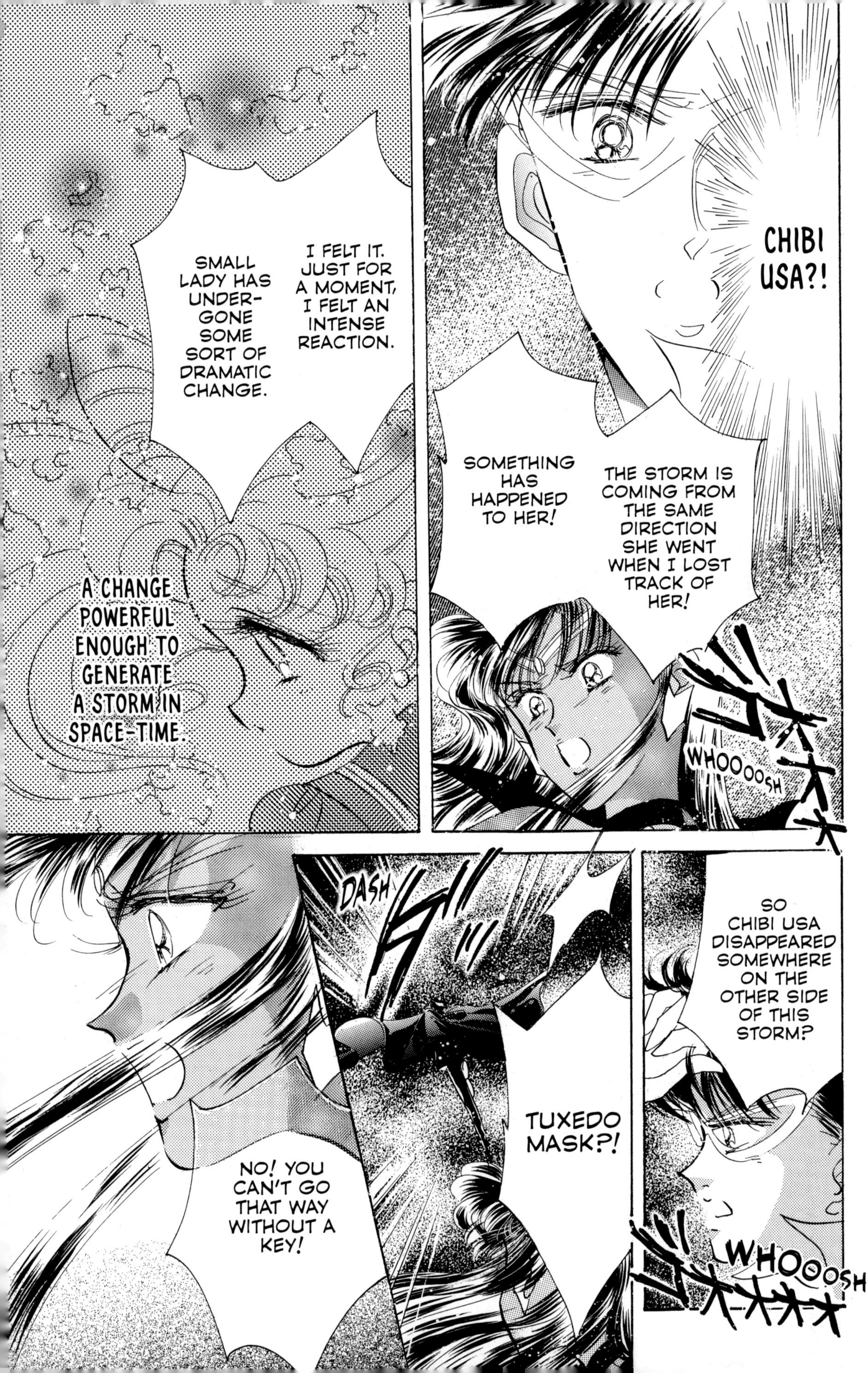
CHIBI USA?!
SOMETHING HAS HAPPENED TO HER!
THE STORM IS COMING FROM THE SAME DIRECTION SHE WENT WHEN I LOST TRACK OF HER!
WHOOOOSH
I FELT IT. JUST FOR A MOMENT, I FELT AN INTENSE REACTION.
SMALL LADY HAS UNDERGONE SOME SORT OF DRAMATIC CHANGE.
A CHANGE POWERFUL ENOUGH TO GENERATE A STORM IN SPACE-TIME.
SO CHIBI USA DISAPPEARED SOMEWHERE ON THE OTHER SIDE OF THIS STORM?
WHOOOOSH
DASH
TUXEDO MASK?!
NO! YOU CAN'T GO THAT WAY WITHOUT A KEY!

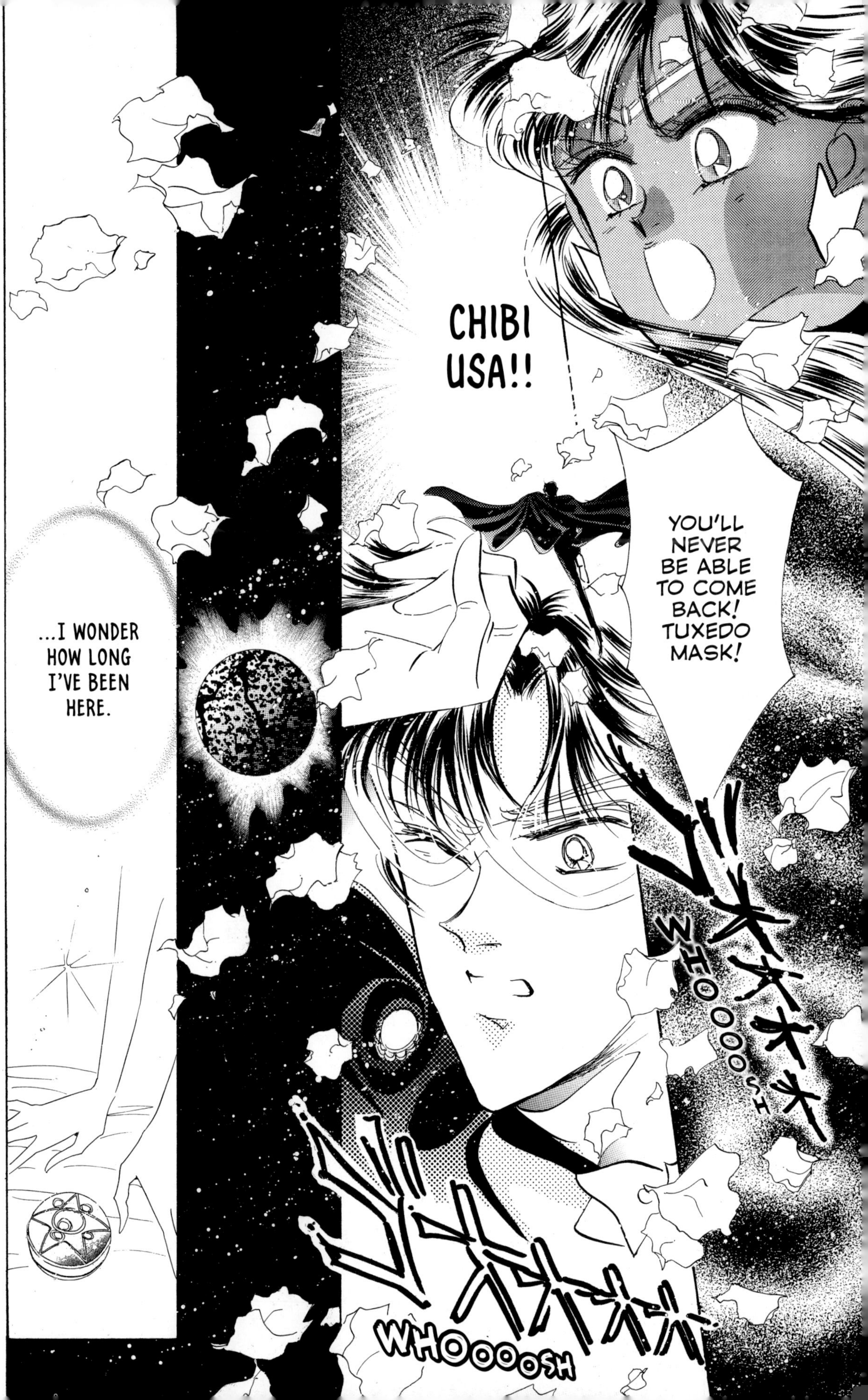
CHIBI USA!!
YOU'LL NEVER BE ABLE TO COME BACK! TUXEDO MASK!
WHOOOOOSH!
WHOOOOSH
...I WONDER HOW LONG I'VE BEEN HERE.

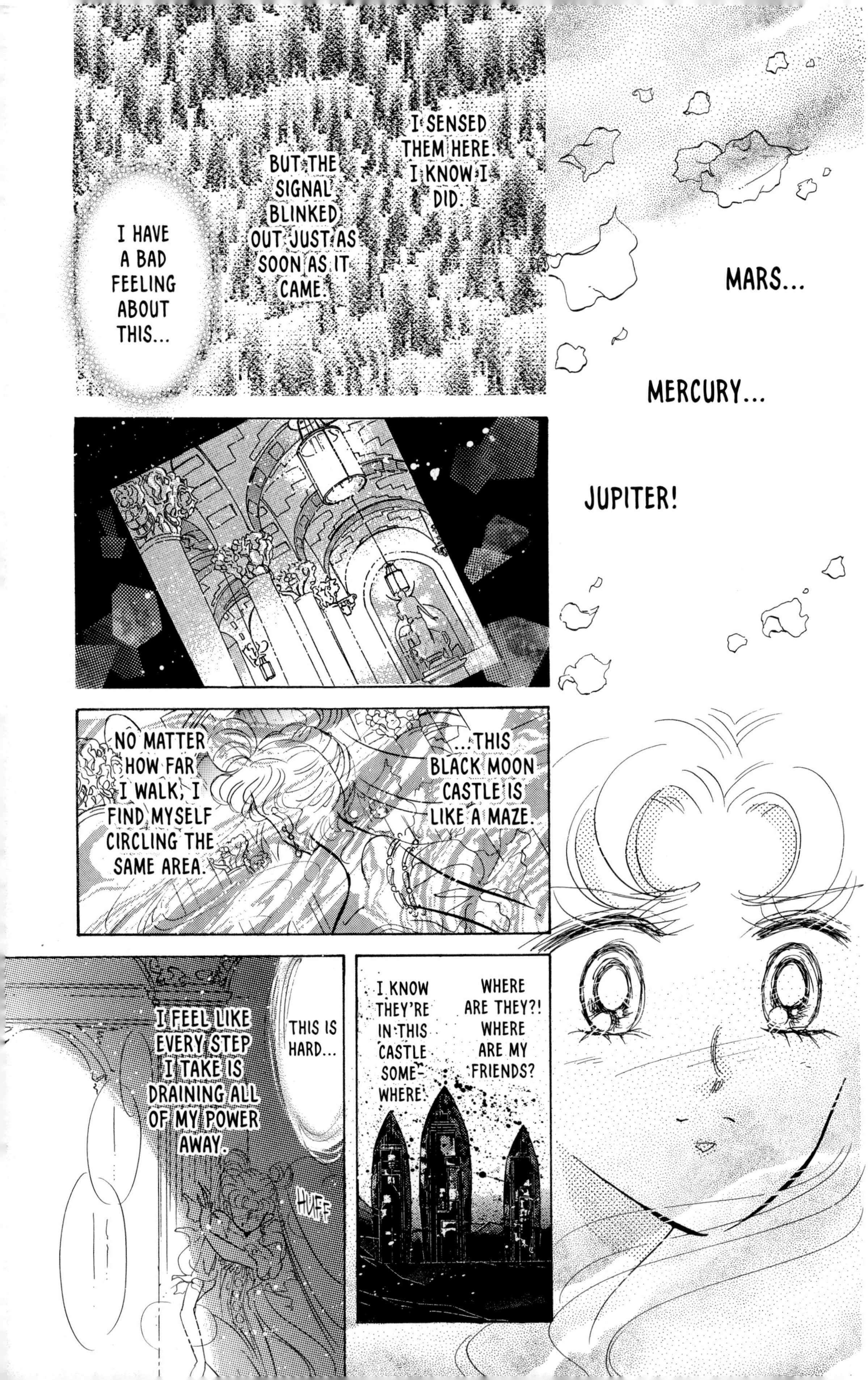
MARS...
MERCURY...
JUPITER!
I SENSED THEM HERE. I KNOW I DID.
BUT THE SIGNAL BLINKED OUT JUST AS SOON AS IT CAME.
I HAVE A BAD FEELING ABOUT THIS...
...THIS BLACK MOON CASTLE IS LIKE A MAZE.
NO MATTER HOW FAR I WALK, I FIND MYSELF CIRCLING THE SAME AREA.
WHERE ARE THEY?! WHERE ARE MY FRIENDS?
I KNOW THEY'RE IN THIS CASTLE SOME-WHERE.
THIS IS HARD...
I FEEL LIKE EVERY STEP I TAKE IS DRAINING ALL OF MY POWER AWAY.
HUFF

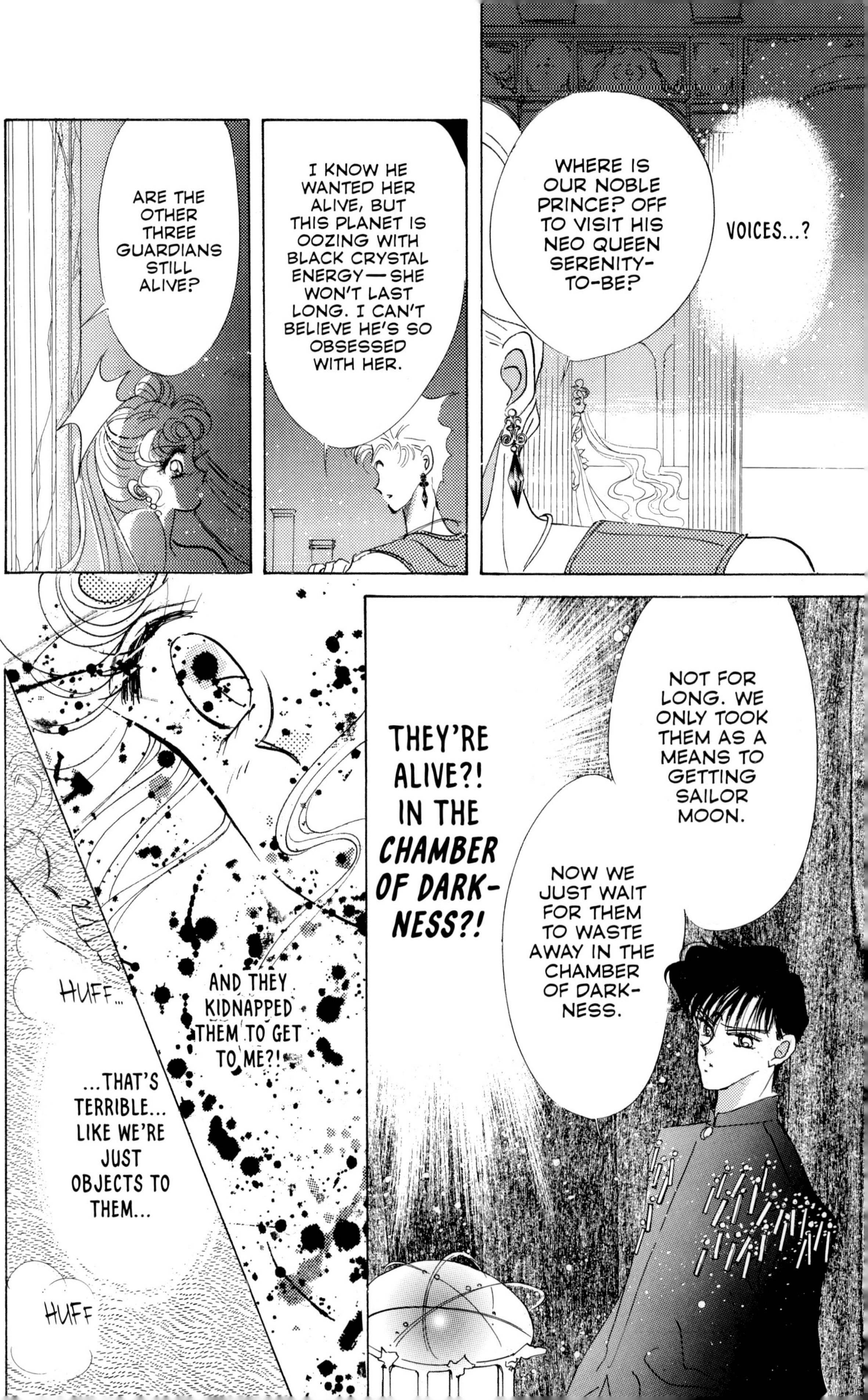
VOICES...?
WHERE IS OUR NOBLE PRINCE? OFF TO VISIT HIS NEO QUEEN SERENITY-TO-BE?
I KNOW HE WANTED HER ALIVE, BUT THIS PLANET IS OOZING WITH BLACK CRYSTAL ENERGY—SHE WON'T LAST LONG. I CAN'T BELIEVE HE'S SO OBSESSED WITH HER.
ARE THE OTHER THREE GUARDIANS STILL ALIVE?
NOT FOR LONG. WE ONLY TOOK THEM AS A MEANS TO GETTING SAILOR MOON.
NOW WE JUST WAIT FOR THEM TO WASTE AWAY IN THE CHAMBER OF DARK-NESS.
THEY'RE ALIVE?! IN THE *CHAMBER OF DARK-NESS?!*
AND THEY KIDNAPPED THEM TO GET TO ME?!
HUFF...
...THAT'S TERRIBLE... LIKE WE'RE JUST OBJECTS TO THEM...
HUFF

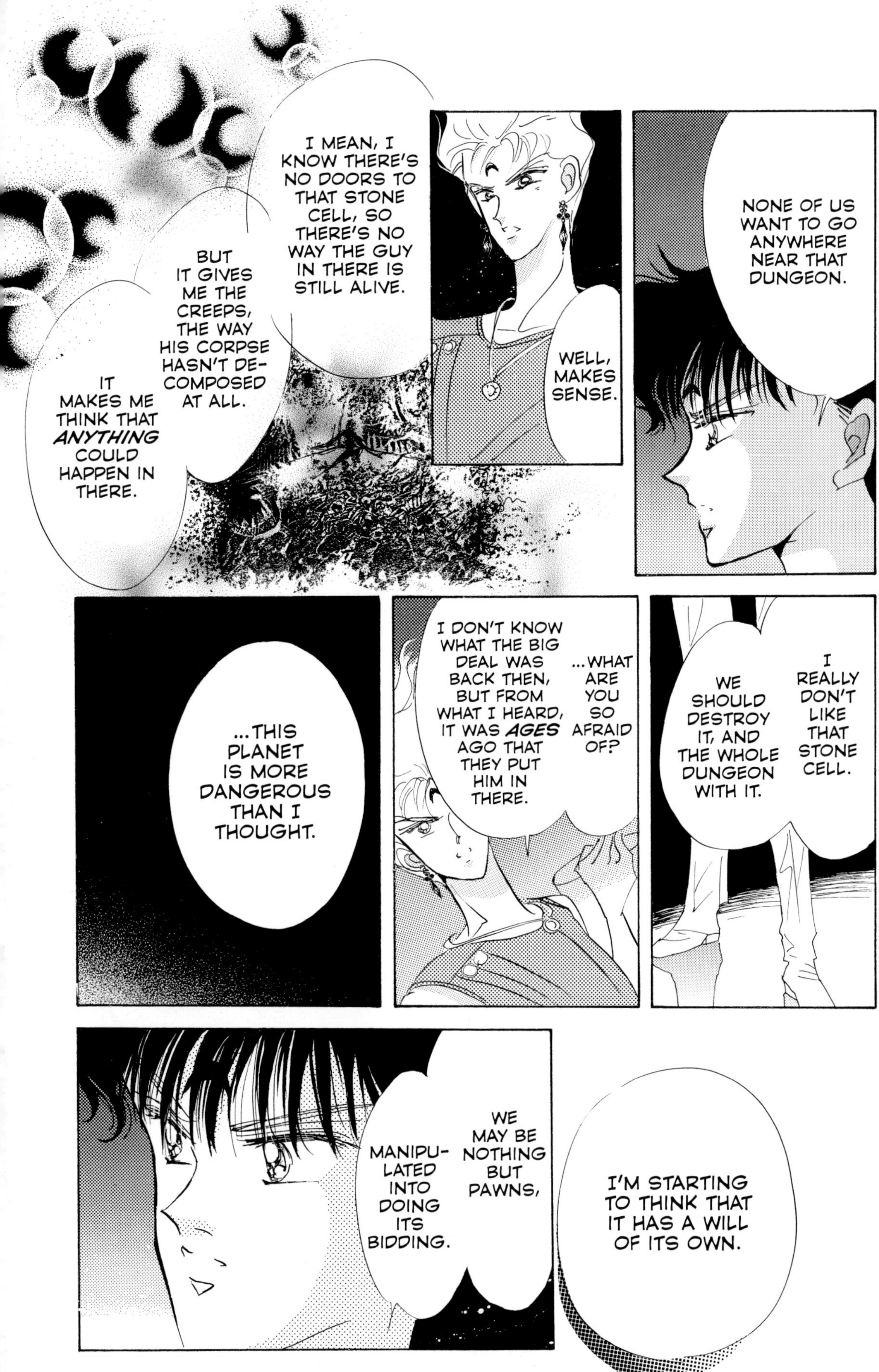
NONE OF US WANT TO GO ANYWHERE NEAR THAT DUNGEON.
WELL, MAKES SENSE.
I MEAN, I KNOW THERE'S NO DOORS TO THAT STONE CELL, SO THERE'S NO WAY THE GUY IN THERE IS STILL ALIVE.
BUT IT GIVES ME THE CREEPS, THE WAY HIS CORPSE HASN'T DE-COMPOSED AT ALL.
IT MAKES ME THINK THAT *ANYTHING* COULD HAPPEN IN THERE.
I REALLY DON'T LIKE THAT STONE CELL.
WE SHOULD DESTROY IT, AND THE WHOLE DUNGEON WITH IT.
...WHAT ARE YOU SO AFRAID OF?
I DON'T KNOW WHAT THE BIG DEAL WAS BACK THEN, BUT FROM WHAT I HEARD, IT WAS *AGES* AGO THAT THEY PUT HIM IN THERE.
...THIS PLANET IS MORE DANGEROUS THAN I THOUGHT.
I'M STARTING TO THINK THAT IT HAS A WILL OF ITS OWN.
WE MAY BE NOTHING BUT PAWNS,
MANIPU-LATED INTO DOING ITS BIDDING.

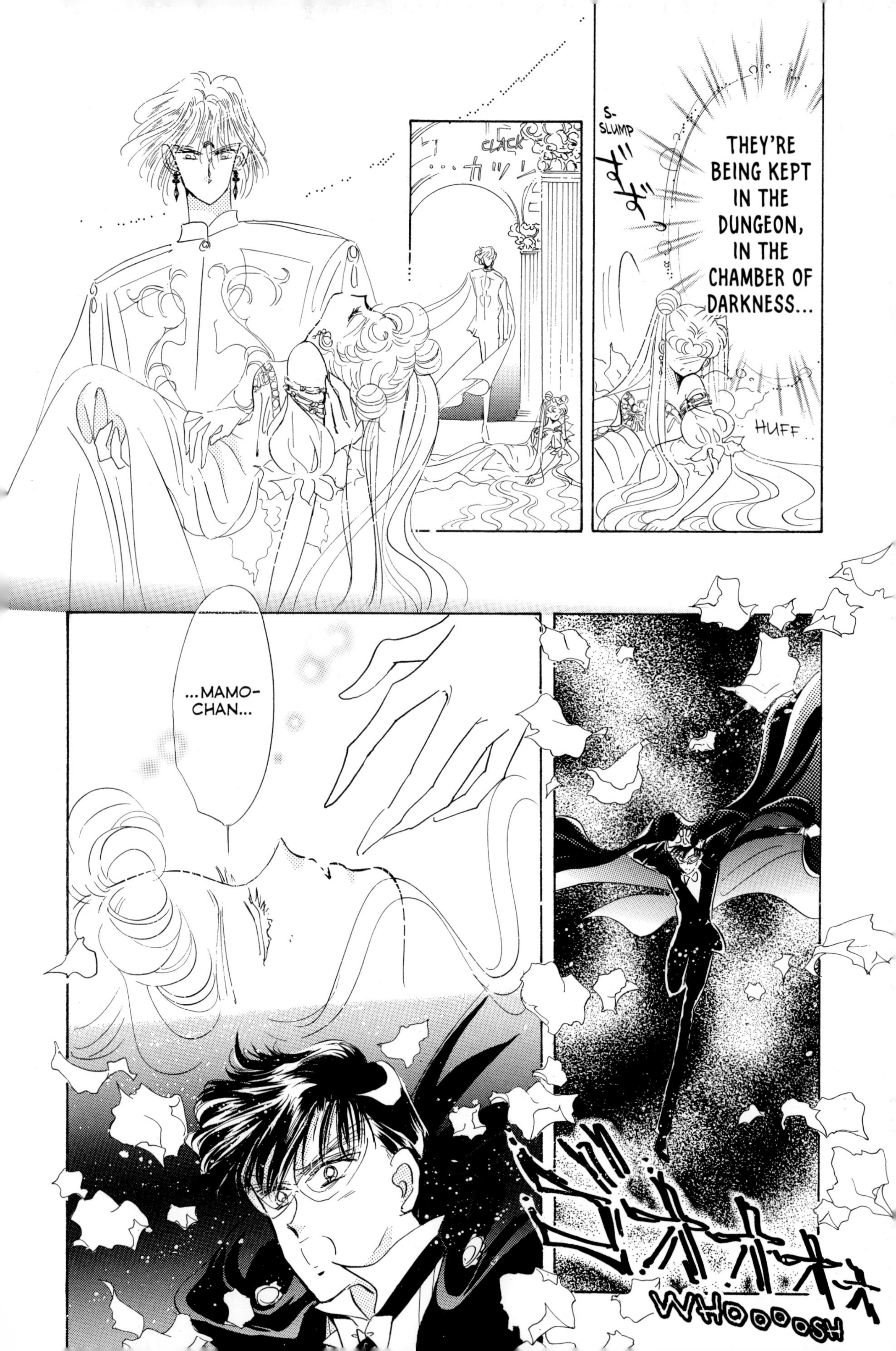
THEY'RE BEING KEPT IN THE DUNGEON, IN THE CHAMBER OF DARKNESS...
S-SLUMP
HUFF...
CLACK
WHOOOOSH
...MAMO-CHAN...

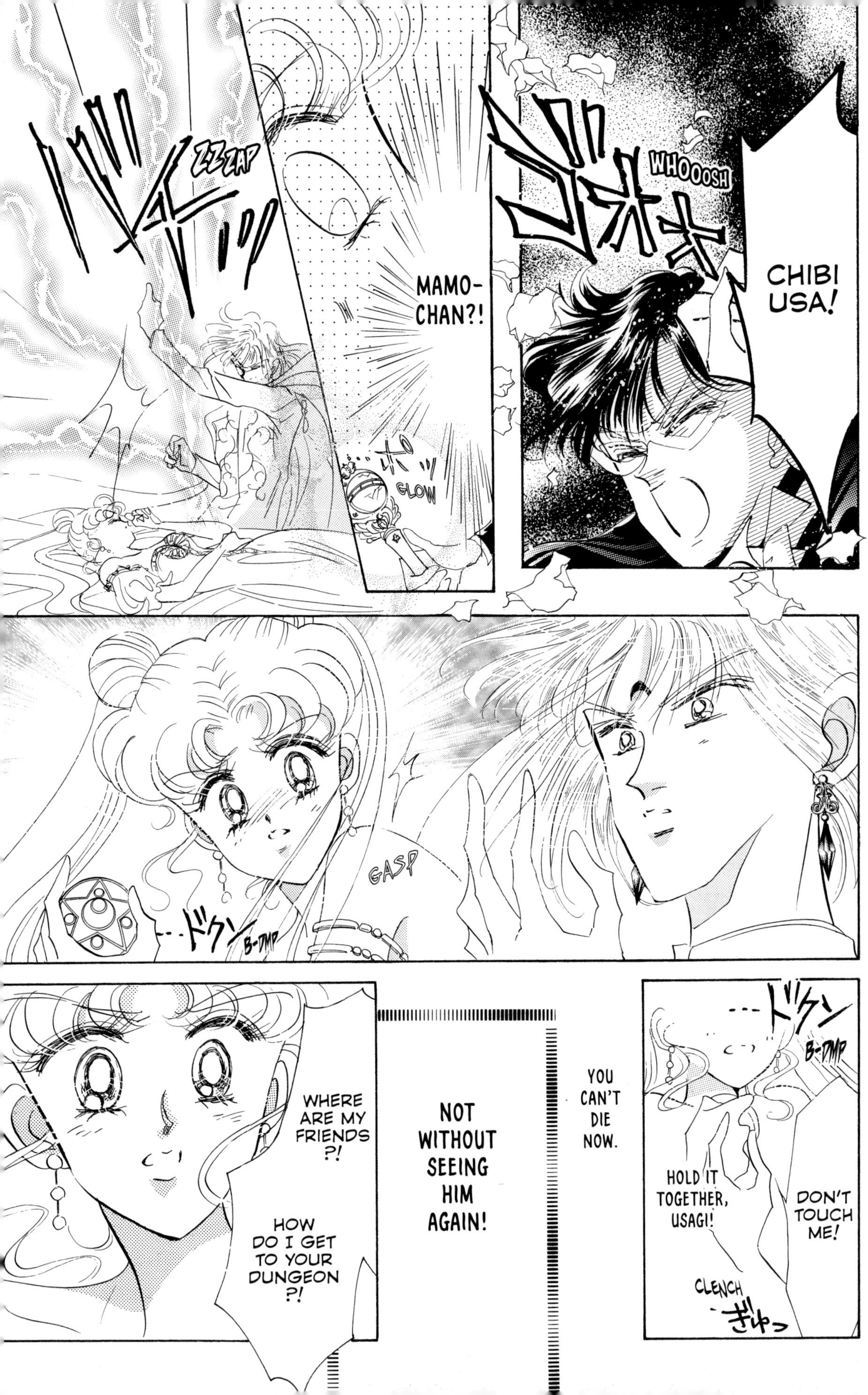
WHOOOSH
CHIBI USA!
MAMO-CHAN?!
GLOW
ZZZAP
GASP
B-DMP
B-DMP
DON'T TOUCH ME!
HOLD IT TOGETHER, USAGI!
CLENCH
YOU CAN'T DIE NOW.
NOT WITHOUT SEEING HIM AGAIN!
WHERE ARE MY FRIENDS?!
HOW DO I GET TO YOUR DUNGEON?!

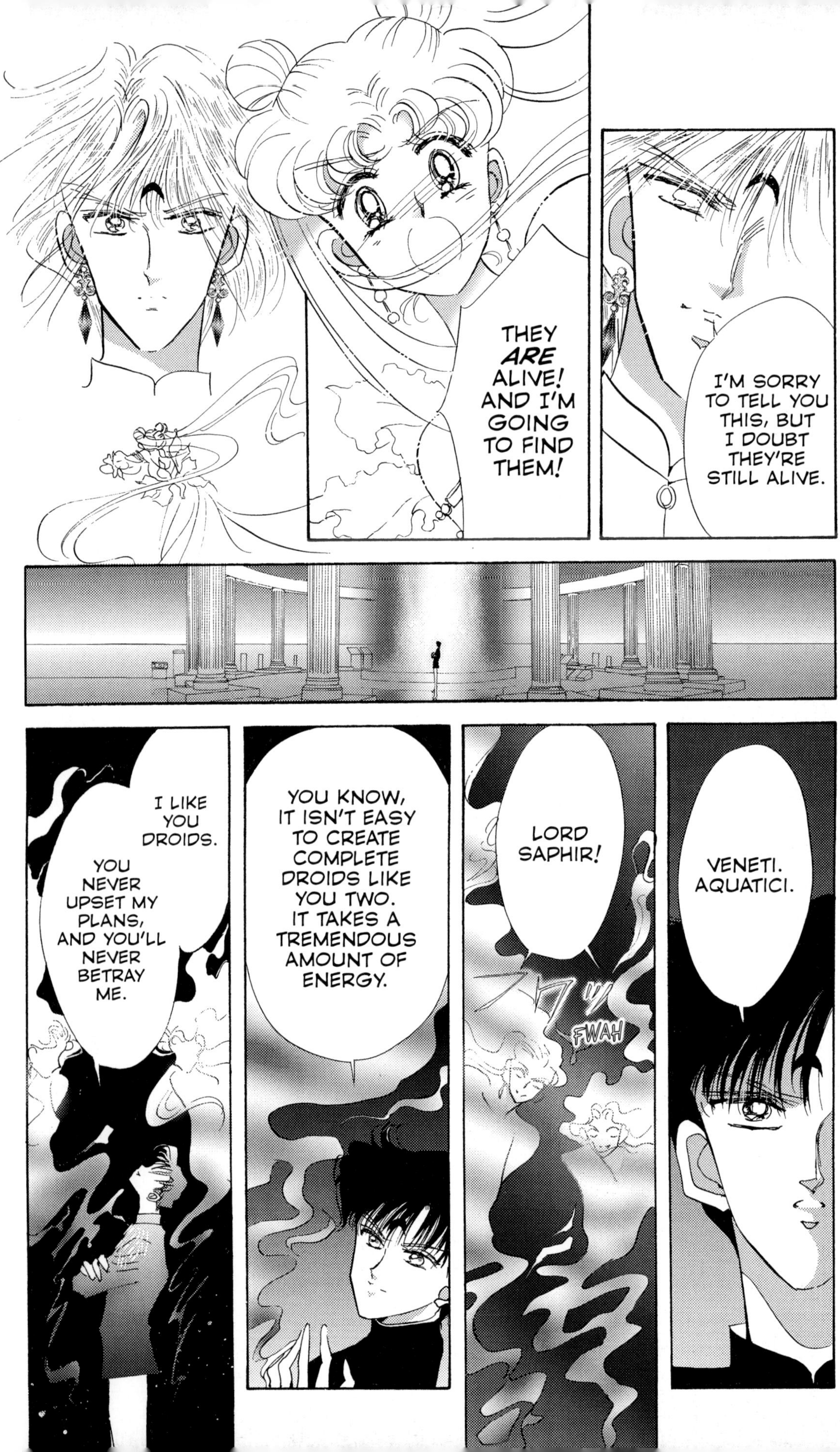
I'M SORRY TO TELL YOU THIS, BUT I DOUBT THEY'RE STILL ALIVE.
THEY *ARE* ALIVE! AND I'M GOING TO FIND THEM!
VENETI. AQUATICI.
LORD SAPHIR!
FWAH
YOU KNOW, IT ISN'T EASY TO CREATE COMPLETE DROIDS LIKE YOU TWO. IT TAKES A TREMENDOUS AMOUNT OF ENERGY.
I LIKE YOU DROIDS.
YOU NEVER UPSET MY PLANS, AND YOU'LL NEVER BETRAY ME.

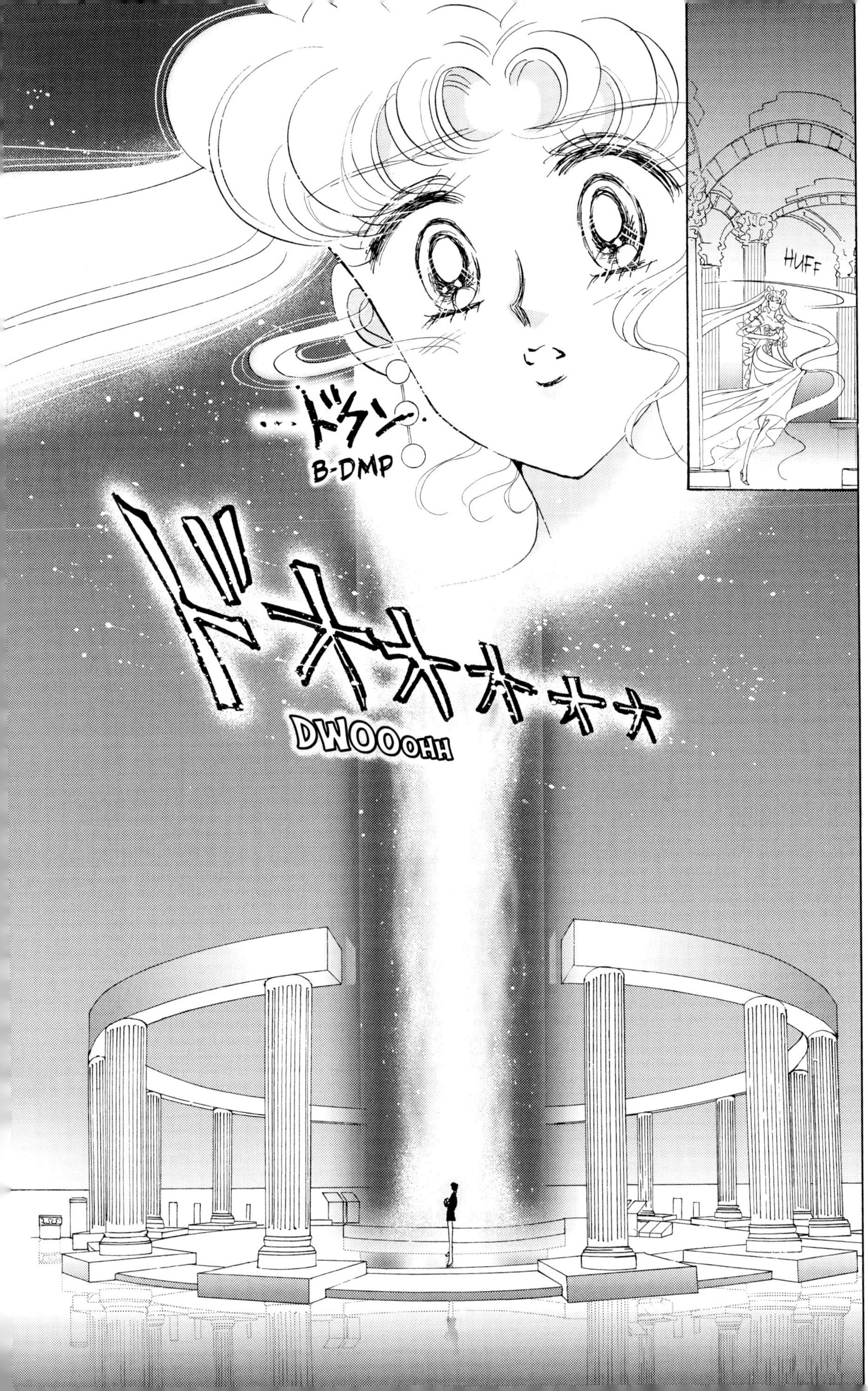
HUFF
ドクン
B-DMP
ドオオオォォ
DWOOOOHH

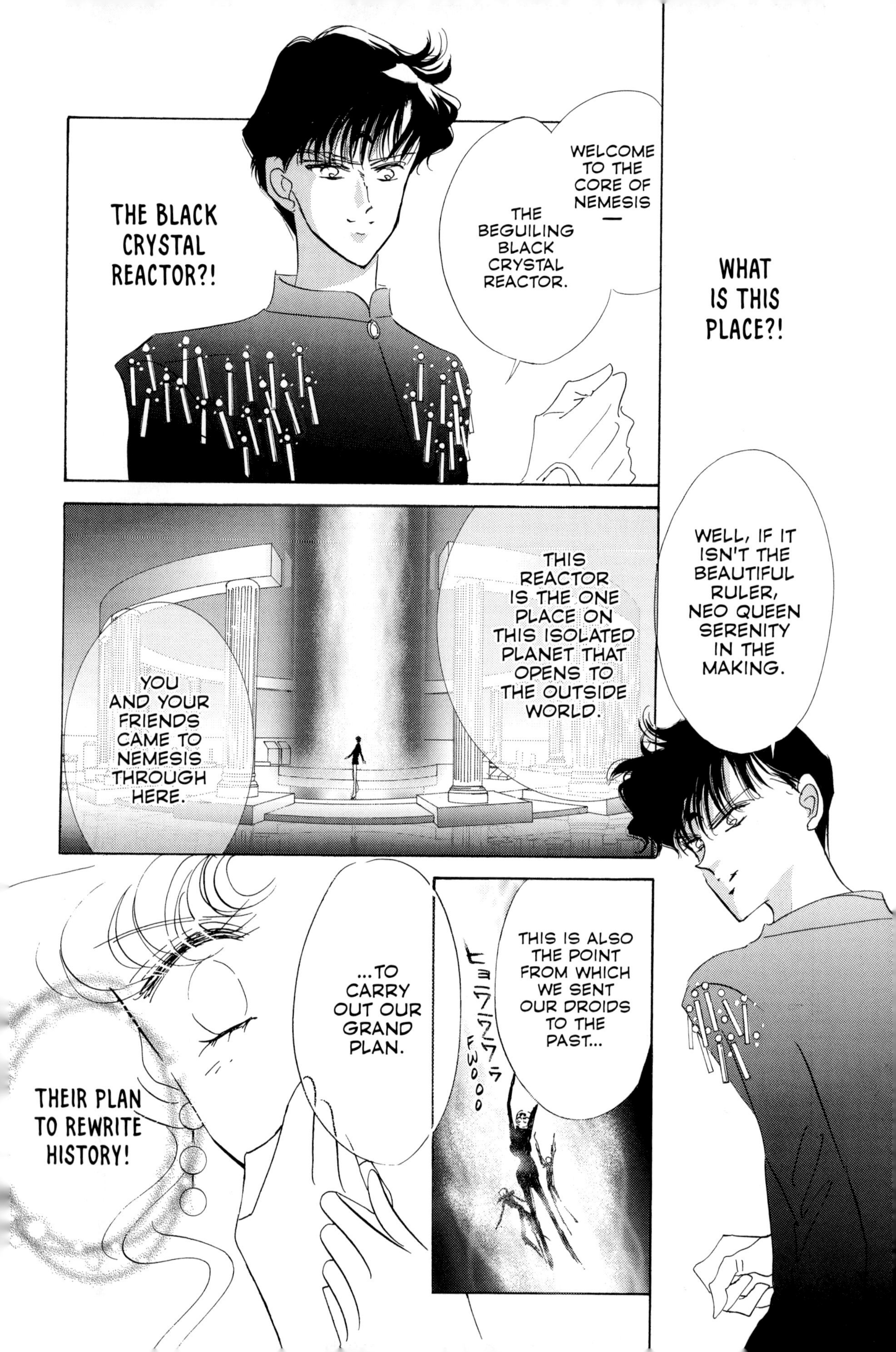
WHAT IS THIS PLACE?!
WELCOME TO THE CORE OF NEMESIS —
THE BEGUILING BLACK CRYSTAL REACTOR.
THE BLACK CRYSTAL REACTOR?!
WELL, IF IT ISN'T THE BEAUTIFUL RULER, NEO QUEEN SERENITY IN THE MAKING.
THIS REACTOR IS THE ONE PLACE ON THIS ISOLATED PLANET THAT OPENS TO THE OUTSIDE WORLD.
YOU AND YOUR FRIENDS CAME TO NEMESIS THROUGH HERE.
THIS IS ALSO THE POINT FROM WHICH WE SENT OUR DROIDS TO THE PAST...
ヒョララララ
FWOOO
...TO CARRY OUT OUR GRAND PLAN.
THEIR PLAN TO REWRITE HISTORY!

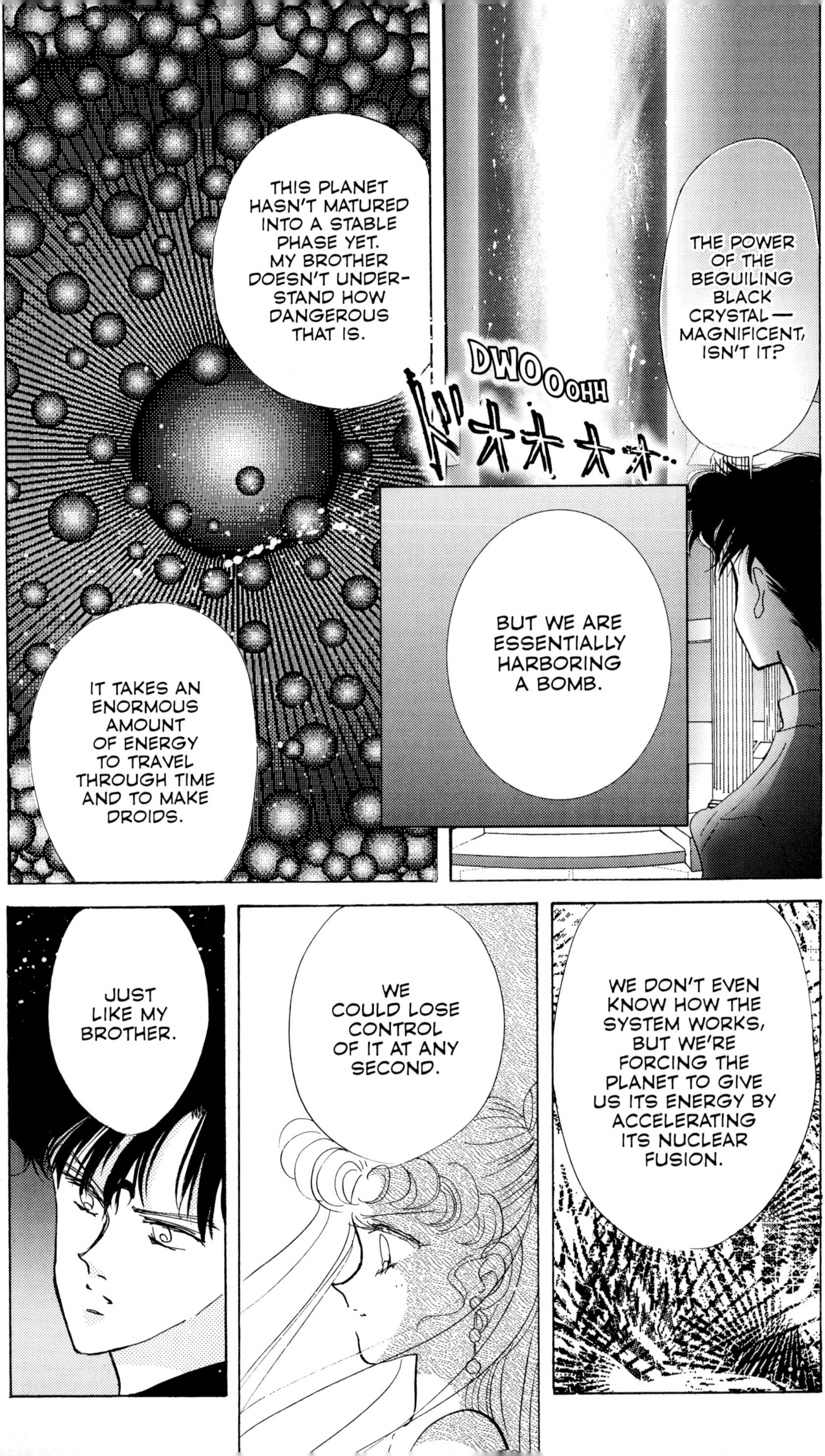
THE POWER OF THE BEGUILING BLACK CRYSTAL—MAGNIFICENT, ISN'T IT?
DWOOoohh
THIS PLANET HASN'T MATURED INTO A STABLE PHASE YET. MY BROTHER DOESN'T UNDER-STAND HOW DANGEROUS THAT IS.
IT TAKES AN ENORMOUS AMOUNT OF ENERGY TO TRAVEL THROUGH TIME AND TO MAKE DROIDS.
BUT WE ARE ESSENTIALLY HARBORING A BOMB.
WE DON'T EVEN KNOW HOW THE SYSTEM WORKS, BUT WE'RE FORCING THE PLANET TO GIVE US ITS ENERGY BY ACCELERATING ITS NUCLEAR FUSION.
WE COULD LOSE CONTROL OF IT AT ANY SECOND.
JUST LIKE MY BROTHER.

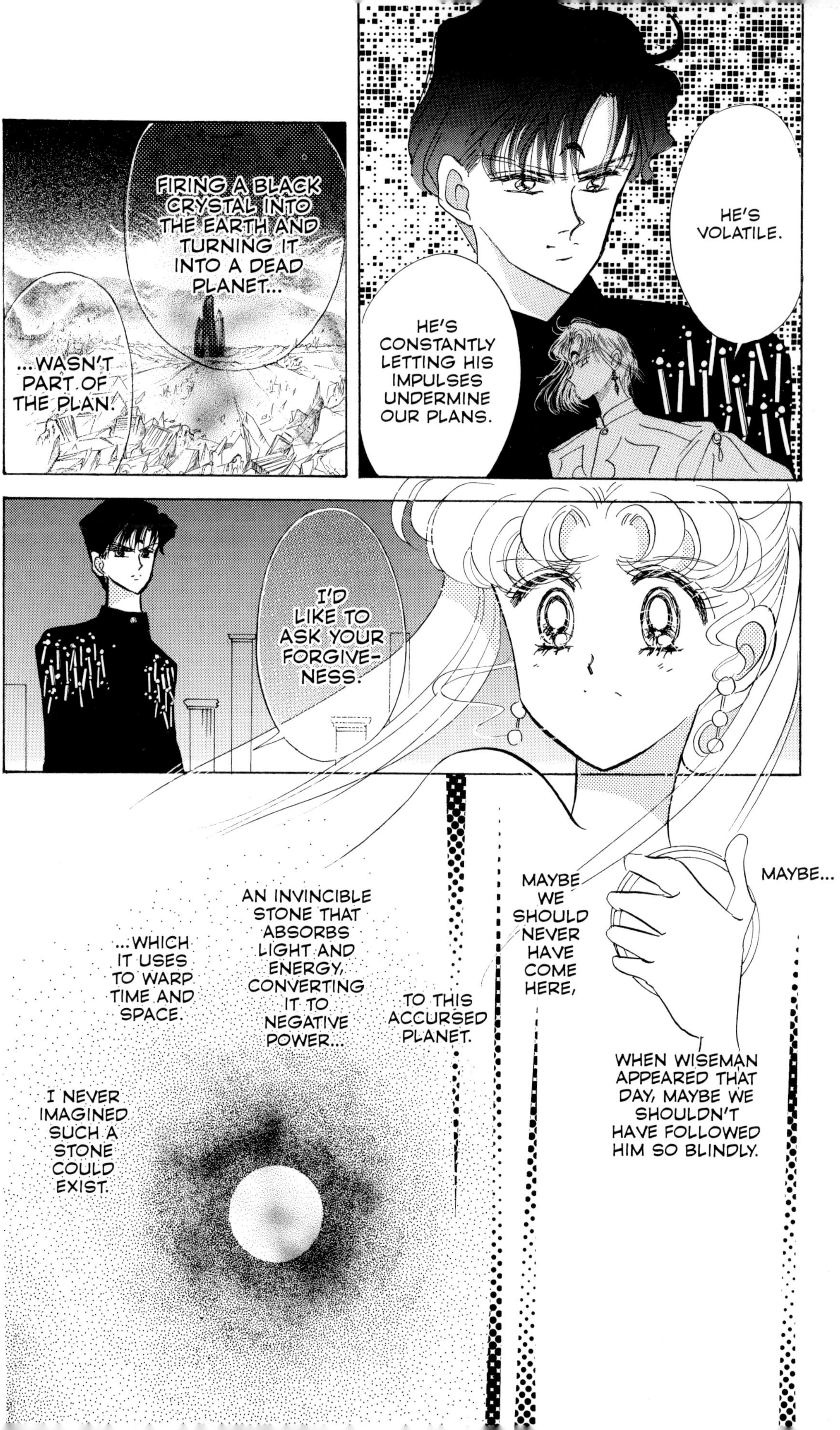
HE'S VOLATILE.
HE'S CONSTANTLY LETTING HIS IMPULSES UNDERMINE OUR PLANS.
FIRING A BLACK CRYSTAL INTO THE EARTH AND TURNING IT INTO A DEAD PLANET...
...WASN'T PART OF THE PLAN.
I'D LIKE TO ASK YOUR FORGIVE-NESS.
MAYBE...
MAYBE WE SHOULD NEVER HAVE COME HERE,
TO THIS ACCURSED PLANET.
WHEN WISEMAN APPEARED THAT DAY, MAYBE WE SHOULDN'T HAVE FOLLOWED HIM SO BLINDLY.
AN INVINCIBLE STONE THAT ABSORBS LIGHT AND ENERGY, CONVERTING IT TO NEGATIVE POWER...
...WHICH IT USES TO WARP TIME AND SPACE.
I NEVER IMAGINED SUCH A STONE COULD EXIST.

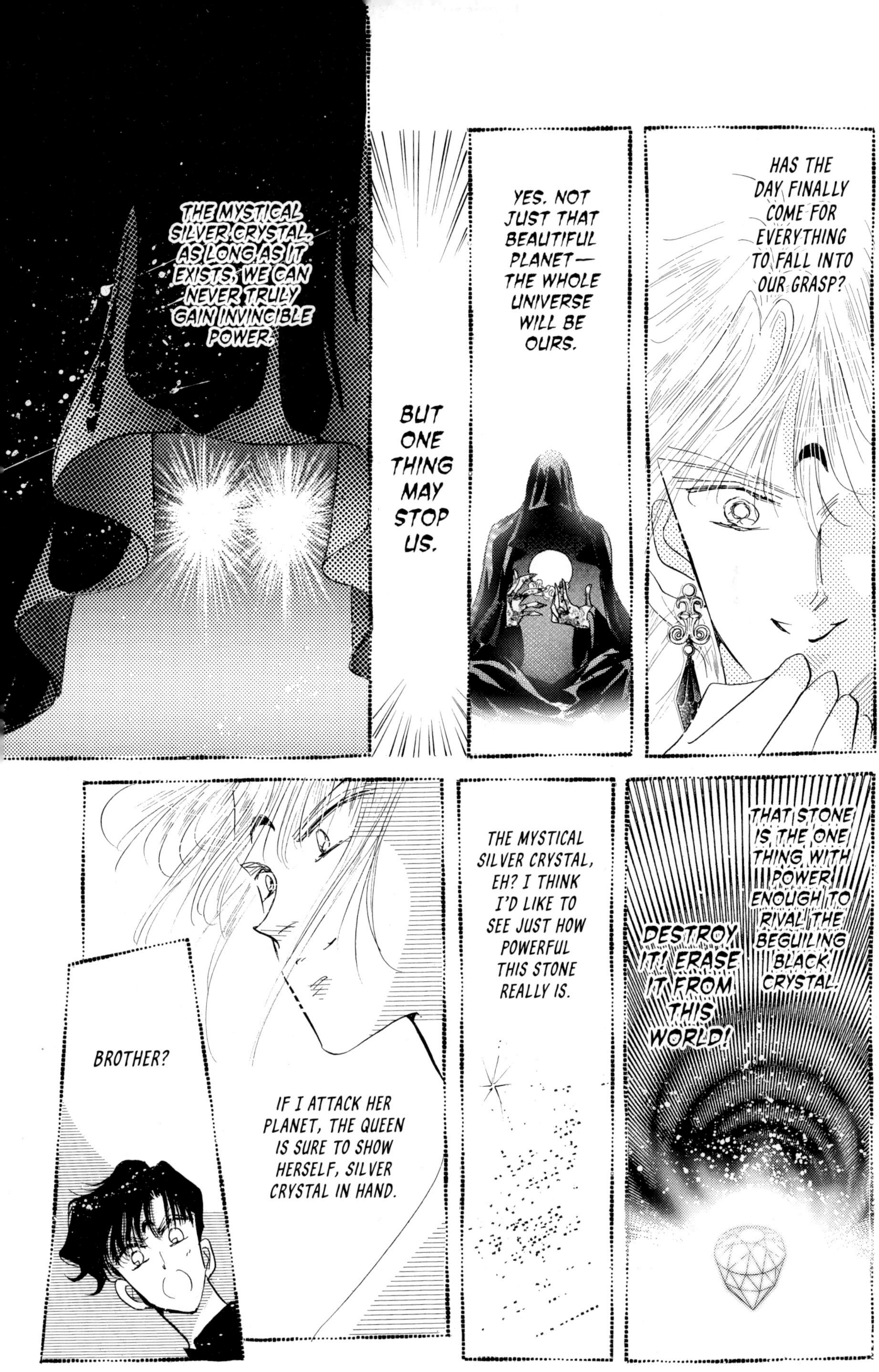
HAS THE DAY FINALLY COME FOR EVERYTHING TO FALL INTO OUR GRASP?
YES. NOT JUST THAT BEAUTIFUL PLANET— THE WHOLE UNIVERSE WILL BE OURS.
BUT ONE THING MAY STOP US.
THE MYSTICAL SILVER CRYSTAL. AS LONG AS IT EXISTS, WE CAN NEVER TRULY GAIN INVINCIBLE POWER.
THAT STONE IS THE ONE THING WITH POWER ENOUGH TO RIVAL THE BEGUILING BLACK CRYSTAL.
DESTROY IT! ERASE IT FROM THIS WORLD!
THE MYSTICAL SILVER CRYSTAL, EH? I THINK I'D LIKE TO SEE JUST HOW POWERFUL THIS STONE REALLY IS.
IF I ATTACK HER PLANET, THE QUEEN IS SURE TO SHOW HERSELF, SILVER CRYSTAL IN HAND.
BROTHER?

AND WHAT BETTER OPPORTUNITY TO SEE THE OVERWHELMING MIGHT...

...OF THE BEGUILING BLACK CRYSTAL?

MY BROTHER HAS BEEN POSSESSED— BY THIS PLANET AND ITS BEGUILING BLACK CRYSTAL. NO ONE CAN STOP HIM NOW.

...CLENCH

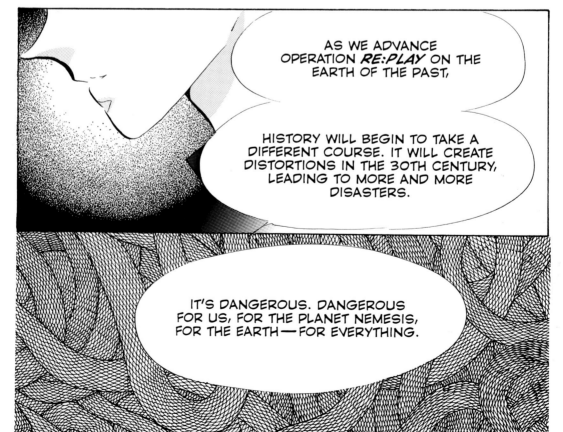

AS WE ADVANCE OPERATION *RE:PLAY* ON THE EARTH OF THE PAST,

HISTORY WILL BEGIN TO TAKE A DIFFERENT COURSE. IT WILL CREATE DISTORTIONS IN THE 30TH CENTURY, LEADING TO MORE AND MORE DISASTERS.

IT'S DANGEROUS. DANGEROUS FOR US, FOR THE PLANET NEMESIS, FOR THE EARTH—FOR EVERYTHING.

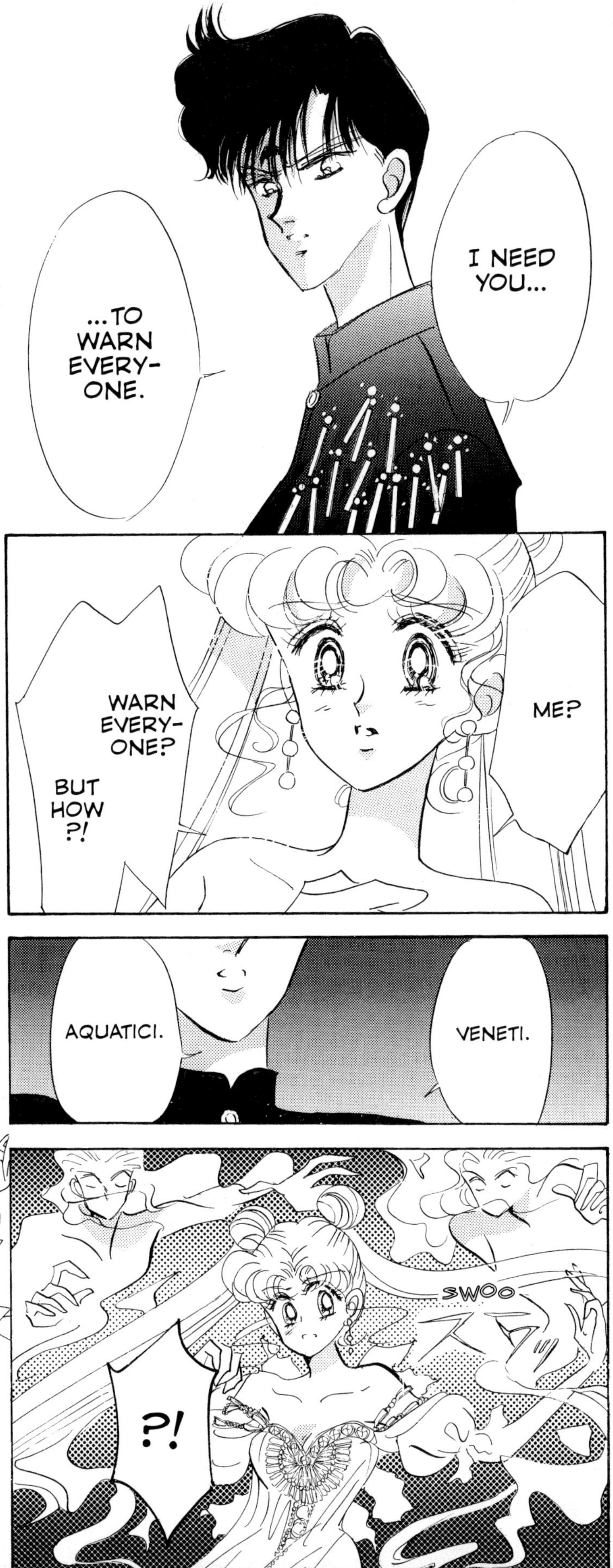
I NEED YOU...
...TO WARN EVERY-ONE.
ME?
WARN EVERY-ONE?
BUT HOW ?!
VENETI.
AQUATICI.
SWOO
?!

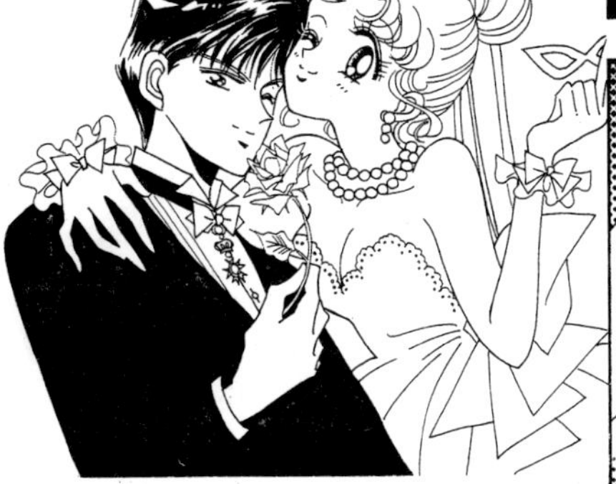

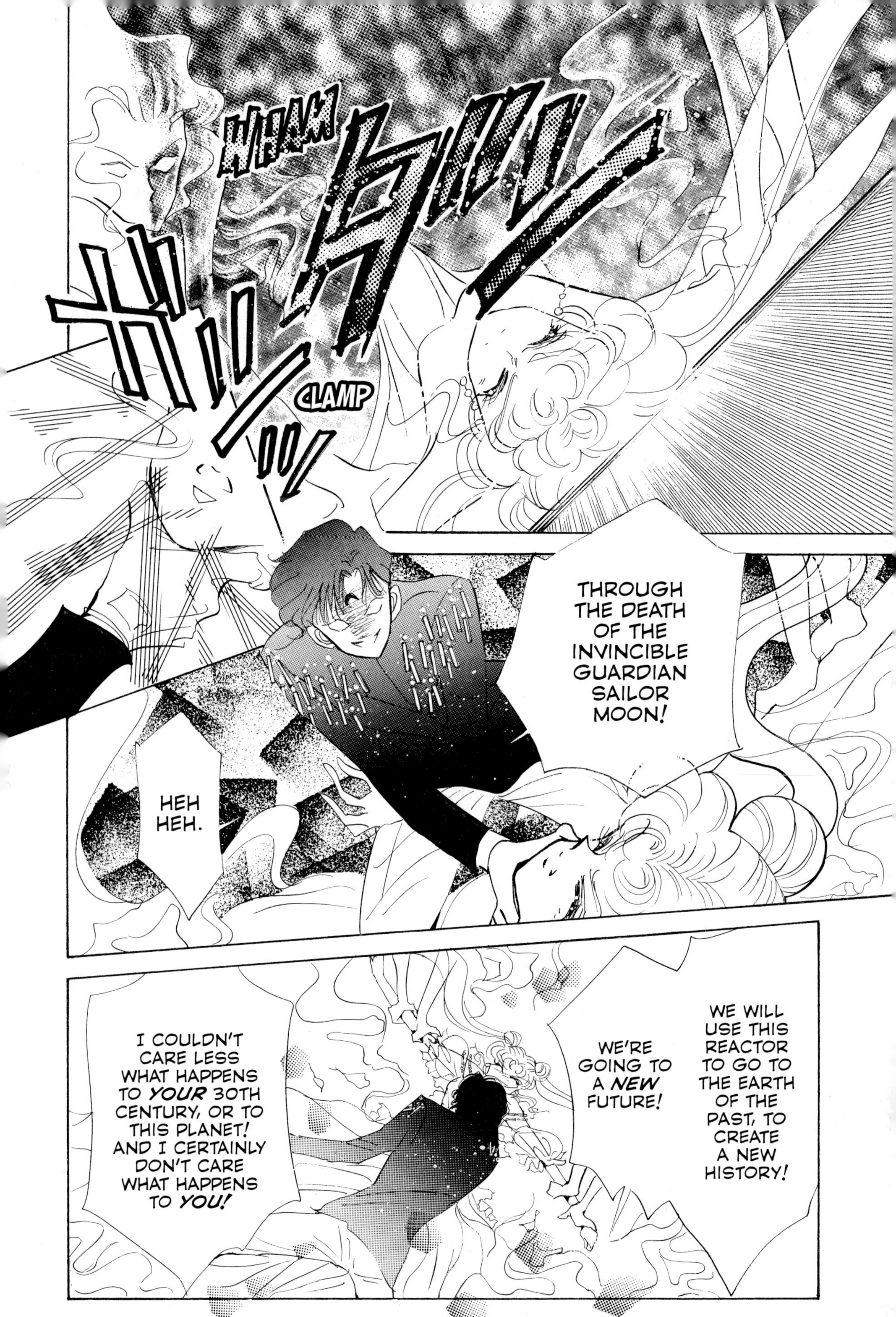
WHAM
CLAMP
THROUGH THE DEATH OF THE INVINCIBLE GUARDIAN SAILOR MOON!
HEH HEH.
WE WILL USE THIS REACTOR TO GO TO THE EARTH OF THE PAST, TO CREATE A NEW HISTORY!
WE'RE GOING TO A *NEW* FUTURE!
I COULDN'T CARE LESS WHAT HAPPENS TO *YOUR* 30TH CENTURY, OR TO THIS PLANET! AND I CERTAINLY DON'T CARE WHAT HAPPENS TO *YOU!*

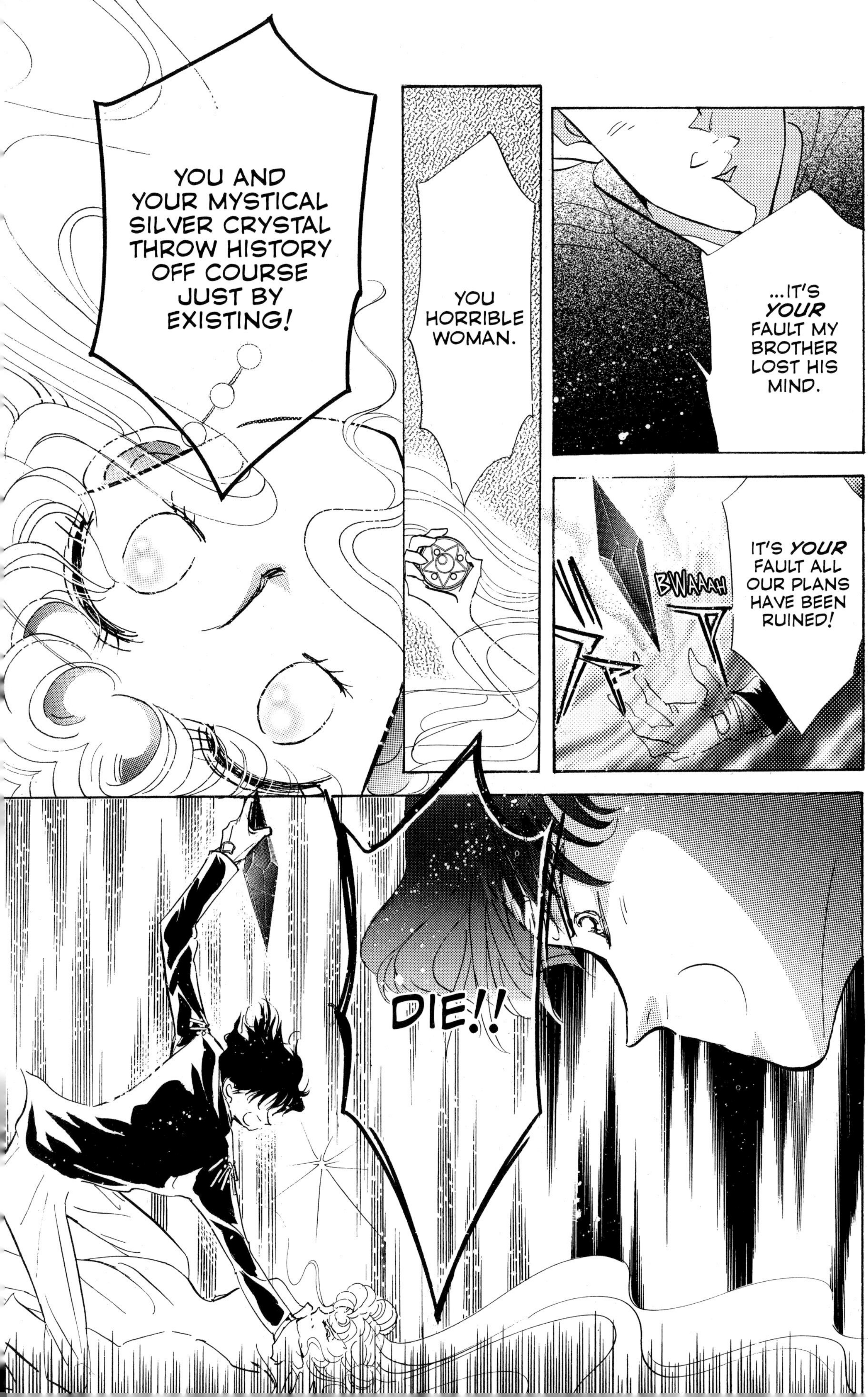
...IT'S *YOUR* FAULT MY BROTHER LOST HIS MIND.
IT'S *YOUR* FAULT ALL OUR PLANS HAVE BEEN RUINED!
BWAAAH
YOU HORRIBLE WOMAN.
YOU AND YOUR MYSTICAL SILVER CRYSTAL THROW HISTORY OFF COURSE JUST BY EXISTING!
DIE!!

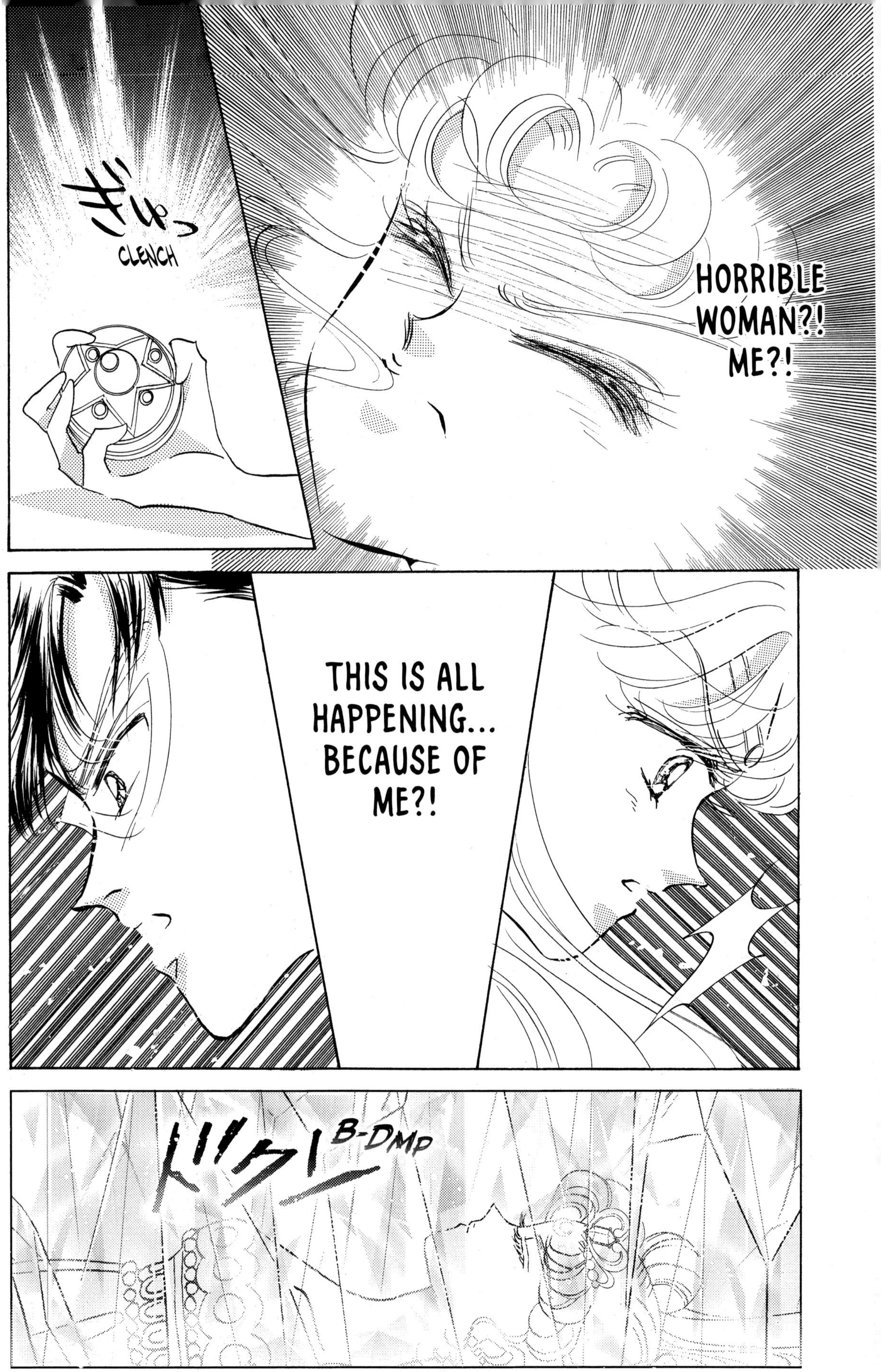
HORRIBLE WOMAN?! ME?!
ぎゅっ
CLENCH
THIS IS ALL HAPPENING... BECAUSE OF ME?!
B-DMP

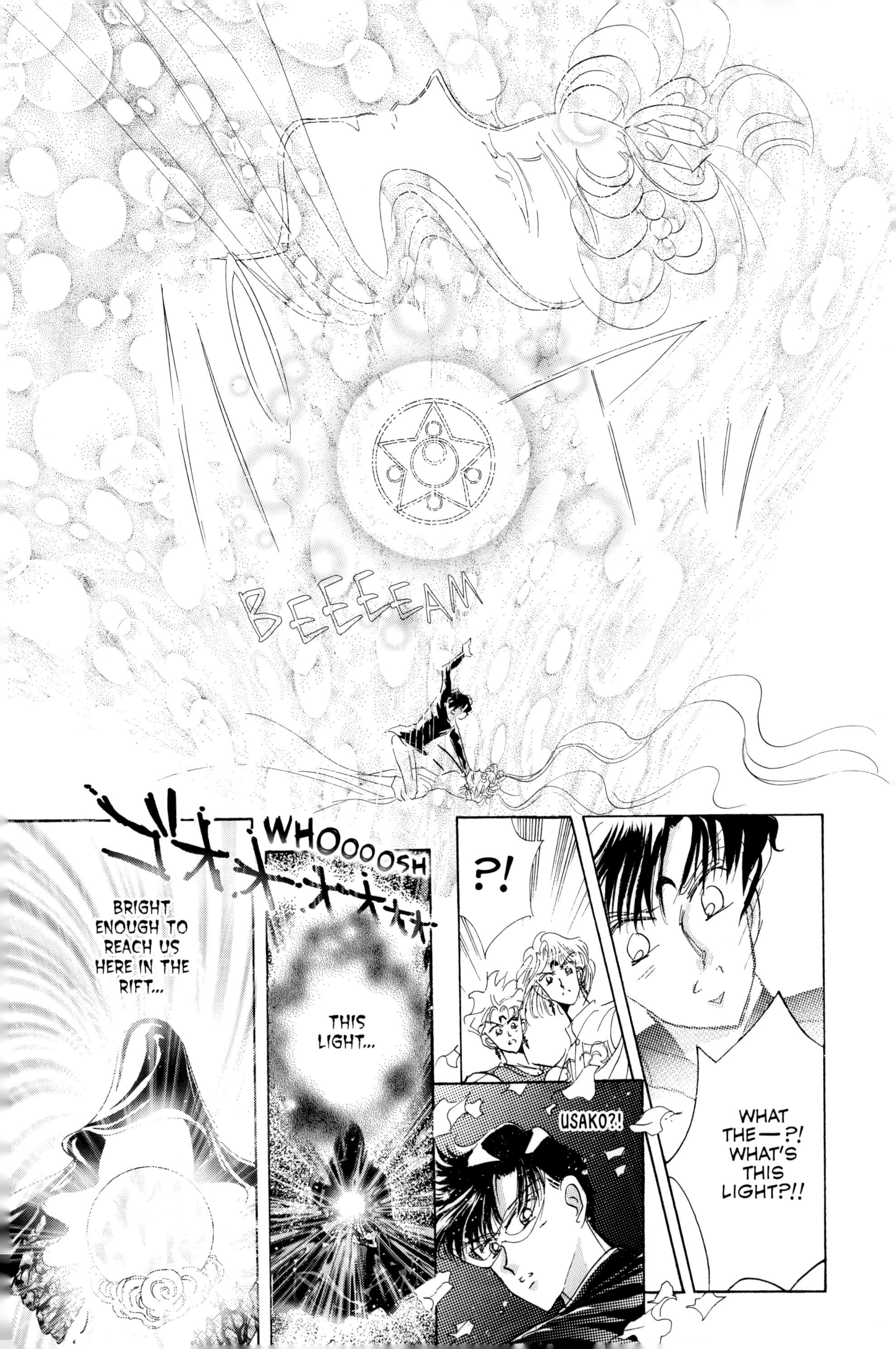

BEEEEAM
WHAT THE—?! WHAT'S THIS LIGHT?!!
?!
USAKO?!
WHOOOOSH
THIS LIGHT...
BRIGHT ENOUGH TO REACH US HERE IN THE RIFT...

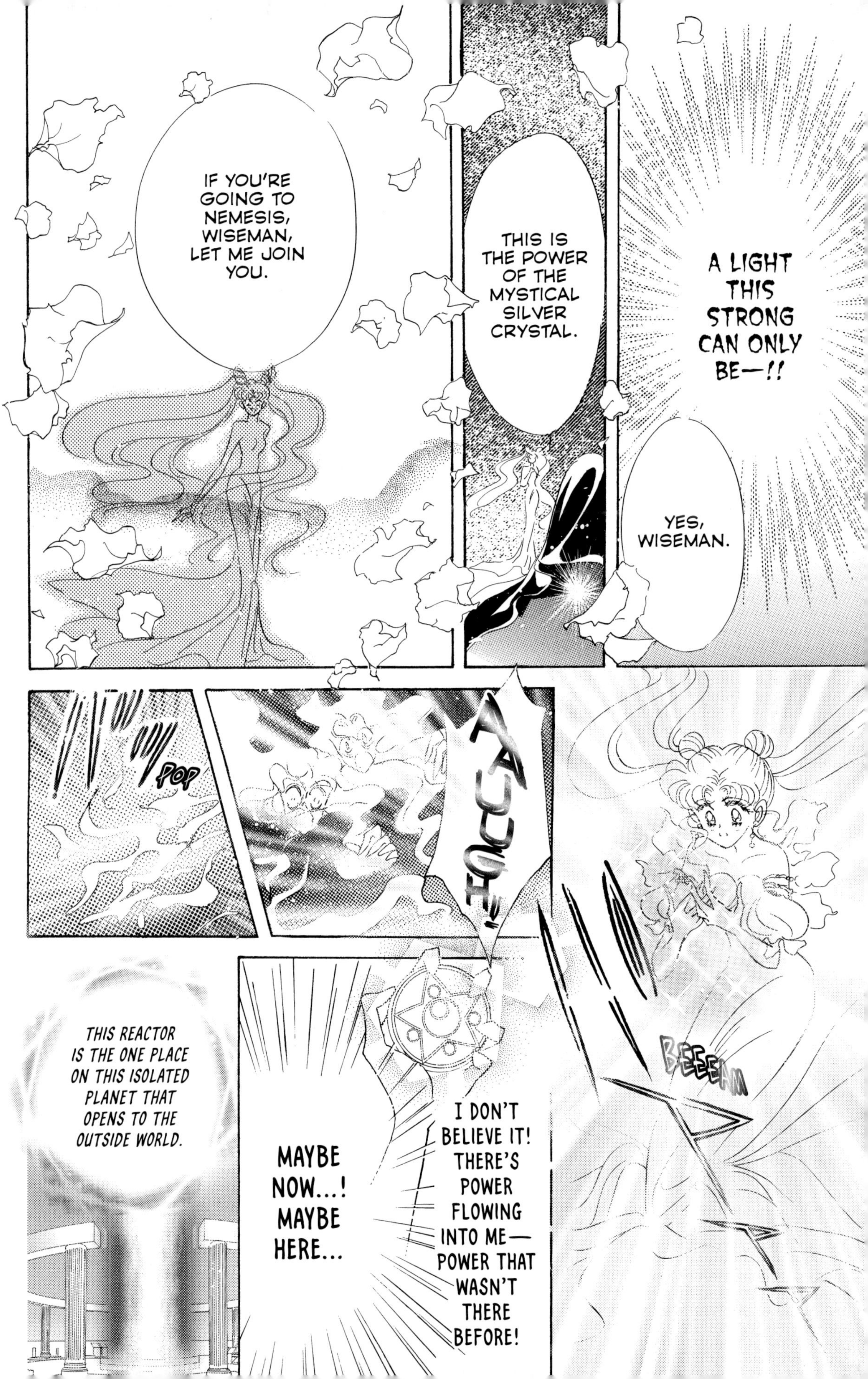
A LIGHT THIS STRONG CAN ONLY BE—!!
YES, WISEMAN.
THIS IS THE POWER OF THE MYSTICAL SILVER CRYSTAL.
IF YOU'RE GOING TO NEMESIS, WISEMAN, LET ME JOIN YOU.
BEEEAM
AAUGH!!
POP
I DON'T BELIEVE IT! THERE'S POWER FLOWING INTO ME— POWER THAT WASN'T THERE BEFORE!
MAYBE NOW...! MAYBE HERE...
THIS REACTOR IS THE ONE PLACE ON THIS ISOLATED PLANET THAT OPENS TO THE OUTSIDE WORLD.

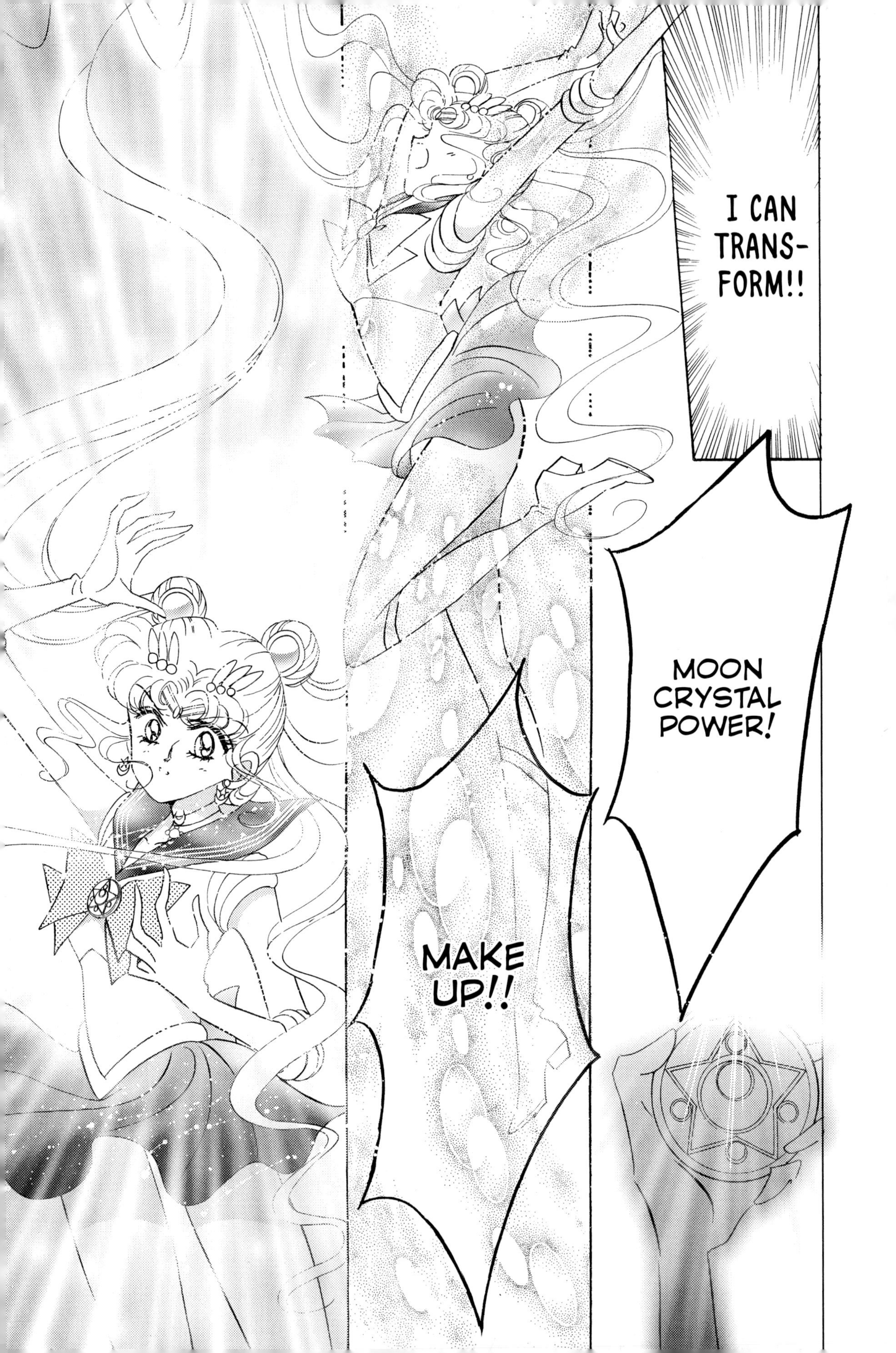
I CAN TRANS-FORM!!
MOON CRYSTAL POWER!
MAKE UP!!

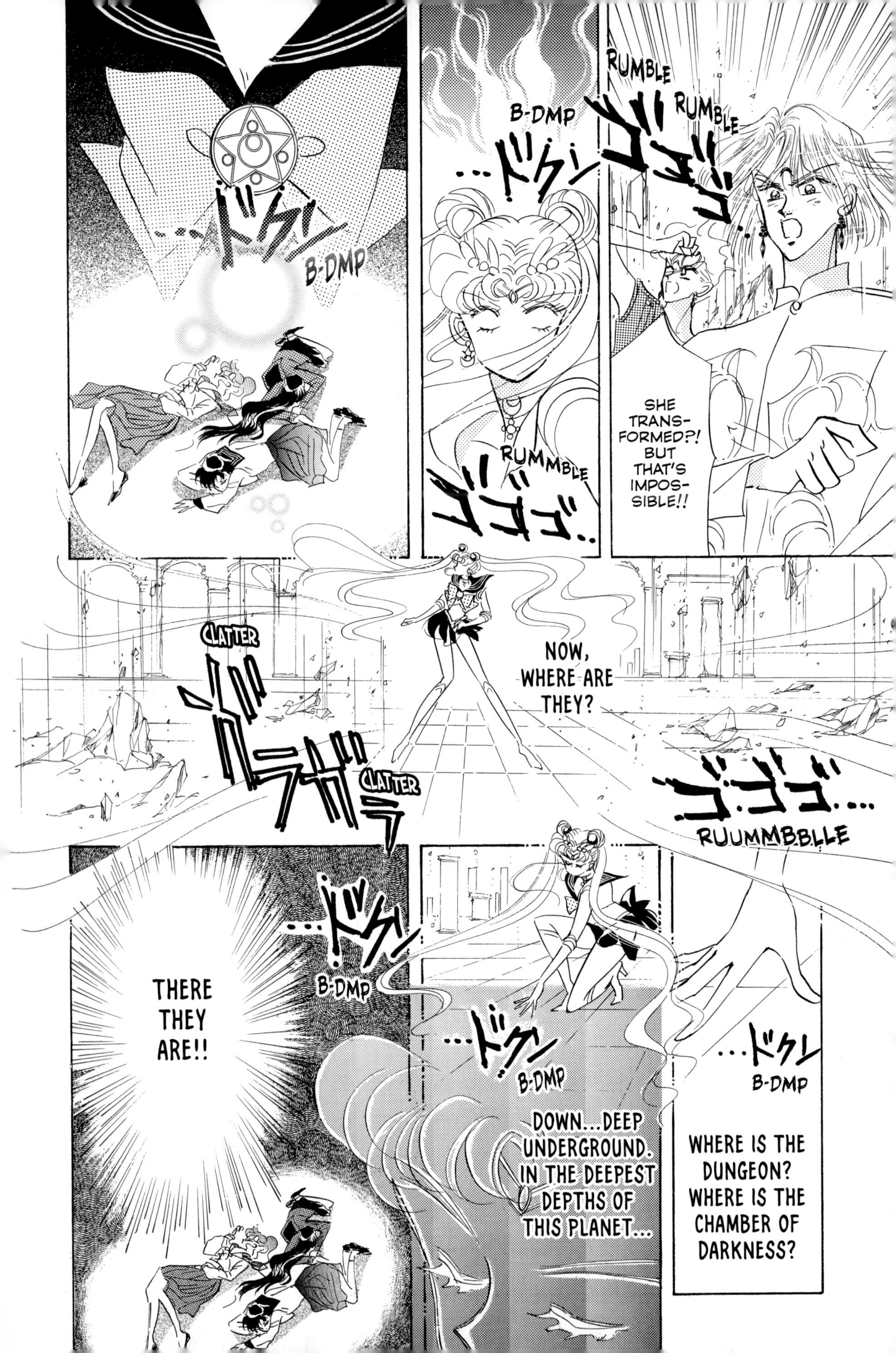
RUMBLE
RUMBLE
ゴゴゴ
SHE TRANSFORMED?! BUT THAT'S IMPOSSIBLE!!
B-DMP
...ドクン
RUMMBLE
ゴゴゴ...
...ドクン
B-DMP
NOW, WHERE ARE THEY?
ゴゴゴ....
RUUMMBBLLE
CLATTER
ガラガラ
CLATTER
...ドクン
B-DMP
WHERE IS THE DUNGEON? WHERE IS THE CHAMBER OF DARKNESS?
...ドクン
B-DMP
DOWN...DEEP UNDERGROUND. IN THE DEEPEST DEPTHS OF THIS PLANET...
...ドクン
B-DMP
THERE THEY ARE!!

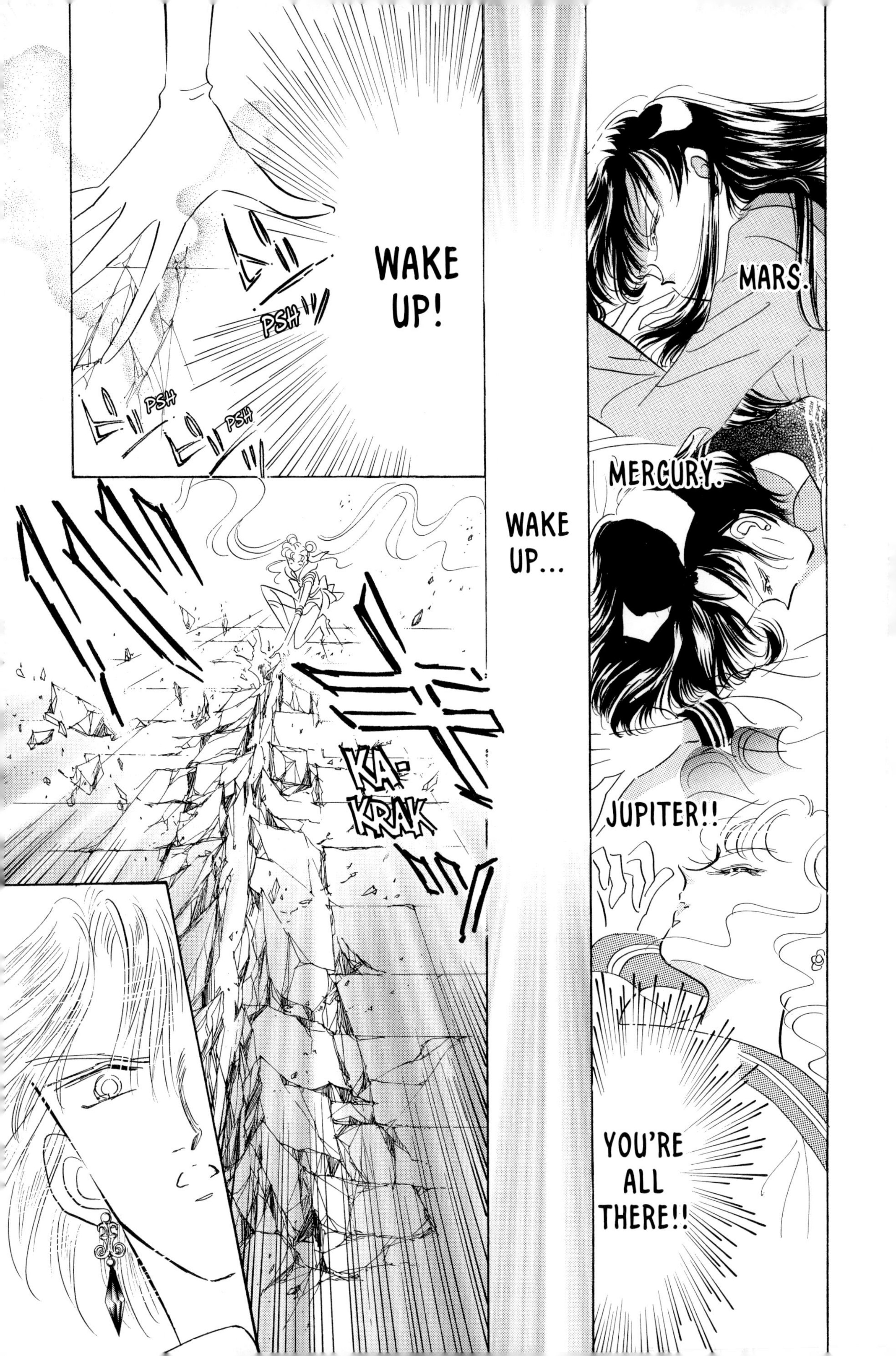
MARS.
MERCURY.
JUPITER!!
YOU'RE ALL THERE!!
WAKE UP...
WAKE UP!
PSH
PSH
PSH
KA-KRAK

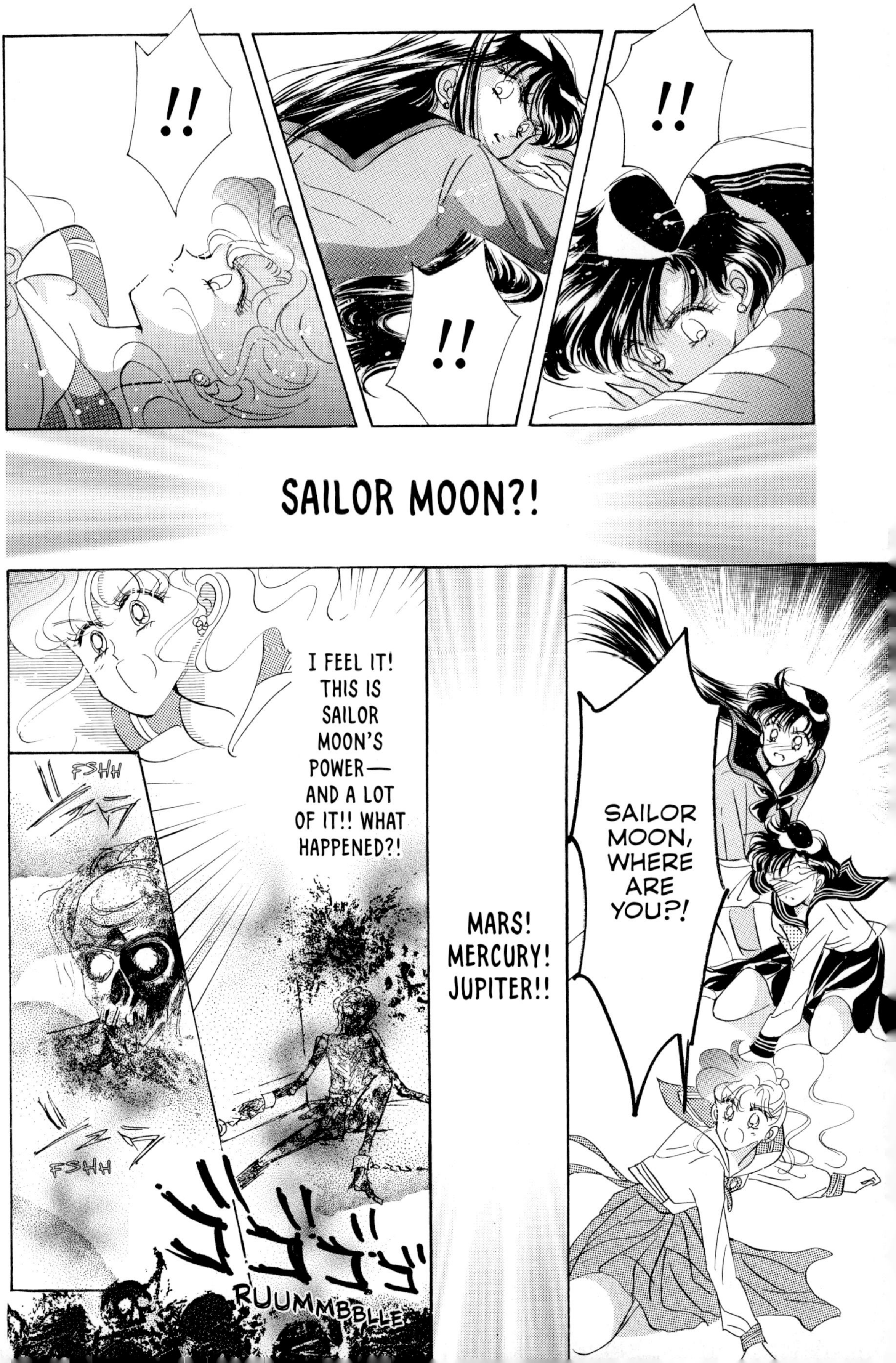
!!
!!
!!
SAILOR MOON?!
SAILOR MOON, WHERE ARE YOU?!
MARS! MERCURY! JUPITER!!
I FEEL IT! THIS IS SAILOR MOON'S POWER—AND A LOT OF IT!! WHAT HAPPENED?!
FSHH
FSHH
RUUMMBBLLE

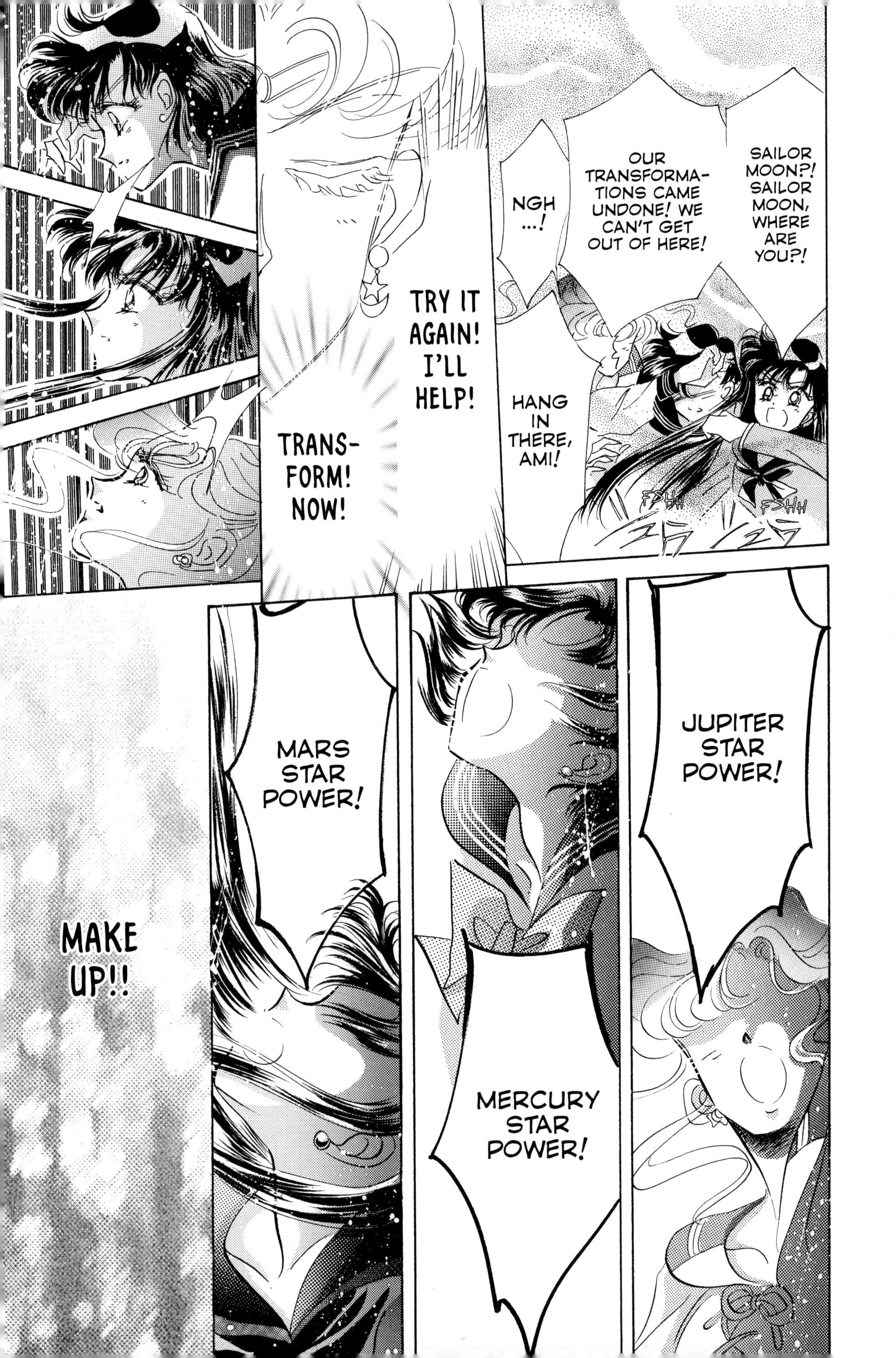
SAILOR MOON?! SAILOR MOON, WHERE ARE YOU?!
OUR TRANSFORMATIONS CAME UNDONE! WE CAN'T GET OUT OF HERE!
NGH ...!
HANG IN THERE, AMI!
FSHH
FSHH
TRY IT AGAIN! I'LL HELP!
TRANS-FORM! NOW!
JUPITER STAR POWER!
MERCURY STAR POWER!
MARS STAR POWER!
MAKE UP!!

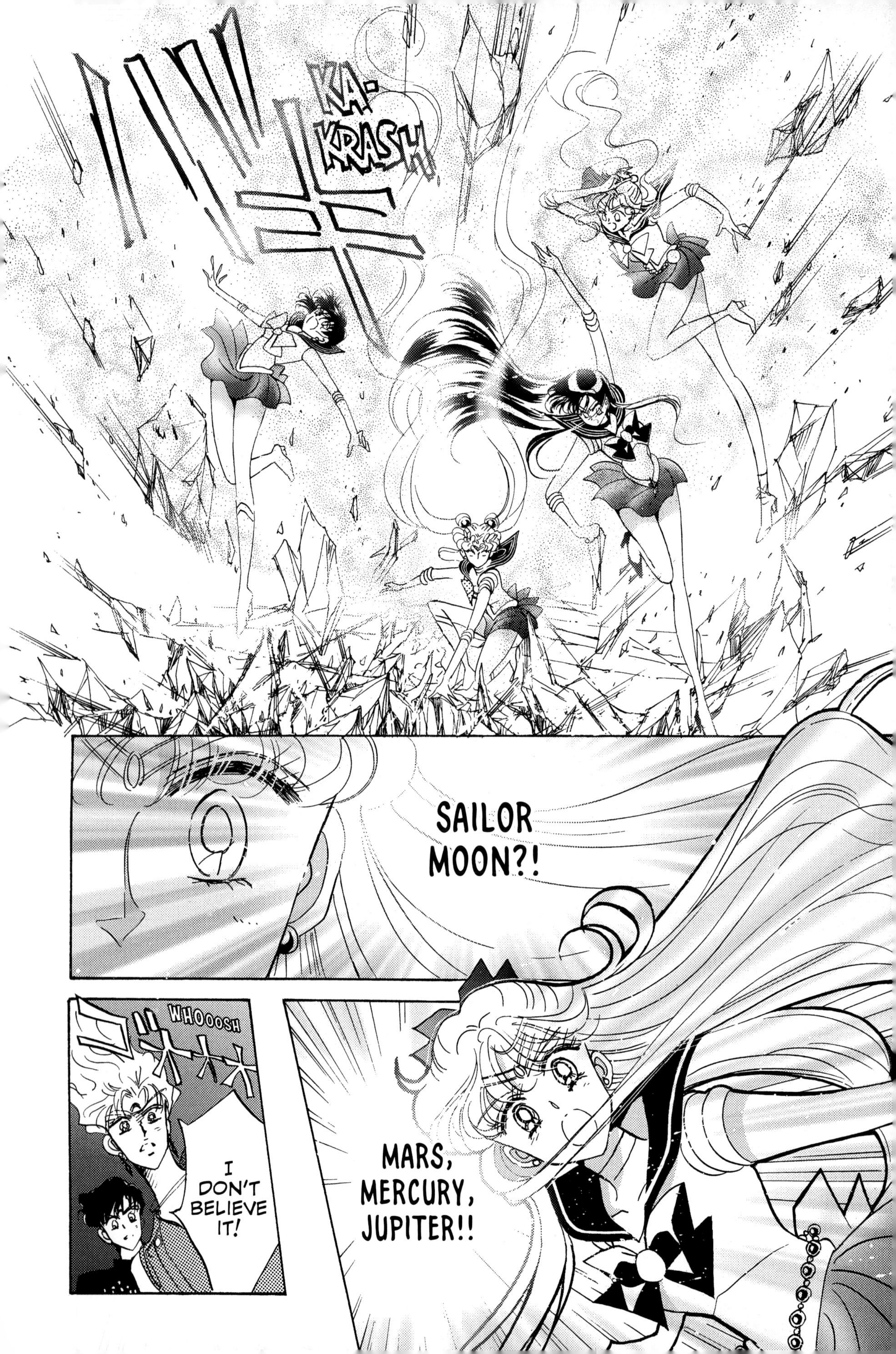
KA-KRASH
SAILOR MOON?!
MARS, MERCURY, JUPITER!!
WHOOOSH
I DON'T BELIEVE IT!

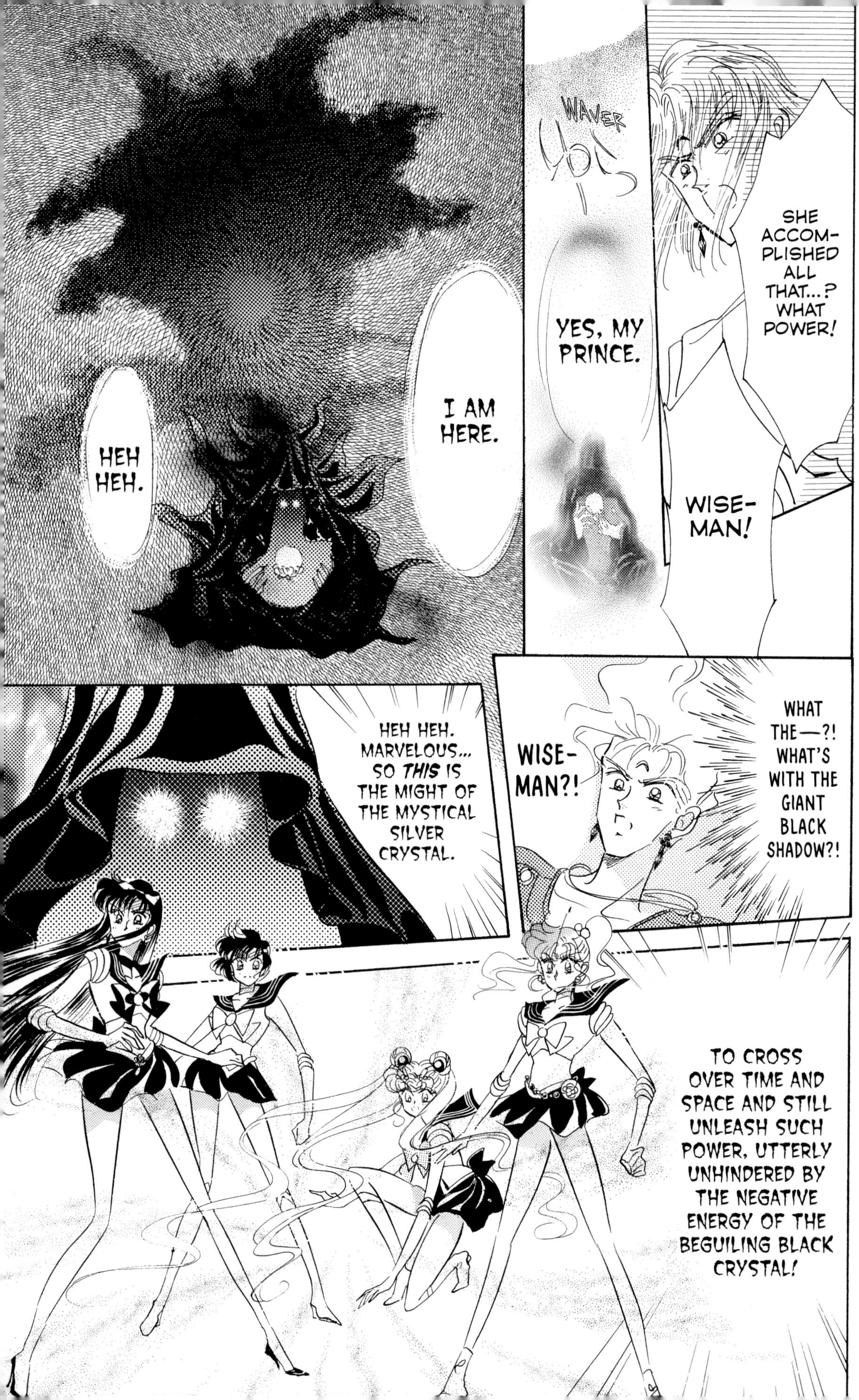
SHE ACCOMPLISHED ALL THAT...? WHAT POWER!
WISE-MAN!
WAVER
YES, MY PRINCE.
I AM HERE.
HEH HEH.
WHAT THE—?! WHAT'S WITH THE GIANT BLACK SHADOW?!
WISE-MAN?!
HEH HEH. MARVELOUS... SO *THIS* IS THE MIGHT OF THE MYSTICAL SILVER CRYSTAL.
TO CROSS OVER TIME AND SPACE AND STILL UNLEASH SUCH POWER, UTTERLY UNHINDERED BY THE NEGATIVE ENERGY OF THE BEGUILING BLACK CRYSTAL!

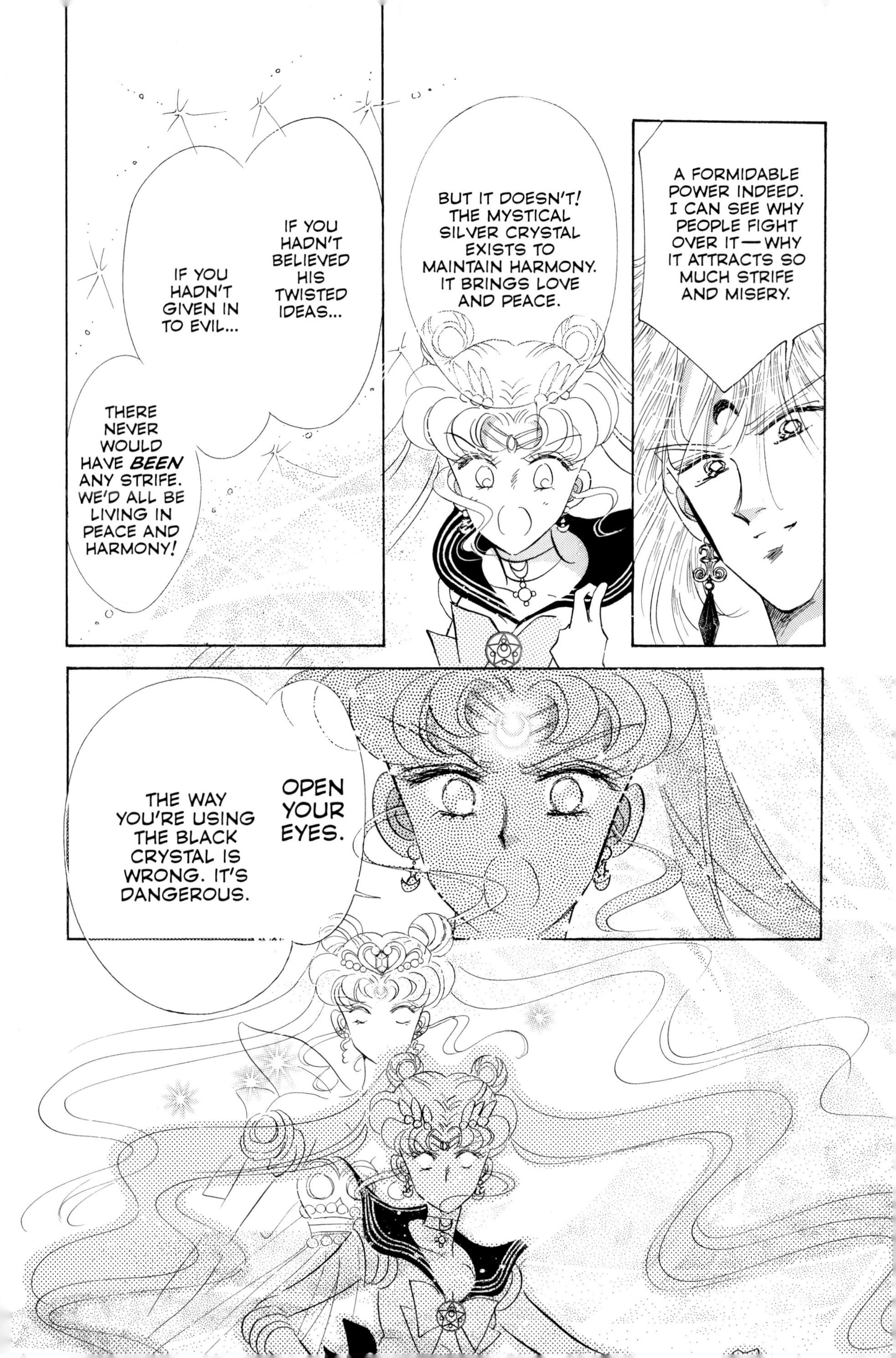
A FORMIDABLE POWER INDEED. I CAN SEE WHY PEOPLE FIGHT OVER IT—WHY IT ATTRACTS SO MUCH STRIFE AND MISERY.
BUT IT DOESN'T! THE MYSTICAL SILVER CRYSTAL EXISTS TO MAINTAIN HARMONY. IT BRINGS LOVE AND PEACE.
IF YOU HADN'T BELIEVED HIS TWISTED IDEAS...
IF YOU HADN'T GIVEN IN TO EVIL...
THERE NEVER WOULD HAVE *BEEN* ANY STRIFE. WE'D ALL BE LIVING IN PEACE AND HARMONY!
OPEN YOUR EYES.
THE WAY YOU'RE USING THE BLACK CRYSTAL IS WRONG. IT'S DANGEROUS.

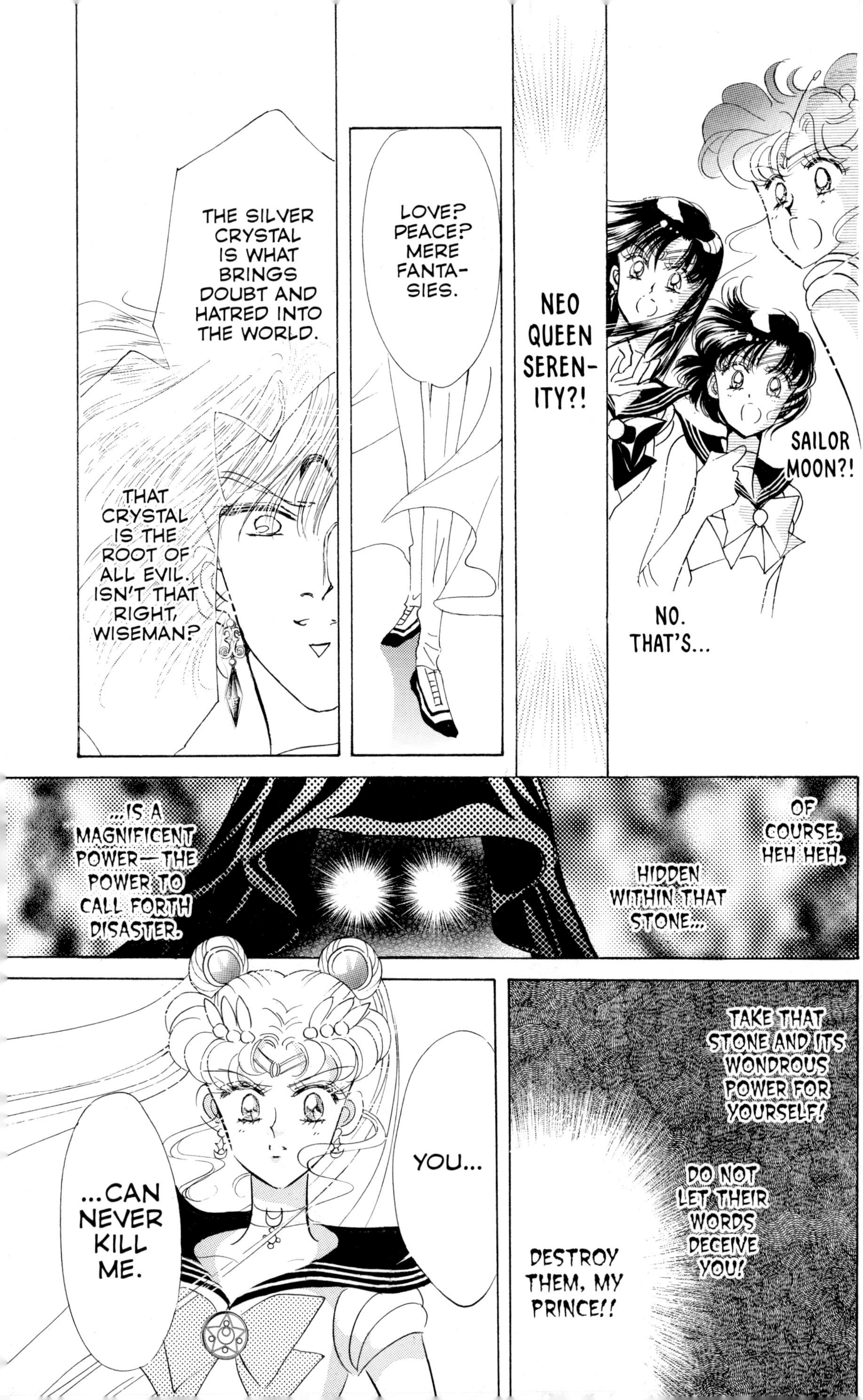
SAILOR MOON?!
NO. THAT'S...
NEO QUEEN SEREN-ITY?!
LOVE? PEACE? MERE FANTA-SIES.
THE SILVER CRYSTAL IS WHAT BRINGS DOUBT AND HATRED INTO THE WORLD.
THAT CRYSTAL IS THE ROOT OF ALL EVIL. ISN'T THAT RIGHT, WISEMAN?
OF COURSE. HEH HEH.
HIDDEN WITHIN THAT STONE...
...IS A MAGNIFICENT POWER—THE POWER TO CALL FORTH DISASTER.
TAKE THAT STONE AND ITS WONDROUS POWER FOR YOURSELF!
DO NOT LET THEIR WORDS DECEIVE YOU!
DESTROY THEM, MY PRINCE!!
YOU...
...CAN NEVER KILL ME.

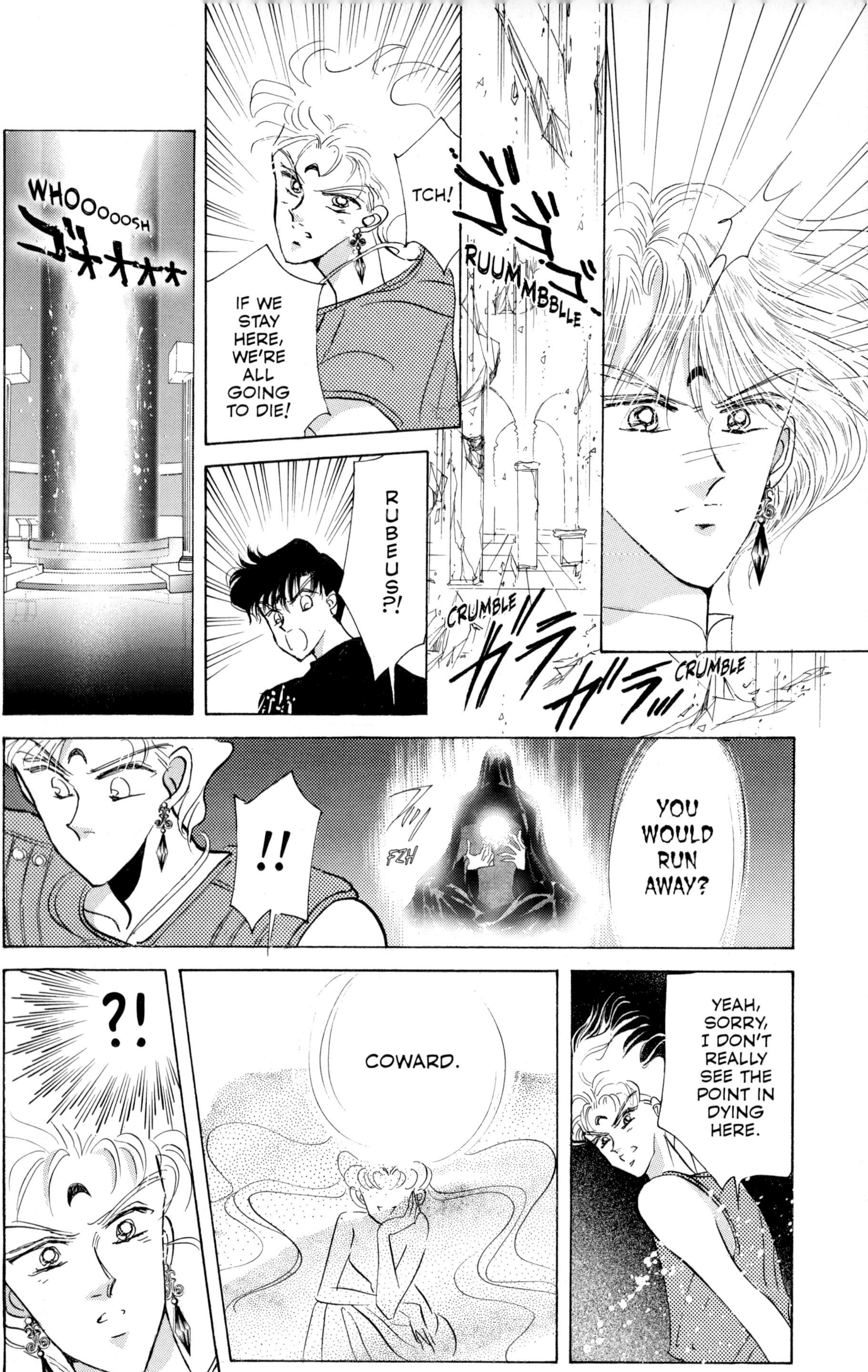
RUUMMBBLLE
CRUMBLE
CRUMBLE
TCH!
IF WE STAY HERE, WE'RE ALL GOING TO DIE!
RUBEUS?!
WHOOOOOSH
YOU WOULD RUN AWAY?
FZH
!!
YEAH, SORRY, I DON'T REALLY SEE THE POINT IN DYING HERE.
COWARD.
?!

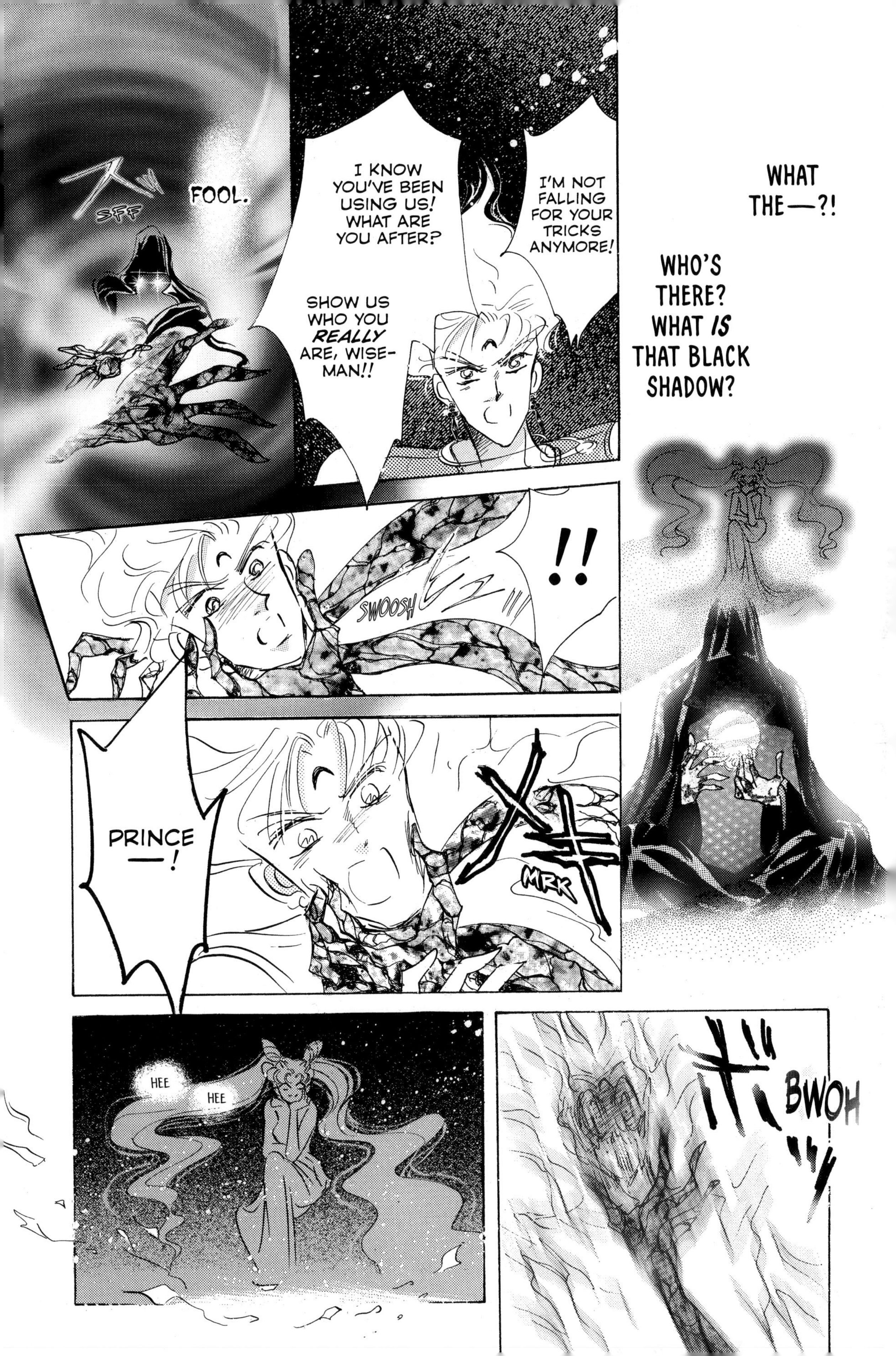

WHAT THE—?!
WHO'S THERE? WHAT *IS* THAT BLACK SHADOW?
I'M NOT FALLING FOR YOUR TRICKS ANYMORE!
I KNOW YOU'VE BEEN USING US! WHAT ARE YOU AFTER?
SHOW US WHO YOU *REALLY* ARE, WISE-MAN!!
FOOL.
SFF
!!
SWOOSH
MRK
PRINCE—!
BWOH
HEE
HEE

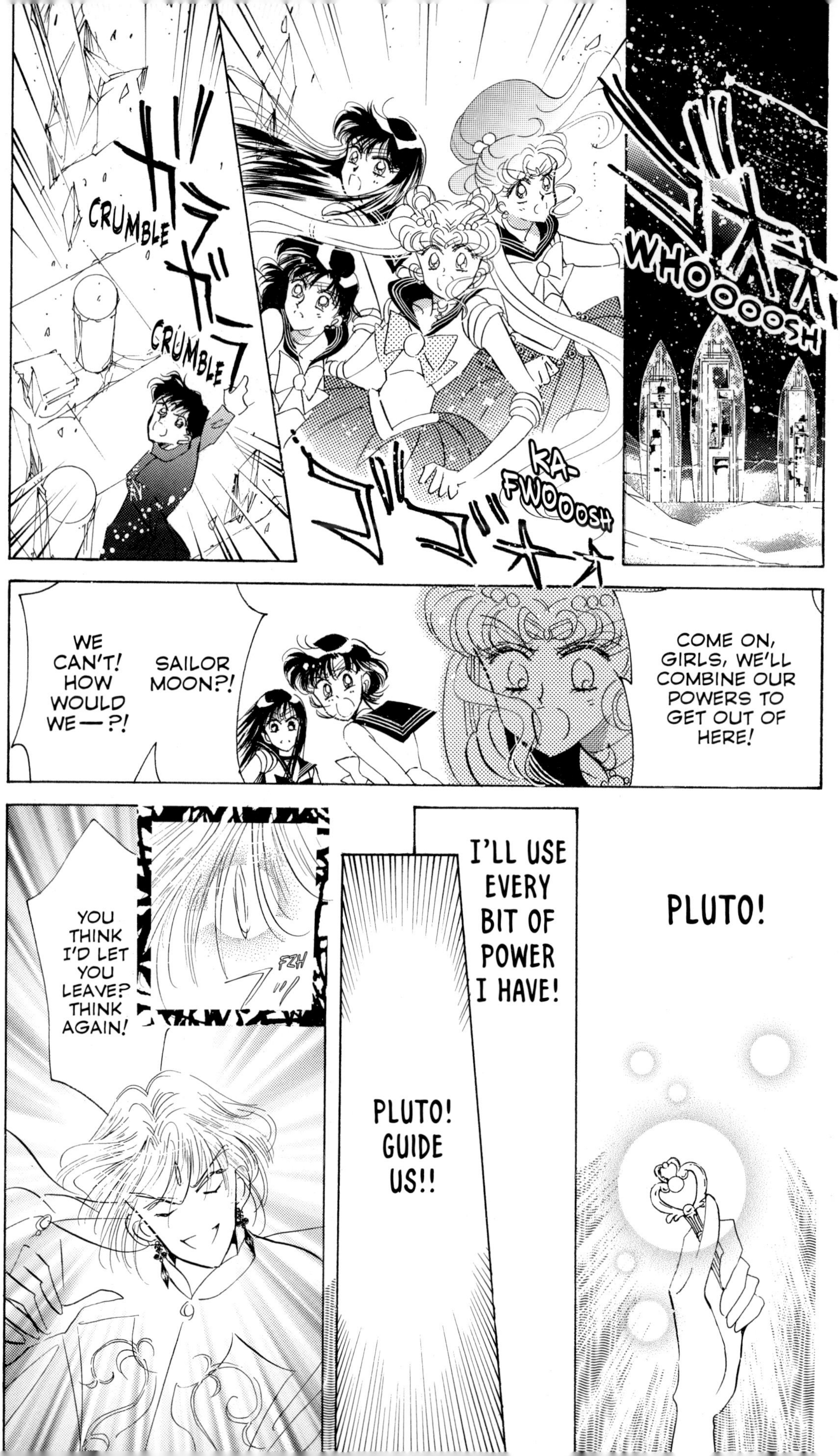
WHOOOOOSH
KA-FWOOOOSH
CRUMBLE
CRUMBLE
COME ON, GIRLS, WE'LL COMBINE OUR POWERS TO GET OUT OF HERE!
SAILOR MOON?!
WE CAN'T! HOW WOULD WE—?!
PLUTO!
I'LL USE EVERY BIT OF POWER I HAVE!
PLUTO! GUIDE US!!
FZH
YOU THINK I'D LET YOU LEAVE? THINK AGAIN!

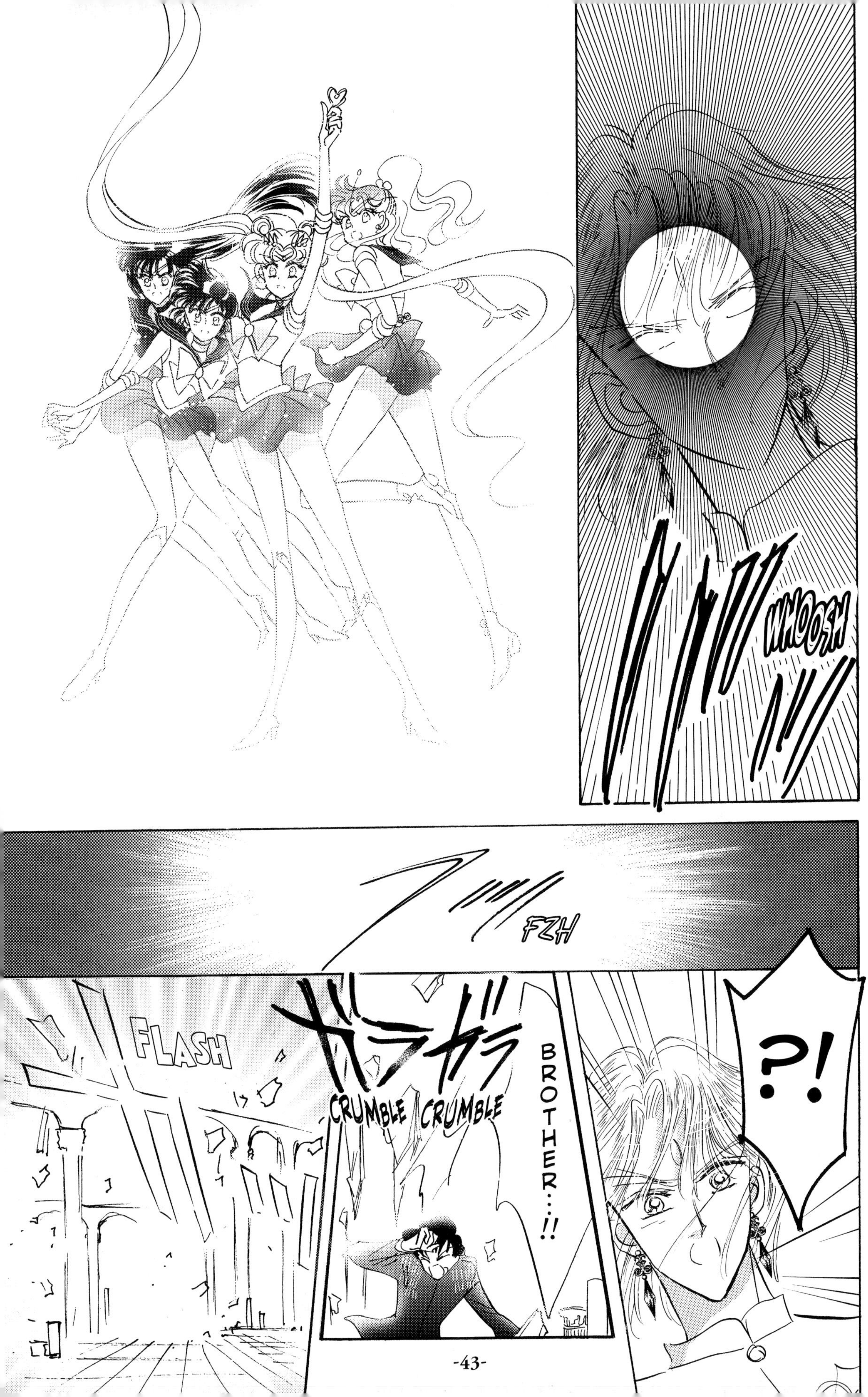

WHOOSH
FZH
?!
ガラガラ
CRUMBLE CRUMBLE
BROTHER…!!
FLASH

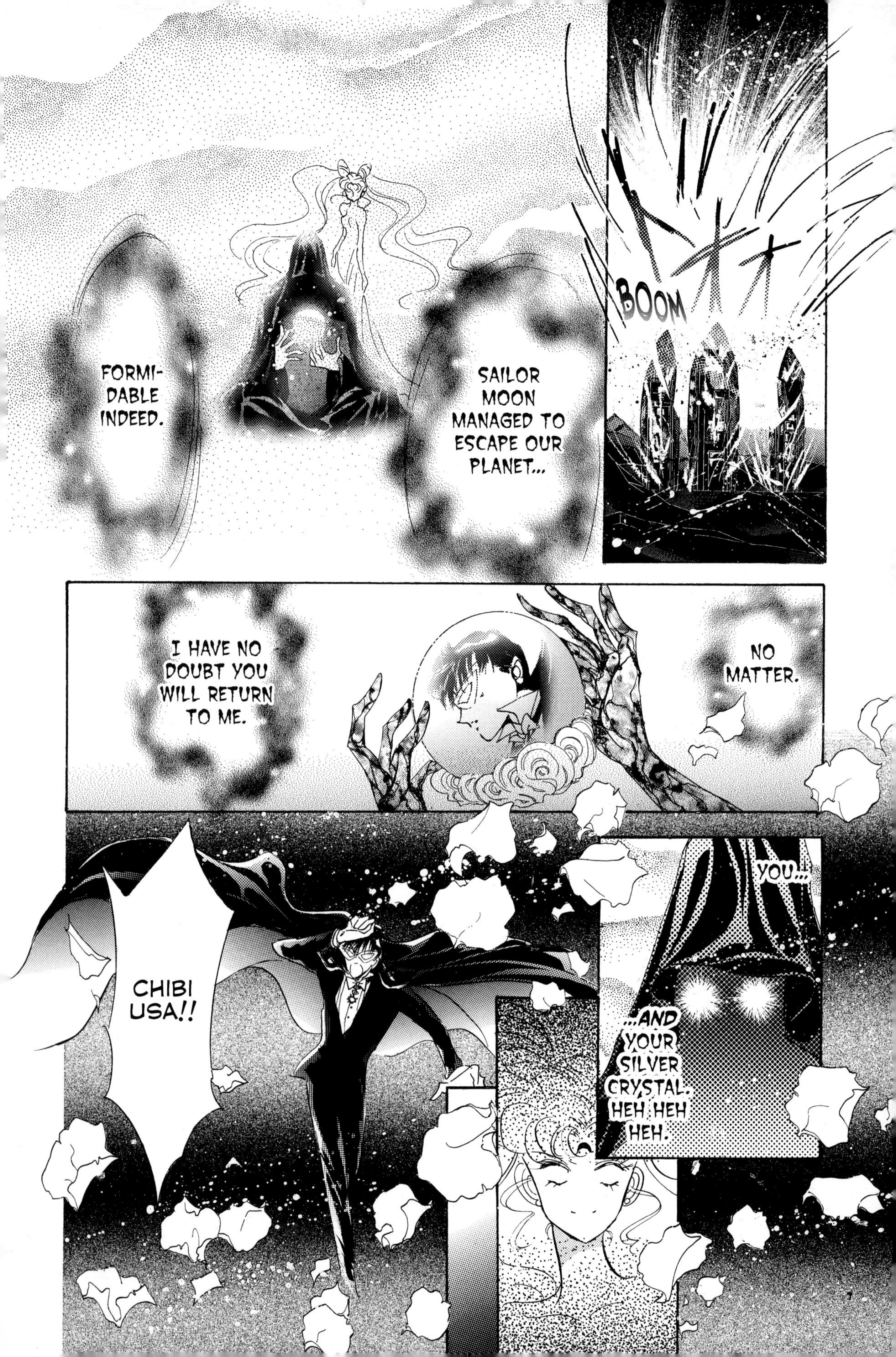
BOOM
SAILOR MOON MANAGED TO ESCAPE OUR PLANET...
FORMI-DABLE INDEED.
NO MATTER.
I HAVE NO DOUBT YOU WILL RETURN TO ME.
YOU...
...AND YOUR SILVER CRYSTAL. HEH HEH HEH.
CHIBI USA!!

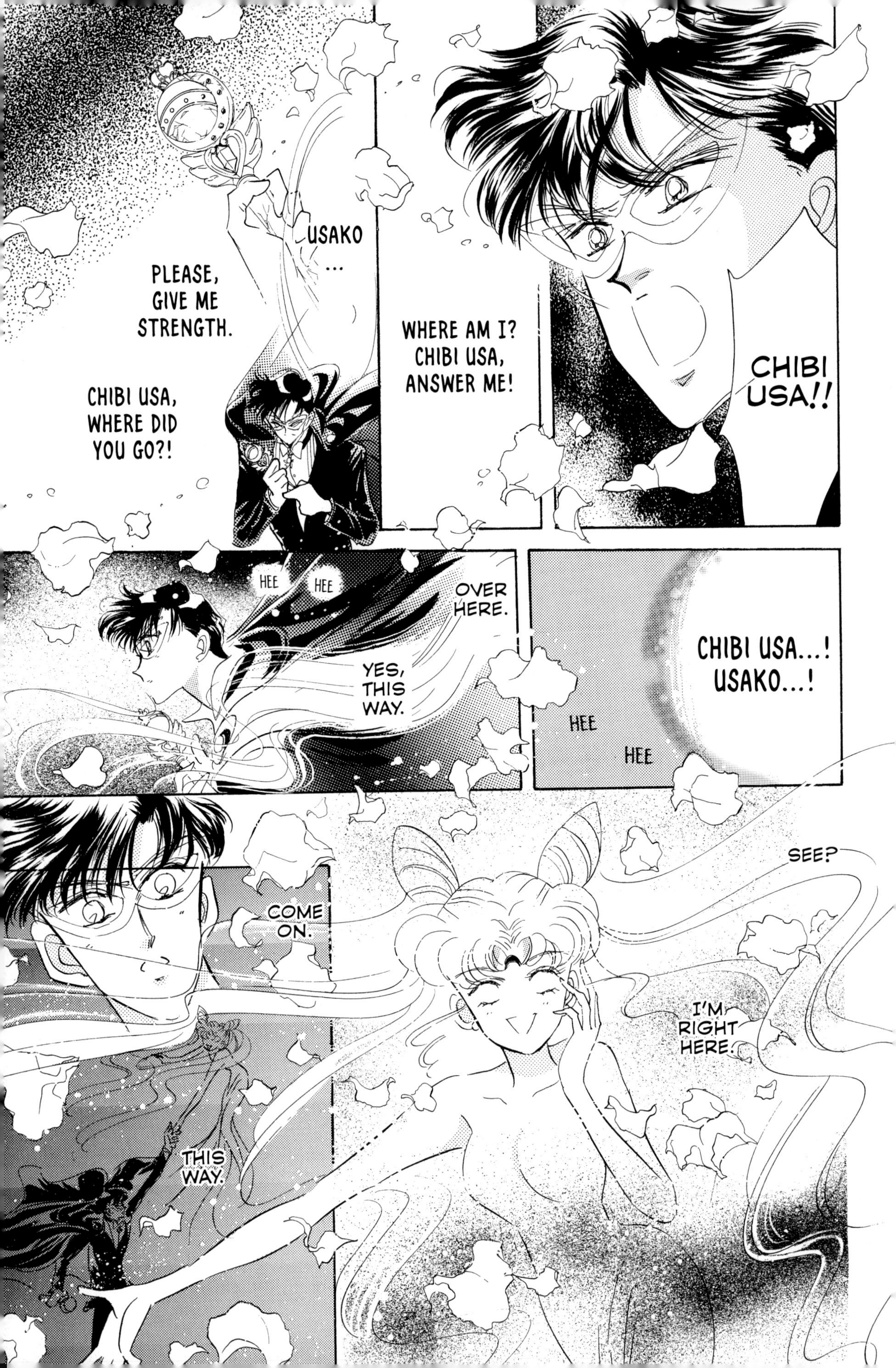
CHIBI USA!!
WHERE AM I? CHIBI USA, ANSWER ME!
USAKO ...
PLEASE, GIVE ME STRENGTH.
CHIBI USA, WHERE DID YOU GO?!
CHIBI USA...! USAKO...!
HEE
HEE
OVER HERE.
HEE
HEE
YES, THIS WAY.
SEE?
I'M RIGHT HERE.
COME ON.
THIS WAY.

WHOOOOOSH

HEE
HEE

GLOW

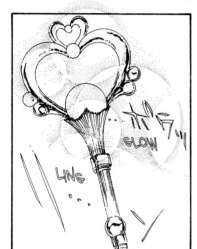

GLOW

LING

SAILOR
MOON!!

BWAH

PLUTO!

LING

LING

GASP

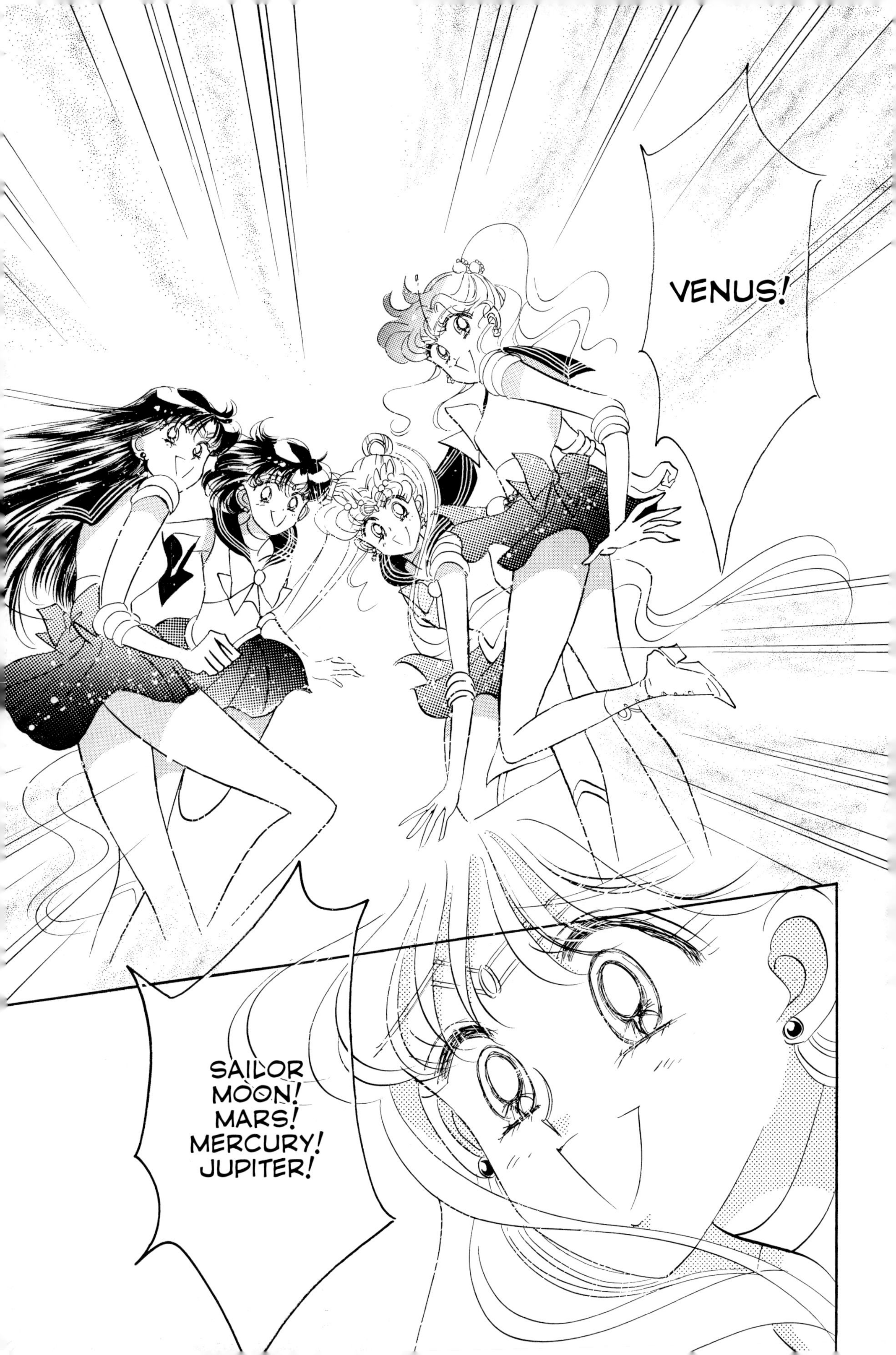
VENUS!
SAILOR MOON! MARS! MERCURY! JUPITER!

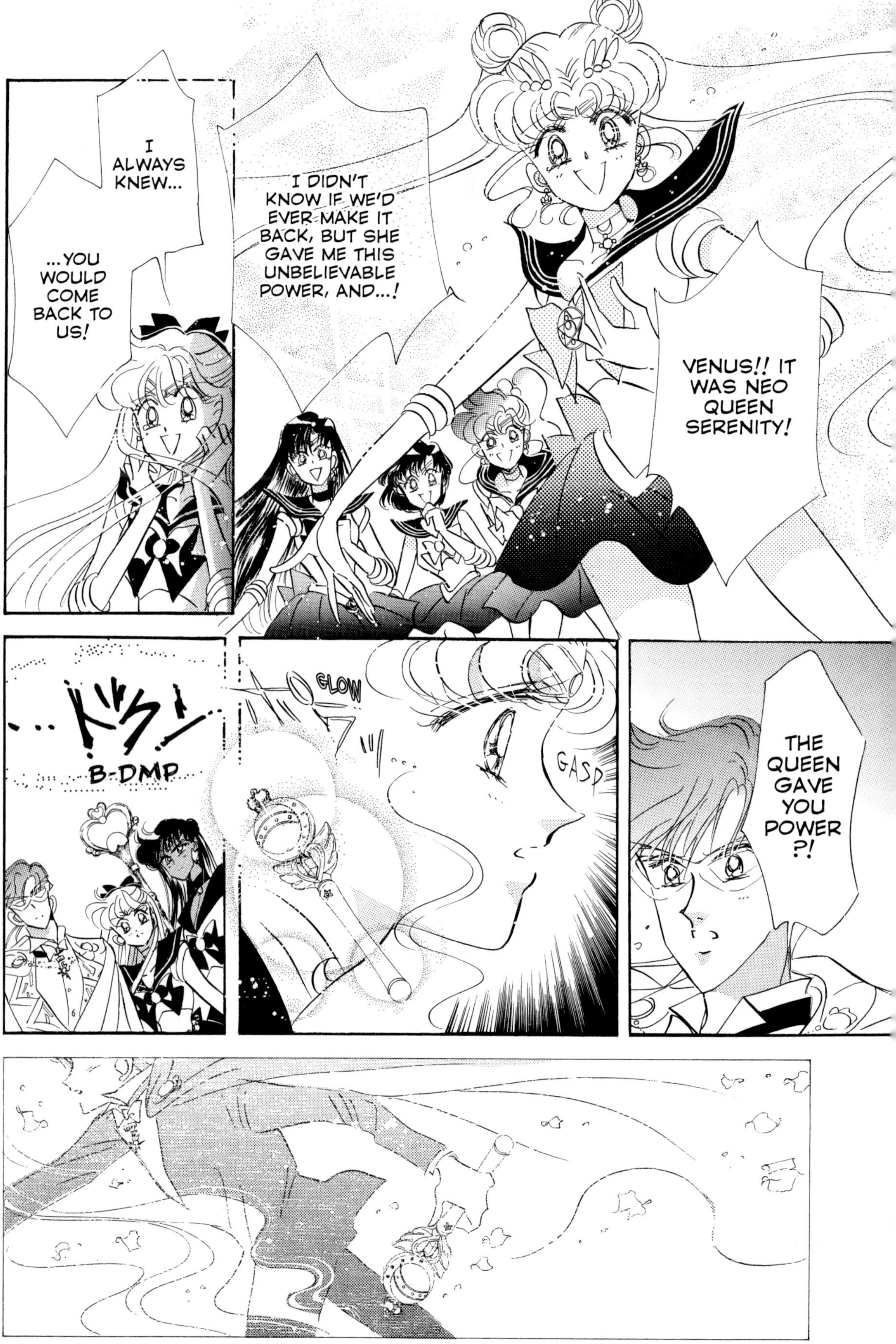
VENUS!! IT WAS NEO QUEEN SERENITY!
I DIDN'T KNOW IF WE'D EVER MAKE IT BACK, BUT SHE GAVE ME THIS UNBELIEVABLE POWER, AND...!
I ALWAYS KNEW...
...YOU WOULD COME BACK TO US!
THE QUEEN GAVE YOU POWER ?!
GLOW
GASP
B-DMP

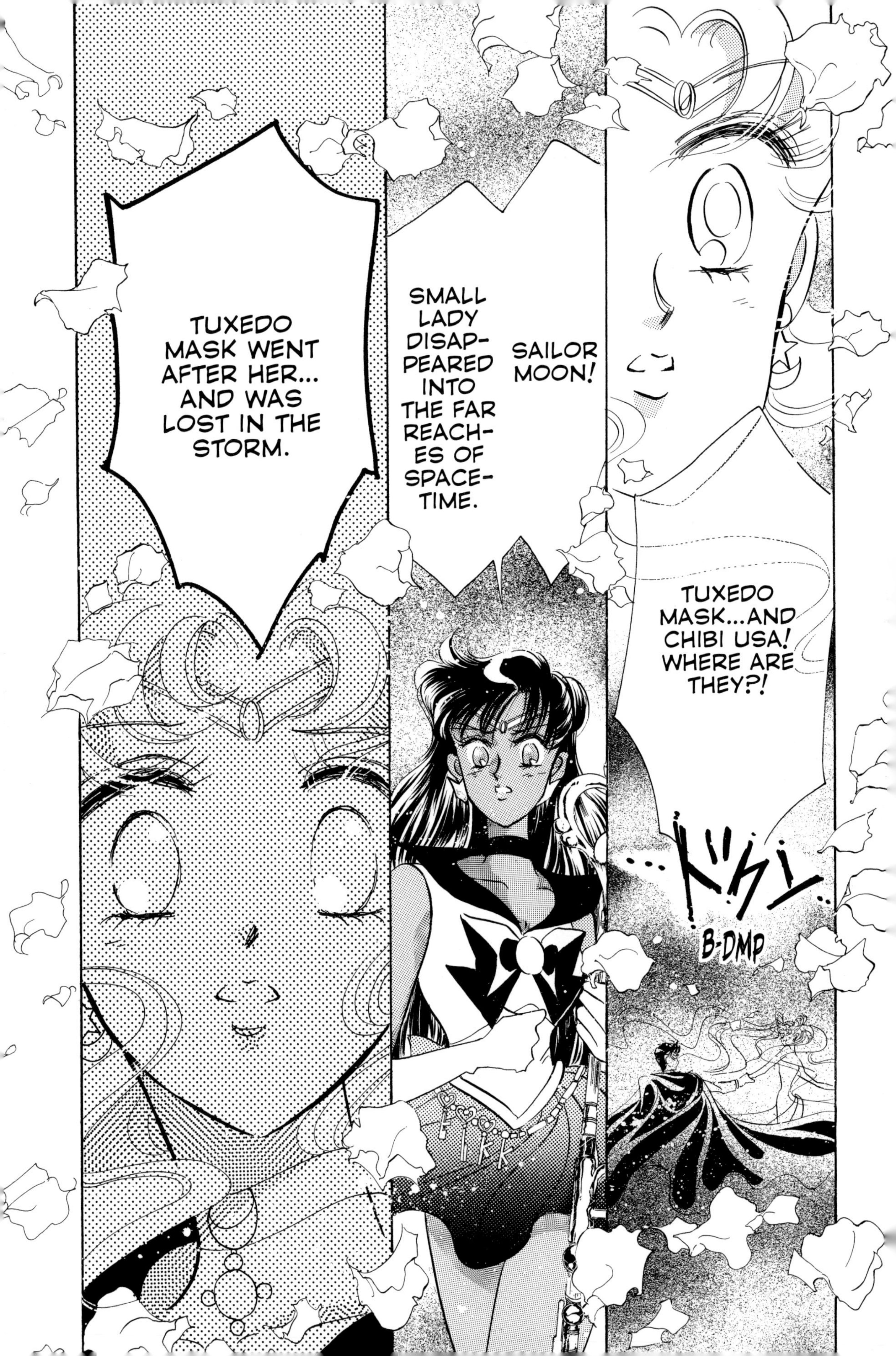
TUXEDO MASK...AND CHIBI USA! WHERE ARE THEY?!
B-DMP
SAILOR MOON!
SMALL LADY DISAPPEARED INTO THE FAR REACHES OF SPACE-TIME.
TUXEDO MASK WENT AFTER HER... AND WAS LOST IN THE STORM.

Pretty Guardian

Sailor Moon

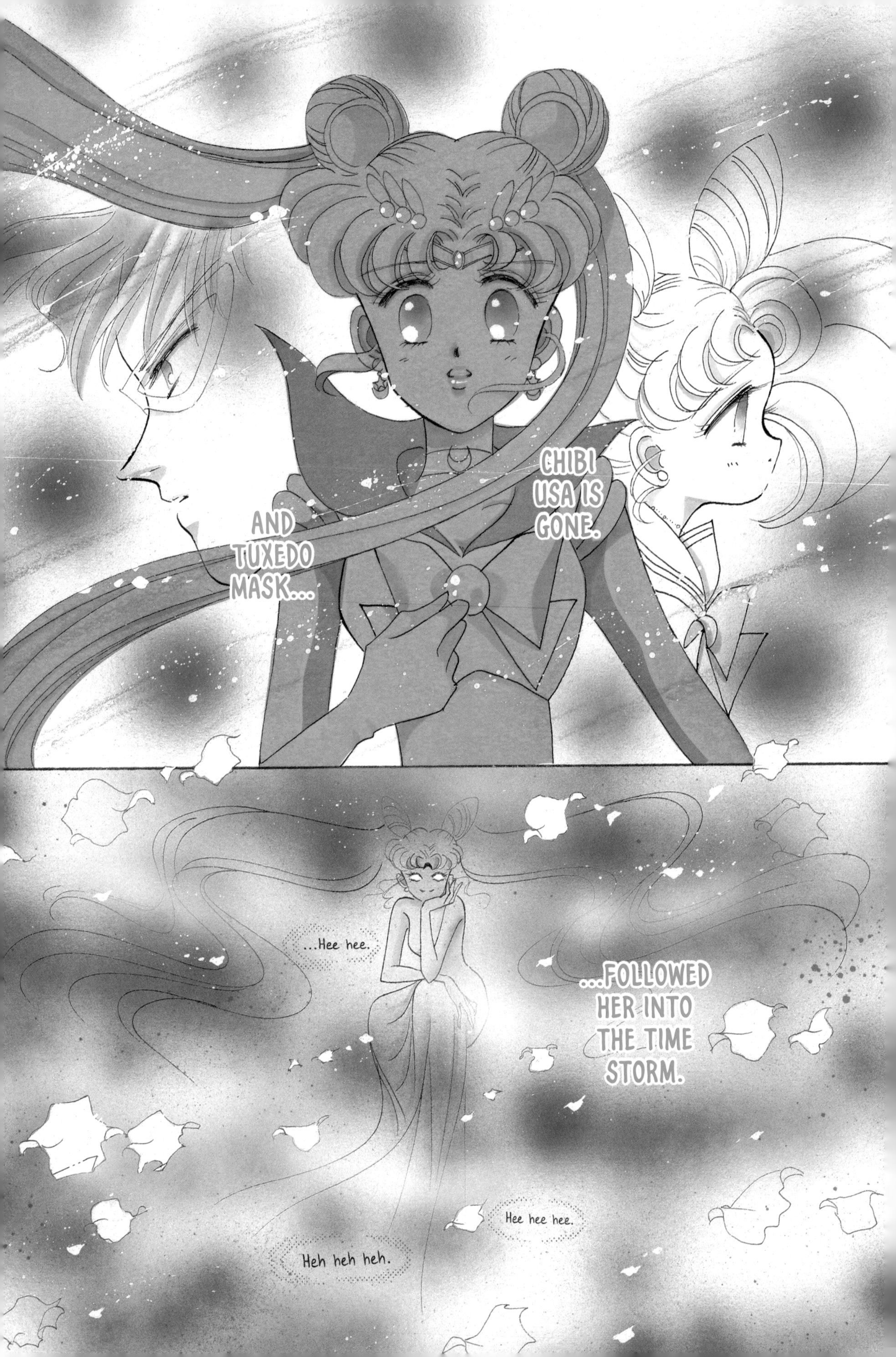
CHIBI USA IS GONE.
AND TUXEDO MASK...
...FOLLOWED HER INTO THE TIME STORM.
...Hee hee.
Hee hee hee.
Heh heh heh.

Act.23 Puppet Master: Wiseman

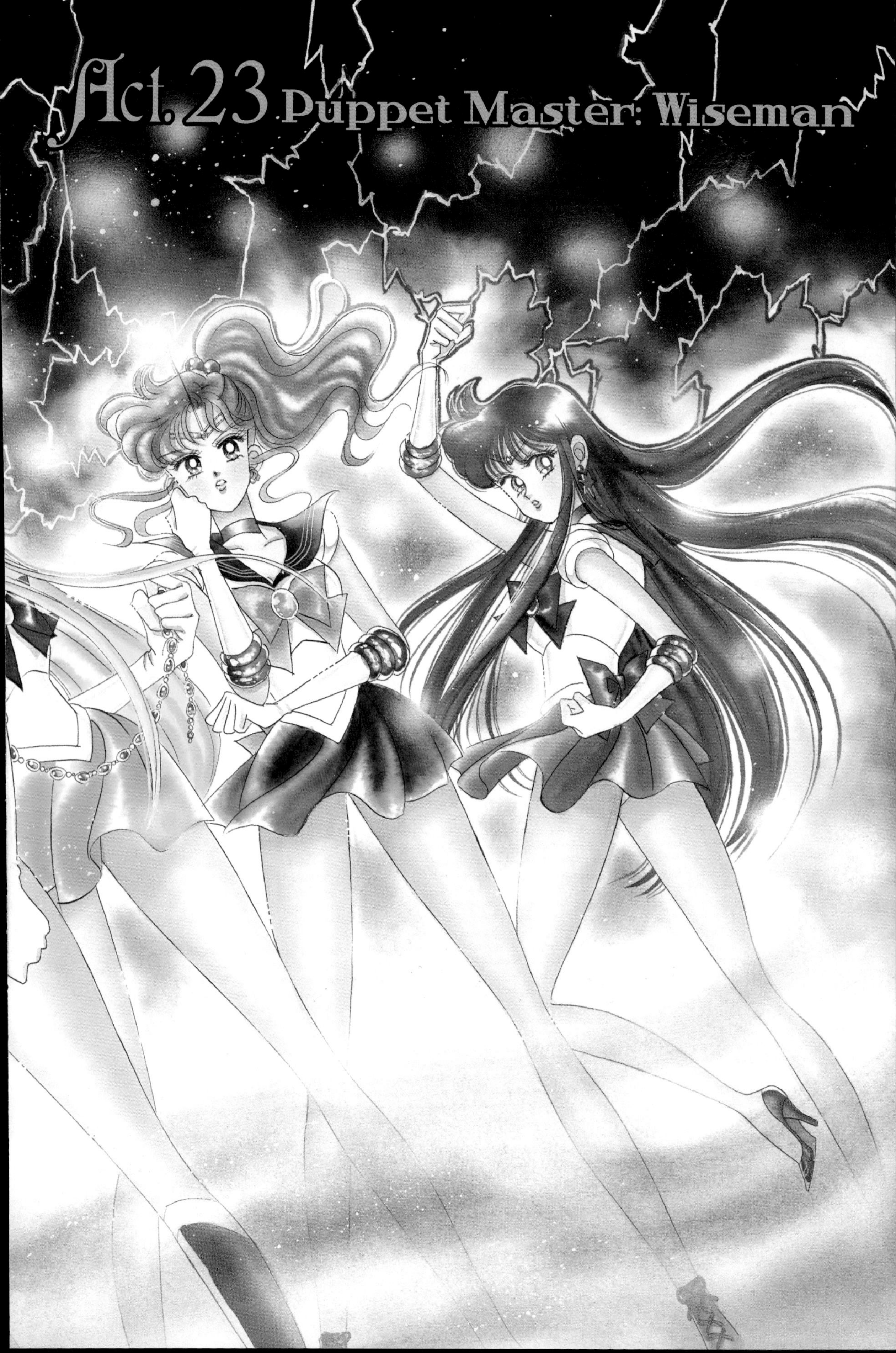

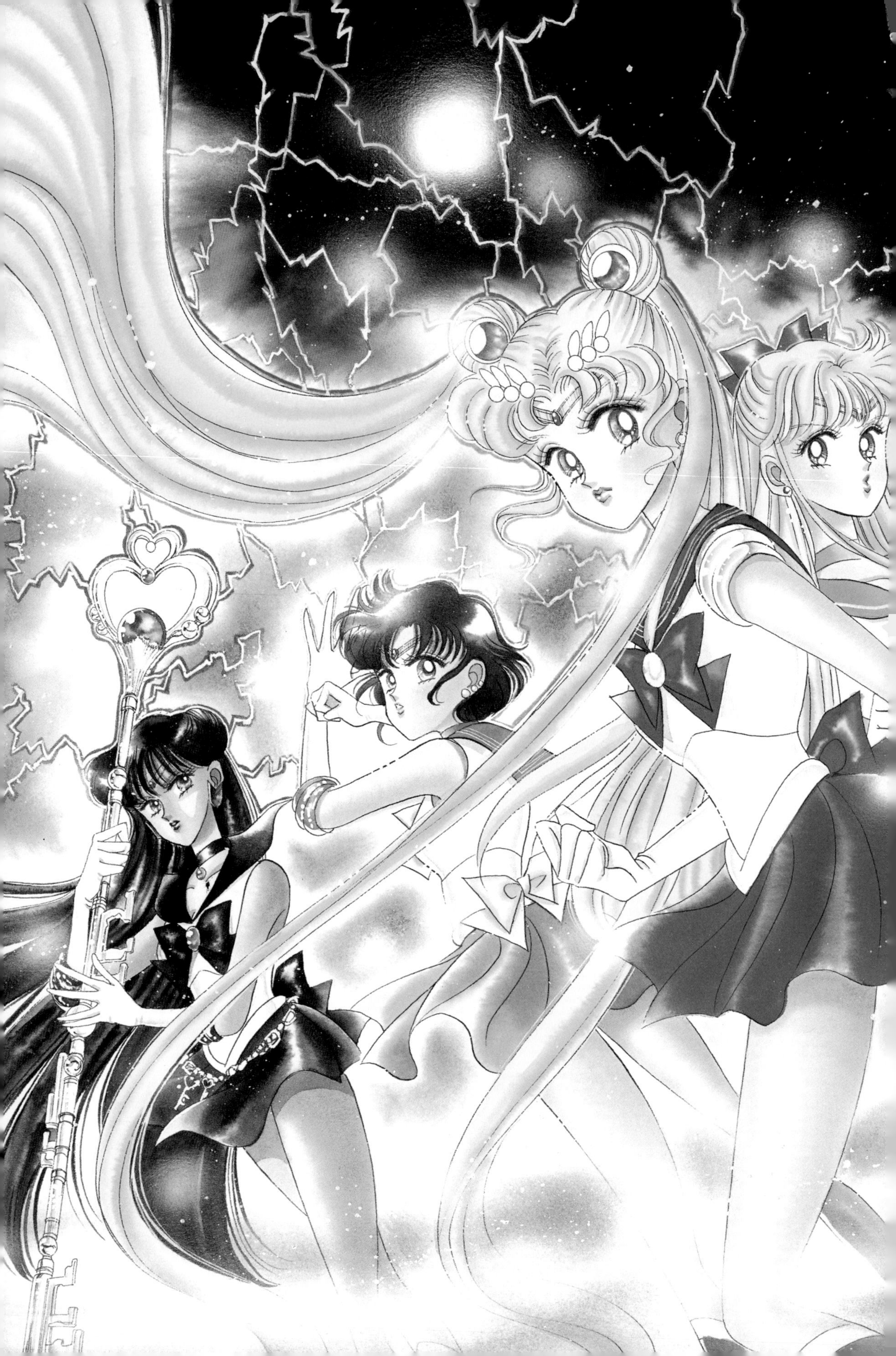

Pretty Guardian
Sailor Moon

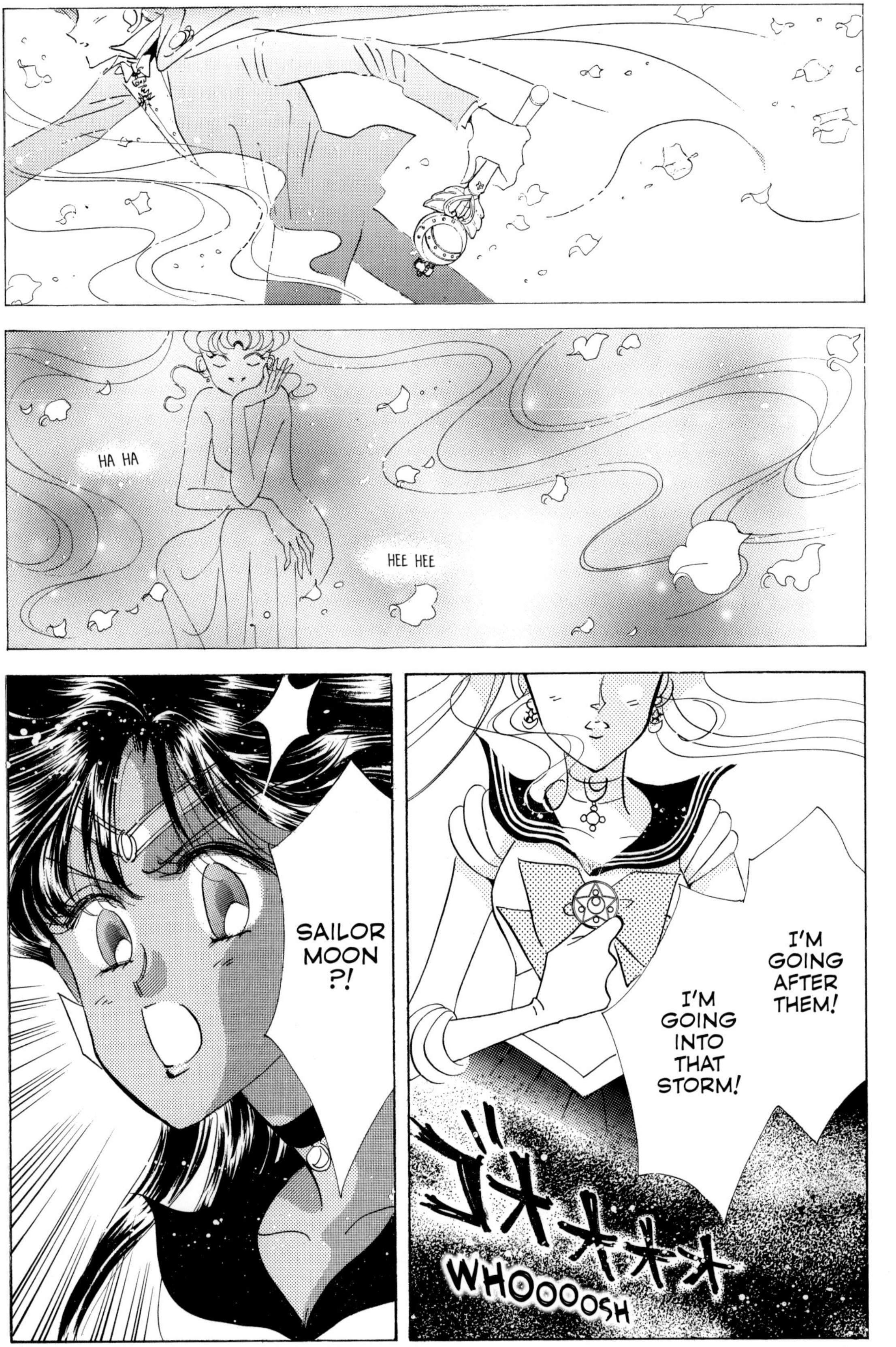
HA HA
HEE HEE
I'M GOING AFTER THEM!
I'M GOING INTO THAT STORM!
WHOOOOSH
SAILOR MOON ?!

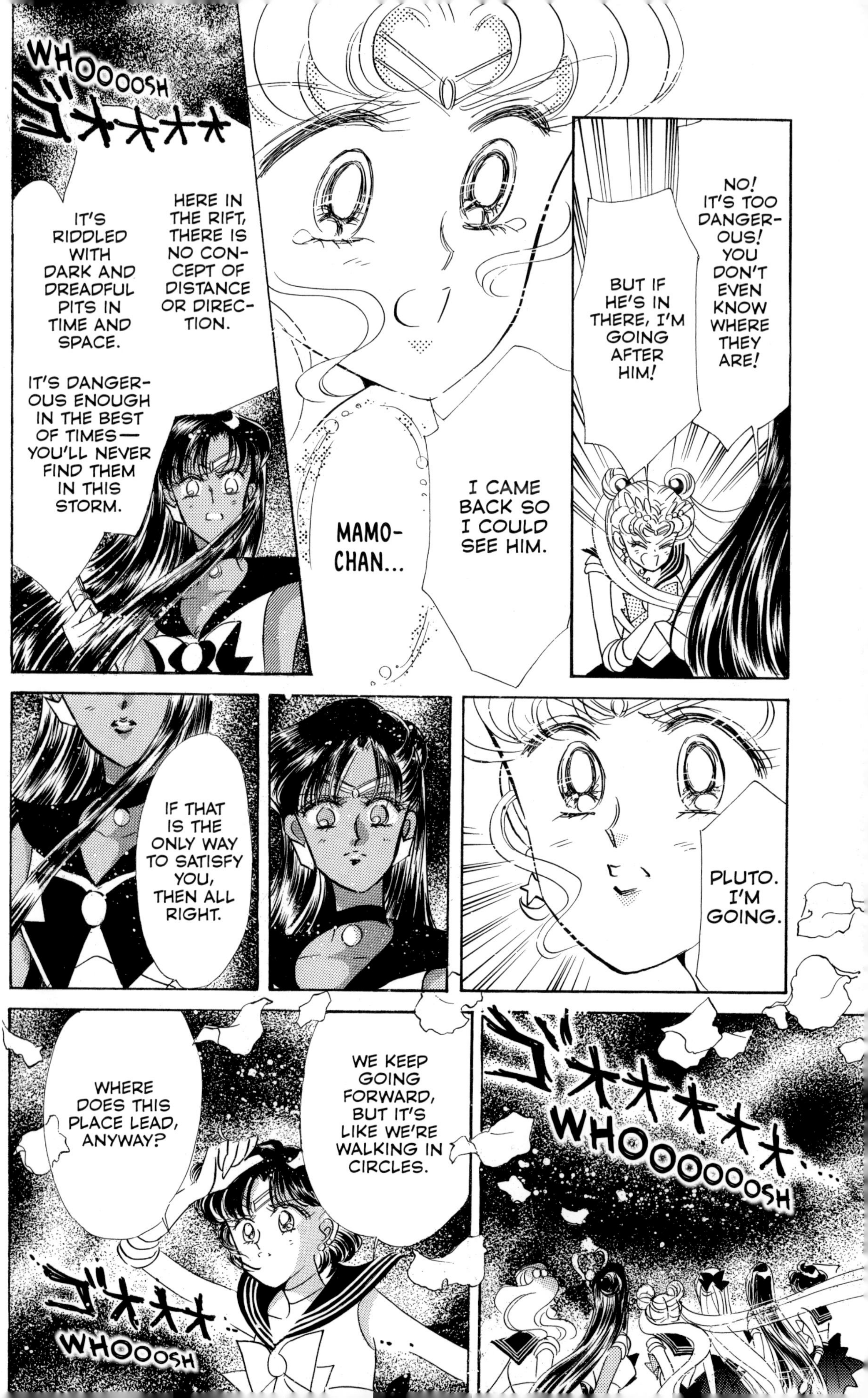
NO! IT'S TOO DANGER-OUS! YOU DON'T EVEN KNOW WHERE THEY ARE!
BUT IF HE'S IN THERE, I'M GOING AFTER HIM!
I CAME BACK SO I COULD SEE HIM.
MAMO-CHAN...
WHOOOOSH
HERE IN THE RIFT, THERE IS NO CON-CEPT OF DISTANCE OR DIREC-TION.
IT'S RIDDLED WITH DARK AND DREADFUL PITS IN TIME AND SPACE.
IT'S DANGER-OUS ENOUGH IN THE BEST OF TIMES—YOU'LL NEVER FIND THEM IN THIS STORM.
PLUTO. I'M GOING.
IF THAT IS THE ONLY WAY TO SATISFY YOU, THEN ALL RIGHT.
WHOOOOOOOSH
WE KEEP GOING FORWARD, BUT IT'S LIKE WE'RE WALKING IN CIRCLES.
WHERE DOES THIS PLACE LEAD, ANYWAY?
WHOOOSH

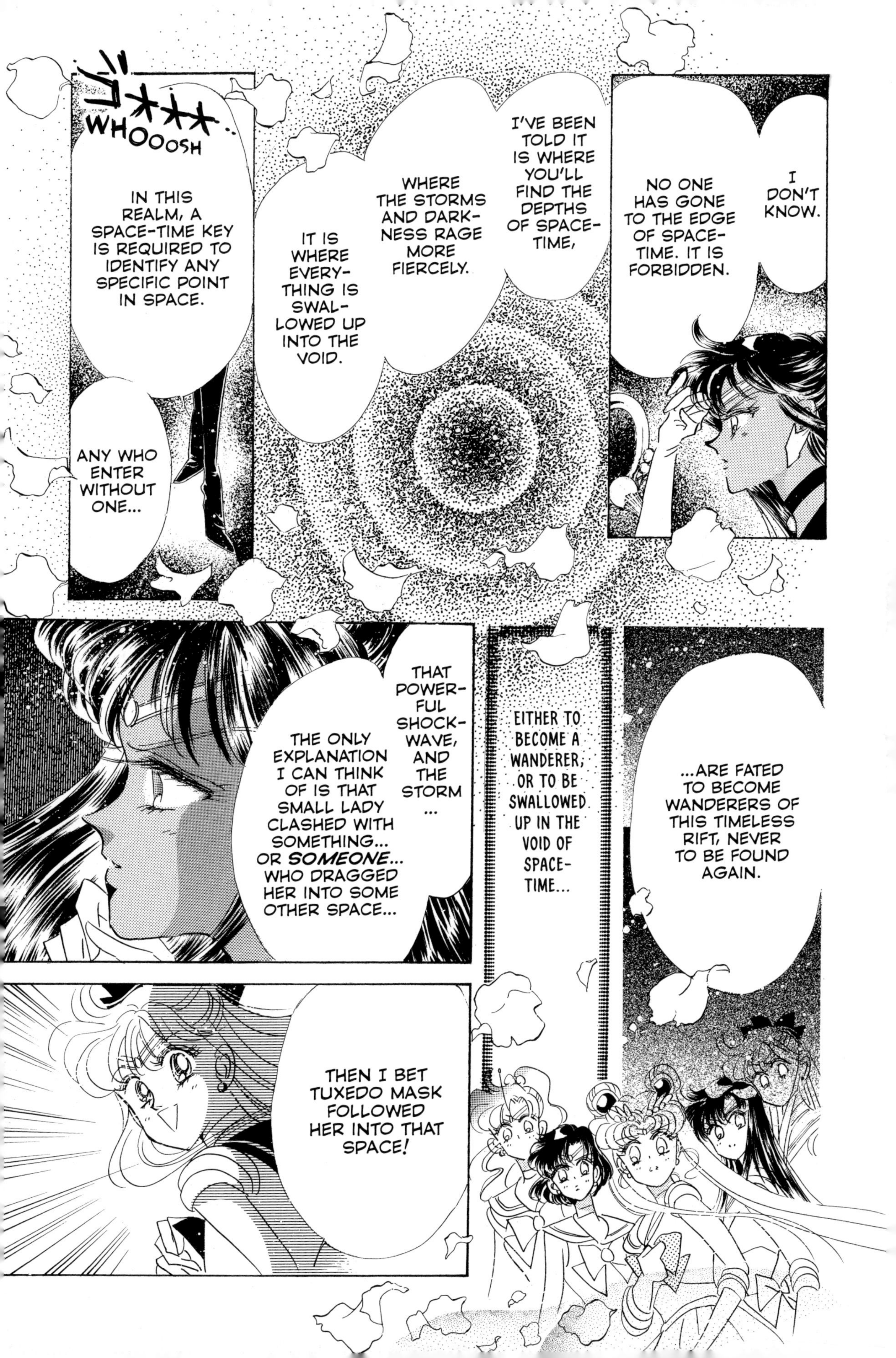
I DON'T KNOW.
NO ONE HAS GONE TO THE EDGE OF SPACE-TIME. IT IS FORBIDDEN.
I'VE BEEN TOLD IT IS WHERE YOU'LL FIND THE DEPTHS OF SPACE-TIME,
WHERE THE STORMS AND DARKNESS RAGE MORE FIERCELY.
IT IS WHERE EVERYTHING IS SWALLOWED UP INTO THE VOID.
WHOOOSH
IN THIS REALM, A SPACE-TIME KEY IS REQUIRED TO IDENTIFY ANY SPECIFIC POINT IN SPACE.
ANY WHO ENTER WITHOUT ONE...
...ARE FATED TO BECOME WANDERERS OF THIS TIMELESS RIFT, NEVER TO BE FOUND AGAIN.
EITHER TO BECOME A WANDERER, OR TO BE SWALLOWED UP IN THE VOID OF SPACE-TIME...
THAT POWERFUL SHOCKWAVE, AND THE STORM...
THE ONLY EXPLANATION I CAN THINK OF IS THAT SMALL LADY CLASHED WITH SOMETHING... OR *SOMEONE*... WHO DRAGGED HER INTO SOME OTHER SPACE...
THEN I BET TUXEDO MASK FOLLOWED HER INTO THAT SPACE!

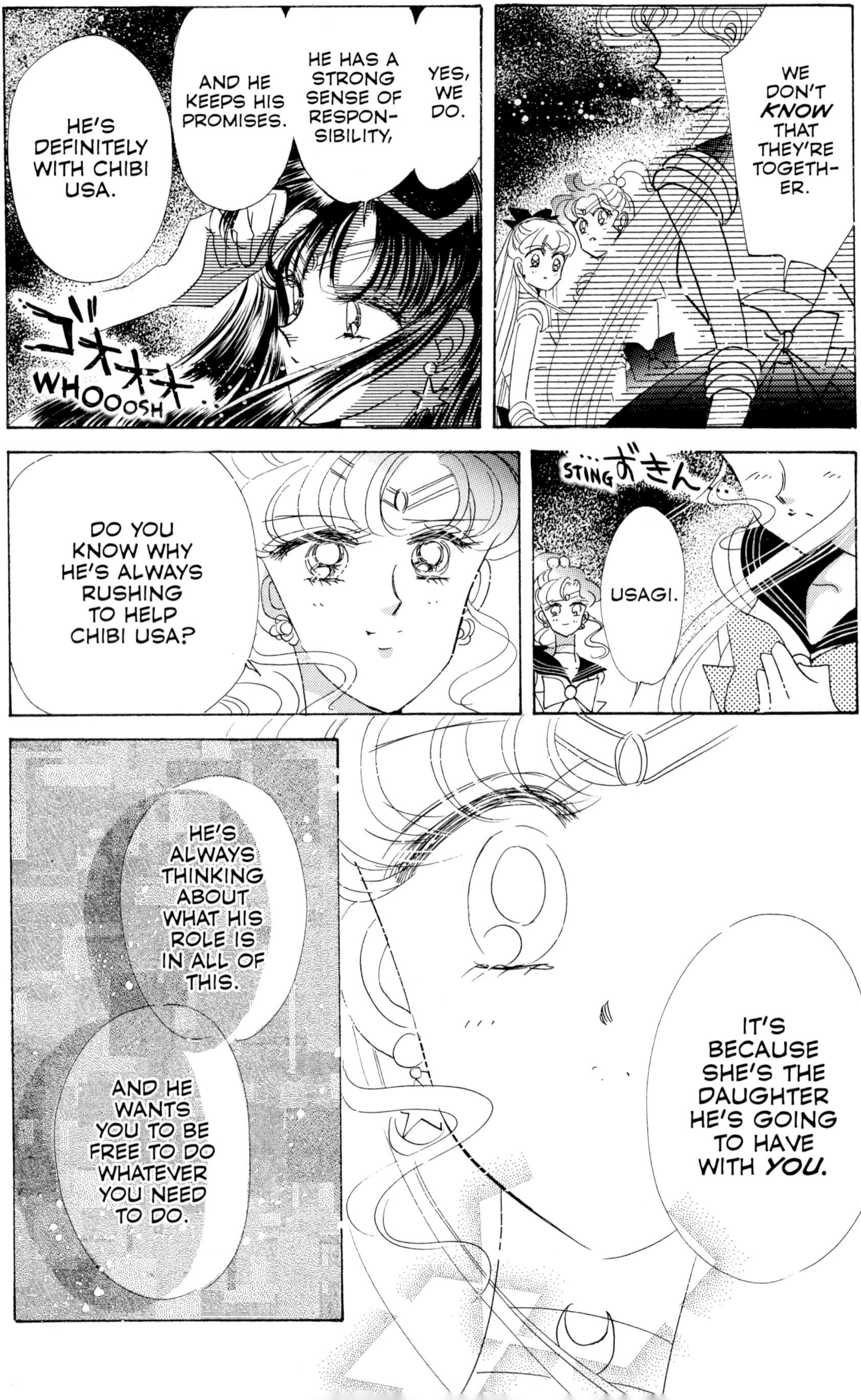
WE DON'T *KNOW* THAT THEY'RE TOGETHER.
YES, WE DO.
HE HAS A STRONG SENSE OF RESPONSIBILITY,
AND HE KEEPS HIS PROMISES.
HE'S DEFINITELY WITH CHIBI USA.
ゴオオオオ
WHOOOSH
STING ずきん
USAGI.
DO YOU KNOW WHY HE'S ALWAYS RUSHING TO HELP CHIBI USA?
IT'S BECAUSE SHE'S THE DAUGHTER HE'S GOING TO HAVE WITH *YOU*.
HE'S ALWAYS THINKING ABOUT WHAT HIS ROLE IS IN ALL OF THIS.
AND HE WANTS YOU TO BE FREE TO DO WHATEVER YOU NEED TO DO.

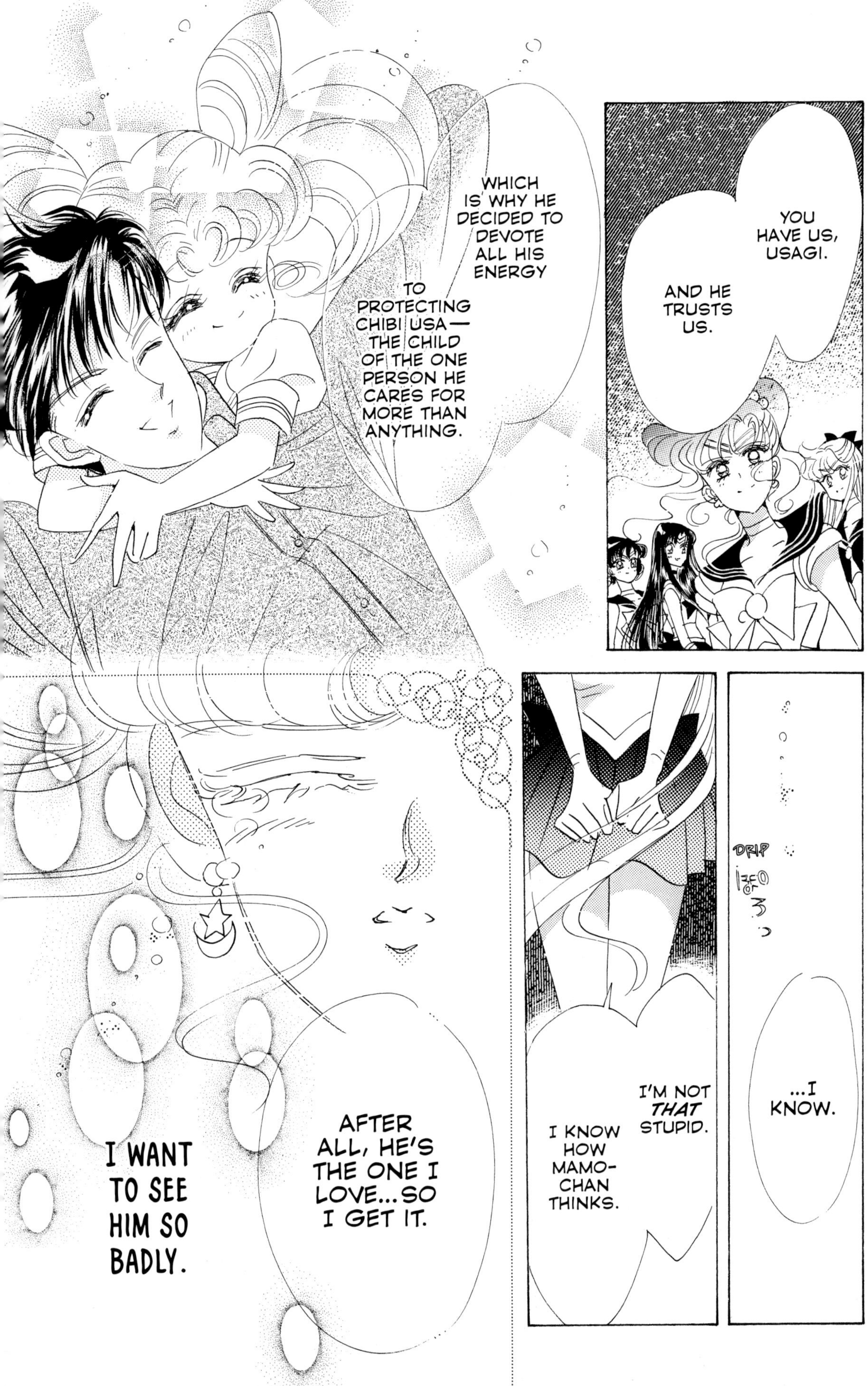
YOU HAVE US, USAGI.
AND HE TRUSTS US.
WHICH IS WHY HE DECIDED TO DEVOTE ALL HIS ENERGY
TO PROTECTING CHIBI USA—THE CHILD OF THE ONE PERSON HE CARES FOR MORE THAN ANYTHING.
DRIP
...I KNOW.
I'M NOT *THAT* STUPID.
I KNOW HOW MAMO-CHAN THINKS.
AFTER ALL, HE'S THE ONE I LOVE...SO I GET IT.
I WANT TO SEE HIM SO BADLY.

HOW CAN GOD BE SO CRUEL?

I MISS HIM SO MUCH.

I THOUGHT WE'D FINALLY, *FINALLY* BE TOGETHER AGAIN.

BUT WE'RE STILL TORN APART.

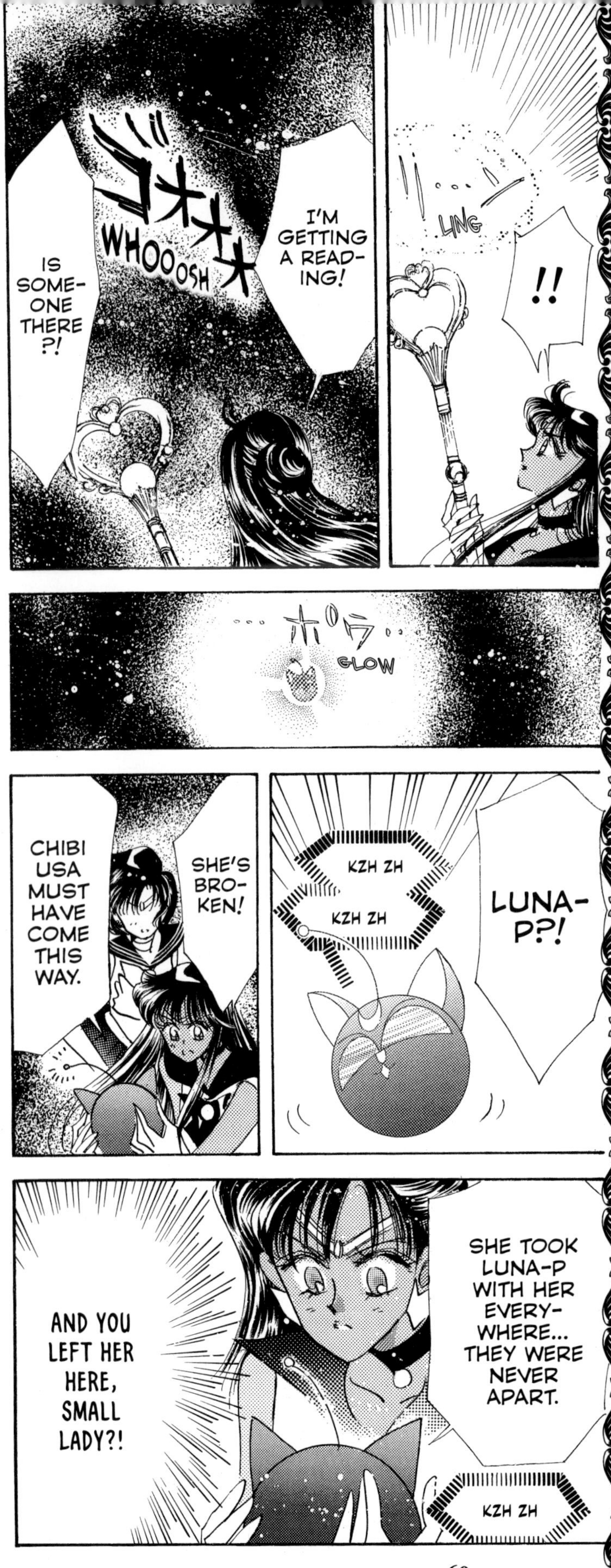
LING
!!
WHOOOSH
I'M GETTING A READING!
IS SOMEONE THERE?!
GLOW
KZH ZH
KZH ZH
LUNA-P?!
SHE'S BROKEN!
CHIBI USA MUST HAVE COME THIS WAY.
SHE TOOK LUNA-P WITH HER EVERYWHERE... THEY WERE NEVER APART.
AND YOU LEFT HER HERE, SMALL LADY?!
KZH ZH

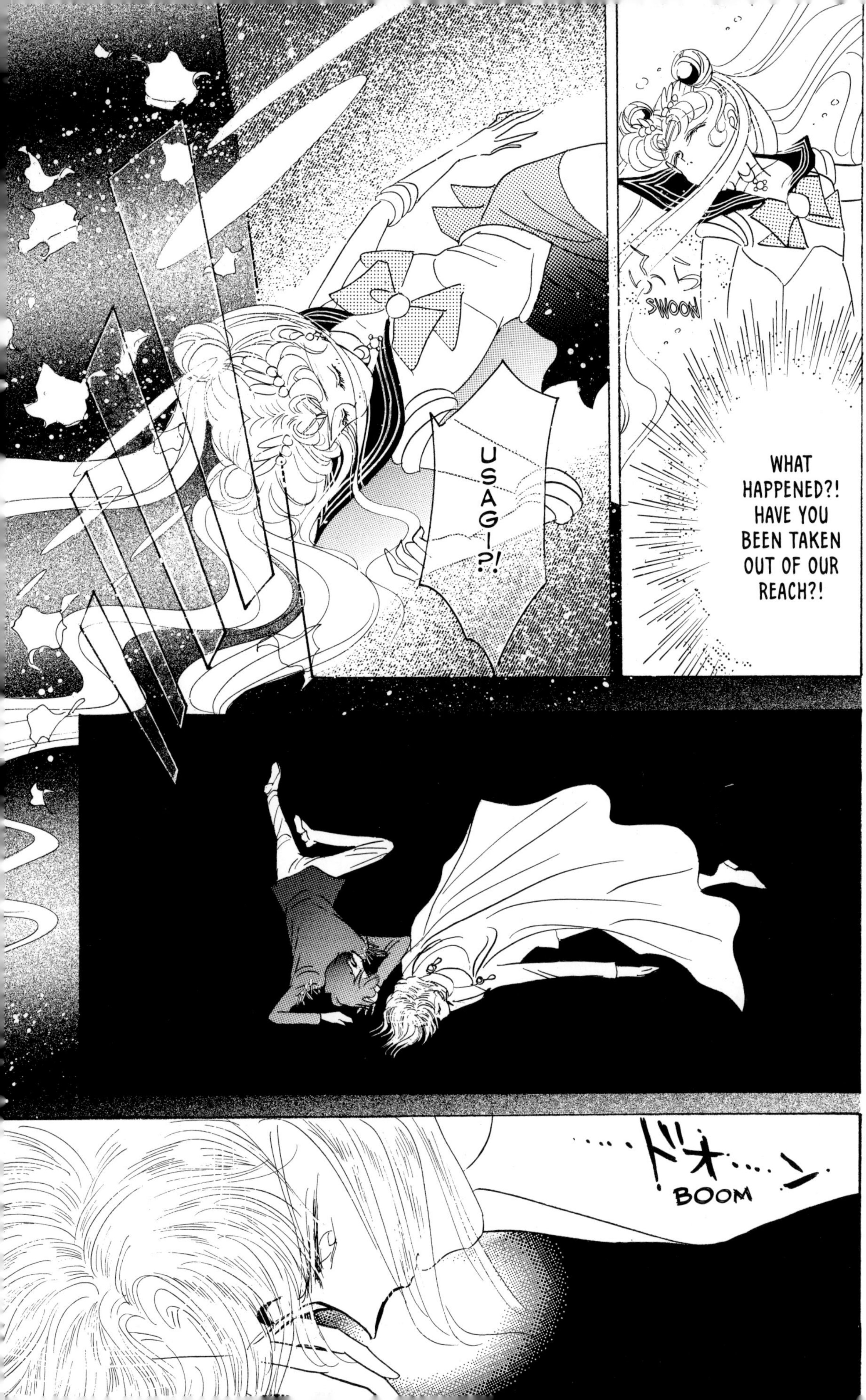
WHAT HAPPENED?! HAVE YOU BEEN TAKEN OUT OF OUR REACH?!
SWOON
USAGI?!
……ドオ……ン
BOOM

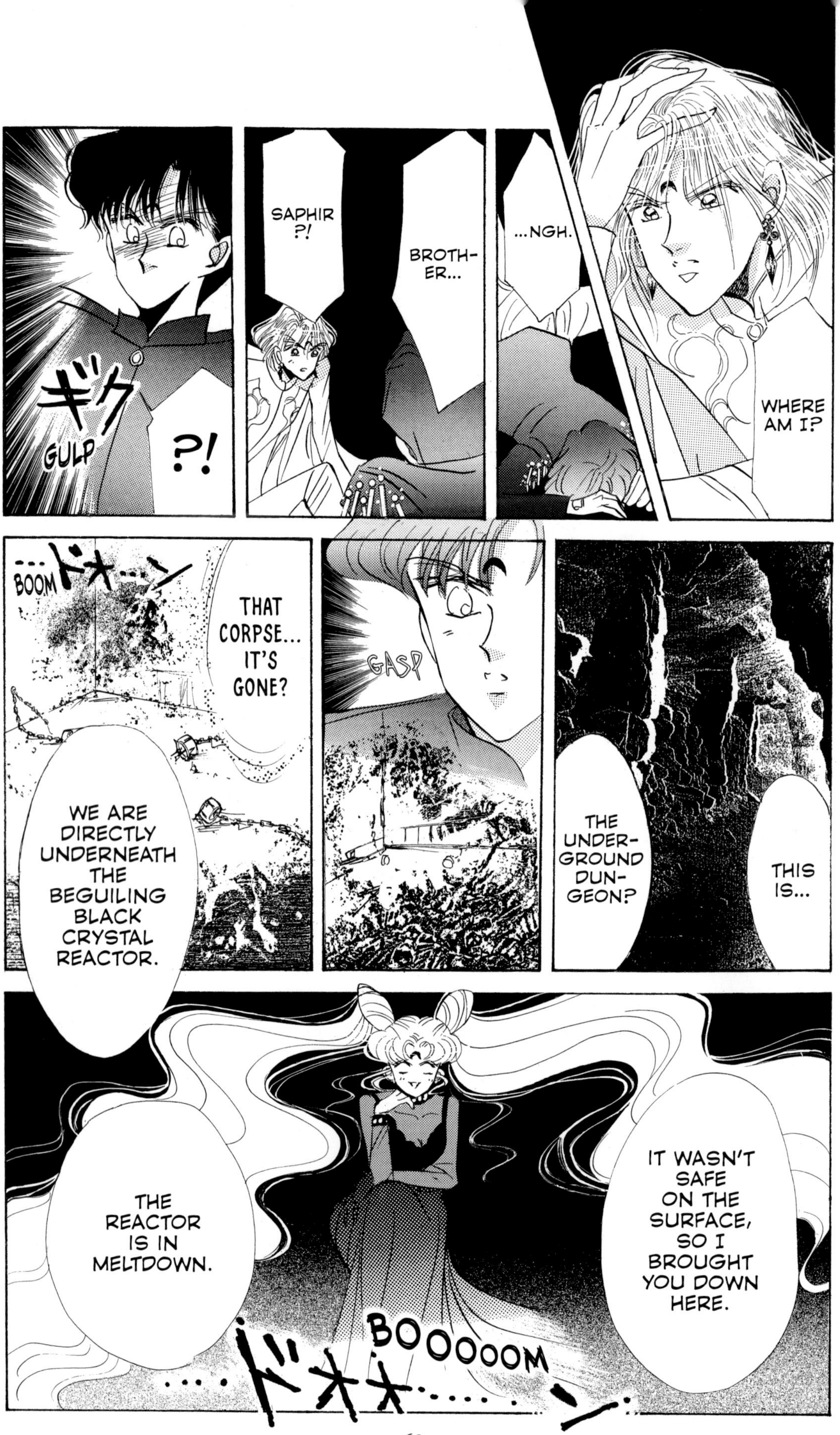
...NGH.
WHERE AM I?
BROTH-
ER...
SAPHIR
?!
ギク
GULP
?!
THIS
IS...
THE
UNDER-
GROUND
DUN-
GEON?
GASP
THAT
CORPSE...
IT'S
GONE?
...BOOM
ドオ…ン
WE ARE
DIRECTLY
UNDERNEATH
THE
BEGUILING
BLACK
CRYSTAL
REACTOR.
IT WASN'T
SAFE
ON THE
SURFACE,
SO I
BROUGHT
YOU DOWN
HERE.
THE
REACTOR
IS IN
MELTDOWN.
BOOOOOM
....ドォォ........ン

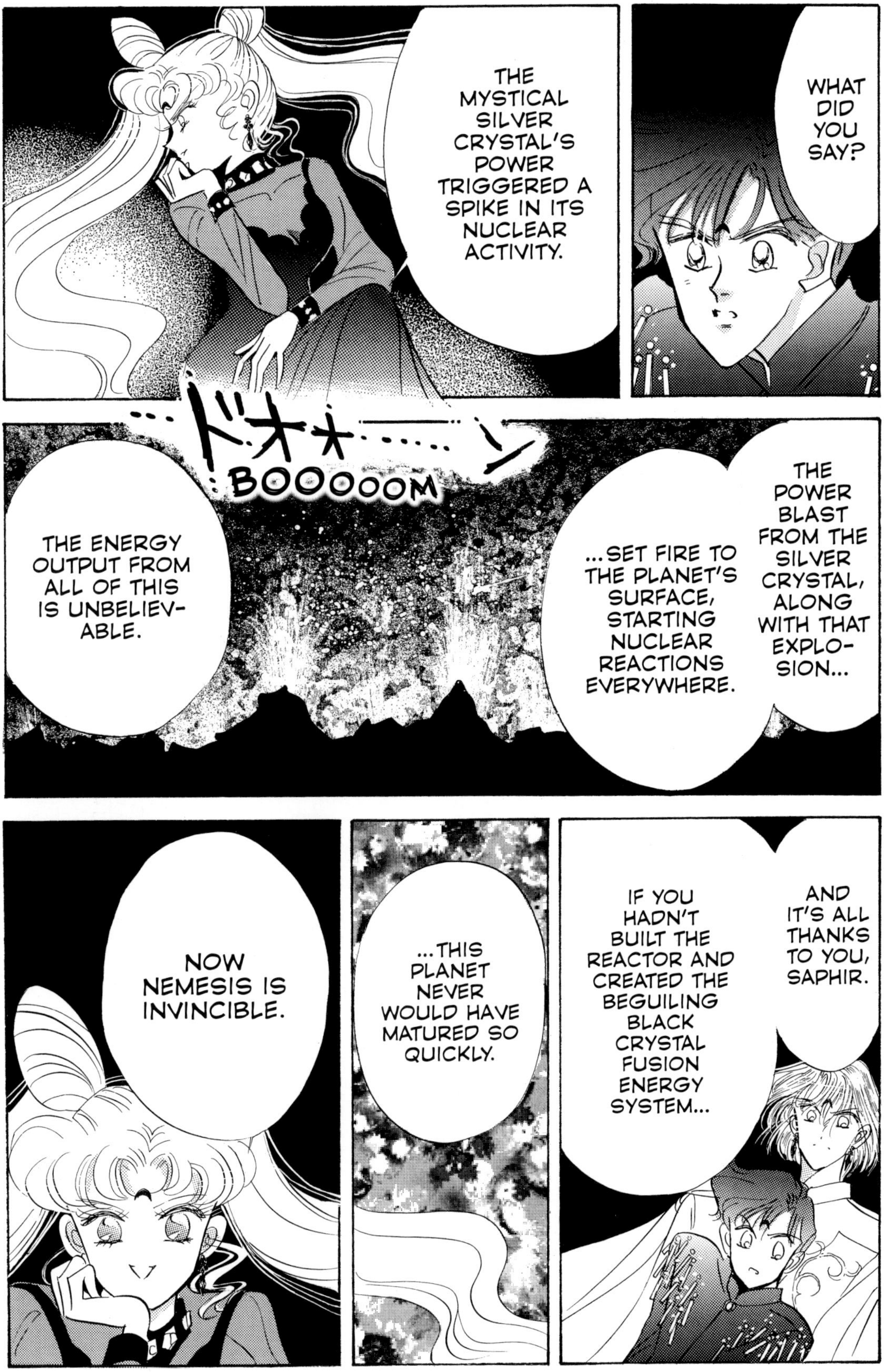
WHAT DID YOU SAY?
THE MYSTICAL SILVER CRYSTAL'S POWER TRIGGERED A SPIKE IN ITS NUCLEAR ACTIVITY.
THE POWER BLAST FROM THE SILVER CRYSTAL, ALONG WITH THAT EXPLOSION...
...SET FIRE TO THE PLANET'S SURFACE, STARTING NUCLEAR REACTIONS EVERYWHERE.
…ドオオ――ン
BOOOOOM
THE ENERGY OUTPUT FROM ALL OF THIS IS UNBELIEVABLE.
AND IT'S ALL THANKS TO YOU, SAPHIR.
IF YOU HADN'T BUILT THE REACTOR AND CREATED THE BEGUILING BLACK CRYSTAL FUSION ENERGY SYSTEM...
...THIS PLANET NEVER WOULD HAVE MATURED SO QUICKLY.
NOW NEMESIS IS INVINCIBLE.

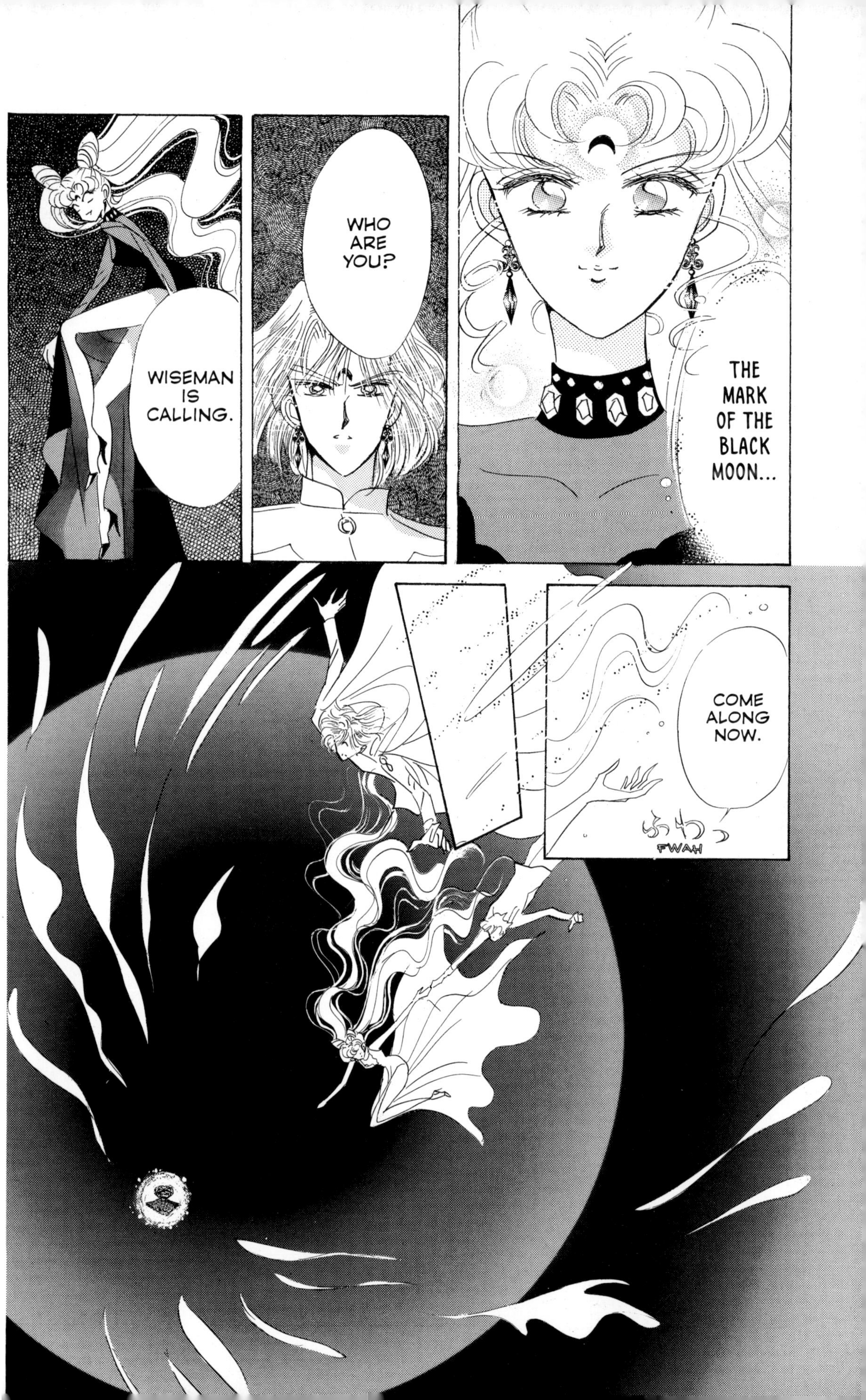
THE MARK OF THE BLACK MOON...
WHO ARE YOU?
WISEMAN IS CALLING.
COME ALONG NOW.
FWAH

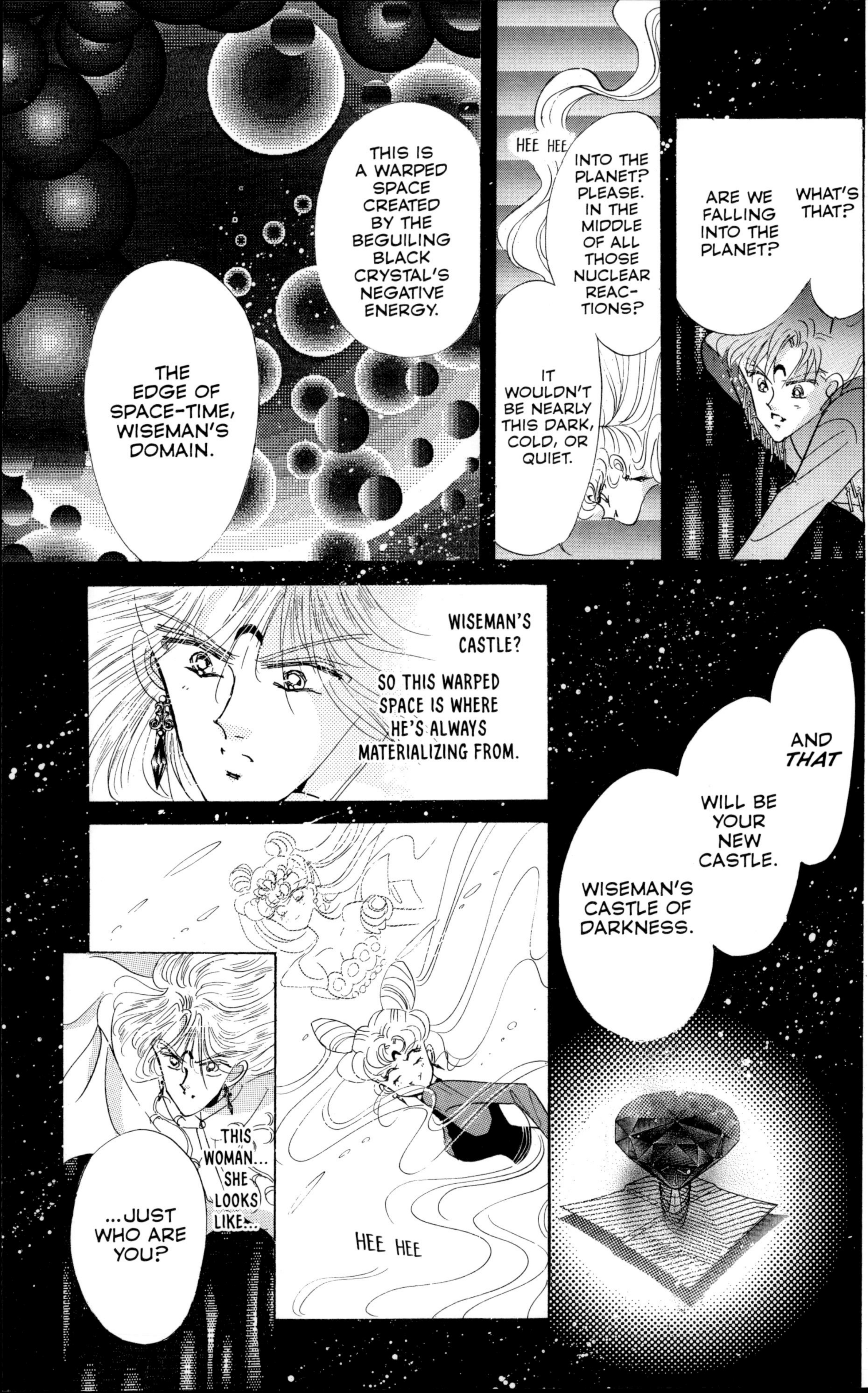
WHAT'S THAT?
ARE WE FALLING INTO THE PLANET?
HEE HEE
INTO THE PLANET? PLEASE. IN THE MIDDLE OF ALL THOSE NUCLEAR REACTIONS?
IT WOULDN'T BE NEARLY THIS DARK, COLD, OR QUIET.
THIS IS A WARPED SPACE CREATED BY THE BEGUILING BLACK CRYSTAL'S NEGATIVE ENERGY.
THE EDGE OF SPACE-TIME, WISEMAN'S DOMAIN.
AND *THAT*
WILL BE YOUR NEW CASTLE.
WISEMAN'S CASTLE OF DARKNESS.
WISEMAN'S CASTLE?
SO THIS WARPED SPACE IS WHERE HE'S ALWAYS MATERIALIZING FROM.
HEE HEE
THIS WOMAN... SHE LOOKS LIKE...
...JUST WHO ARE YOU?

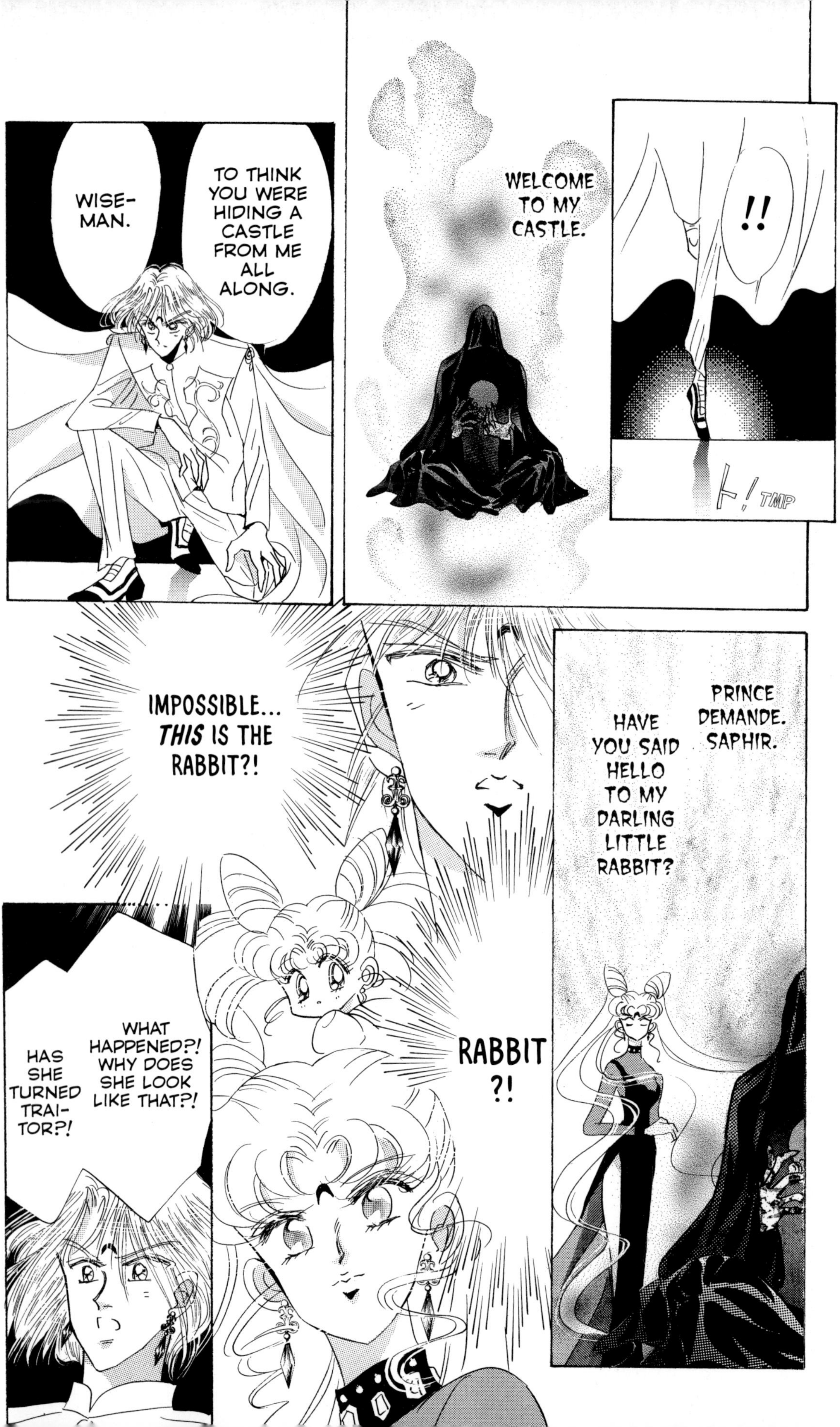
!!
ト!
TMP
WELCOME TO MY CASTLE.
TO THINK YOU WERE HIDING A CASTLE FROM ME ALL ALONG.
WISE-MAN.
PRINCE DEMANDE. SAPHIR.
HAVE YOU SAID HELLO TO MY DARLING LITTLE RABBIT?
RABBIT ?!
IMPOSSIBLE... *THIS* IS THE RABBIT?!
......
WHAT HAPPENED?! WHY DOES SHE LOOK LIKE THAT?!
HAS SHE TURNED TRAI-TOR?!

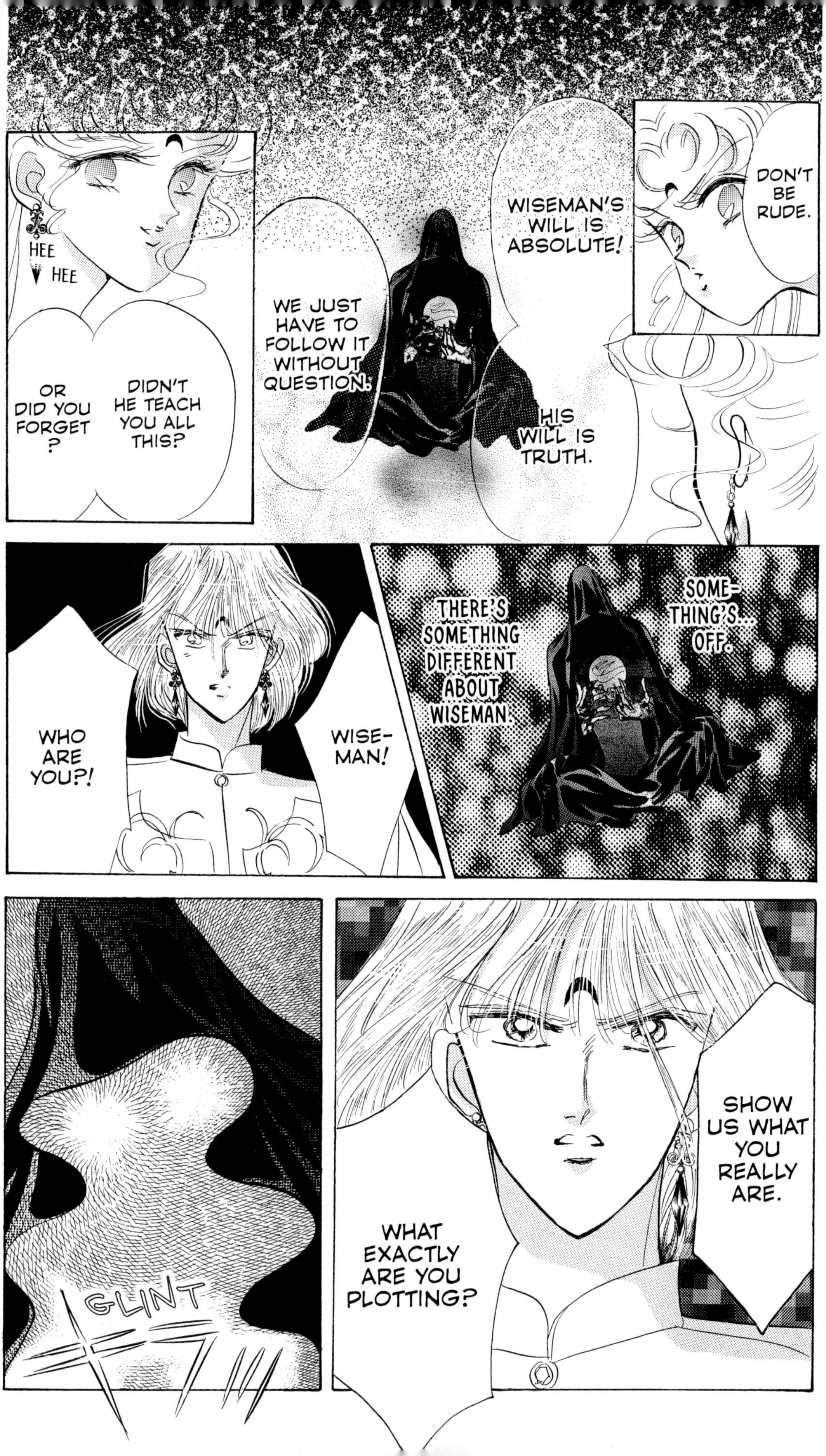
DON'T BE RUDE.
WISEMAN'S WILL IS ABSOLUTE!
HIS WILL IS TRUTH.
WE JUST HAVE TO FOLLOW IT WITHOUT QUESTION.
HEE HEE
DIDN'T HE TEACH YOU ALL THIS?
OR DID YOU FORGET?
SOME-THING'S... OFF.
THERE'S SOMETHING DIFFERENT ABOUT WISEMAN.
WISE-MAN!
WHO ARE YOU?!
SHOW US WHAT YOU REALLY ARE.
WHAT EXACTLY ARE YOU PLOTTING?
GLINT

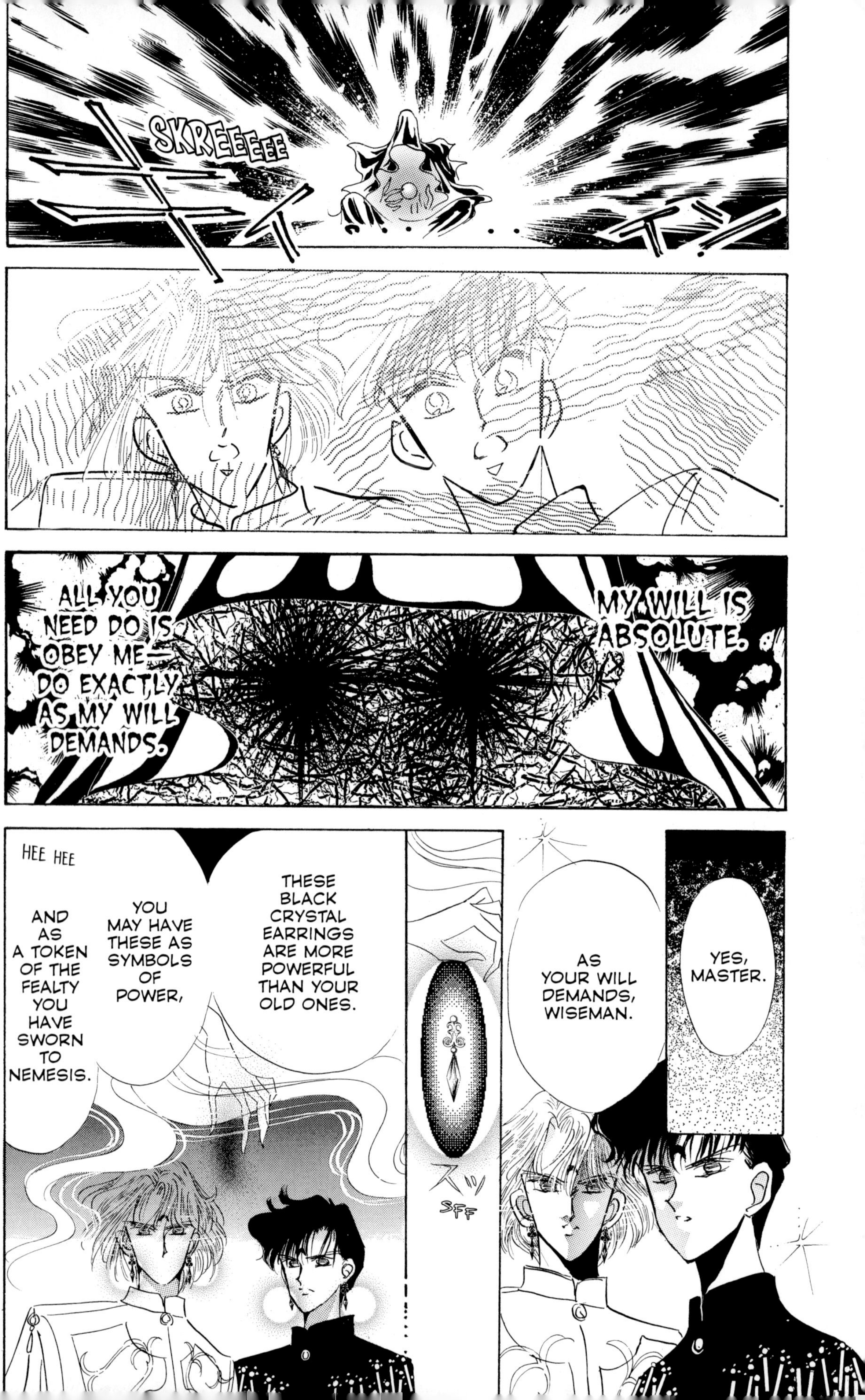
SKREEEEEE
MY WILL IS ABSOLUTE.
ALL YOU NEED DO IS OBEY ME— DO EXACTLY AS MY WILL DEMANDS.
YES, MASTER.
AS YOUR WILL DEMANDS, WISEMAN.
SFF
THESE BLACK CRYSTAL EARRINGS ARE MORE POWERFUL THAN YOUR OLD ONES.
YOU MAY HAVE THESE AS SYMBOLS OF POWER,
AND AS A TOKEN OF THE FEALTY YOU HAVE SWORN TO NEMESIS.
HEE HEE

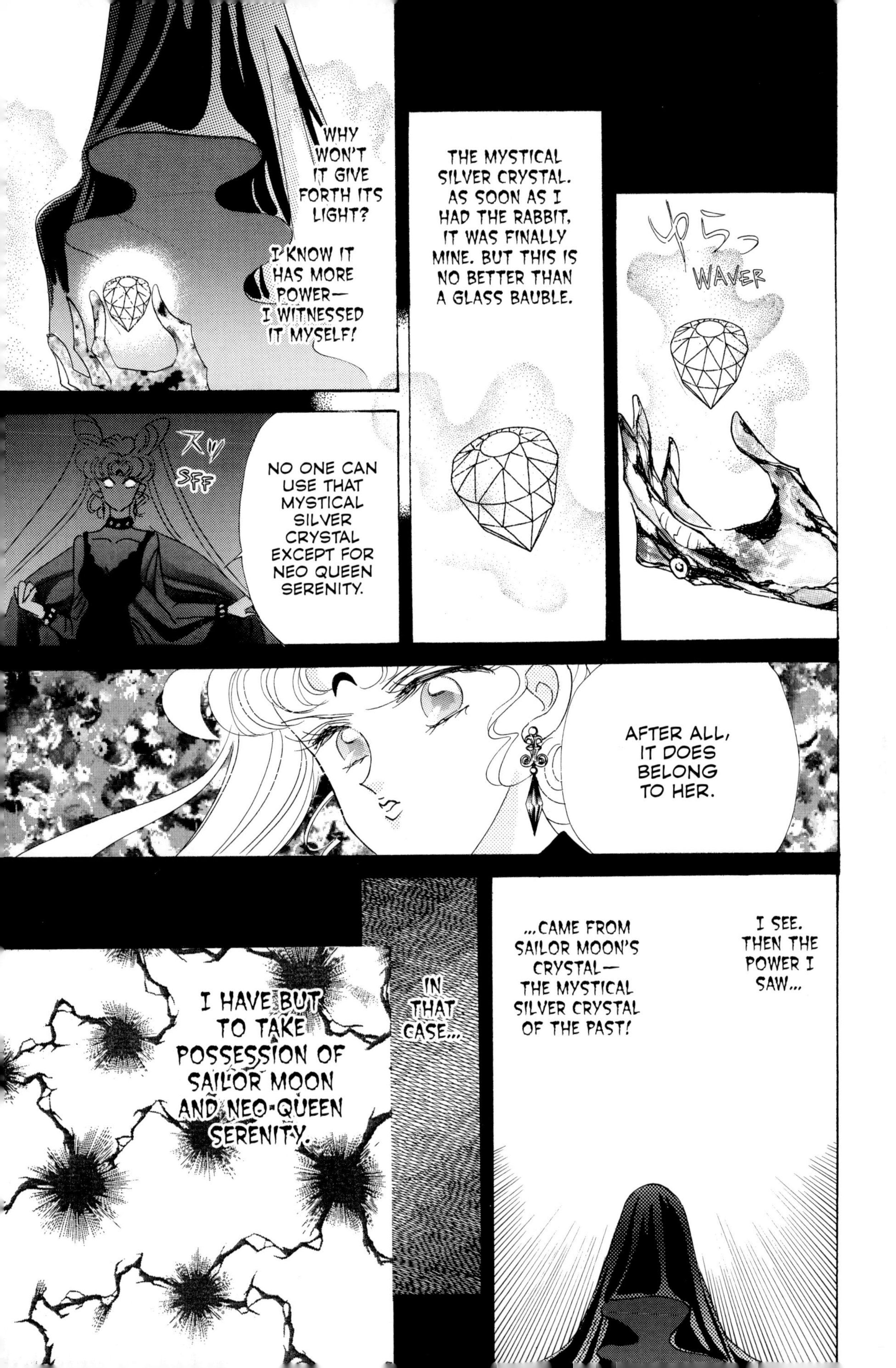
ゆらっ
WAVER
THE MYSTICAL SILVER CRYSTAL. AS SOON AS I HAD THE RABBIT, IT WAS FINALLY MINE. BUT THIS IS NO BETTER THAN A GLASS BAUBLE.
WHY WON'T IT GIVE FORTH ITS LIGHT?
I KNOW IT HAS MORE POWER— I WITNESSED IT MYSELF!
スッ
SFF
NO ONE CAN USE THAT MYSTICAL SILVER CRYSTAL EXCEPT FOR NEO QUEEN SERENITY.
AFTER ALL, IT DOES BELONG TO HER.
I SEE. THEN THE POWER I SAW...
...CAME FROM SAILOR MOON'S CRYSTAL— THE MYSTICAL SILVER CRYSTAL OF THE PAST!
IN THAT CASE...
I HAVE BUT TO TAKE POSSESSION OF SAILOR MOON AND NEO-QUEEN SERENITY.

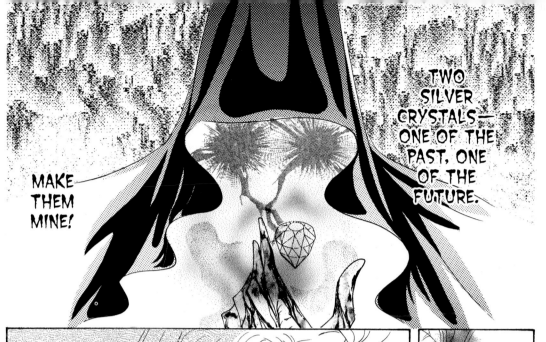

TWO SILVER CRYSTALS—ONE OF THE PAST, ONE OF THE FUTURE.
MAKE THEM MINE!
SUCH A TASK SHOULD BE CHILD'S PLAY FOR YOU.
YES, WISE-MAN.
IT *WILL* BE EASY.
THE TWO CRYSTALS WILL BE YOURS BEFORE YOU KNOW IT.
PLEASE. IT WILL BE FAR FROM EASY...
...TO OVER-THROW NEO QUEEN SERENITY'S PALACE.
BESIDES, YOU MAY HAVE GOTTEN THAT BAUBLE FROM THE RABBIT,
BUT I HAVE MY DOUBTS AS TO WHETHER OR NOT IT'S REALLY THE MYSTICAL SILVER CRYSTAL.
RAGE
ARE YOU SURE WE SHOULD TRUST HER SO READILY, WISEMAN?

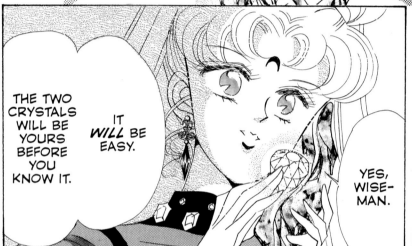

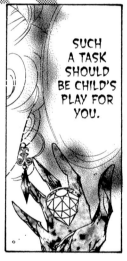

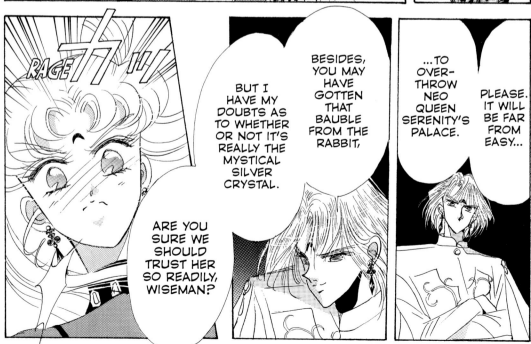

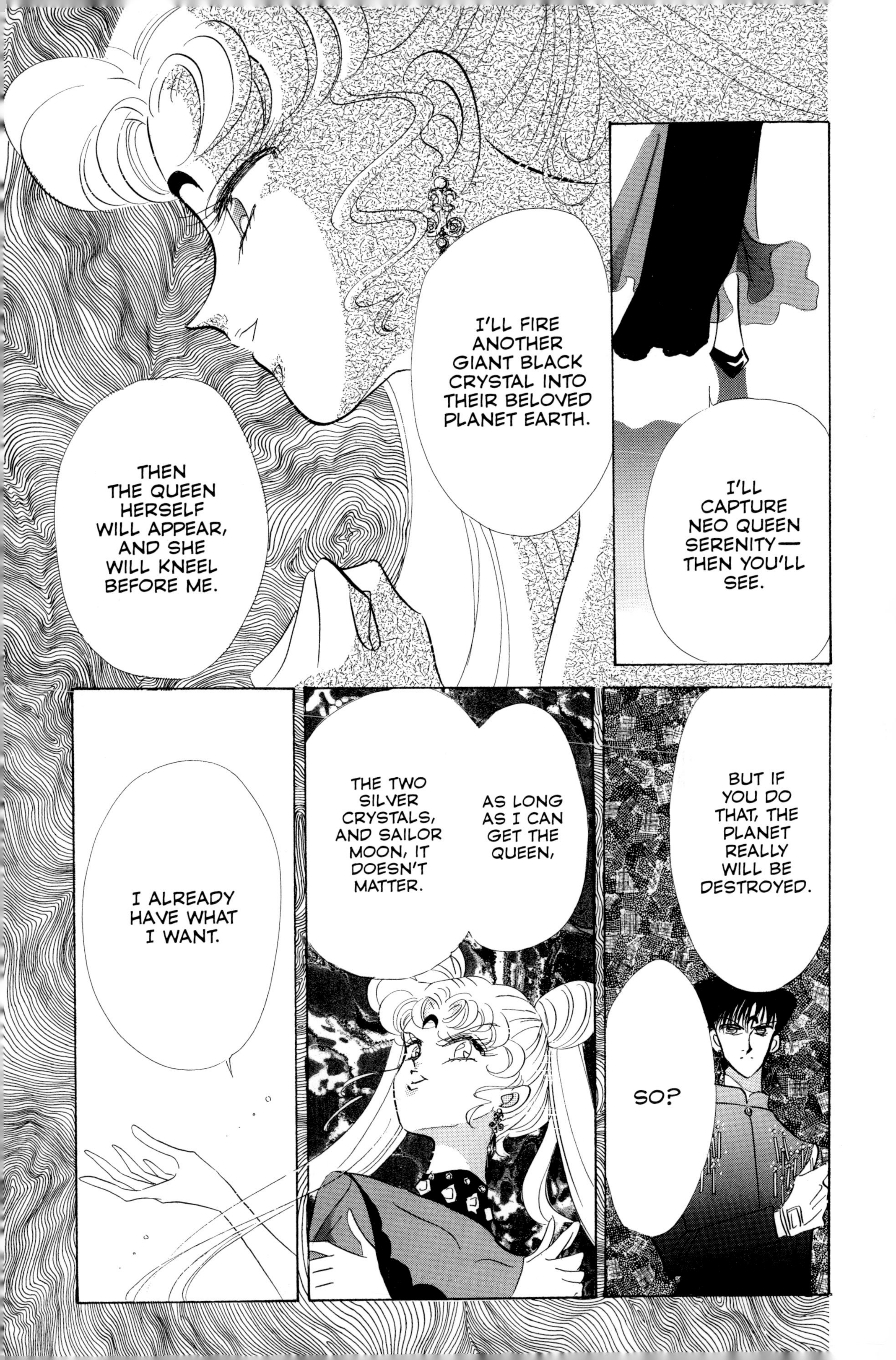
I'LL CAPTURE NEO QUEEN SERENITY—THEN YOU'LL SEE.
I'LL FIRE ANOTHER GIANT BLACK CRYSTAL INTO THEIR BELOVED PLANET EARTH.
THEN THE QUEEN HERSELF WILL APPEAR, AND SHE WILL KNEEL BEFORE ME.
BUT IF YOU DO THAT, THE PLANET REALLY WILL BE DESTROYED.
SO?
AS LONG AS I CAN GET THE QUEEN,
THE TWO SILVER CRYSTALS, AND SAILOR MOON, IT DOESN'T MATTER.
I ALREADY HAVE WHAT I WANT.

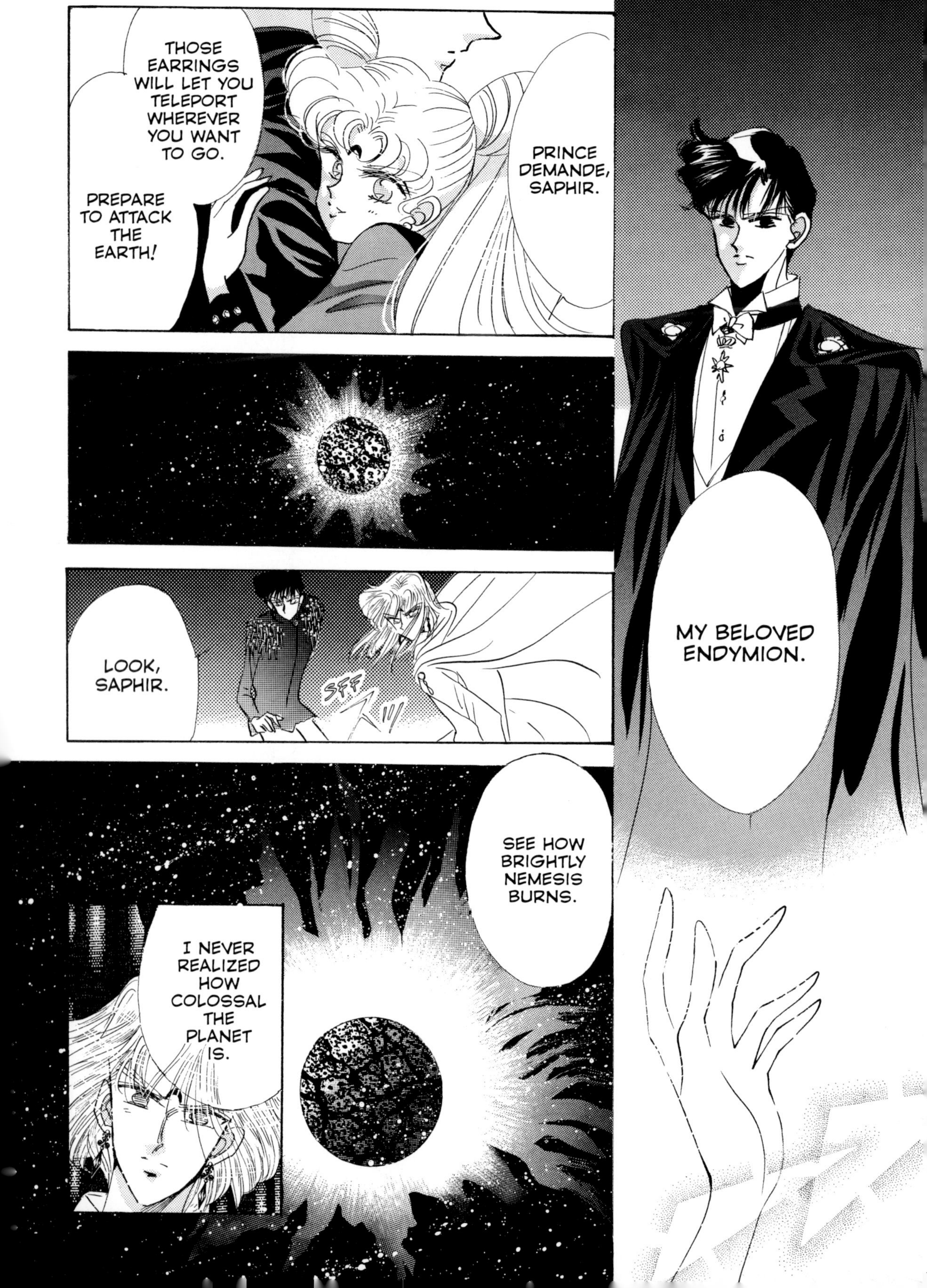
MY BELOVED ENDYMION.
PRINCE DEMANDE, SAPHIR.
THOSE EARRINGS WILL LET YOU TELEPORT WHEREVER YOU WANT TO GO.
PREPARE TO ATTACK THE EARTH!
LOOK, SAPHIR.
SFF
SEE HOW BRIGHTLY NEMESIS BURNS.
I NEVER REALIZED HOW COLOSSAL THE PLANET IS.

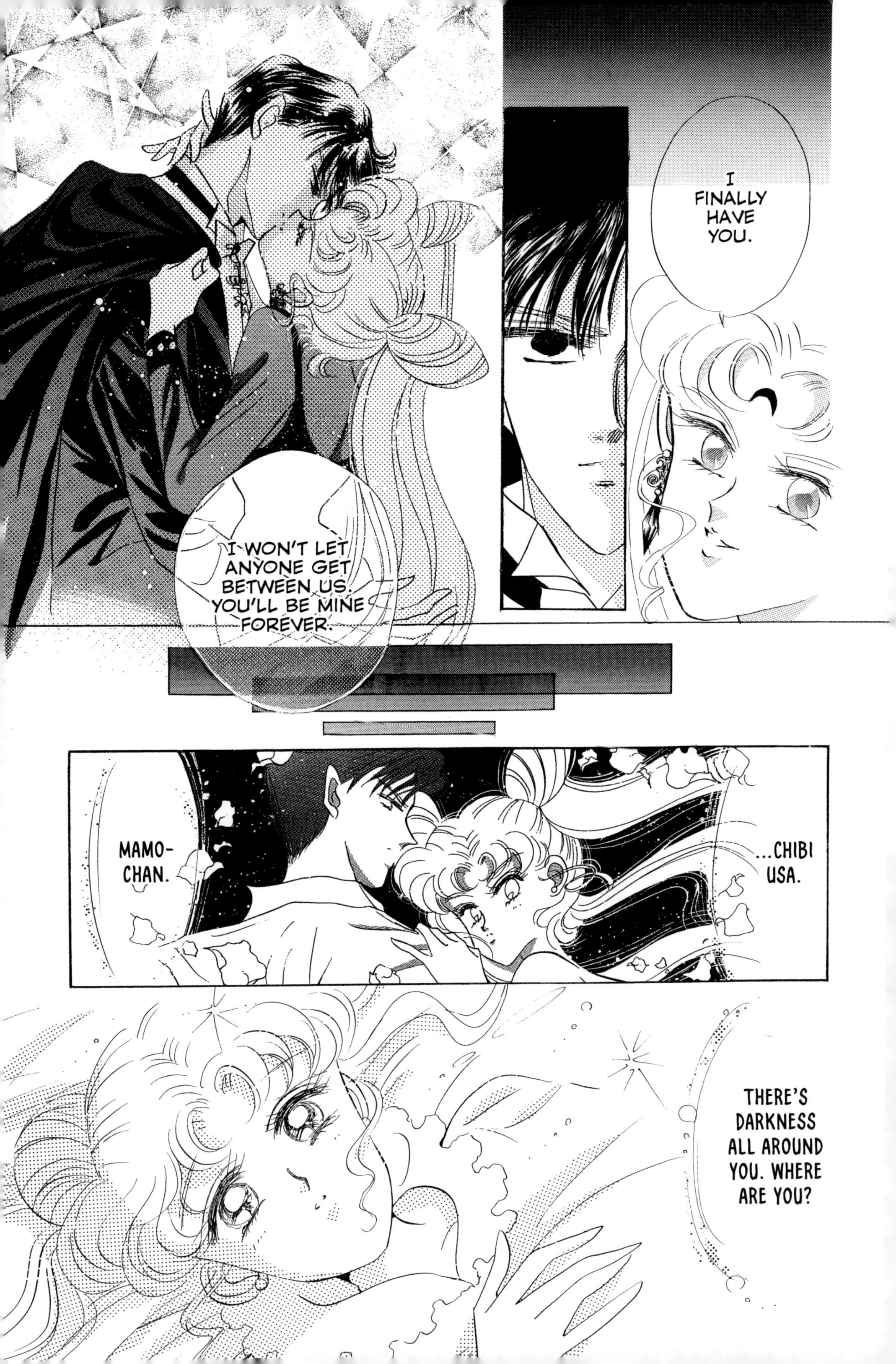
I FINALLY HAVE YOU.
I WON'T LET ANYONE GET BETWEEN US. YOU'LL BE MINE FOREVER.
...CHIBI USA.
MAMO-CHAN.
THERE'S DARKNESS ALL AROUND YOU. WHERE ARE YOU?

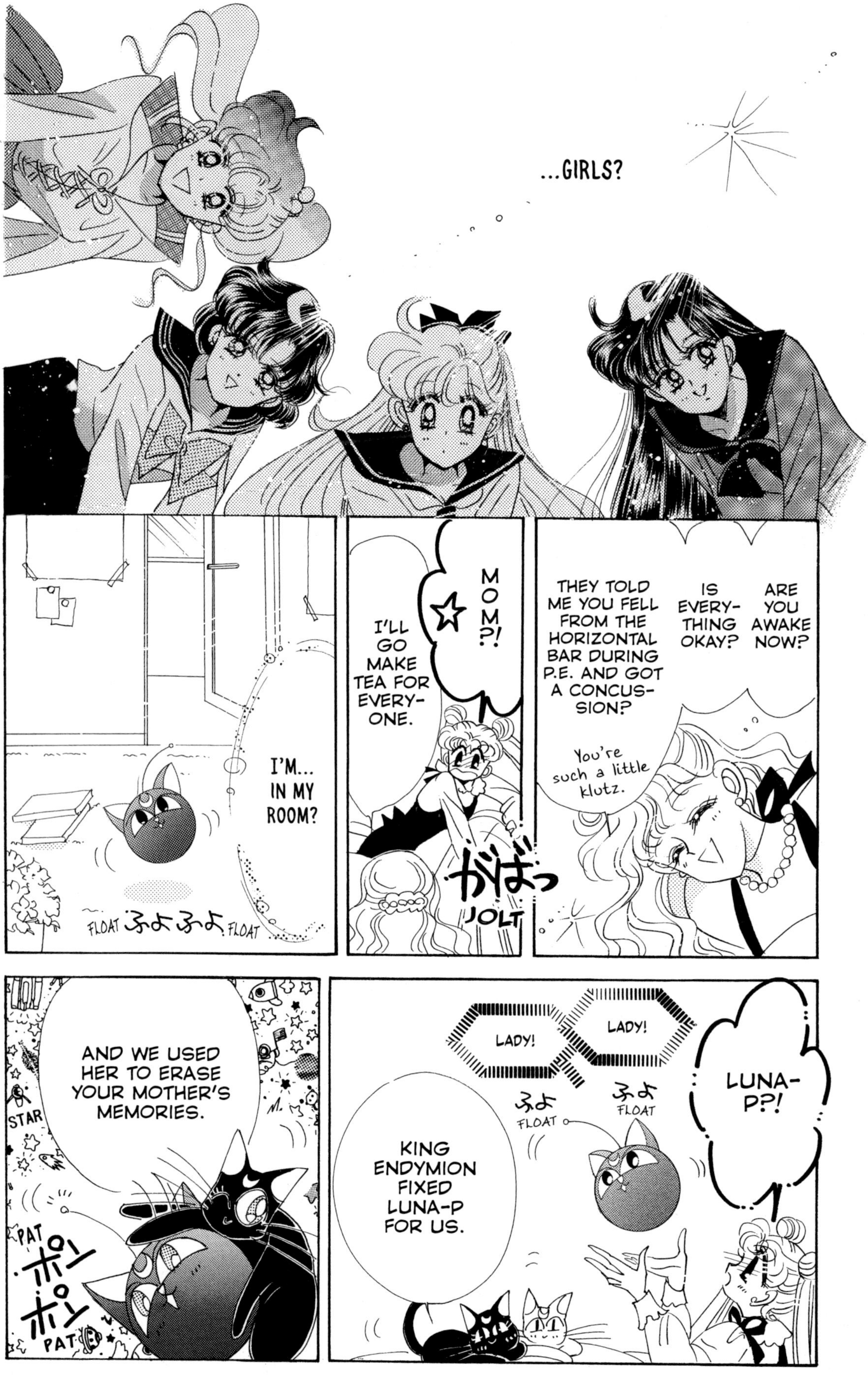
...GIRLS?
ARE YOU AWAKE NOW?
IS EVERY-THING OKAY?
THEY TOLD ME YOU FELL FROM THE HORIZONTAL BAR DURING P.E. AND GOT A CONCUS-SION?
You're such a little klutz.
MOM?!
I'LL GO MAKE TEA FOR EVERY-ONE.
がばっ
JOLT
I'M... IN MY ROOM?
FLOAT ふよふよ FLOAT
LUNA-P?!
LADY!
LADY!
ふよ
FLOAT
ふよ
FLOAT
KING ENDYMION FIXED LUNA-P FOR US.
AND WE USED HER TO ERASE YOUR MOTHER'S MEMORIES.
STAR
PAT
ポン
ポン
PAT

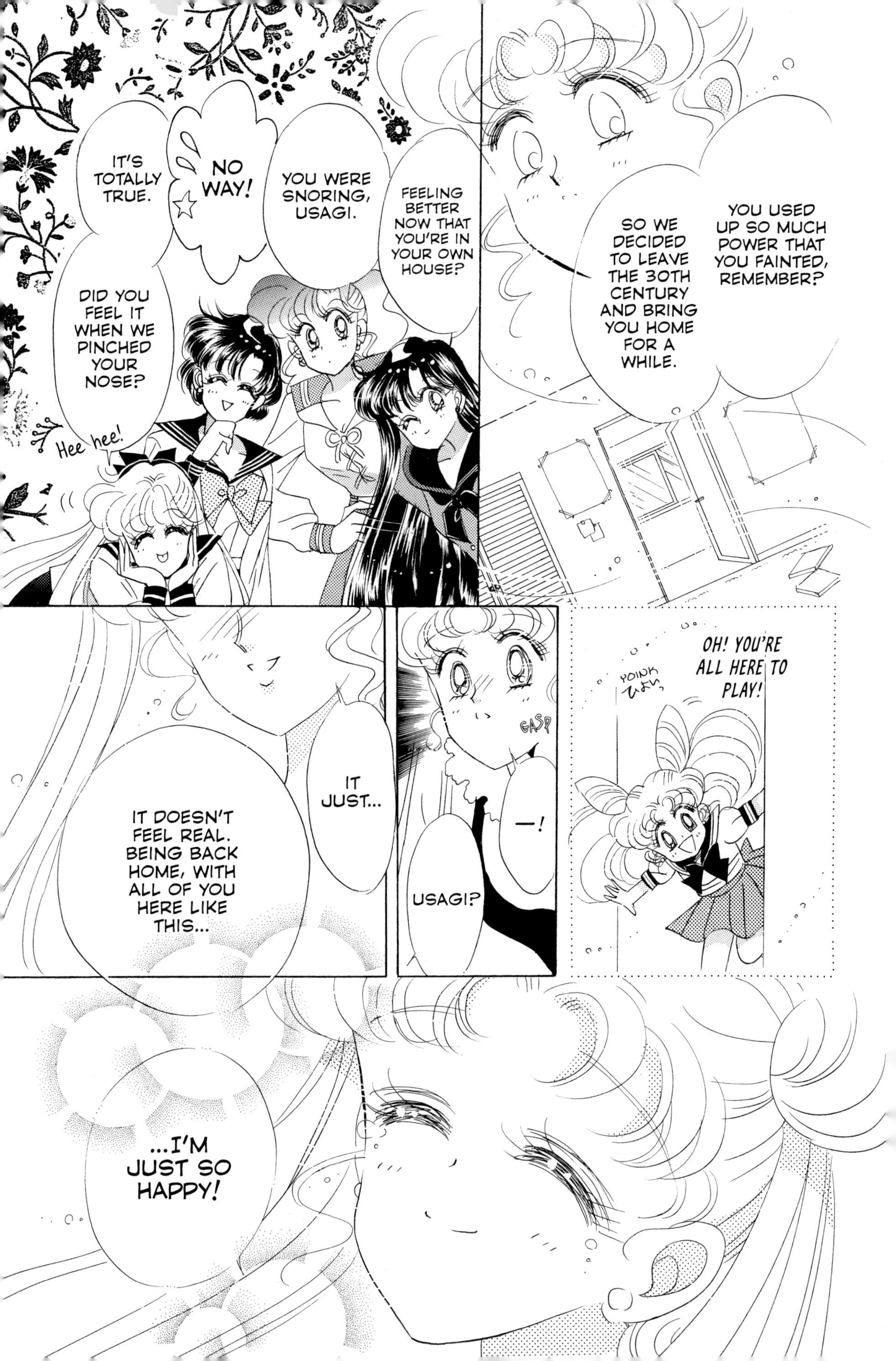
YOU USED UP SO MUCH POWER THAT YOU FAINTED, REMEMBER?
SO WE DECIDED TO LEAVE THE 30TH CENTURY AND BRING YOU HOME FOR A WHILE.
FEELING BETTER NOW THAT YOU'RE IN YOUR OWN HOUSE?
YOU WERE SNORING, USAGI.
NO WAY!
IT'S TOTALLY TRUE.
DID YOU FEEL IT WHEN WE PINCHED YOUR NOSE?
Hee hee!
OH! YOU'RE ALL HERE TO PLAY!
YOINK
GASP
—!
USAGI?
IT JUST...
IT DOESN'T FEEL REAL. BEING BACK HOME, WITH ALL OF YOU HERE LIKE THIS...
...I'M JUST SO HAPPY!

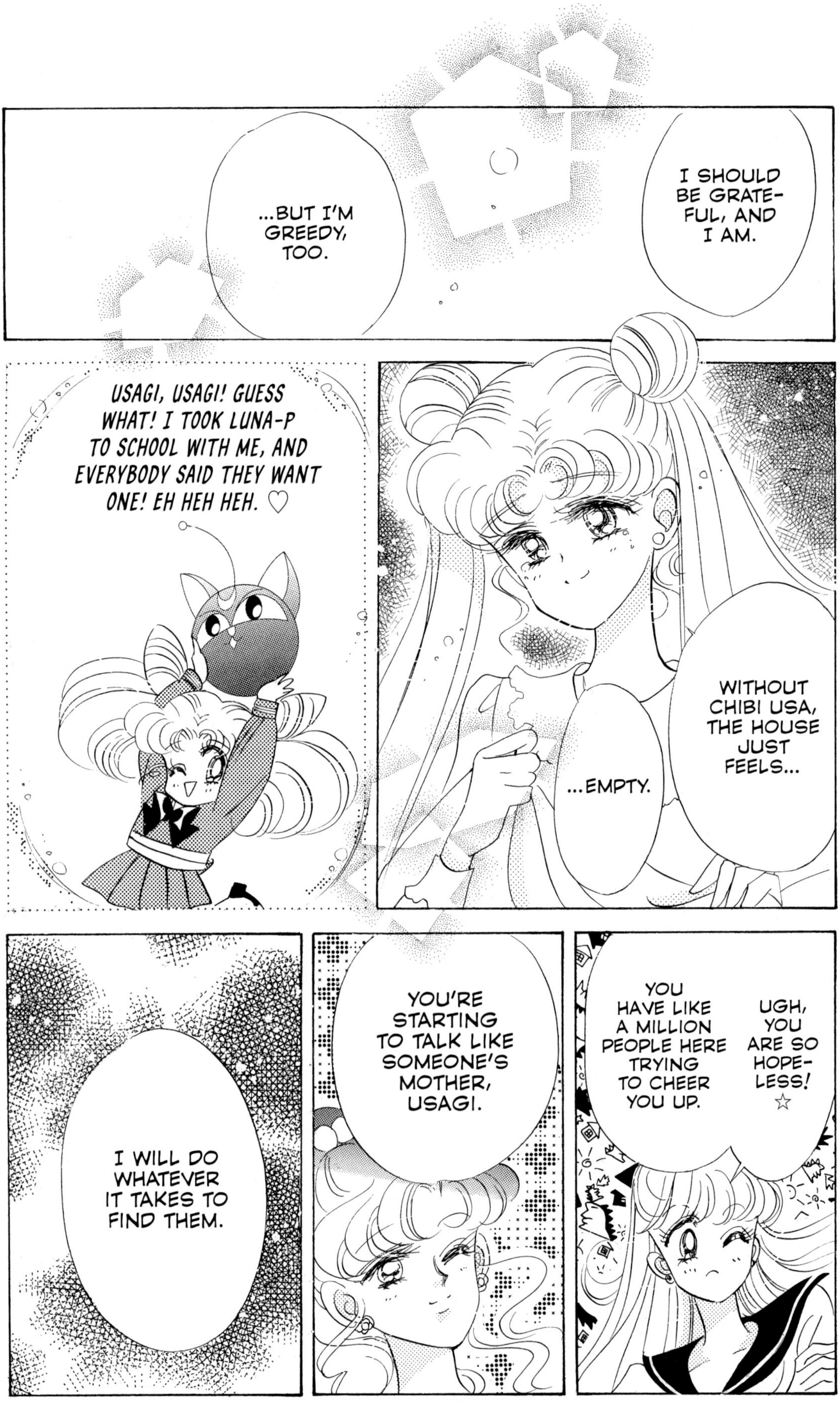
I SHOULD BE GRATEFUL, AND I AM.
...BUT I'M GREEDY, TOO.
WITHOUT CHIBI USA, THE HOUSE JUST FEELS...
...EMPTY.
USAGI, USAGI! GUESS WHAT! I TOOK LUNA-P TO SCHOOL WITH ME, AND EVERYBODY SAID THEY WANT ONE! EH HEH HEH. ♡
UGH, YOU ARE SO HOPELESS! ☆
YOU HAVE LIKE A MILLION PEOPLE HERE TRYING TO CHEER YOU UP.
YOU'RE STARTING TO TALK LIKE SOMEONE'S MOTHER, USAGI.
I WILL DO WHATEVER IT TAKES TO FIND THEM.

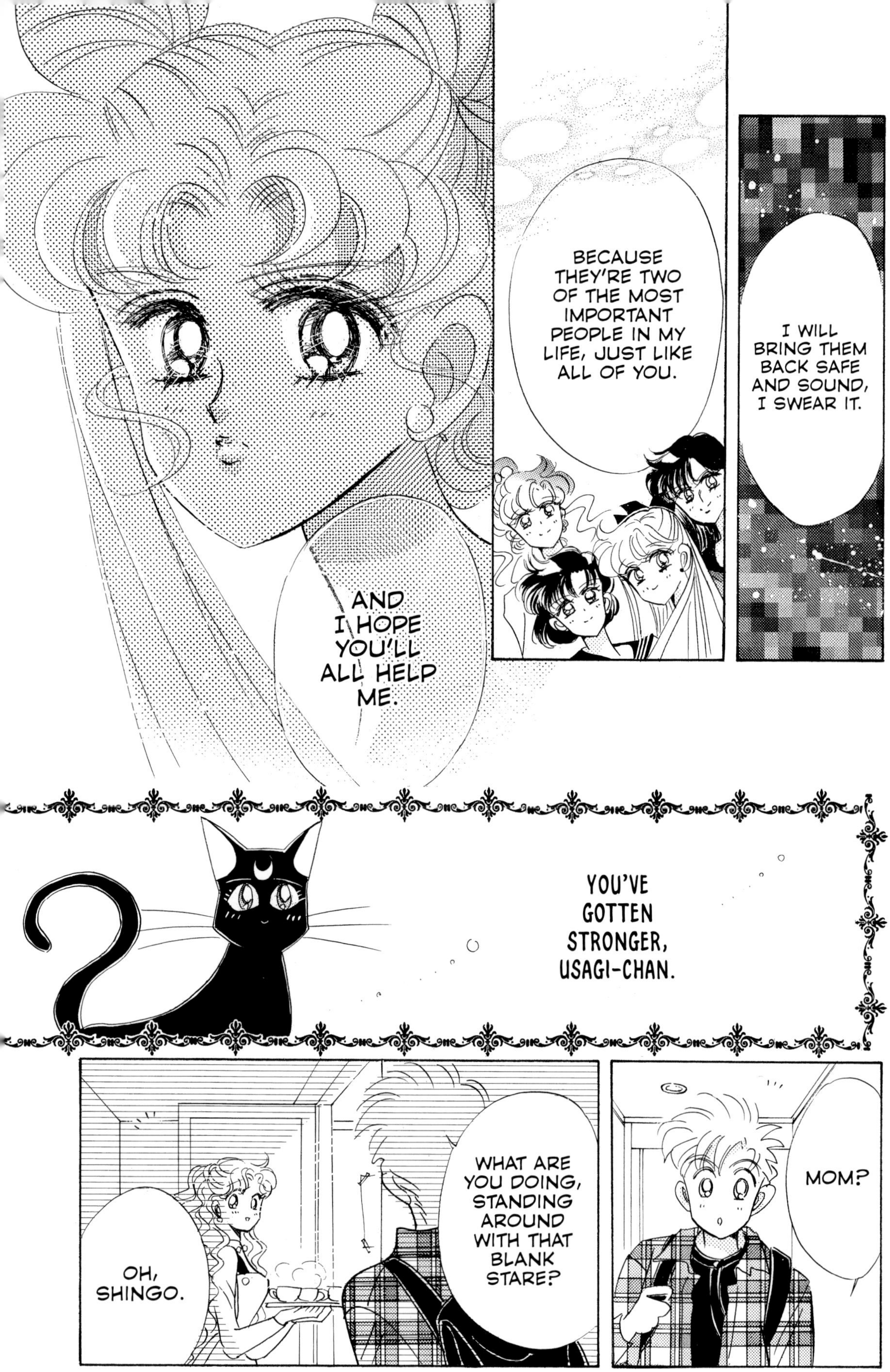
I WILL BRING THEM BACK SAFE AND SOUND, I SWEAR IT.
BECAUSE THEY'RE TWO OF THE MOST IMPORTANT PEOPLE IN MY LIFE, JUST LIKE ALL OF YOU.
AND I HOPE YOU'LL ALL HELP ME.
YOU'VE GOTTEN STRONGER, USAGI-CHAN.
MOM?
WHAT ARE YOU DOING, STANDING AROUND WITH THAT BLANK STARE?
OH, SHINGO.

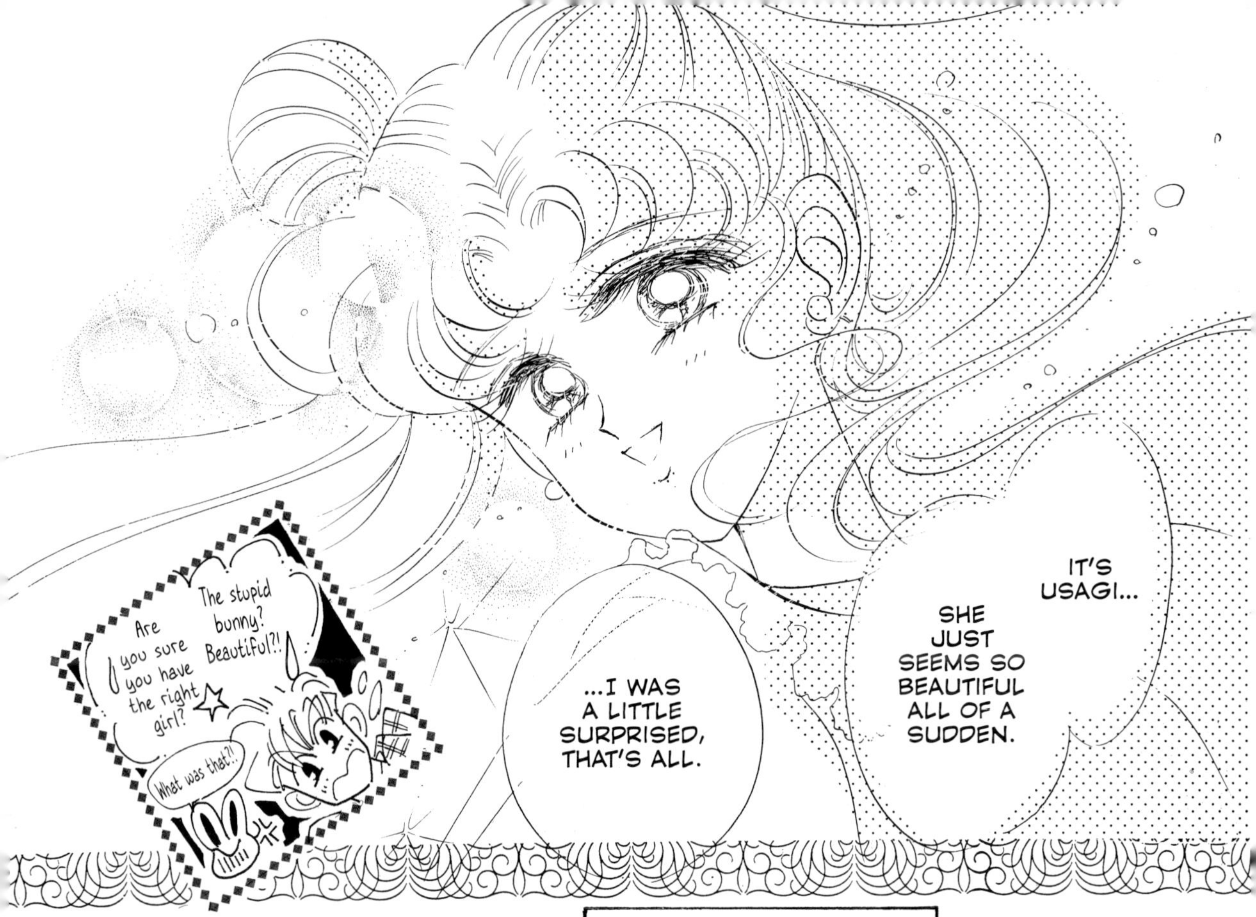
IT'S USAGI...
SHE JUST SEEMS SO BEAUTIFUL ALL OF A SUDDEN.
...I WAS A LITTLE SURPRISED, THAT'S ALL.
The stupid bunny? Beautiful?!
Are you sure you have the right girl?
What was that?!

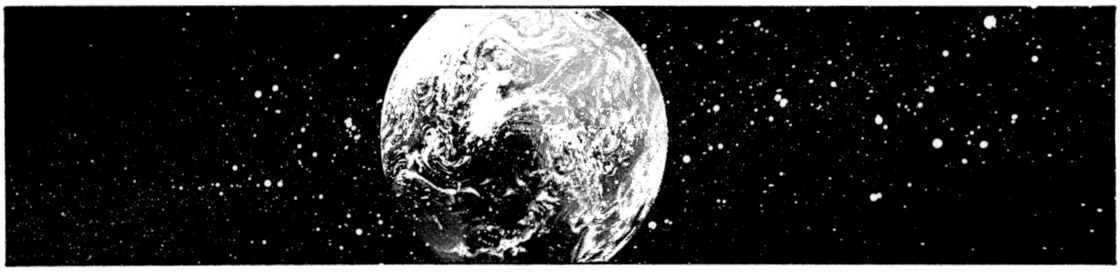

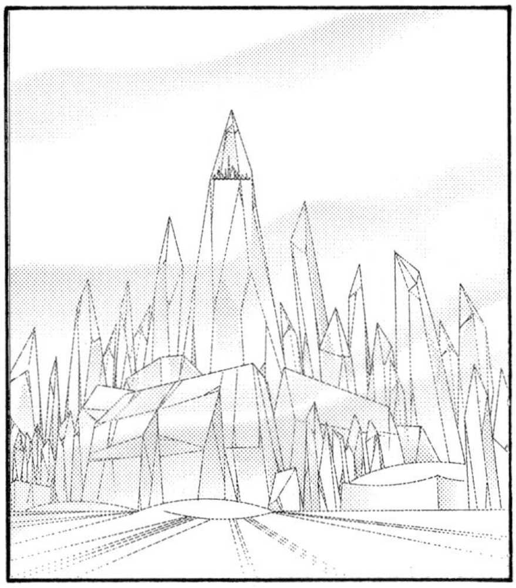

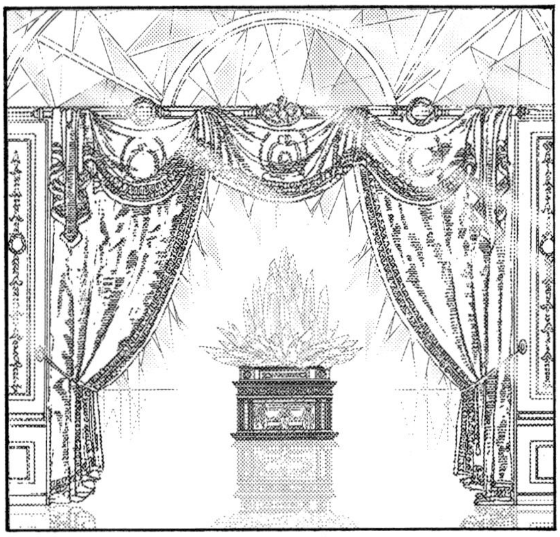

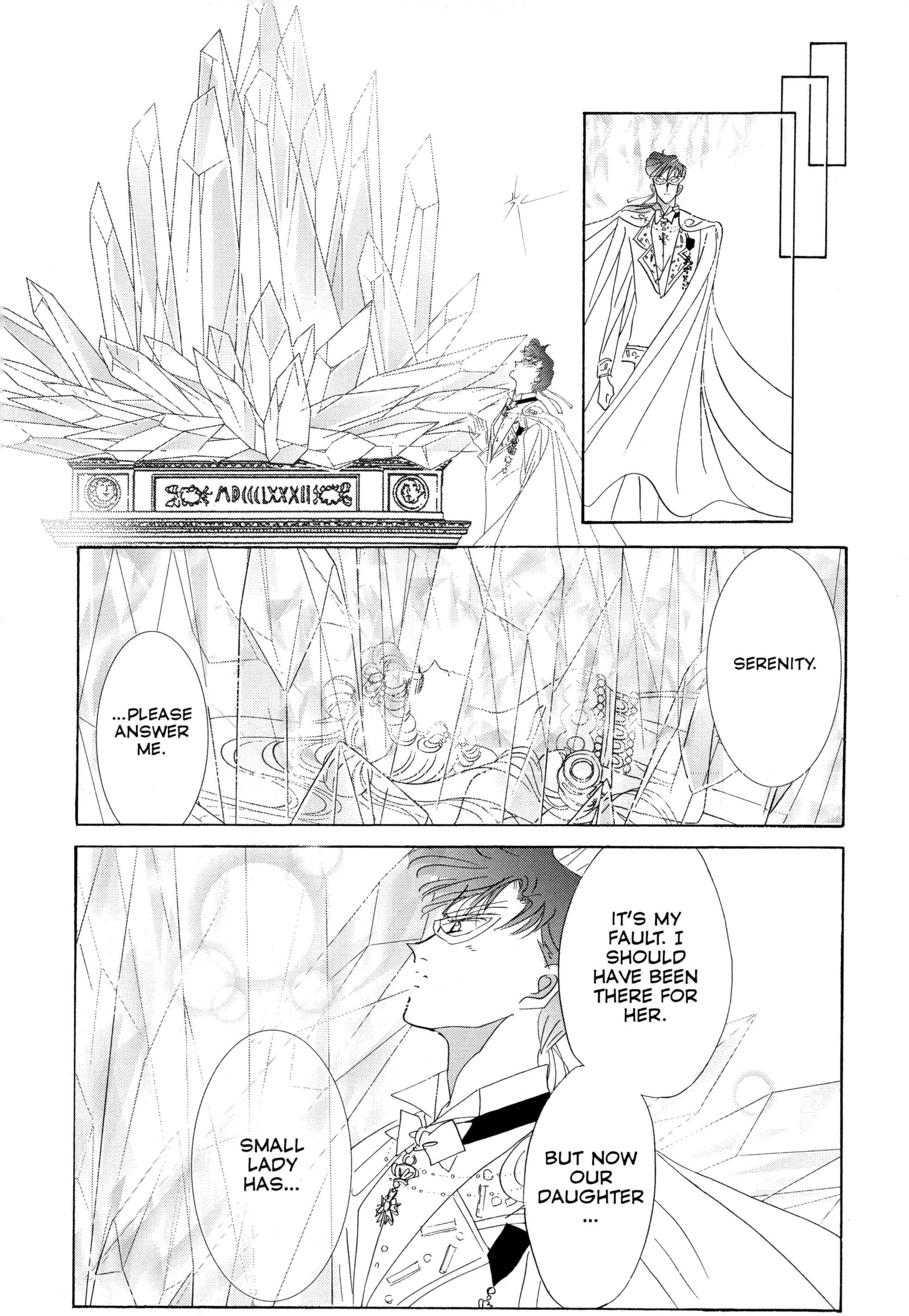
SERENITY.
...PLEASE ANSWER ME.
IT'S MY FAULT. I SHOULD HAVE BEEN THERE FOR HER.
BUT NOW OUR DAUGHTER ...
SMALL LADY HAS...

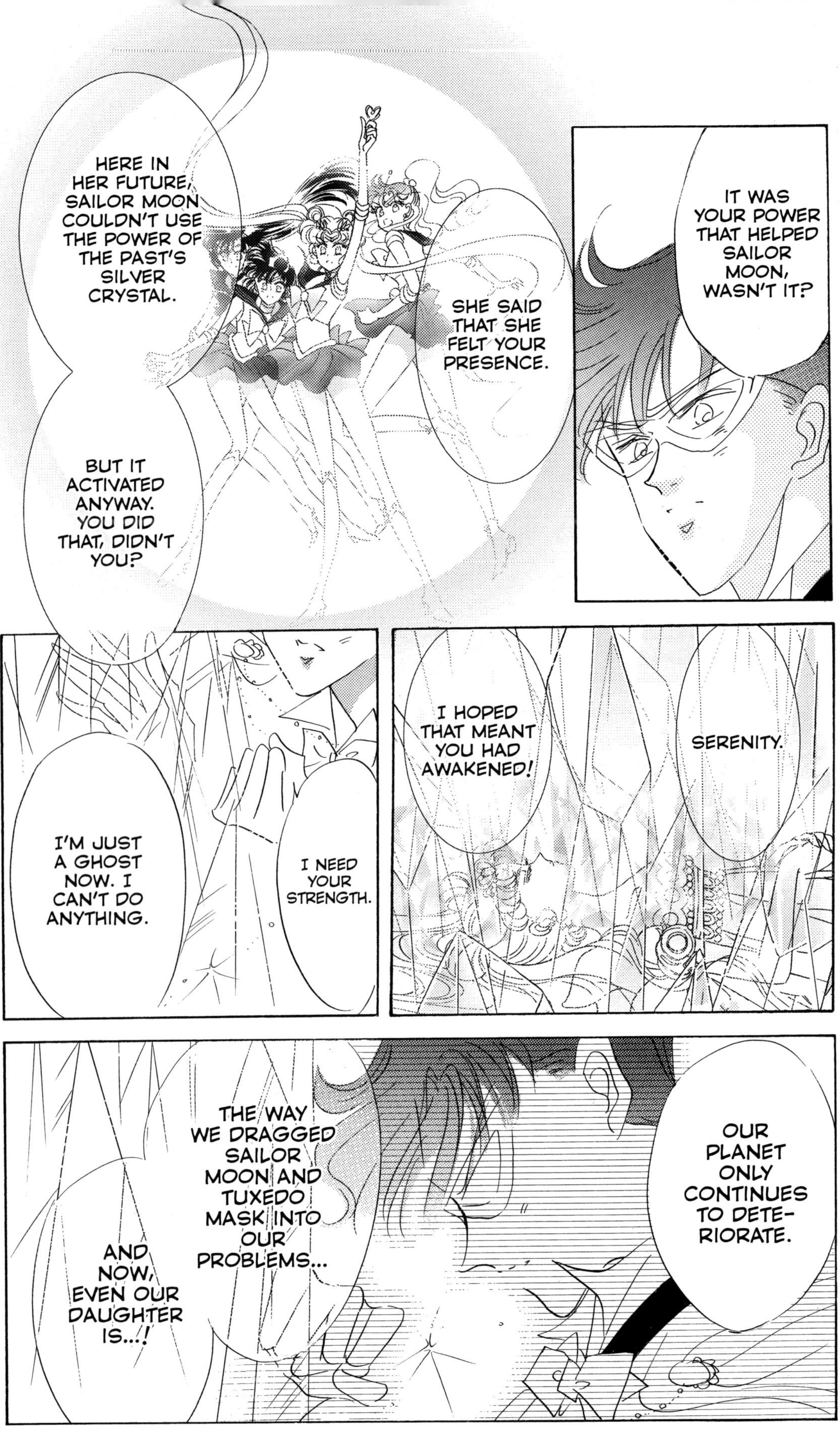
IT WAS YOUR POWER THAT HELPED SAILOR MOON, WASN'T IT?
SHE SAID THAT SHE FELT YOUR PRESENCE.
HERE IN HER FUTURE, SAILOR MOON COULDN'T USE THE POWER OF THE PAST'S SILVER CRYSTAL.
BUT IT ACTIVATED ANYWAY. YOU DID THAT, DIDN'T YOU?
SERENITY.
I HOPED THAT MEANT YOU HAD AWAKENED!
I NEED YOUR STRENGTH.
I'M JUST A GHOST NOW. I CAN'T DO ANYTHING.
OUR PLANET ONLY CONTINUES TO DETE-RIORATE.
THE WAY WE DRAGGED SAILOR MOON AND TUXEDO MASK INTO OUR PROBLEMS...
AND NOW, EVEN OUR DAUGHTER IS...!

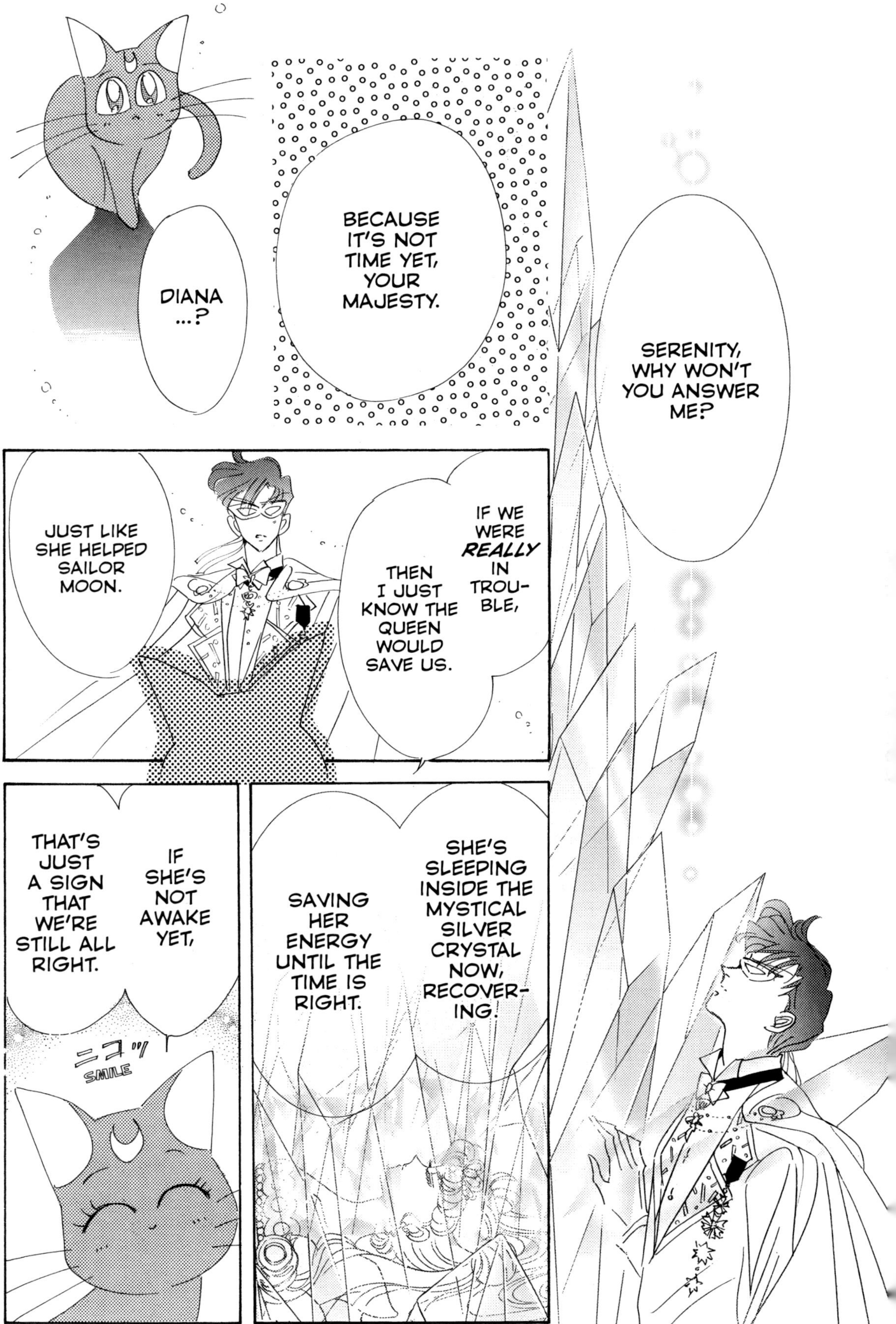
SERENITY, WHY WON'T YOU ANSWER ME?
BECAUSE IT'S NOT TIME YET, YOUR MAJESTY.
DIANA ...?
IF WE WERE *REALLY* IN TROUBLE,
THEN I JUST KNOW THE QUEEN WOULD SAVE US.
JUST LIKE SHE HELPED SAILOR MOON.
SHE'S SLEEPING INSIDE THE MYSTICAL SILVER CRYSTAL NOW, RECOVERING.
SAVING HER ENERGY UNTIL THE TIME IS RIGHT.
IF SHE'S NOT AWAKE YET,
THAT'S JUST A SIGN THAT WE'RE STILL ALL RIGHT.
ニコッ
SMILE

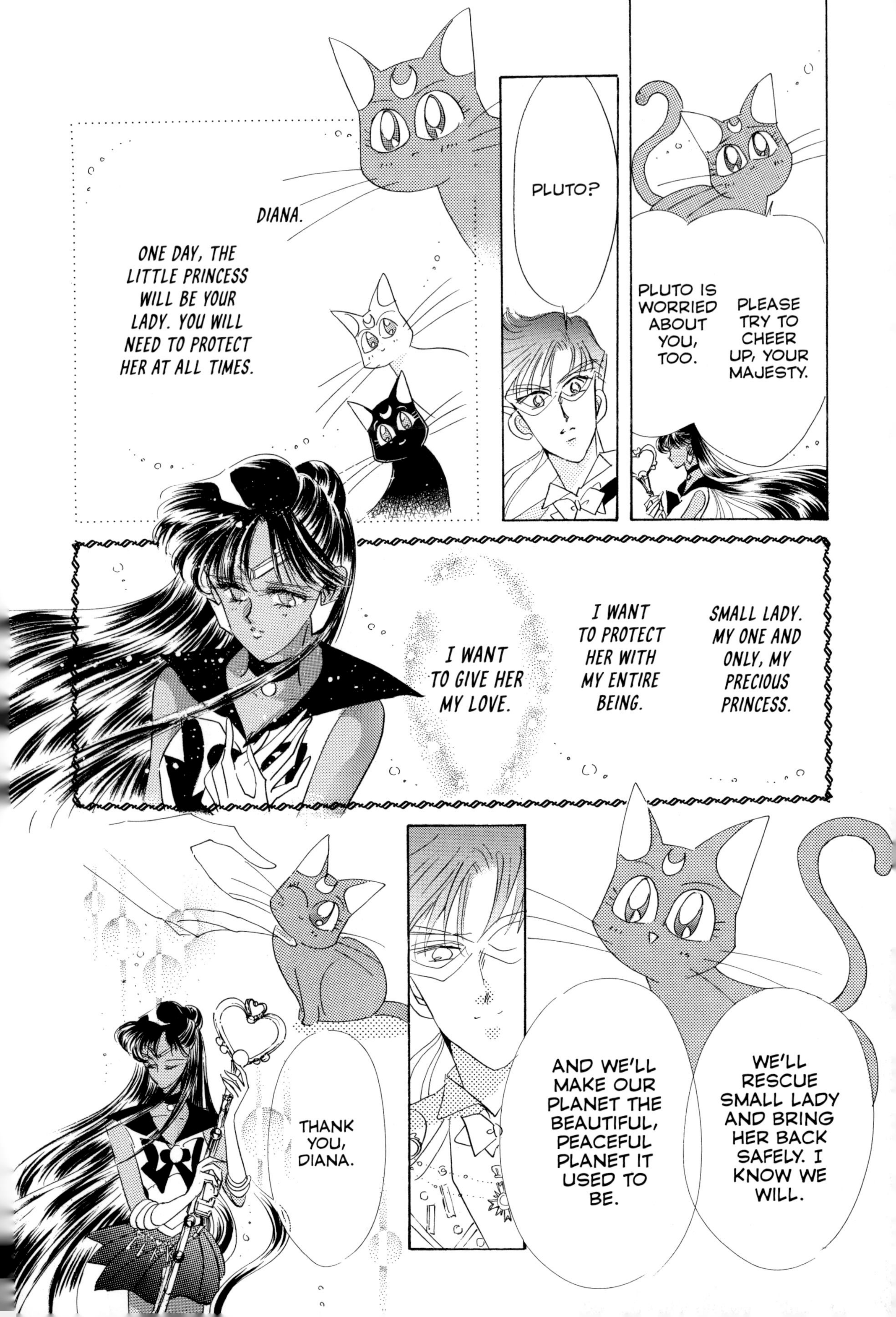
PLEASE TRY TO CHEER UP, YOUR MAJESTY.
PLUTO IS WORRIED ABOUT YOU, TOO.
PLUTO?
DIANA.
ONE DAY, THE LITTLE PRINCESS WILL BE YOUR LADY. YOU WILL NEED TO PROTECT HER AT ALL TIMES.
SMALL LADY. MY ONE AND ONLY, MY PRECIOUS PRINCESS.
I WANT TO PROTECT HER WITH MY ENTIRE BEING.
I WANT TO GIVE HER MY LOVE.
WE'LL RESCUE SMALL LADY AND BRING HER BACK SAFELY. I KNOW WE WILL.
AND WE'LL MAKE OUR PLANET THE BEAUTIFUL, PEACEFUL PLANET IT USED TO BE.
THANK YOU, DIANA.

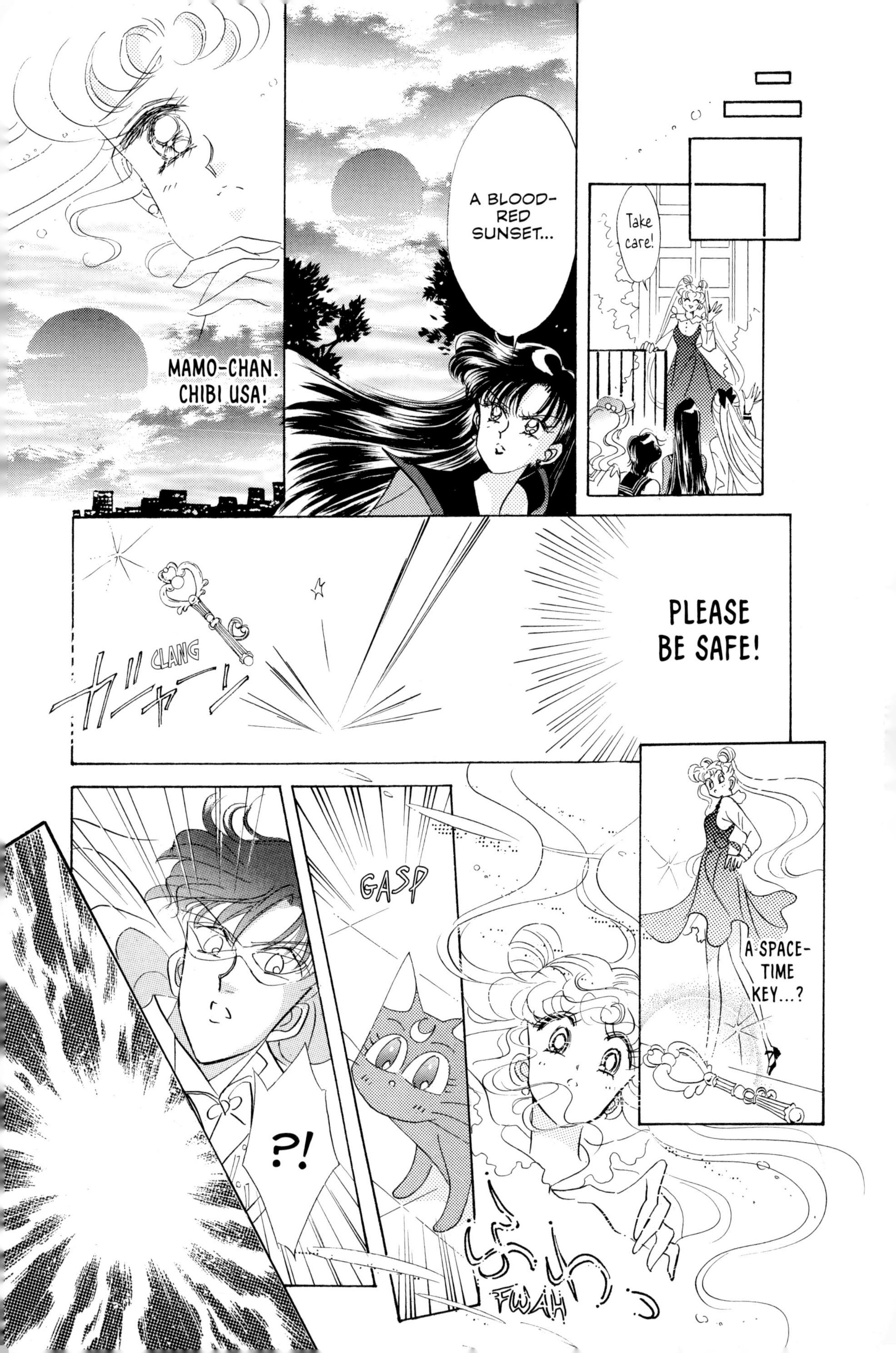

Take care!
A BLOOD-RED SUNSET...
MAMO-CHAN. CHIBI USA!
PLEASE BE SAFE!
ガシャーン
CLANG
A SPACE-TIME KEY...?
FWAH
GASP
?!

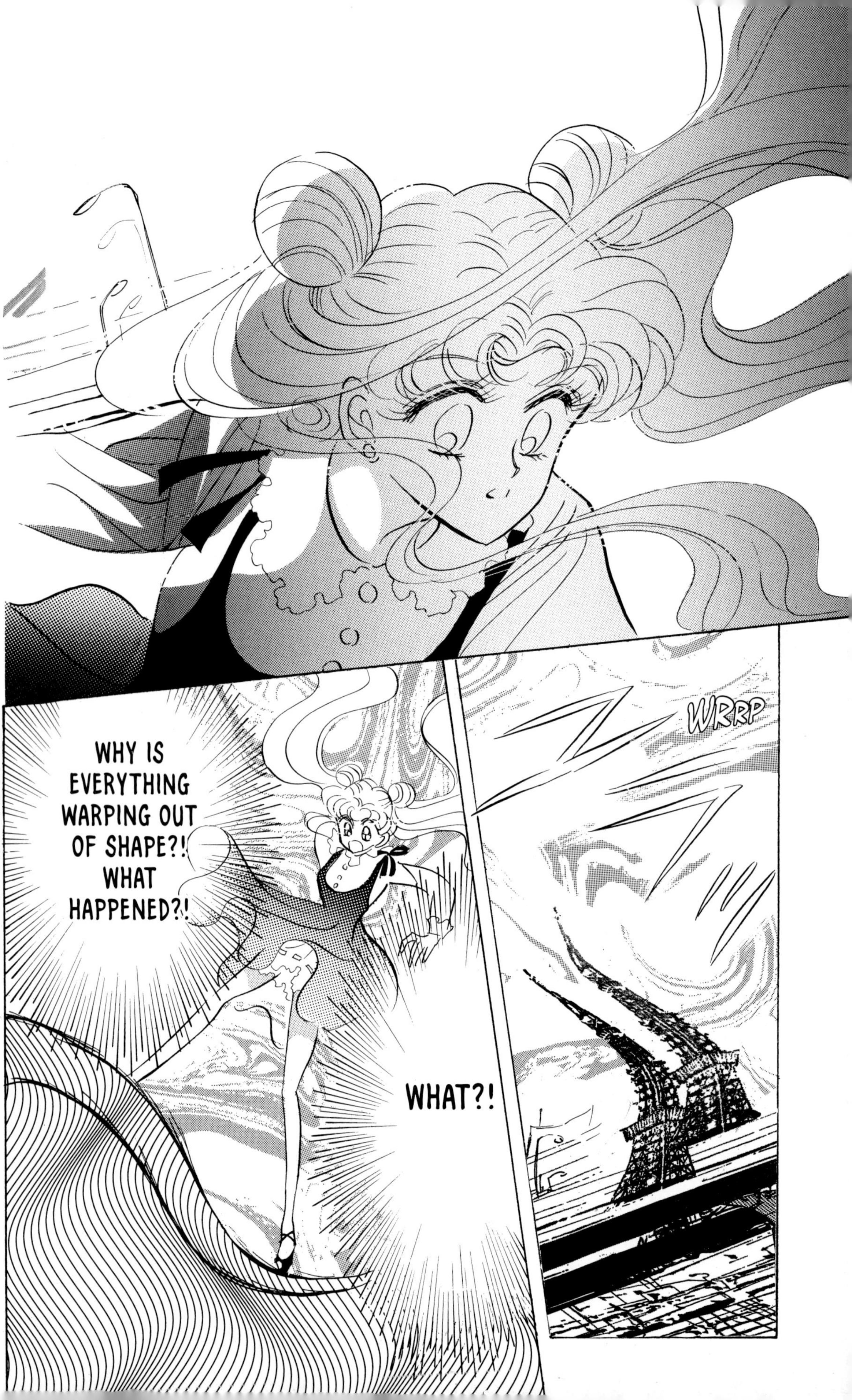
WRRP
WHY IS EVERYTHING WARPING OUT OF SHAPE?! WHAT HAPPENED?!
WHAT?!

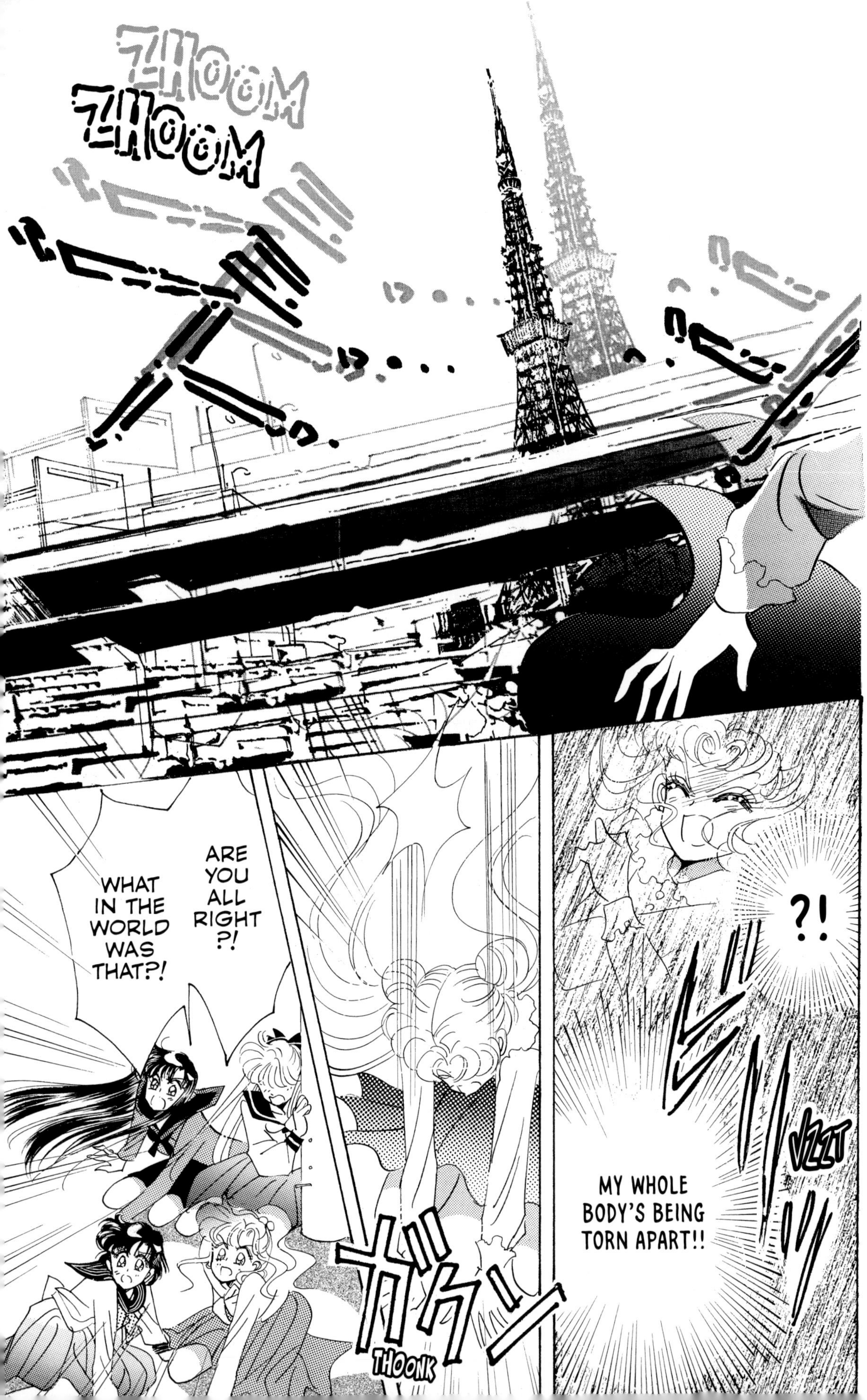
ZHOOM
ZHOOM
?!
VZZT
MY WHOLE BODY'S BEING TORN APART!!
ARE YOU ALL RIGHT?!
WHAT IN THE WORLD WAS THAT?!
THOONK

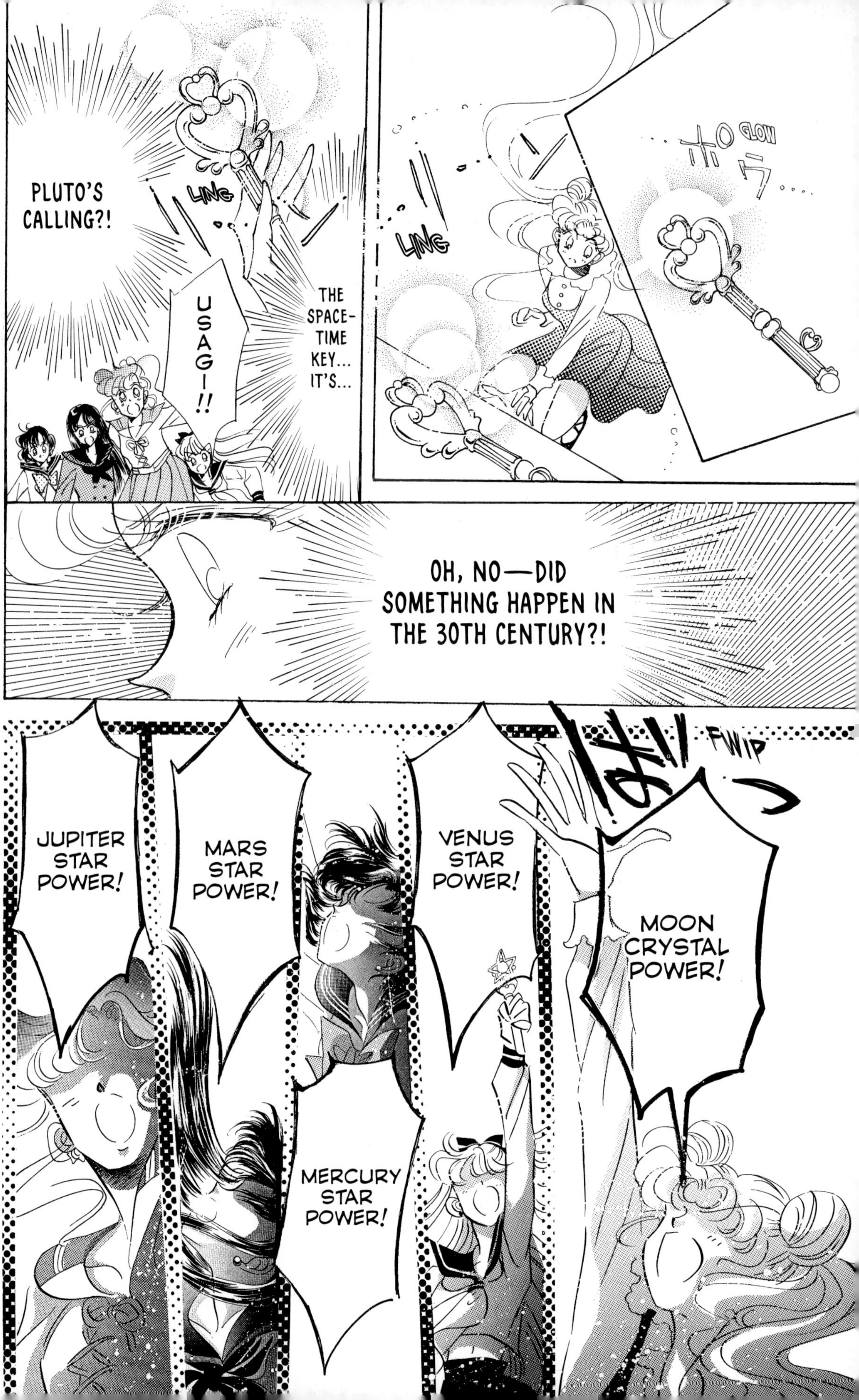
ホ ラ GLOW
LING
THE SPACE-TIME KEY... IT'S...
LING
USAGI!!
PLUTO'S CALLING?!
OH, NO—DID SOMETHING HAPPEN IN THE 30TH CENTURY?!
FWIP
MOON CRYSTAL POWER!
VENUS STAR POWER!
MERCURY STAR POWER!
MARS STAR POWER!
JUPITER STAR POWER!

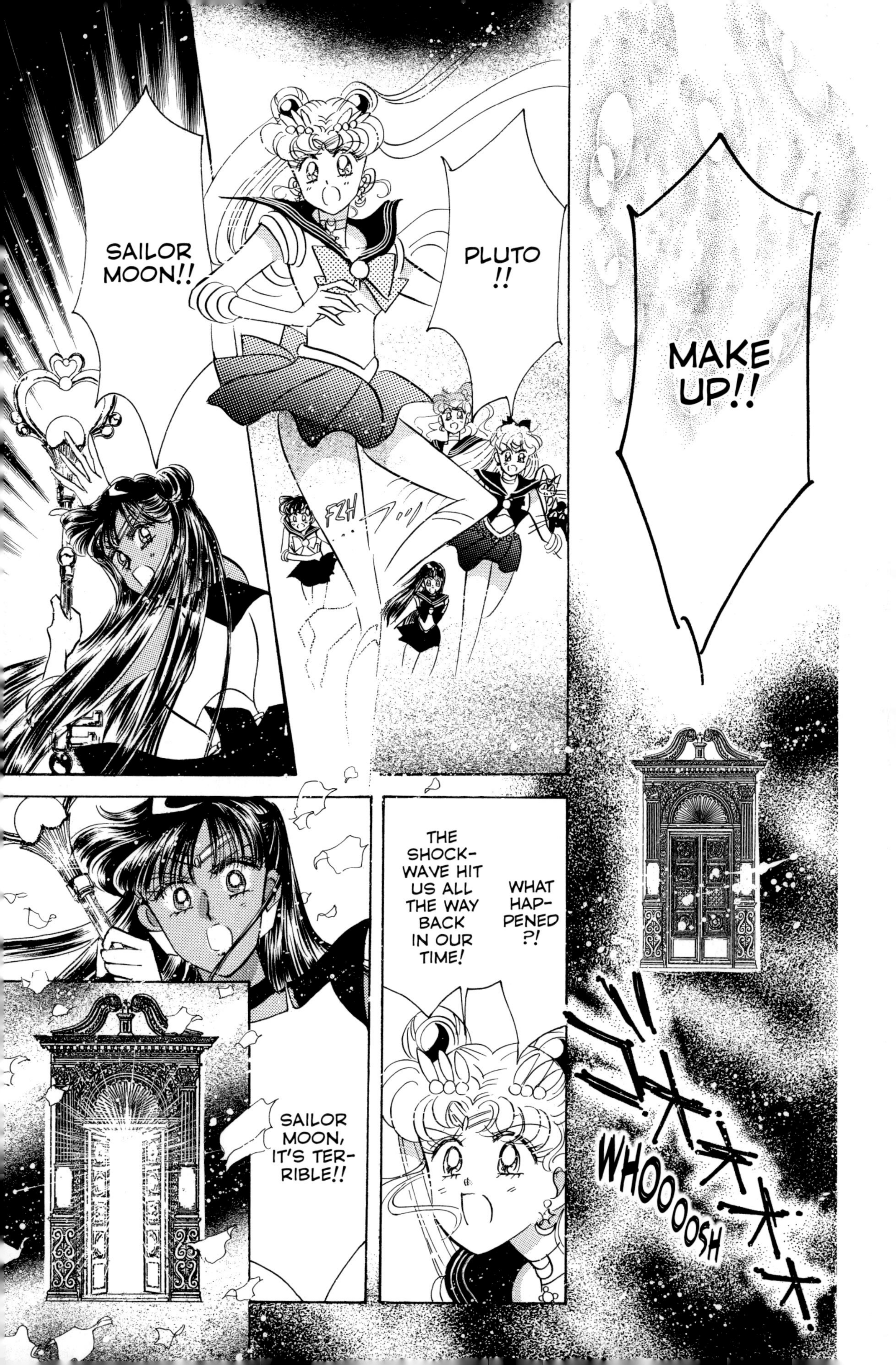
MAKE UP!!
WHOOOOSH
PLUTO!!
SAILOR MOON!!
FZH
WHAT HAPPENED?!
THE SHOCKWAVE HIT US ALL THE WAY BACK IN OUR TIME!
SAILOR MOON, IT'S TERRIBLE!!

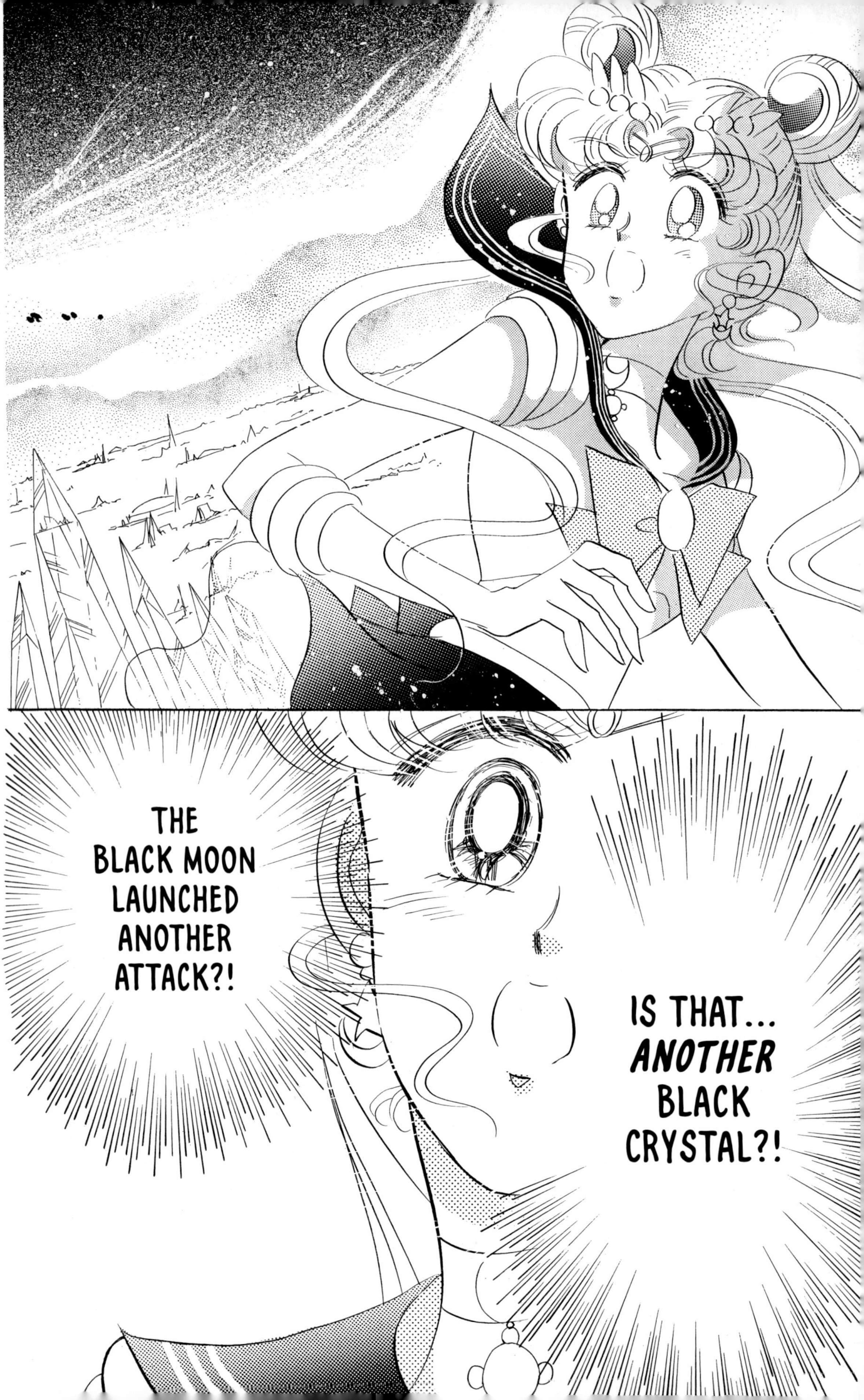
IS THAT... *ANOTHER* BLACK CRYSTAL?!
THE BLACK MOON LAUNCHED ANOTHER ATTACK?!

WHOOOOOSH

SFF

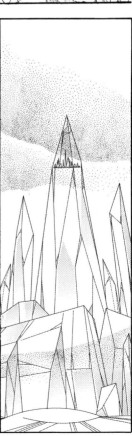

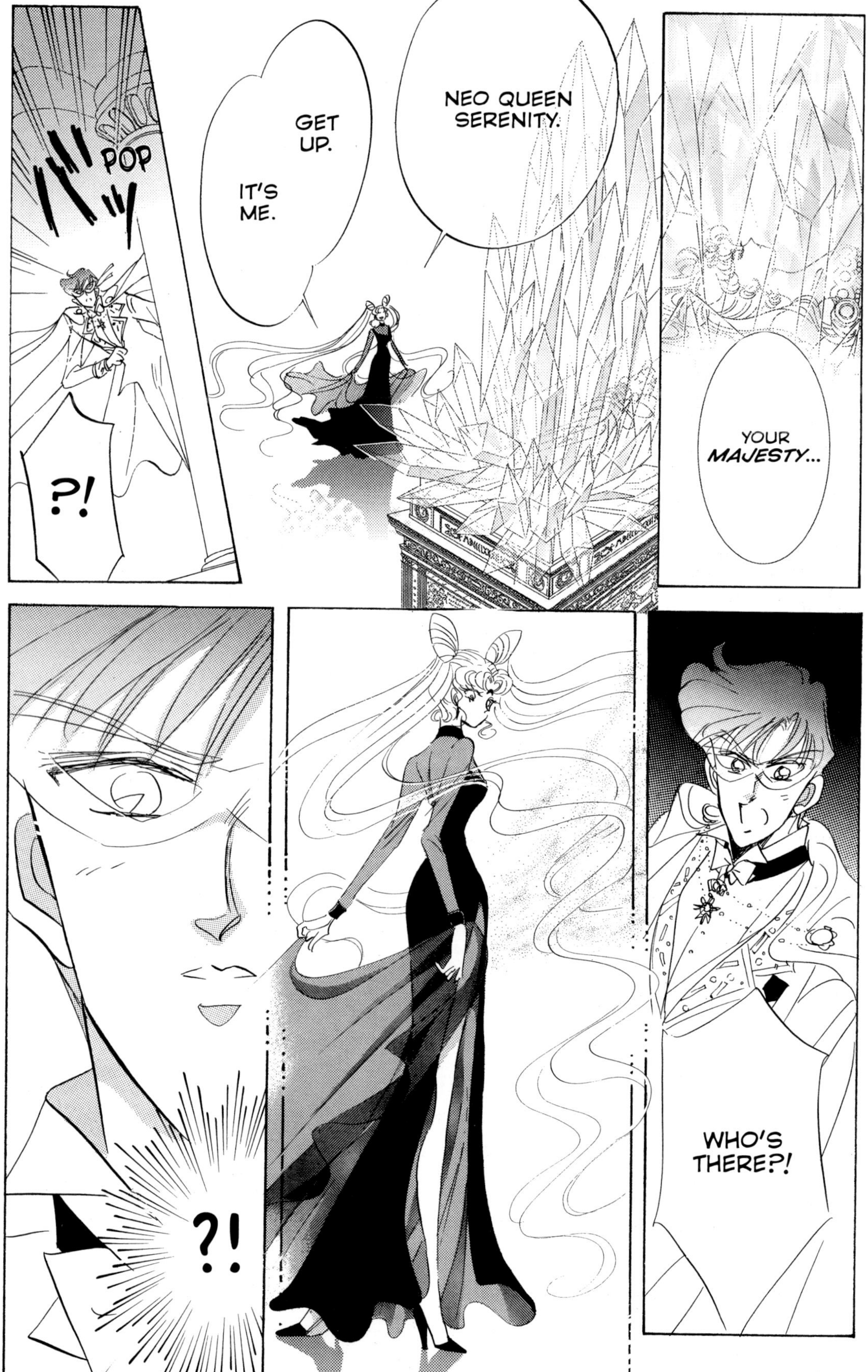
YOUR MAJESTY...
NEO QUEEN SERENITY.
GET UP.
IT'S ME.
POP
?!
WHO'S THERE?!
?!

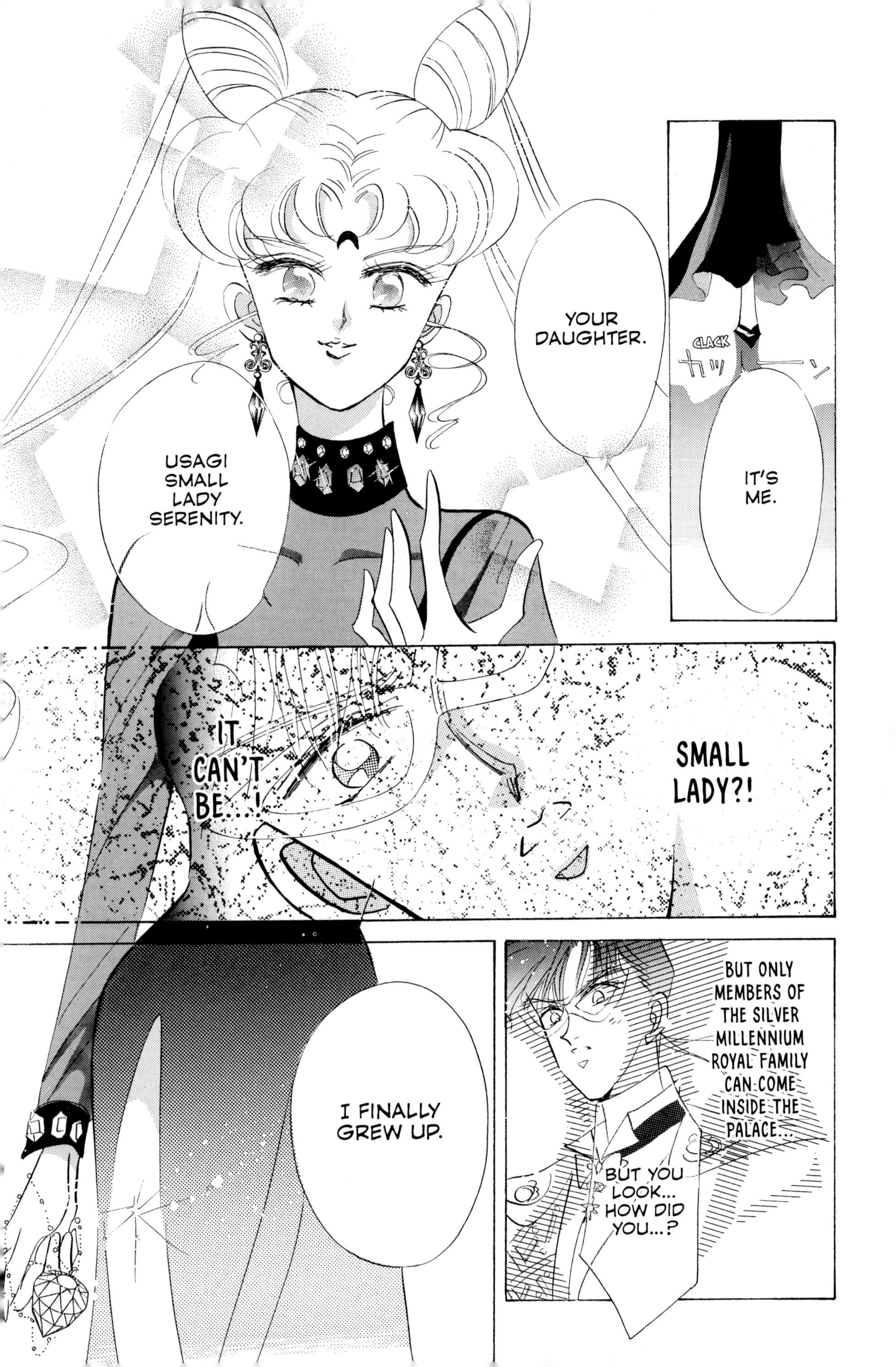

CLACK
カッ
IT'S ME.
YOUR DAUGHTER.
USAGI SMALL LADY SERENITY.
SMALL LADY?!
IT CAN'T BE...!
BUT ONLY MEMBERS OF THE SILVER MILLENNIUM ROYAL FAMILY CAN COME INSIDE THE PALACE...
BUT YOU LOOK... HOW DID YOU...?
I FINALLY GREW UP.

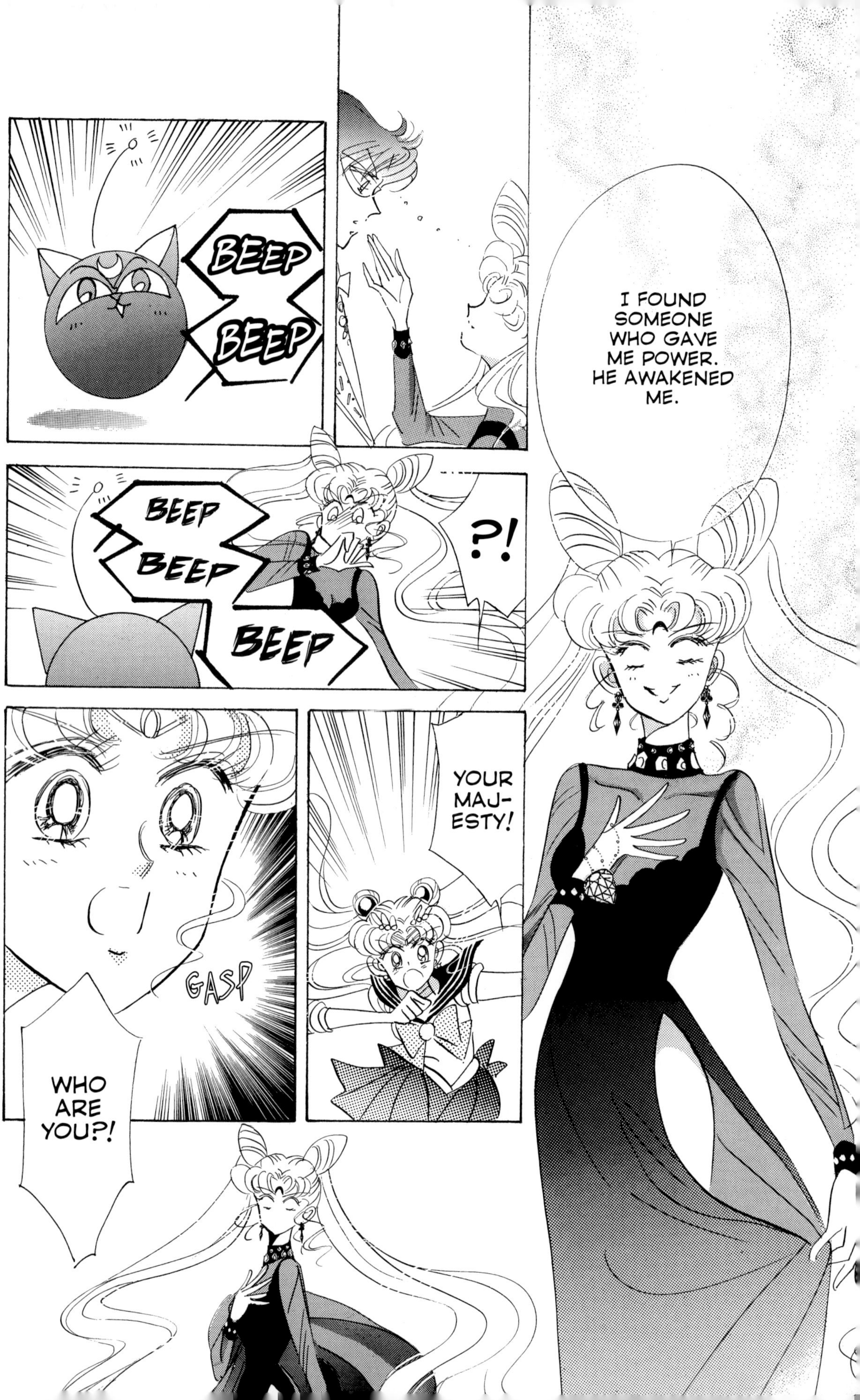
I FOUND SOMEONE WHO GAVE ME POWER. HE AWAKENED ME.
BEEP
BEEP
?!
BEEP
BEEP
BEEP
YOUR MAJ-ESTY!
GASP
WHO ARE YOU?!

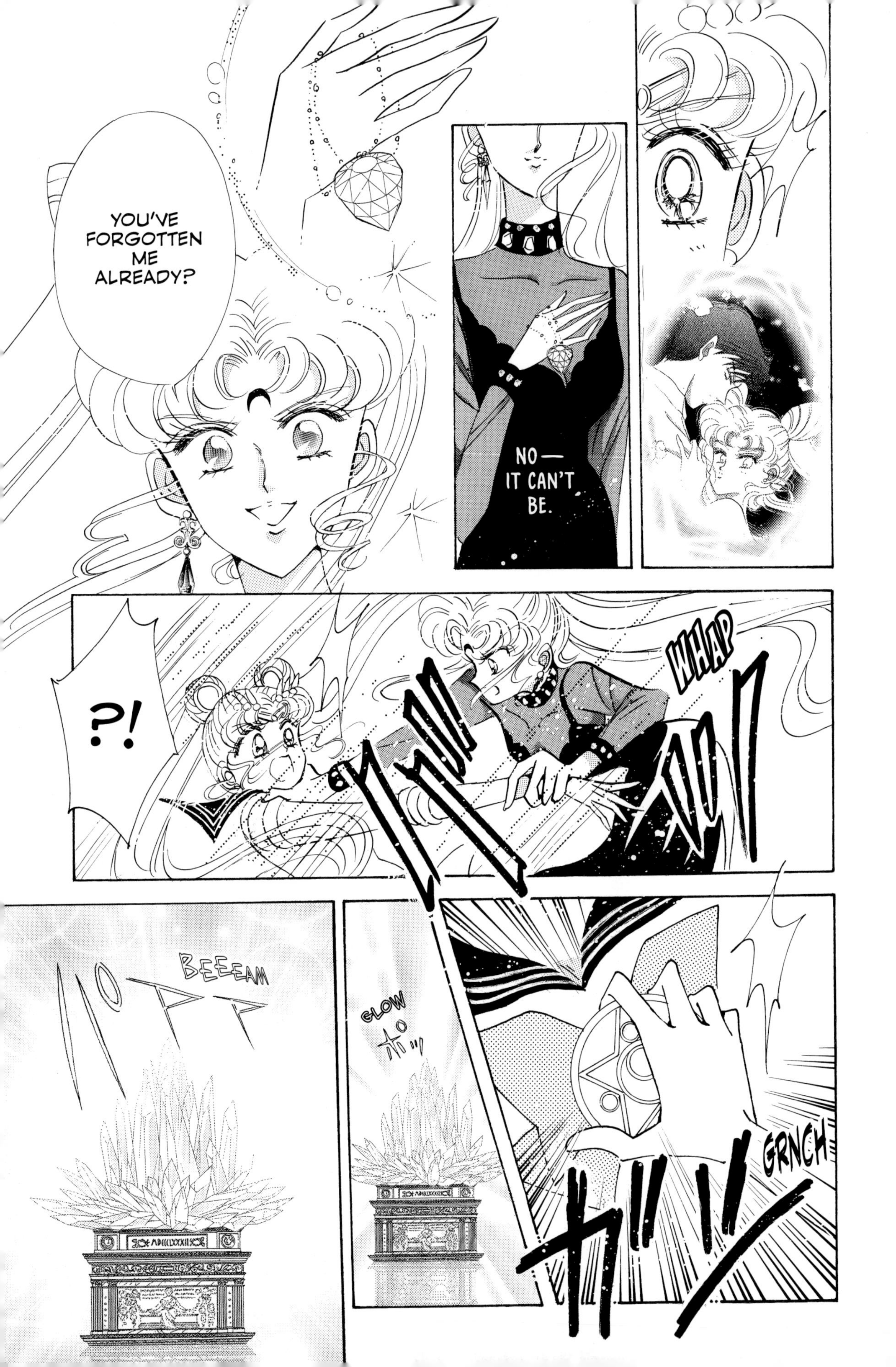
NO— IT CAN'T BE.
YOU'VE FORGOTTEN ME ALREADY?
WHAP
?!
GRNCH
GLOW
BEEEAM

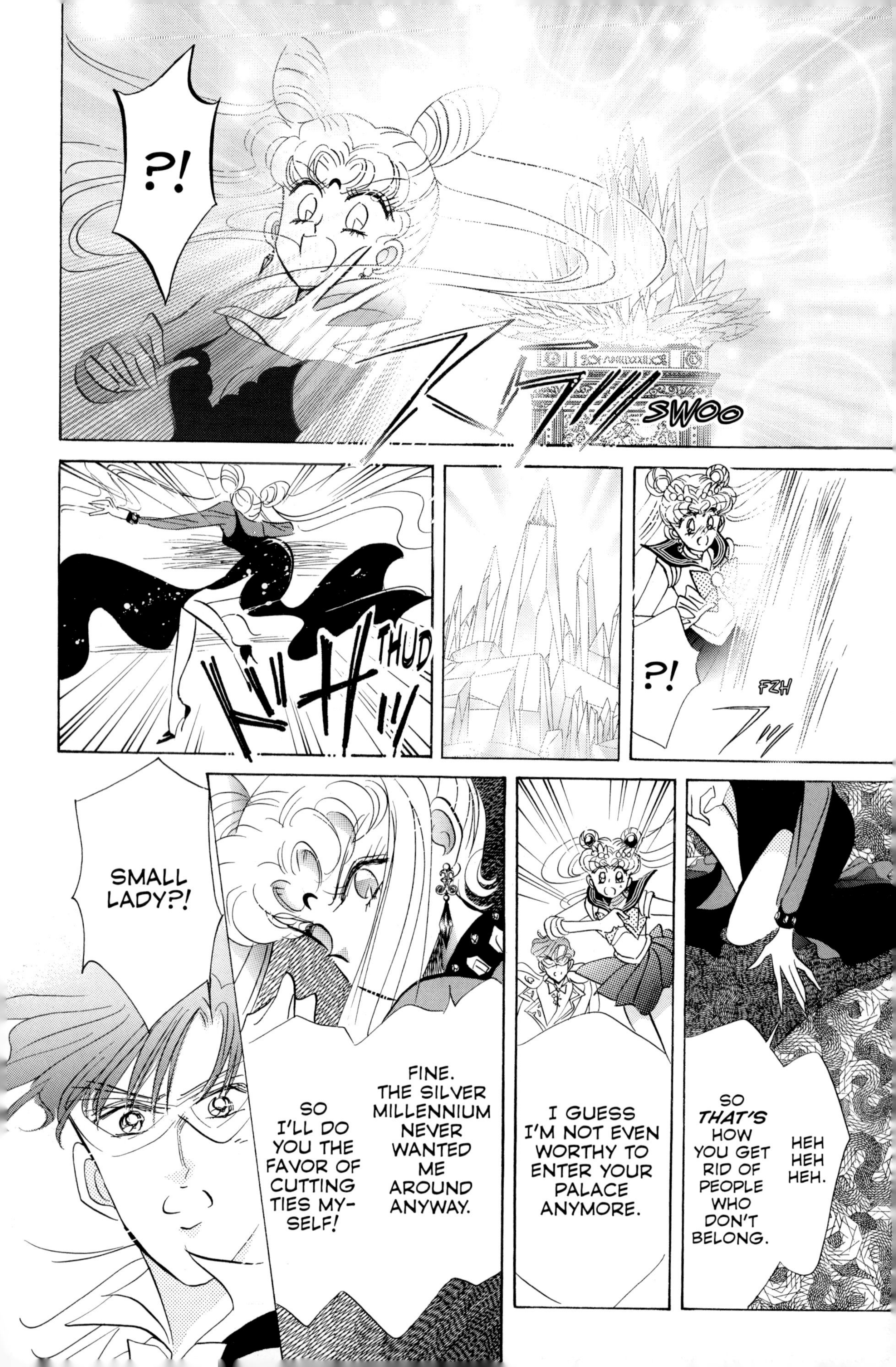
?!
SWOO
?!
FZH
THUD
SO *THAT'S* HOW YOU GET RID OF PEOPLE WHO DON'T BELONG.
HEH HEH HEH.
I GUESS I'M NOT EVEN WORTHY TO ENTER YOUR PALACE ANYMORE.
FINE. THE SILVER MILLENNIUM NEVER WANTED ME AROUND ANYWAY.
SO I'LL DO YOU THE FAVOR OF CUTTING TIES MY-SELF!
SMALL LADY?!

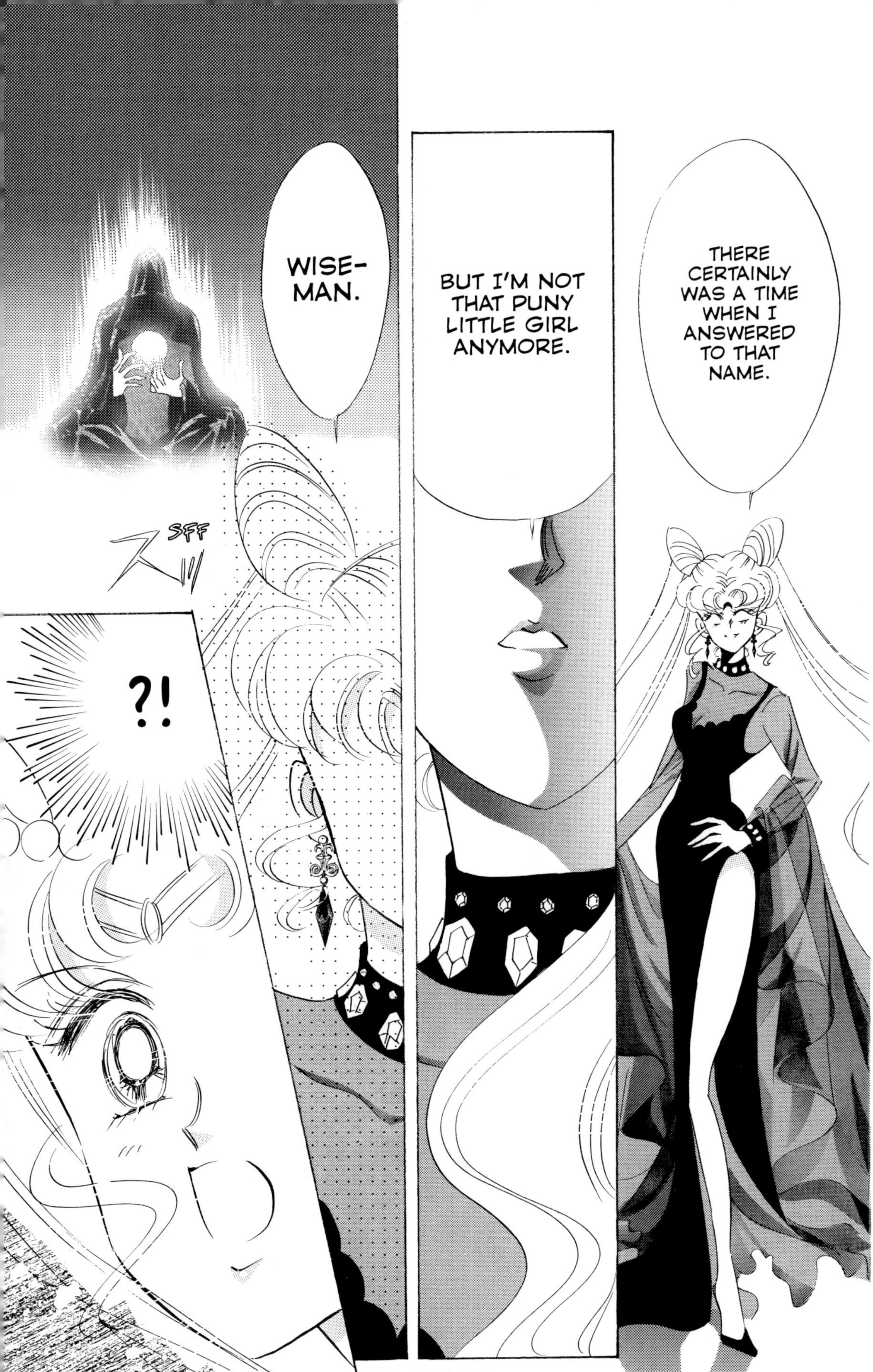
THERE CERTAINLY WAS A TIME WHEN I ANSWERED TO THAT NAME.
BUT I'M NOT THAT PUNY LITTLE GIRL ANYMORE.
WISE-MAN.
SFF
?!

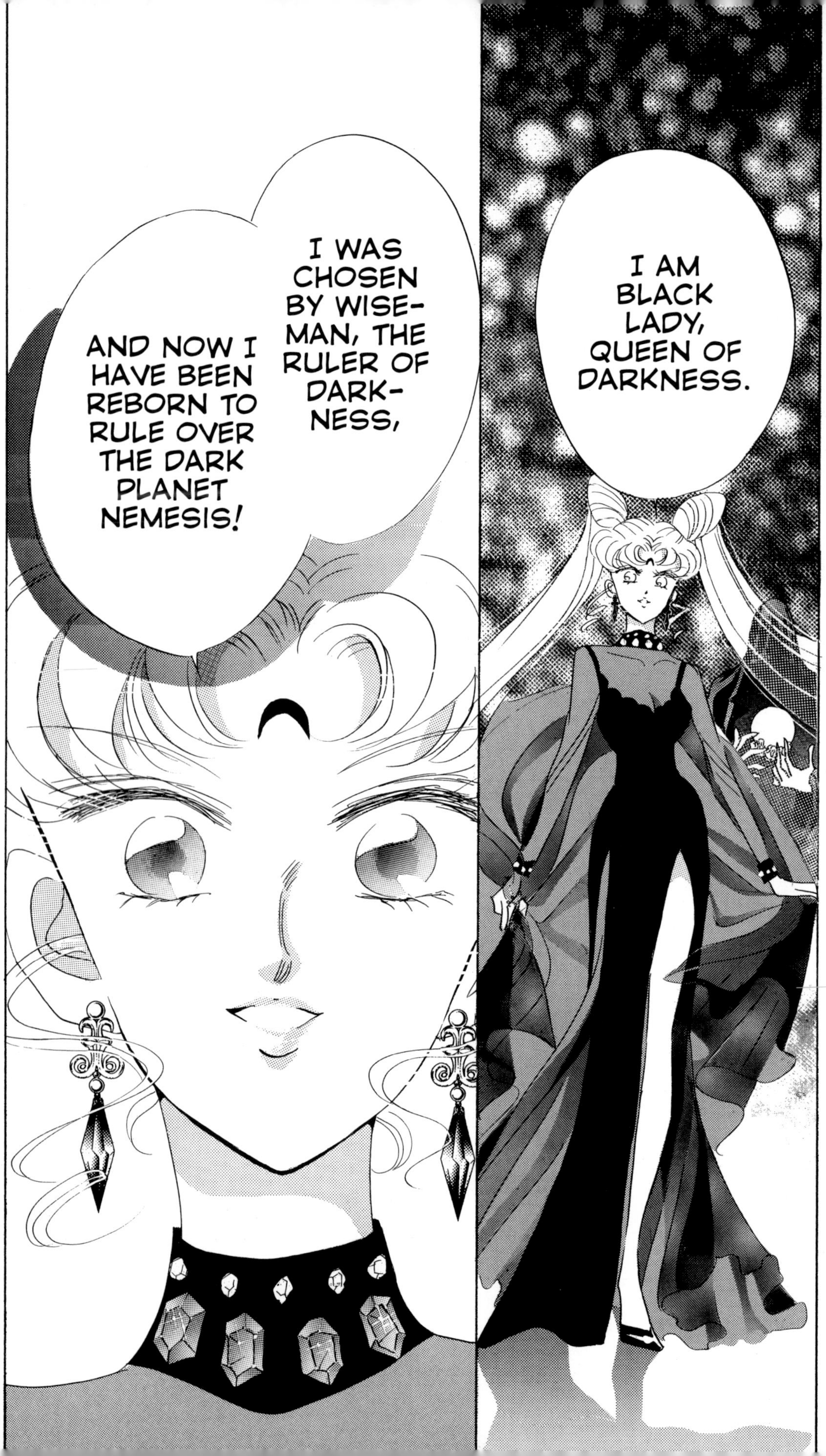
I AM BLACK LADY, QUEEN OF DARKNESS.
I WAS CHOSEN BY WISE-MAN, THE RULER OF DARK-NESS,
AND NOW I HAVE BEEN REBORN TO RULE OVER THE DARK PLANET NEMESIS!

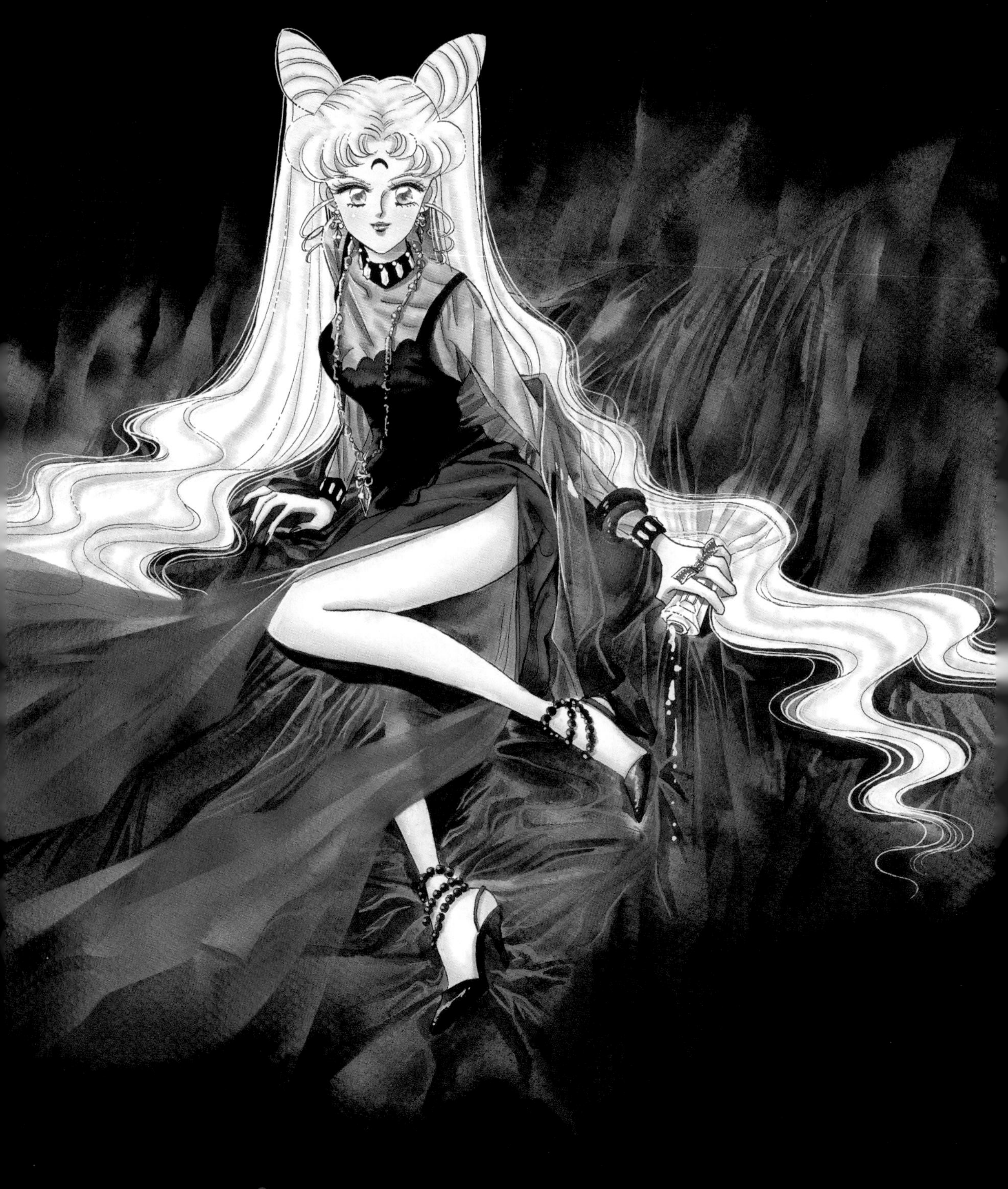

Act. 24 Attack: Black Lady

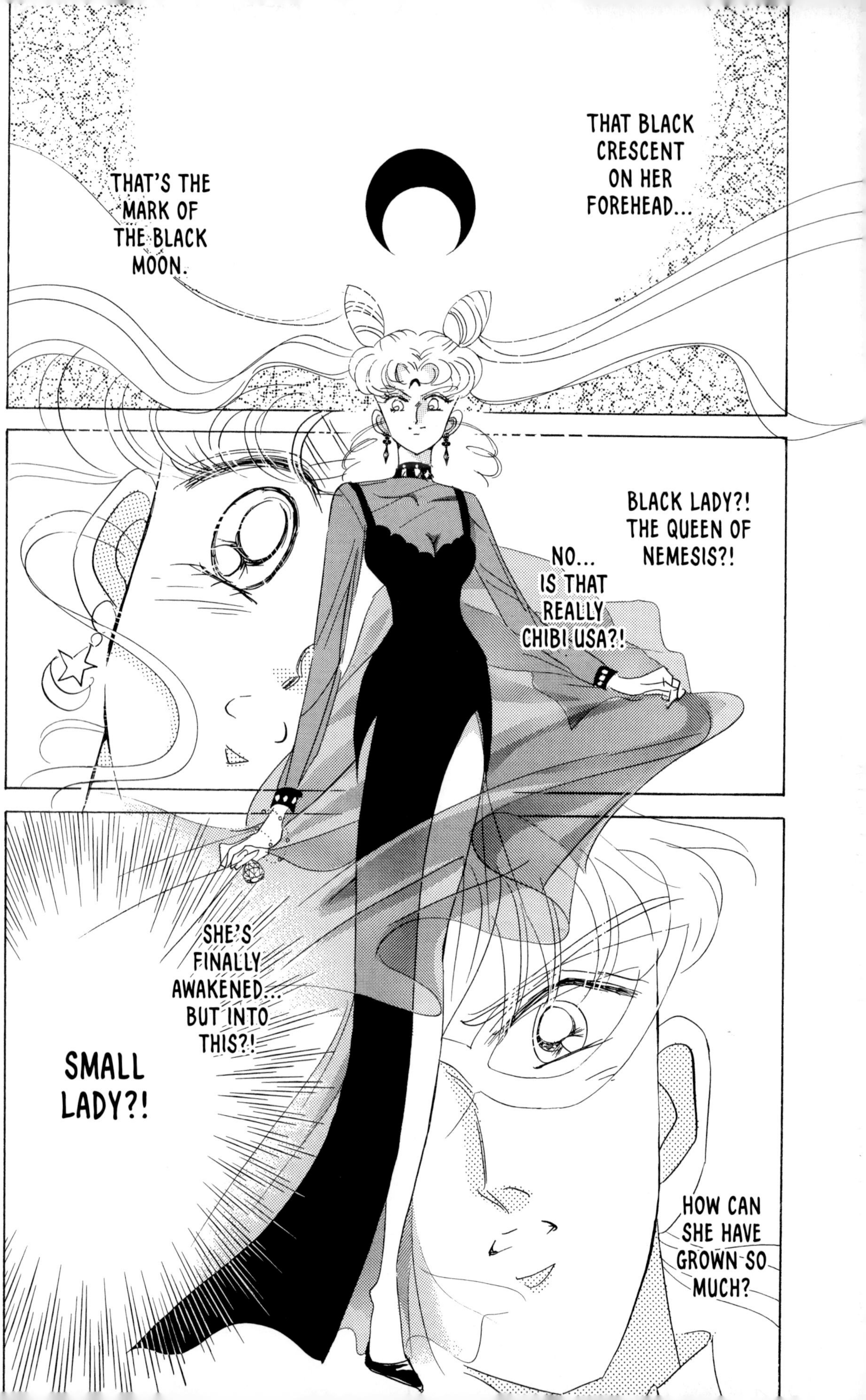
THAT BLACK CRESCENT ON HER FOREHEAD...
THAT'S THE MARK OF THE BLACK MOON.
BLACK LADY?! THE QUEEN OF NEMESIS?!
NO... IS THAT REALLY CHIBI USA?!
SHE'S FINALLY AWAKENED... BUT INTO THIS?!
SMALL LADY?!
HOW CAN SHE HAVE GROWN SO MUCH?

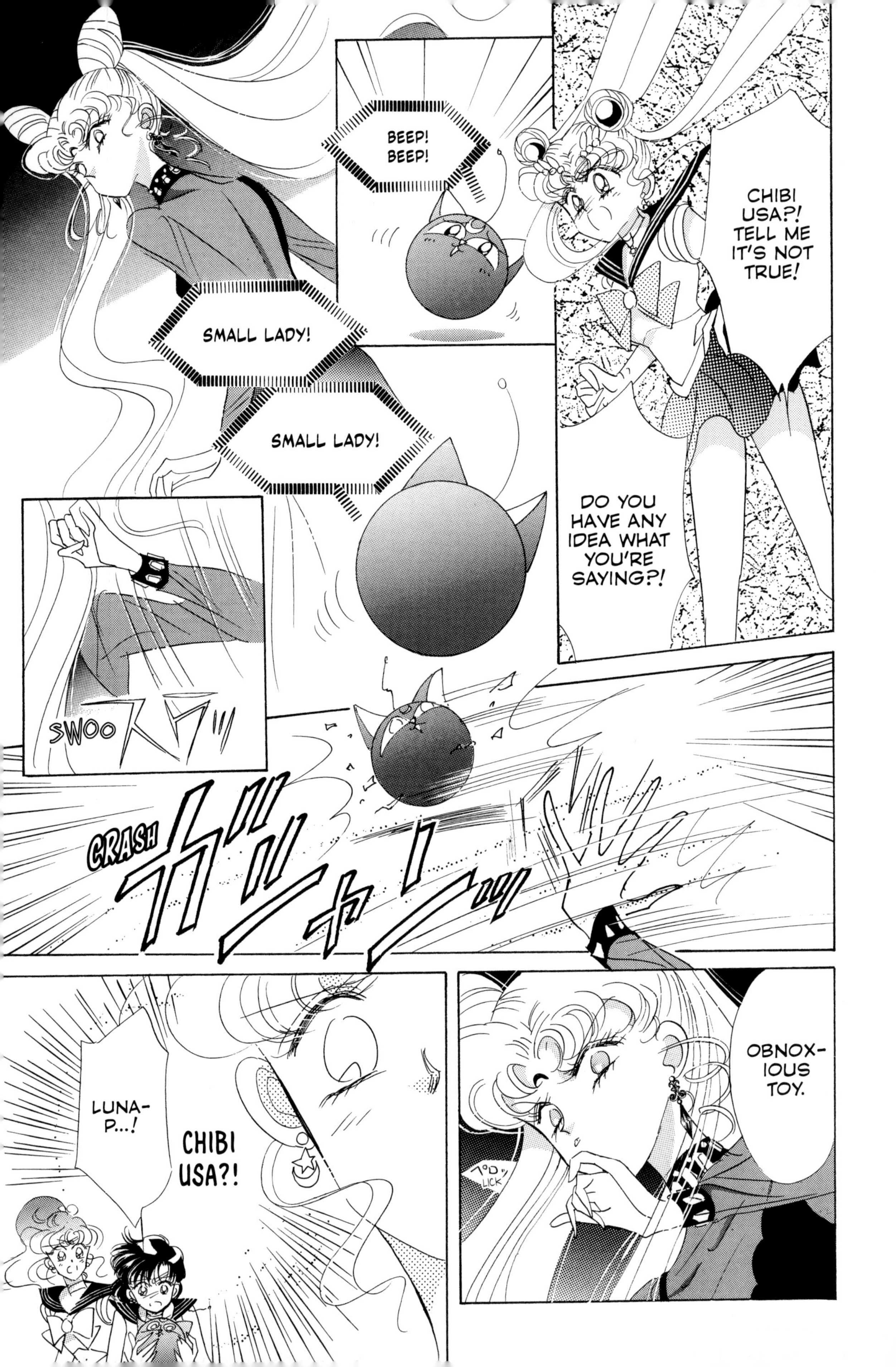
CHIBI USA?! TELL ME IT'S NOT TRUE!
DO YOU HAVE ANY IDEA WHAT YOU'RE SAYING?!
BEEP! BEEP!
SMALL LADY!
SMALL LADY!
SWOO
CRASH
OBNOXIOUS TOY.
LICK
CHIBI USA?!
LUNA-P...!

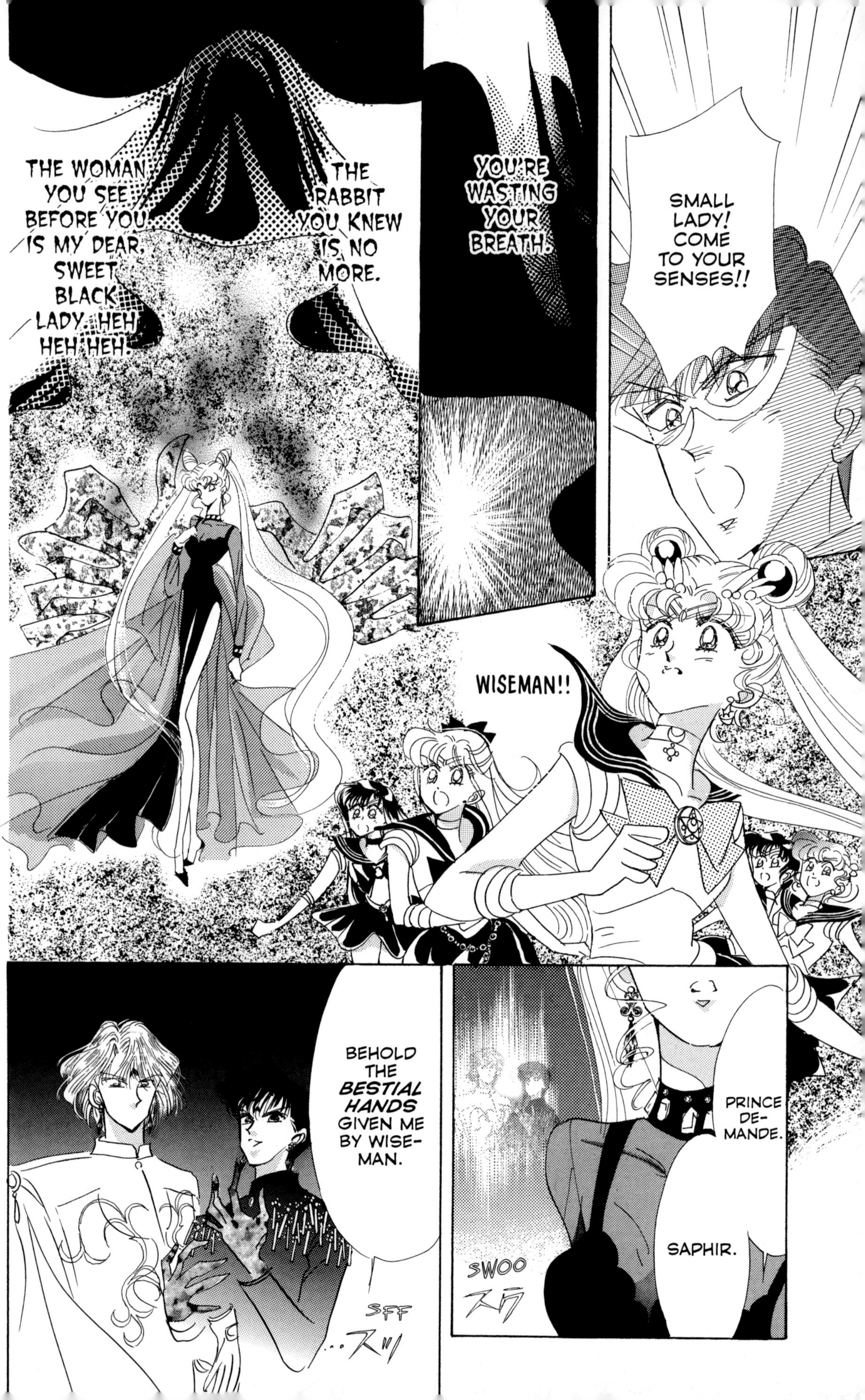
SMALL LADY! COME TO YOUR SENSES!!
YOU'RE WASTING YOUR BREATH.
THE RABBIT YOU KNEW IS NO MORE.
THE WOMAN YOU SEE BEFORE YOU IS MY DEAR, SWEET BLACK LADY. HEH HEH HEH.
WISEMAN!!
PRINCE DE-MANDE.
SAPHIR.
SWOO
スウ
BEHOLD THE *BESTIAL HANDS* GIVEN ME BY WISE-MAN.
SFF
...スッ

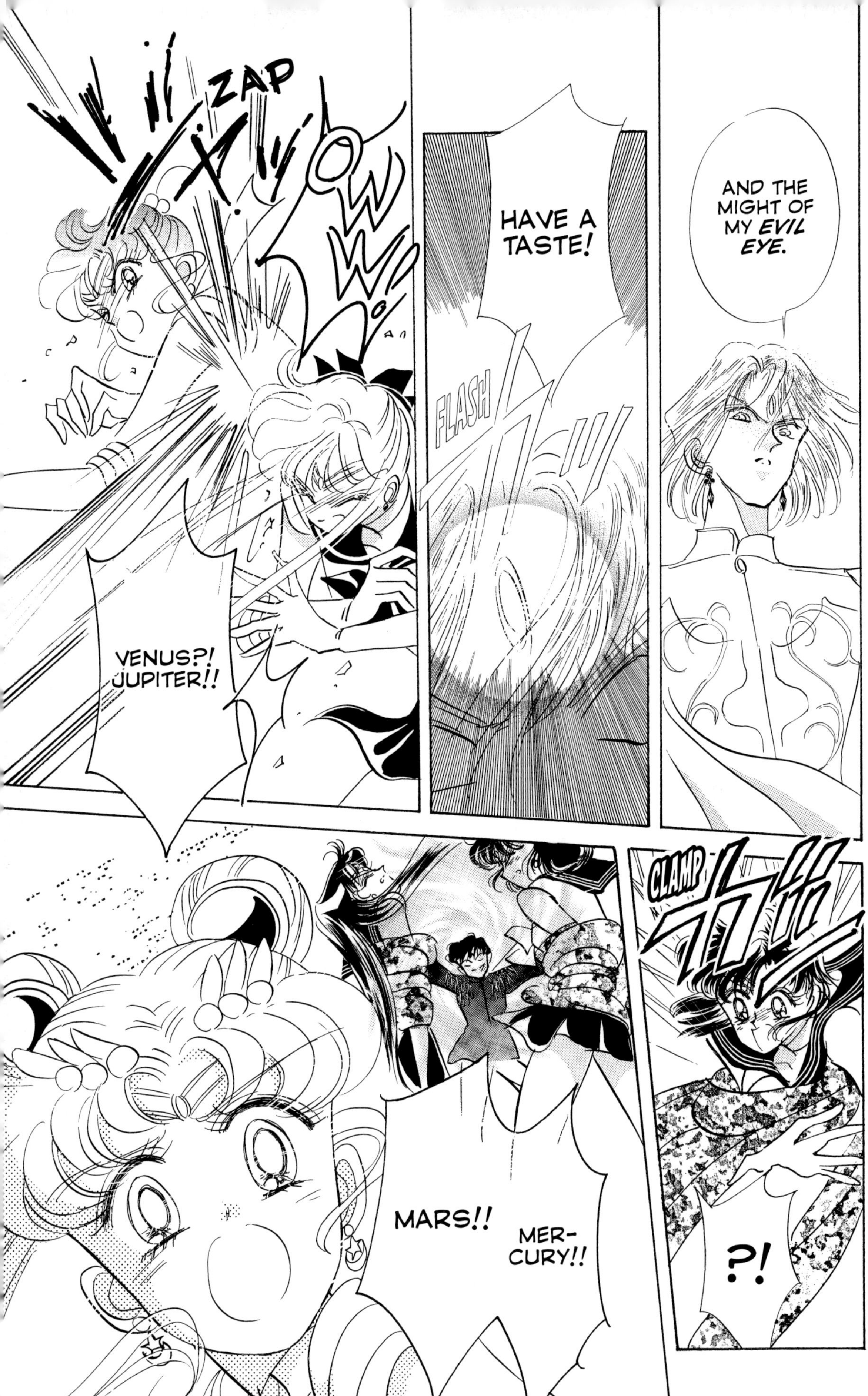
AND THE MIGHT OF MY EVIL EYE.
HAVE A TASTE!
FLASH
ZAP
VENUS?! JUPITER!!
CLAMP
?!
MARS!!
MER-CURY!!

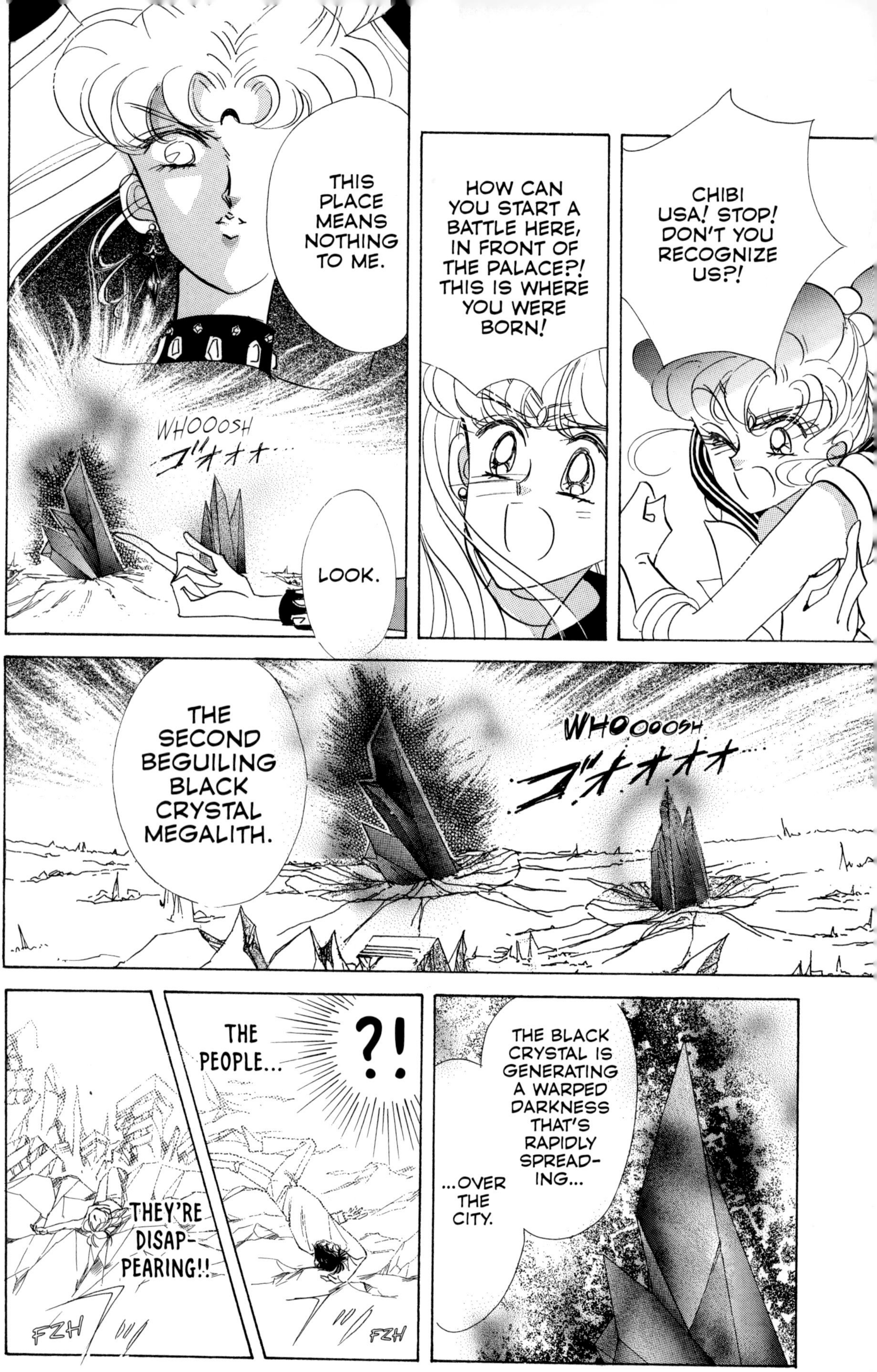
CHIBI USA! STOP! DON'T YOU RECOGNIZE US?!
HOW CAN YOU START A BATTLE HERE, IN FRONT OF THE PALACE?! THIS IS WHERE YOU WERE BORN!
THIS PLACE MEANS NOTHING TO ME.
WHOOOSH
ゴオオオ…
LOOK.
THE SECOND BEGUILING BLACK CRYSTAL MEGALITH.
WHOOOOOSH
ゴオオオオ…
THE BLACK CRYSTAL IS GENERATING A WARPED DARKNESS THAT'S RAPIDLY SPREAD-ING...
...OVER THE CITY.
?!
THE PEOPLE...
FZH
THEY'RE DISAP-PEARING!!
FZH

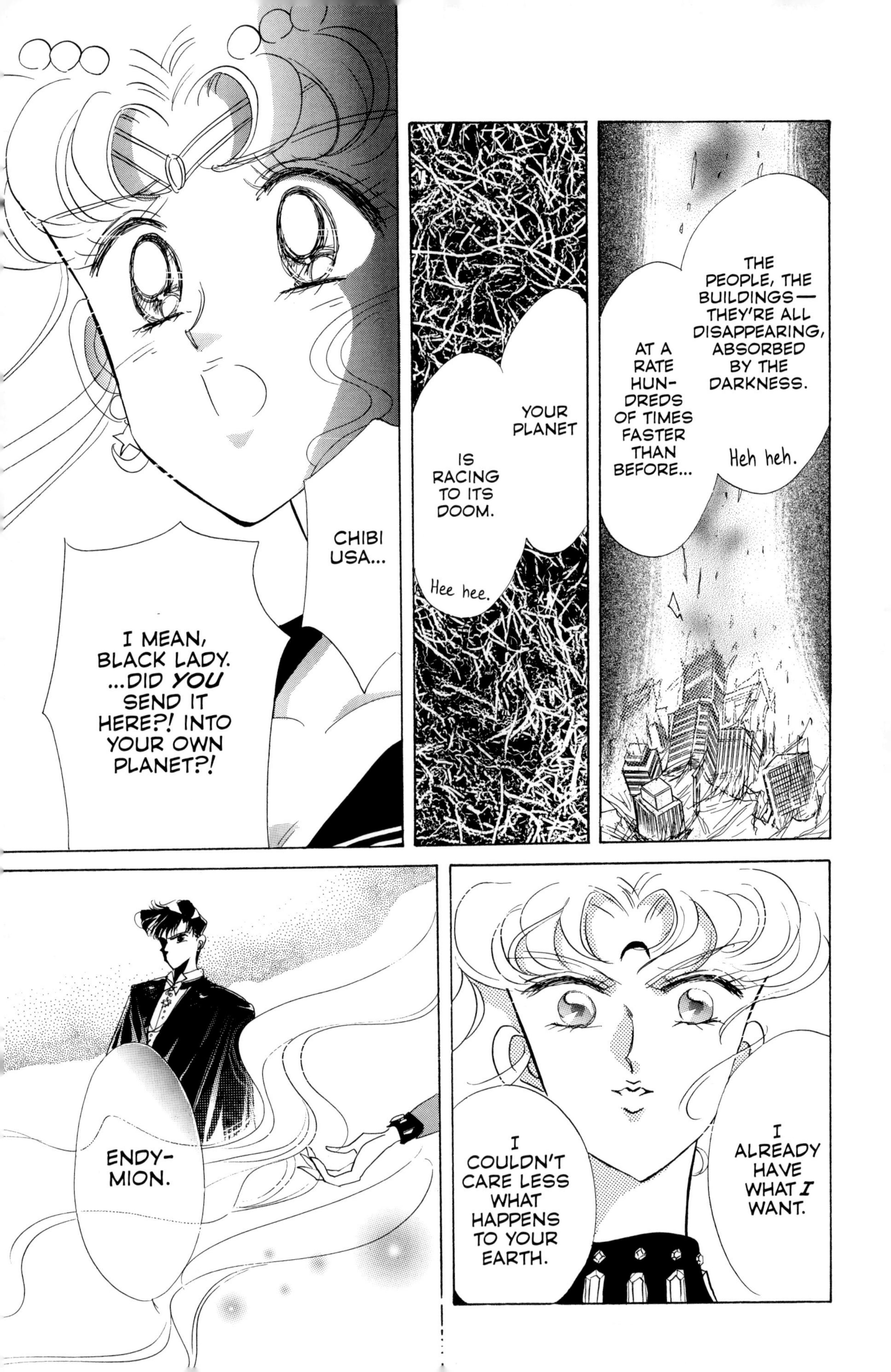
THE PEOPLE, THE BUILDINGS— THEY'RE ALL DISAPPEARING, ABSORBED BY THE DARKNESS.
AT A RATE HUN-DREDS OF TIMES FASTER THAN BEFORE...
Heh heh.
YOUR PLANET
IS RACING TO ITS DOOM.
Hee hee.
CHIBI USA...
I MEAN, BLACK LADY. ...DID *YOU* SEND IT HERE?! INTO YOUR OWN PLANET?!
I ALREADY HAVE WHAT *I* WANT.
I COULDN'T CARE LESS WHAT HAPPENS TO YOUR EARTH.
ENDY-MION.

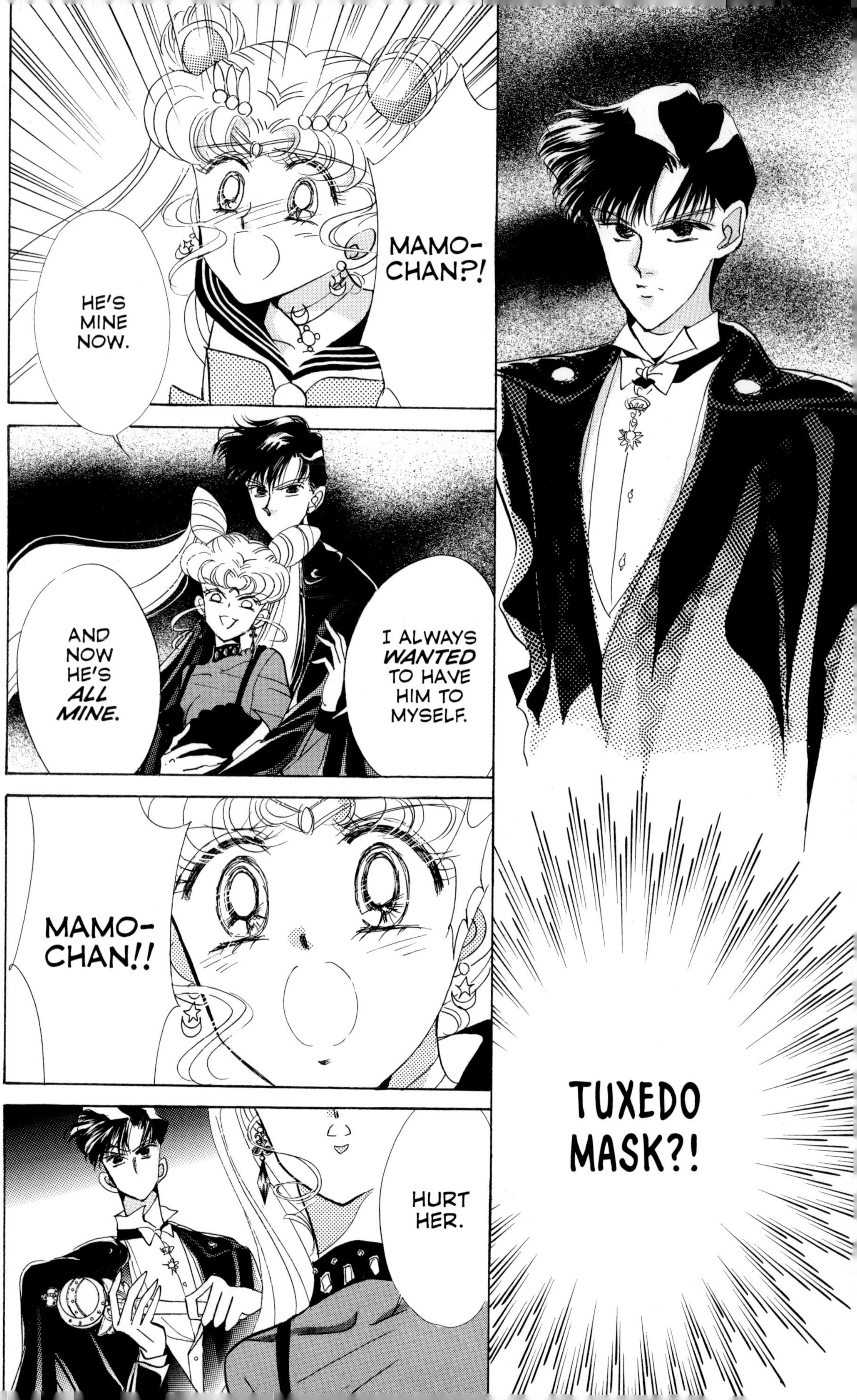
TUXEDO MASK?!
MAMO-CHAN?!
HE'S MINE NOW.
I ALWAYS *WANTED* TO HAVE HIM TO MYSELF.
AND NOW HE'S *ALL MINE*.
MAMO-CHAN!!
HURT HER.

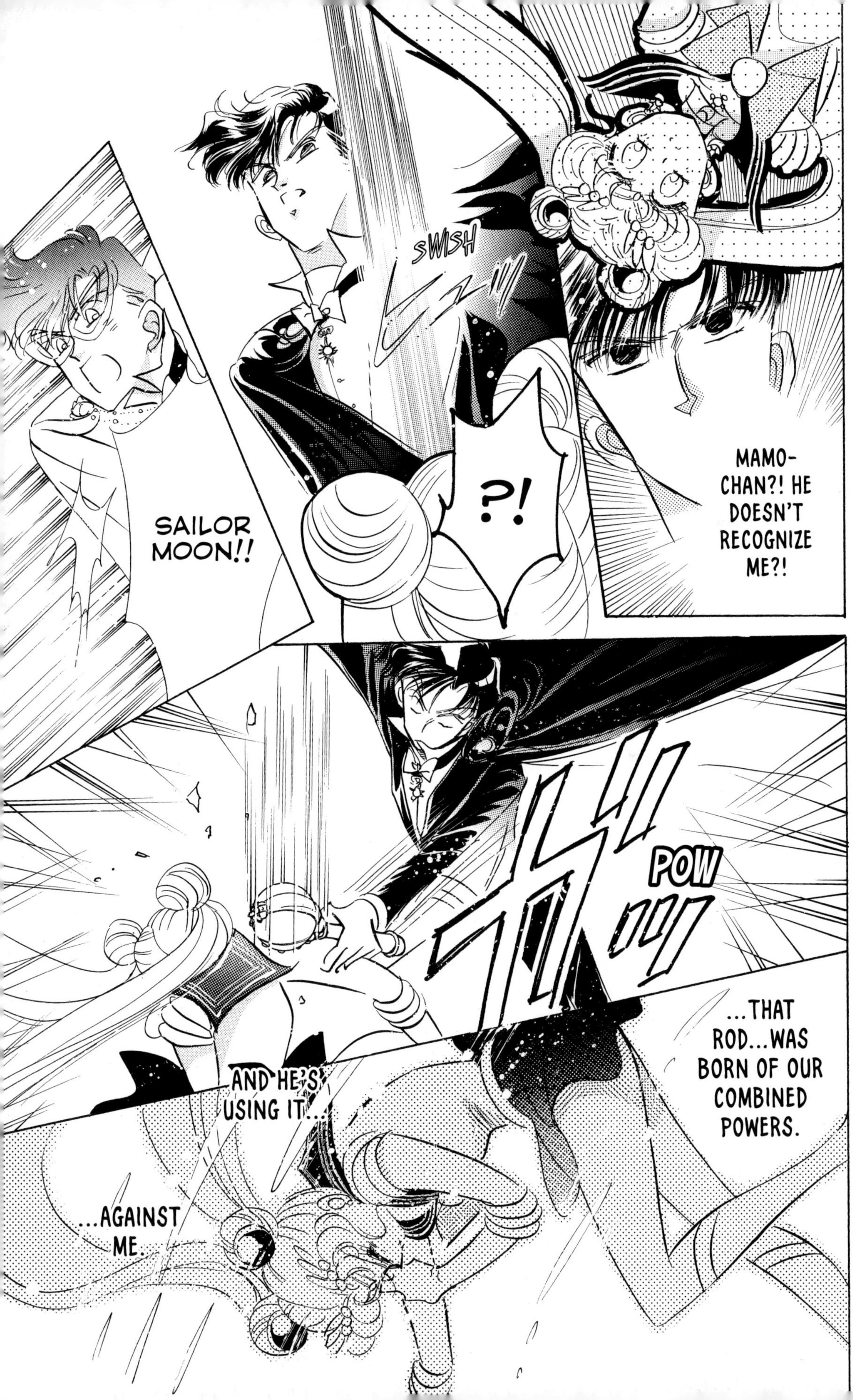
MAMO-CHAN?! HE DOESN'T RECOGNIZE ME?!
SWISH
?!
SAILOR MOON!!
POW
...THAT ROD...WAS BORN OF OUR COMBINED POWERS.
AND HE'S USING IT...
...AGAINST ME.

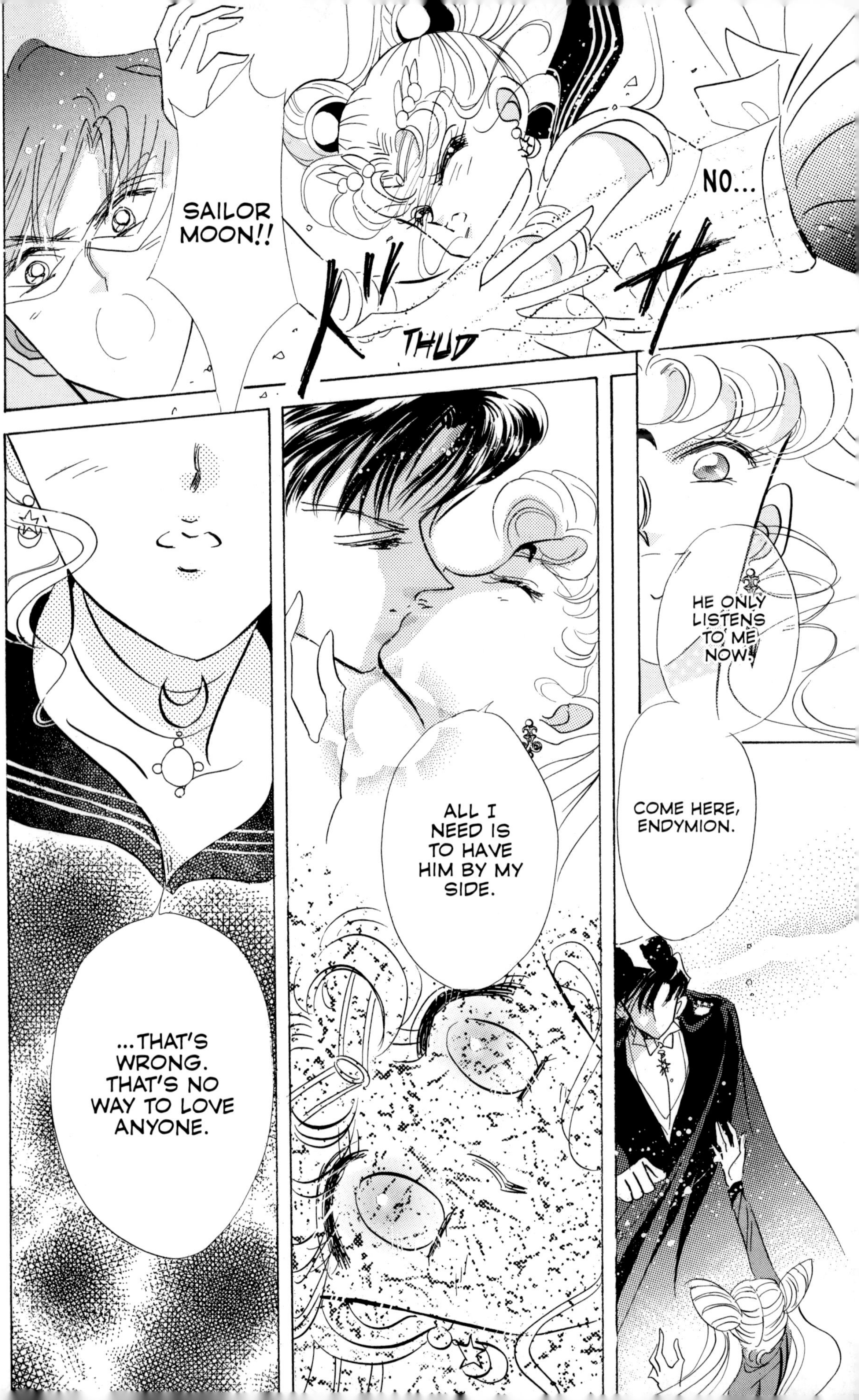
NO...
SAILOR MOON!!
THUD
HE ONLY LISTENS TO ME NOW!
COME HERE, ENDYMION.
ALL I NEED IS TO HAVE HIM BY MY SIDE.
...THAT'S WRONG. THAT'S NO WAY TO LOVE ANYONE.

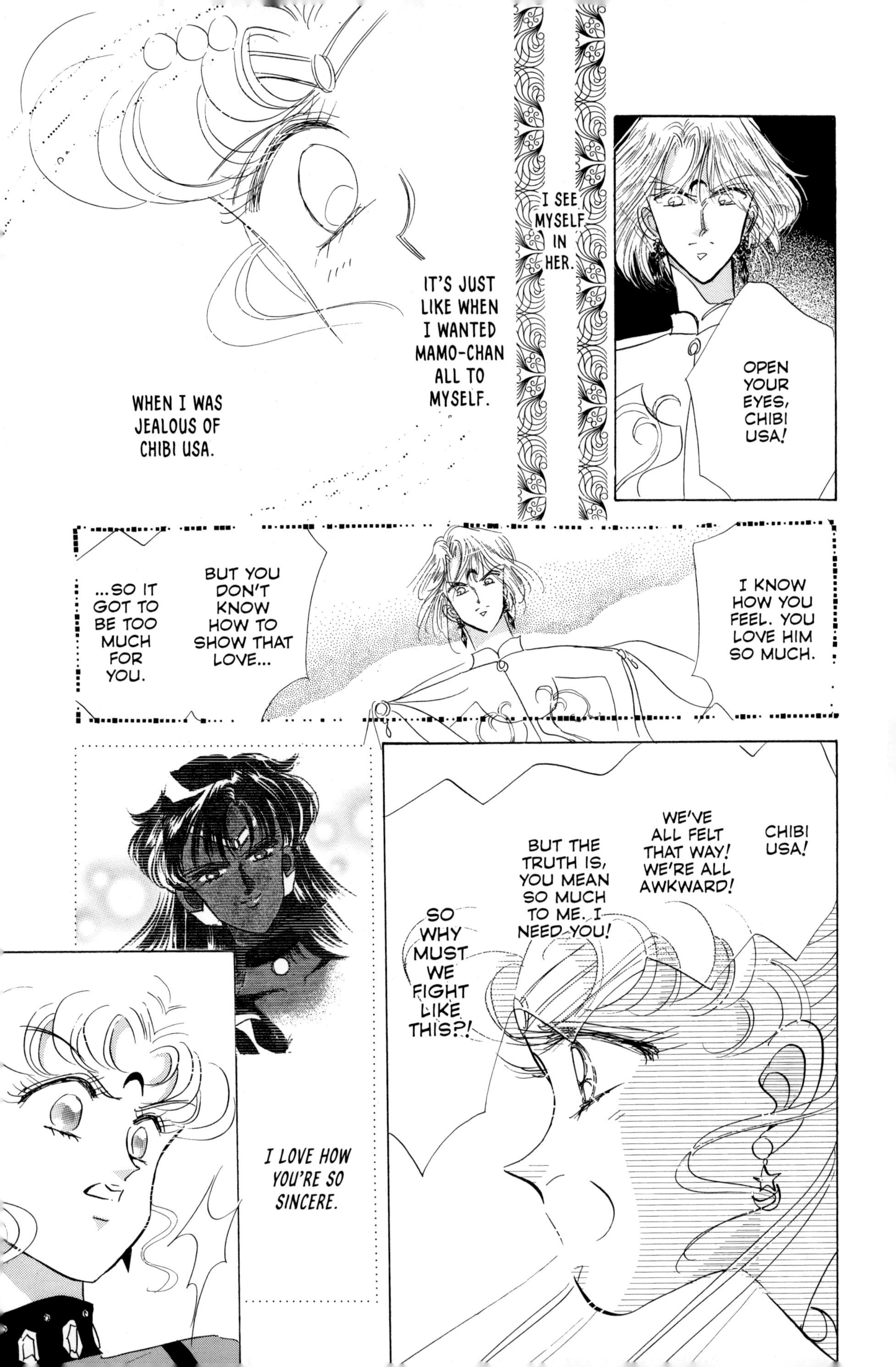
OPEN YOUR EYES, CHIBI USA!
I SEE MYSELF IN HER.
IT'S JUST LIKE WHEN I WANTED MAMO-CHAN ALL TO MYSELF.
WHEN I WAS JEALOUS OF CHIBI USA.
I KNOW HOW YOU FEEL. YOU LOVE HIM SO MUCH.
BUT YOU DON'T KNOW HOW TO SHOW THAT LOVE...
...SO IT GOT TO BE TOO MUCH FOR YOU.
CHIBI USA!
WE'VE ALL FELT THAT WAY! WE'RE ALL AWKWARD!
BUT THE TRUTH IS, YOU MEAN SO MUCH TO ME. I NEED YOU!
SO WHY MUST WE FIGHT LIKE THIS?!
I LOVE HOW YOU'RE SO SINCERE.

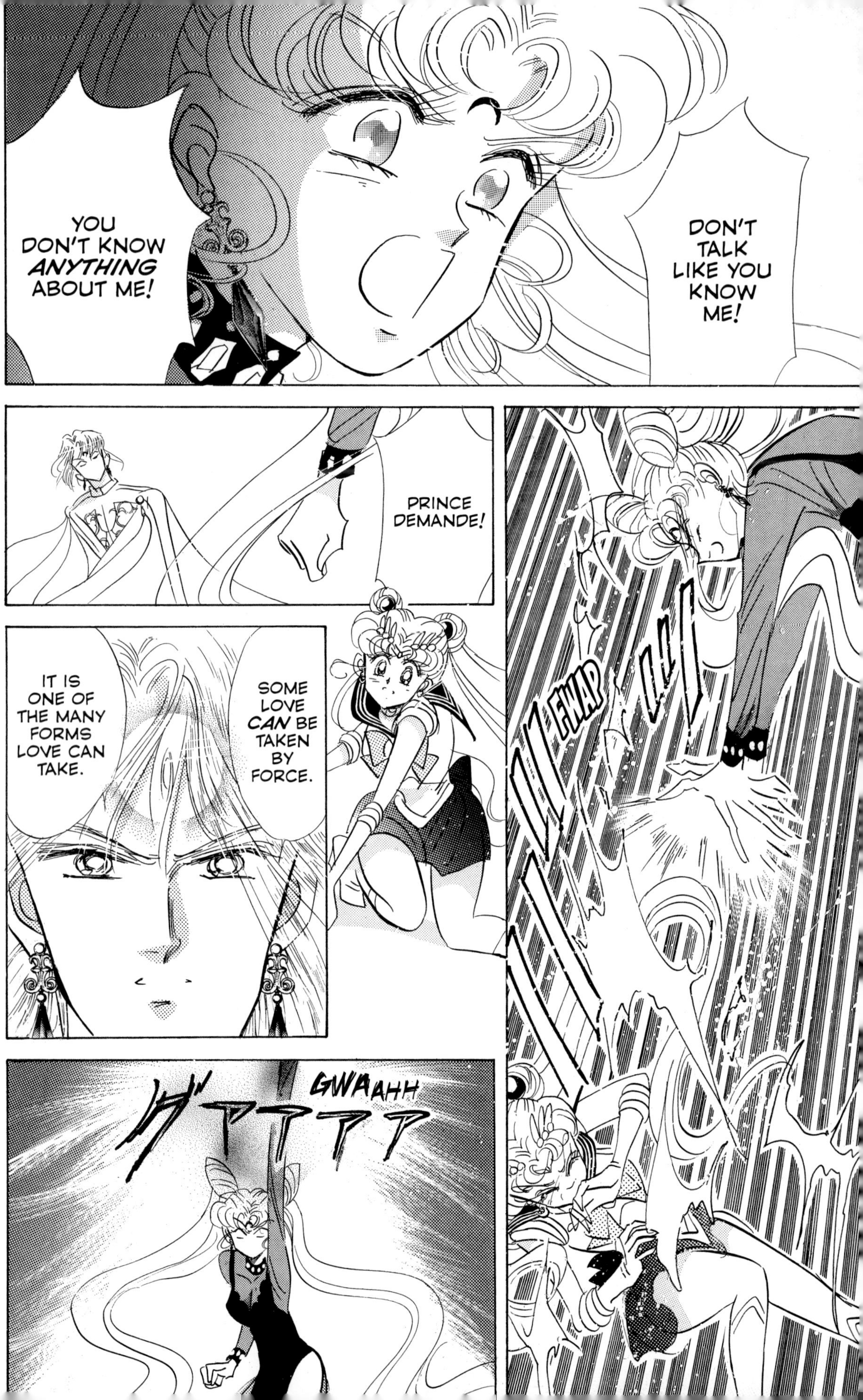
DON'T TALK LIKE YOU KNOW ME!
YOU DON'T KNOW ANYTHING ABOUT ME!
FWAP
PRINCE DEMANDE!
SOME LOVE CAN BE TAKEN BY FORCE.
IT IS ONE OF THE MANY FORMS LOVE CAN TAKE.
GWAAHH

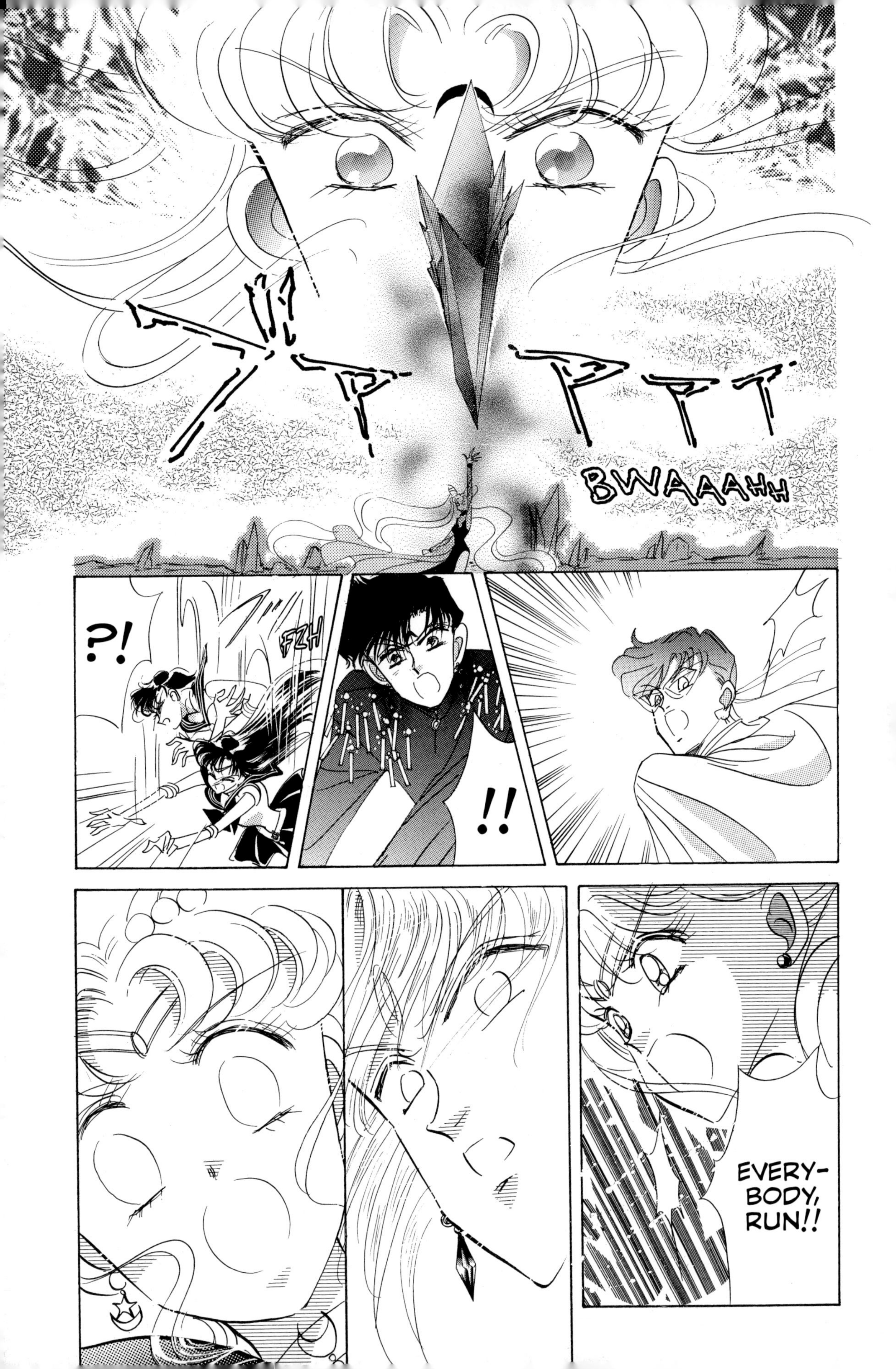
BWAAAAHH
!!
?!
FZH
EVERY-
BODY,
RUN!!

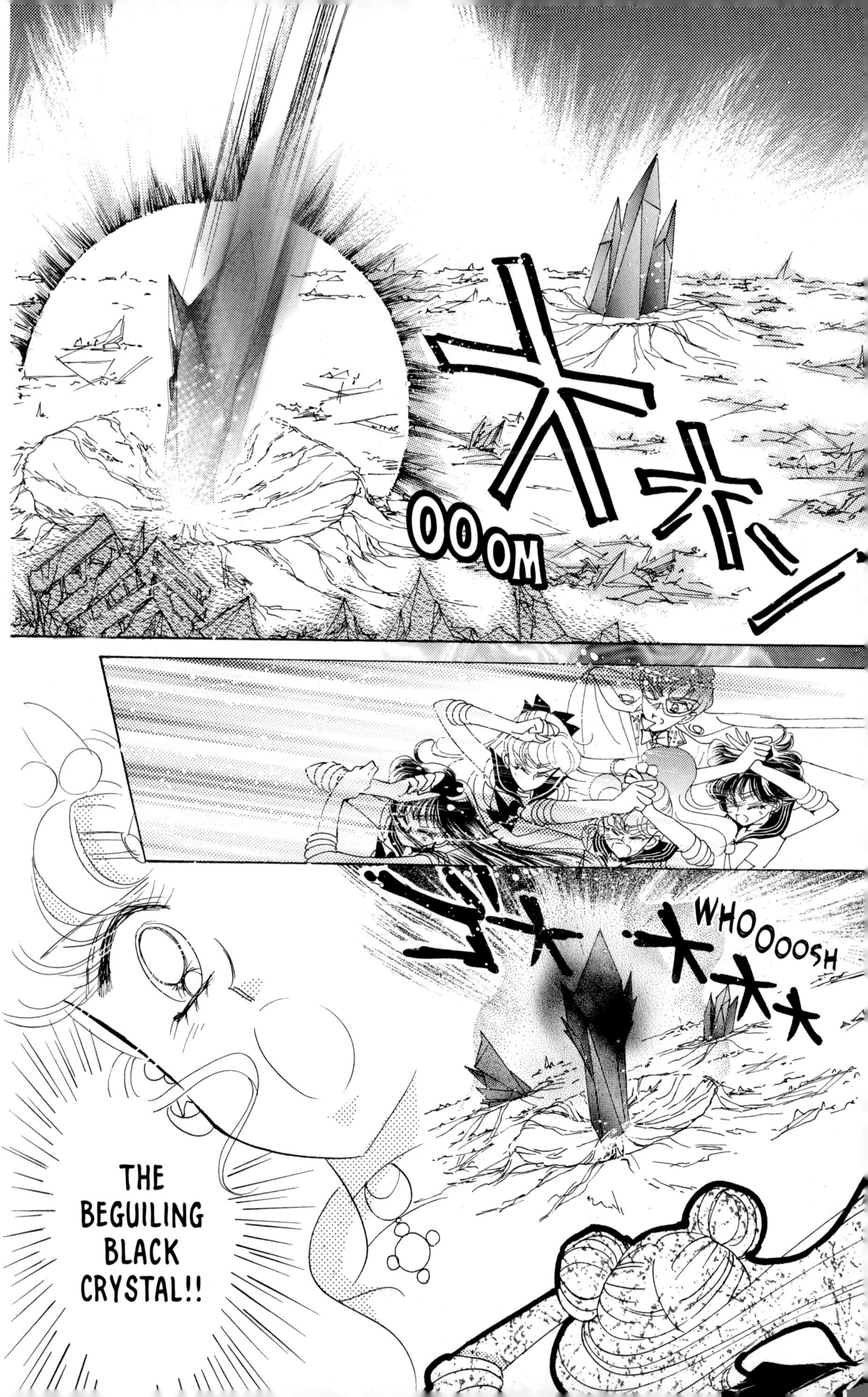
OOOM
WHOOOOSH
THE BEGUILING BLACK CRYSTAL!!

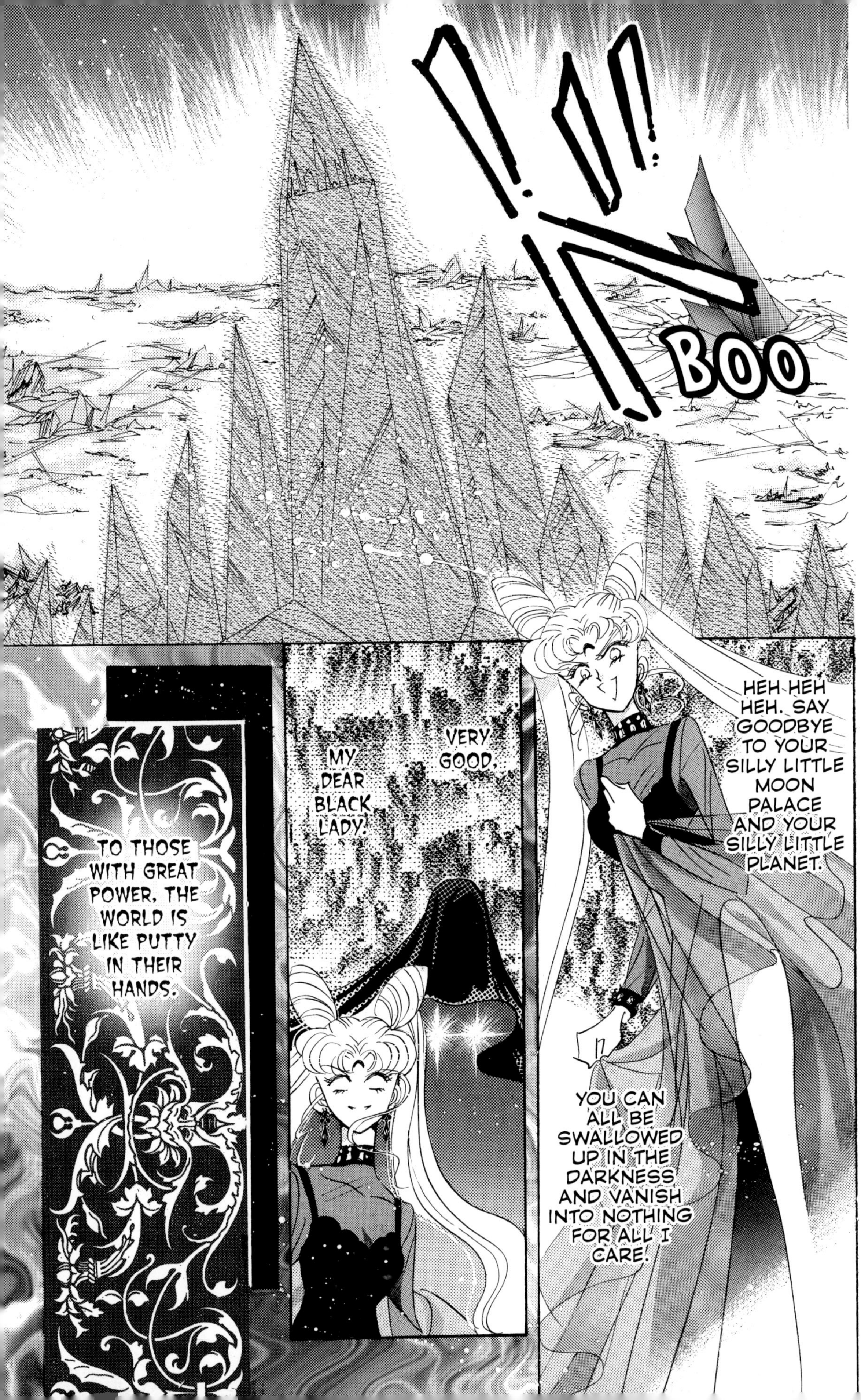

BOO
HEH HEH HEH. SAY GOODBYE TO YOUR SILLY LITTLE MOON PALACE AND YOUR SILLY LITTLE PLANET.
YOU CAN ALL BE SWALLOWED UP IN THE DARKNESS AND VANISH INTO NOTHING FOR ALL I CARE.
VERY GOOD,
MY DEAR BLACK LADY.
TO THOSE WITH GREAT POWER, THE WORLD IS LIKE PUTTY IN THEIR HANDS.

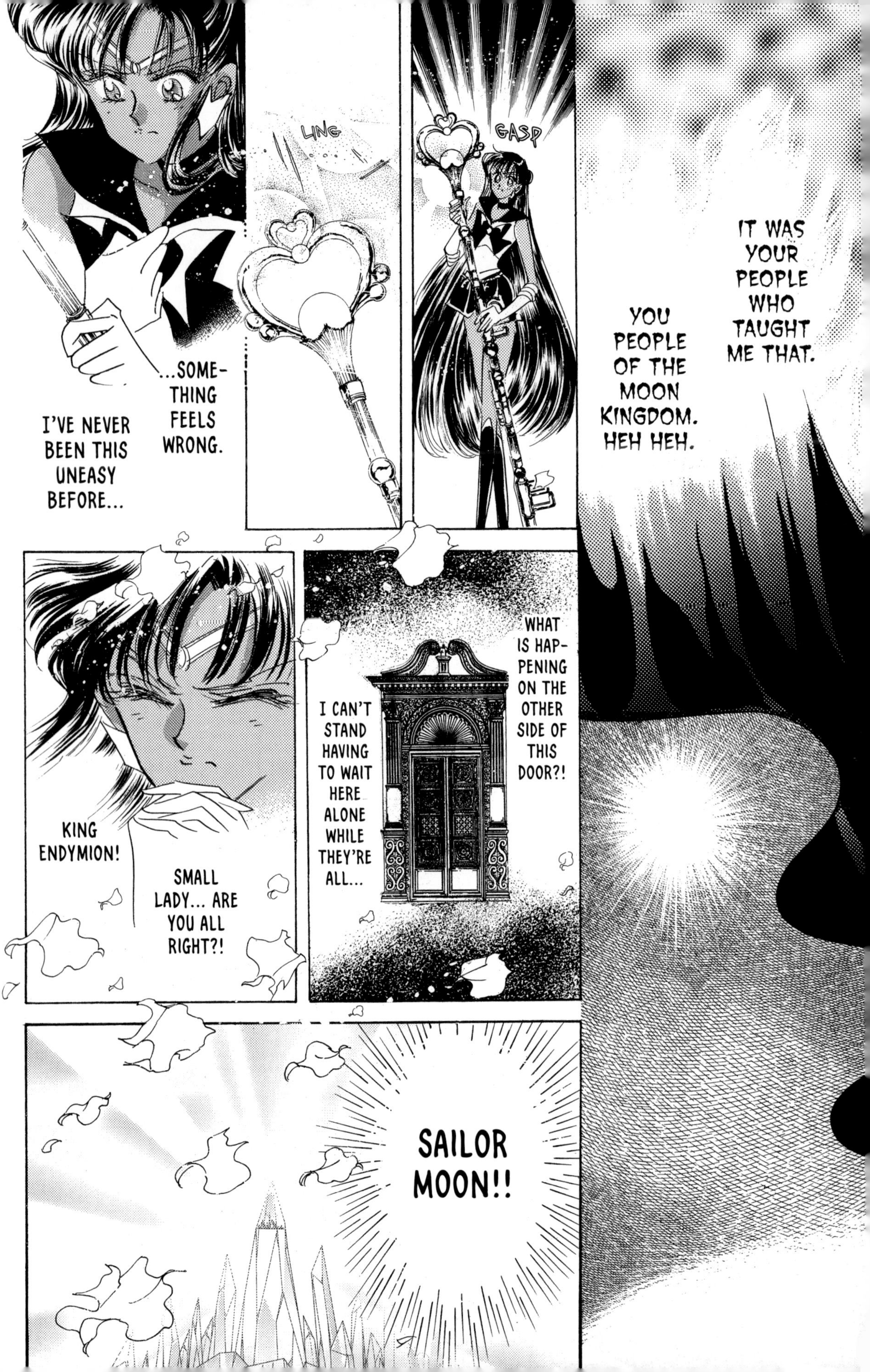

IT WAS YOUR PEOPLE WHO TAUGHT ME THAT.
YOU PEOPLE OF THE MOON KINGDOM. HEH HEH.
GASP
LING
...SOME-THING FEELS WRONG.
I'VE NEVER BEEN THIS UNEASY BEFORE...
WHAT IS HAP-PENING ON THE OTHER SIDE OF THIS DOOR?!
I CAN'T STAND HAVING TO WAIT HERE ALONE WHILE THEY'RE ALL...
SMALL LADY... ARE YOU ALL RIGHT?!
KING ENDYMION!
SAILOR MOON!!

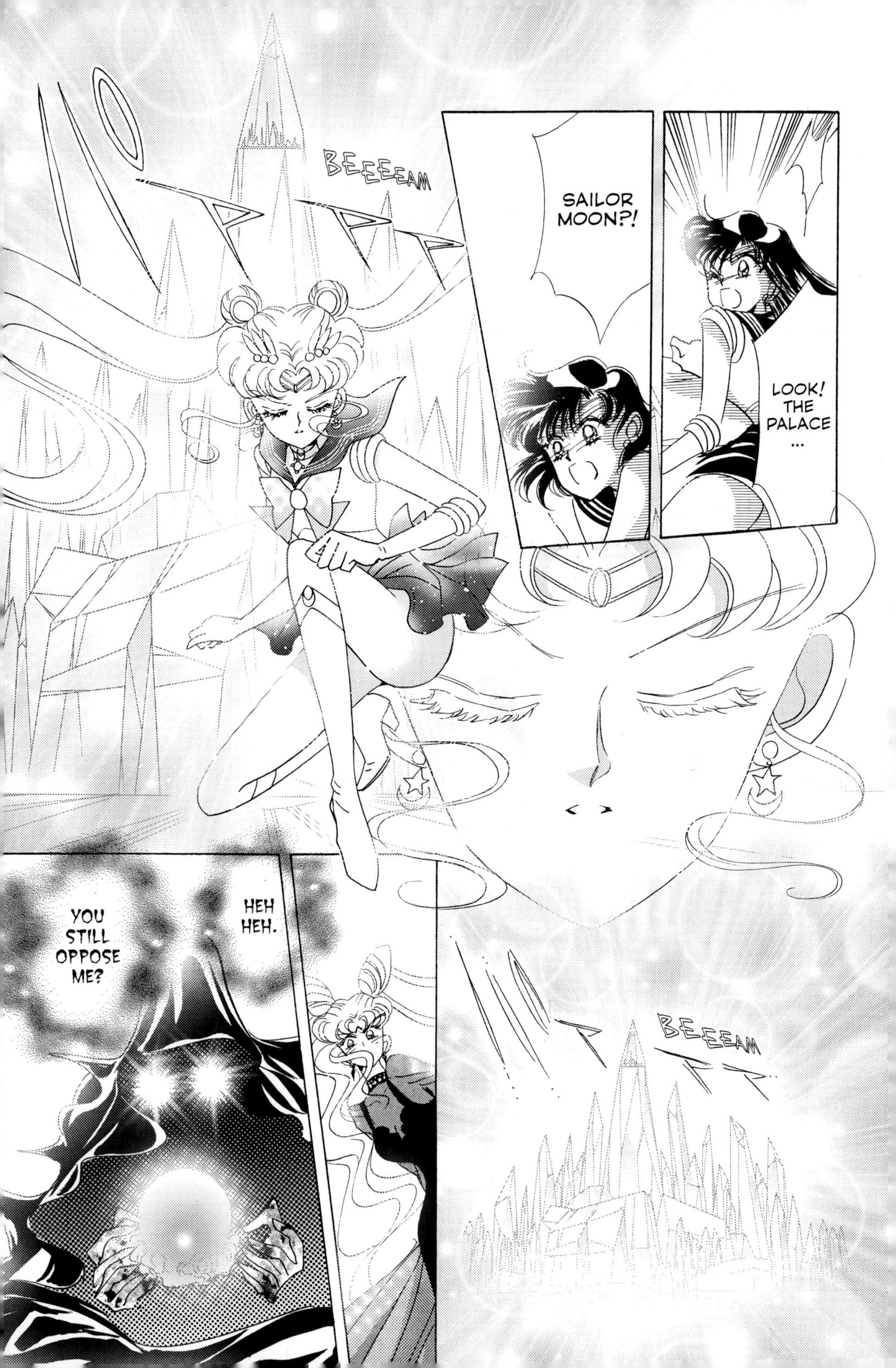
LOOK! THE PALACE ...
SAILOR MOON?!
BEEEEEAM
BEEEAM
HEH HEH.
YOU STILL OPPOSE ME?

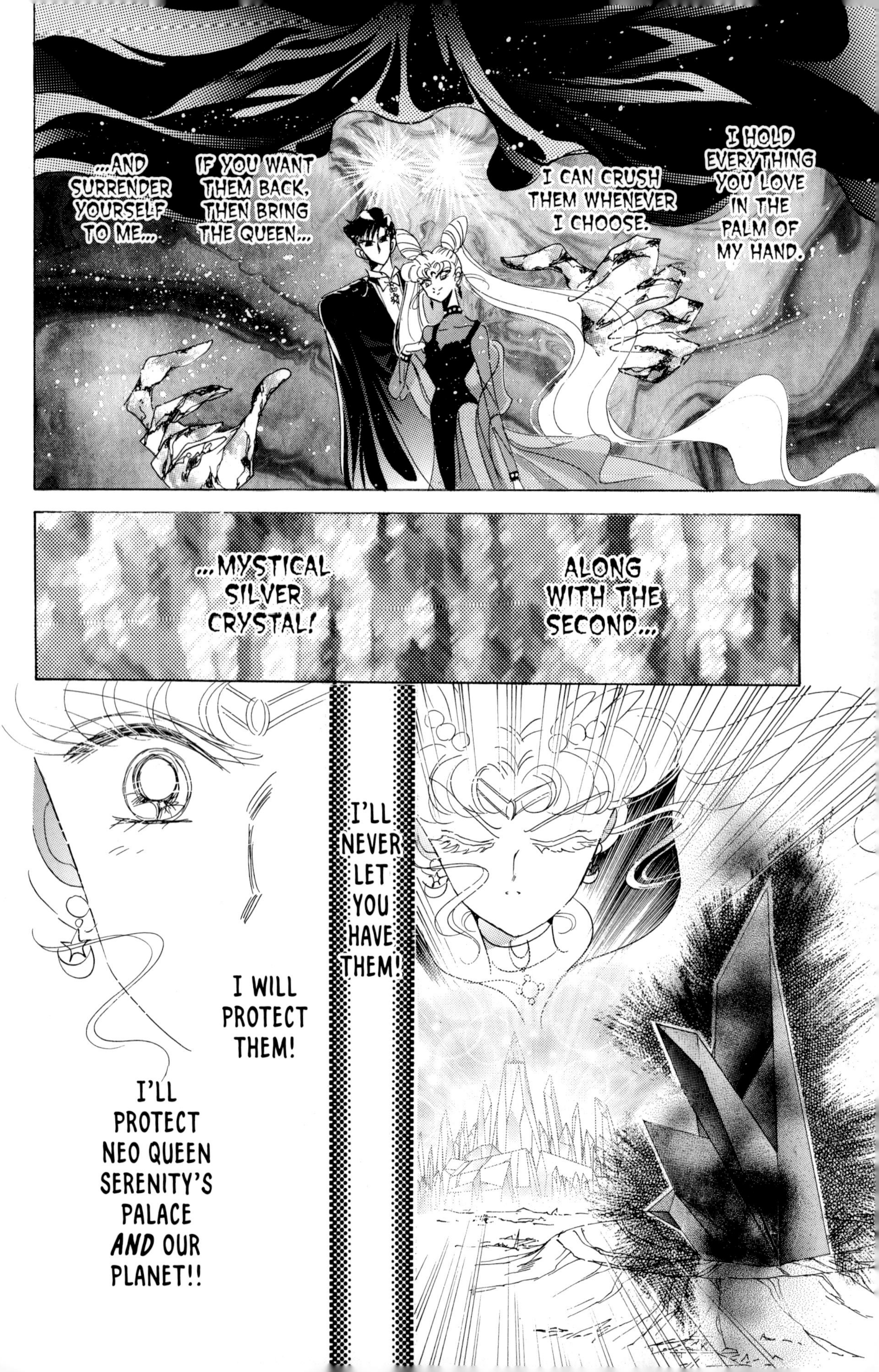

I HOLD EVERYTHING YOU LOVE IN THE PALM OF MY HAND.
I CAN CRUSH THEM WHENEVER I CHOOSE.
IF YOU WANT THEM BACK, THEN BRING THE QUEEN...
...AND SURRENDER YOURSELF TO ME...
ALONG WITH THE SECOND...
...MYSTICAL SILVER CRYSTAL!
I'LL NEVER LET YOU HAVE THEM!
I WILL PROTECT THEM!
I'LL PROTECT NEO QUEEN SERENITY'S PALACE *AND* OUR PLANET!!

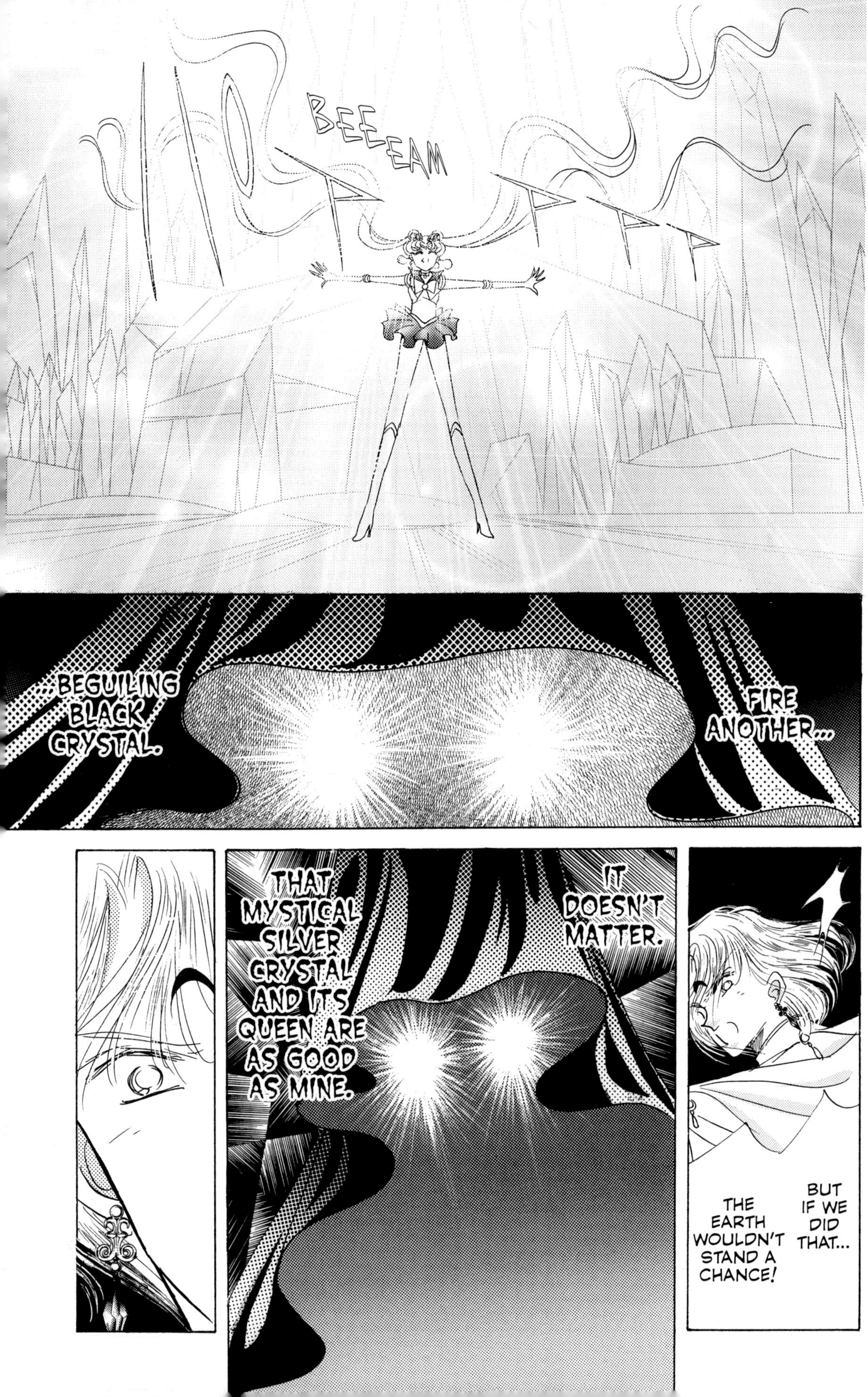
BEEEAM
FIRE ANOTHER...
...BEGUILING BLACK CRYSTAL.
BUT IF WE DID THAT...
THE EARTH WOULDN'T STAND A CHANCE!
IT DOESN'T MATTER.
THAT MYSTICAL SILVER CRYSTAL AND ITS QUEEN ARE AS GOOD AS MINE.

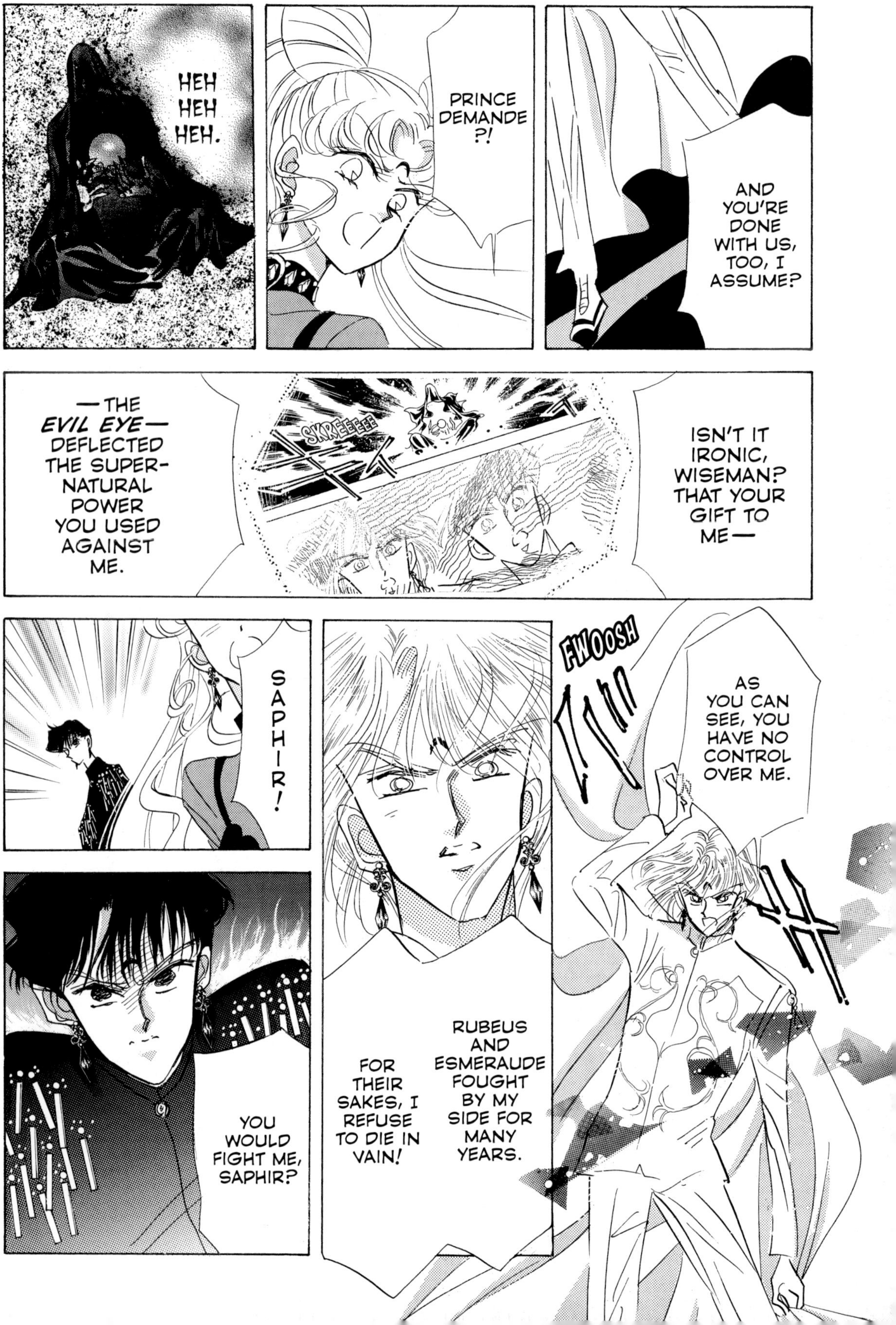
AND YOU'RE DONE WITH US, TOO, I ASSUME?
PRINCE DEMANDE ?!
HEH HEH HEH.
ISN'T IT IRONIC, WISEMAN? THAT YOUR GIFT TO ME—
SKREEEEEE
—THE *EVIL EYE*— DEFLECTED THE SUPER-NATURAL POWER YOU USED AGAINST ME.
FWOOSH
AS YOU CAN SEE, YOU HAVE NO CONTROL OVER ME.
RUBEUS AND ESMERAUDE FOUGHT BY MY SIDE FOR MANY YEARS.
FOR THEIR SAKES, I REFUSE TO DIE IN VAIN!
SAPHIR!
YOU WOULD FIGHT ME, SAPHIR?

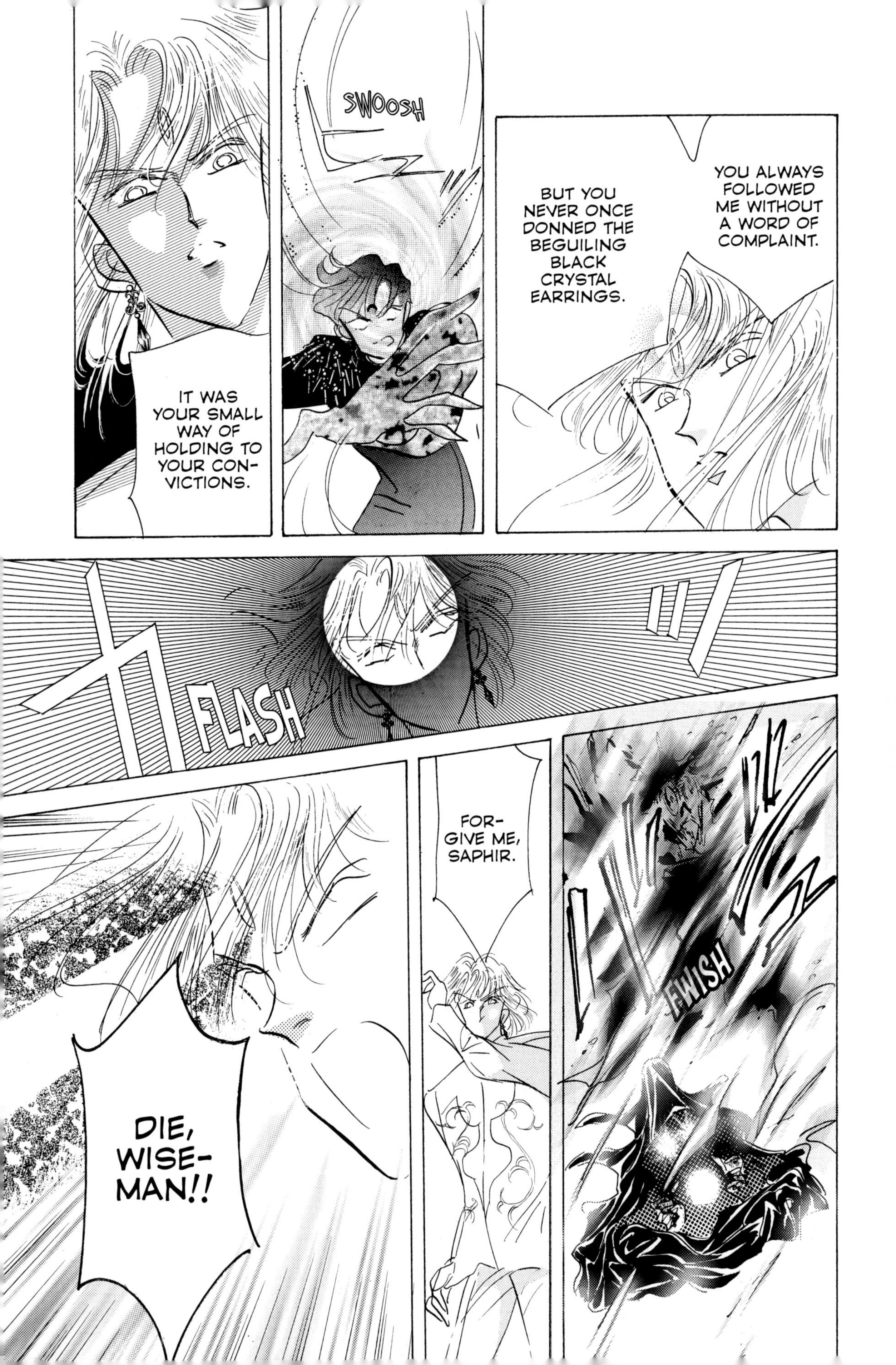
YOU ALWAYS FOLLOWED ME WITHOUT A WORD OF COMPLAINT.
BUT YOU NEVER ONCE DONNED THE BEGUILING BLACK CRYSTAL EARRINGS.
SWOOSH
IT WAS YOUR SMALL WAY OF HOLDING TO YOUR CON-VICTIONS.
FLASH
FWISH
FOR-GIVE ME, SAPHIR.
DIE, WISE-MAN!!

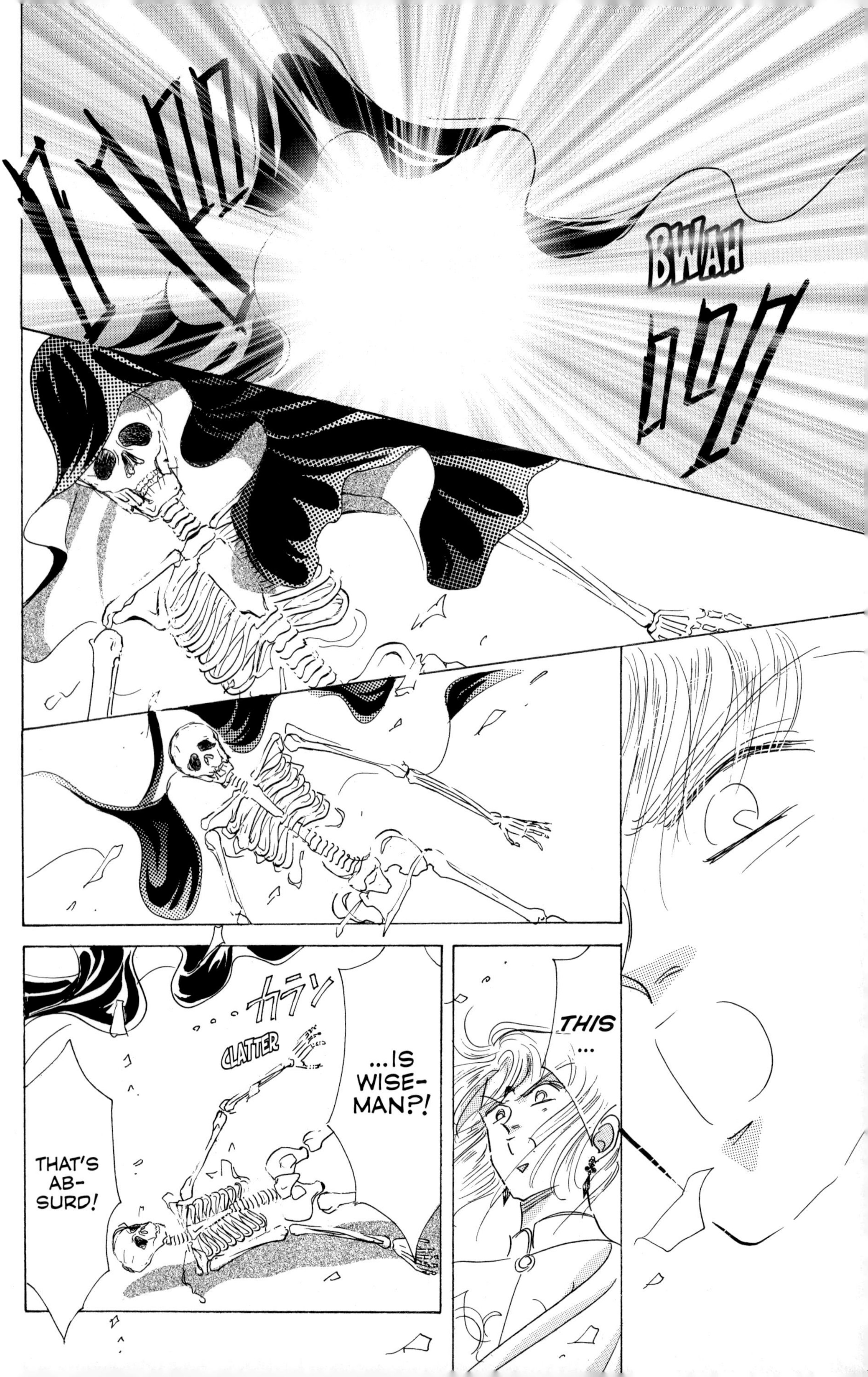
BWAH
THIS ...
...IS WISE-MAN?!
カラン
CLATTER
THAT'S AB-SURD!

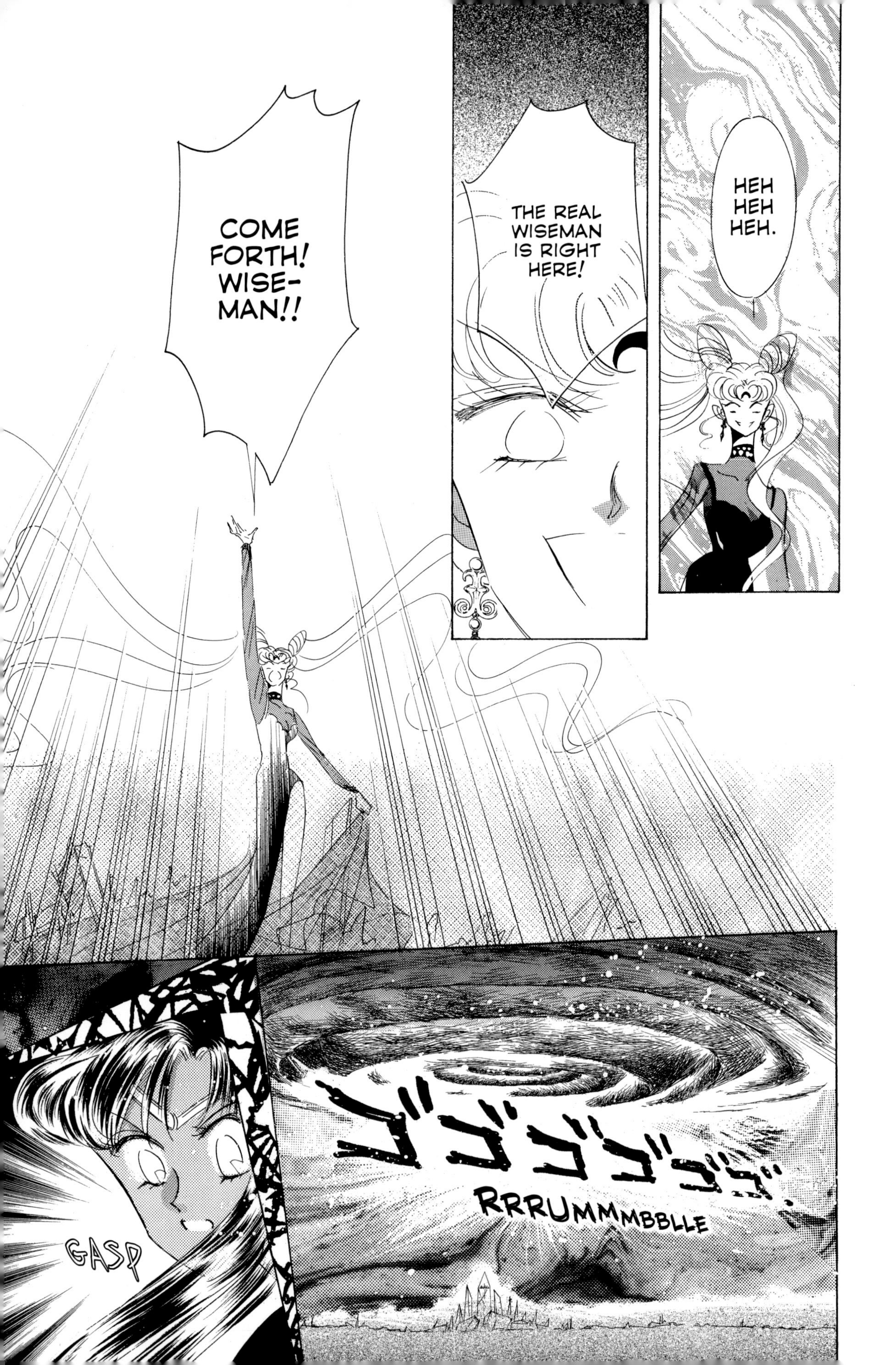
HEH HEH HEH.
THE REAL WISEMAN IS RIGHT HERE!
COME FORTH! WISE-MAN!!
RRRUMMMBBLLE
GASP

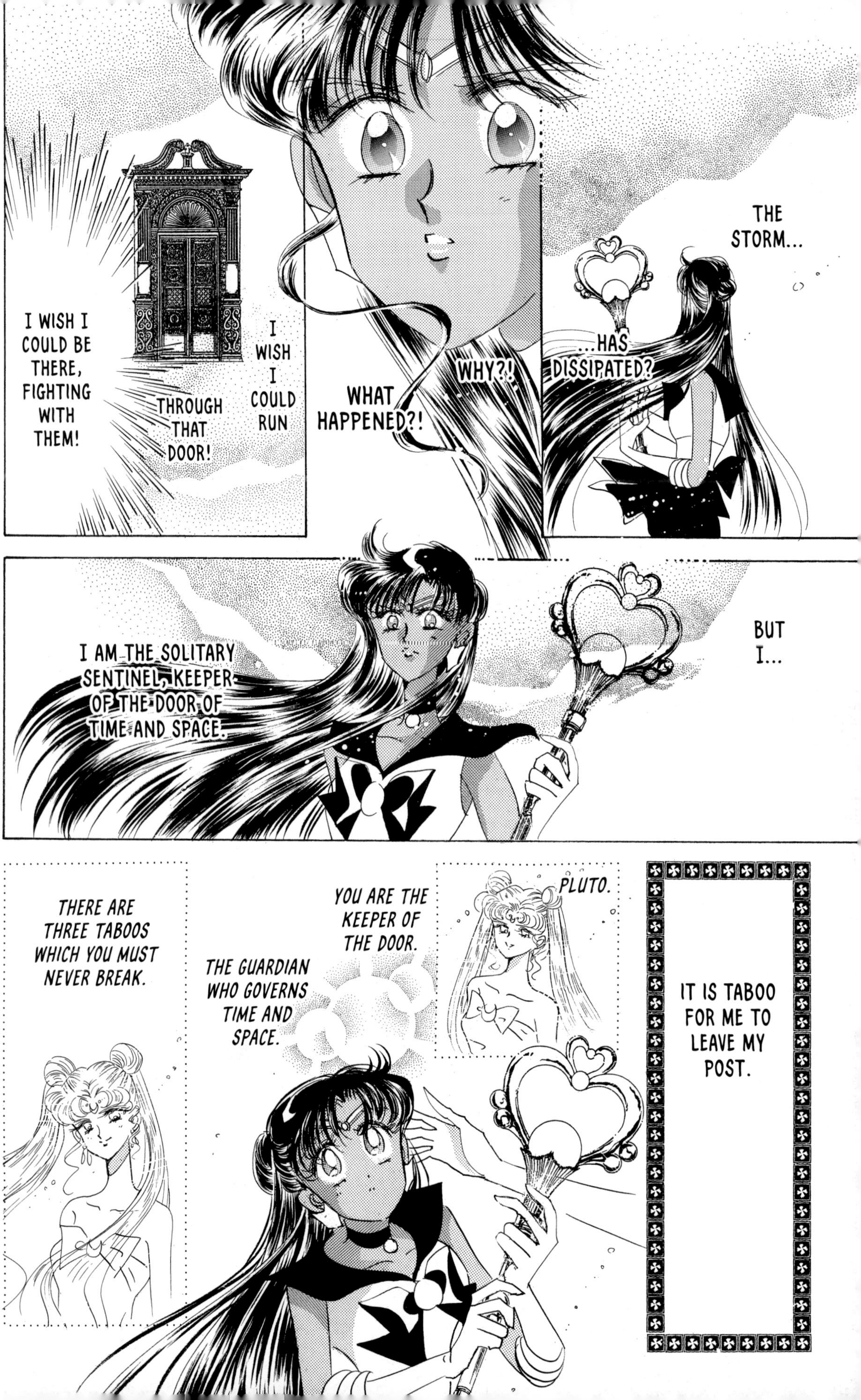
THE STORM...
...HAS DISSIPATED?
WHY?!
WHAT HAPPENED?!
I WISH I COULD RUN
THROUGH THAT DOOR!
I WISH I COULD BE THERE, FIGHTING WITH THEM!
BUT I...
I AM THE SOLITARY SENTINEL, KEEPER OF THE DOOR OF TIME AND SPACE.
IT IS TABOO FOR ME TO LEAVE MY POST.
PLUTO.
YOU ARE THE KEEPER OF THE DOOR.
THE GUARDIAN WHO GOVERNS TIME AND SPACE.
THERE ARE THREE TABOOS WHICH YOU MUST NEVER BREAK.

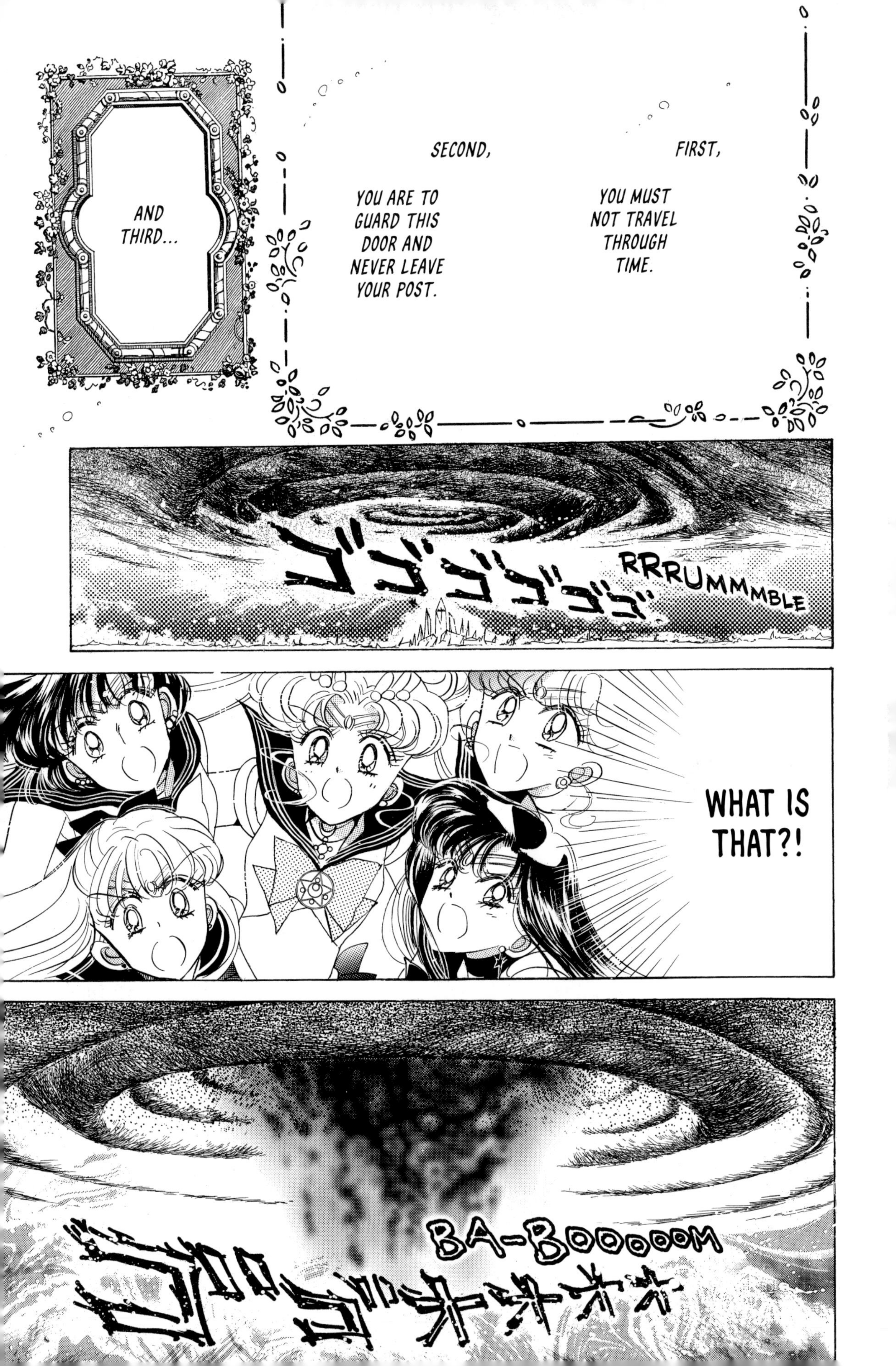
FIRST,
YOU MUST NOT TRAVEL THROUGH TIME.
SECOND,
YOU ARE TO GUARD THIS DOOR AND NEVER LEAVE YOUR POST.
AND THIRD...
RRRUMMMBLE
WHAT IS THAT?!
BA-BOOOOOM

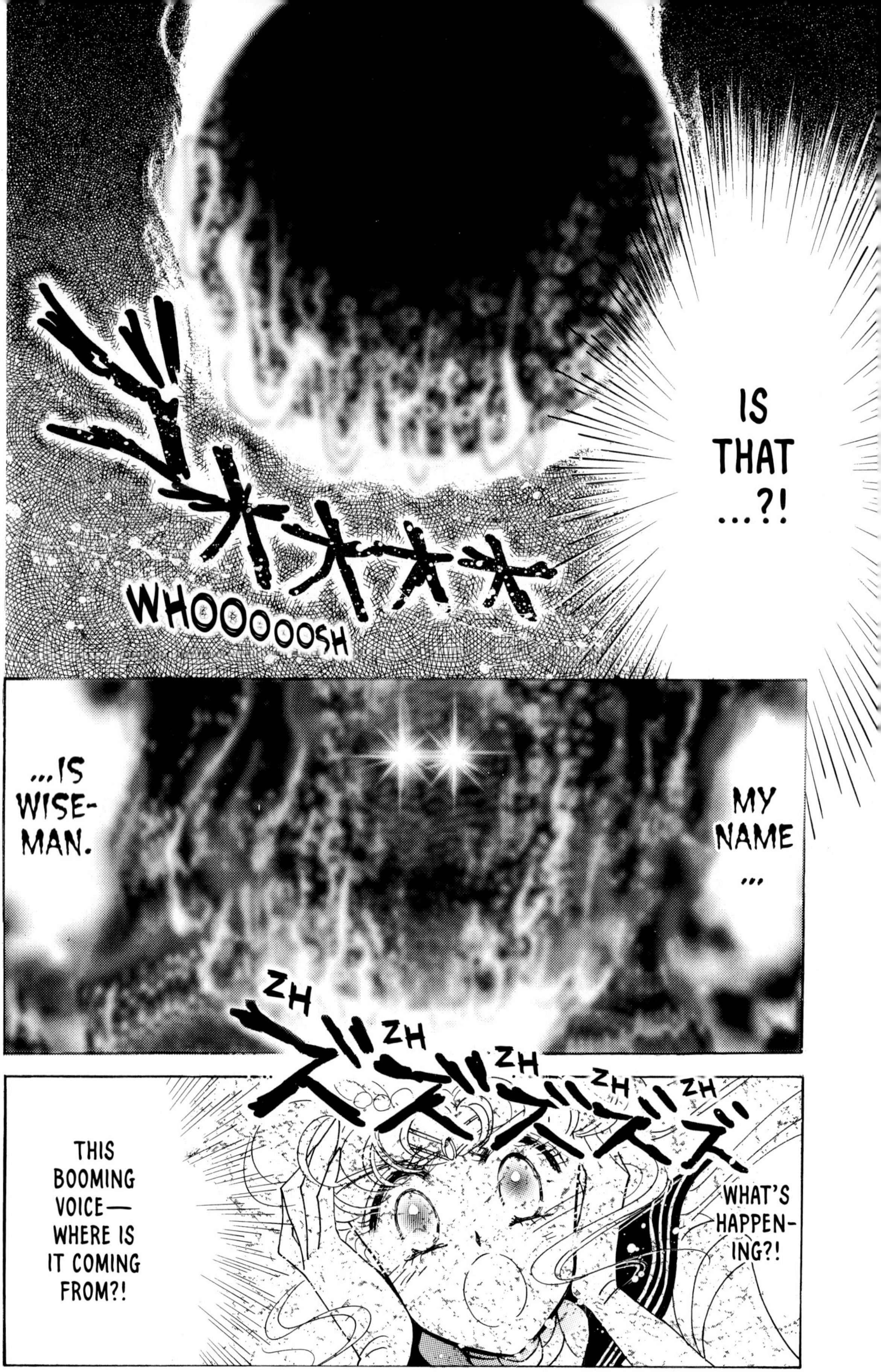
IS THAT ...?!
WHOOOOOSH
MY NAME ...
...IS WISE-MAN.
ZH ZH ZH ZH ZH
WHAT'S HAPPEN-ING?!
THIS BOOMING VOICE— WHERE IS IT COMING FROM?!

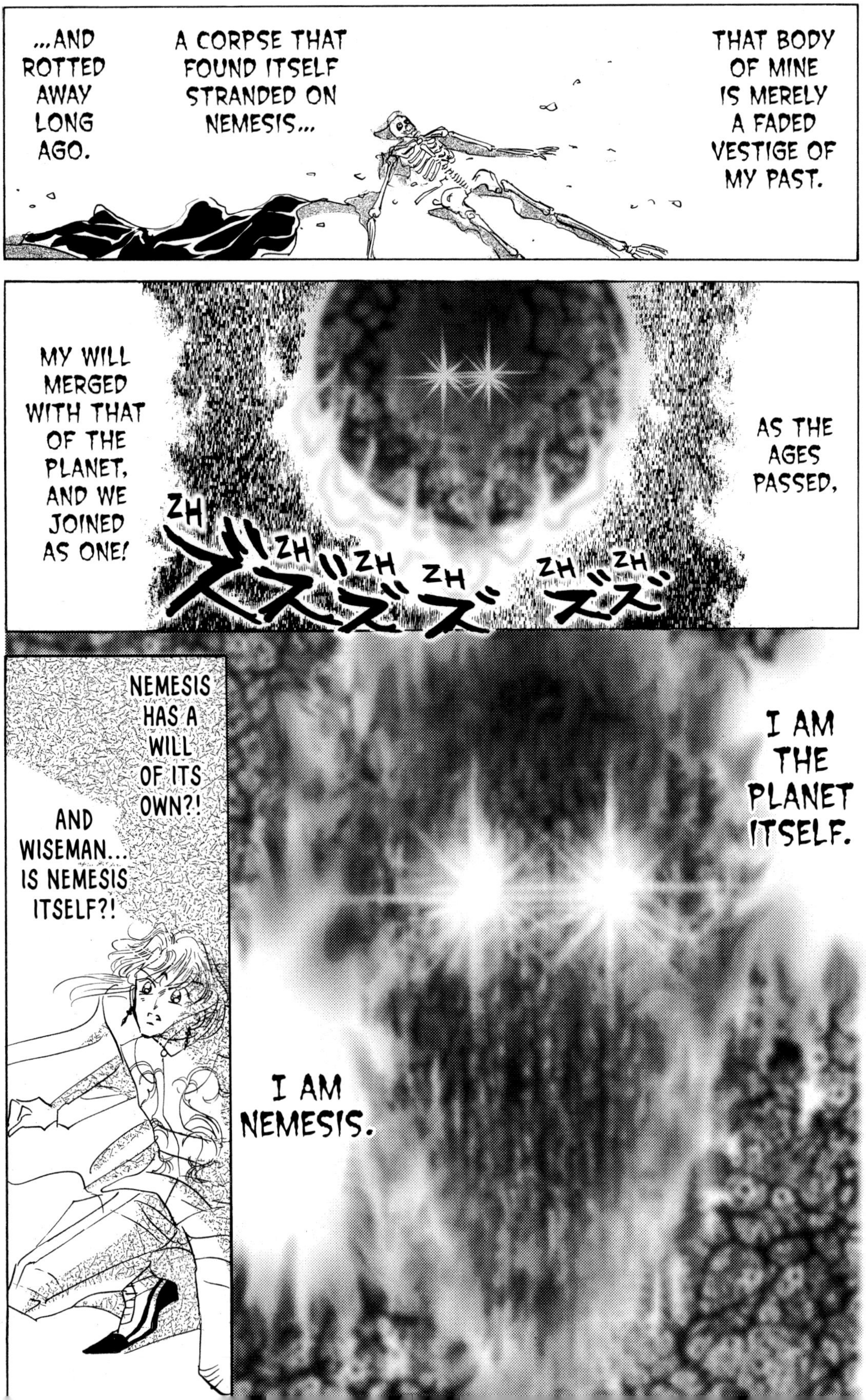
THAT BODY OF MINE IS MERELY A FADED VESTIGE OF MY PAST.
A CORPSE THAT FOUND ITSELF STRANDED ON NEMESIS...
...AND ROTTED AWAY LONG AGO.
AS THE AGES PASSED,
MY WILL MERGED WITH THAT OF THE PLANET, AND WE JOINED AS ONE!
ZH ZH ZH ZH ZH ZH
ズズズズ ズズ
I AM THE PLANET ITSELF.
I AM NEMESIS.
NEMESIS HAS A WILL OF ITS OWN?!
AND WISEMAN... IS NEMESIS ITSELF?!

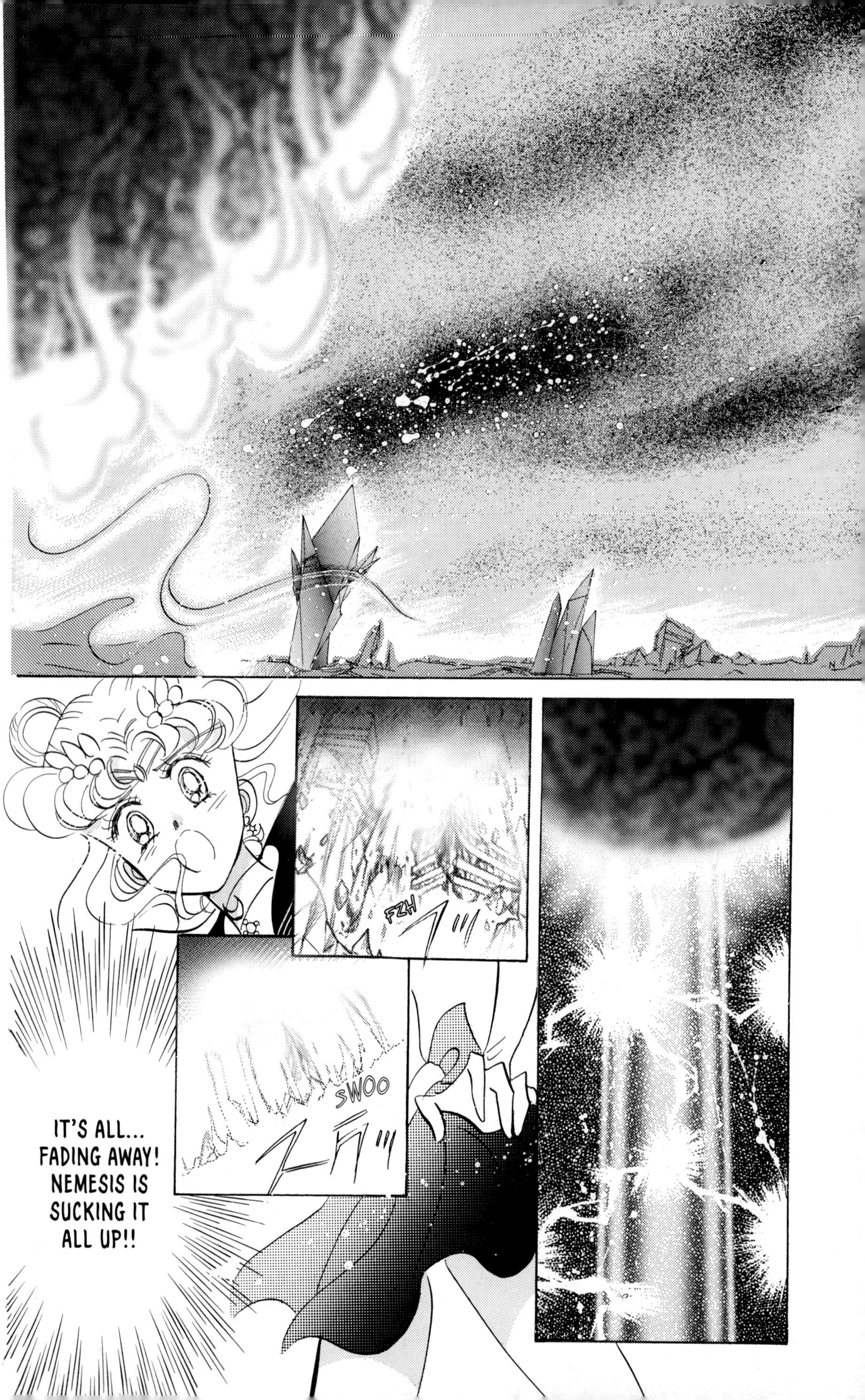
FZH
SWOO
IT'S ALL... FADING AWAY! NEMESIS IS SUCKING IT ALL UP!!

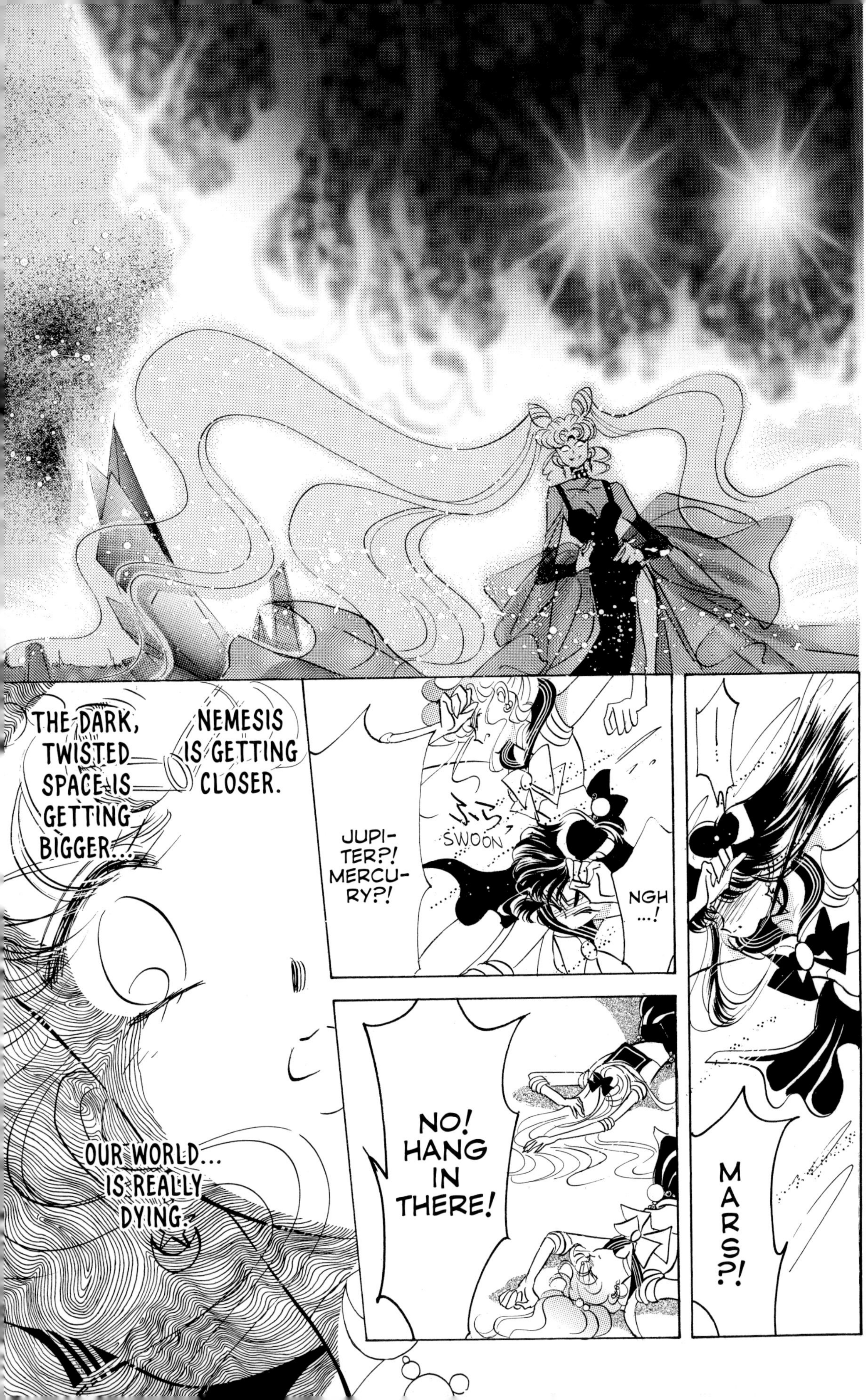
!
MARS?!
NGH ...!
ふら SWOON
JUPITER?! MERCURY?!
NO! HANG IN THERE!
NEMESIS IS GETTING CLOSER.
THE DARK, TWISTED SPACE IS GETTING BIGGER...
OUR WORLD... IS REALLY DYING.

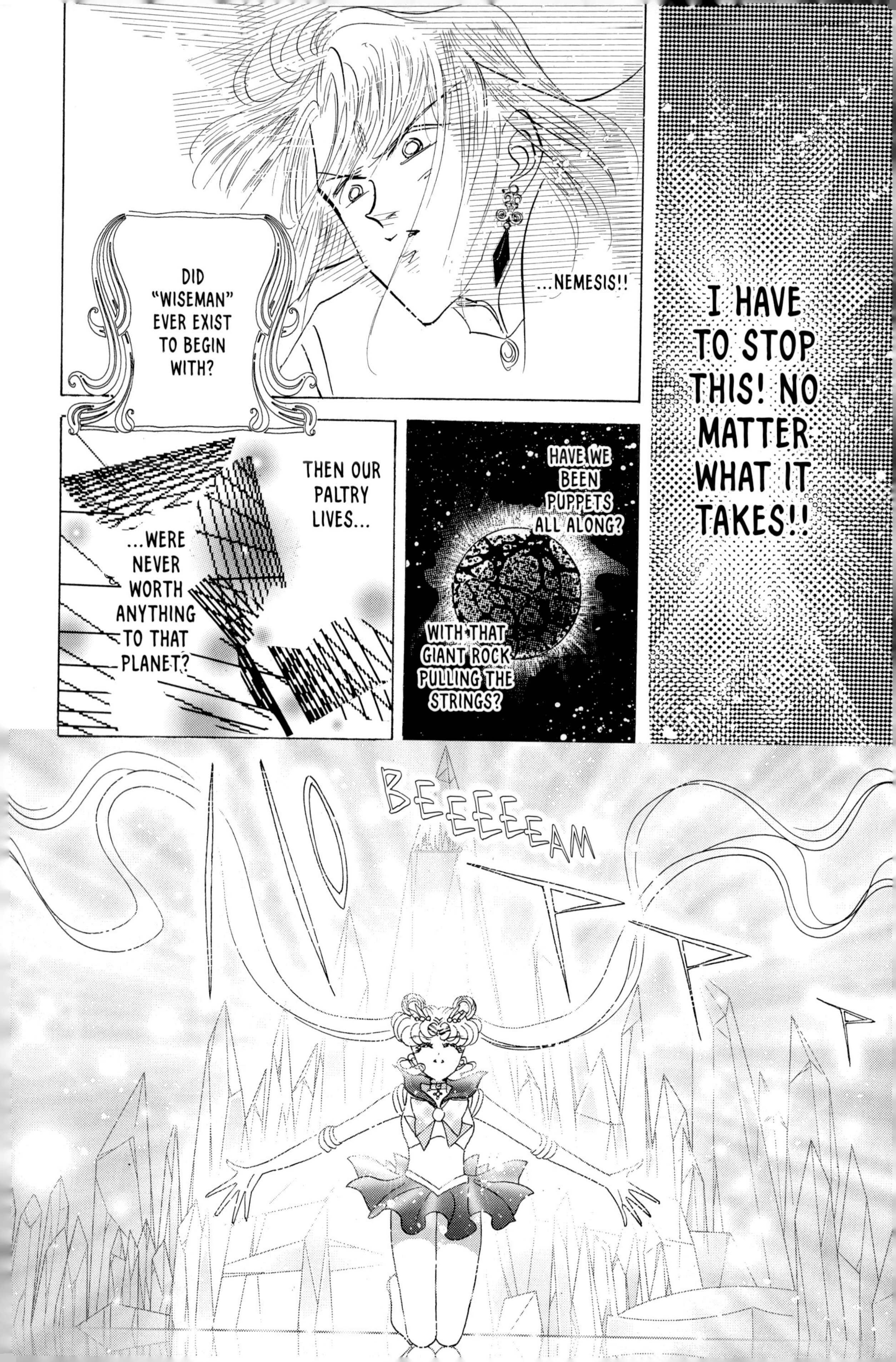
I HAVE TO STOP THIS! NO MATTER WHAT IT TAKES!!
...NEMESIS!!
DID "WISEMAN" EVER EXIST TO BEGIN WITH?
HAVE WE BEEN PUPPETS ALL ALONG?
WITH THAT GIANT ROCK PULLING THE STRINGS?
THEN OUR PALTRY LIVES...
...WERE NEVER WORTH ANYTHING TO THAT PLANET?
BEEEEEAM

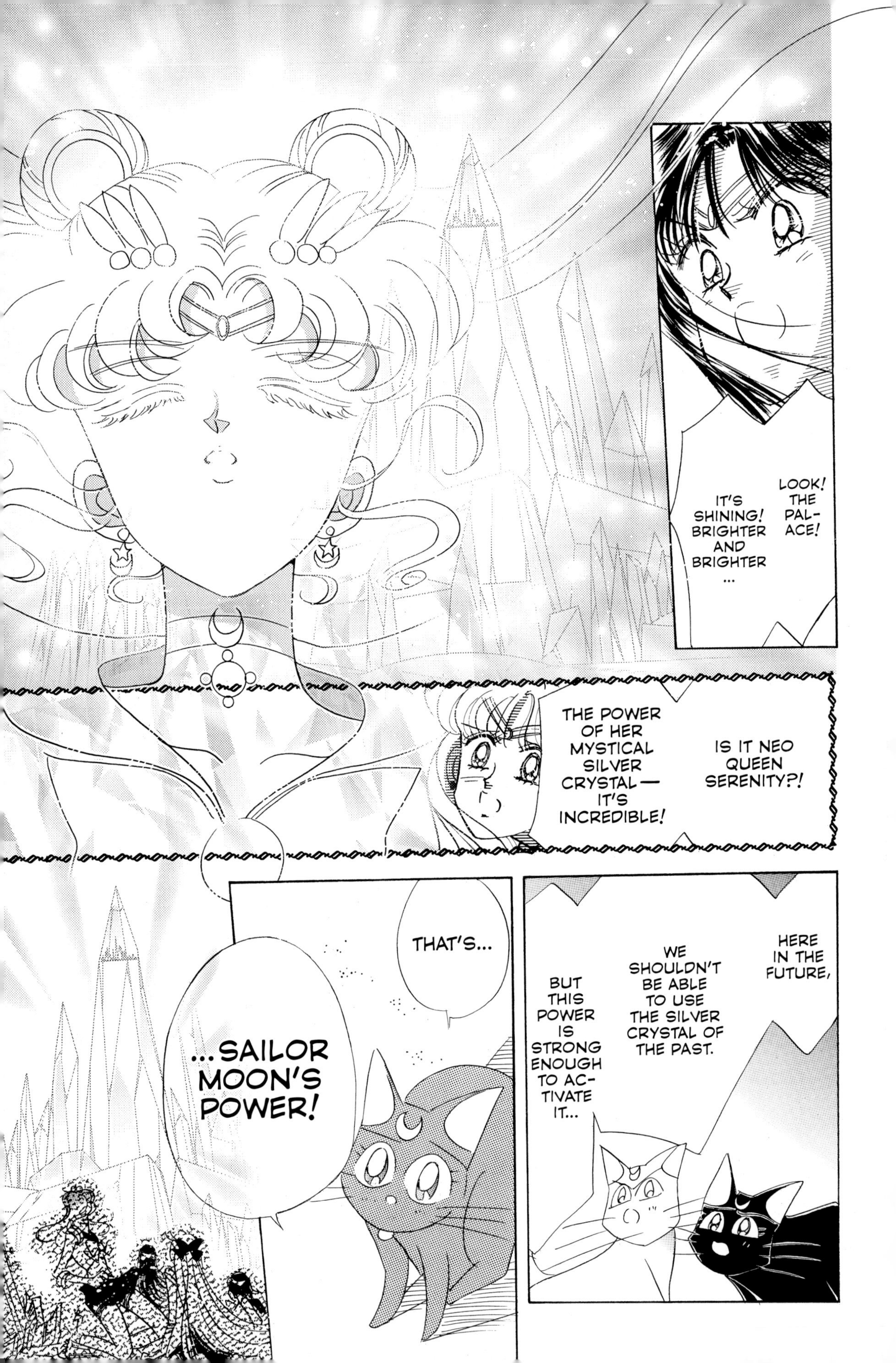
LOOK! THE PAL-ACE!
IT'S SHINING! BRIGHTER AND BRIGHTER ...
IS IT NEO QUEEN SERENITY?!
THE POWER OF HER MYSTICAL SILVER CRYSTAL— IT'S INCREDIBLE!
HERE IN THE FUTURE,
WE SHOULDN'T BE ABLE TO USE THE SILVER CRYSTAL OF THE PAST.
BUT THIS POWER IS STRONG ENOUGH TO AC-TIVATE IT...
THAT'S...
...SAILOR MOON'S POWER!

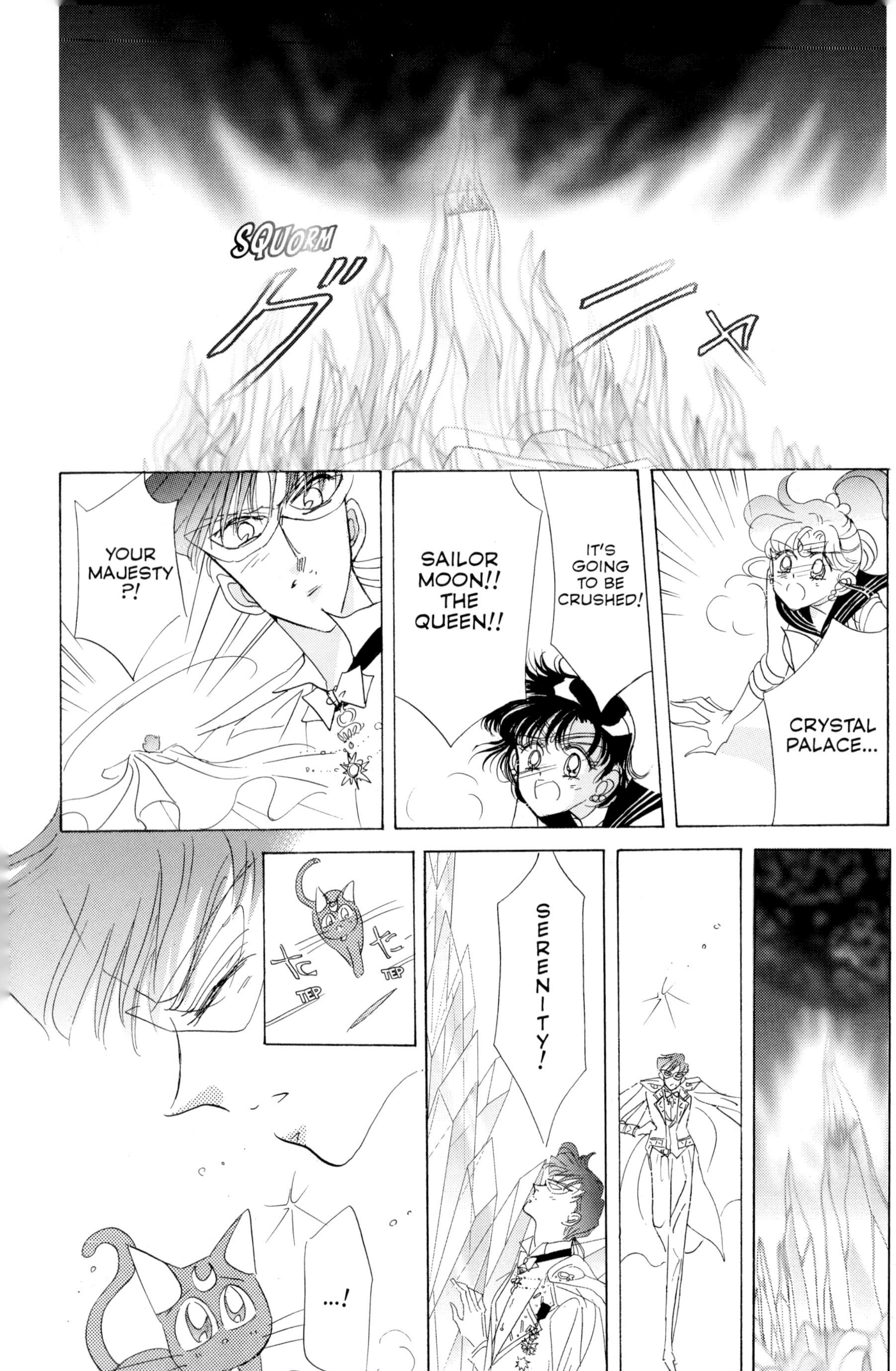

SQUORM
グニャ
CRYSTAL PALACE...
IT'S GOING TO BE CRUSHED!
SAILOR MOON!! THE QUEEN!!
YOUR MAJESTY ?!
SERENITY!
TEP
TEP
...!

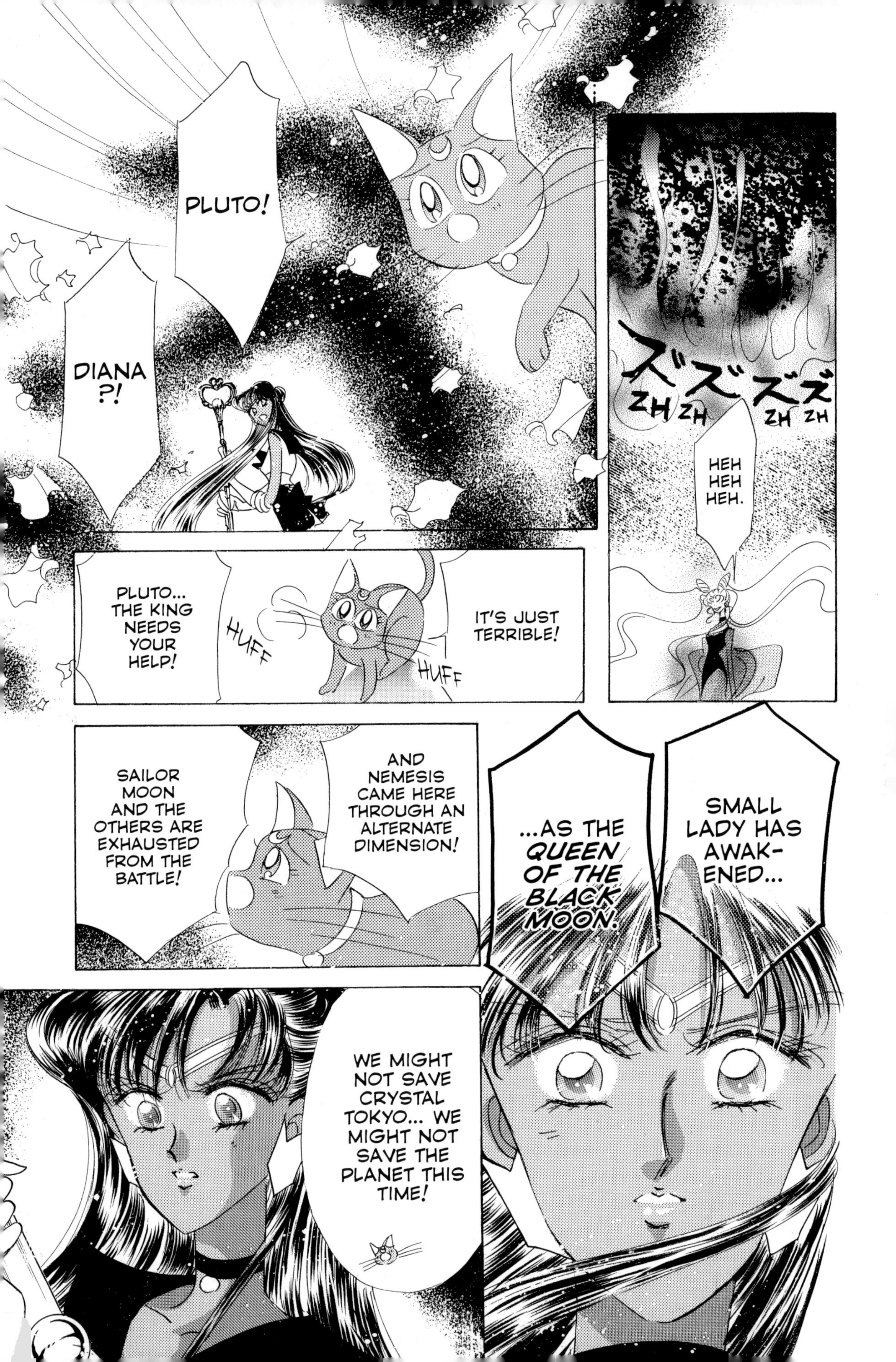
ズズズズ
ZH ZH ZH ZH
HEH HEH HEH.
PLUTO!
DIANA ?!
IT'S JUST TERRIBLE!
HUFF
HUFF
PLUTO... THE KING NEEDS YOUR HELP!
SMALL LADY HAS AWAK-ENED...
...AS THE *QUEEN OF THE BLACK MOON.*
AND NEMESIS CAME HERE THROUGH AN ALTERNATE DIMENSION!
SAILOR MOON AND THE OTHERS ARE EXHAUSTED FROM THE BATTLE!
WE MIGHT NOT SAVE CRYSTAL TOKYO... WE MIGHT NOT SAVE THE PLANET THIS TIME!

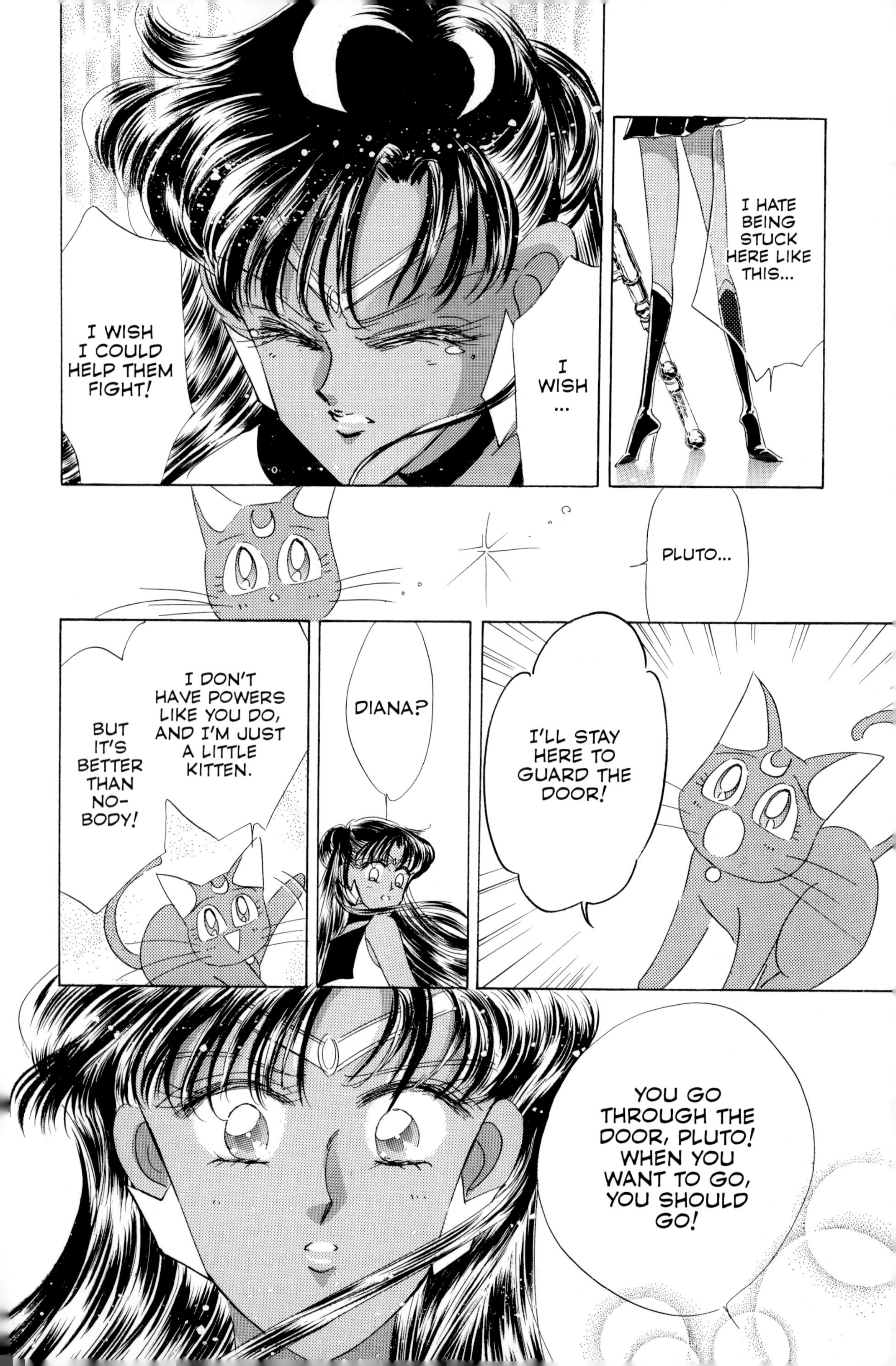
I HATE BEING STUCK HERE LIKE THIS...
I WISH...
I WISH I COULD HELP THEM FIGHT!
PLUTO...
I'LL STAY HERE TO GUARD THE DOOR!
DIANA?
I DON'T HAVE POWERS LIKE YOU DO, AND I'M JUST A LITTLE KITTEN.
BUT IT'S BETTER THAN NO-BODY!
YOU GO THROUGH THE DOOR, PLUTO! WHEN YOU WANT TO GO, YOU SHOULD GO!

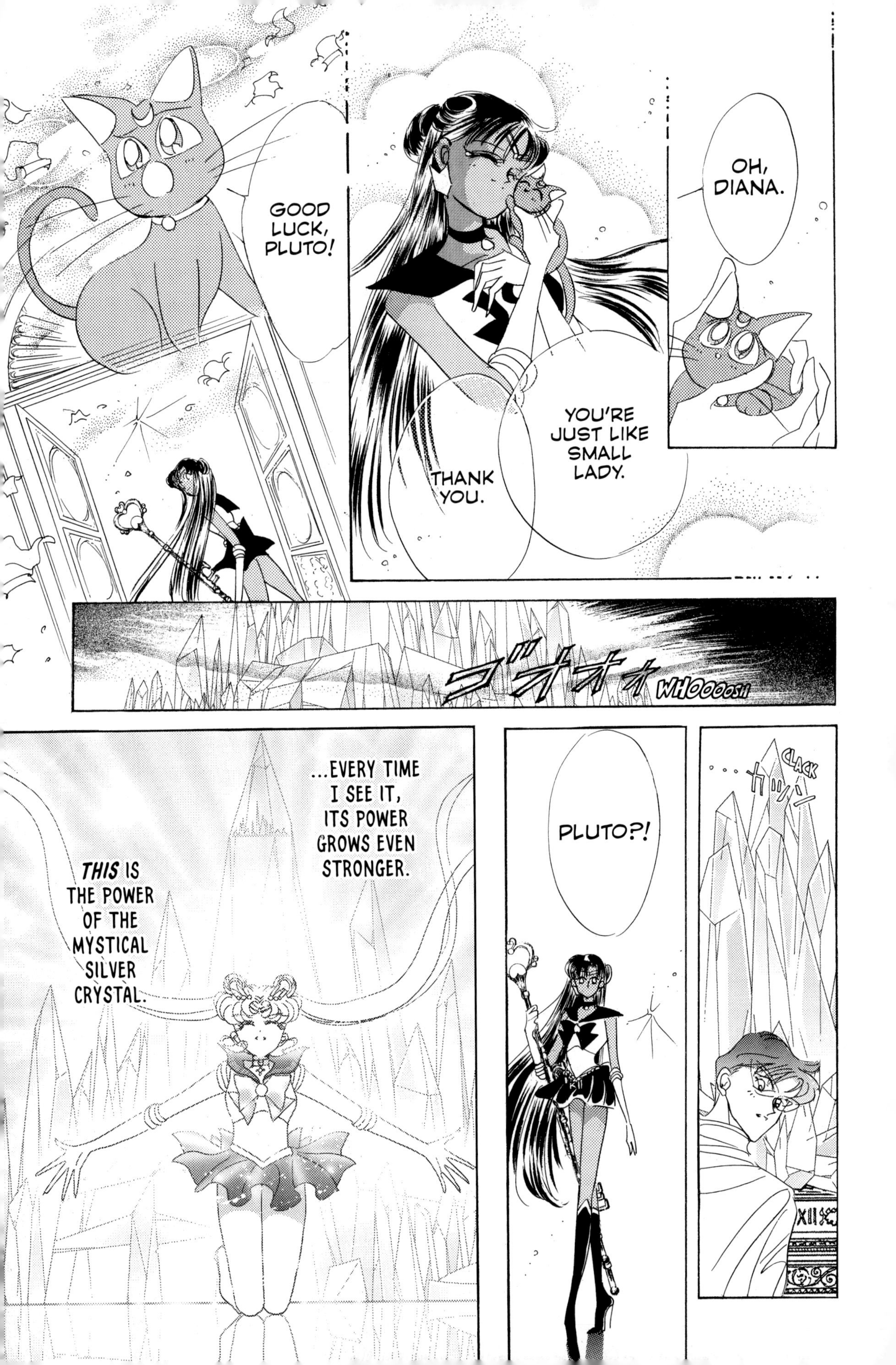
OH, DIANA.
YOU'RE JUST LIKE SMALL LADY.
THANK YOU.
GOOD LUCK, PLUTO!
ゴオオオ
WHOOOOSH!
カツン
CLACK
PLUTO?!
...EVERY TIME I SEE IT, ITS POWER GROWS EVEN STRONGER.
THIS IS THE POWER OF THE MYSTICAL SILVER CRYSTAL.

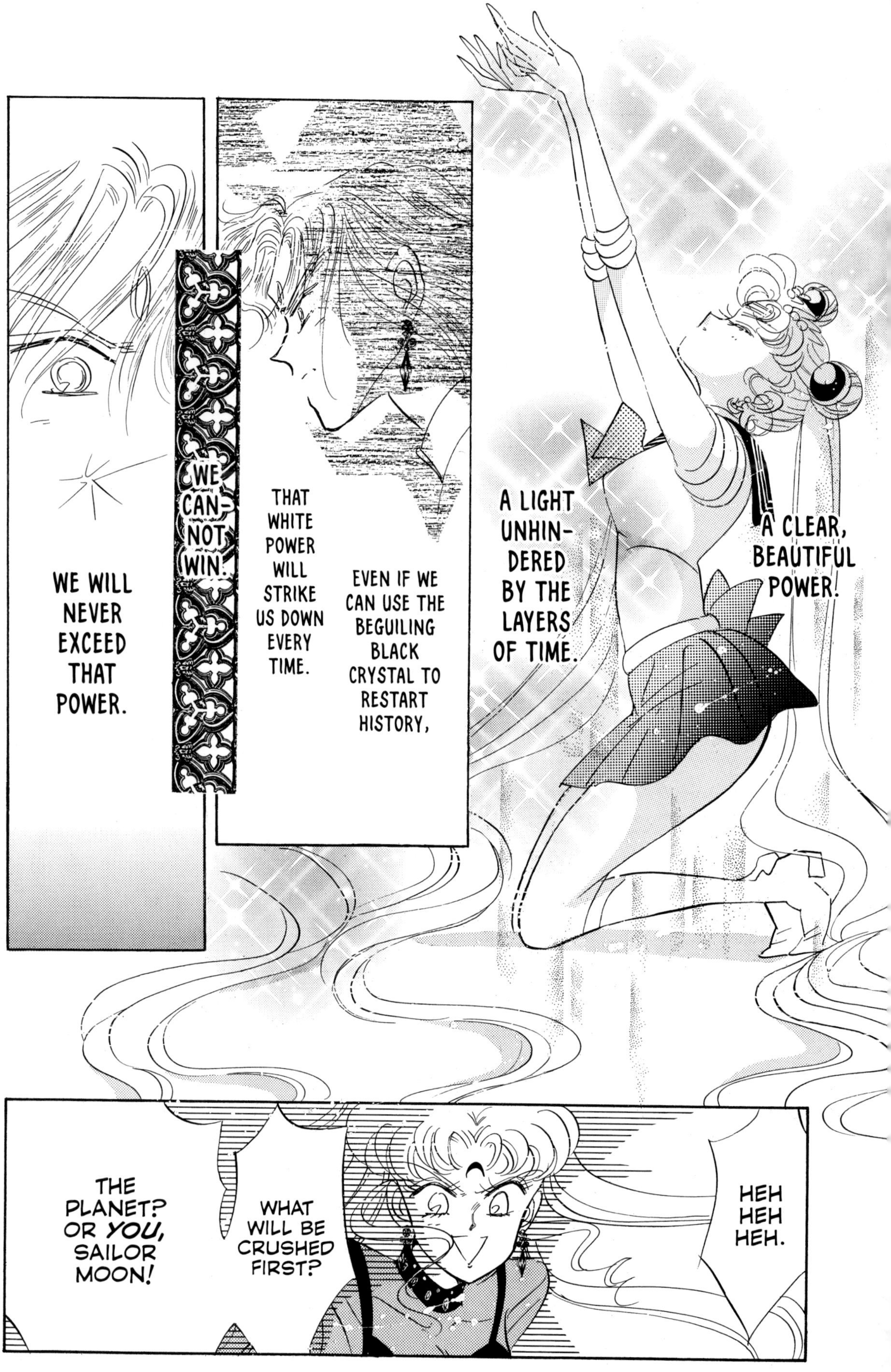
A CLEAR, BEAUTIFUL POWER!
A LIGHT UNHIN-DERED BY THE LAYERS OF TIME.
EVEN IF WE CAN USE THE BEGUILING BLACK CRYSTAL TO RESTART HISTORY,
THAT WHITE POWER WILL STRIKE US DOWN EVERY TIME.
WE CAN-NOT WIN.
WE WILL NEVER EXCEED THAT POWER.
HEH HEH HEH.
WHAT WILL BE CRUSHED FIRST?
THE PLANET? OR *YOU*, SAILOR MOON!

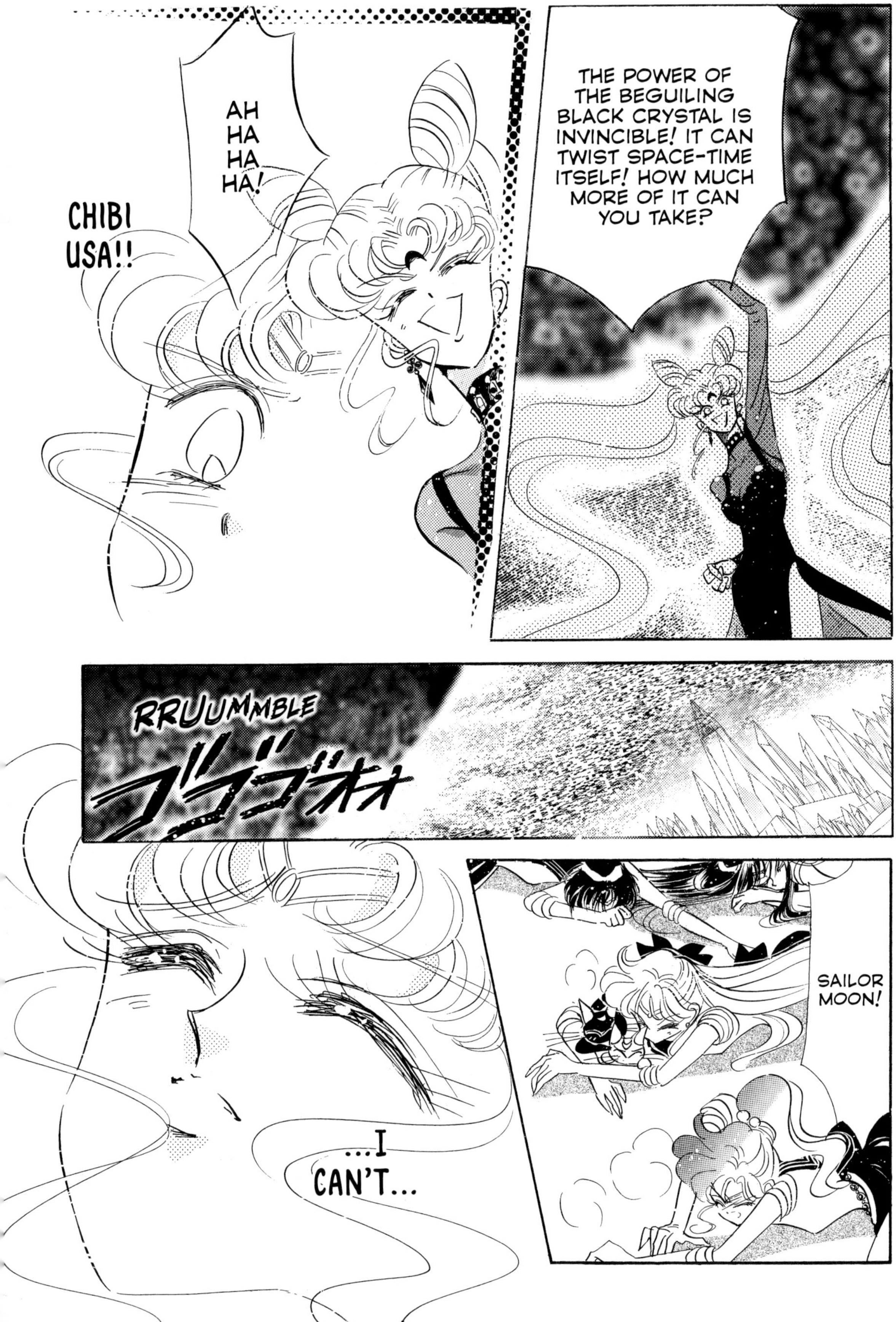
THE POWER OF THE BEGUILING BLACK CRYSTAL IS INVINCIBLE! IT CAN TWIST SPACE-TIME ITSELF! HOW MUCH MORE OF IT CAN YOU TAKE?
AH HA HA HA!
CHIBI USA!!
RRUUMMBLE
SAILOR MOON!
...I CAN'T...

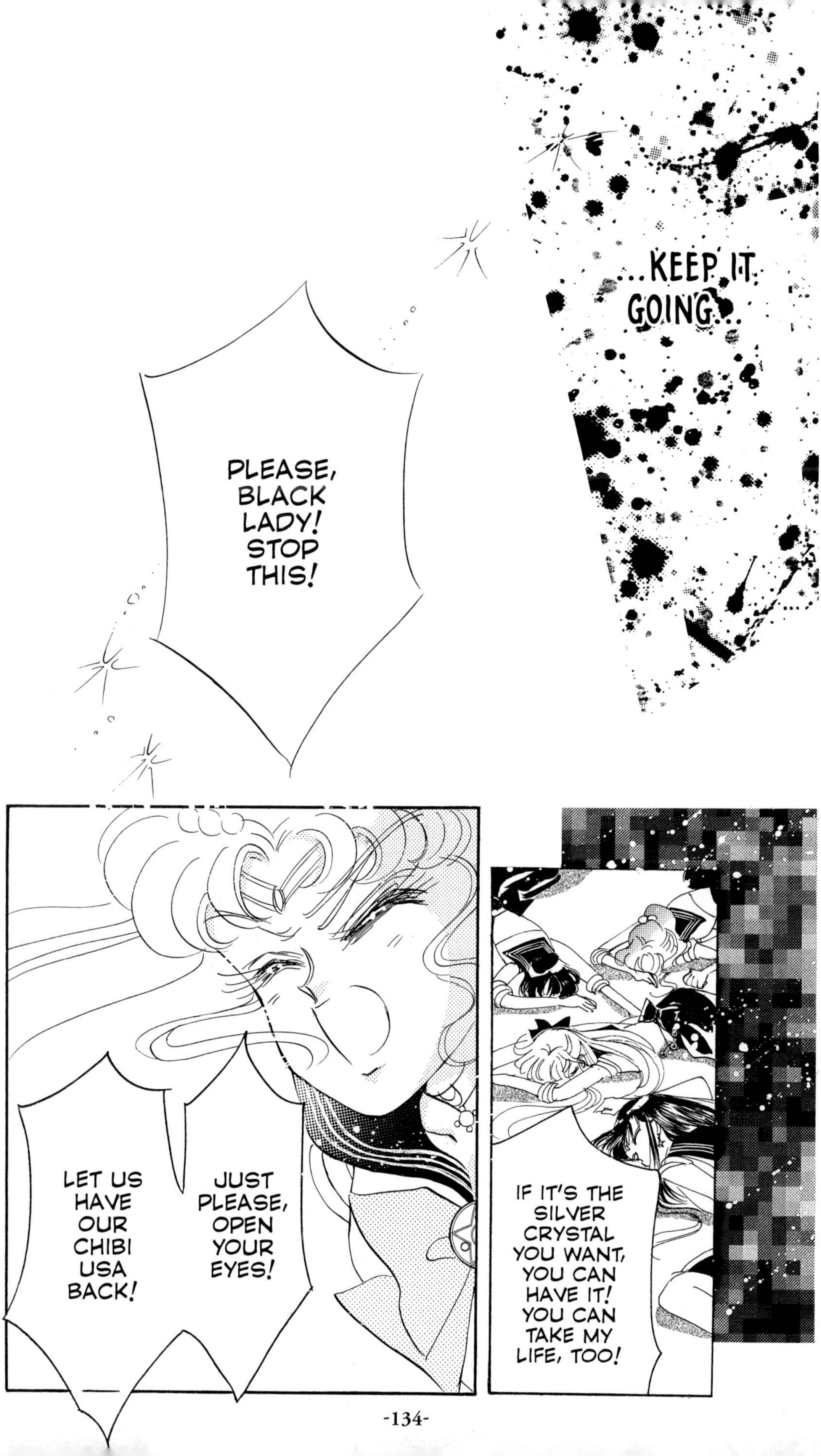
...KEEP IT GOING...
PLEASE, BLACK LADY! STOP THIS!
IF IT'S THE SILVER CRYSTAL YOU WANT, YOU CAN HAVE IT! YOU CAN TAKE MY LIFE, TOO!
JUST PLEASE, OPEN YOUR EYES!
LET US HAVE OUR CHIBI USA BACK!

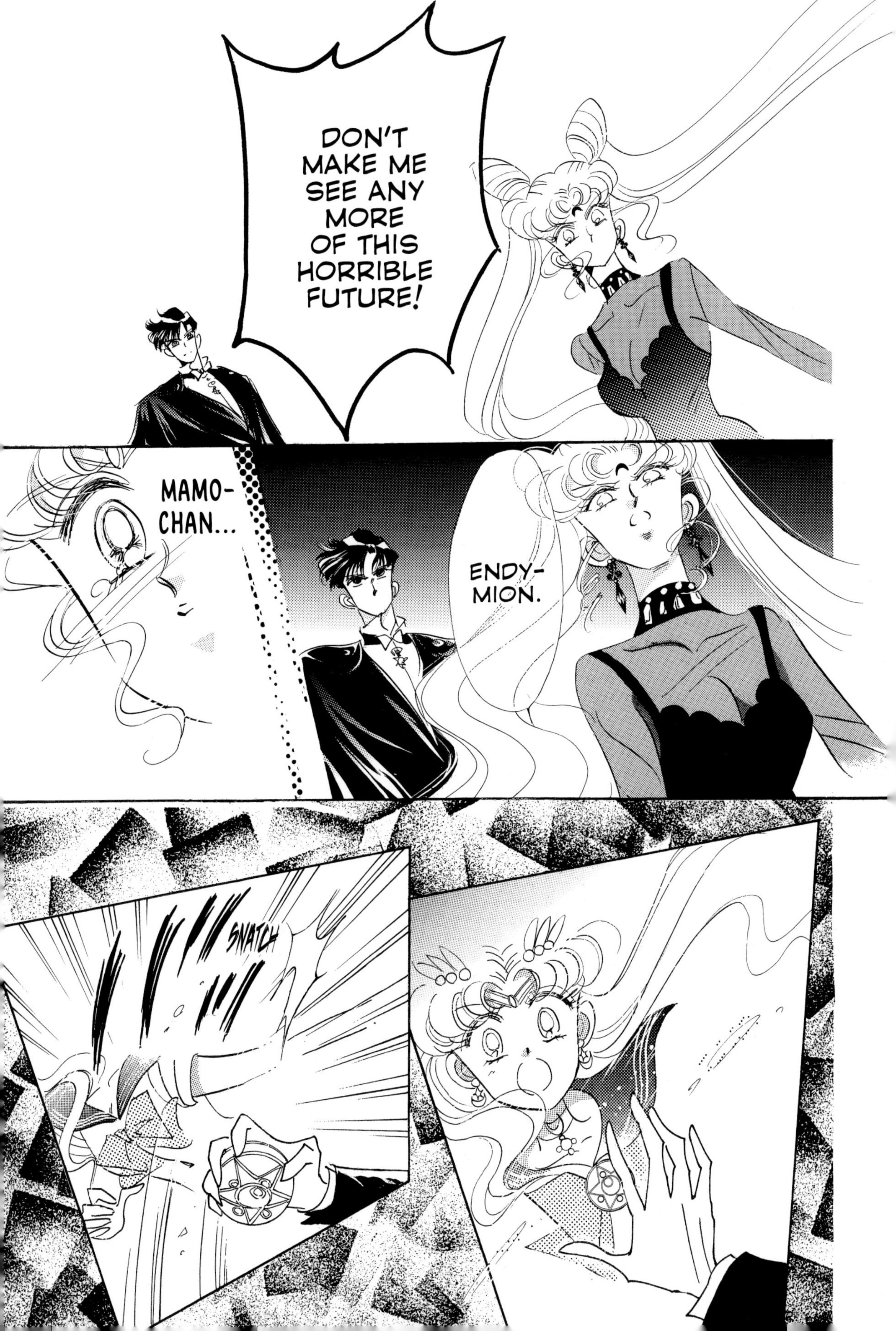
DON'T MAKE ME SEE ANY MORE OF THIS HORRIBLE FUTURE!
ENDY-MION.
MAMO-CHAN...
SNATCH

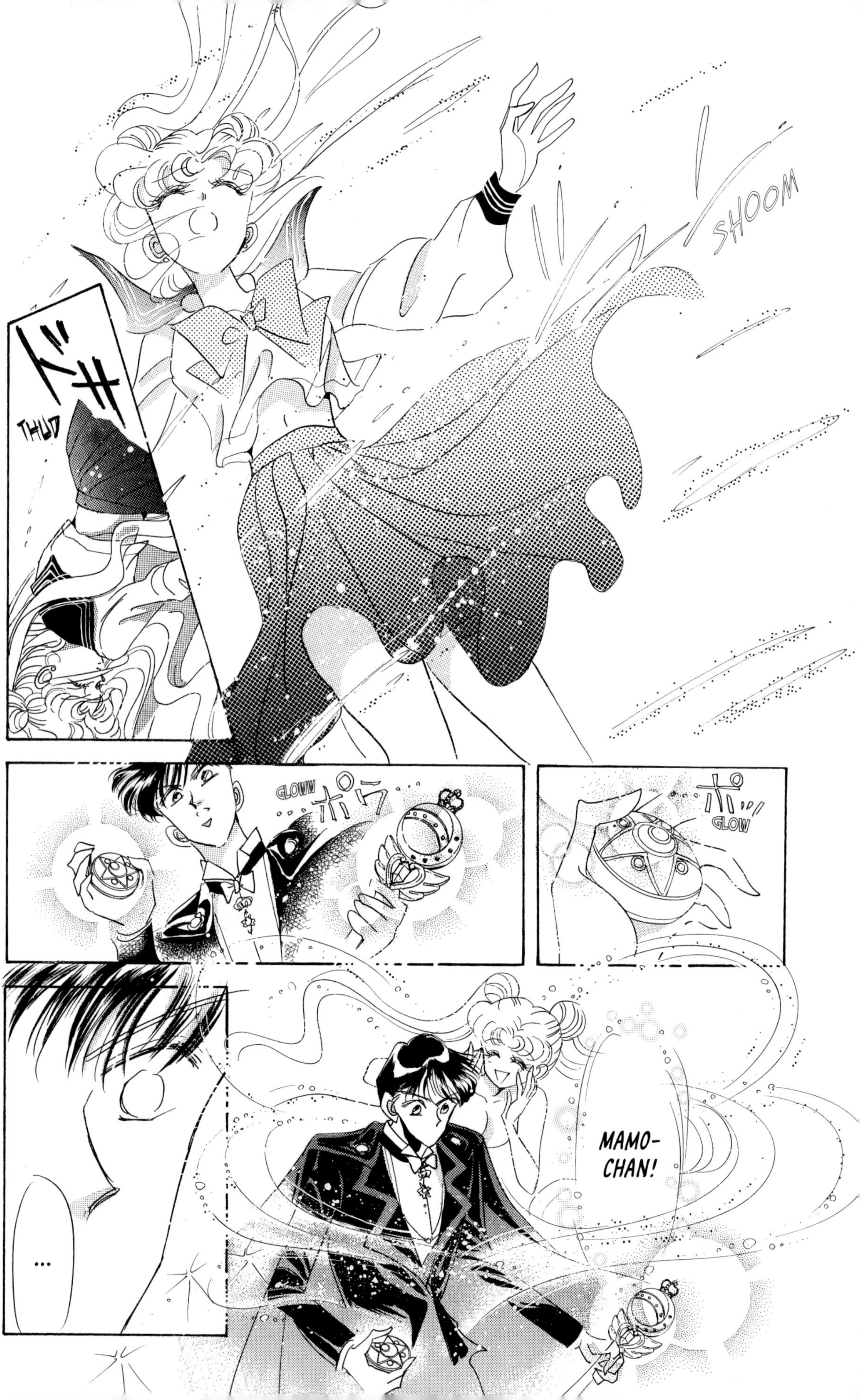
SHOOM
ドサ
THUD
ポ
GLOW
GLOWW
ポウ
MAMO-
CHAN!
...

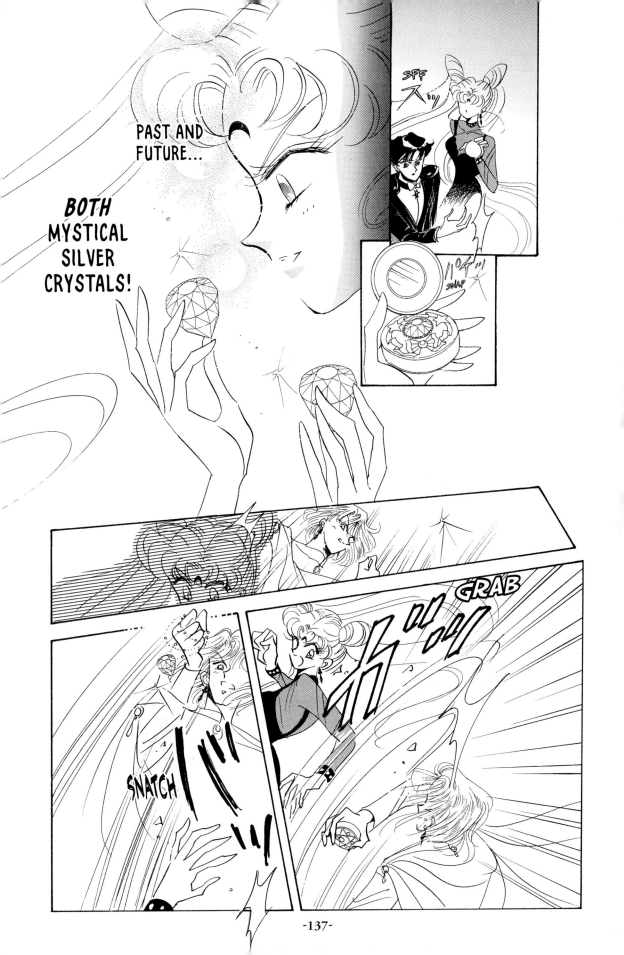

PAST AND FUTURE...

BOTH MYSTICAL SILVER CRYSTALS!

SFF

SNAP

GRAB

SNATCH

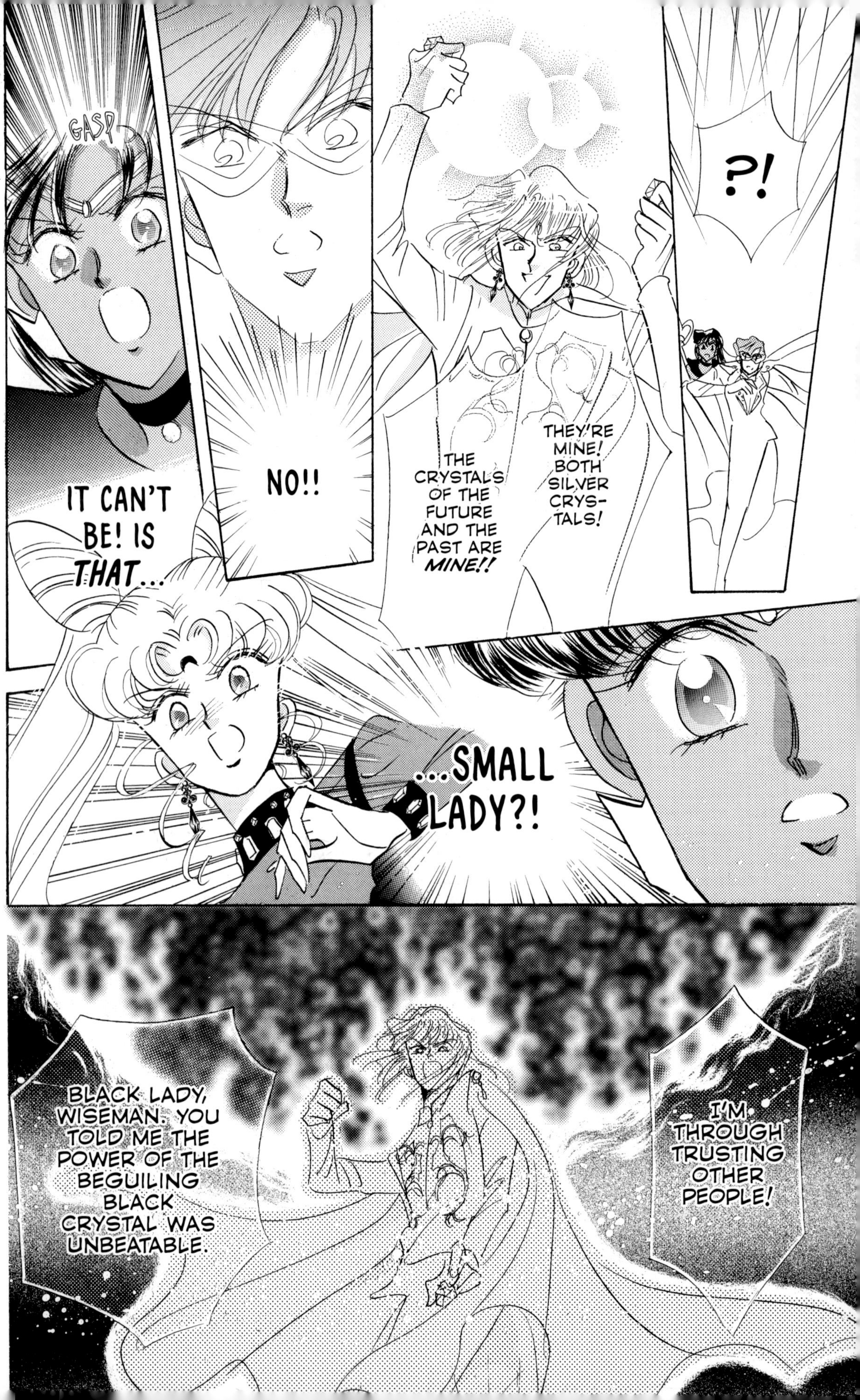

?!
THEY'RE MINE! BOTH SILVER CRYS-TALS!
THE CRYSTALS OF THE FUTURE AND THE PAST ARE *MINE!!*
NO!!
GASP
IT CAN'T BE! IS *THAT*...
...SMALL LADY?!
I'M THROUGH TRUSTING OTHER PEOPLE!
BLACK LADY, WISEMAN. YOU TOLD ME THE POWER OF THE BEGUILING BLACK CRYSTAL WAS UNBEATABLE.

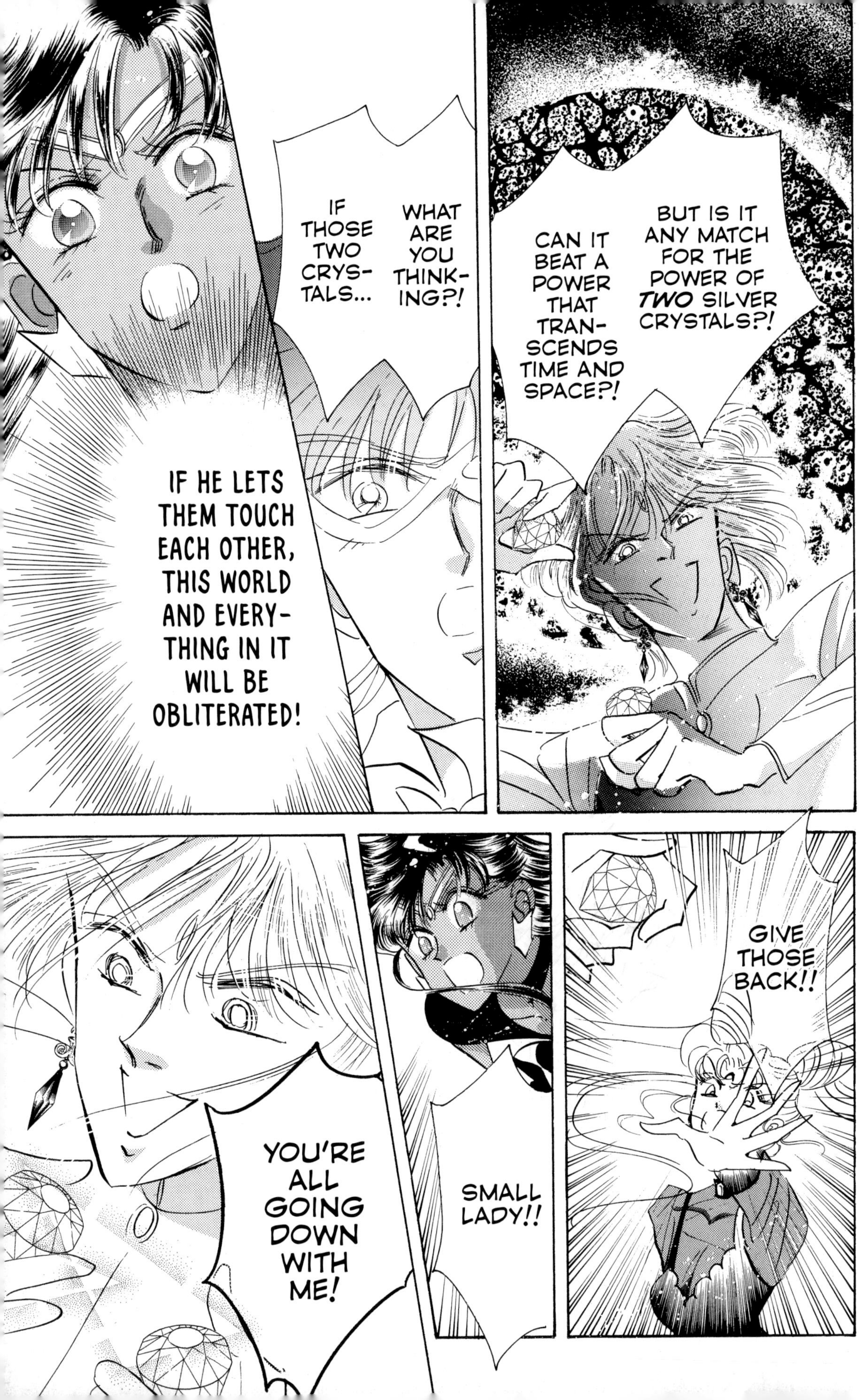
BUT IS IT ANY MATCH FOR THE POWER OF *TWO* SILVER CRYSTALS?!
CAN IT BEAT A POWER THAT TRAN-SCENDS TIME AND SPACE?!
WHAT ARE YOU THINK-ING?!
IF THOSE TWO CRYS-TALS...
IF HE LETS THEM TOUCH EACH OTHER, THIS WORLD AND EVERY-THING IN IT WILL BE OBLITERATED!
GIVE THOSE BACK!!
SMALL LADY!!
YOU'RE ALL GOING DOWN WITH ME!

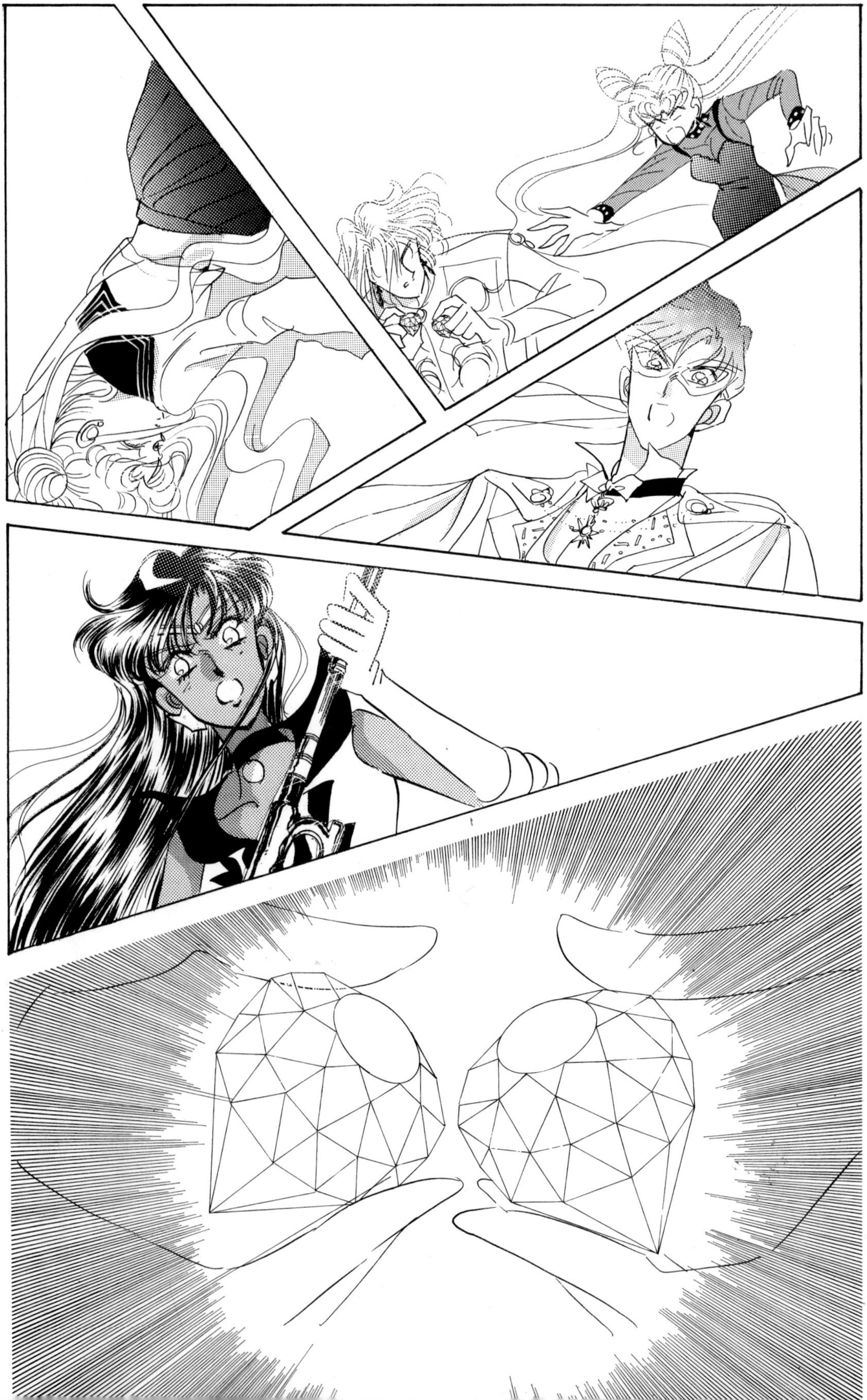

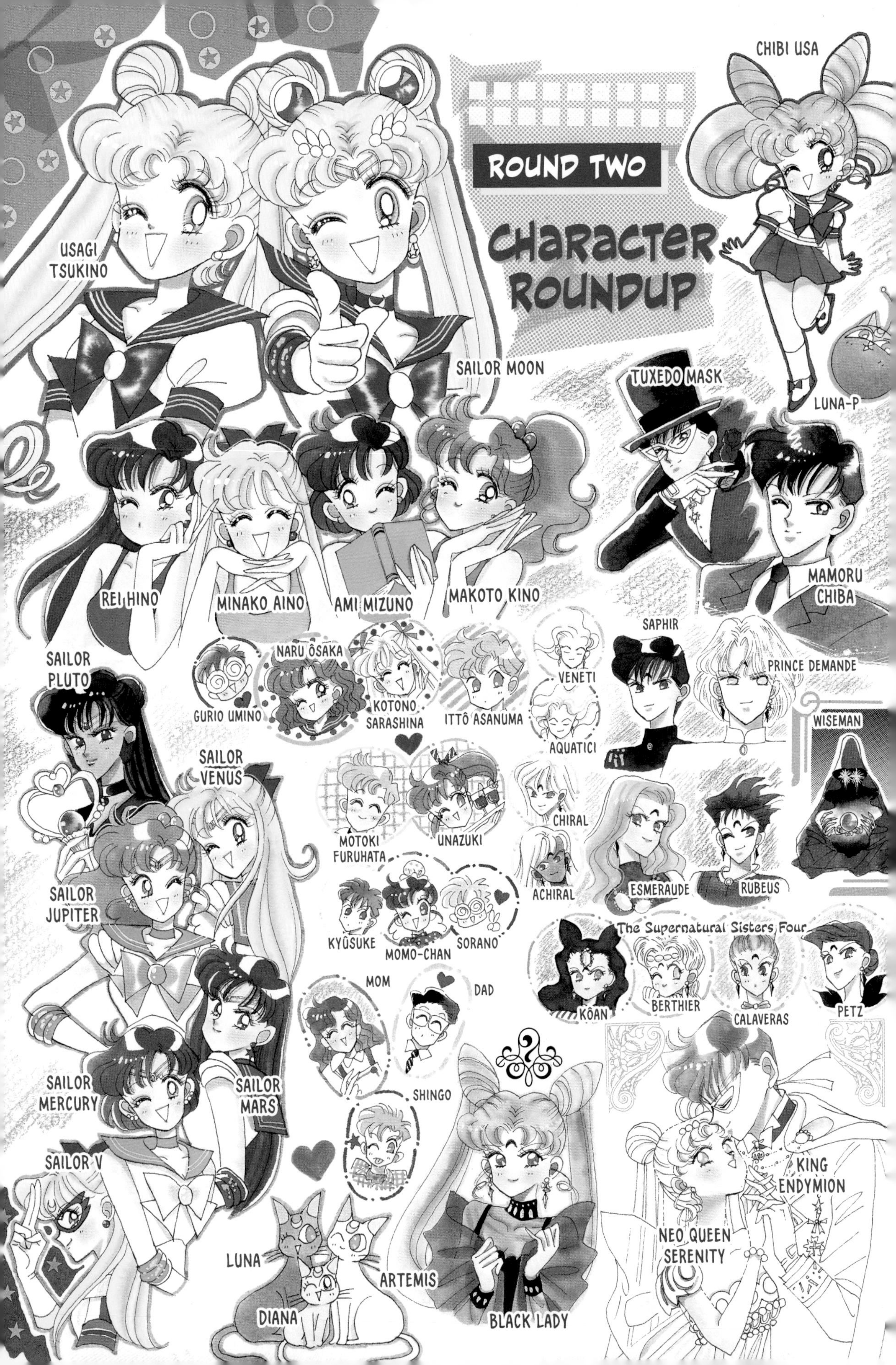
ROUND TWO
Character Roundup
CHIBI USA
USAGI TSUKINO
SAILOR MOON
TUXEDO MASK
LUNA-P
REI HINO
MINAKO AINO
AMI MIZUNO
MAKOTO KINO
MAMORU CHIBA
SAILOR PLUTO
GURIO UMINO
NARU ÔSAKA
KOTONO SARASHINA
ITTÔ ASANUMA
VENETI
AQUATICI
SAPHIR
PRINCE DEMANDE
WISEMAN
SAILOR VENUS
MOTOKI FURUHATA
UNAZUKI
CHIRAL
ACHIRAL
ESMERAUDE
RUBEUS
SAILOR JUPITER
KYÛSUKE
MOMO-CHAN
SORANO
The Supernatural Sisters Four
KÔAN
BERTHIER
CALAVERAS
PETZ
MOM
DAD
SAILOR MERCURY
SAILOR MARS
SHINGO
SAILOR V
KING ENDYMION
NEO QUEEN SERENITY
LUNA
ARTEMIS
DIANA
BLACK LADY

Act. 25 Confrontation: Death Phantom

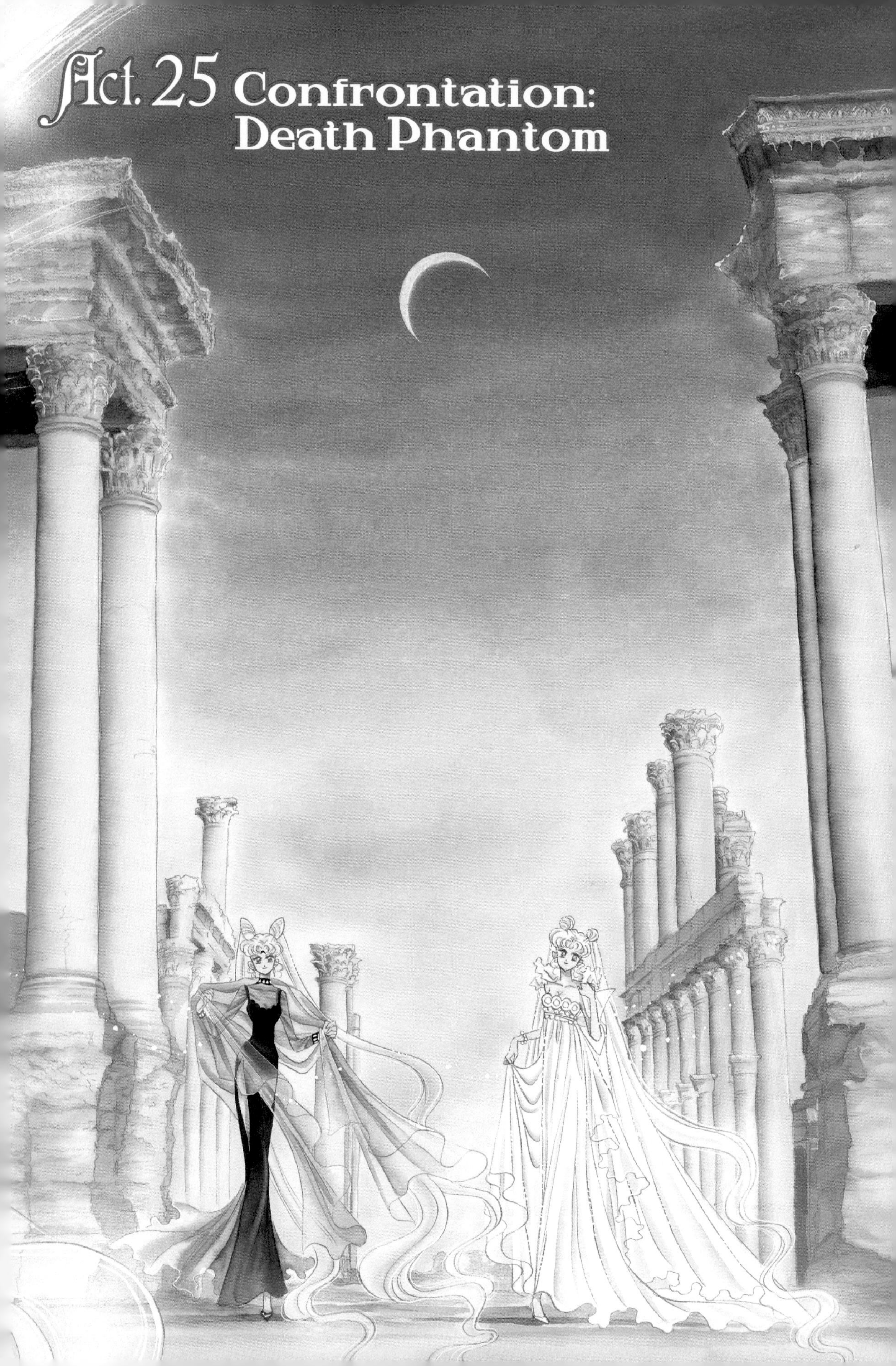

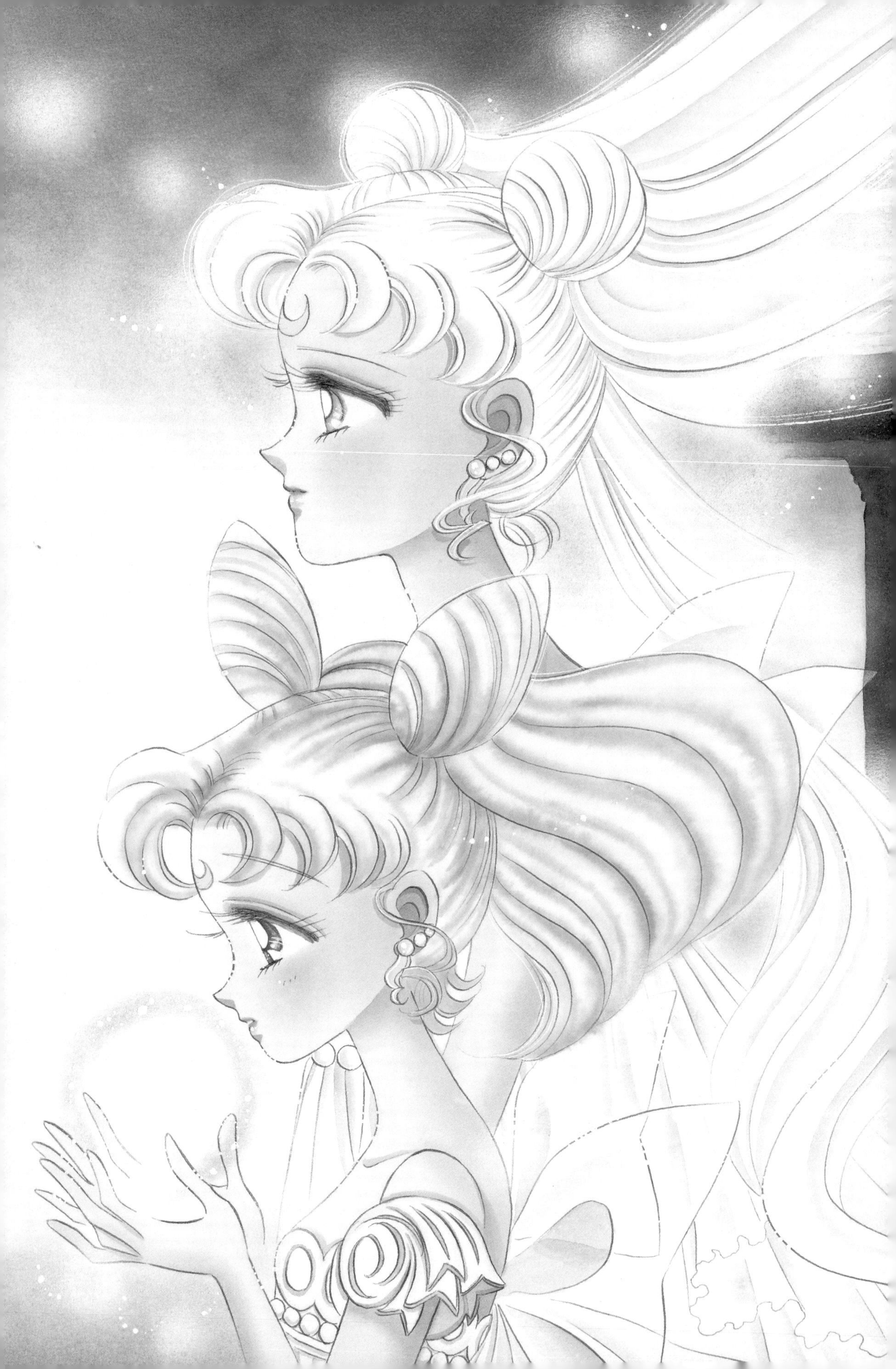

Pretty Guardian
Sailor Moon

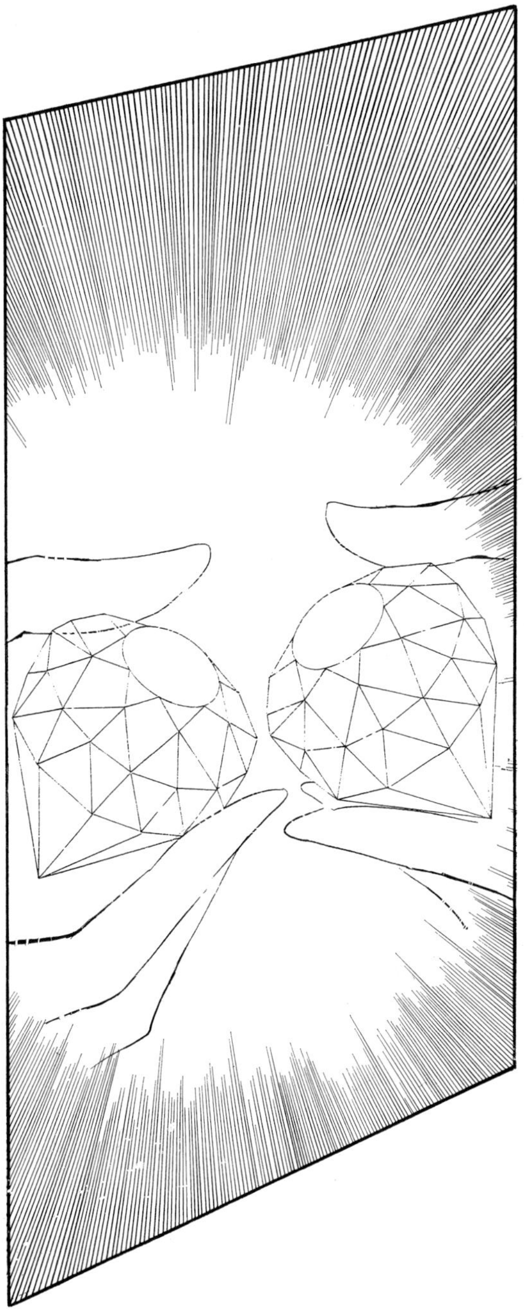

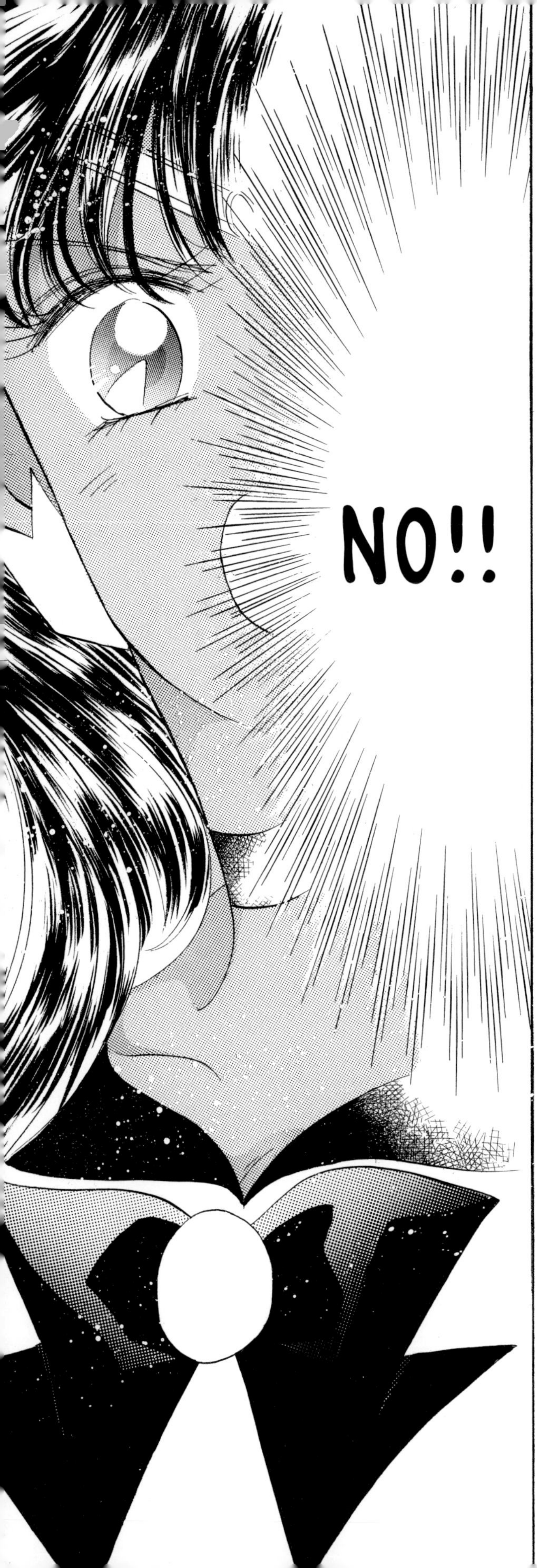
NO!!

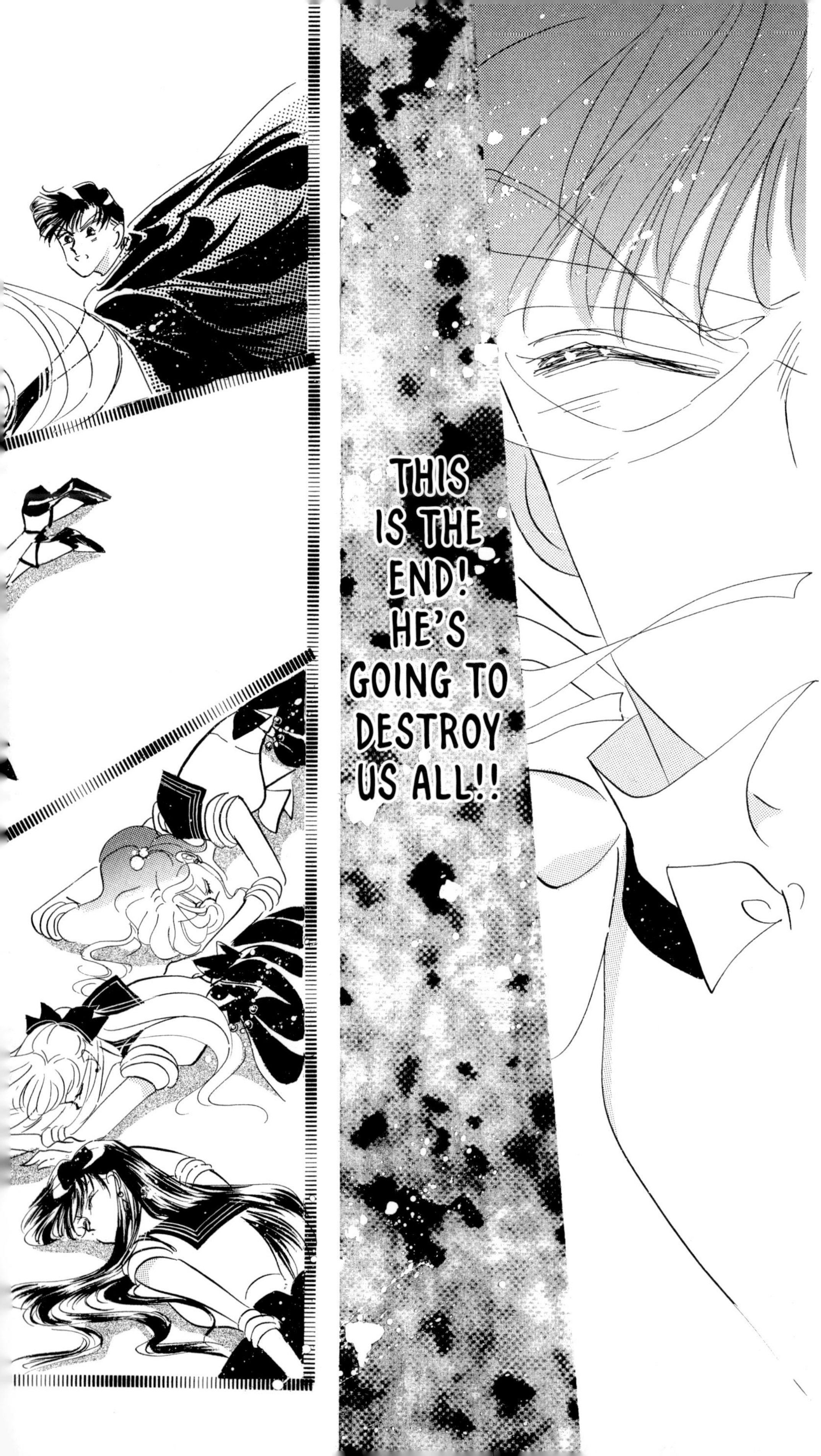
THIS IS THE END! HE'S GOING TO DESTROY US ALL!!

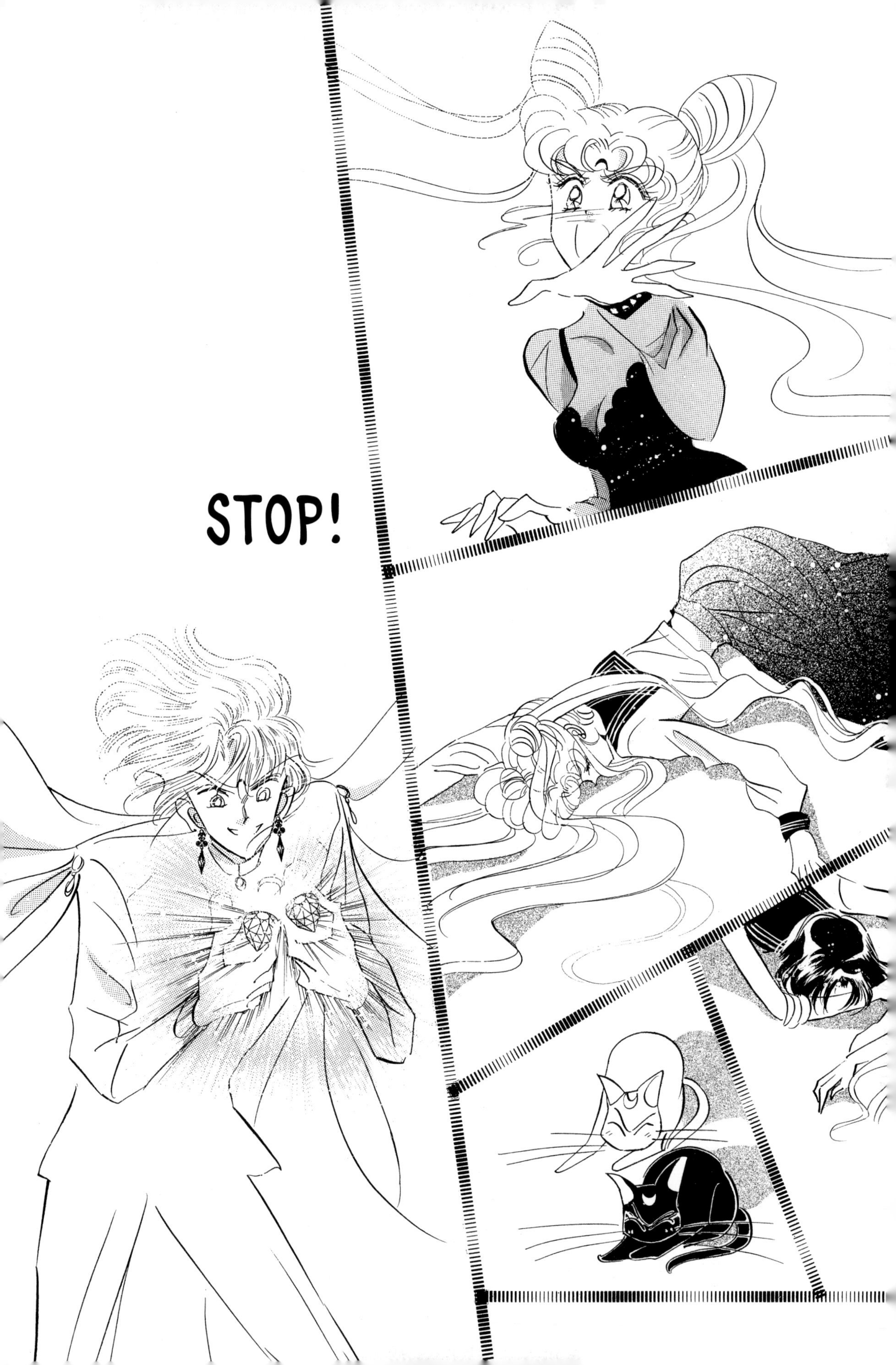
STOP!

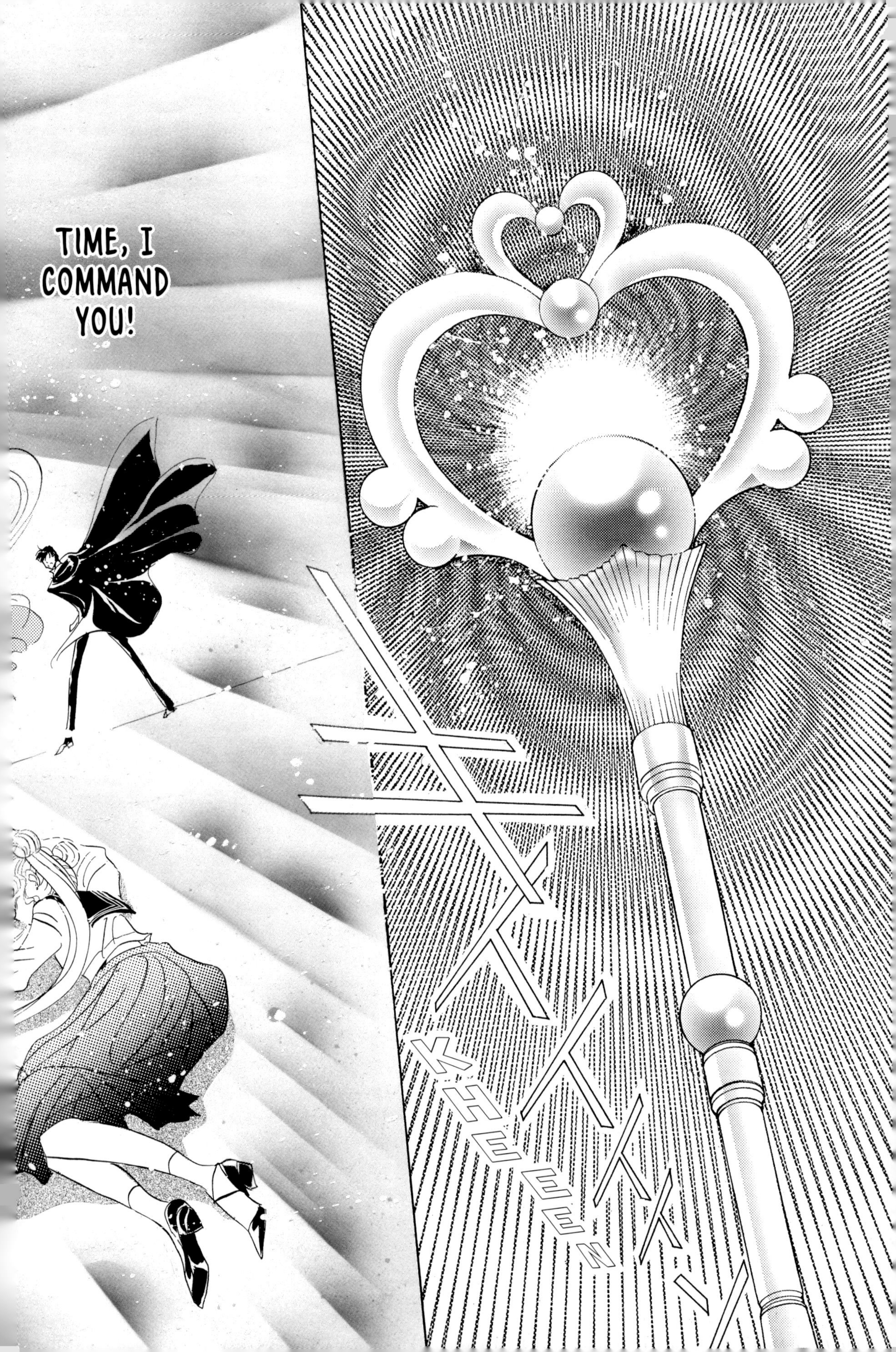
KHEEEN
TIME, I COMMAND YOU!

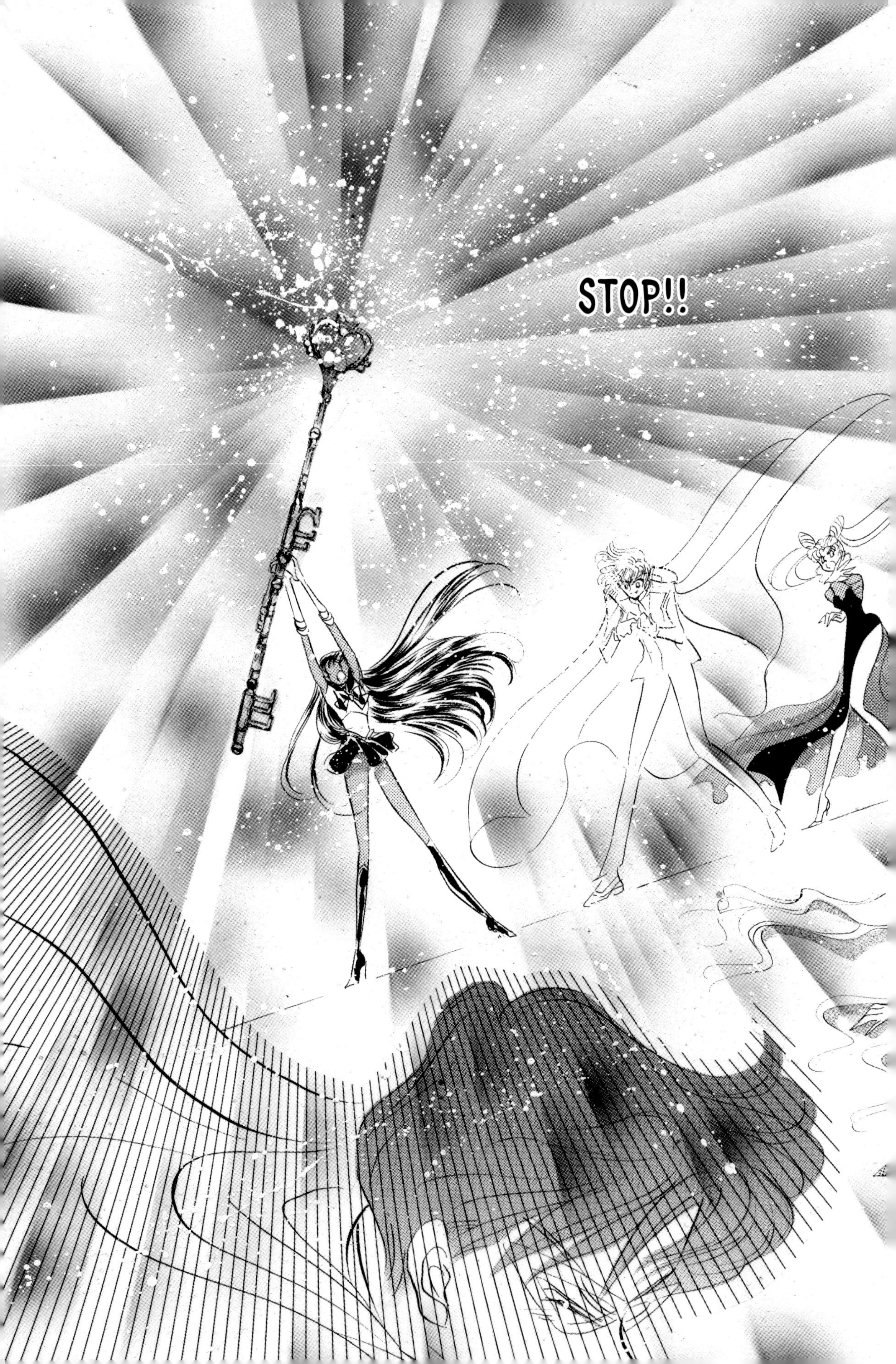
STOP!!

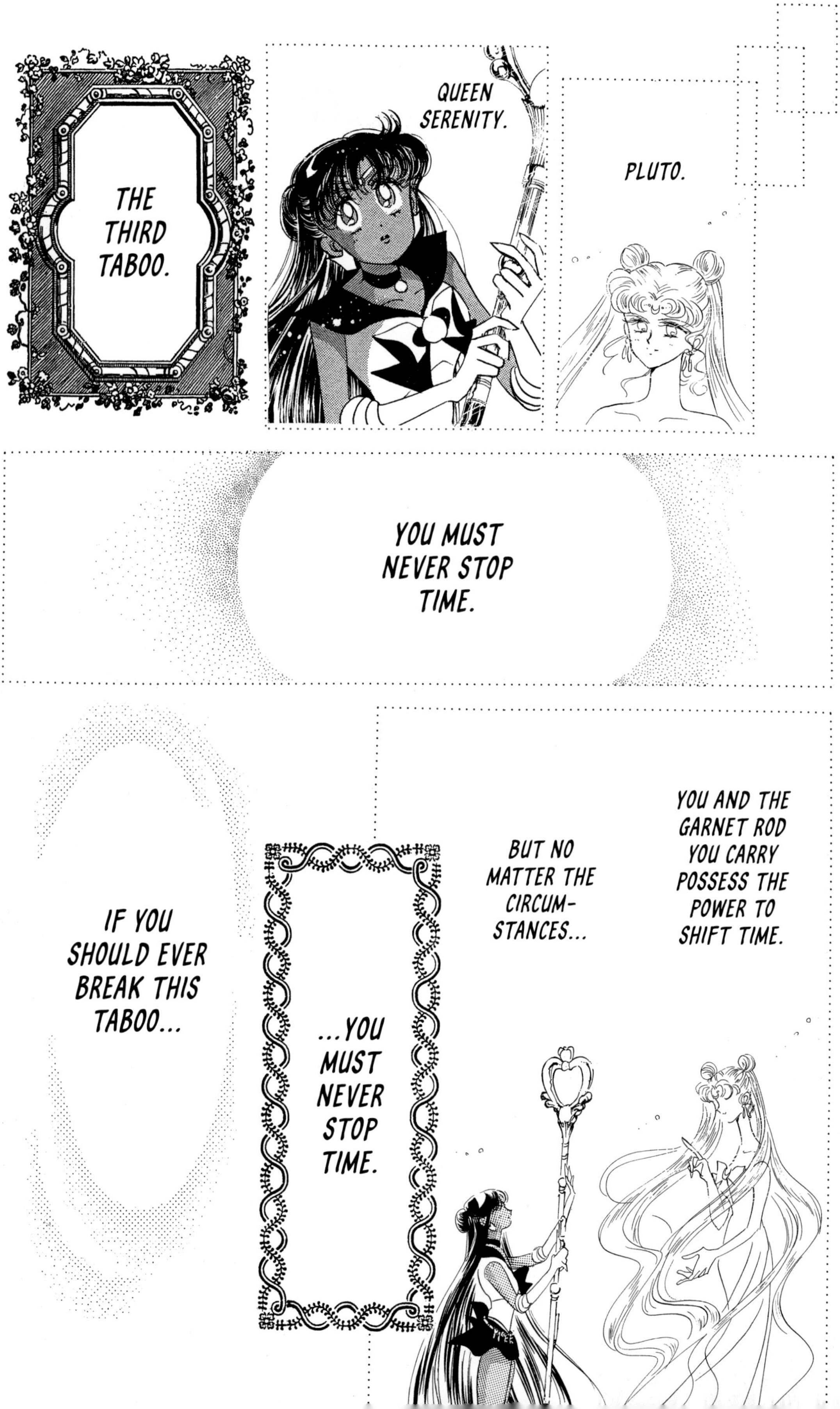
PLUTO.
QUEEN SERENITY.
THE THIRD TABOO.
YOU MUST NEVER STOP TIME.
YOU AND THE GARNET ROD YOU CARRY POSSESS THE POWER TO SHIFT TIME.
BUT NO MATTER THE CIRCUM-STANCES...
...YOU MUST NEVER STOP TIME.
IF YOU SHOULD EVER BREAK THIS TABOO...

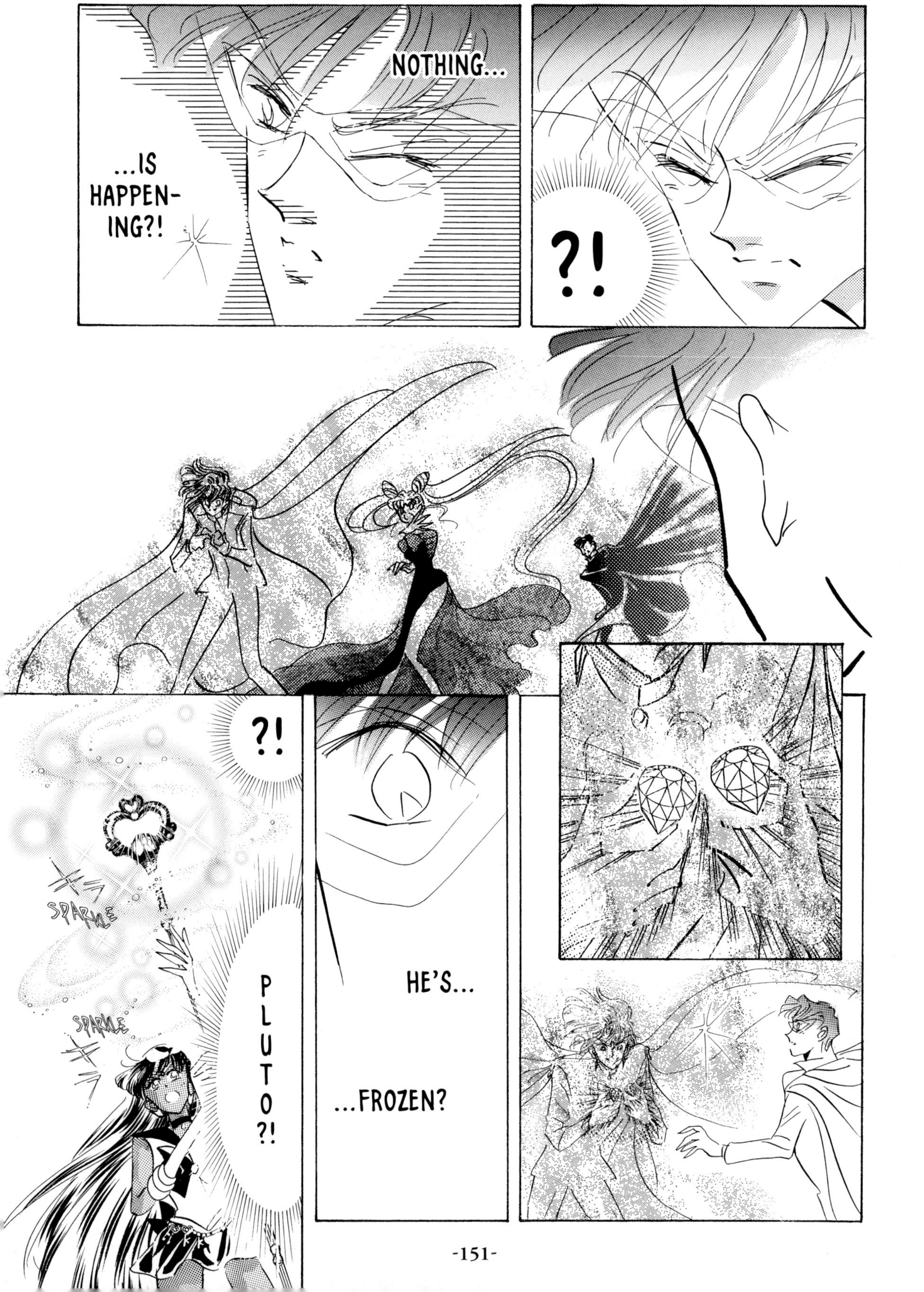
?!
NOTHING...
...IS HAPPEN-ING?!
HE'S...
...FROZEN?
?!
SPARKLE
PLUTO?!
SPARKLE

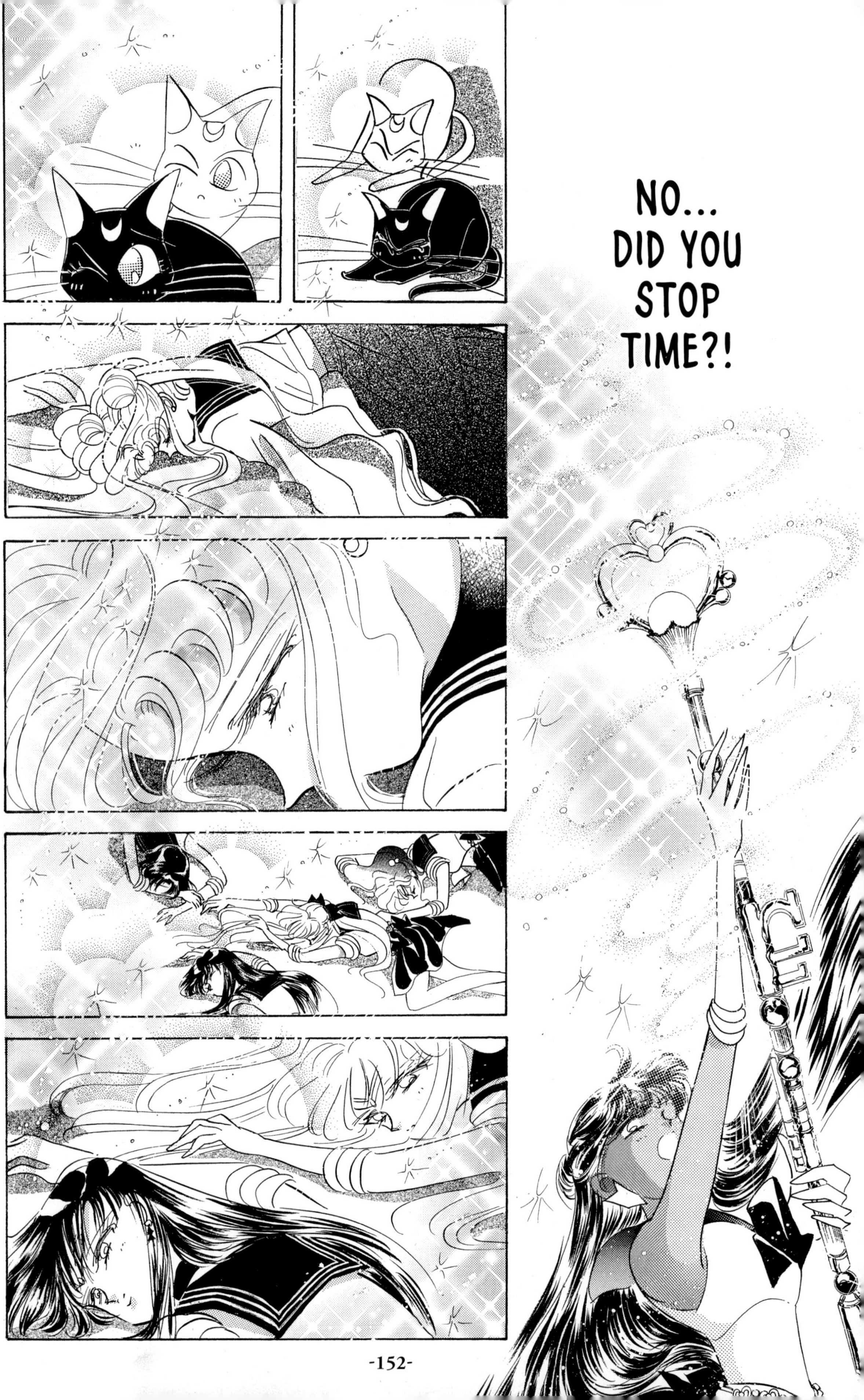
NO... DID YOU STOP TIME?!

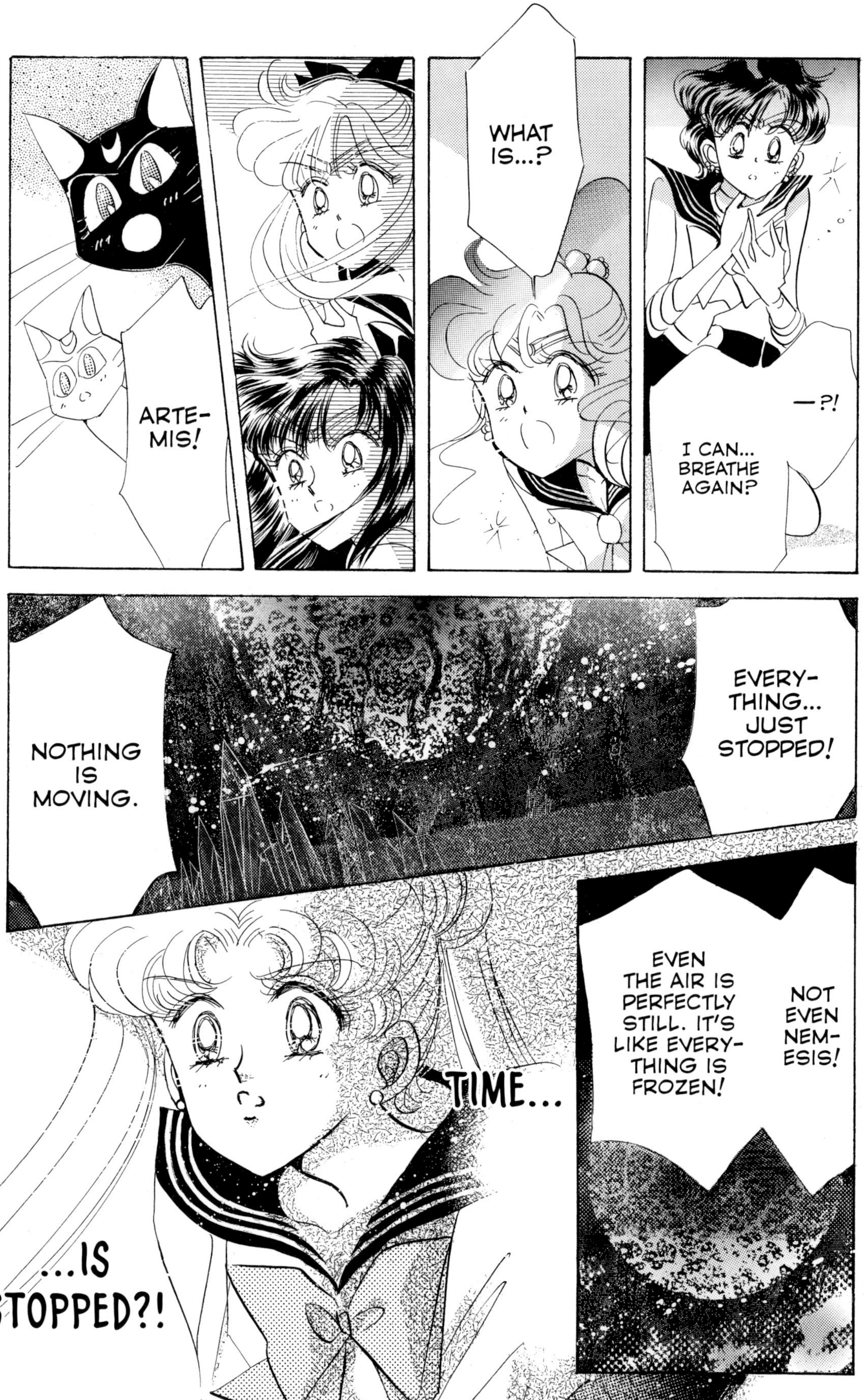
—?!
I CAN... BREATHE AGAIN?
WHAT IS...?
ARTE-MIS!
EVERY-THING... JUST STOPPED!
NOTHING IS MOVING.
NOT EVEN NEM-ESIS!
EVEN THE AIR IS PERFECTLY STILL. IT'S LIKE EVERY-THING IS FROZEN!
TIME...
...IS STOPPED?!

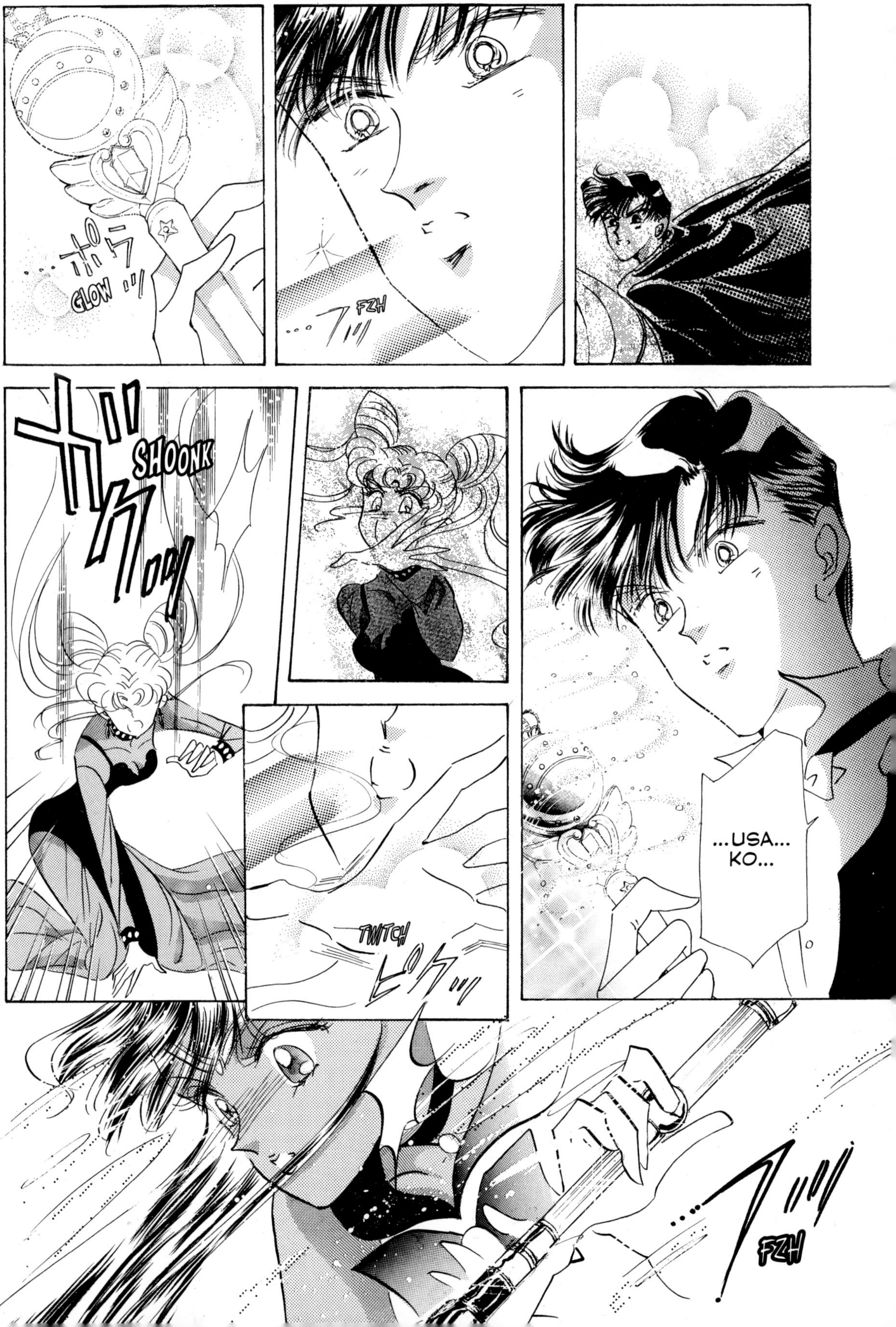
FZH
GLOW
...USA... KO...
TWITCH
SHOONK
FZH

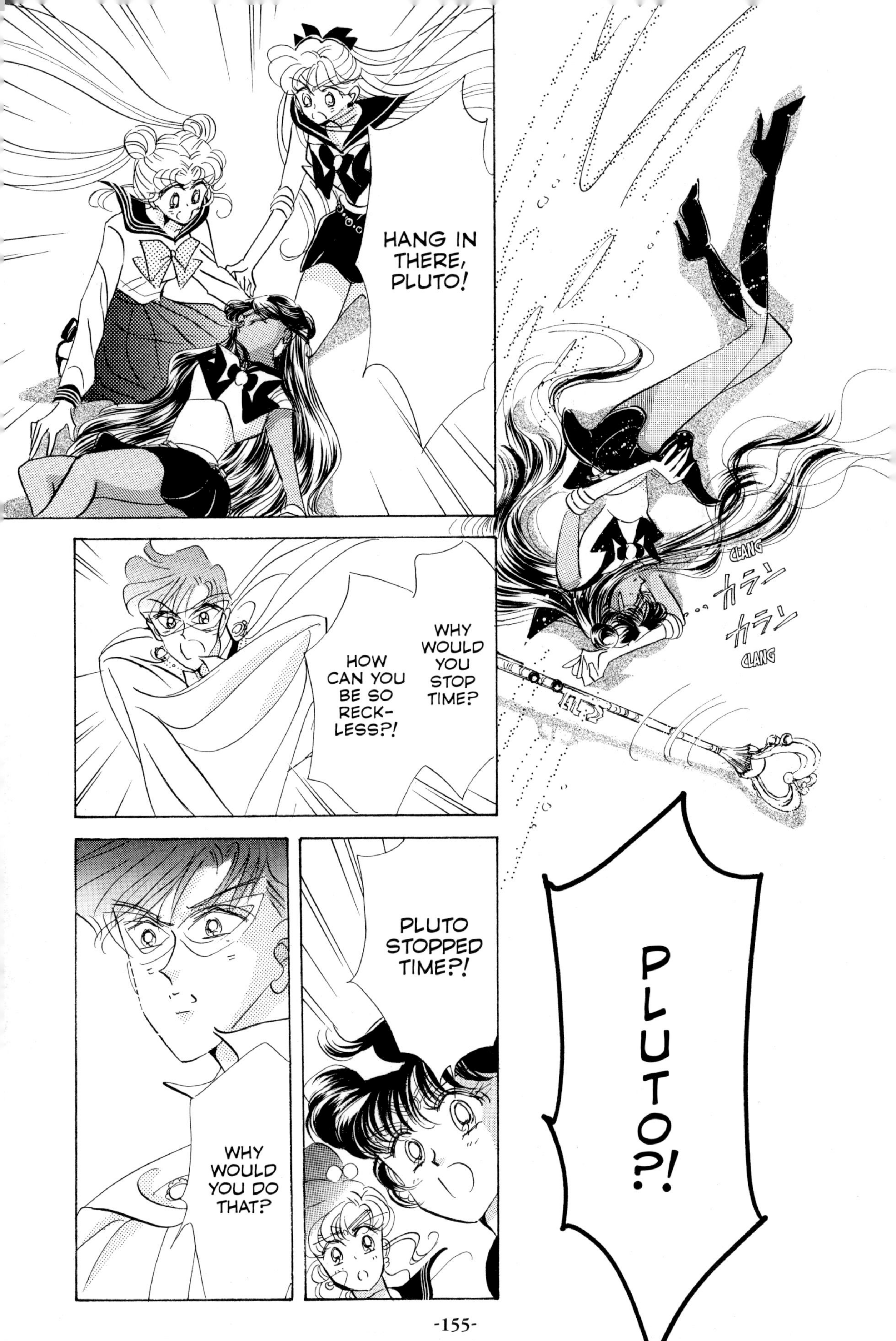
CLANG
カラン
カラン
CLANG
PLUTO?!
HANG IN THERE, PLUTO!
WHY WOULD YOU STOP TIME?
HOW CAN YOU BE SO RECK-LESS?!
PLUTO STOPPED TIME?!
WHY WOULD YOU DO THAT?

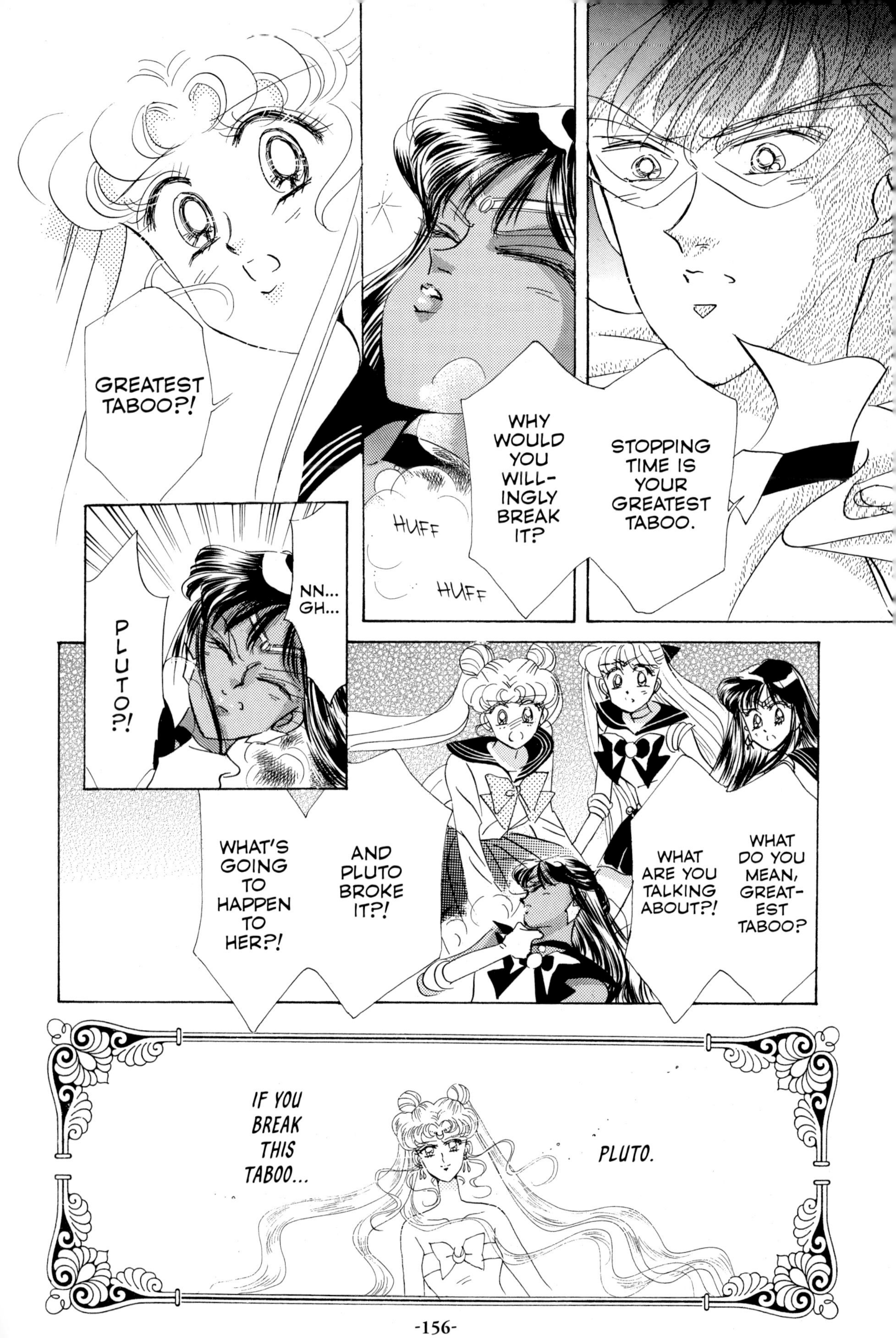
STOPPING TIME IS YOUR GREATEST TABOO.
WHY WOULD YOU WILL-INGLY BREAK IT?
HUFF
HUFF
GREATEST TABOO?!
NN... GH...
PLUTO?!
WHAT DO YOU MEAN, GREAT-EST TABOO?
WHAT ARE YOU TALKING ABOUT?!
AND PLUTO BROKE IT?!
WHAT'S GOING TO HAPPEN TO HER?!
PLUTO.
IF YOU BREAK THIS TABOO...

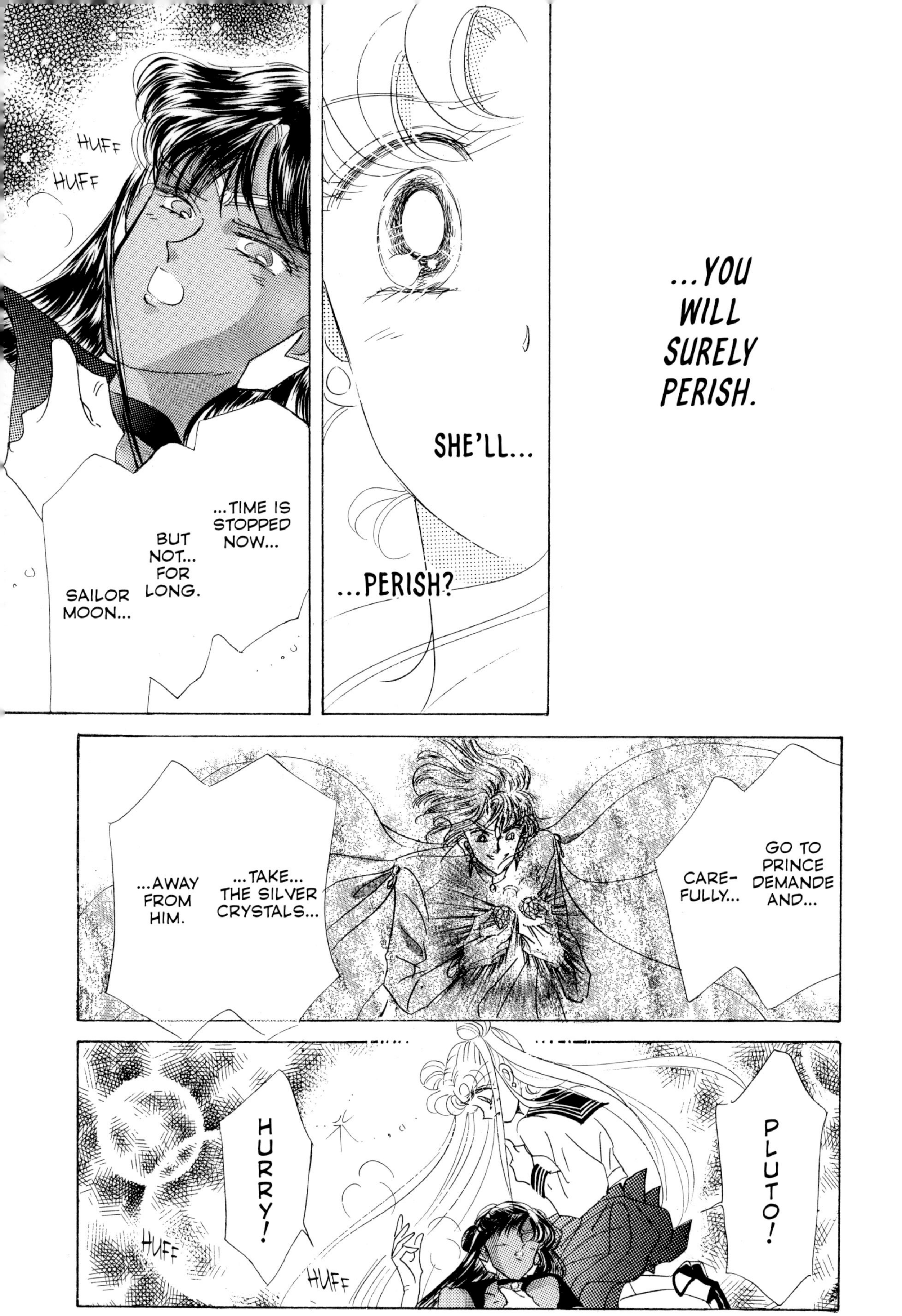
...YOU WILL SURELY PERISH.
SHE'LL...
...PERISH?
HUFF
HUFF
...TIME IS STOPPED NOW...
BUT NOT... FOR LONG.
SAILOR MOON...
GO TO PRINCE DEMANDE AND...
CARE-FULLY...
...TAKE... THE SILVER CRYSTALS...
...AWAY FROM HIM.
PLUTO!
HURRY!
HUFF
HUFF

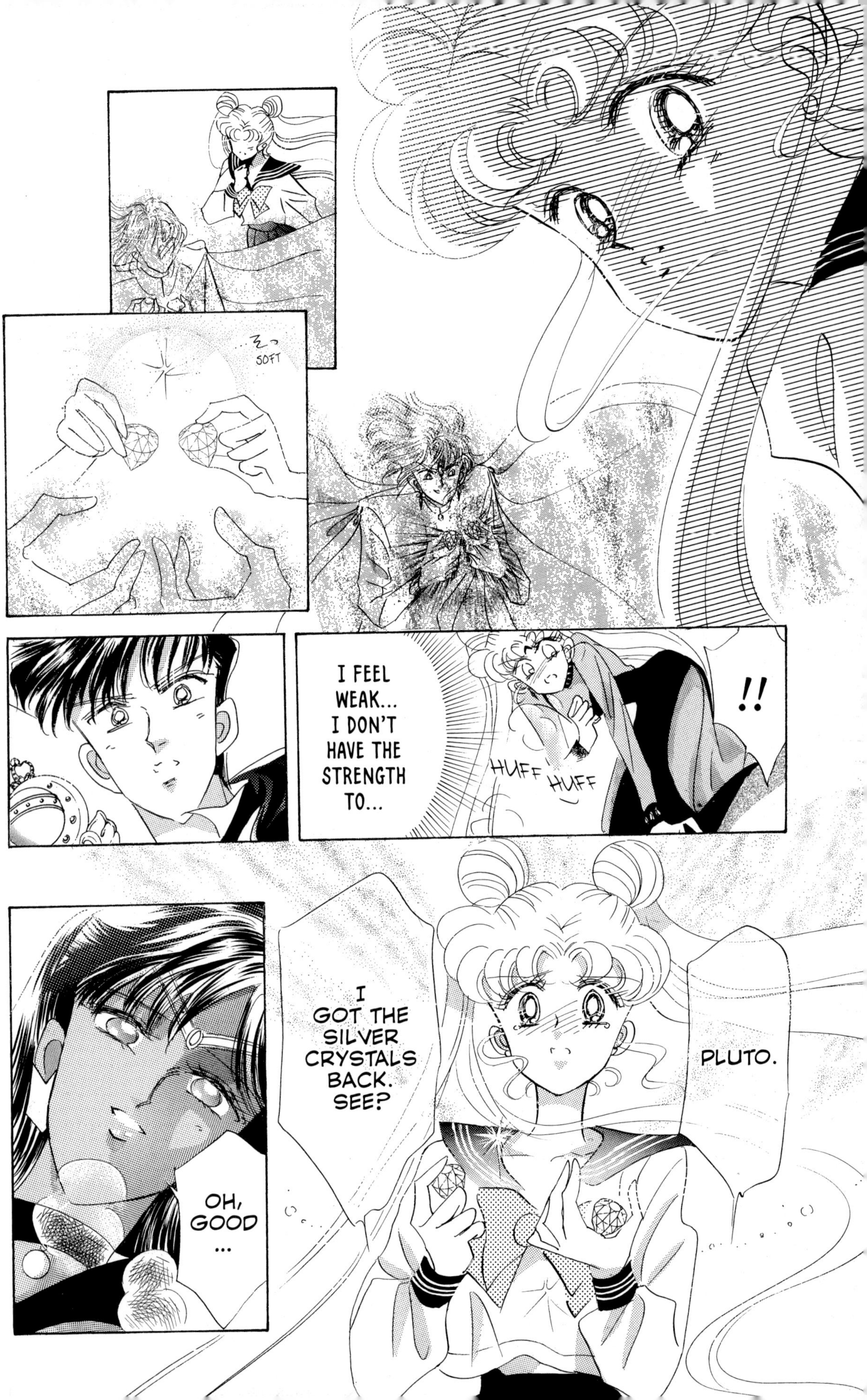
SOFT
!!
I FEEL WEAK... I DON'T HAVE THE STRENGTH TO...
HUFF HUFF
PLUTO.
I GOT THE SILVER CRYSTALS BACK. SEE?
OH, GOOD ...

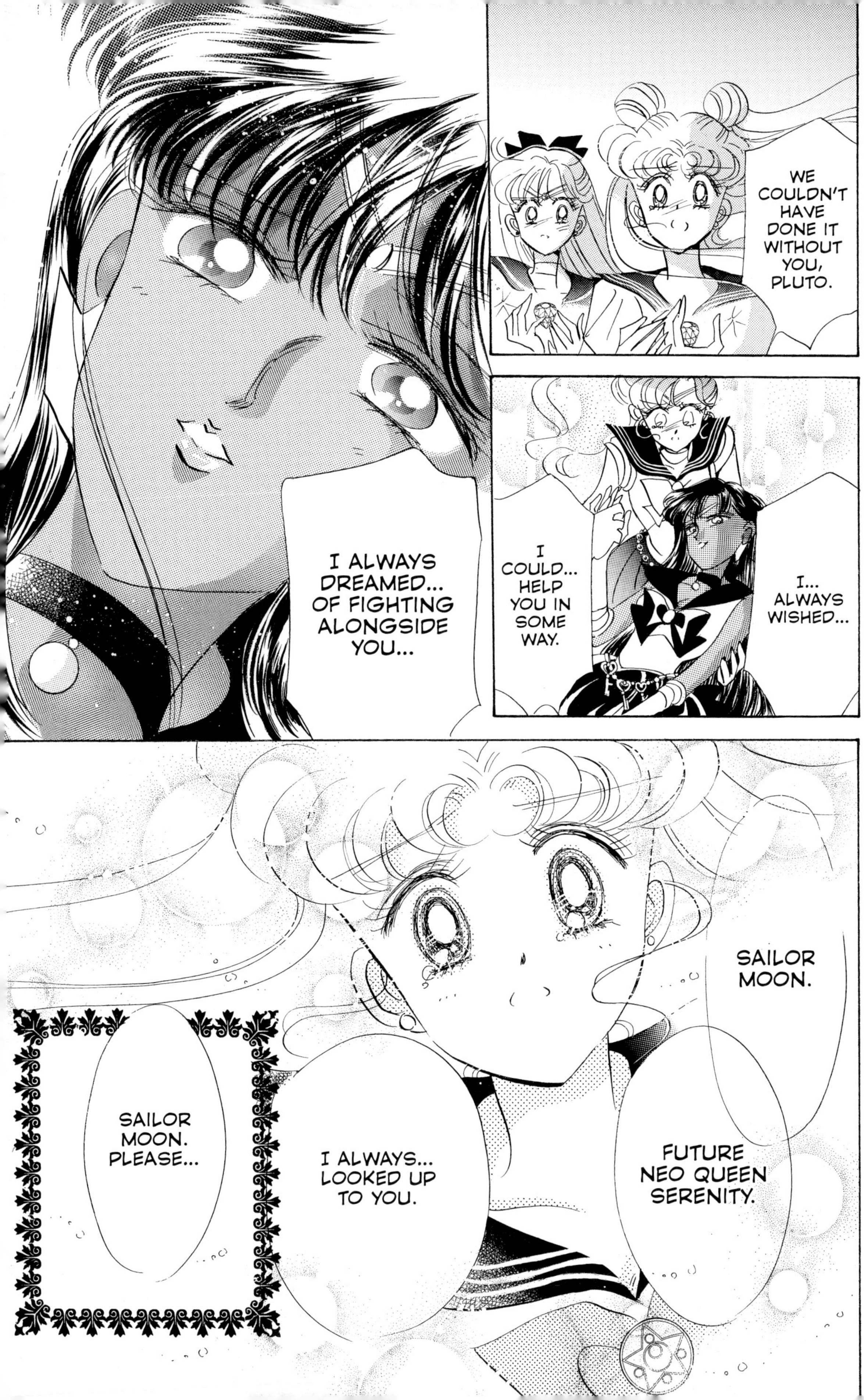
WE COULDN'T HAVE DONE IT WITHOUT YOU, PLUTO.
I... ALWAYS WISHED...
I COULD... HELP YOU IN SOME WAY.
I ALWAYS DREAMED... OF FIGHTING ALONGSIDE YOU...
SAILOR MOON.
FUTURE NEO QUEEN SERENITY.
I ALWAYS... LOOKED UP TO YOU.
SAILOR MOON. PLEASE...

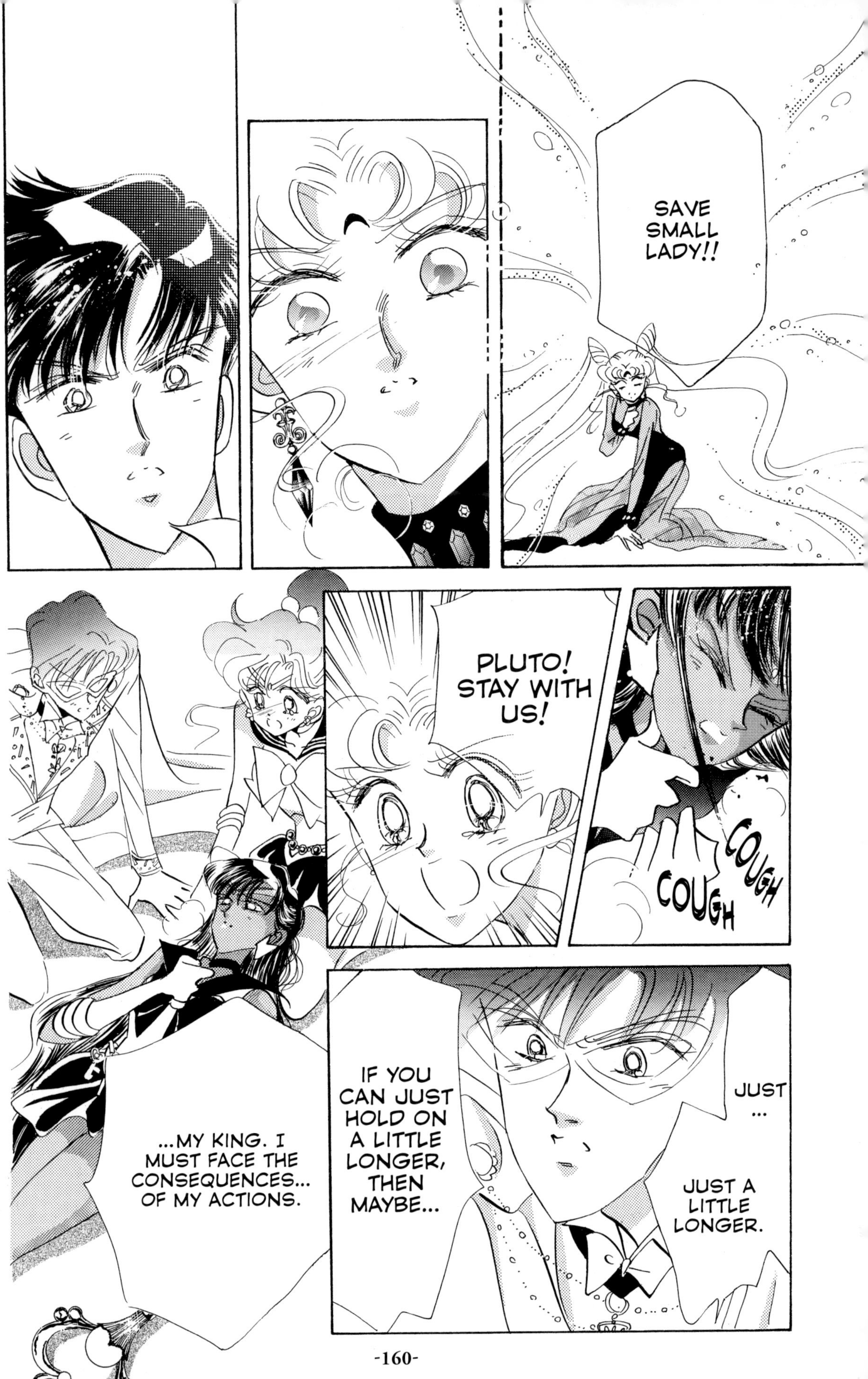
SAVE SMALL LADY!!
COUGH
COUGH
PLUTO! STAY WITH US!
JUST ...
JUST A LITTLE LONGER.
IF YOU CAN JUST HOLD ON A LITTLE LONGER, THEN MAYBE...
...MY KING. I MUST FACE THE CONSEQUENCES... OF MY ACTIONS.

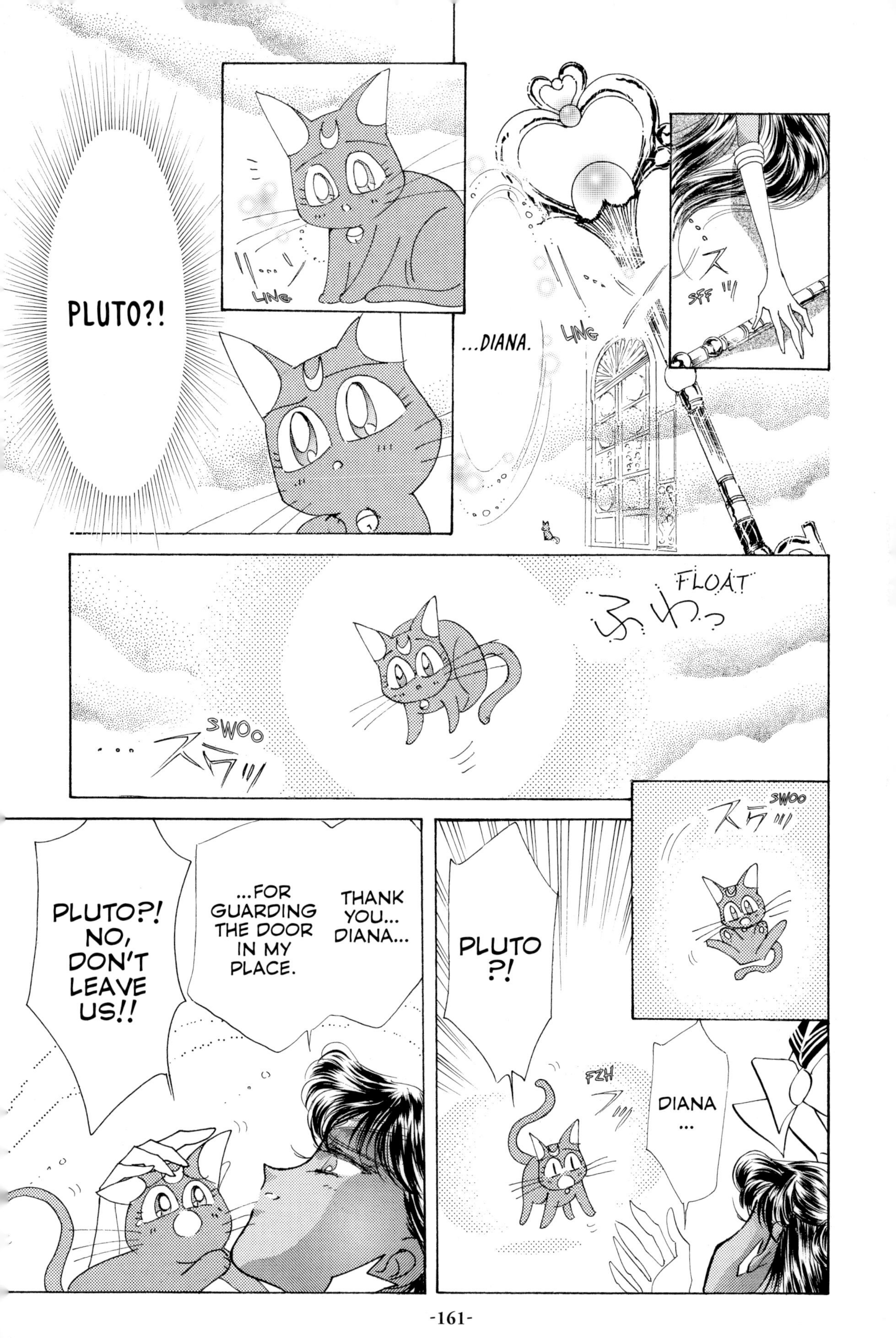

ス
SFF
...DIANA.
LING
LING
PLUTO?!
FLOAT
ふわっ
...
SWOO
スラッ
SWOO
スラッ
PLUTO
?!
FZH
フ
DIANA
...
THANK YOU... DIANA...
...FOR GUARDING THE DOOR IN MY PLACE.
PLUTO?! NO, DON'T LEAVE US!!

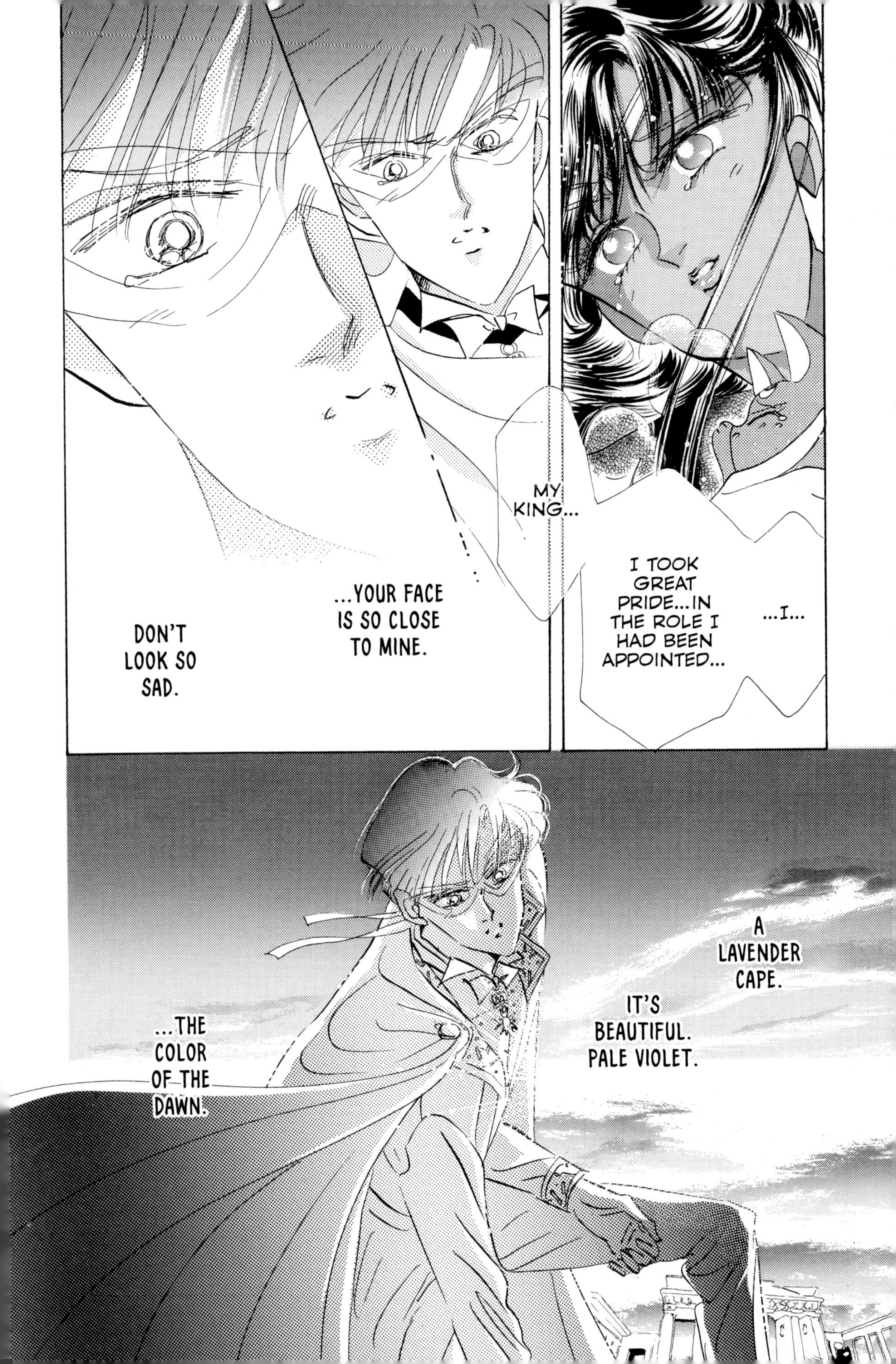
MY KING...
...I...
I TOOK GREAT PRIDE...IN THE ROLE I HAD BEEN APPOINTED...
...YOUR FACE IS SO CLOSE TO MINE.
DON'T LOOK SO SAD.
A LAVENDER CAPE.
IT'S BEAUTIFUL. PALE VIOLET.
...THE COLOR OF THE DAWN.

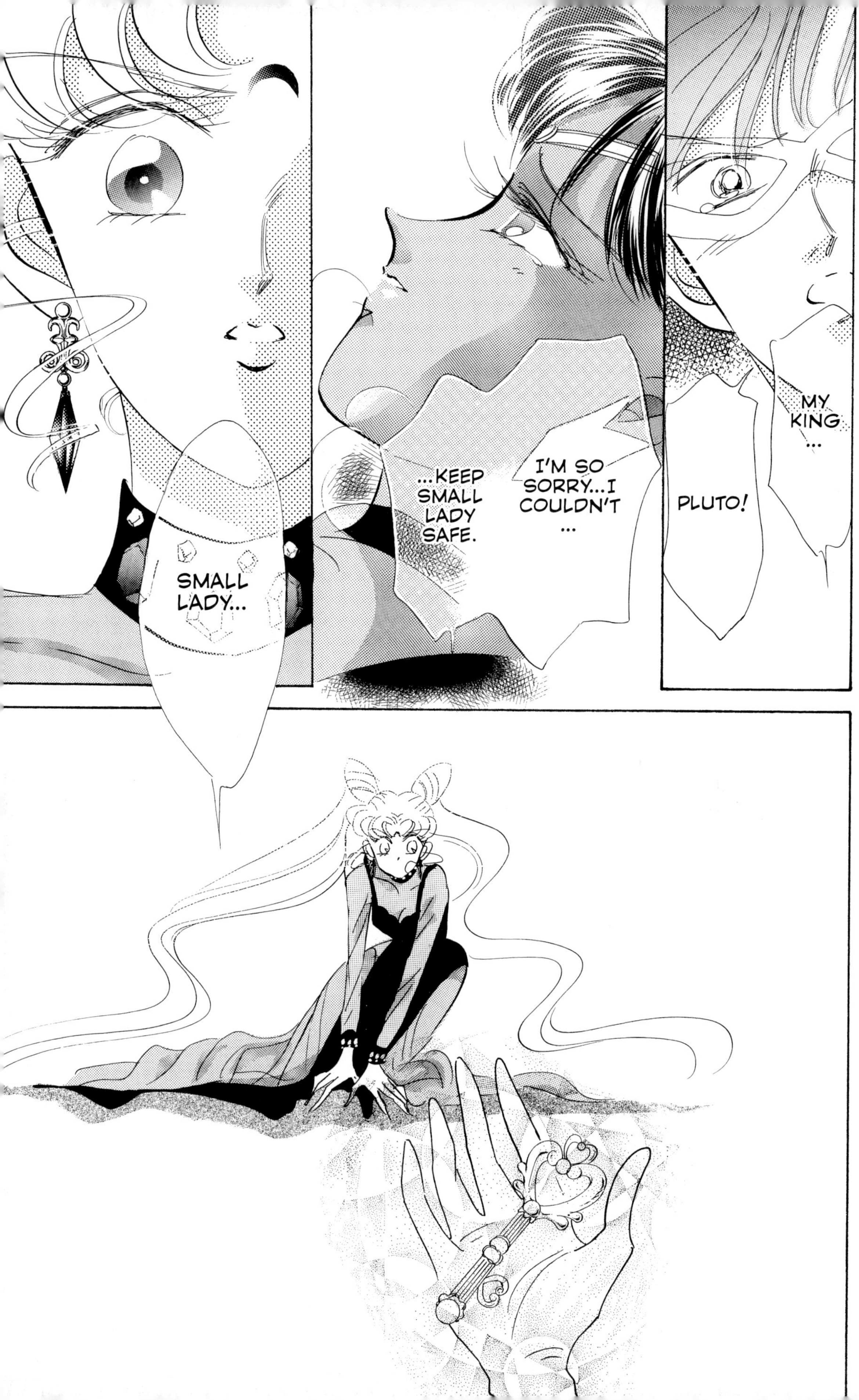
MY KING ...
PLUTO!
I'M SO SORRY...I COULDN'T ...
...KEEP SMALL LADY SAFE.
SMALL LADY...

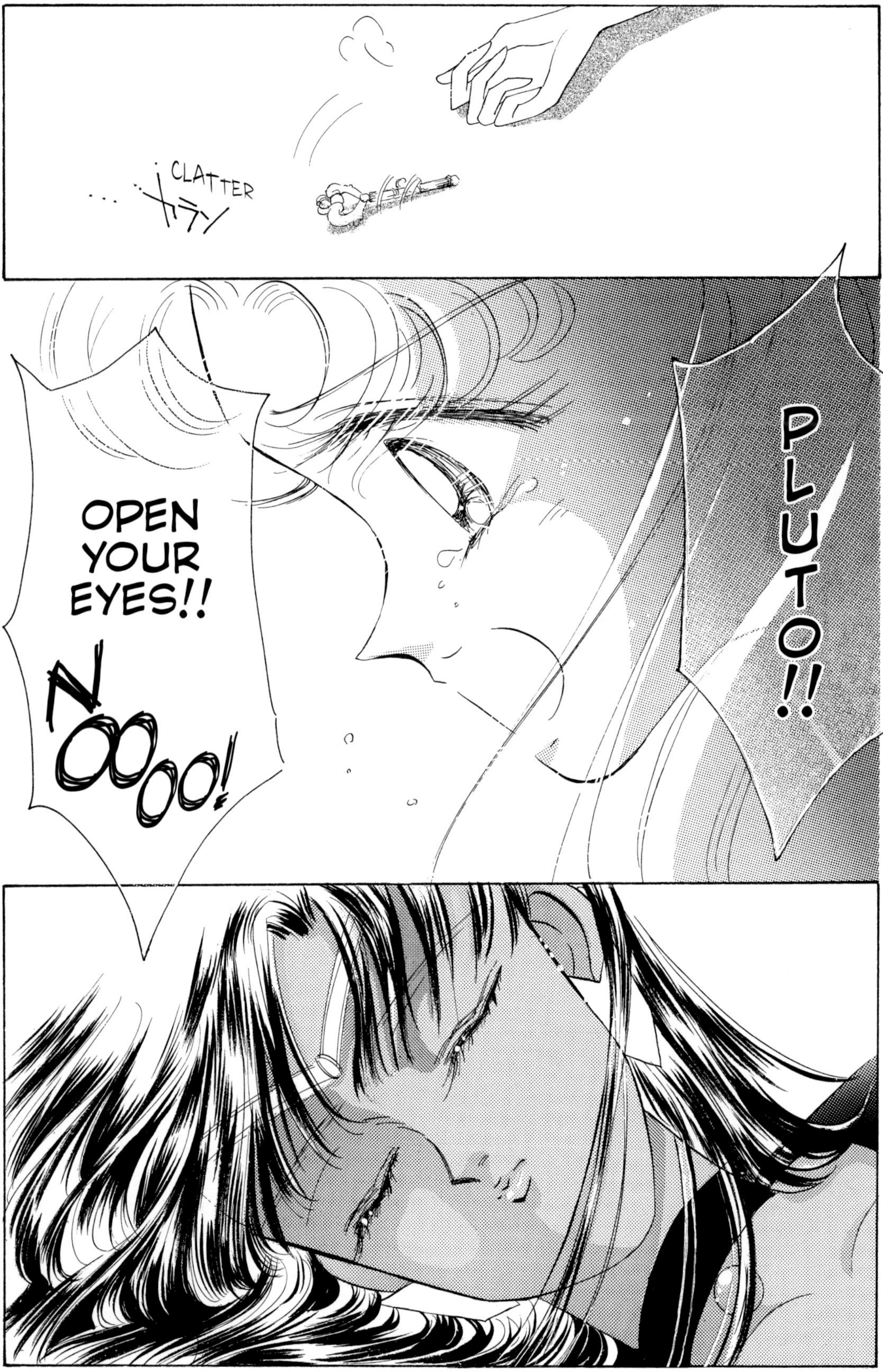
. . .
CLATTER
カラン
PLUTO!!
OPEN YOUR EYES!!
NOOOO!

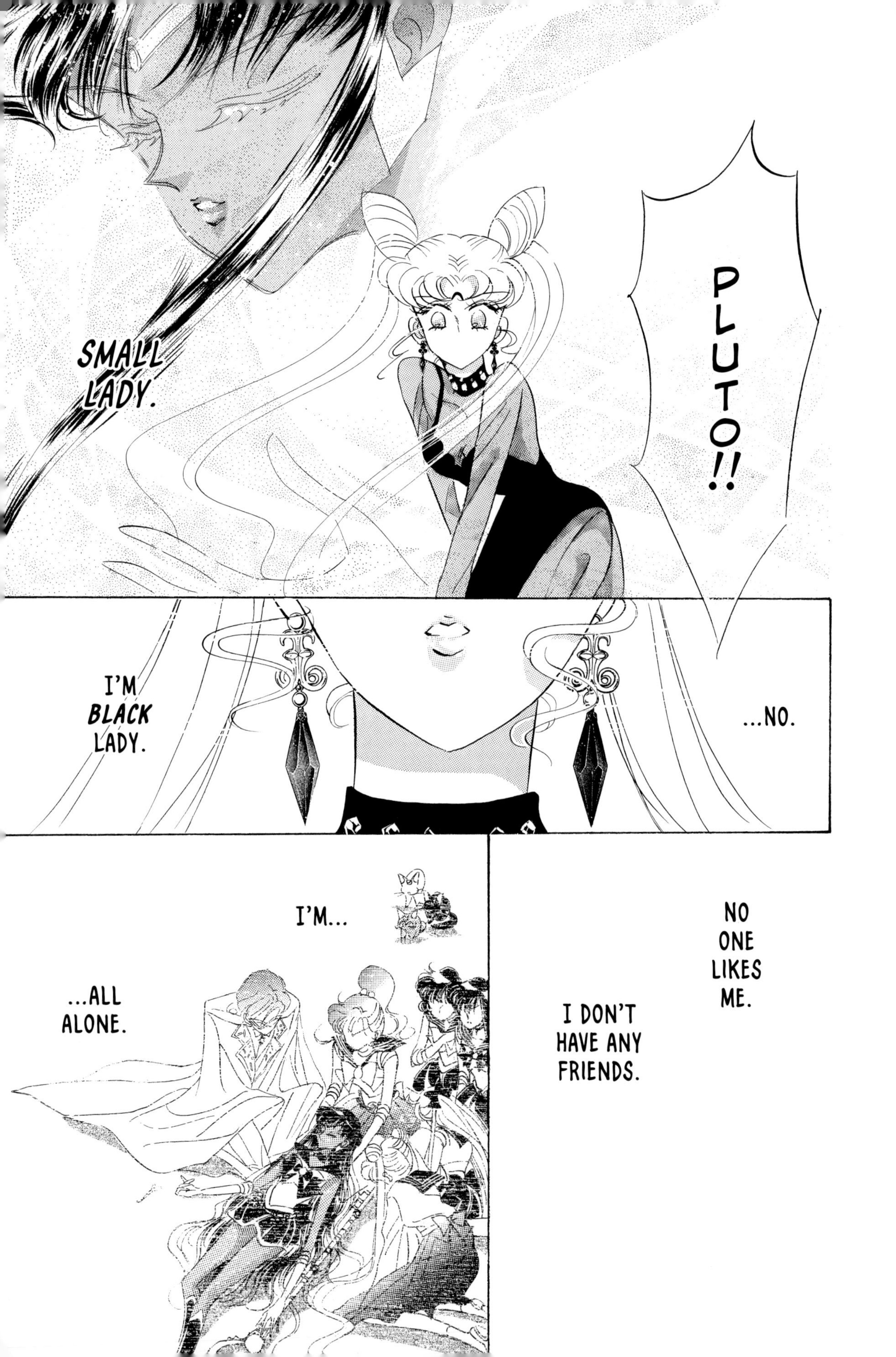
PLUTO!!
SMALL LADY.
...NO.
I'M BLACK LADY.
NO ONE LIKES ME.
I DON'T HAVE ANY FRIENDS.
I'M...
...ALL ALONE.

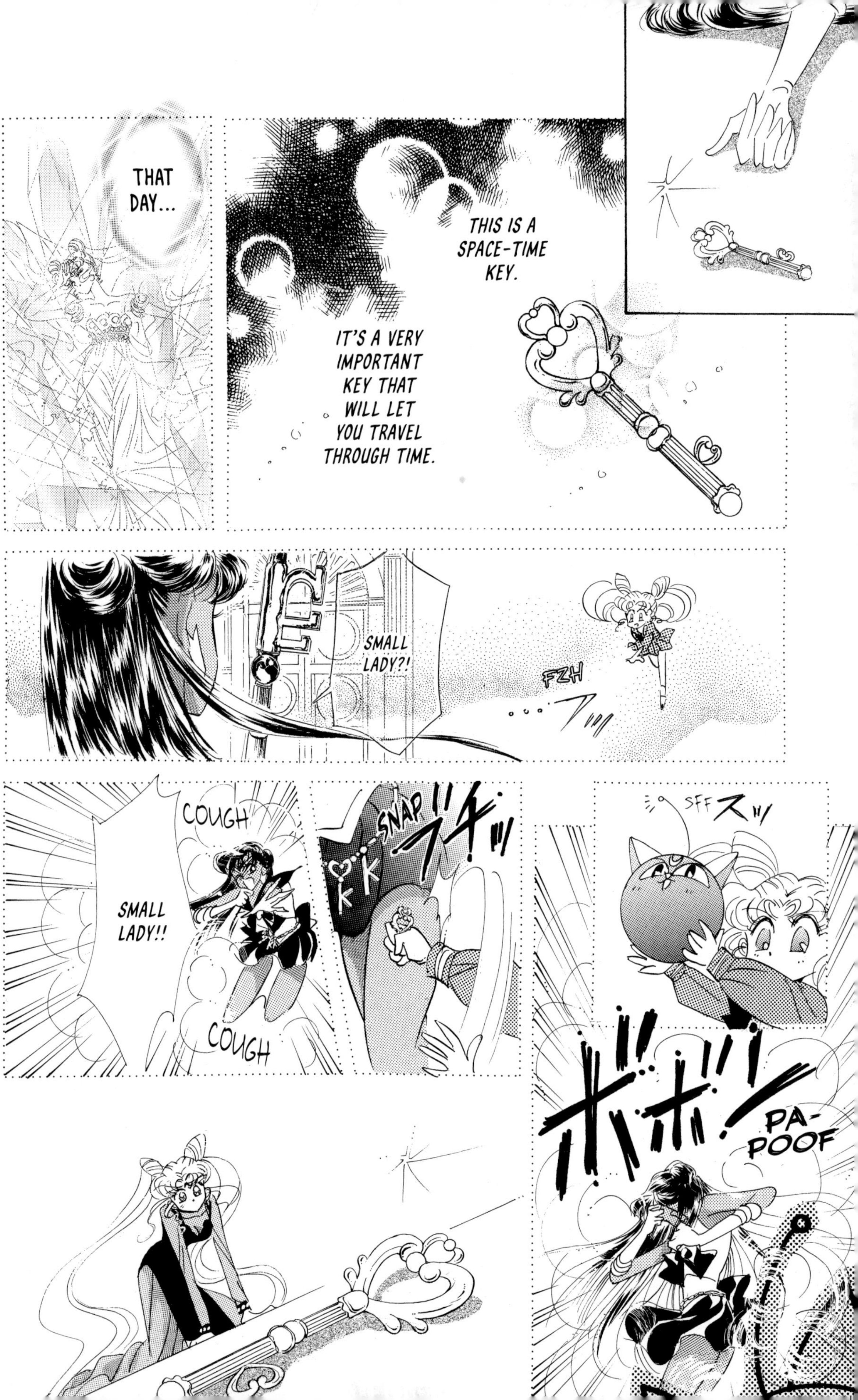
THIS IS A SPACE-TIME KEY.
IT'S A VERY IMPORTANT KEY THAT WILL LET YOU TRAVEL THROUGH TIME.
THAT DAY...
FZH
SMALL LADY?!
SFF
PA-POOF
SNAP
COUGH
SMALL LADY!!
COUGH

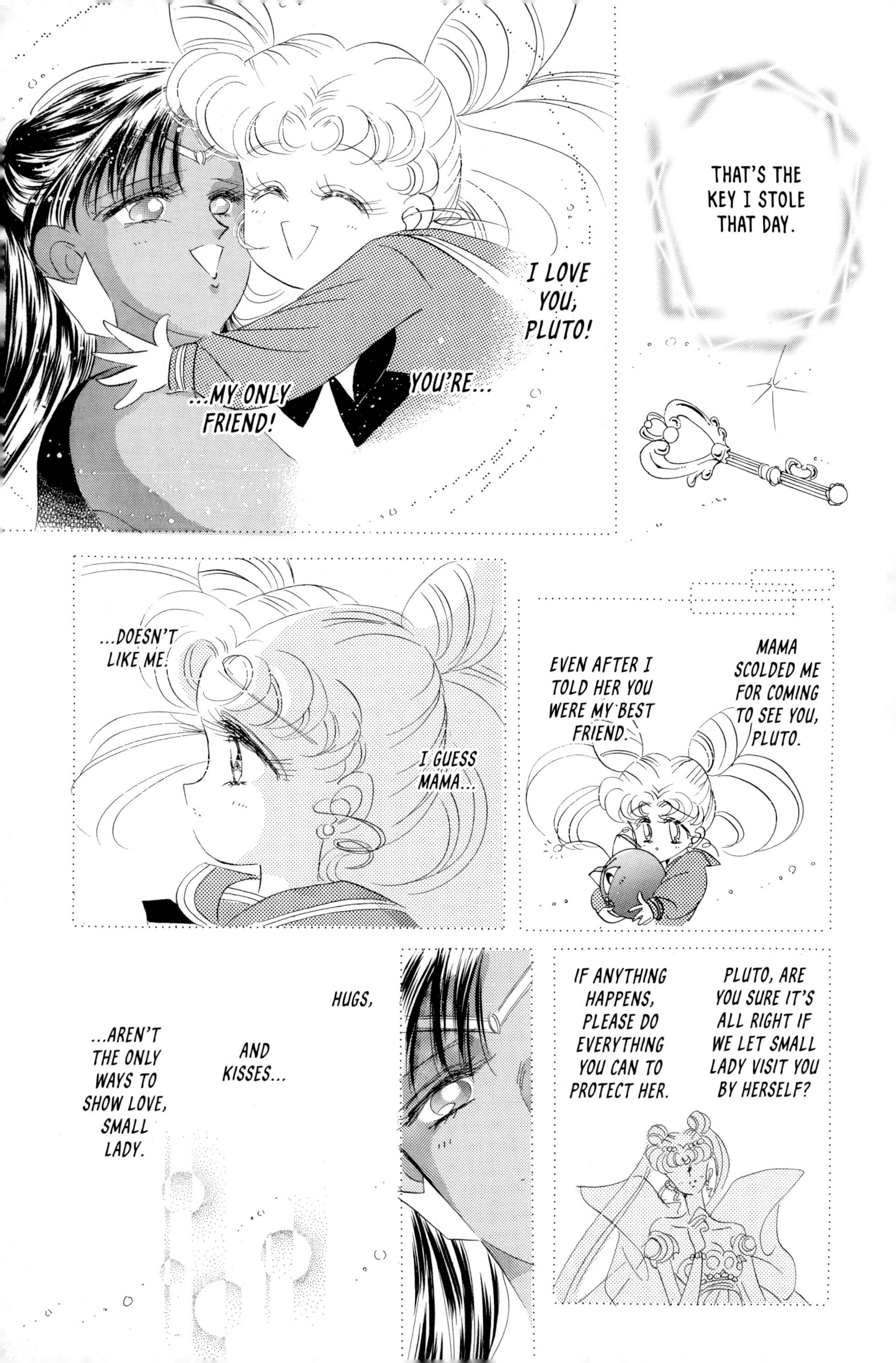
THAT'S THE KEY I STOLE THAT DAY.
I LOVE YOU, PLUTO!
YOU'RE...
...MY ONLY FRIEND!
MAMA SCOLDED ME FOR COMING TO SEE YOU, PLUTO.
EVEN AFTER I TOLD HER YOU WERE MY BEST FRIEND.
I GUESS MAMA...
...DOESN'T LIKE ME.
PLUTO, ARE YOU SURE IT'S ALL RIGHT IF WE LET SMALL LADY VISIT YOU BY HERSELF?
IF ANYTHING HAPPENS, PLEASE DO EVERYTHING YOU CAN TO PROTECT HER.
HUGS,
AND KISSES...
...AREN'T THE ONLY WAYS TO SHOW LOVE, SMALL LADY.

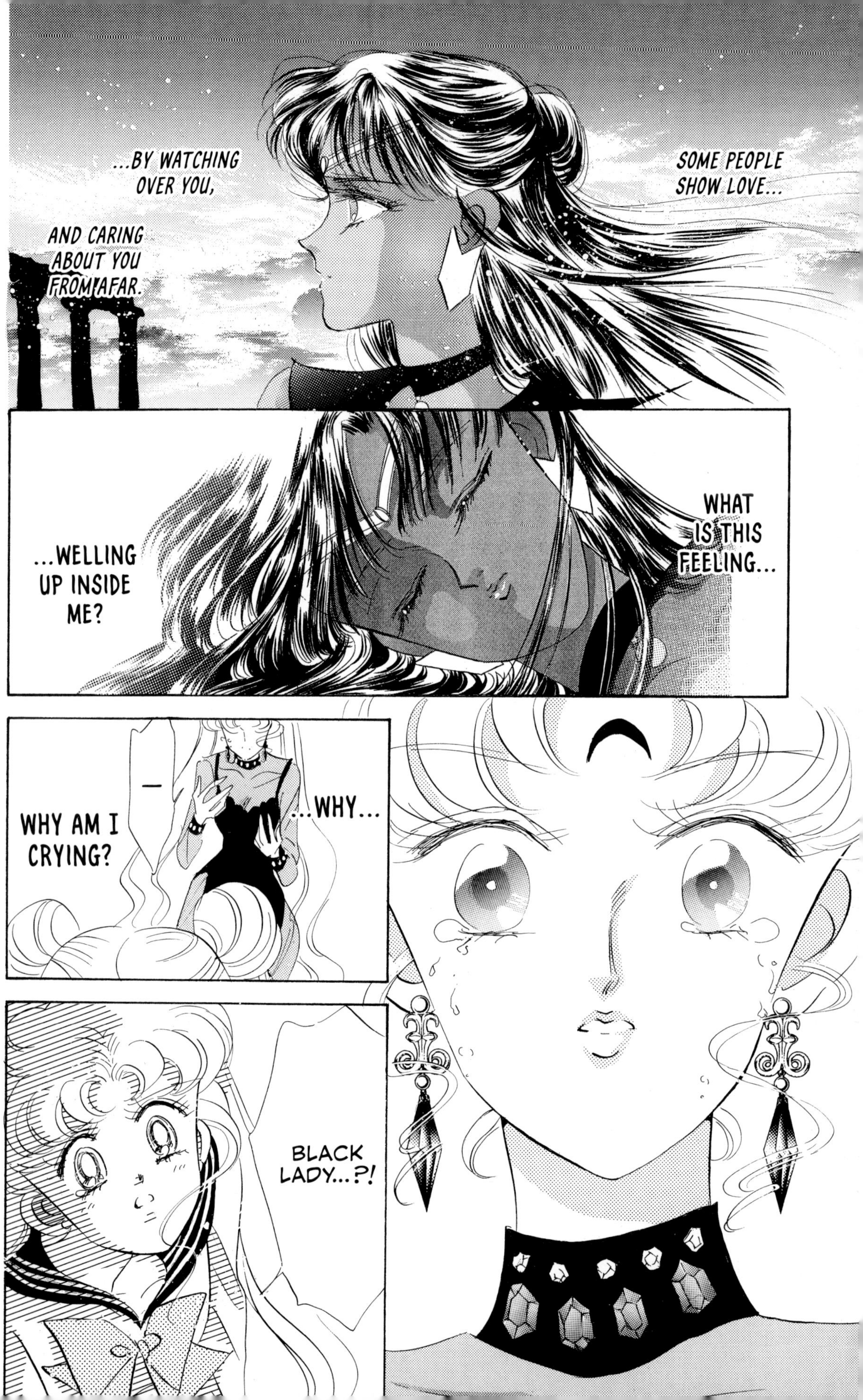
SOME PEOPLE SHOW LOVE...
...BY WATCHING OVER YOU,
AND CARING ABOUT YOU FROM AFAR.
WHAT IS THIS FEELING...
...WELLING UP INSIDE ME?
...WHY...
WHY AM I CRYING?
BLACK LADY...?!

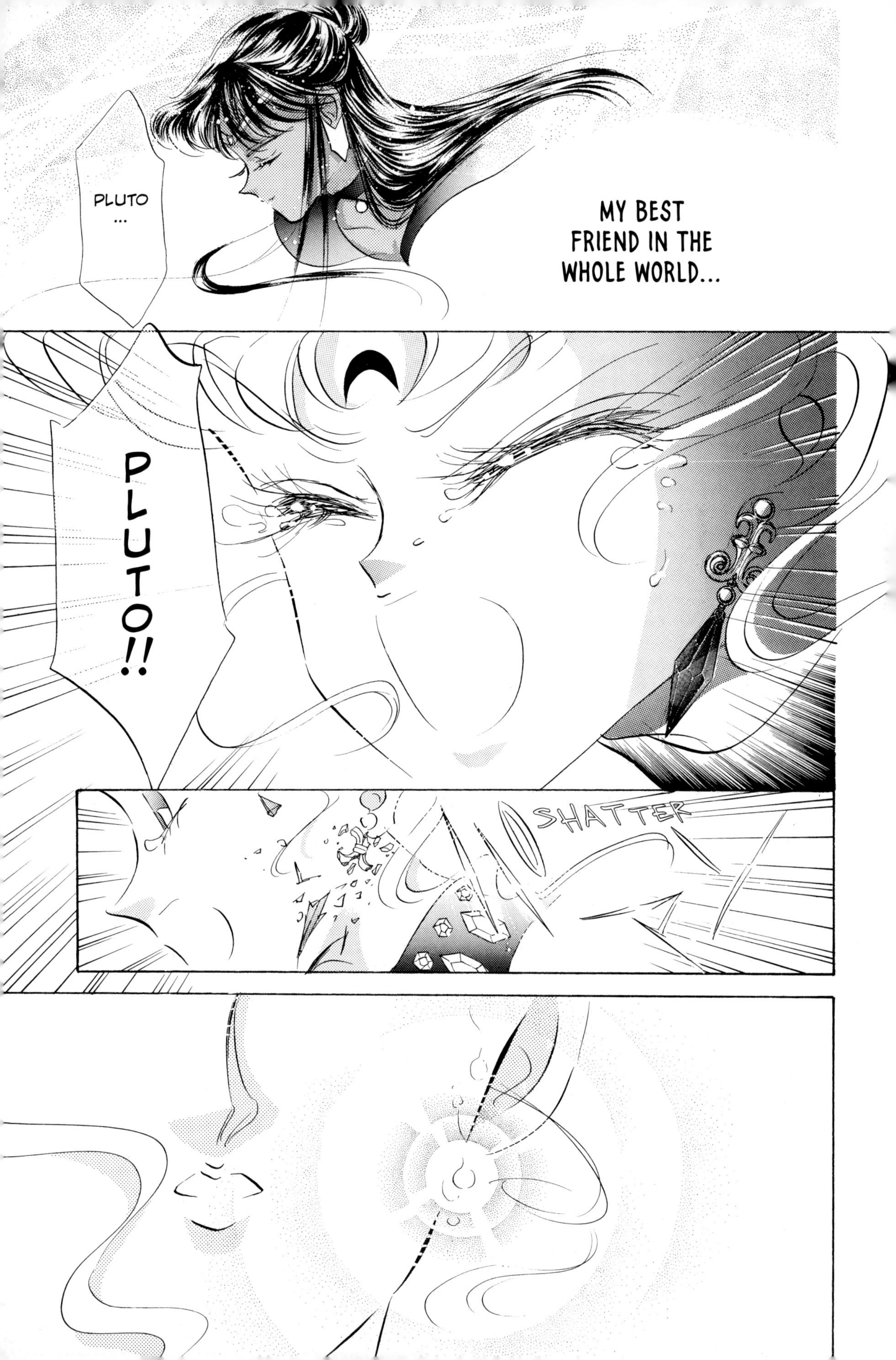

MY BEST FRIEND IN THE WHOLE WORLD...
PLUTO ...
PLUTO!!
SHATTER

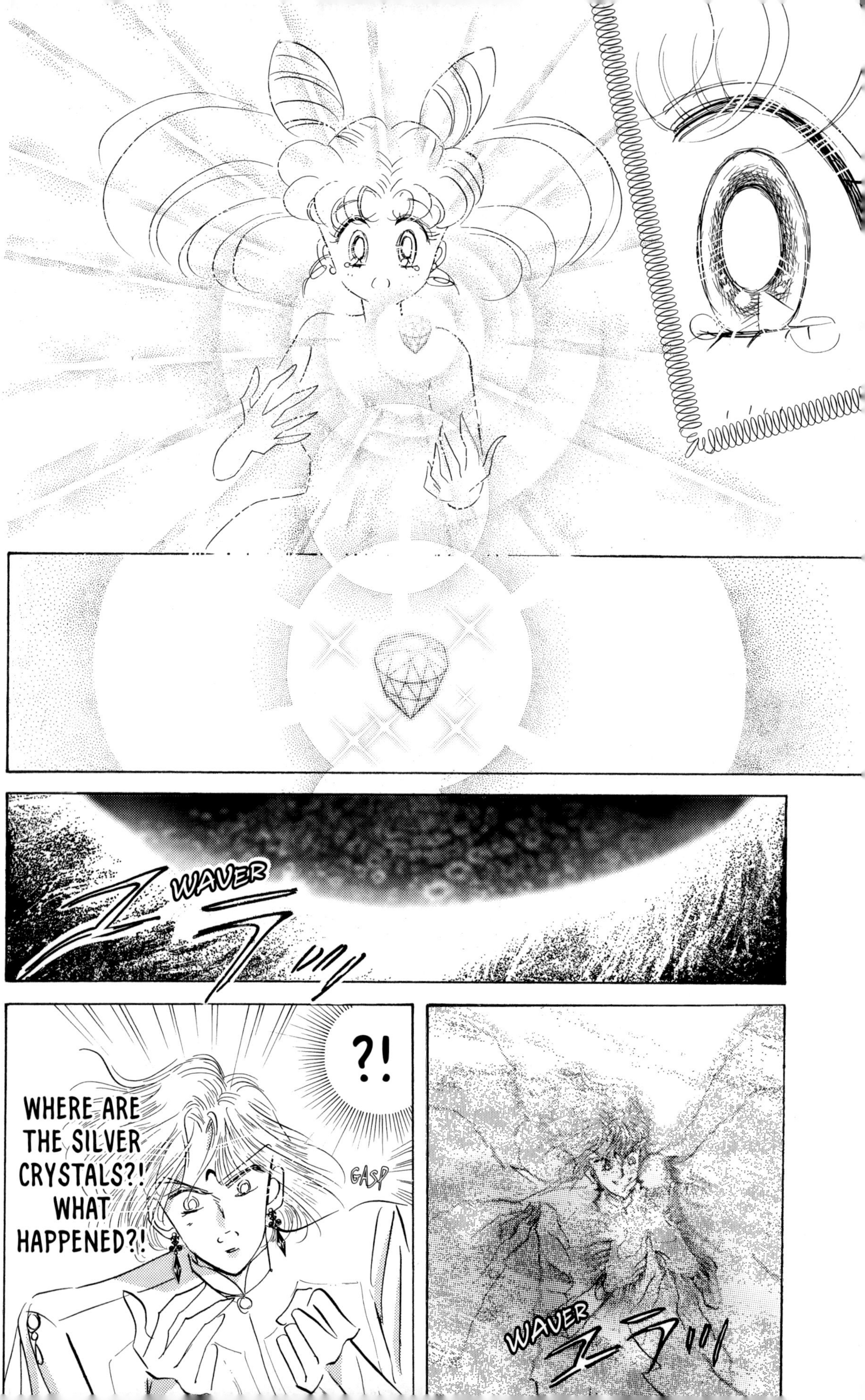
WAVER
WAVER
?!
WHERE ARE THE SILVER CRYSTALS?! WHAT HAPPENED?!
GASP

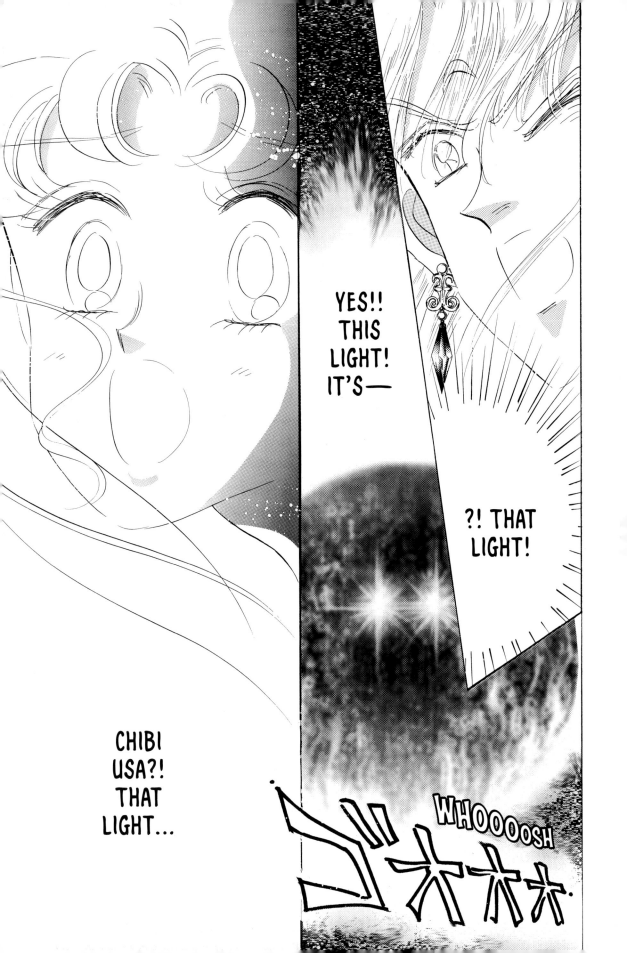

YES!!
THIS
LIGHT!
IT'S—

?! THAT
LIGHT!

CHIBI
USA?!
THAT
LIGHT...

WHOOOOSH

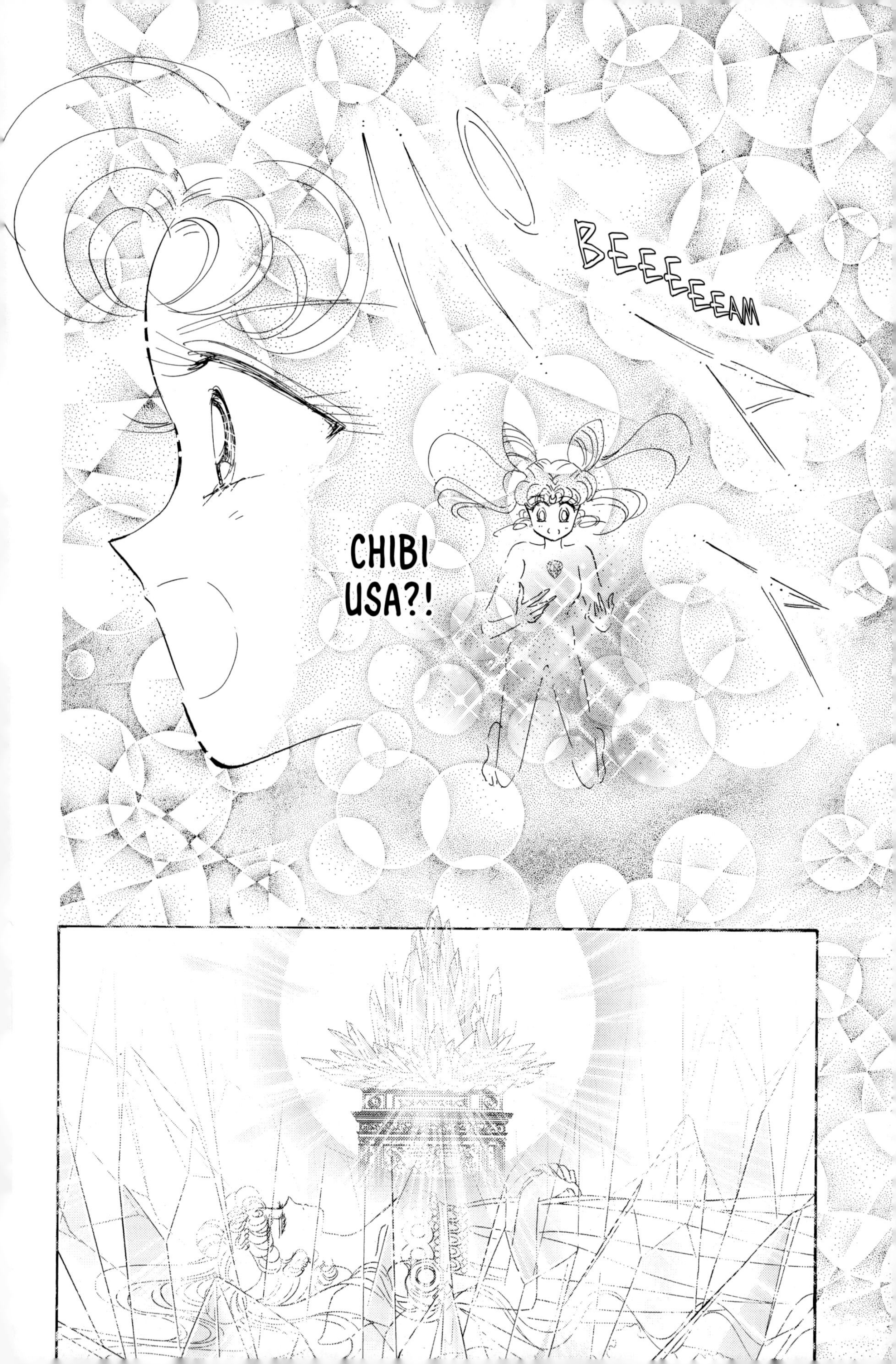
BEEEEEAM
CHIBI USA?!

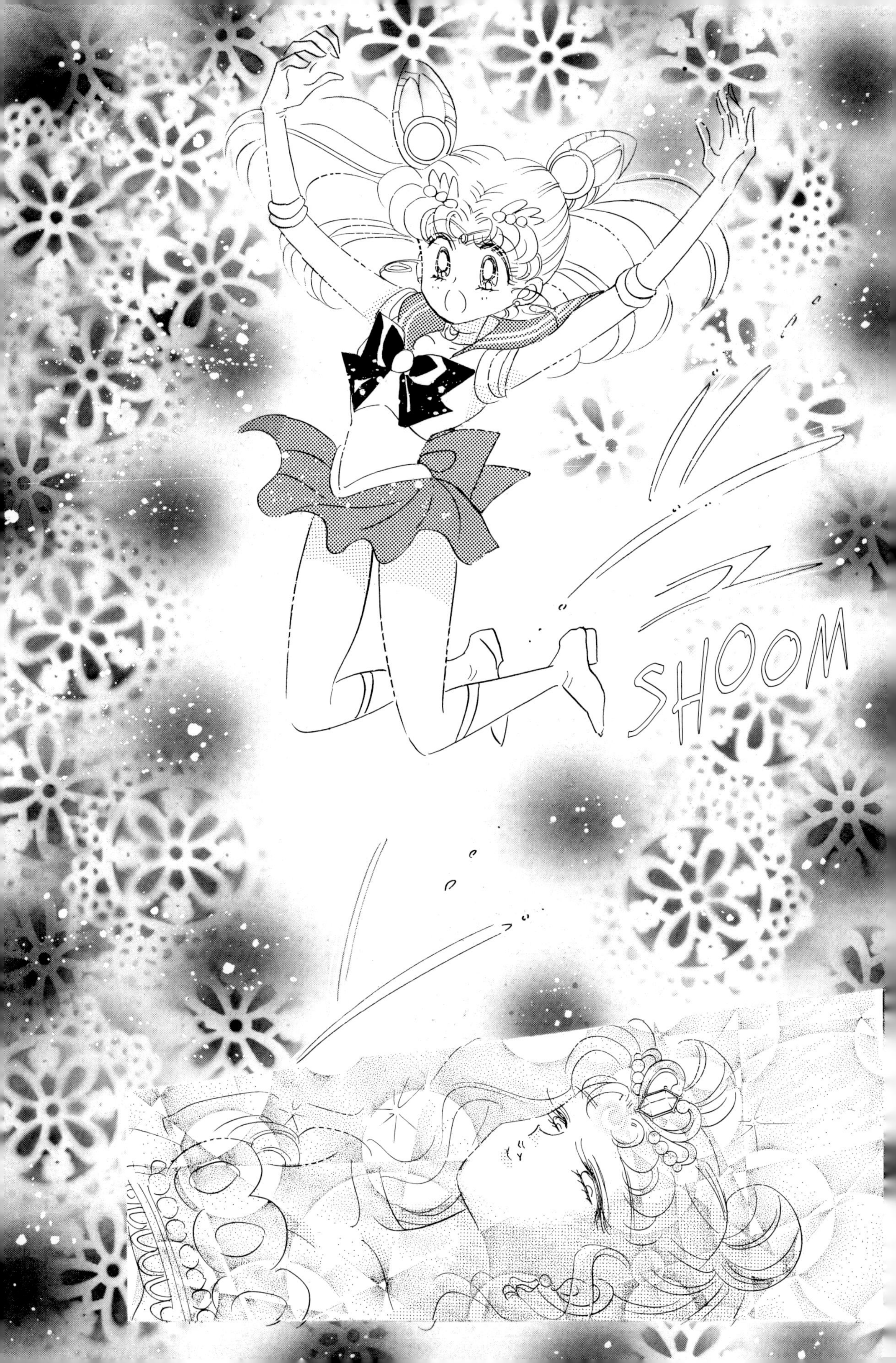
SHOOM

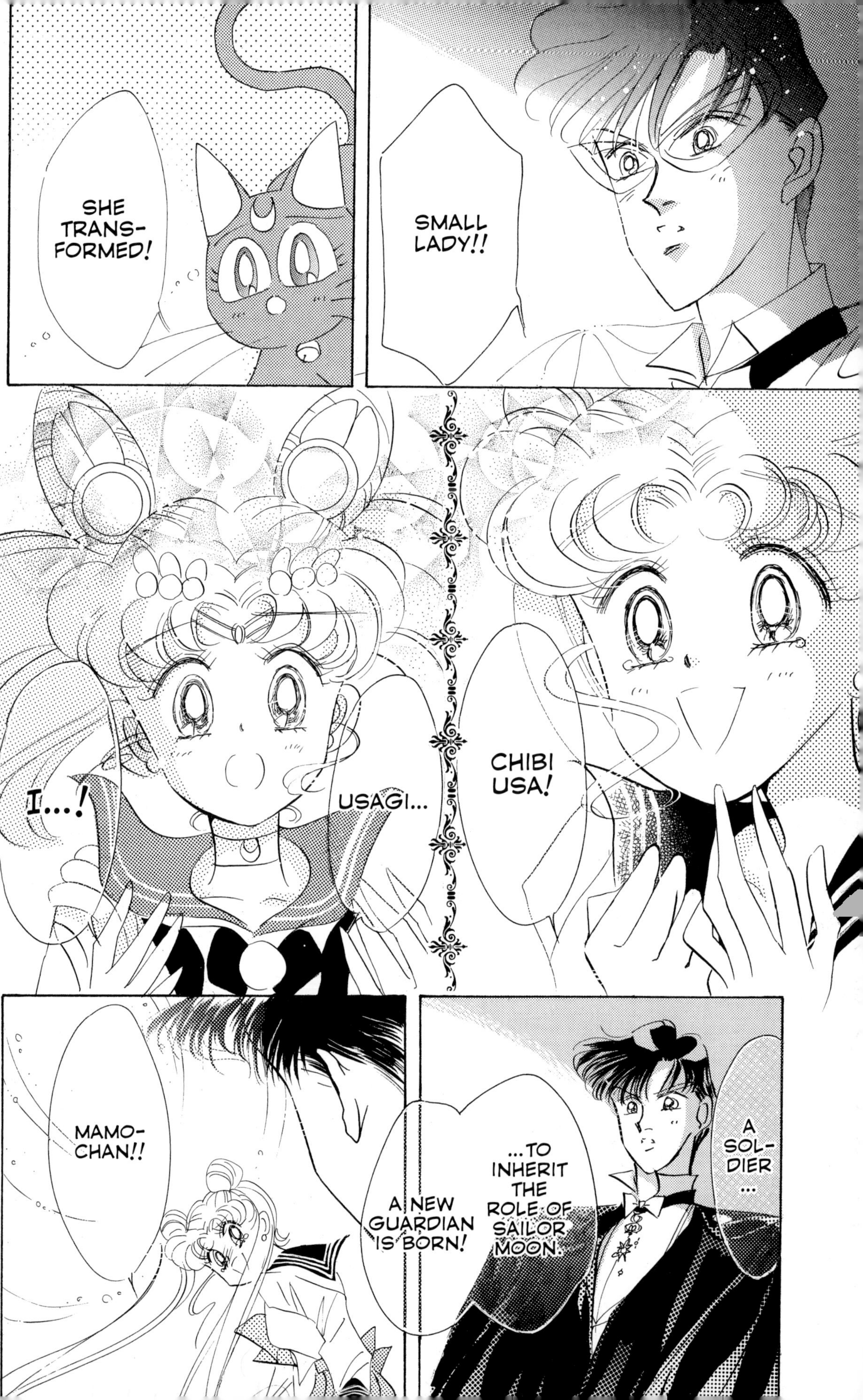
SMALL LADY!!
SHE TRANS-FORMED!
CHIBI USA!
USAGI...
I...!
A SOL-DIER...
...TO INHERIT THE ROLE OF SAILOR MOON.
A NEW GUARDIAN IS BORN!
MAMO-CHAN!!

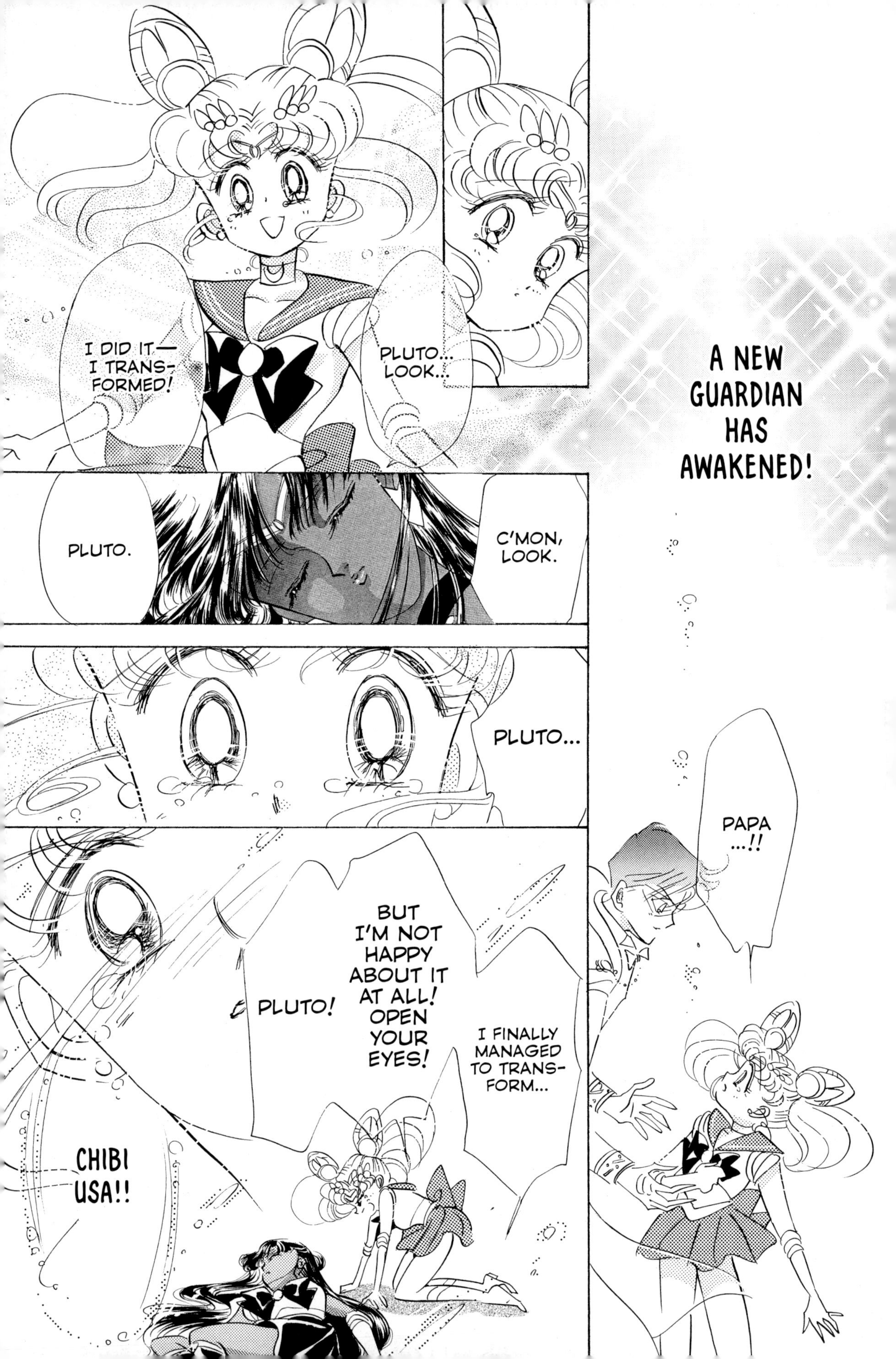
A NEW GUARDIAN HAS AWAKENED!
PAPA ...!!
PLUTO... LOOK...
I DID IT— I TRANSFORMED!
C'MON, LOOK.
PLUTO.
PLUTO...
I FINALLY MANAGED TO TRANSFORM...
BUT I'M NOT HAPPY ABOUT IT AT ALL! OPEN YOUR EYES!
PLUTO!
CHIBI USA!!

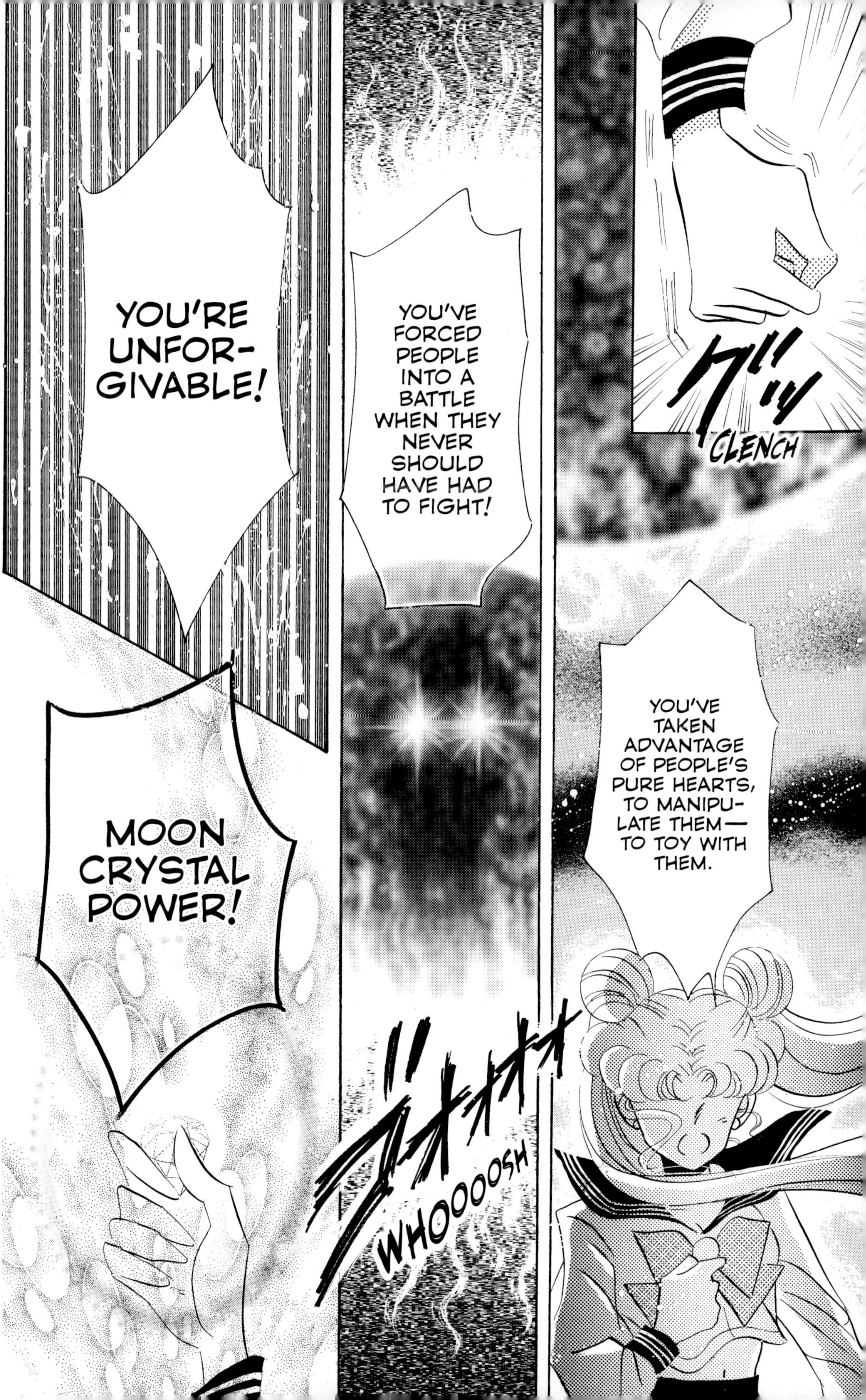
CLENCH
YOU'VE TAKEN ADVANTAGE OF PEOPLE'S PURE HEARTS, TO MANIPULATE THEM—TO TOY WITH THEM.
YOU'VE FORCED PEOPLE INTO A BATTLE WHEN THEY NEVER SHOULD HAVE HAD TO FIGHT!
WHOOOOSH
YOU'RE UNFORGIVABLE!
MOON CRYSTAL POWER!

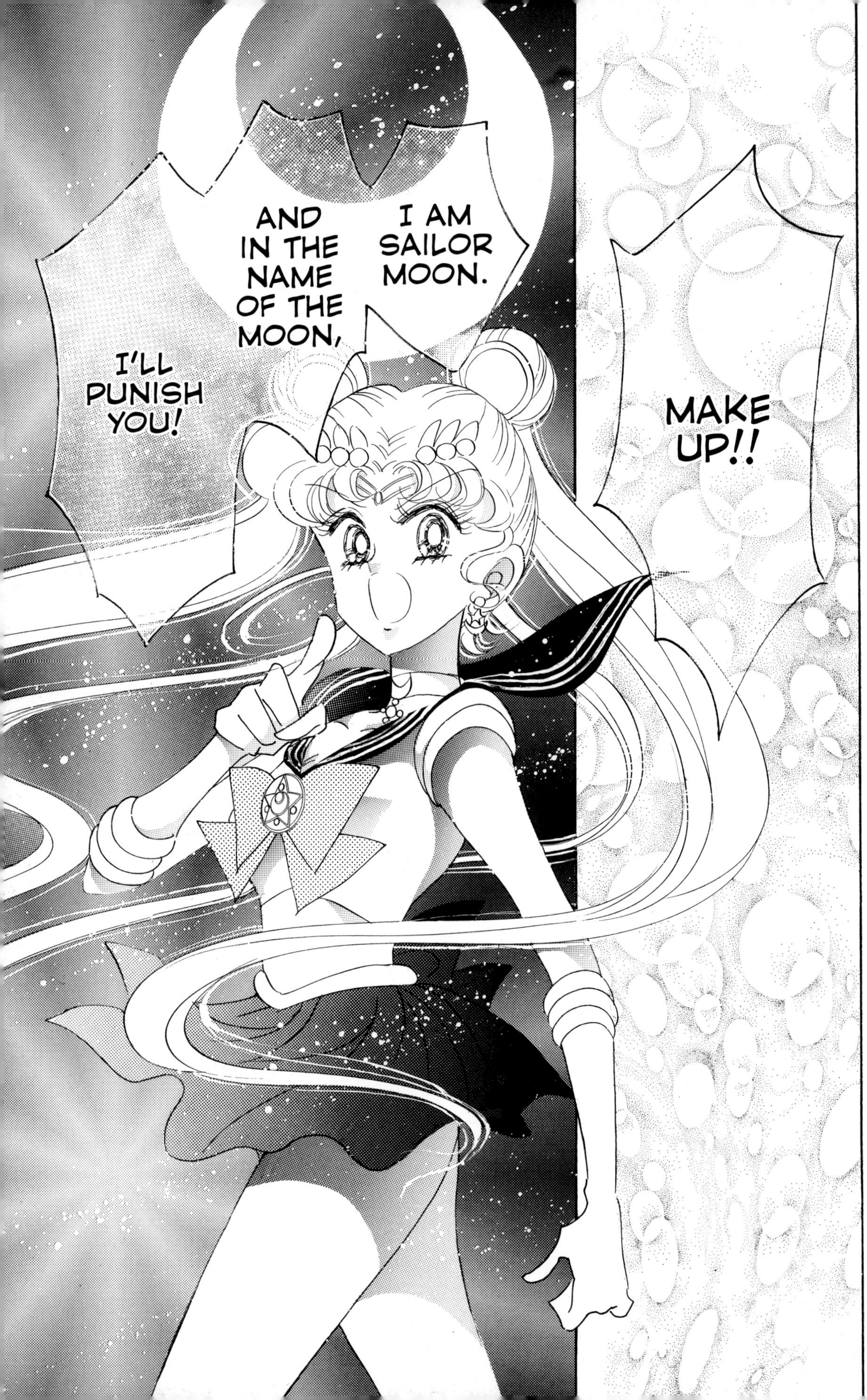
MAKE UP!!
I AM SAILOR MOON.
AND IN THE NAME OF THE MOON,
I'LL PUNISH YOU!

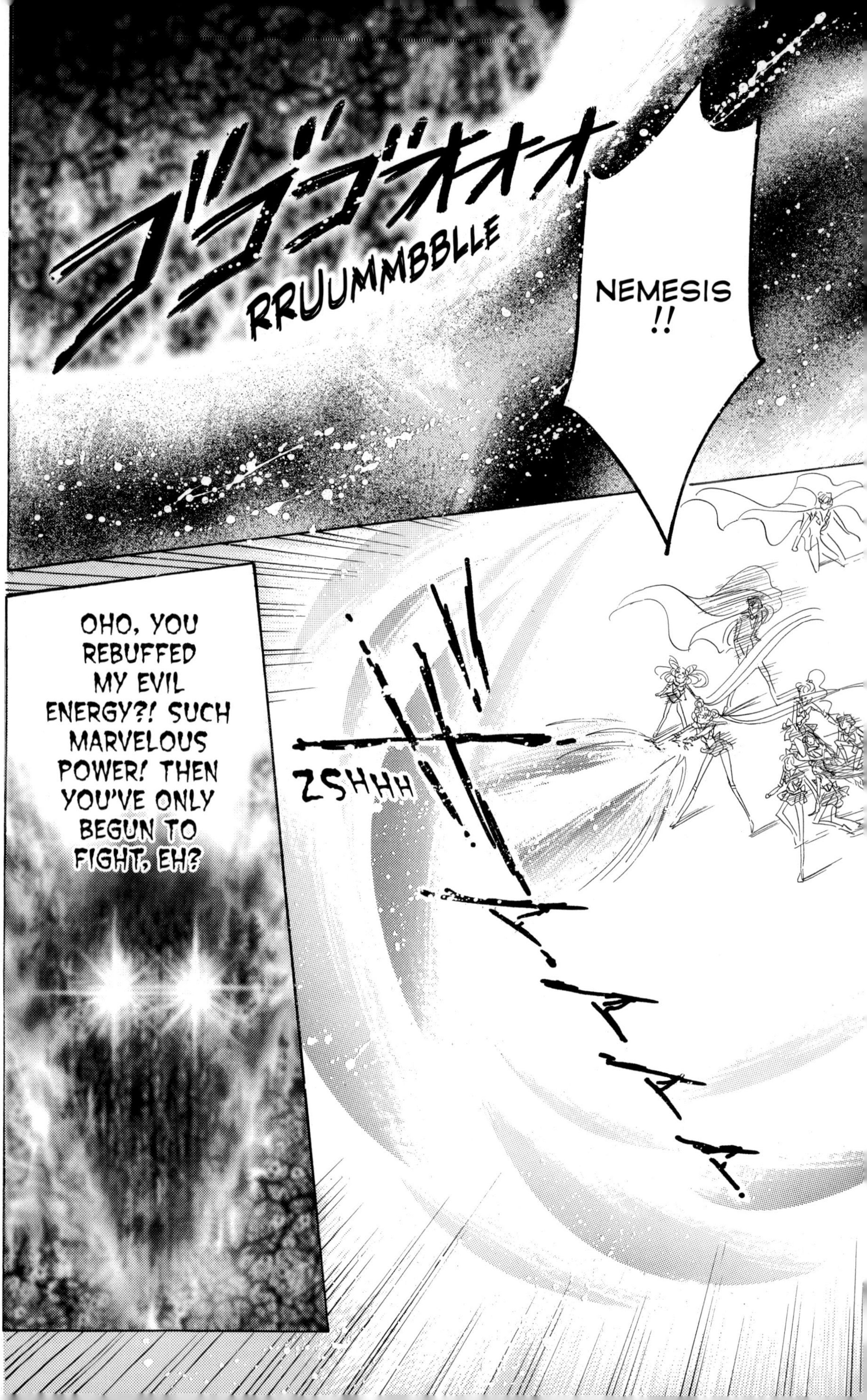
ゴゴゴオオオ
RRUUMMBBLLE
NEMESIS!!
ZSHHH
OHO, YOU REBUFFED MY EVIL ENERGY?! SUCH MARVELOUS POWER! THEN YOU'VE ONLY BEGUN TO FIGHT, EH?

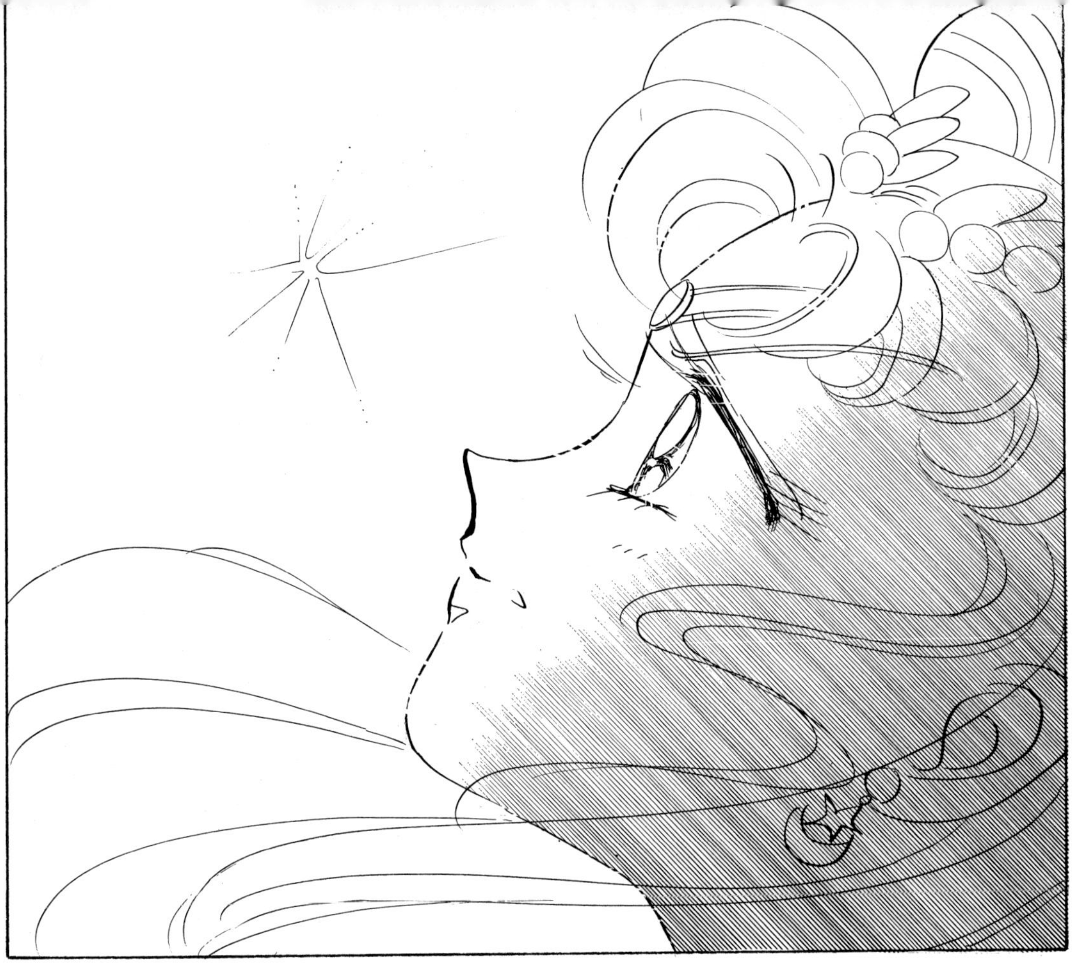

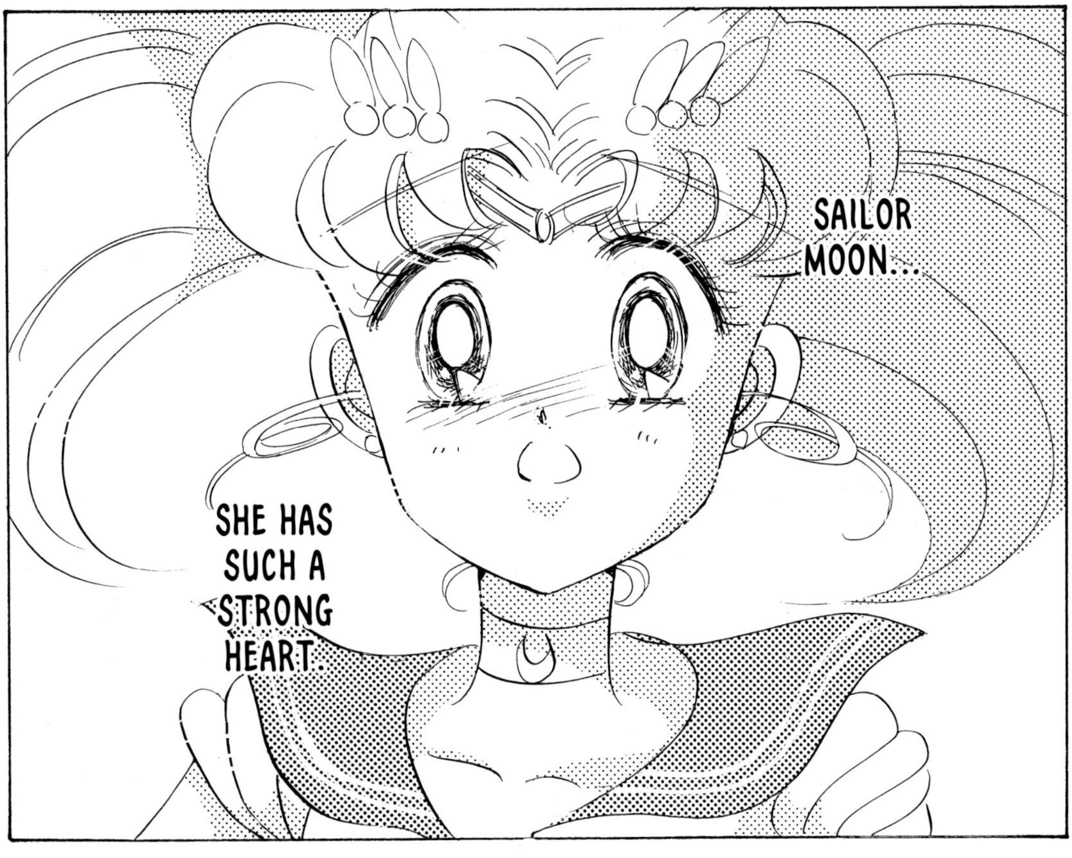
SAILOR MOON...
SHE HAS SUCH A STRONG HEART.

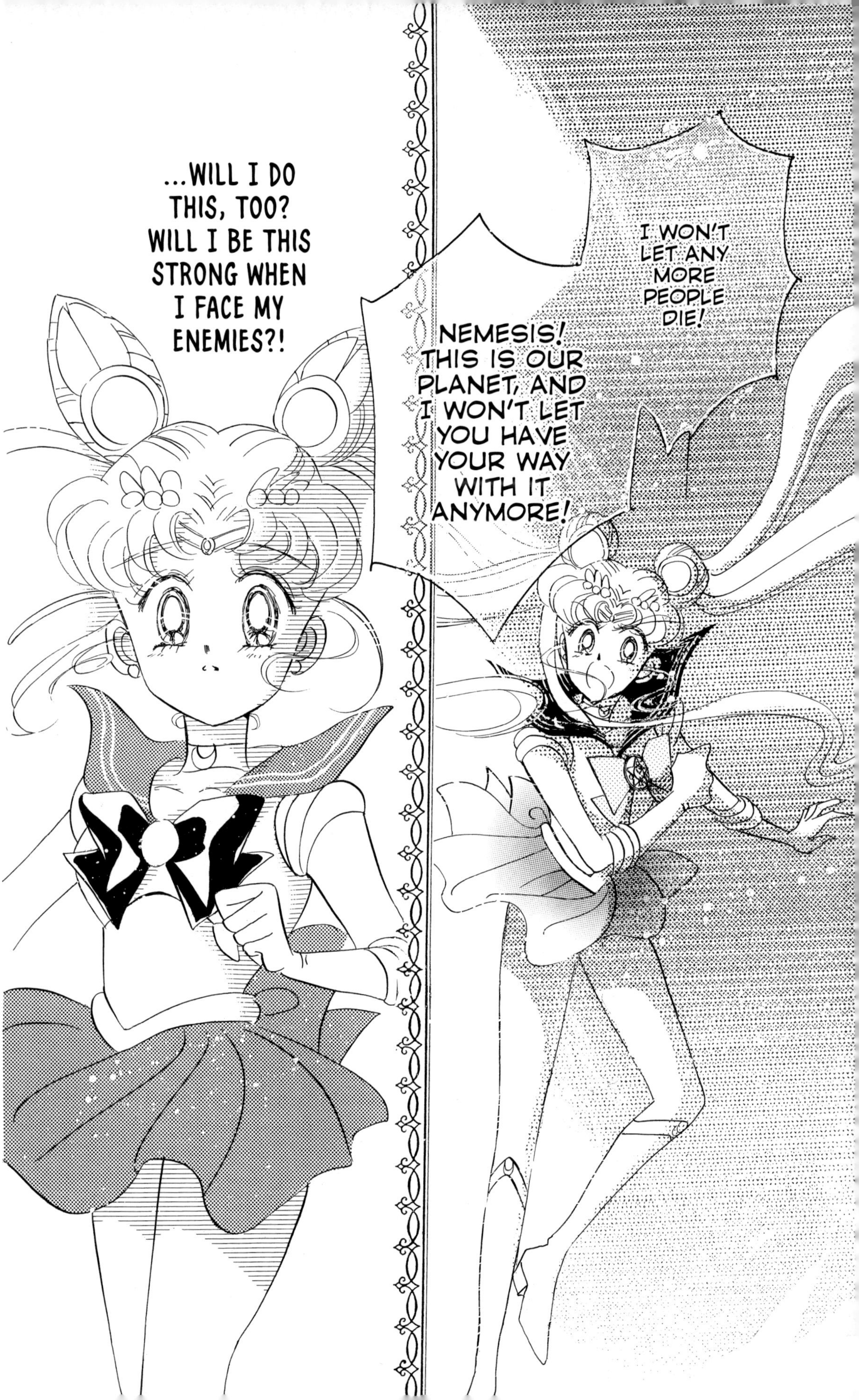
I WON'T LET ANY MORE PEOPLE DIE!
NEMESIS! THIS IS OUR PLANET, AND I WON'T LET YOU HAVE YOUR WAY WITH IT ANYMORE!
...WILL I DO THIS, TOO? WILL I BE THIS STRONG WHEN I FACE MY ENEMIES?!

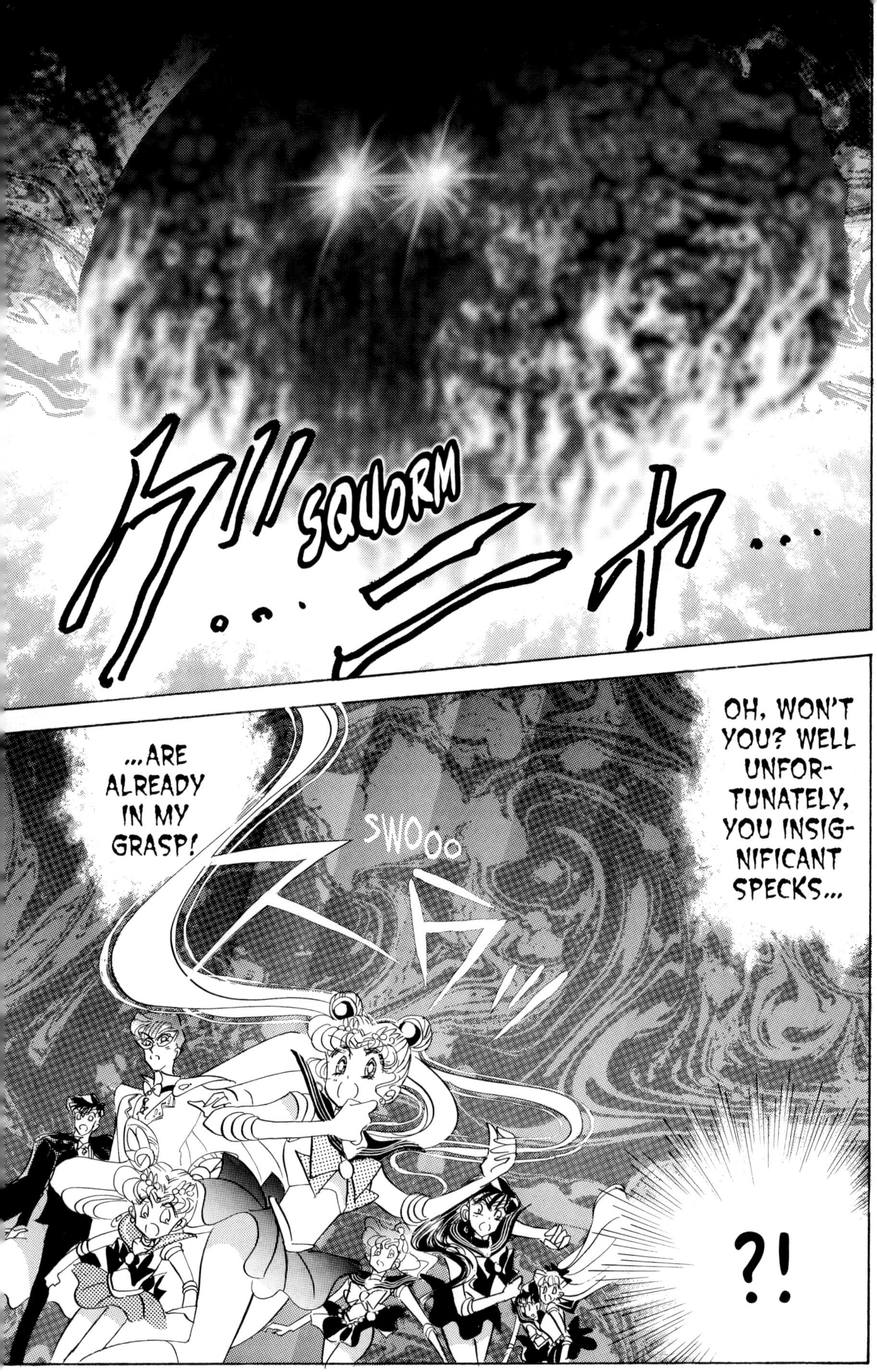
SQUORM
OH, WON'T YOU? WELL UNFORTUNATELY, YOU INSIGNIFICANT SPECKS...
...ARE ALREADY IN MY GRASP!
SWOOO
?!

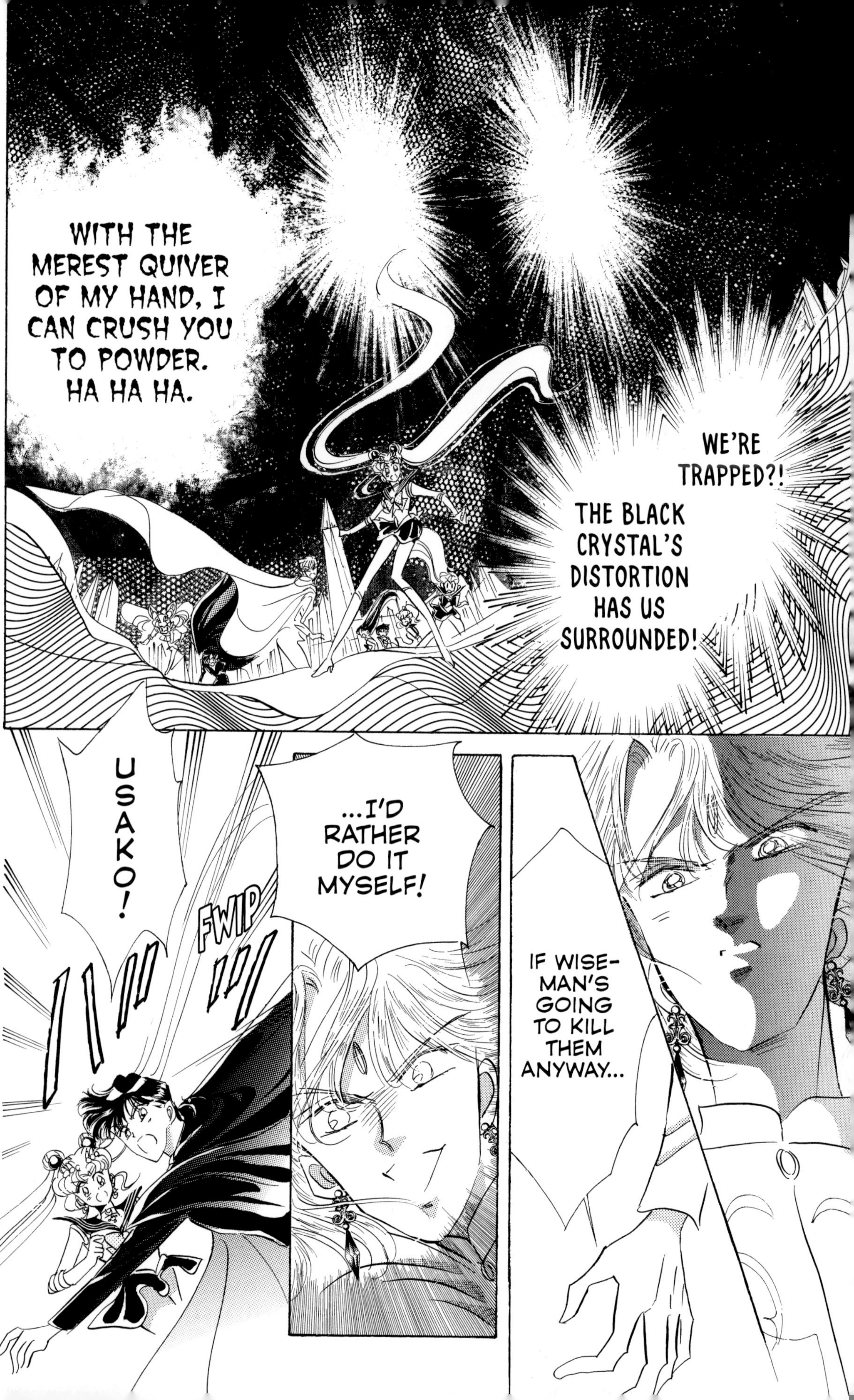
WE'RE TRAPPED?!
THE BLACK CRYSTAL'S DISTORTION HAS US SURROUNDED!
WITH THE MEREST QUIVER OF MY HAND, I CAN CRUSH YOU TO POWDER. HA HA HA.
IF WISE-MAN'S GOING TO KILL THEM ANYWAY...
...I'D RATHER DO IT MYSELF!
USAKO!
FWIP

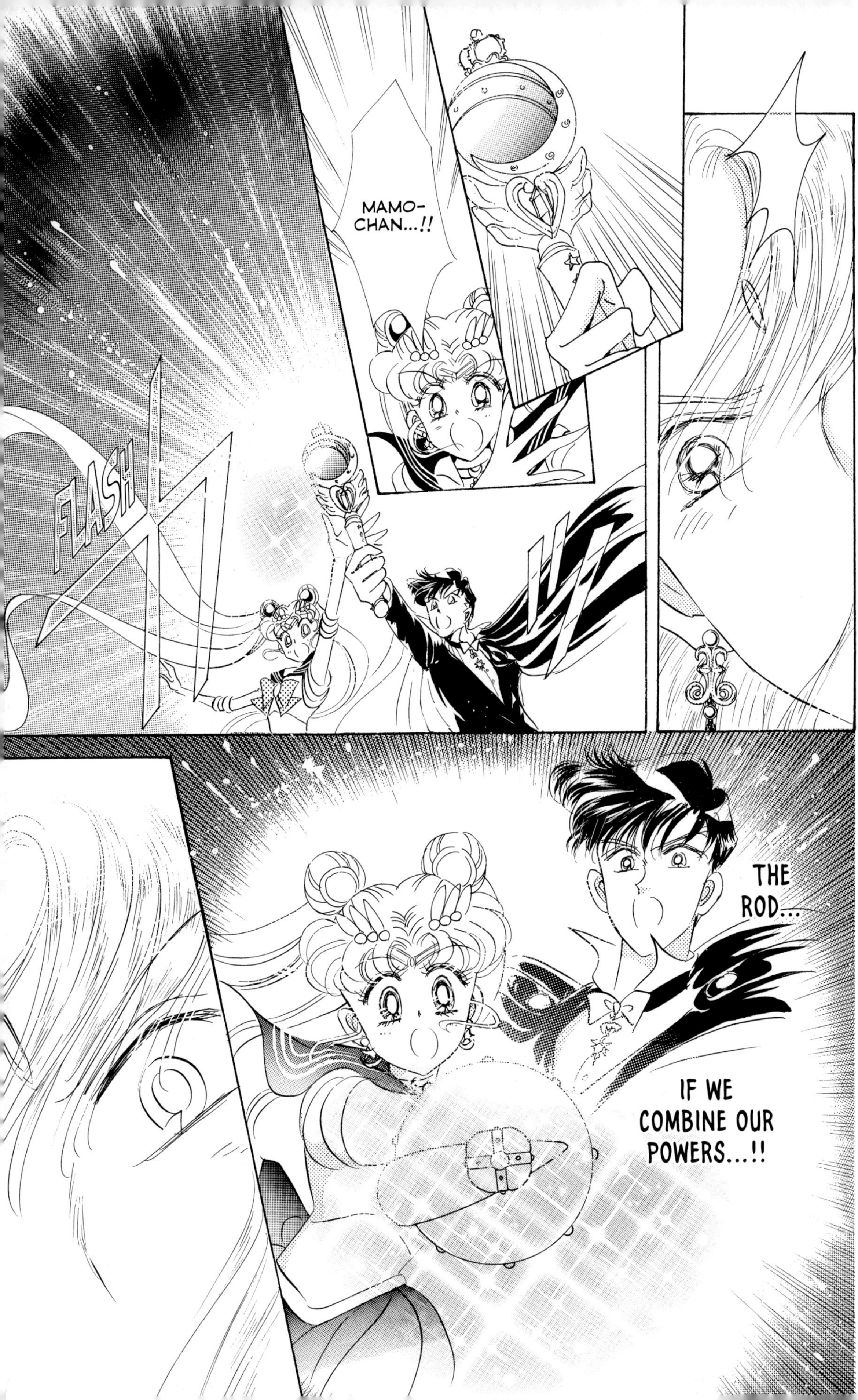
MAMO-
CHAN...!!
FLASH
THE
ROD...
IF WE
COMBINE OUR
POWERS...!!

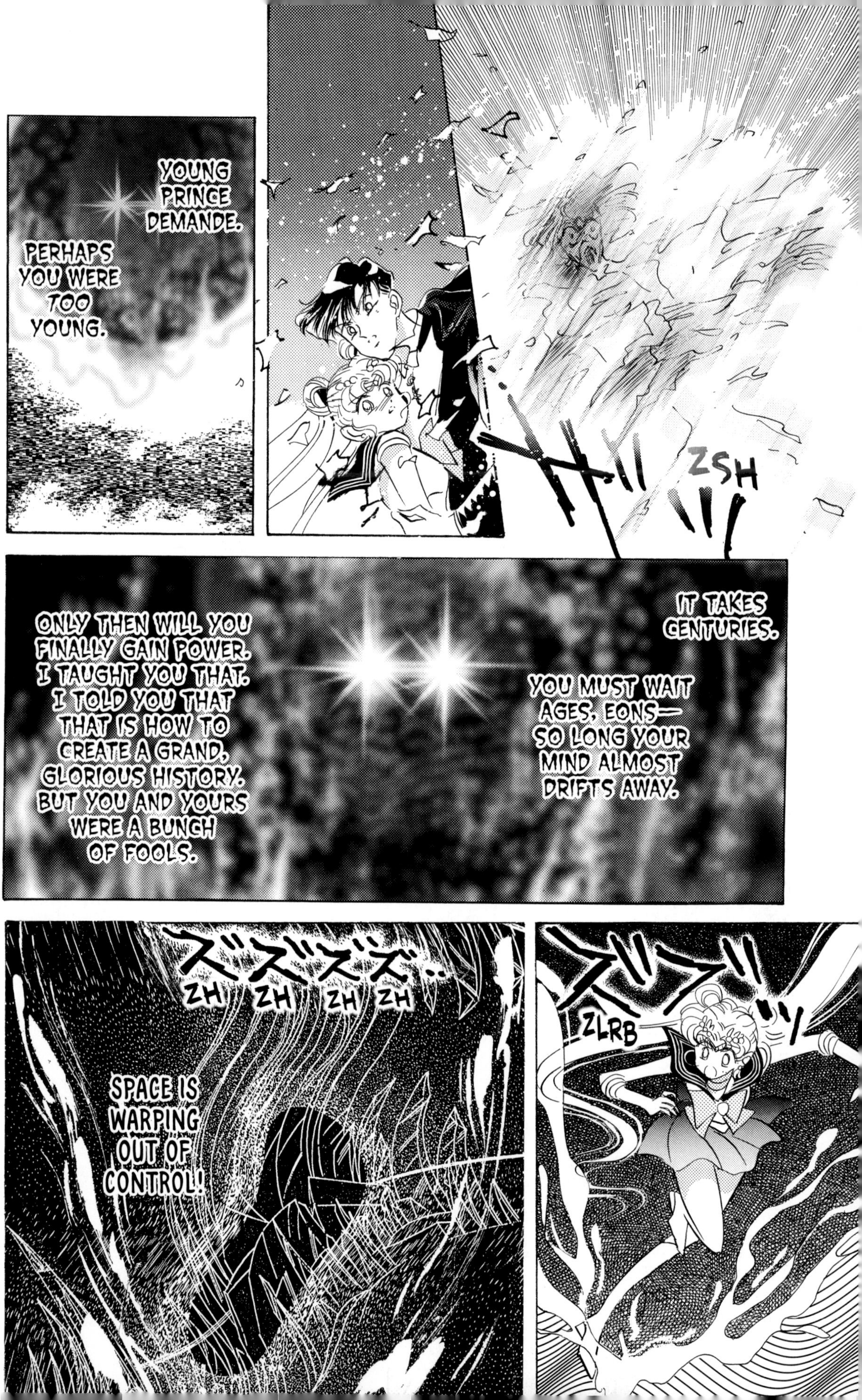
ZSH
YOUNG PRINCE DEMANDE.
PERHAPS YOU WERE TOO YOUNG.
IT TAKES CENTURIES.
YOU MUST WAIT AGES, EONS— SO LONG YOUR MIND ALMOST DRIFTS AWAY.
ONLY THEN WILL YOU FINALLY GAIN POWER. I TAUGHT YOU THAT. I TOLD YOU THAT THAT IS HOW TO CREATE A GRAND, GLORIOUS HISTORY. BUT YOU AND YOURS WERE A BUNCH OF FOOLS.
ZLRB
ズズズズ..
ZH ZH ZH ZH
SPACE IS WARPING OUT OF CONTROL!

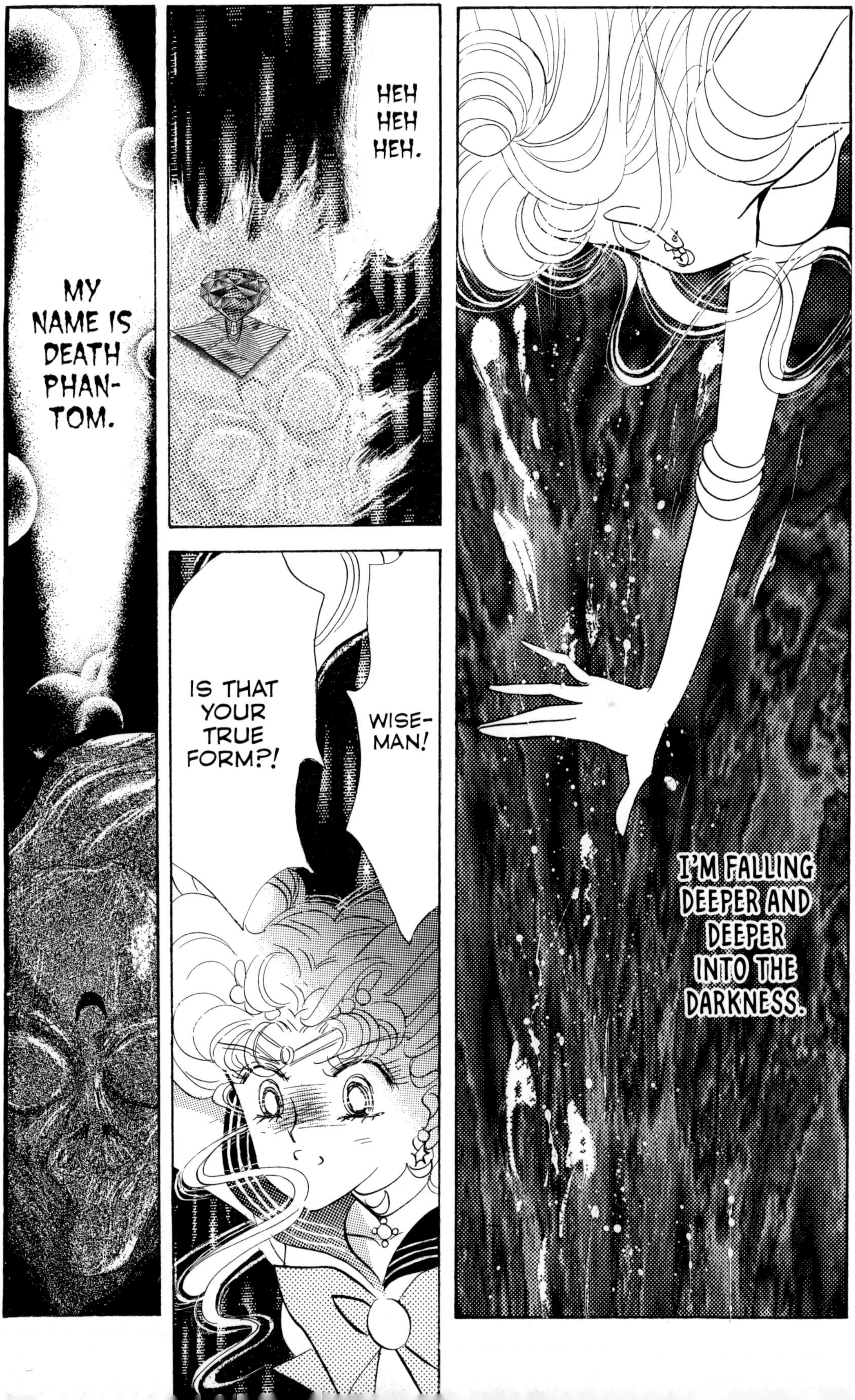
I'M FALLING DEEPER AND DEEPER INTO THE DARKNESS.
HEH HEH HEH.
WISE-MAN!
IS THAT YOUR TRUE FORM?!
MY NAME IS DEATH PHANTOM.

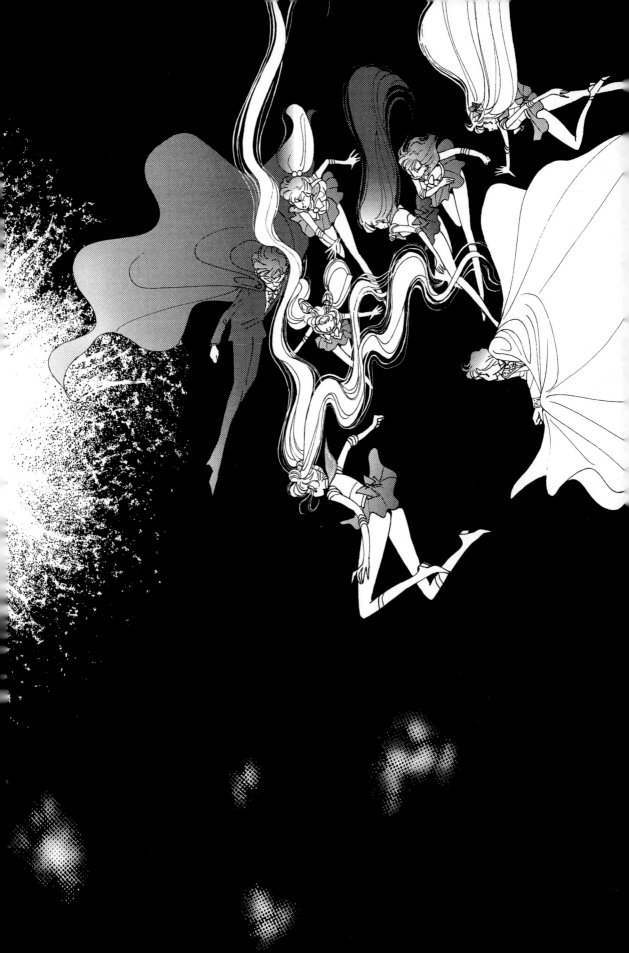

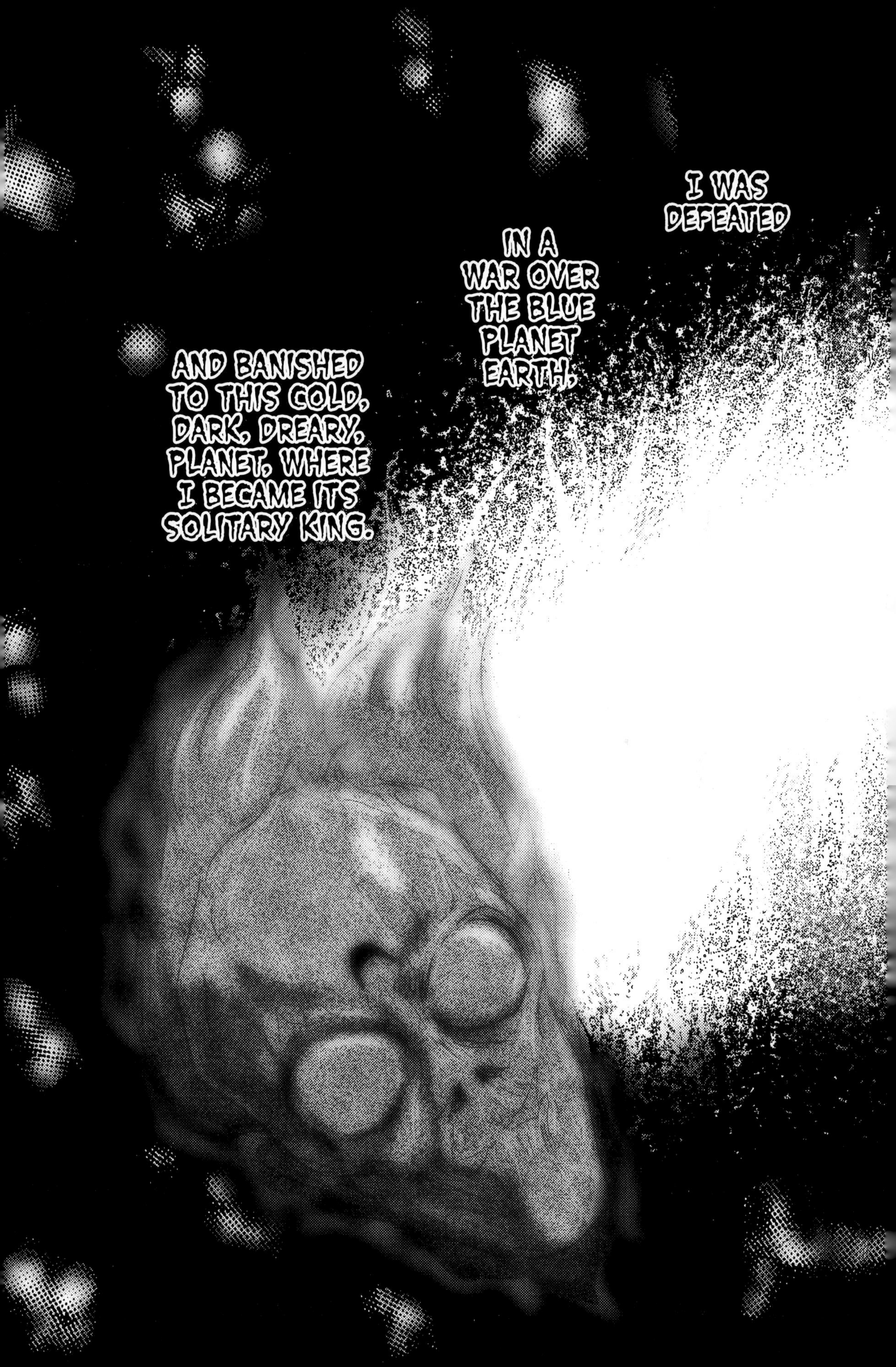
I WAS DEFEATED
IN A WAR OVER THE BLUE PLANET EARTH,
AND BANISHED TO THIS COLD, DARK, DREARY, PLANET, WHERE I BECAME ITS SOLITARY KING.

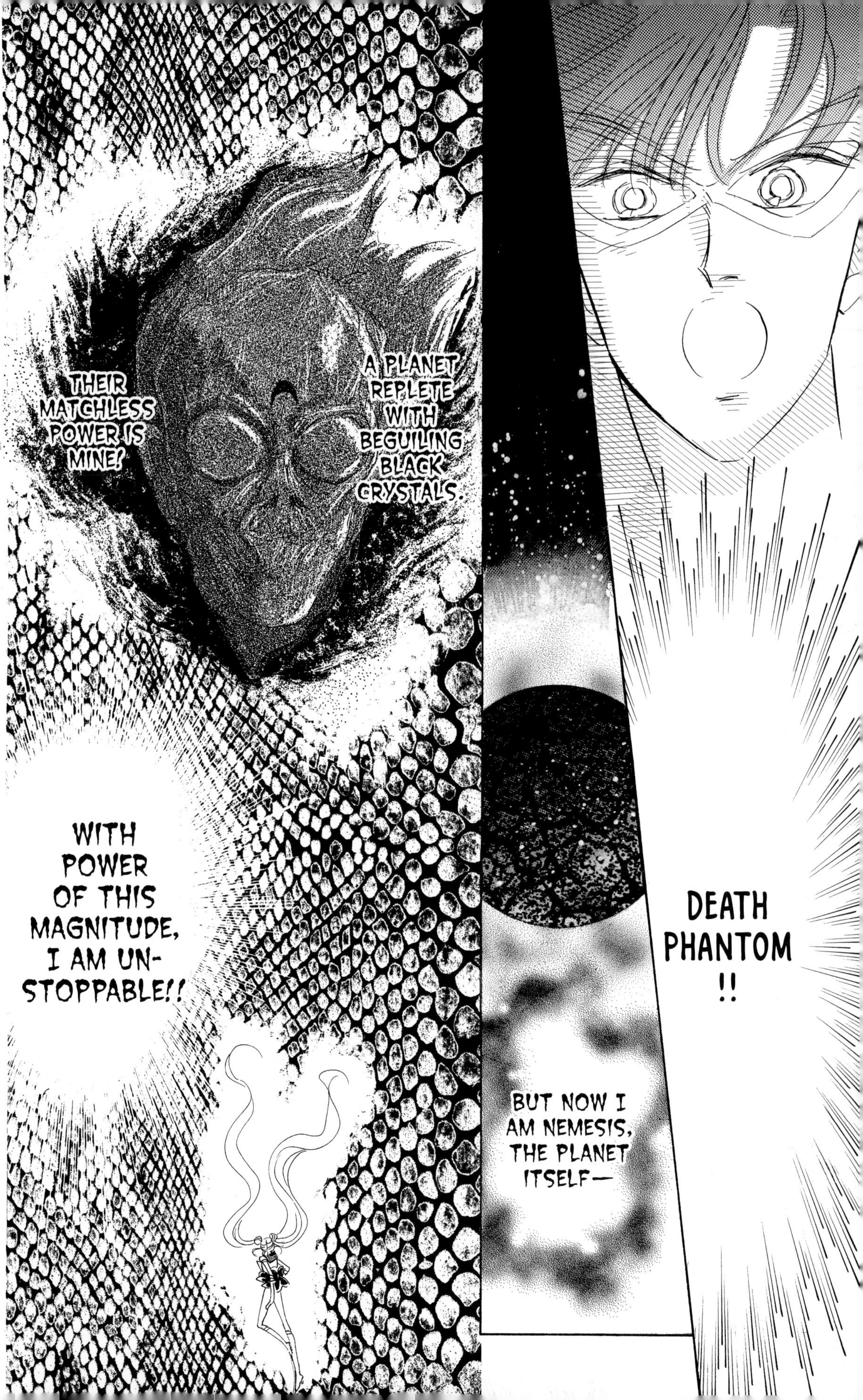
DEATH PHANTOM !!
BUT NOW I AM NEMESIS, THE PLANET ITSELF—
A PLANET REPLETE WITH BEGUILING BLACK CRYSTALS.
THEIR MATCHLESS POWER IS MINE!
WITH POWER OF THIS MAGNITUDE, I AM UN-STOPPABLE!!

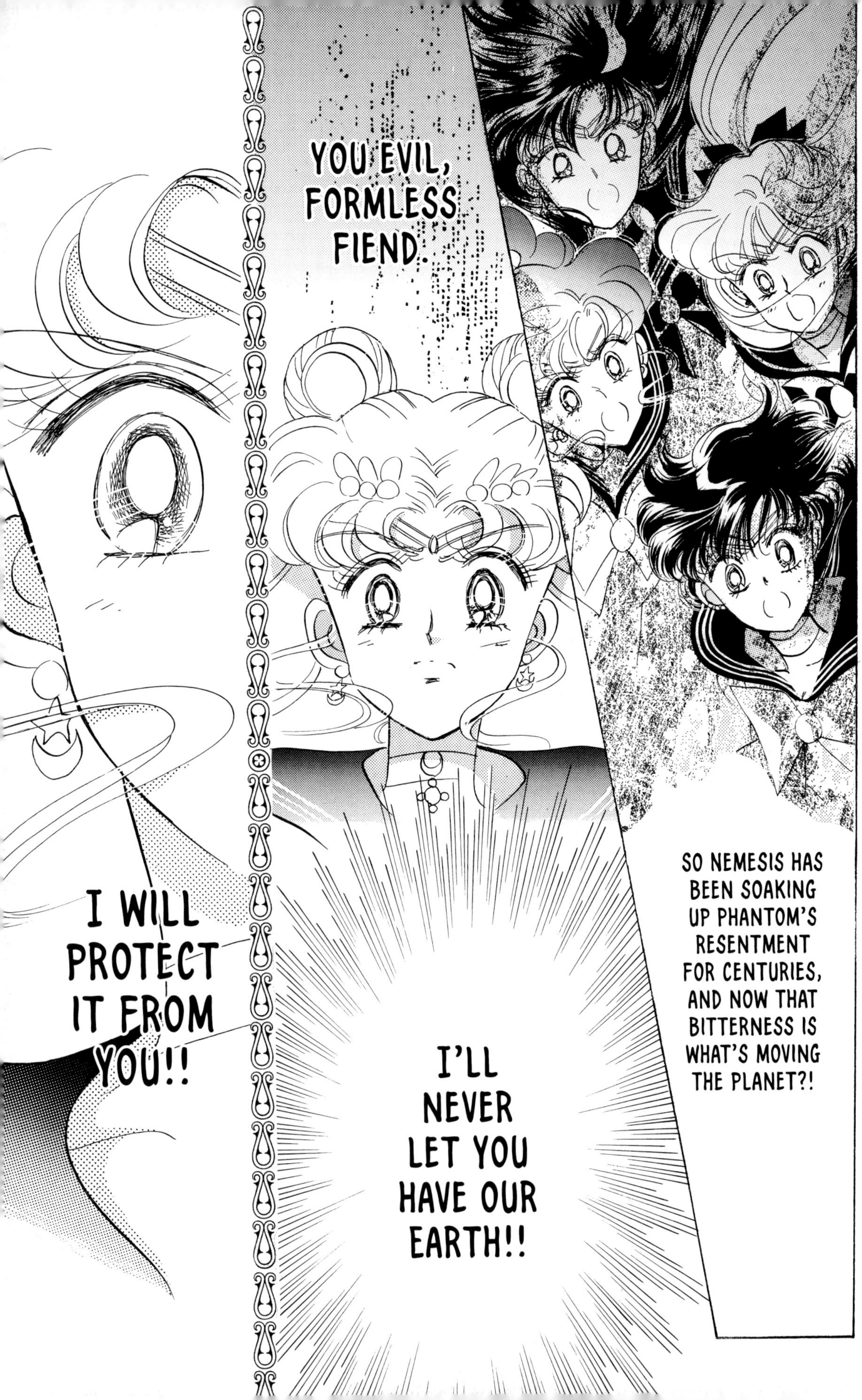
SO NEMESIS HAS BEEN SOAKING UP PHANTOM'S RESENTMENT FOR CENTURIES, AND NOW THAT BITTERNESS IS WHAT'S MOVING THE PLANET?!
YOU EVIL, FORMLESS FIEND.
I'LL NEVER LET YOU HAVE OUR EARTH!!
I WILL PROTECT IT FROM YOU!!

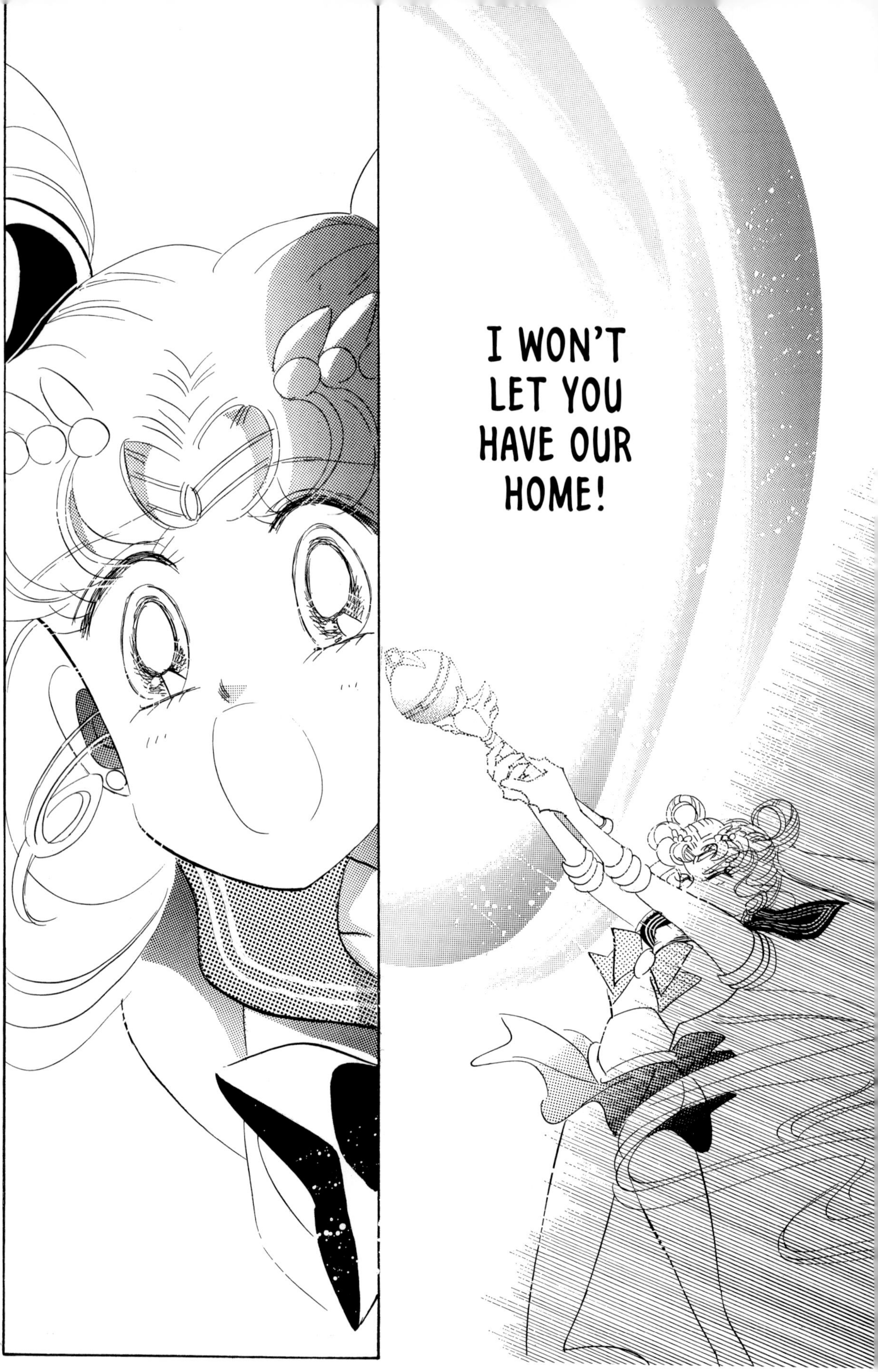
I WON'T LET YOU HAVE OUR HOME!

Act. 26 Rebirth: Never-Ending

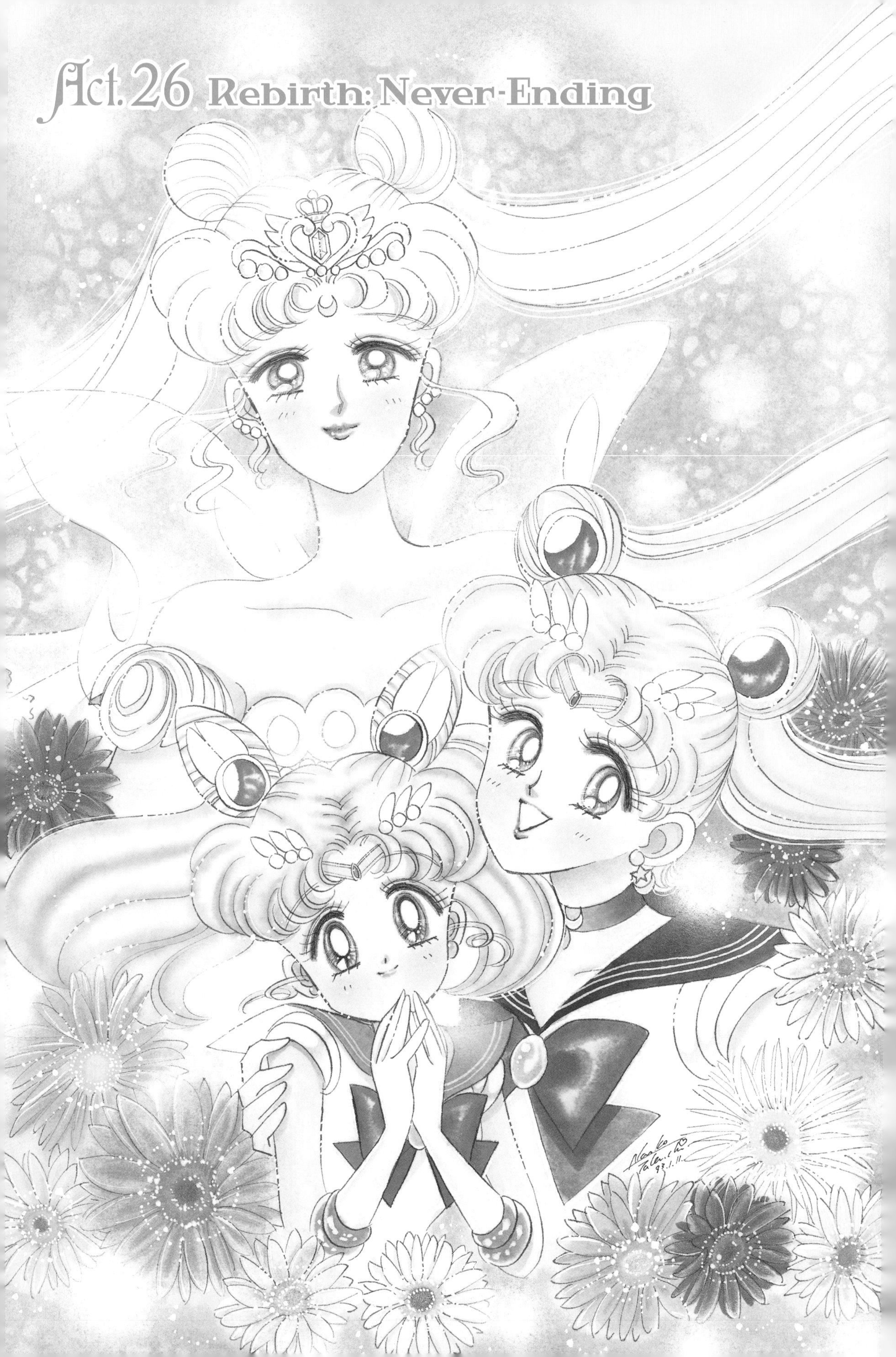

Pretty Guardian
Sailor Moon

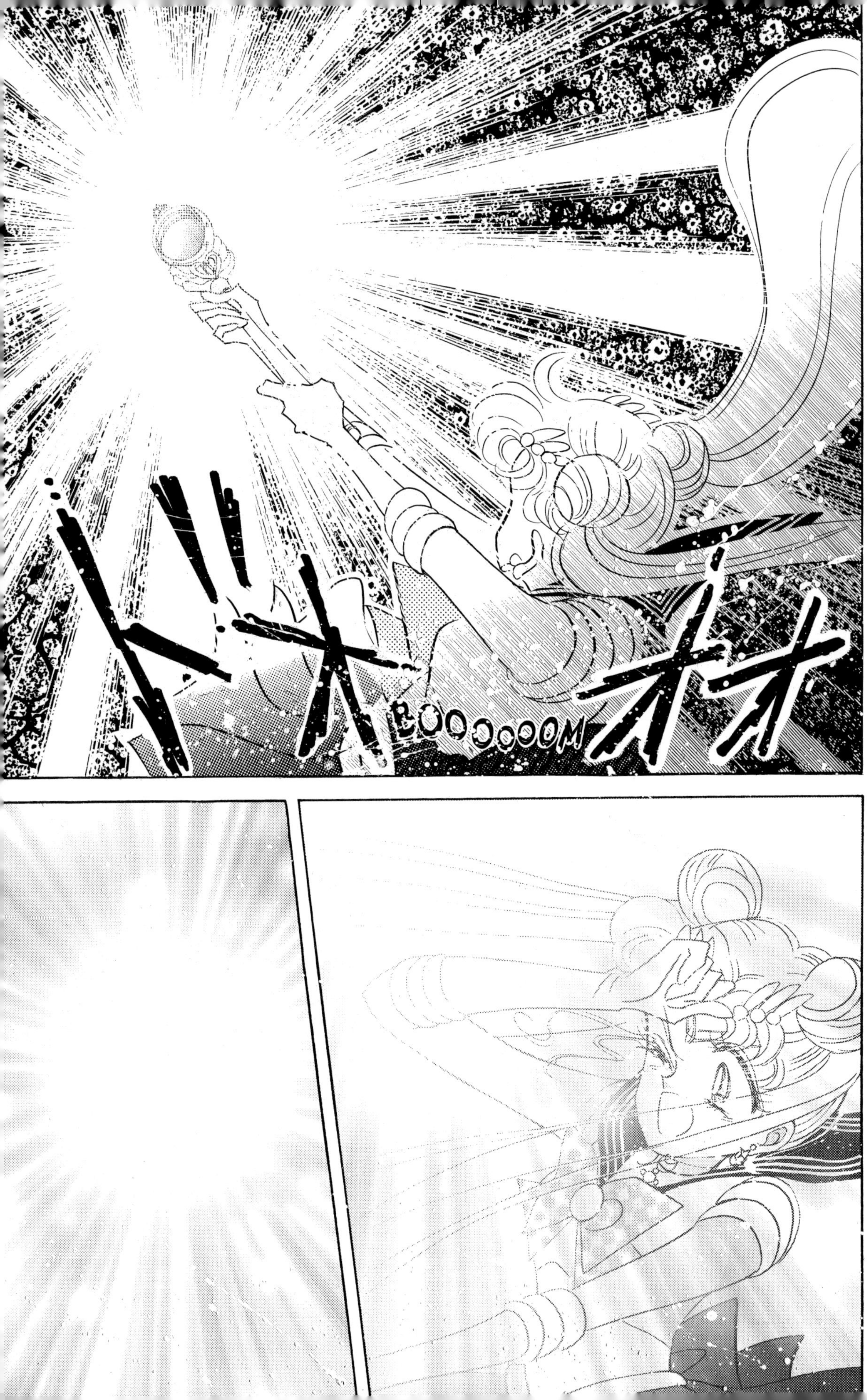
ドオオオ
BOOOoOOM

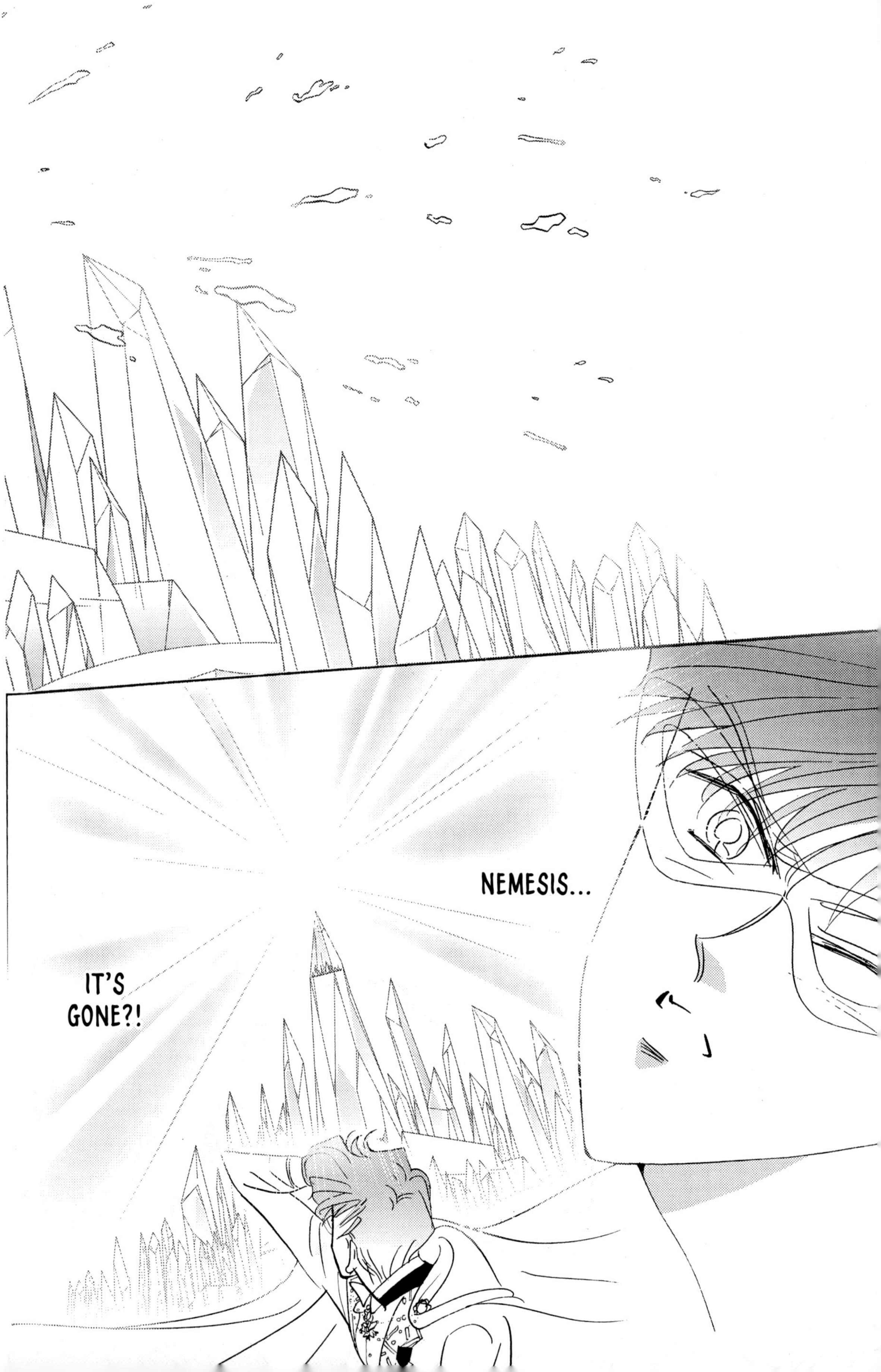
NEMESIS...
IT'S GONE?!

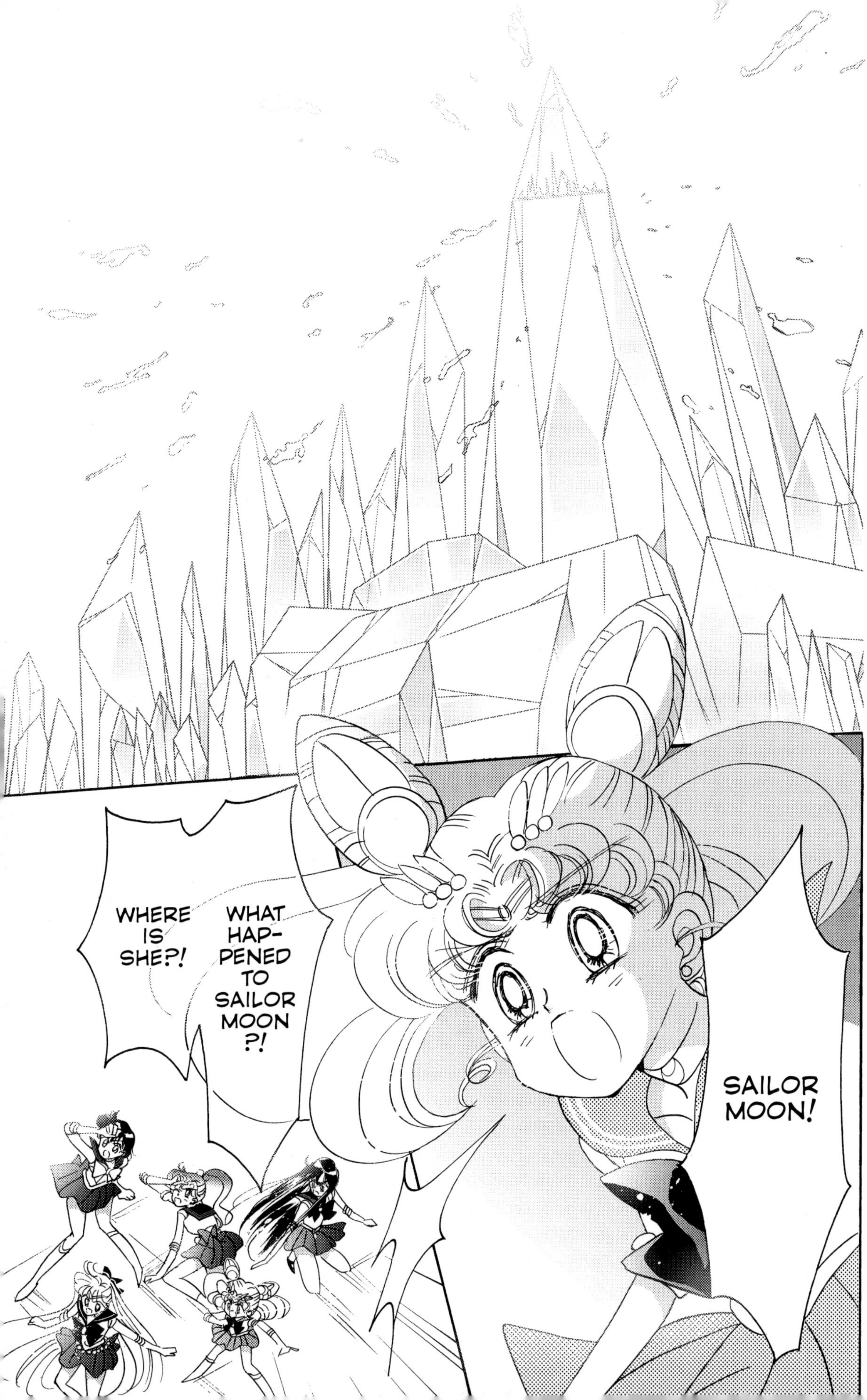
SAILOR MOON!
WHAT HAPPENED TO SAILOR MOON?!
WHERE IS SHE?!

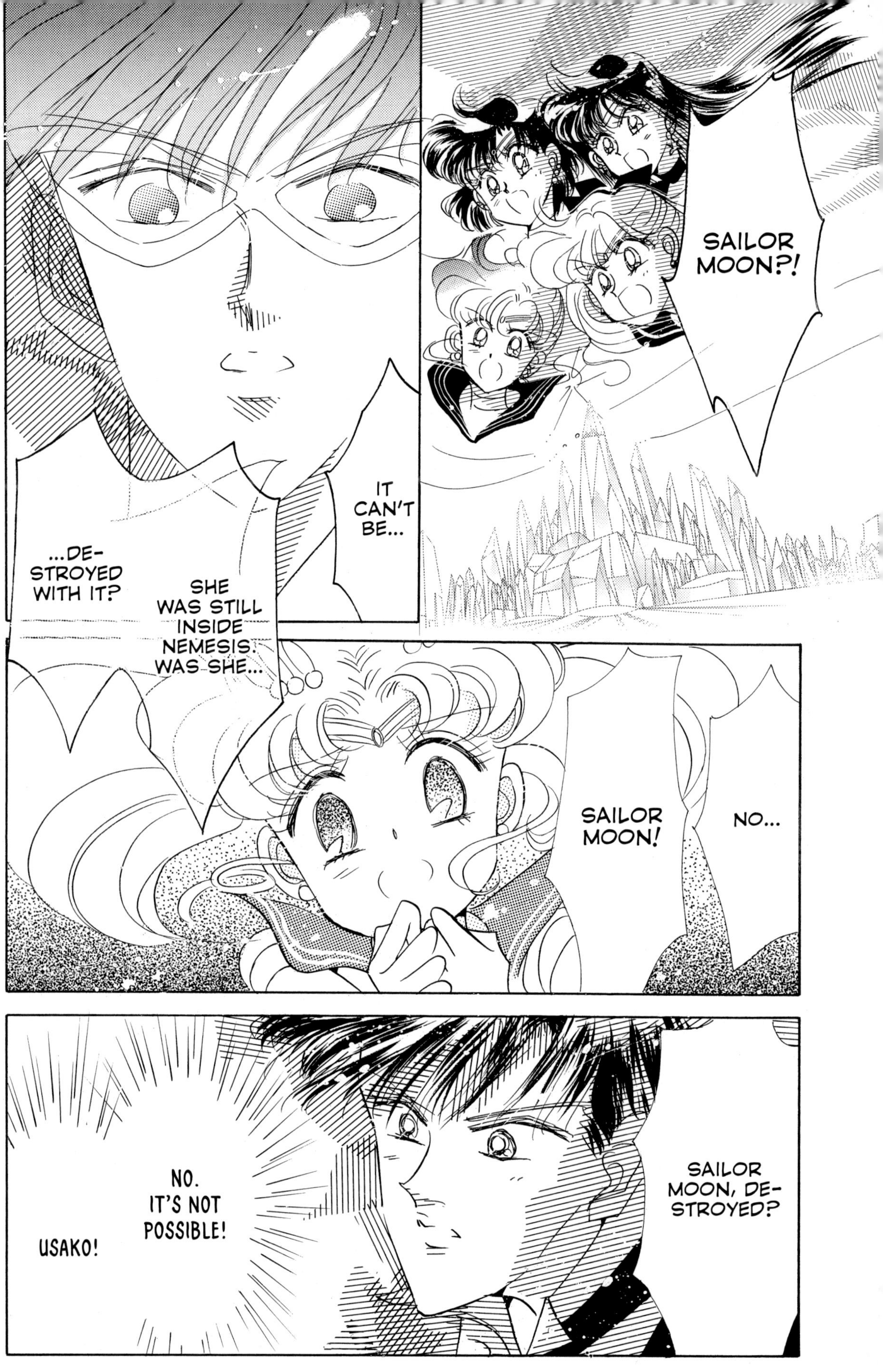
SAILOR MOON?!
IT CAN'T BE...
SHE WAS STILL INSIDE NEMESIS. WAS SHE...
...DE-STROYED WITH IT?
NO...
SAILOR MOON!
SAILOR MOON, DE-STROYED?
NO. IT'S NOT POSSIBLE!
USAKO!

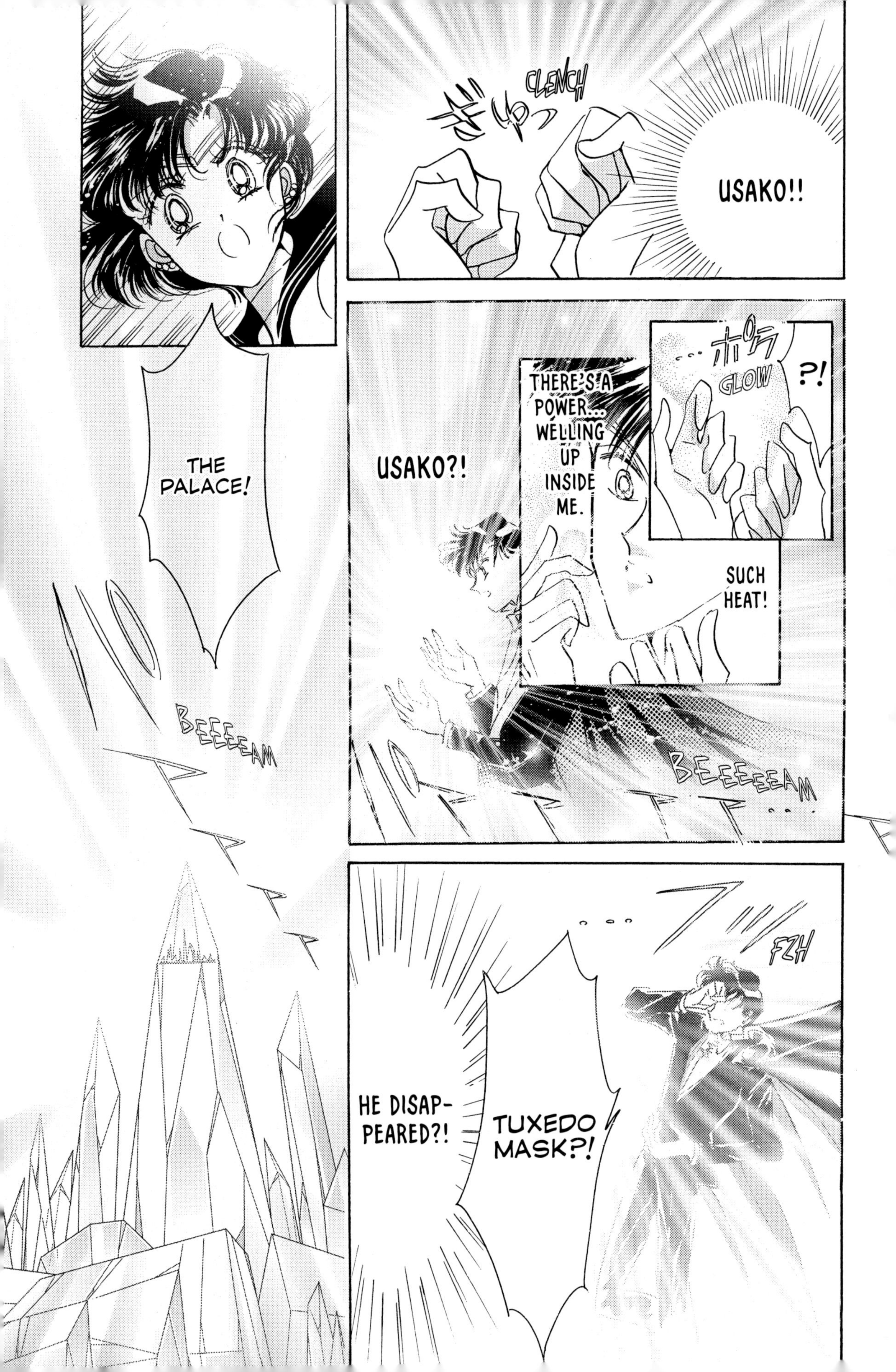

ぎゅっ
CLENCH
USAKO!!
... ポウ
GLOW
?!
THERE'S A POWER... WELLING UP INSIDE ME.
SUCH HEAT!
USAKO?!
BEEEEEEAM...
...
FZH
TUXEDO MASK?!
HE DISAP- PEARED?!
THE PALACE!
BEEEEAM

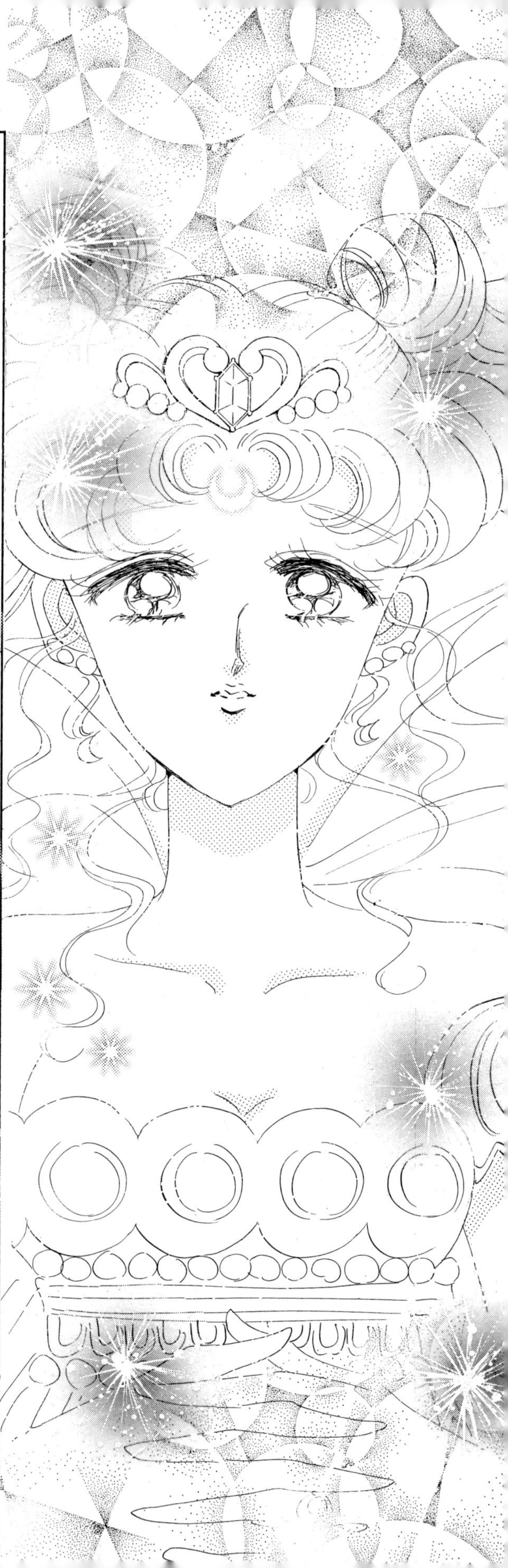
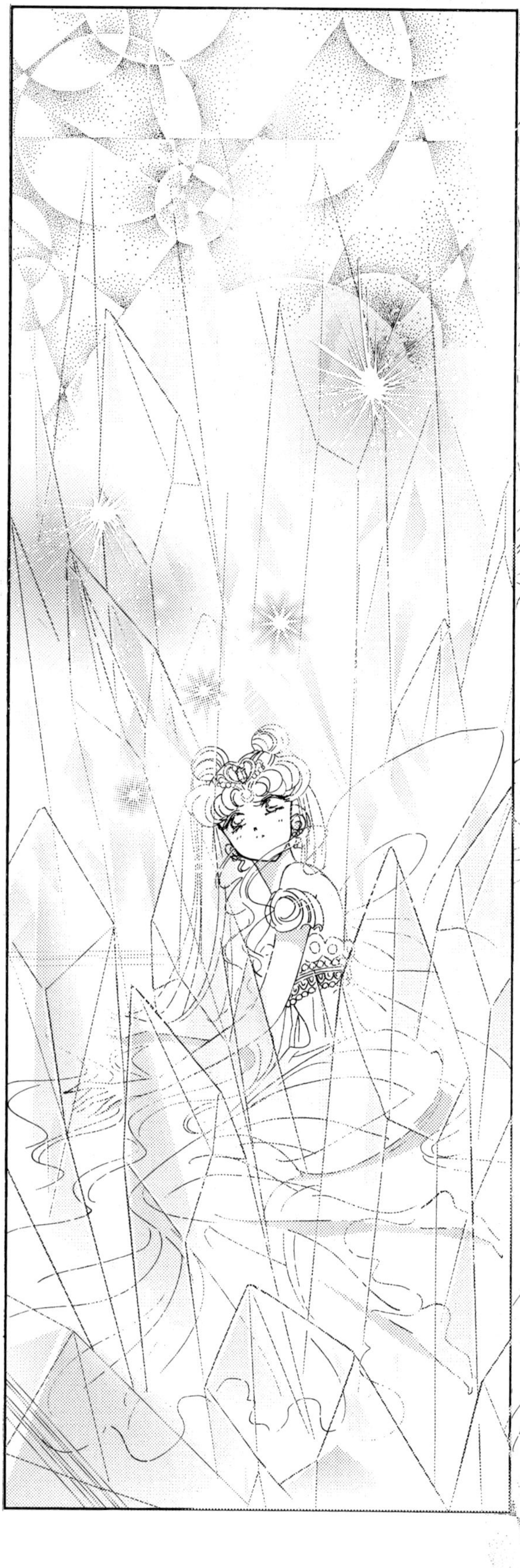

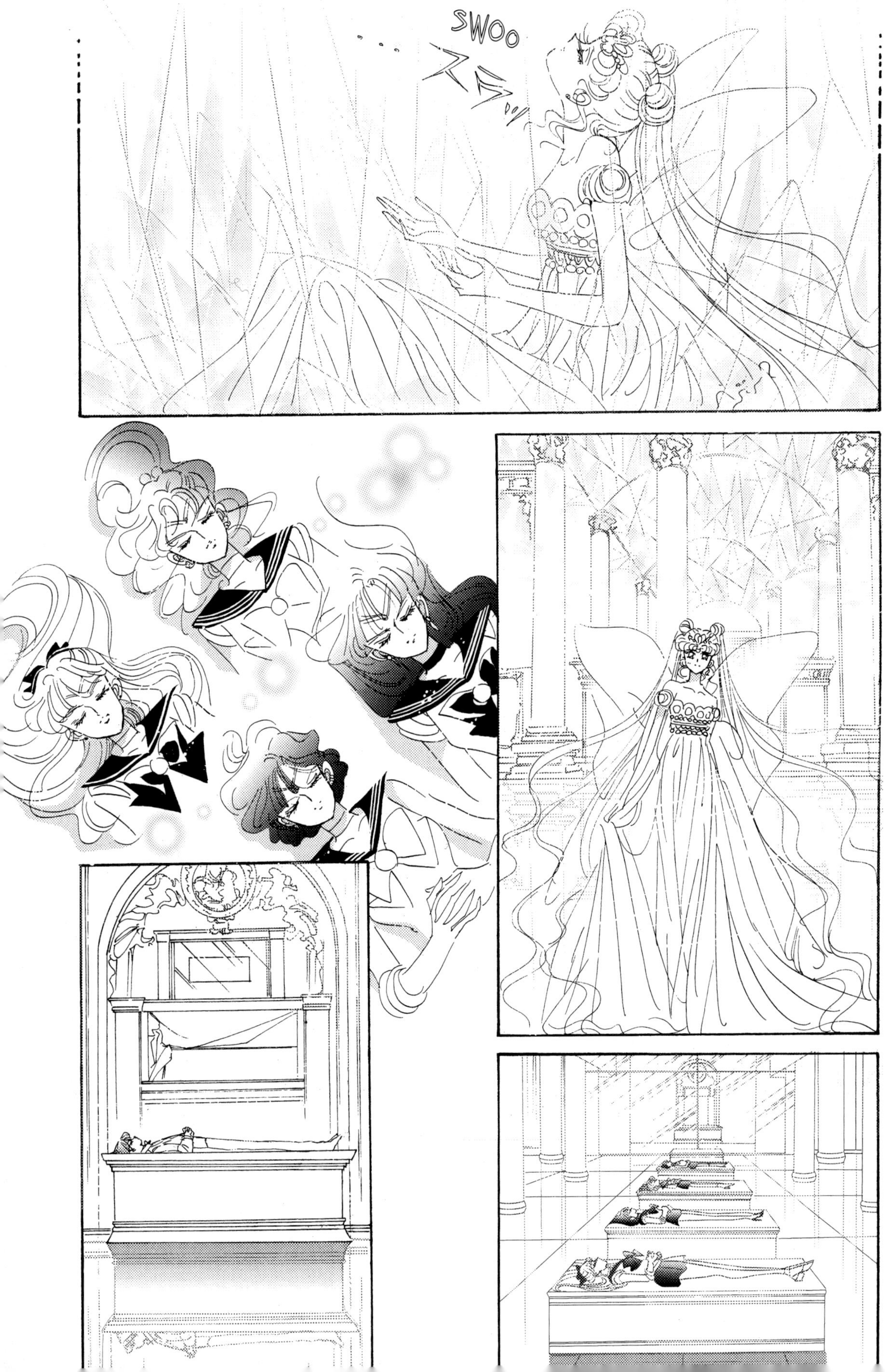
SWOO
スラッ

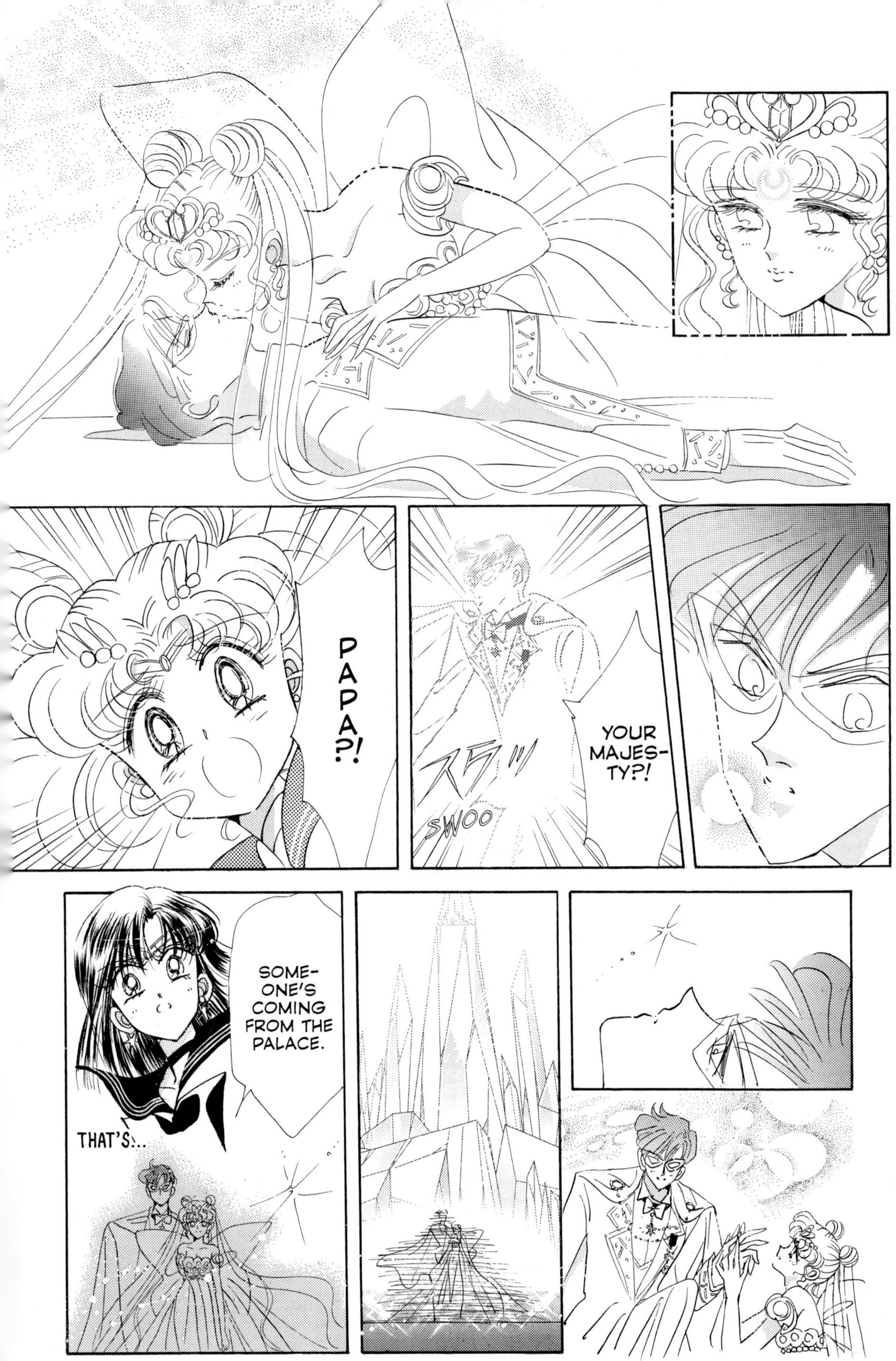
YOUR MAJES-TY?!
スラッ
SWOO
PAPA?!
SOME-ONE'S COMING FROM THE PALACE.
THAT'S...

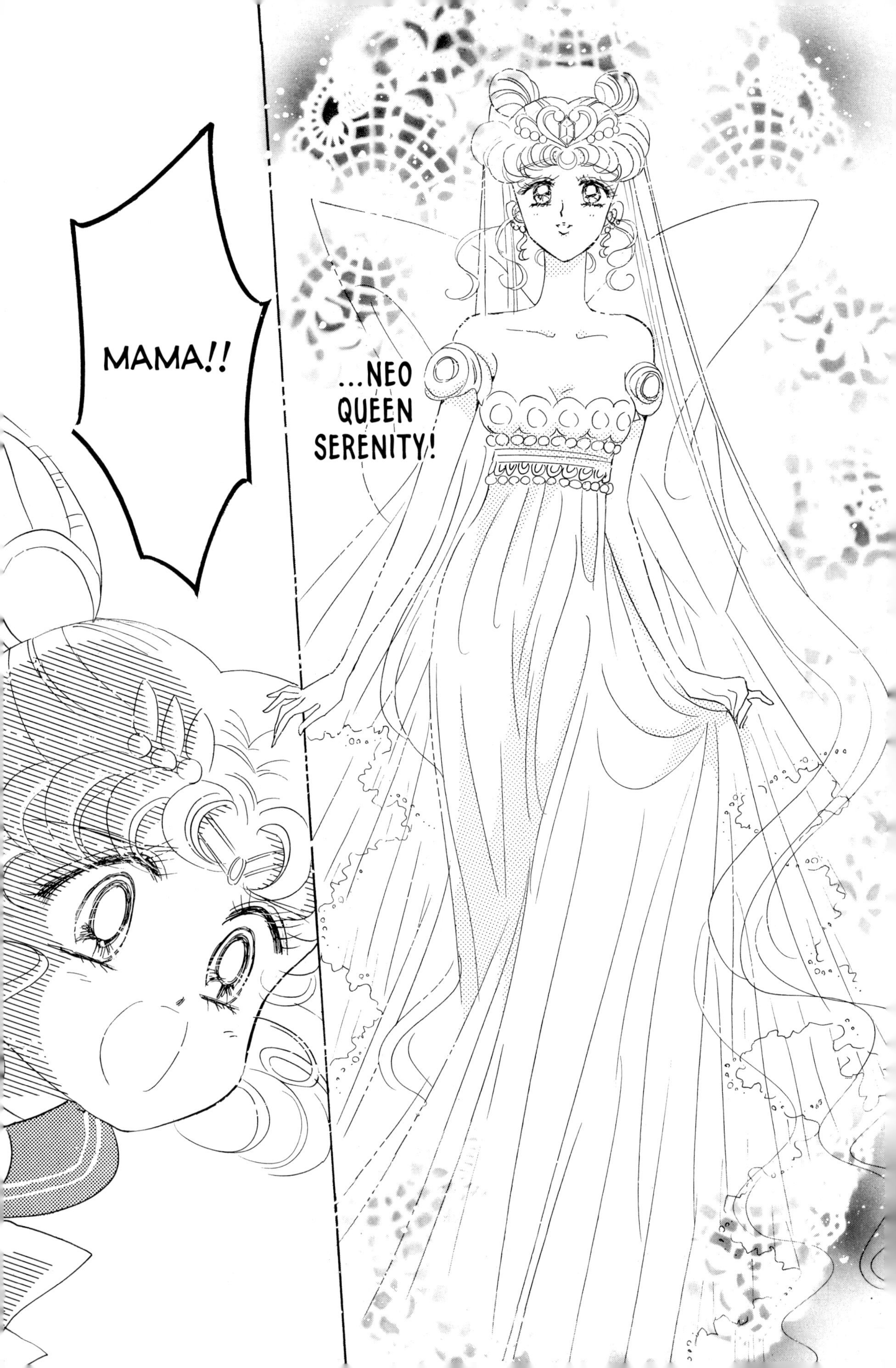
...NEO QUEEN SERENITY!
MAMA!!

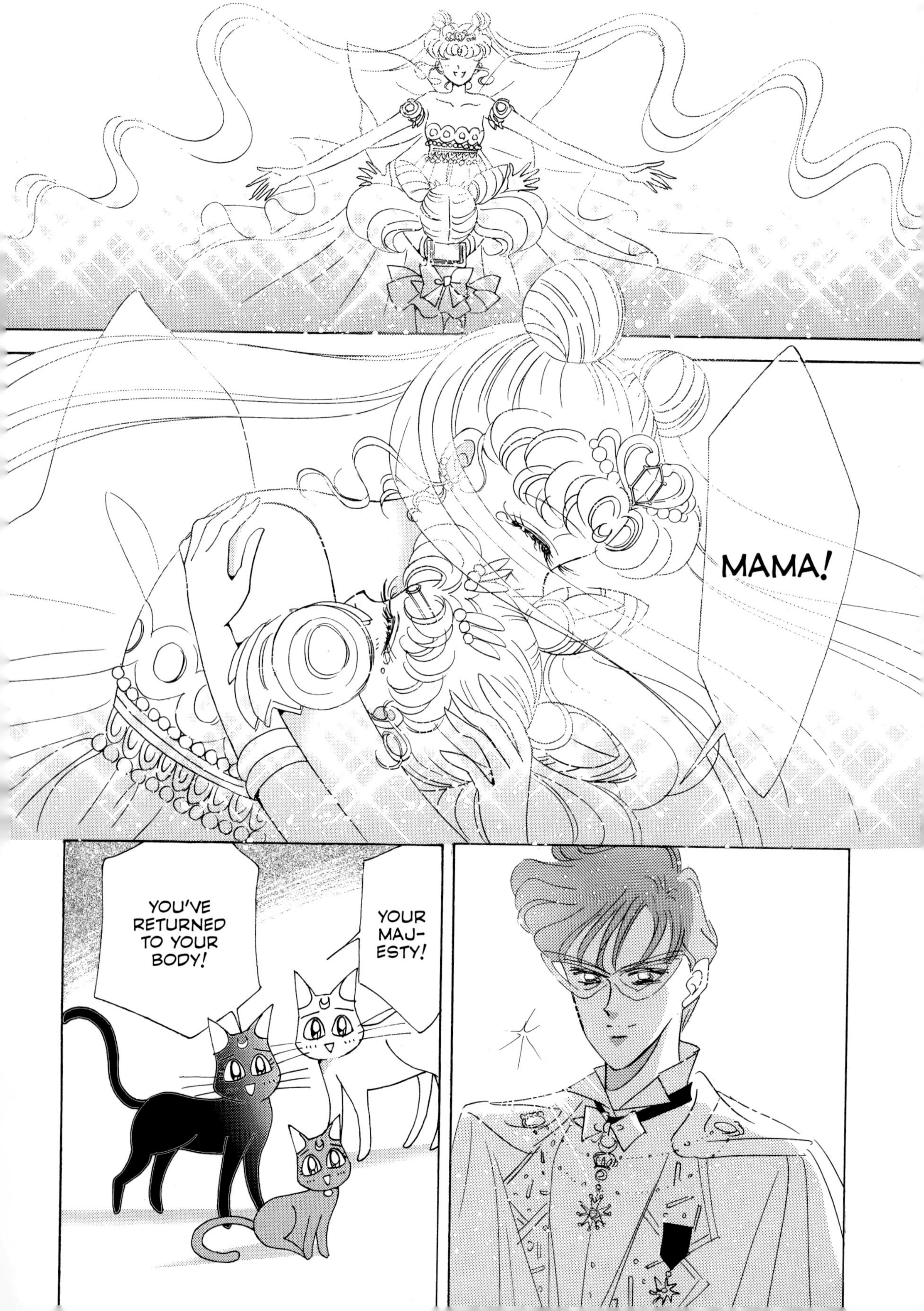
MAMA!
YOUR MAJ-ESTY!
YOU'VE RETURNED TO YOUR BODY!

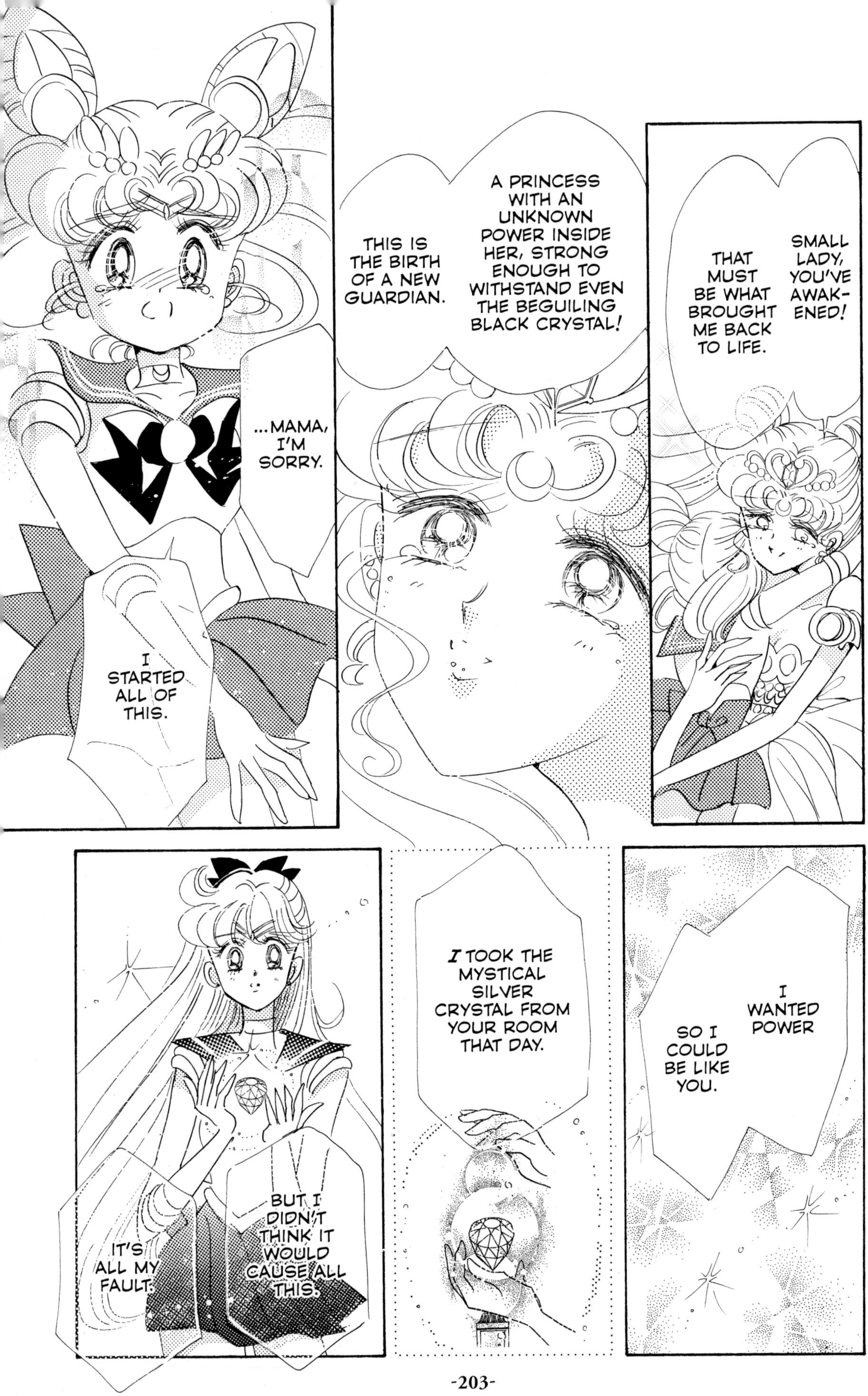

SMALL LADY, YOU'VE AWAK-ENED!
THAT MUST BE WHAT BROUGHT ME BACK TO LIFE.
A PRINCESS WITH AN UNKNOWN POWER INSIDE HER, STRONG ENOUGH TO WITHSTAND EVEN THE BEGUILING BLACK CRYSTAL!
THIS IS THE BIRTH OF A NEW GUARDIAN.
...MAMA, I'M SORRY.
I STARTED ALL OF THIS.
I WANTED POWER
SO I COULD BE LIKE YOU.
I TOOK THE MYSTICAL SILVER CRYSTAL FROM YOUR ROOM THAT DAY.
BUT I DIDN'T THINK IT WOULD CAUSE ALL THIS.
IT'S ALL MY FAULT.

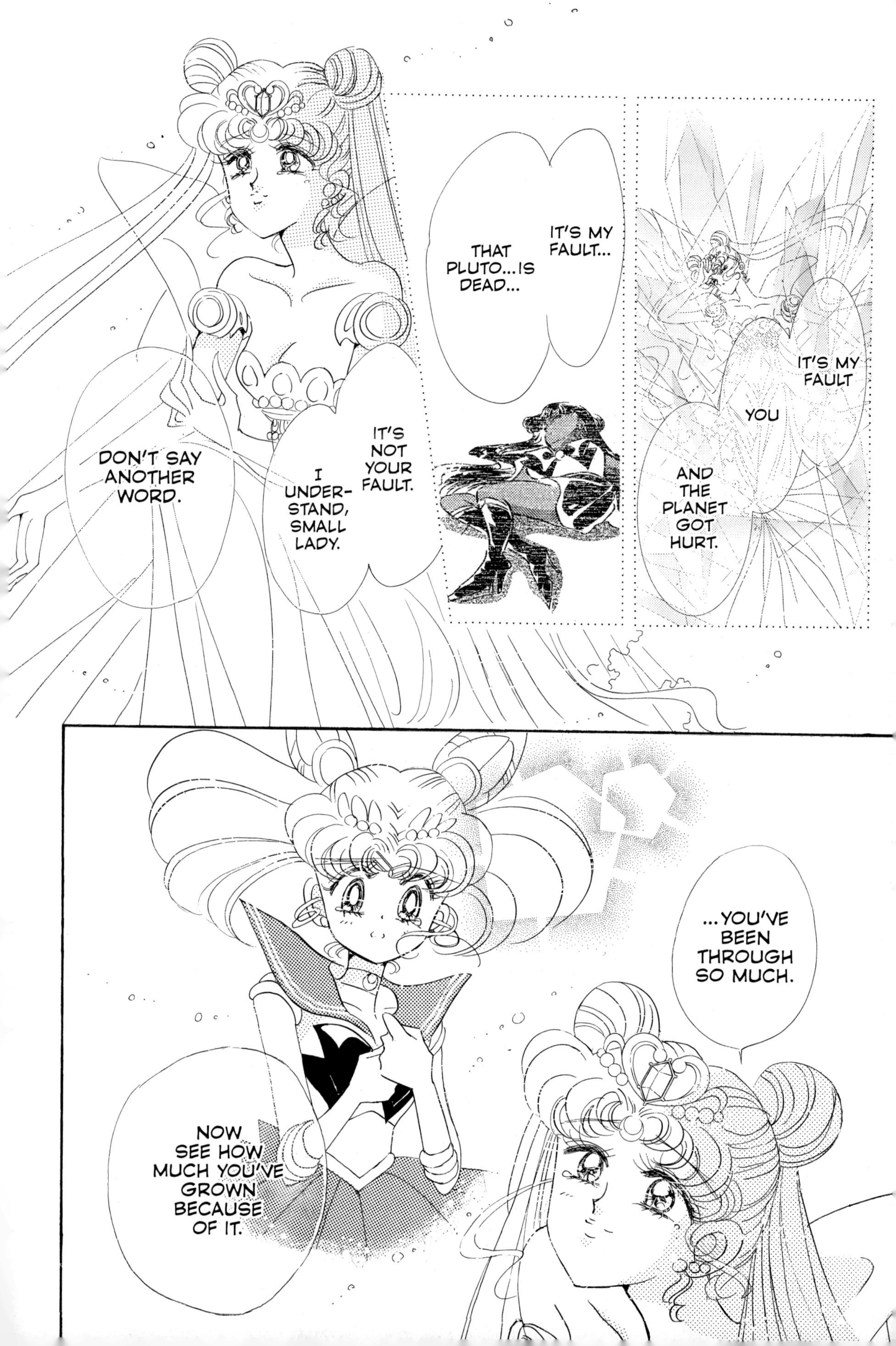
IT'S MY FAULT
YOU
AND THE PLANET GOT HURT.
IT'S MY FAULT...
THAT PLUTO...IS DEAD...
IT'S NOT YOUR FAULT.
I UNDERSTAND, SMALL LADY.
DON'T SAY ANOTHER WORD.
...YOU'VE BEEN THROUGH SO MUCH.
NOW SEE HOW MUCH YOU'VE GROWN BECAUSE OF IT.

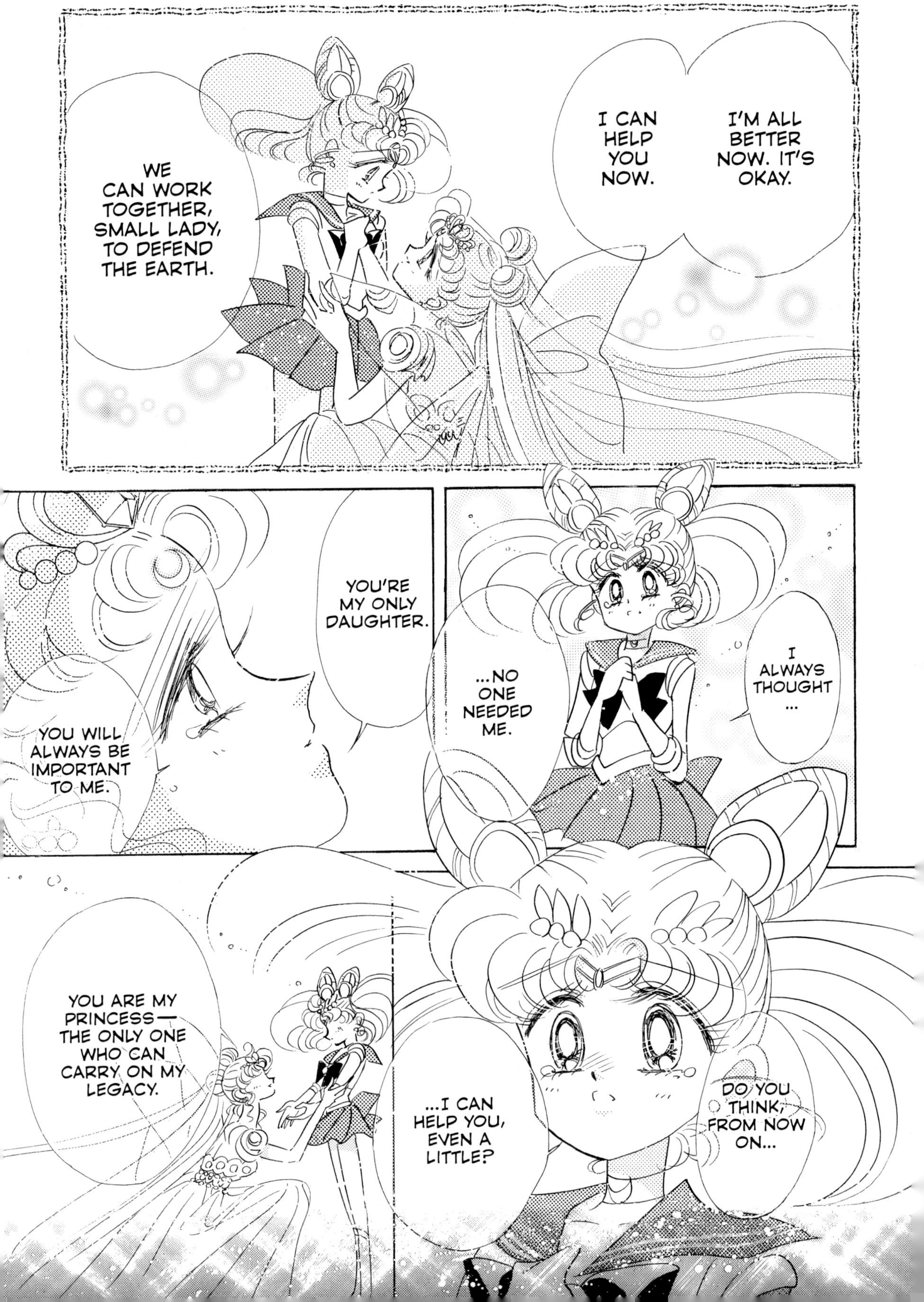
I'M ALL BETTER NOW. IT'S OKAY.
I CAN HELP YOU NOW.
WE CAN WORK TOGETHER, SMALL LADY, TO DEFEND THE EARTH.
I ALWAYS THOUGHT ...
...NO ONE NEEDED ME.
YOU'RE MY ONLY DAUGHTER.
YOU WILL ALWAYS BE IMPORTANT TO ME.
DO YOU THINK, FROM NOW ON...
...I CAN HELP YOU, EVEN A LITTLE?
YOU ARE MY PRINCESS— THE ONLY ONE WHO CAN CARRY ON MY LEGACY.

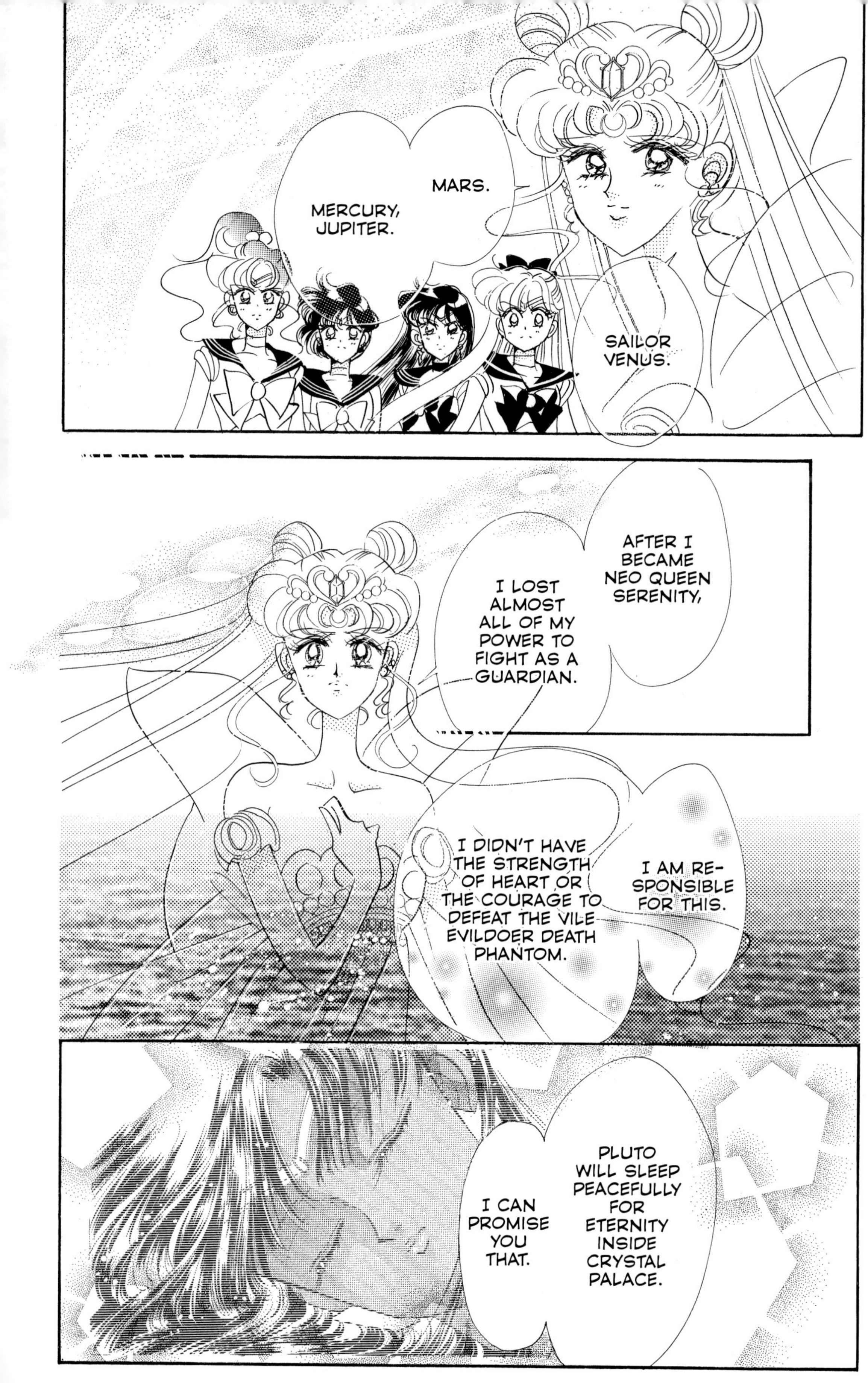
SAILOR VENUS.
MARS.
MERCURY, JUPITER.
AFTER I BECAME NEO QUEEN SERENITY,
I LOST ALMOST ALL OF MY POWER TO FIGHT AS A GUARDIAN.
I AM RE-SPONSIBLE FOR THIS.
I DIDN'T HAVE THE STRENGTH OF HEART OR THE COURAGE TO DEFEAT THE VILE EVILDOER DEATH PHANTOM.
PLUTO WILL SLEEP PEACEFULLY FOR ETERNITY INSIDE CRYSTAL PALACE.
I CAN PROMISE YOU THAT.

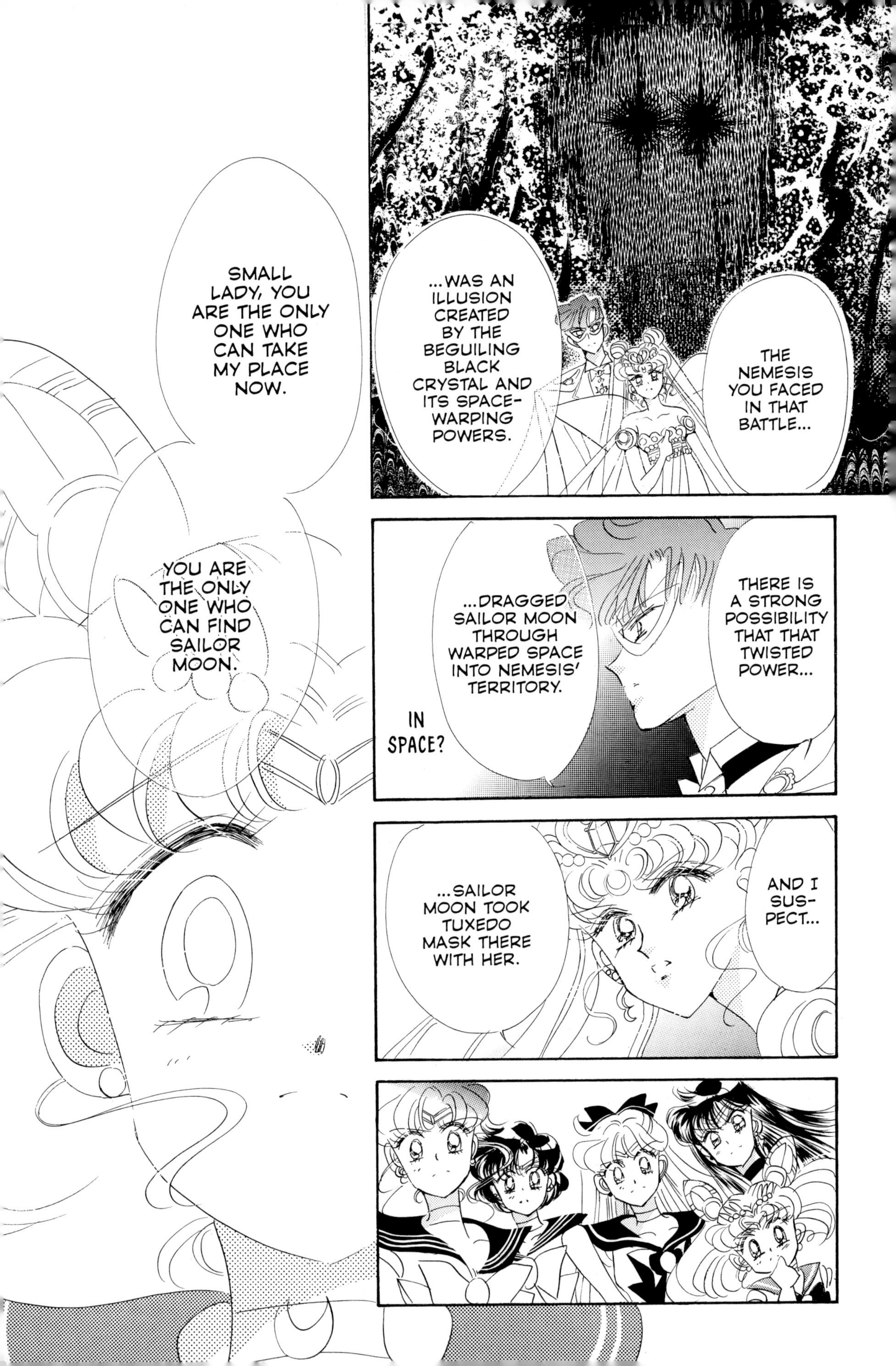
THE NEMESIS YOU FACED IN THAT BATTLE...
...WAS AN ILLUSION CREATED BY THE BEGUILING BLACK CRYSTAL AND ITS SPACE-WARPING POWERS.
THERE IS A STRONG POSSIBILITY THAT THAT TWISTED POWER...
...DRAGGED SAILOR MOON THROUGH WARPED SPACE INTO NEMESIS' TERRITORY.
IN SPACE?
AND I SUSPECT...
...SAILOR MOON TOOK TUXEDO MASK THERE WITH HER.
SMALL LADY, YOU ARE THE ONLY ONE WHO CAN TAKE MY PLACE NOW.
YOU ARE THE ONLY ONE WHO CAN FIND SAILOR MOON.

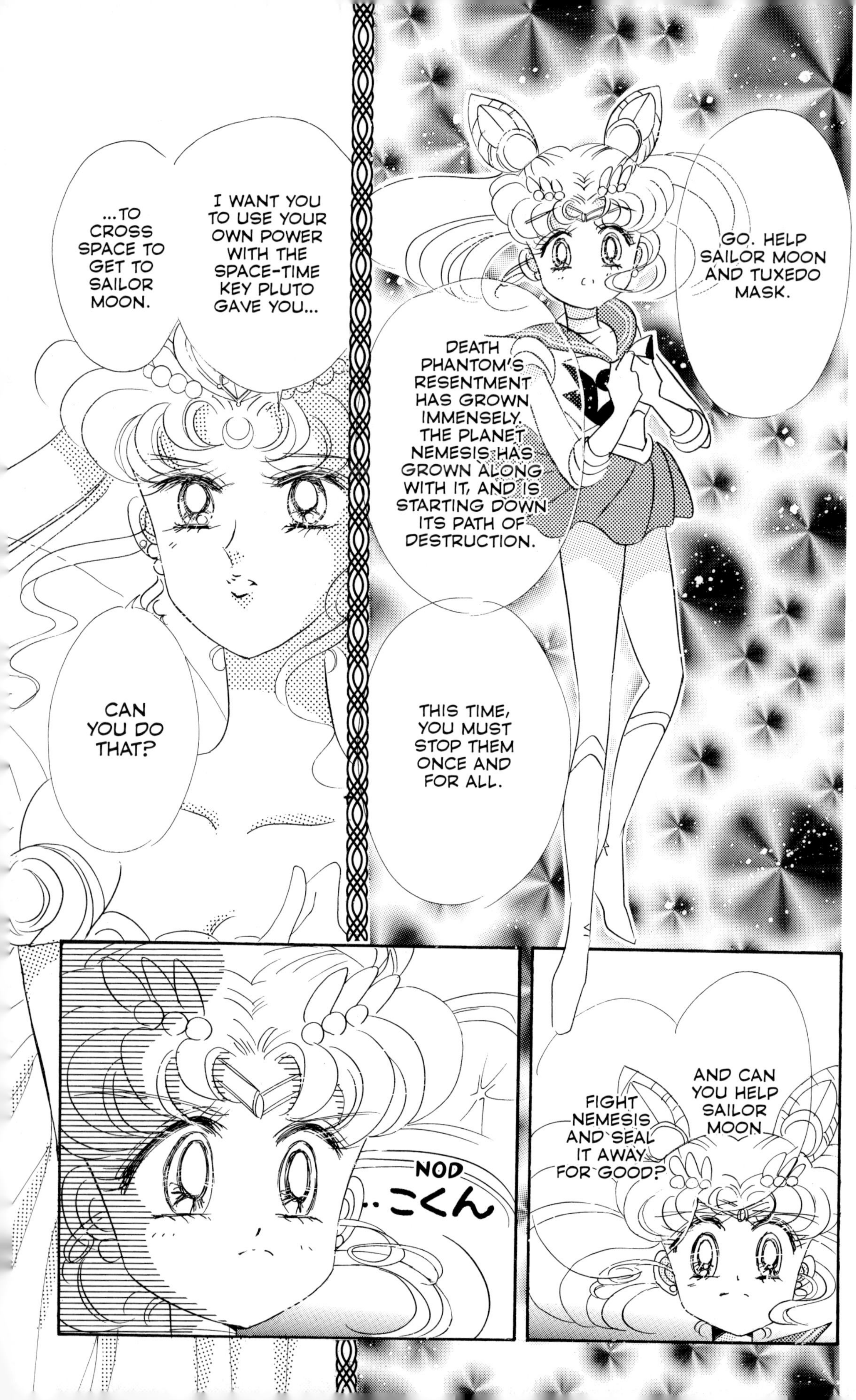
GO. HELP SAILOR MOON AND TUXEDO MASK.
DEATH PHANTOM'S RESENTMENT HAS GROWN IMMENSELY. THE PLANET NEMESIS HAS GROWN ALONG WITH IT, AND IS STARTING DOWN ITS PATH OF DESTRUCTION.
THIS TIME, YOU MUST STOP THEM ONCE AND FOR ALL.
I WANT YOU TO USE YOUR OWN POWER WITH THE SPACE-TIME KEY PLUTO GAVE YOU...
...TO CROSS SPACE TO GET TO SAILOR MOON.
CAN YOU DO THAT?
AND CAN YOU HELP SAILOR MOON
FIGHT NEMESIS AND SEAL IT AWAY FOR GOOD?
NOD
…こくん

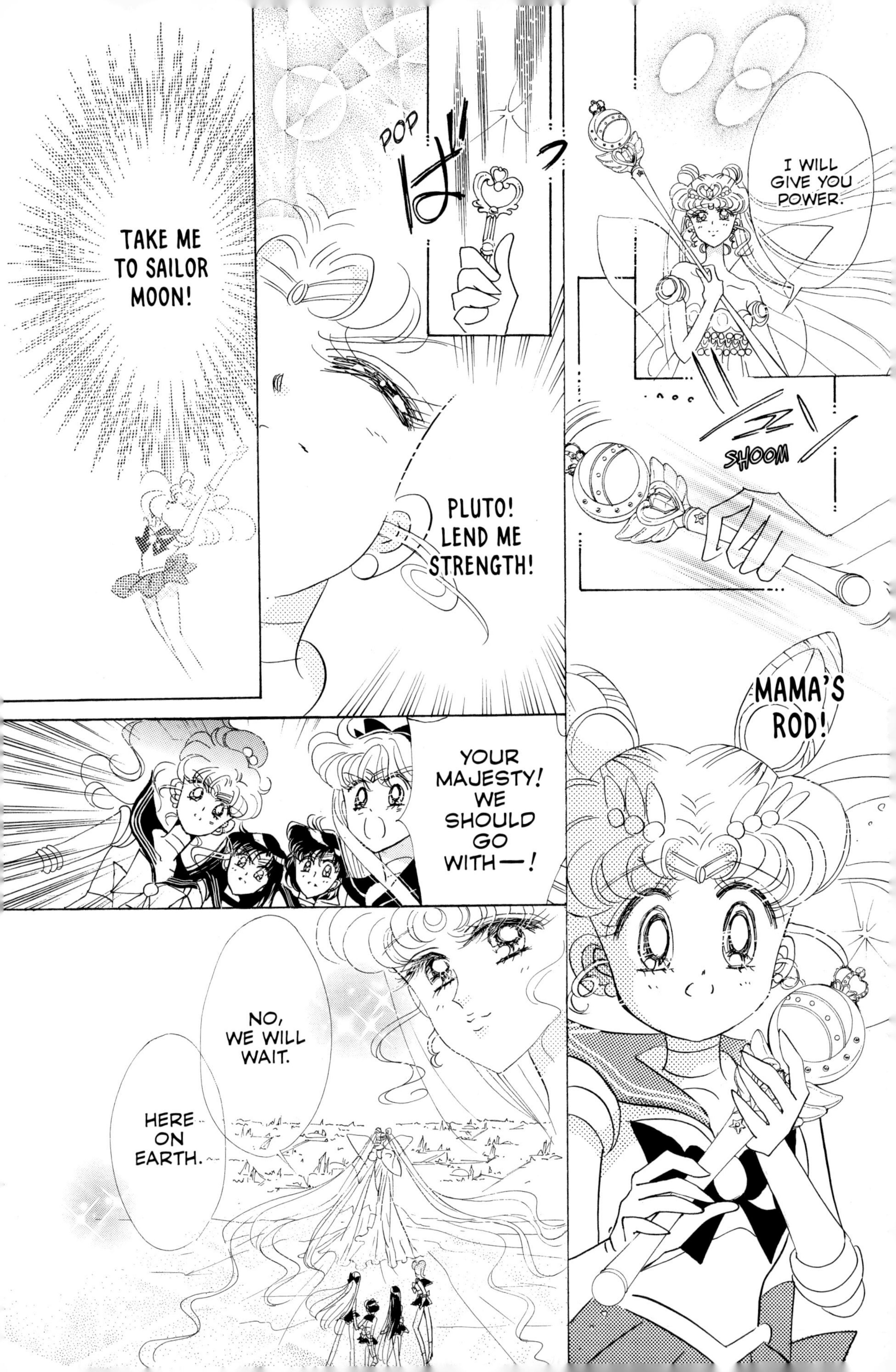
I WILL GIVE YOU POWER.
SHOOM
POP
ぱっ
PLUTO! LEND ME STRENGTH!
TAKE ME TO SAILOR MOON!
MAMA'S ROD!
YOUR MAJESTY! WE SHOULD GO WITH—!
NO, WE WILL WAIT.
HERE ON EARTH.

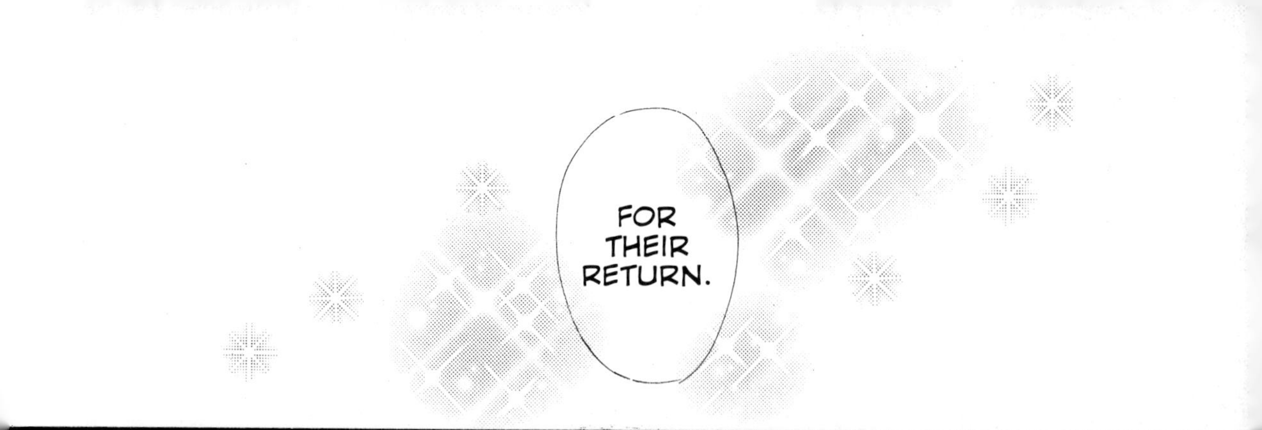
FOR THEIR RETURN.

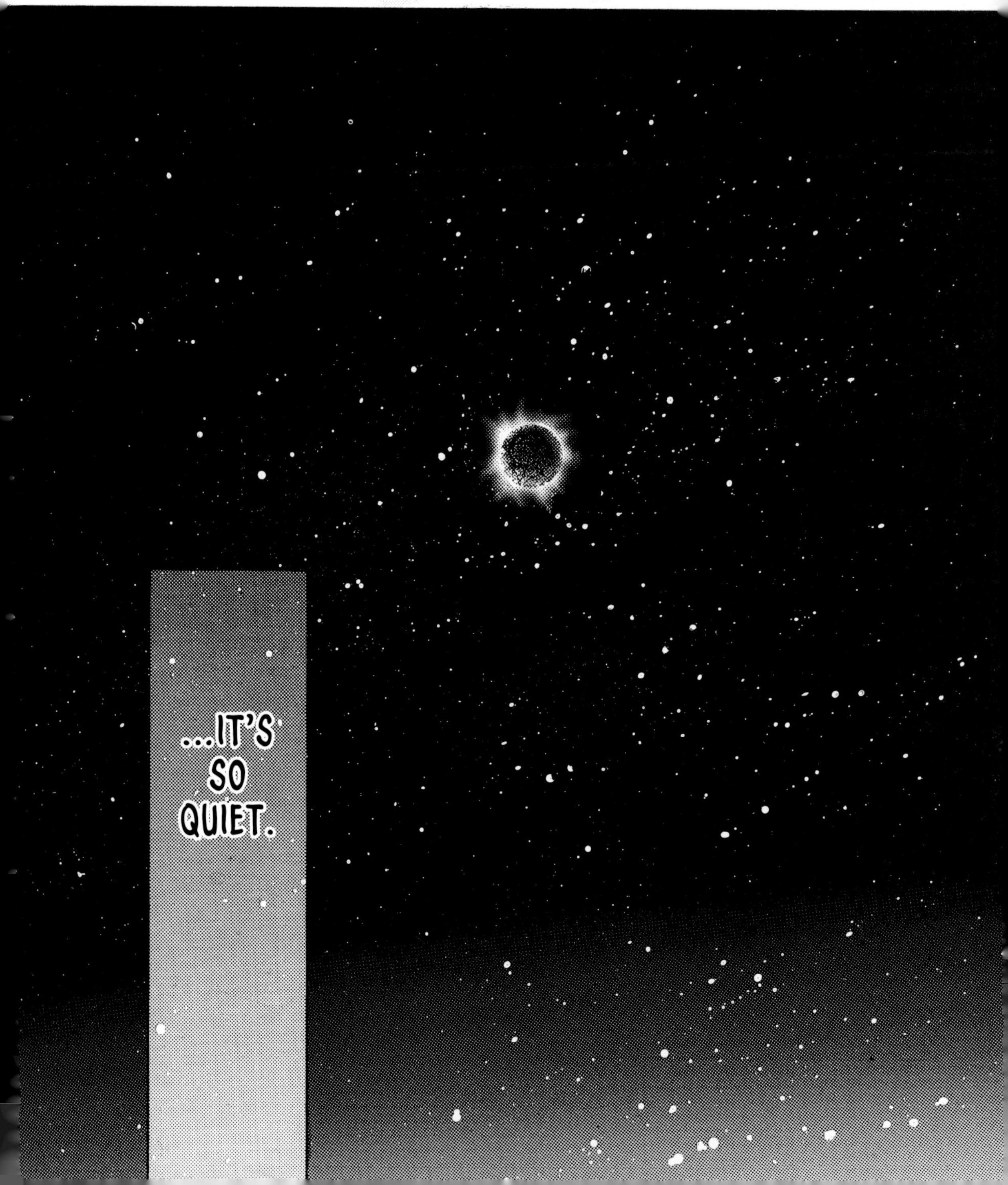
...IT'S SO QUIET.

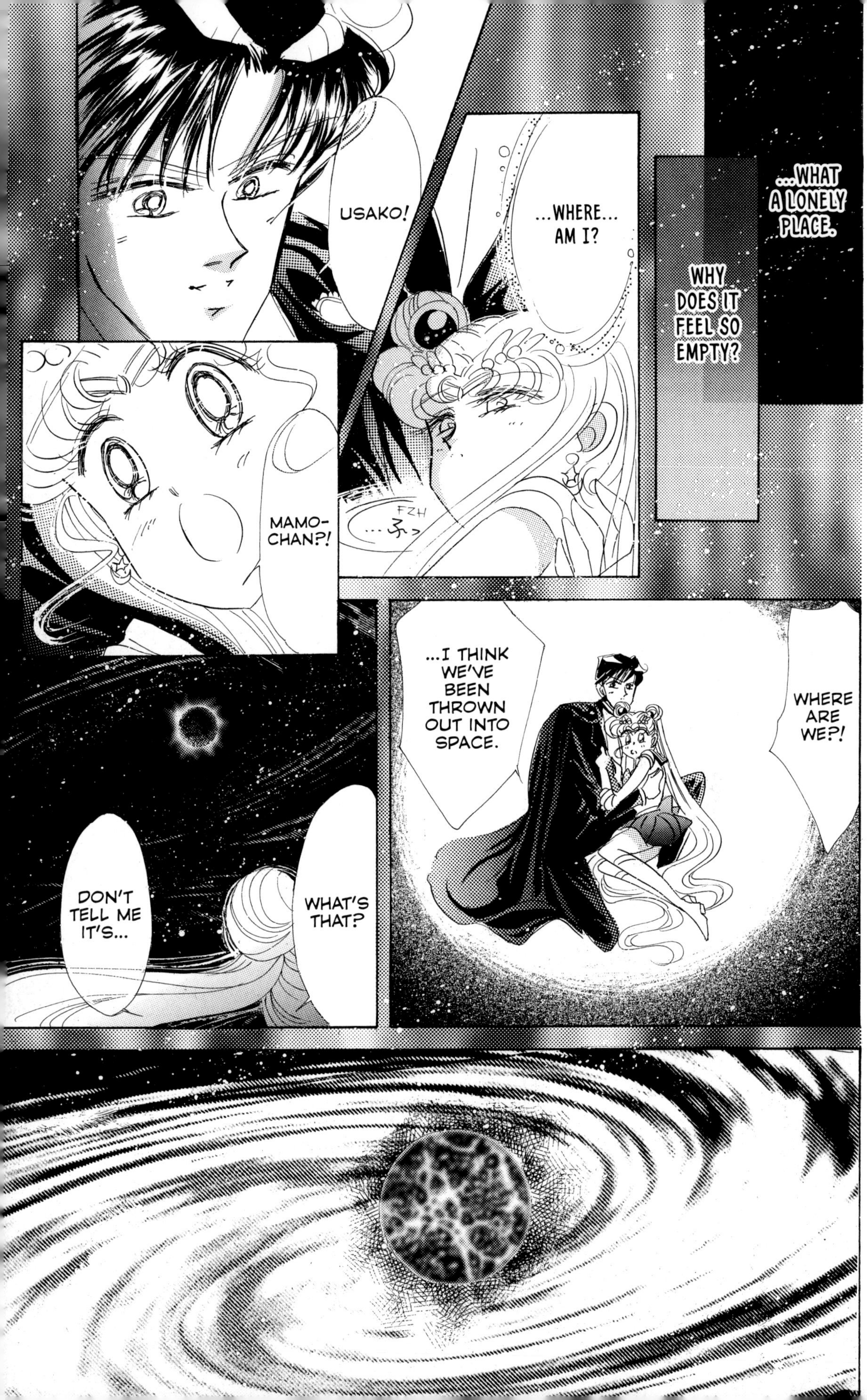
...WHAT A LONELY PLACE.
WHY DOES IT FEEL SO EMPTY?
...WHERE... AM I?
FZH
...ふっ
USAKO!
MAMO-CHAN?!
WHERE ARE WE?!
...I THINK WE'VE BEEN THROWN OUT INTO SPACE.
WHAT'S THAT?
DON'T TELL ME IT'S...

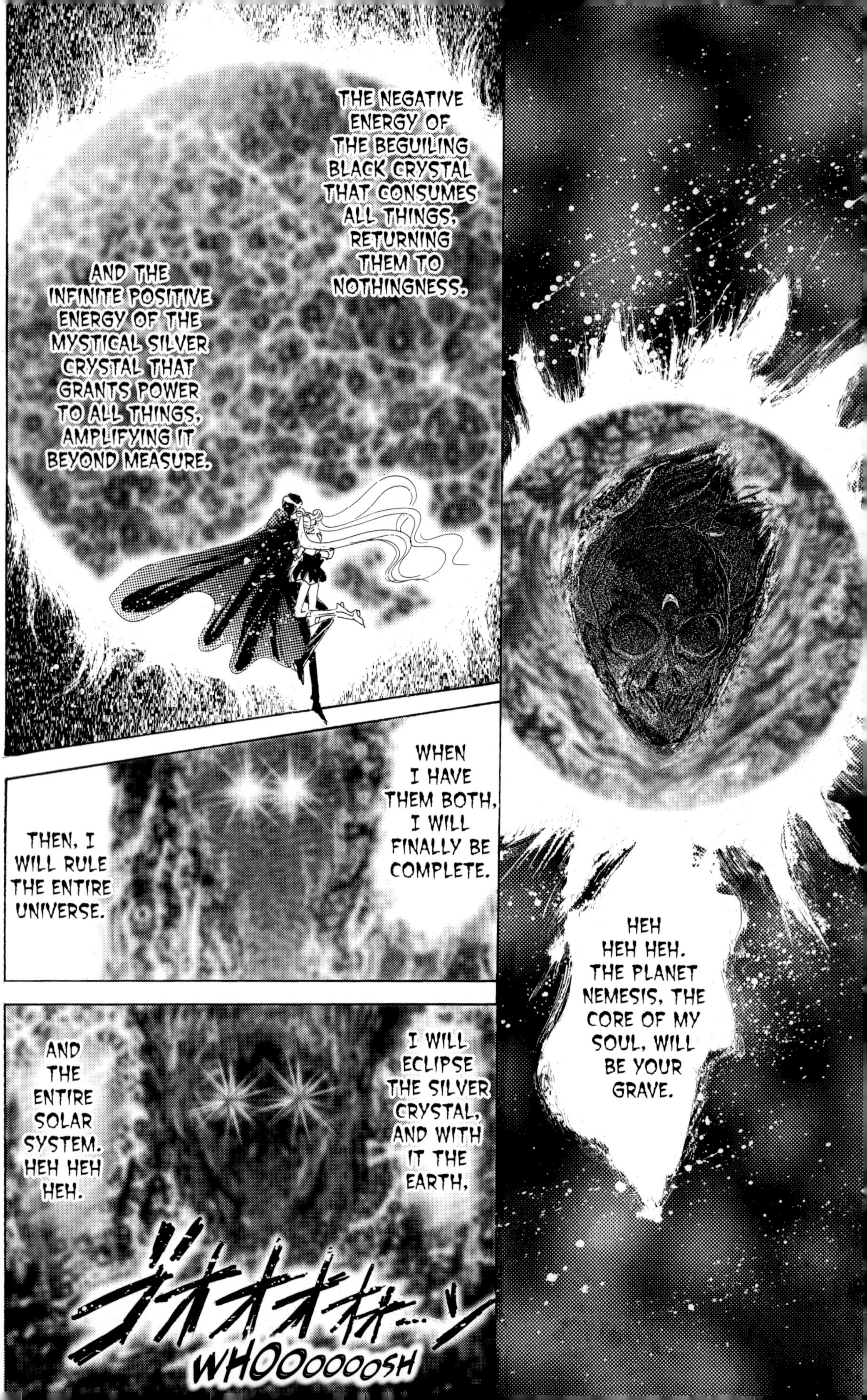

HEH HEH HEH. THE PLANET NEMESIS, THE CORE OF MY SOUL, WILL BE YOUR GRAVE.
THE NEGATIVE ENERGY OF THE BEGUILING BLACK CRYSTAL THAT CONSUMES ALL THINGS, RETURNING THEM TO NOTHINGNESS.
AND THE INFINITE POSITIVE ENERGY OF THE MYSTICAL SILVER CRYSTAL THAT GRANTS POWER TO ALL THINGS, AMPLIFYING IT BEYOND MEASURE.
WHEN I HAVE THEM BOTH, I WILL FINALLY BE COMPLETE.
THEN, I WILL RULE THE ENTIRE UNIVERSE.
I WILL ECLIPSE THE SILVER CRYSTAL, AND WITH IT THE EARTH,
AND THE ENTIRE SOLAR SYSTEM. HEH HEH HEH.
WHOOOOOOSH

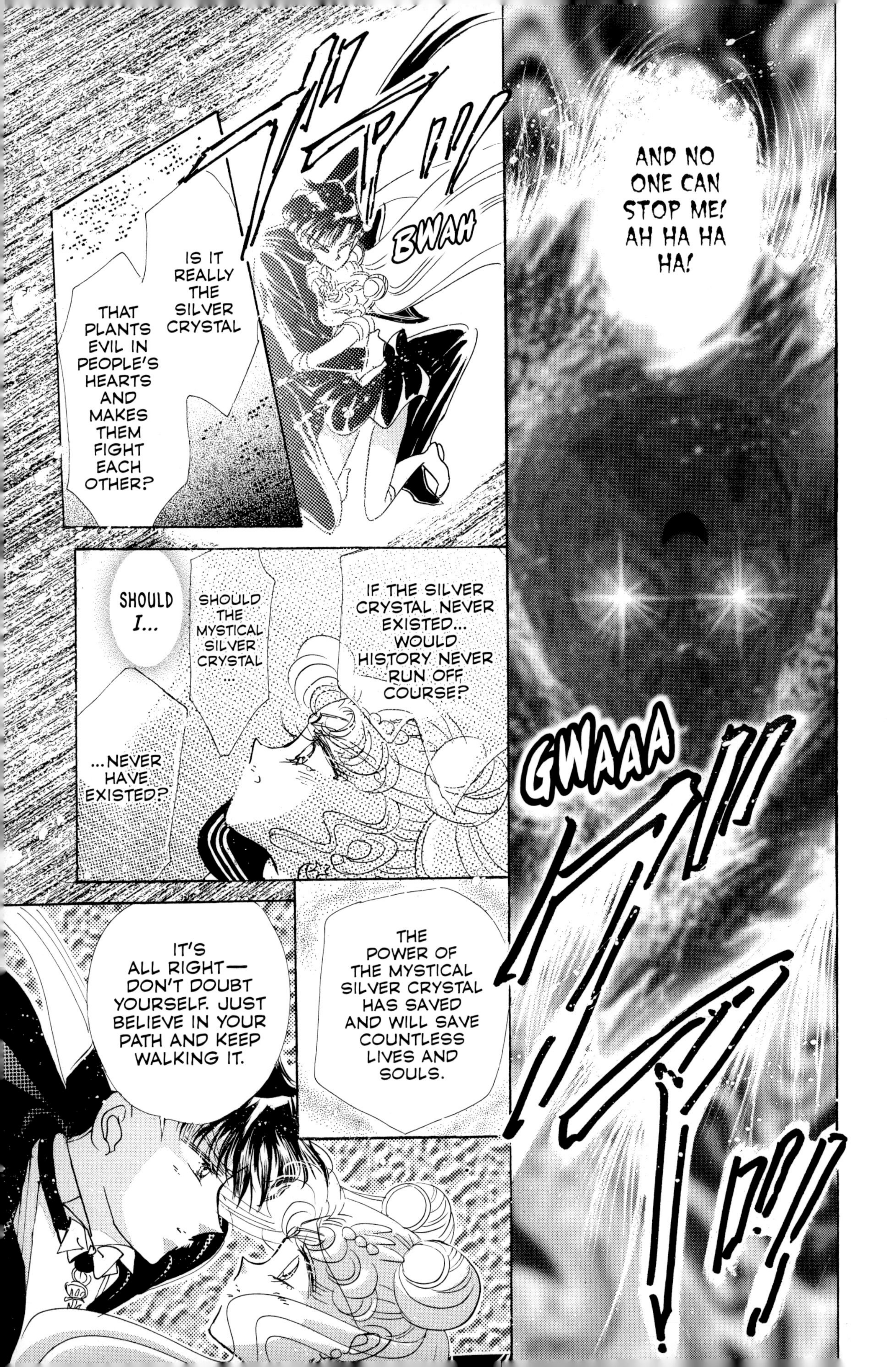
AND NO ONE CAN STOP ME! AH HA HA HA!
GWAAA
BWAH
IS IT REALLY THE SILVER CRYSTAL
THAT PLANTS EVIL IN PEOPLE'S HEARTS AND MAKES THEM FIGHT EACH OTHER?
IF THE SILVER CRYSTAL NEVER EXISTED... WOULD HISTORY NEVER RUN OFF COURSE?
SHOULD THE MYSTICAL SILVER CRYSTAL ...
SHOULD I...
...NEVER HAVE EXISTED?
THE POWER OF THE MYSTICAL SILVER CRYSTAL HAS SAVED AND WILL SAVE COUNTLESS LIVES AND SOULS.
IT'S ALL RIGHT—DON'T DOUBT YOURSELF. JUST BELIEVE IN YOUR PATH AND KEEP WALKING IT.

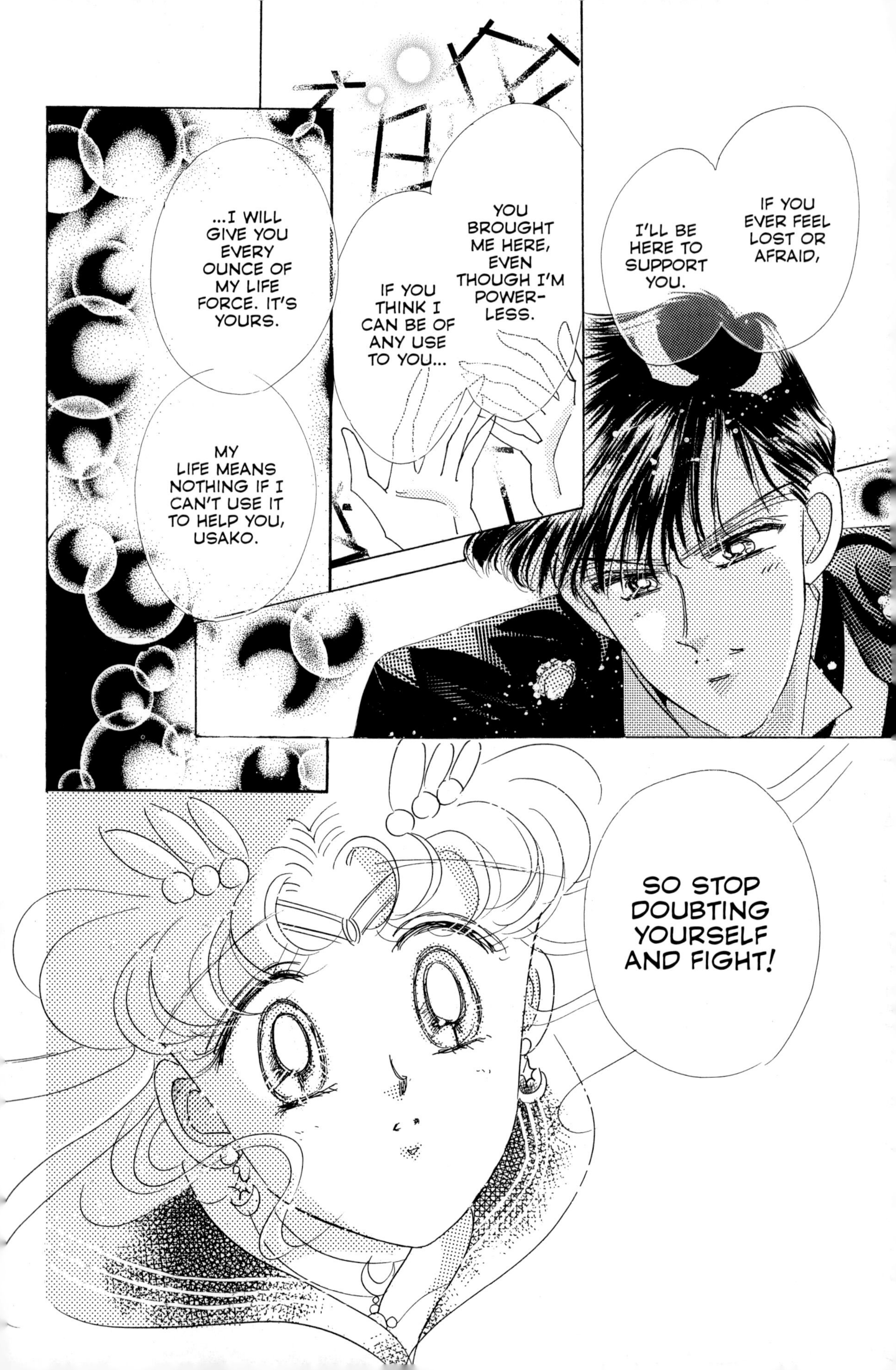
IF YOU EVER FEEL LOST OR AFRAID,
I'LL BE HERE TO SUPPORT YOU.
YOU BROUGHT ME HERE, EVEN THOUGH I'M POWER-LESS.
IF YOU THINK I CAN BE OF ANY USE TO YOU...
...I WILL GIVE YOU EVERY OUNCE OF MY LIFE FORCE. IT'S YOURS.
MY LIFE MEANS NOTHING IF I CAN'T USE IT TO HELP YOU, USAKO.
SO STOP DOUBTING YOURSELF AND FIGHT!

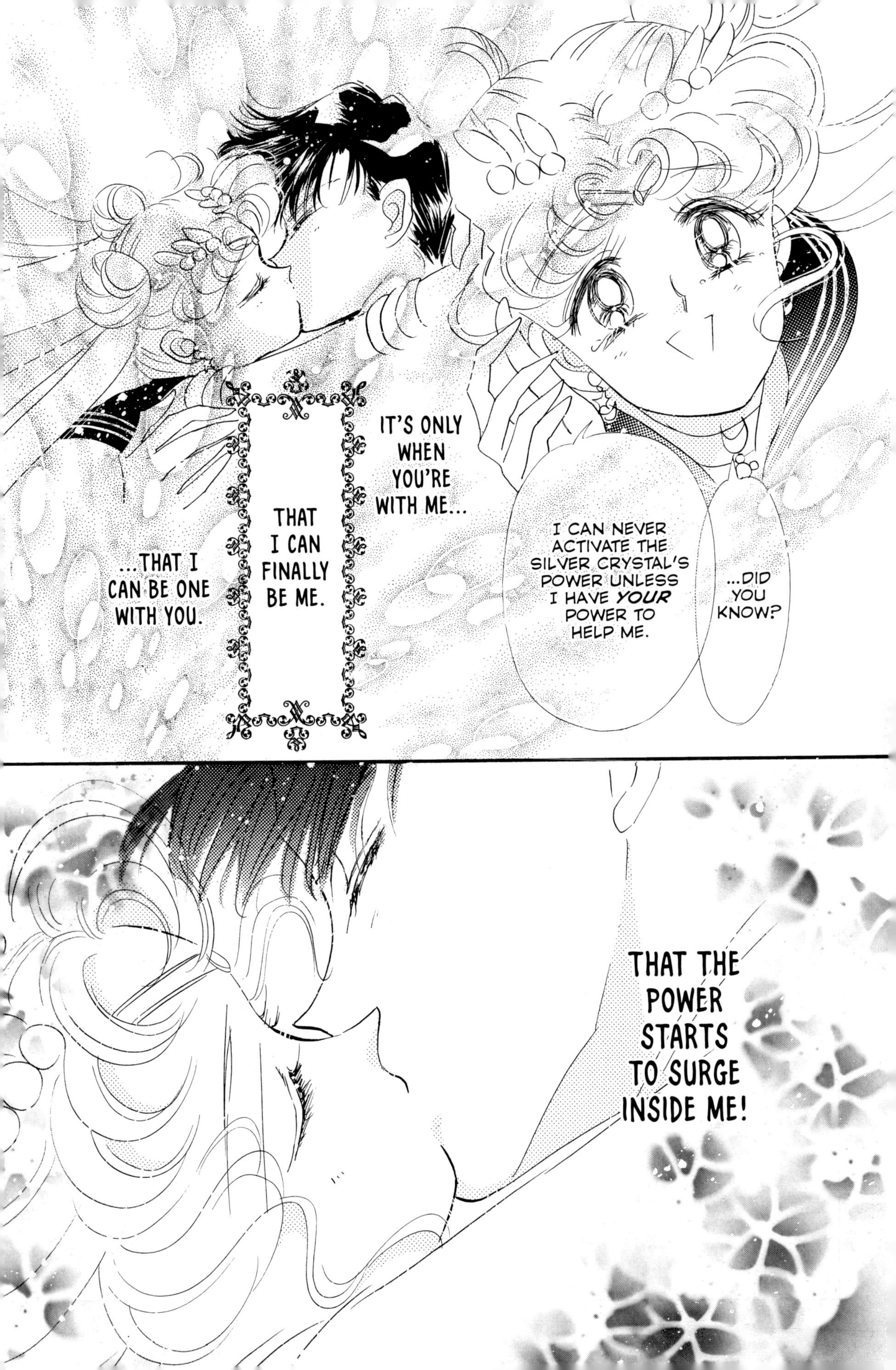
I CAN NEVER ACTIVATE THE SILVER CRYSTAL'S POWER UNLESS I HAVE *YOUR* POWER TO HELP ME.
...DID YOU KNOW?
IT'S ONLY WHEN YOU'RE WITH ME...
THAT I CAN FINALLY BE ME.
...THAT I CAN BE ONE WITH YOU.
THAT THE POWER STARTS TO SURGE INSIDE ME!

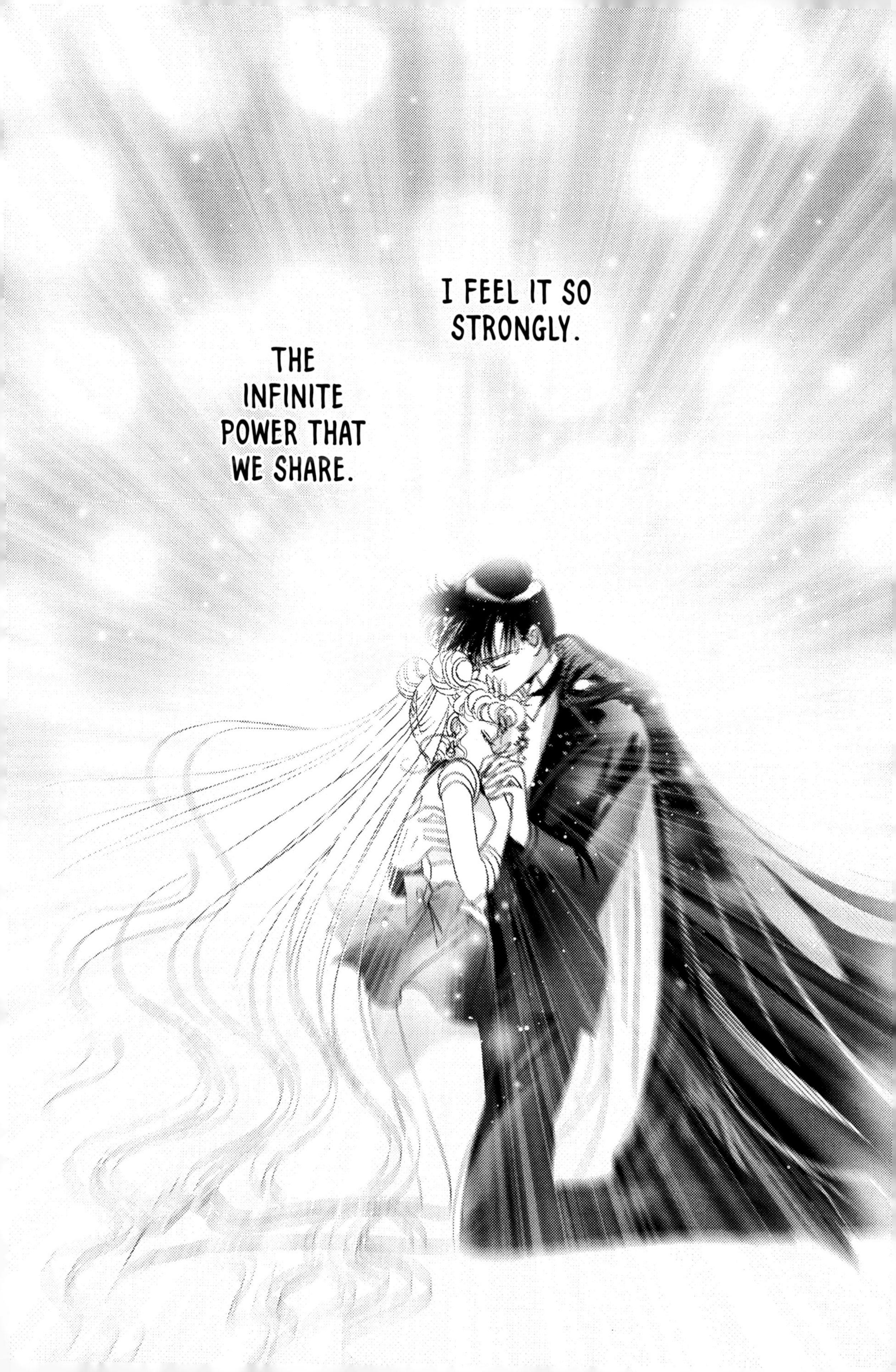
I FEEL IT SO STRONGLY.
THE INFINITE POWER THAT WE SHARE.

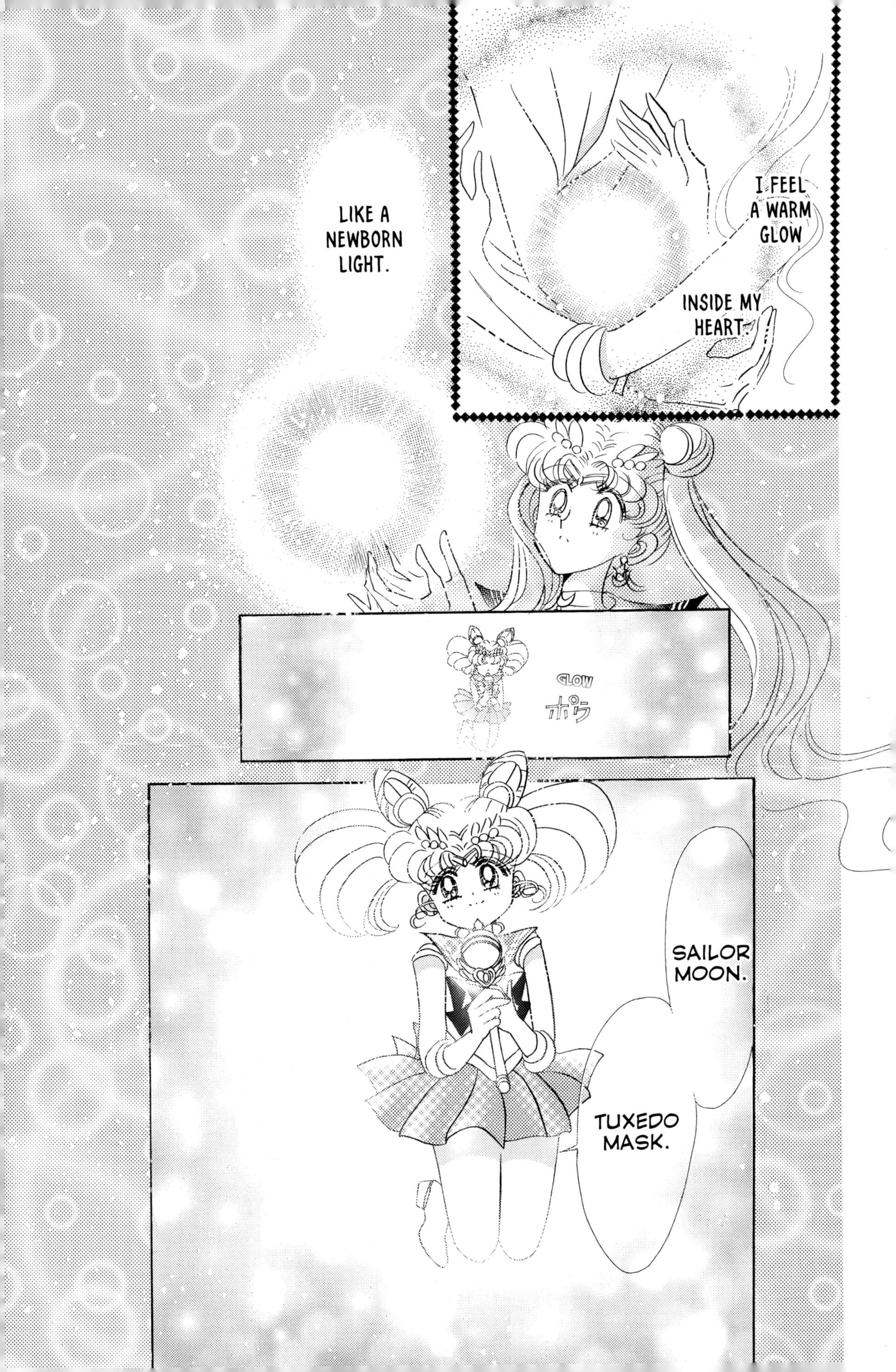
I FEEL A WARM GLOW
INSIDE MY HEART.
LIKE A NEWBORN LIGHT.
GLOW
ポウ
SAILOR MOON.
TUXEDO MASK.

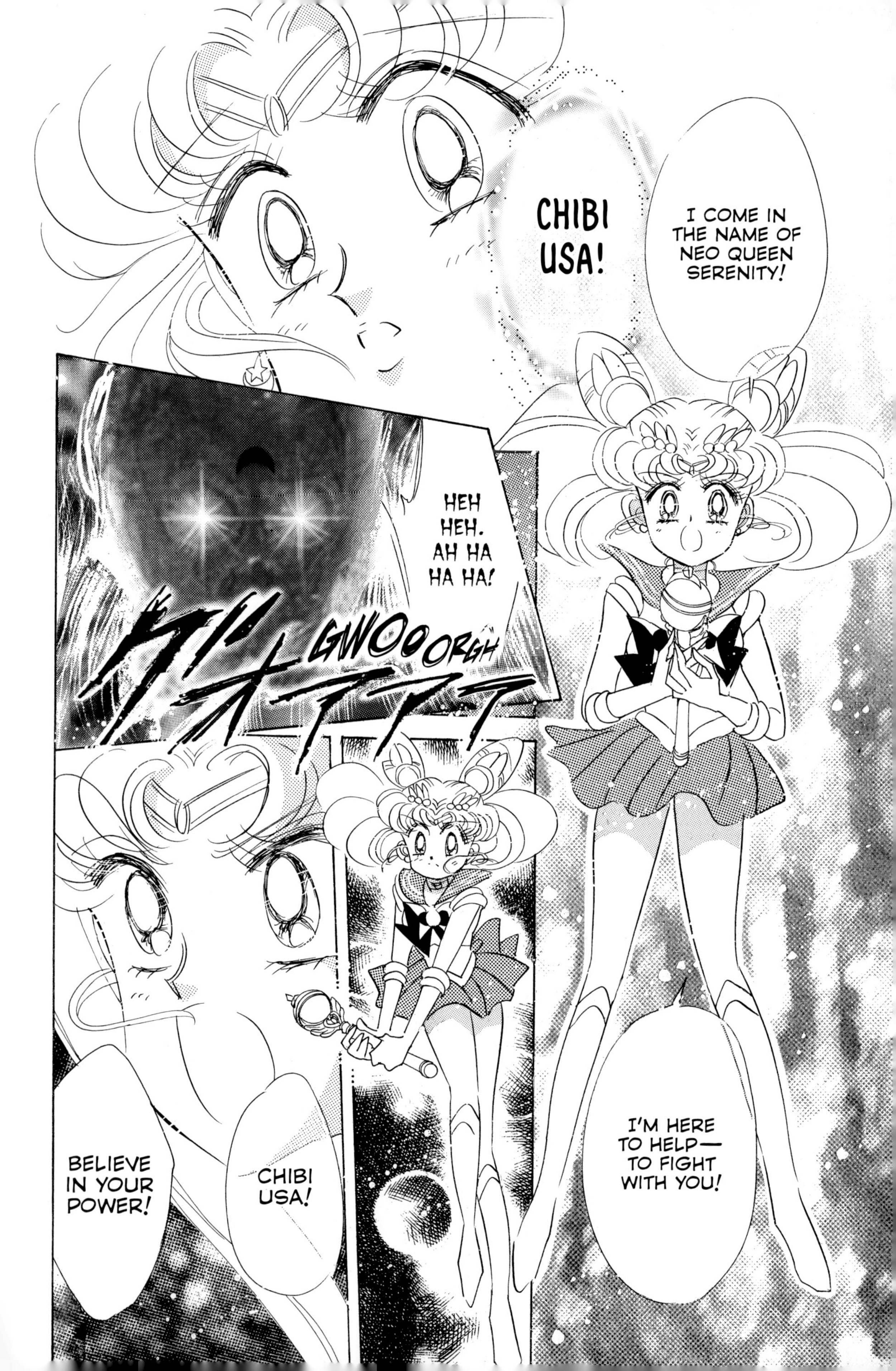

CHIBI USA!
I COME IN THE NAME OF NEO QUEEN SERENITY!
I'M HERE TO HELP— TO FIGHT WITH YOU!
HEH HEH. AH HA HA HA!
GWOOOORGH
CHIBI USA!
BELIEVE IN YOUR POWER!

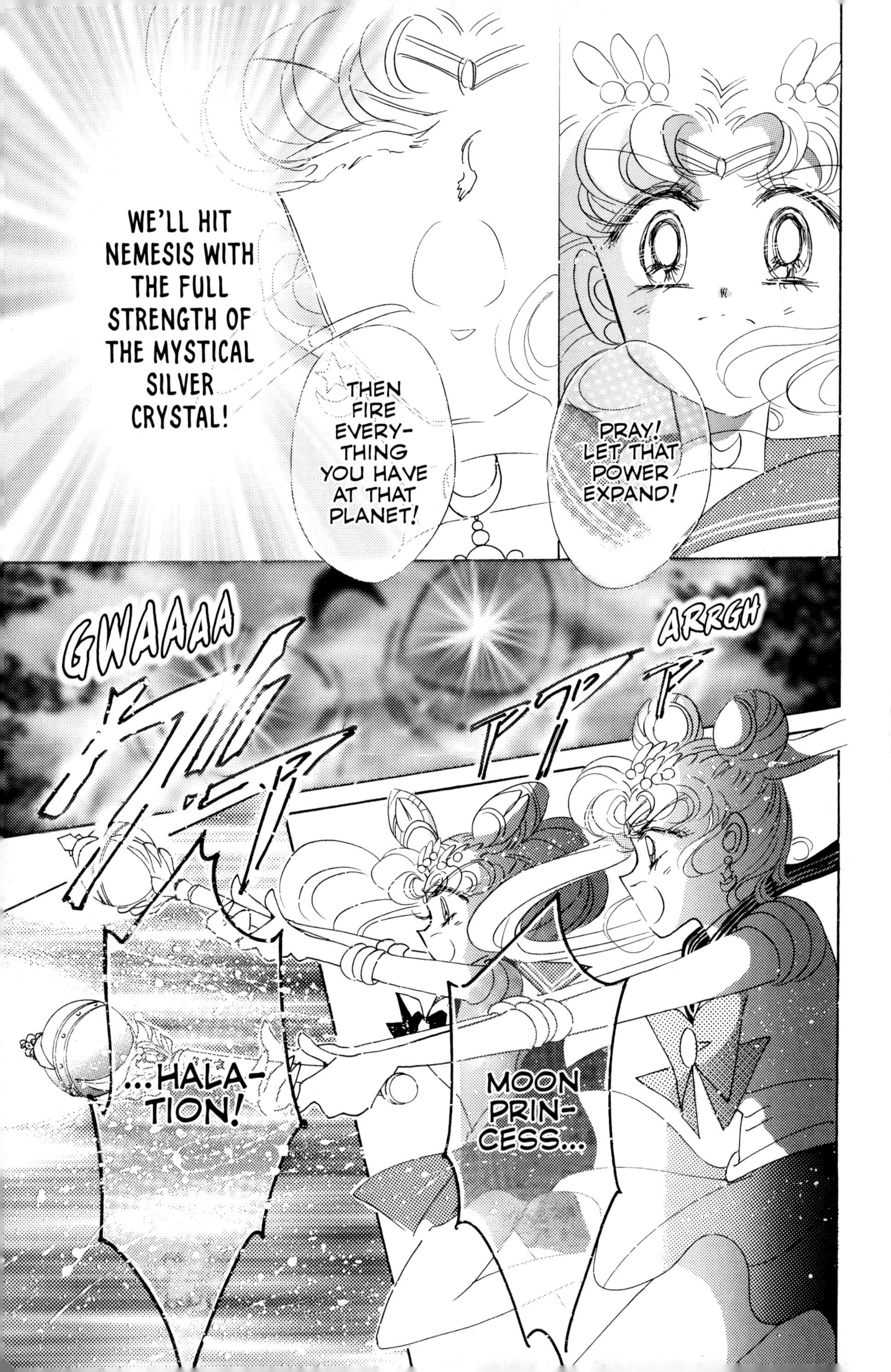
PRAY! LET THAT POWER EXPAND!
WE'LL HIT NEMESIS WITH THE FULL STRENGTH OF THE MYSTICAL SILVER CRYSTAL!
THEN FIRE EVERY-THING YOU HAVE AT THAT PLANET!
ARRGH
GWAAAA
MOON PRIN-CESS...
...HALA-TION!

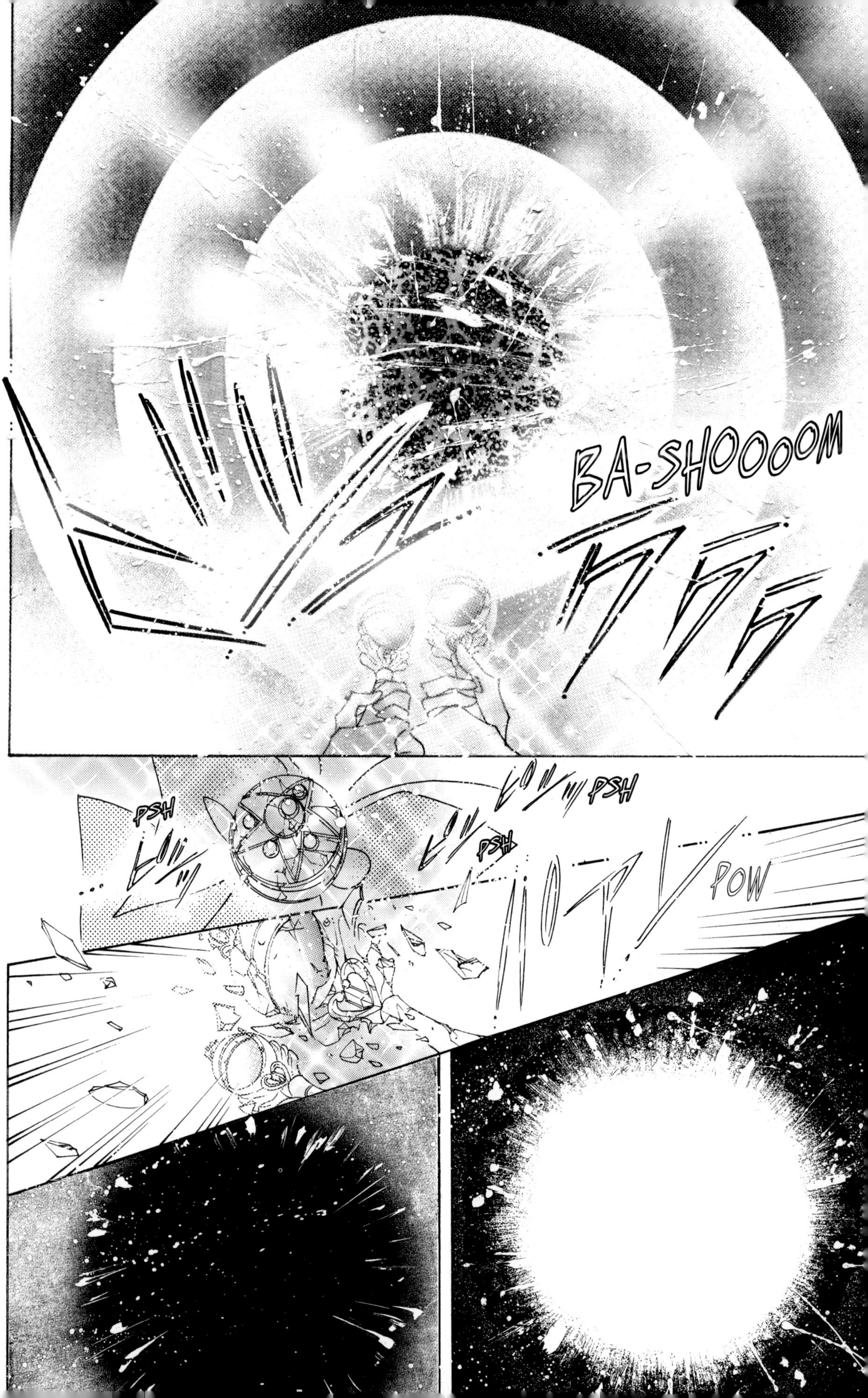
BA-SHOOOOM
PSH
POW
PSH
PSH

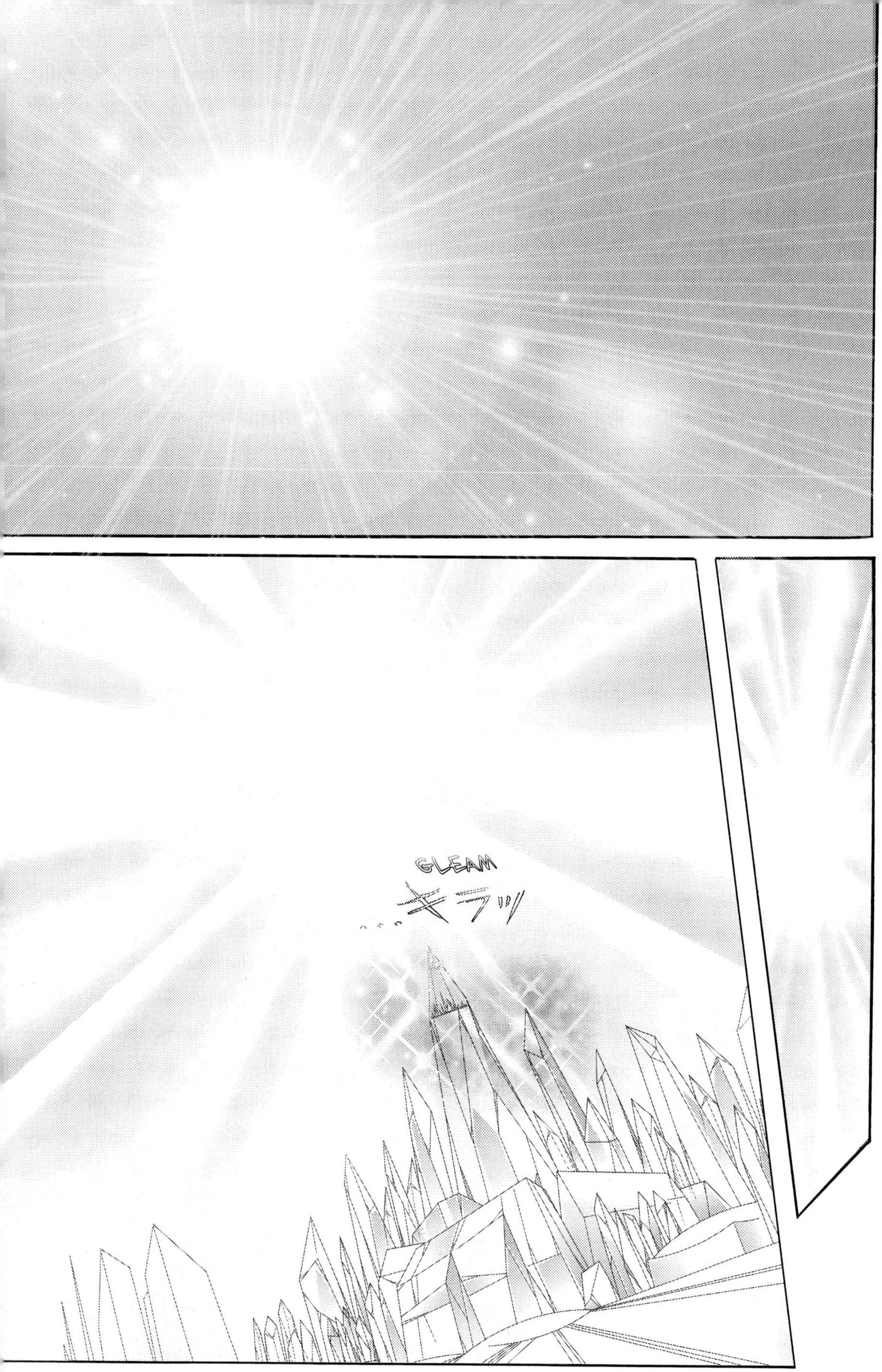
GLEAM
キラッ

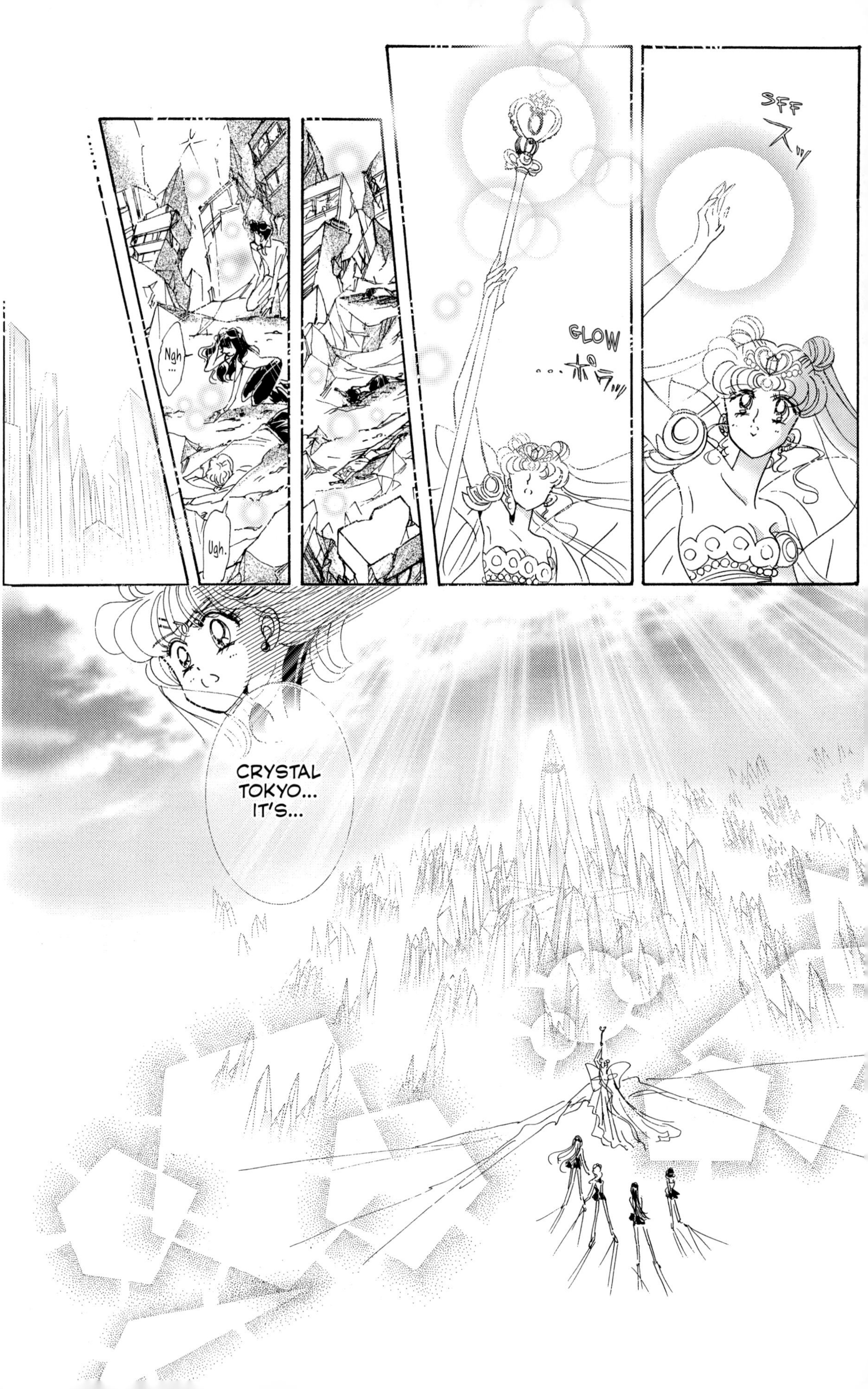
SFF
スッ
GLOW
...ポウッ
Ngh...
Ugh.
CRYSTAL TOKYO... IT'S...

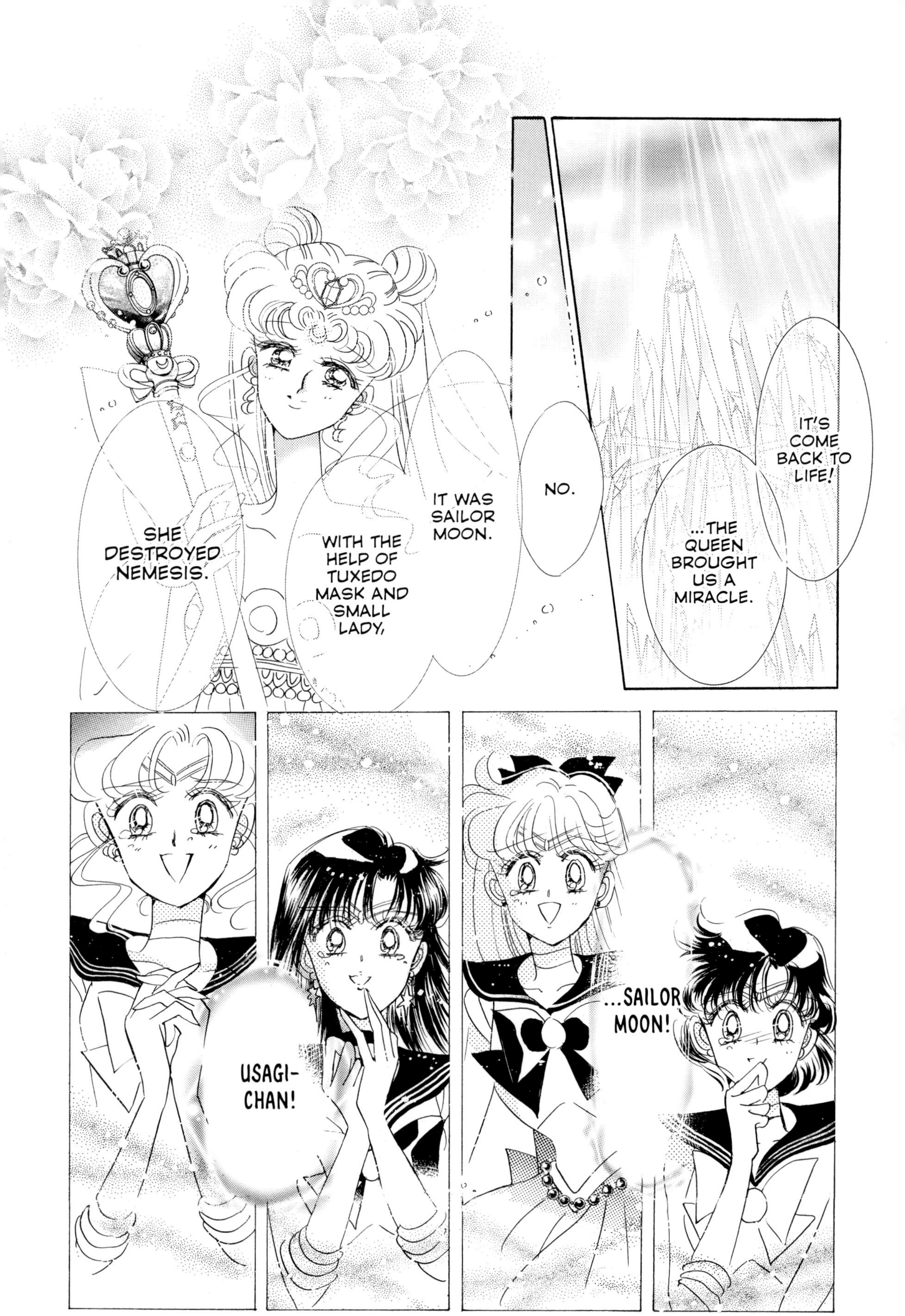
IT'S COME BACK TO LIFE!
...THE QUEEN BROUGHT US A MIRACLE.
NO.
IT WAS SAILOR MOON.
WITH THE HELP OF TUXEDO MASK AND SMALL LADY,
SHE DESTROYED NEMESIS.
...SAILOR MOON!
USAGI-CHAN!

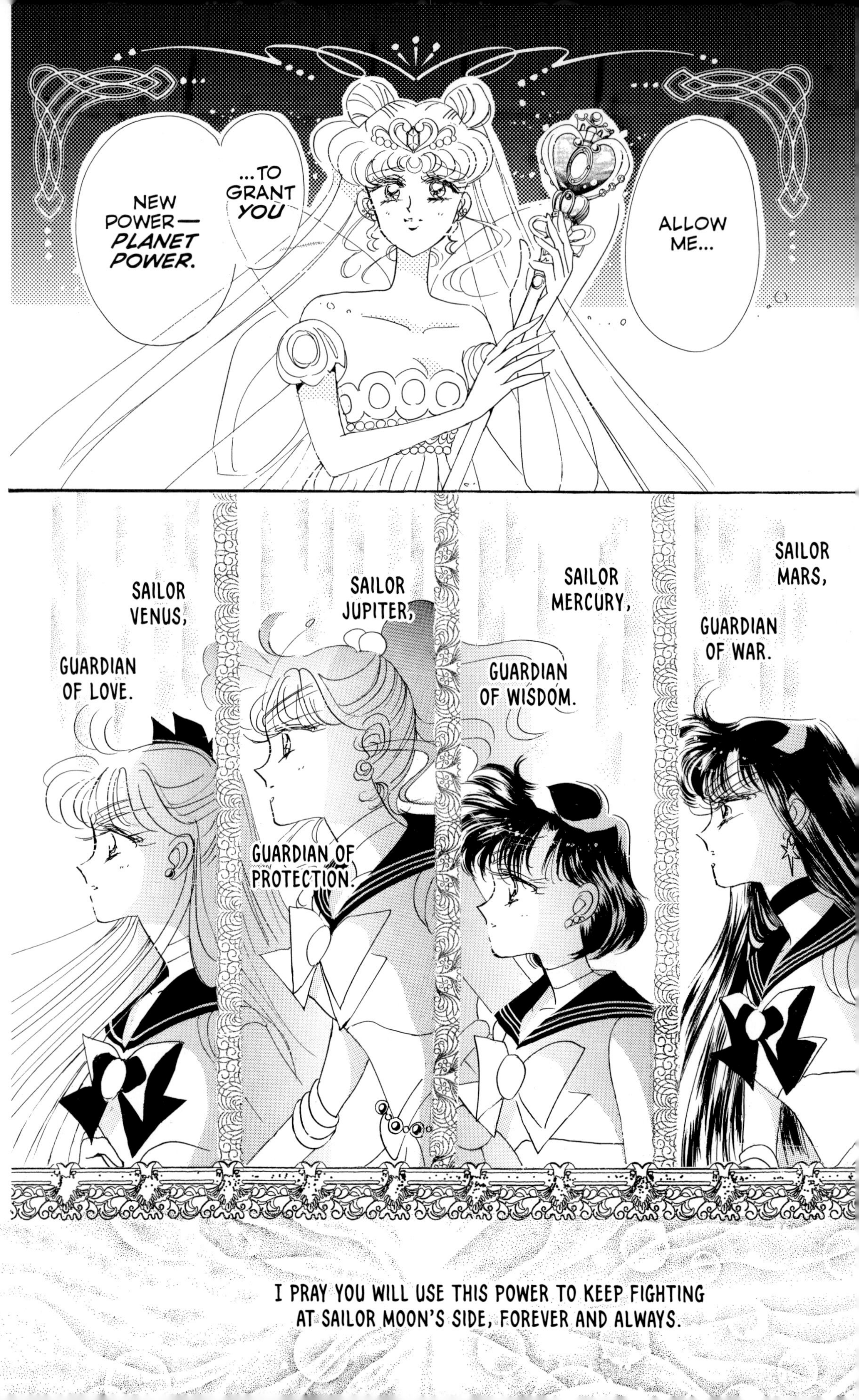
ALLOW ME...
...TO GRANT *YOU*
NEW POWER—*PLANET POWER.*
SAILOR MARS,
GUARDIAN OF WAR.
SAILOR MERCURY,
GUARDIAN OF WISDOM.
SAILOR JUPITER,
GUARDIAN OF PROTECTION.
SAILOR VENUS,
GUARDIAN OF LOVE.
I PRAY YOU WILL USE THIS POWER TO KEEP FIGHTING AT SAILOR MOON'S SIDE, FOREVER AND ALWAYS.

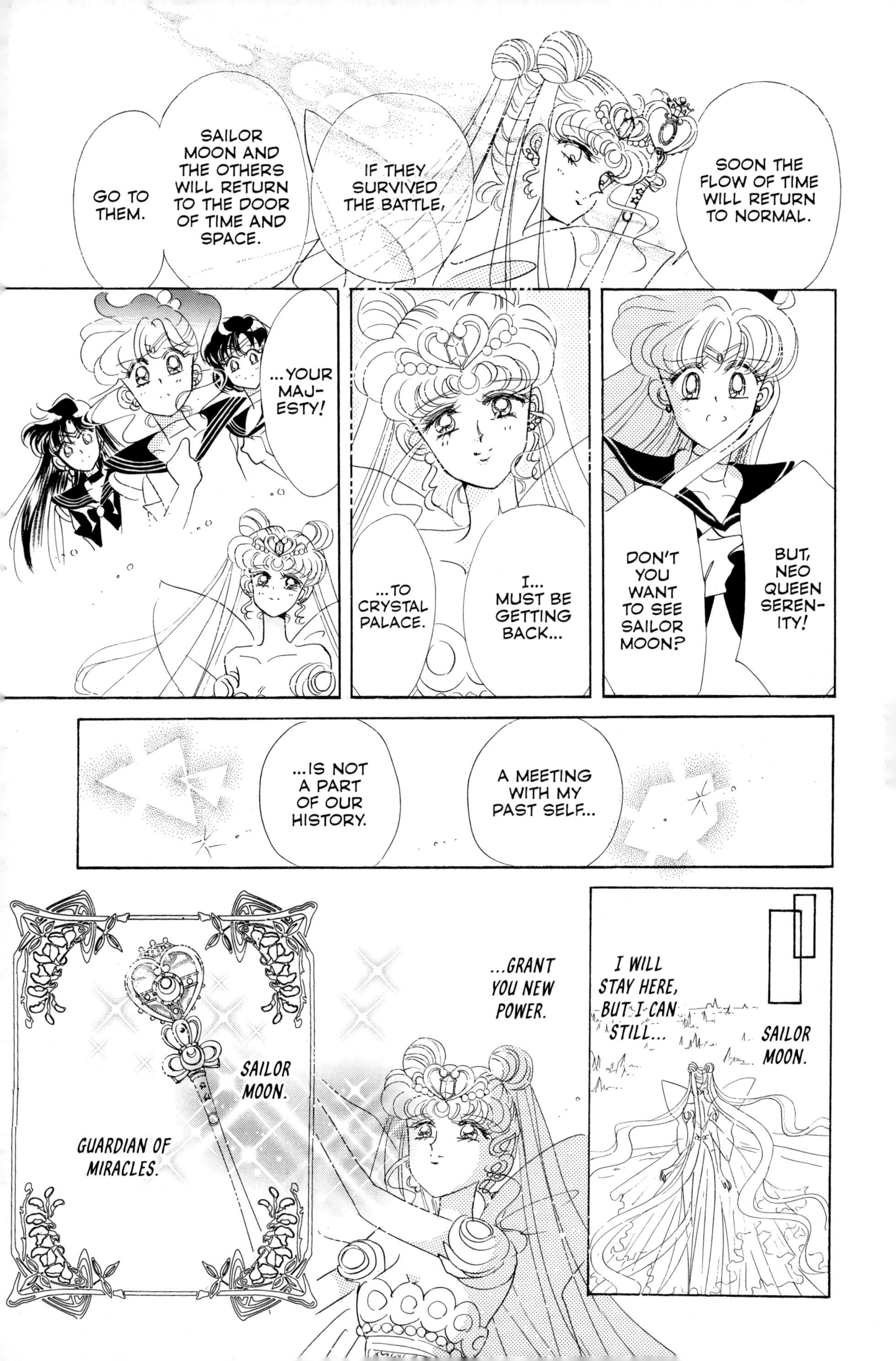
SOON THE FLOW OF TIME WILL RETURN TO NORMAL.
IF THEY SURVIVED THE BATTLE,
SAILOR MOON AND THE OTHERS WILL RETURN TO THE DOOR OF TIME AND SPACE.
GO TO THEM.
BUT, NEO QUEEN SERENITY!
DON'T YOU WANT TO SEE SAILOR MOON?
I... MUST BE GETTING BACK...
...TO CRYSTAL PALACE.
...YOUR MAJESTY!
A MEETING WITH MY PAST SELF...
...IS NOT A PART OF OUR HISTORY.
SAILOR MOON.
I WILL STAY HERE, BUT I CAN STILL...
...GRANT YOU NEW POWER.
SAILOR MOON.
GUARDIAN OF MIRACLES.

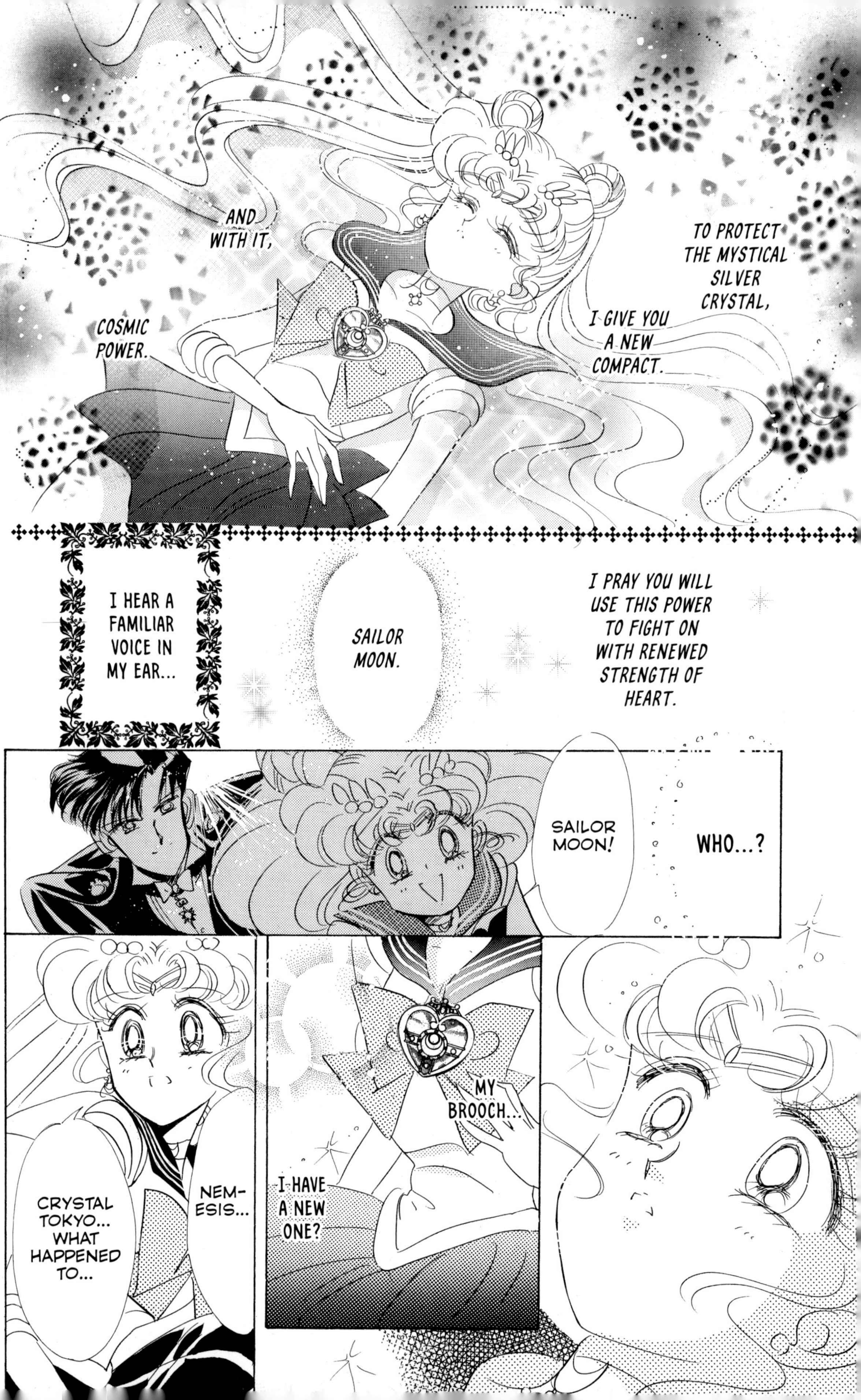
TO PROTECT THE MYSTICAL SILVER CRYSTAL,
I GIVE YOU A NEW COMPACT.
AND WITH IT,
COSMIC POWER.
I PRAY YOU WILL USE THIS POWER TO FIGHT ON WITH RENEWED STRENGTH OF HEART.
SAILOR MOON.
I HEAR A FAMILIAR VOICE IN MY EAR...
WHO...?
SAILOR MOON!
MY BROOCH...
I HAVE A NEW ONE?
NEM-ESIS...
CRYSTAL TOKYO... WHAT HAPPENED TO...

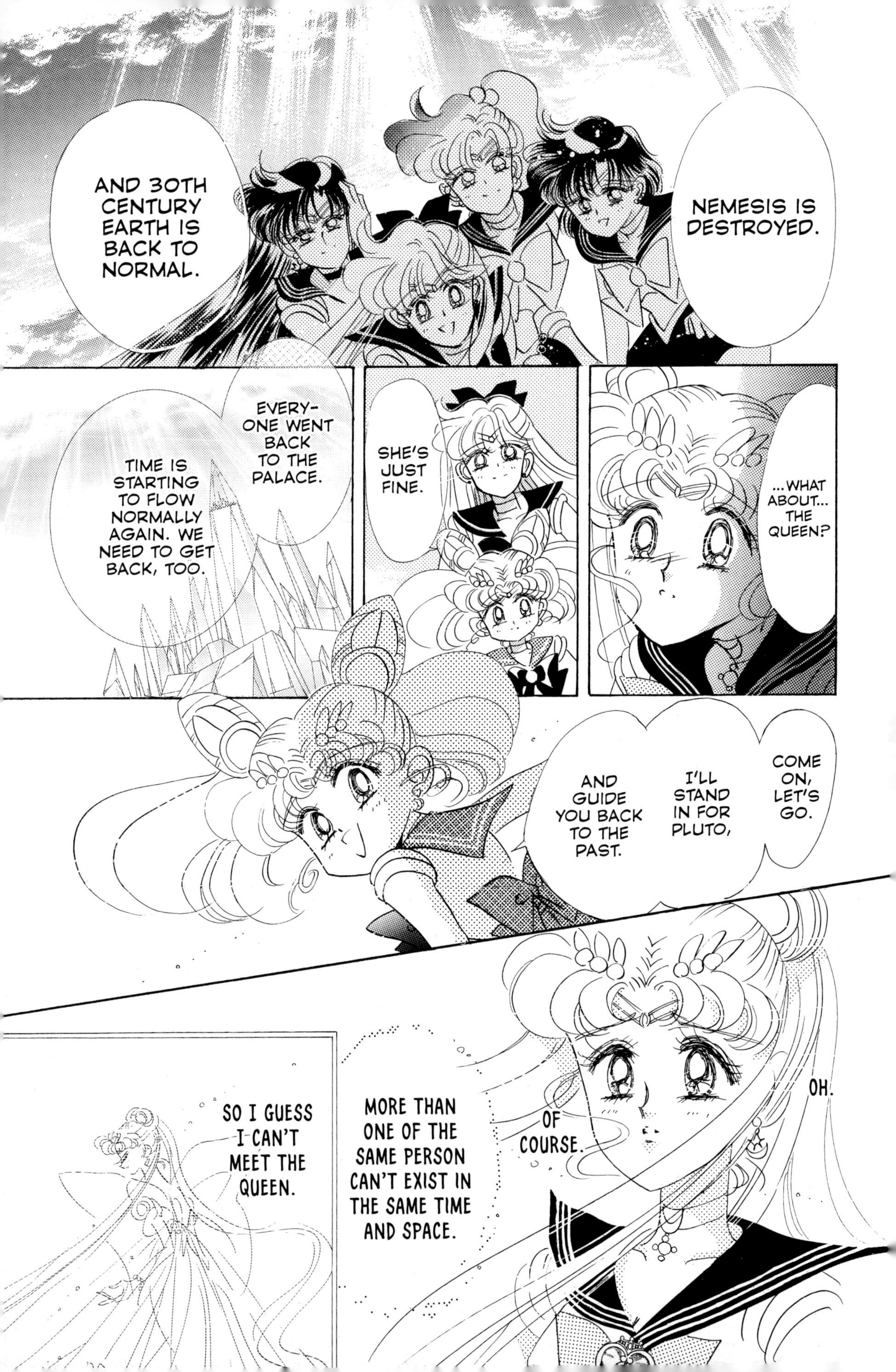
NEMESIS IS DESTROYED.
AND 30TH CENTURY EARTH IS BACK TO NORMAL.
...WHAT ABOUT... THE QUEEN?
SHE'S JUST FINE.
EVERY-ONE WENT BACK TO THE PALACE.
TIME IS STARTING TO FLOW NORMALLY AGAIN. WE NEED TO GET BACK, TOO.
COME ON, LET'S GO.
I'LL STAND IN FOR PLUTO,
AND GUIDE YOU BACK TO THE PAST.
OH.
OF COURSE.
MORE THAN ONE OF THE SAME PERSON CAN'T EXIST IN THE SAME TIME AND SPACE.
SO I GUESS I CAN'T MEET THE QUEEN.

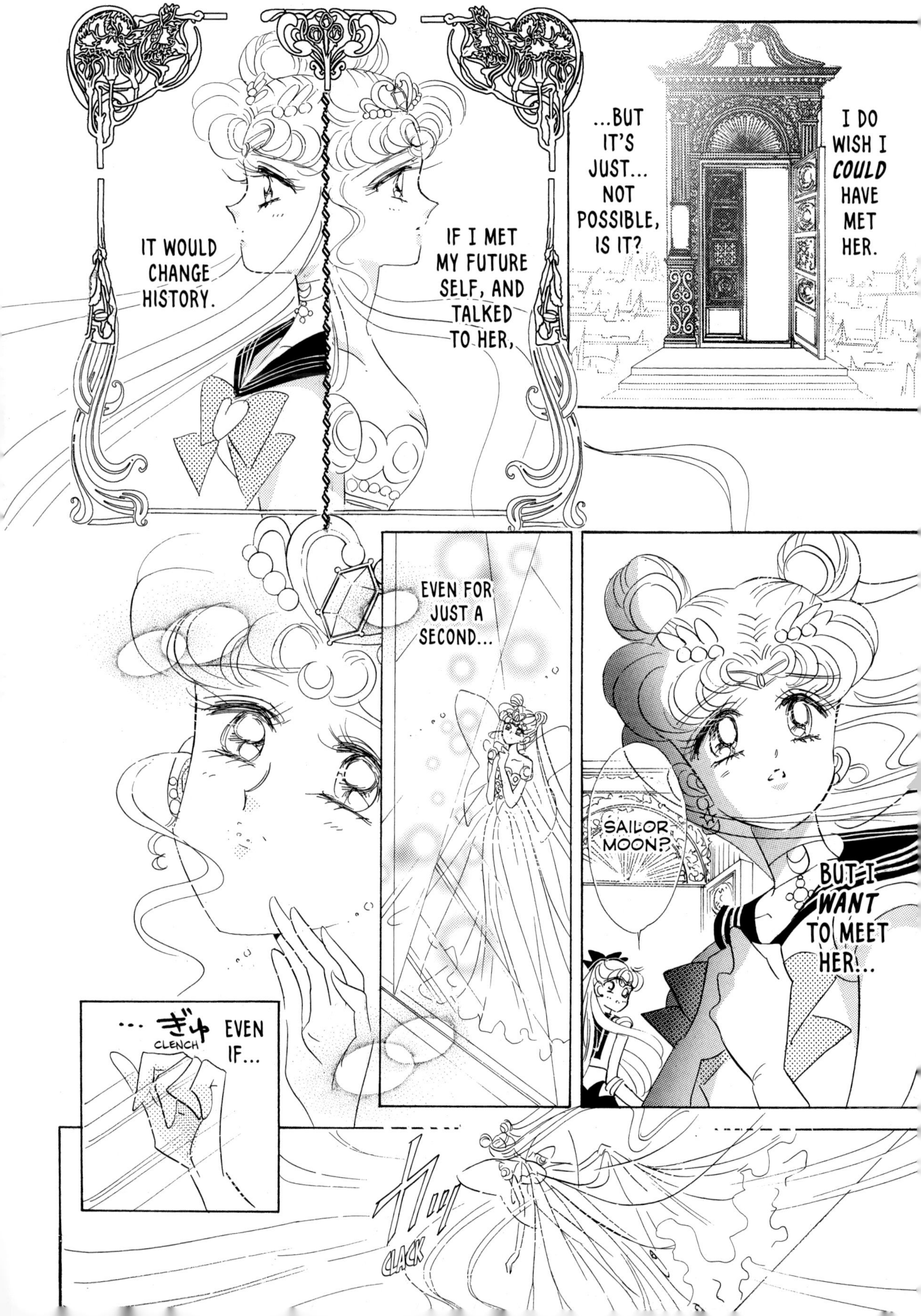
I DO WISH I COULD HAVE MET HER.
...BUT IT'S JUST... NOT POSSIBLE, IS IT?
IF I MET MY FUTURE SELF, AND TALKED TO HER,
IT WOULD CHANGE HISTORY.
SAILOR MOON?
BUT I WANT TO MEET HER...
EVEN FOR JUST A SECOND...
... EVEN IF...
ぎゅ
CLENCH
カッ
CLACK

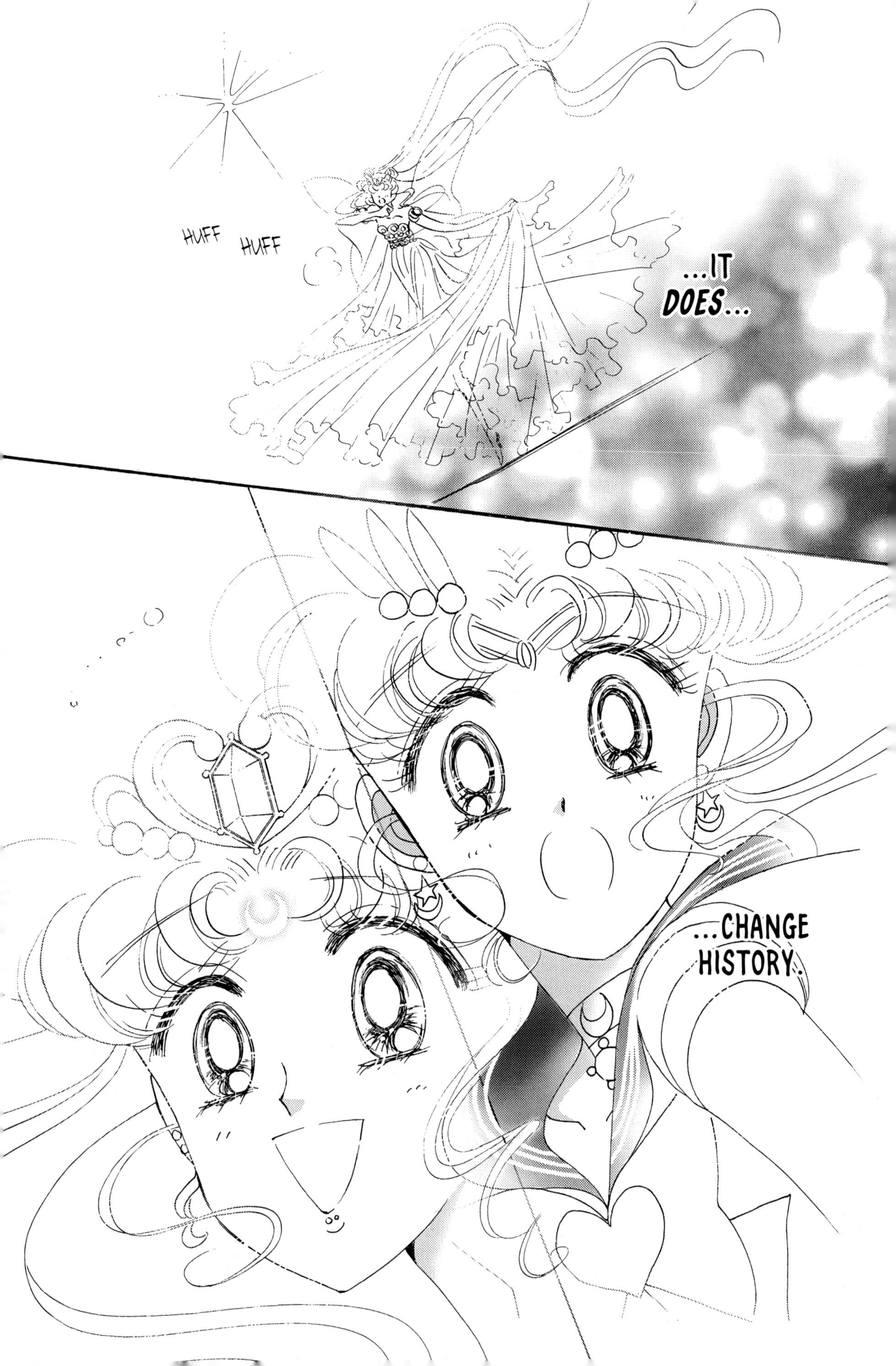
...IT DOES...
HUFF HUFF
...CHANGE HISTORY.

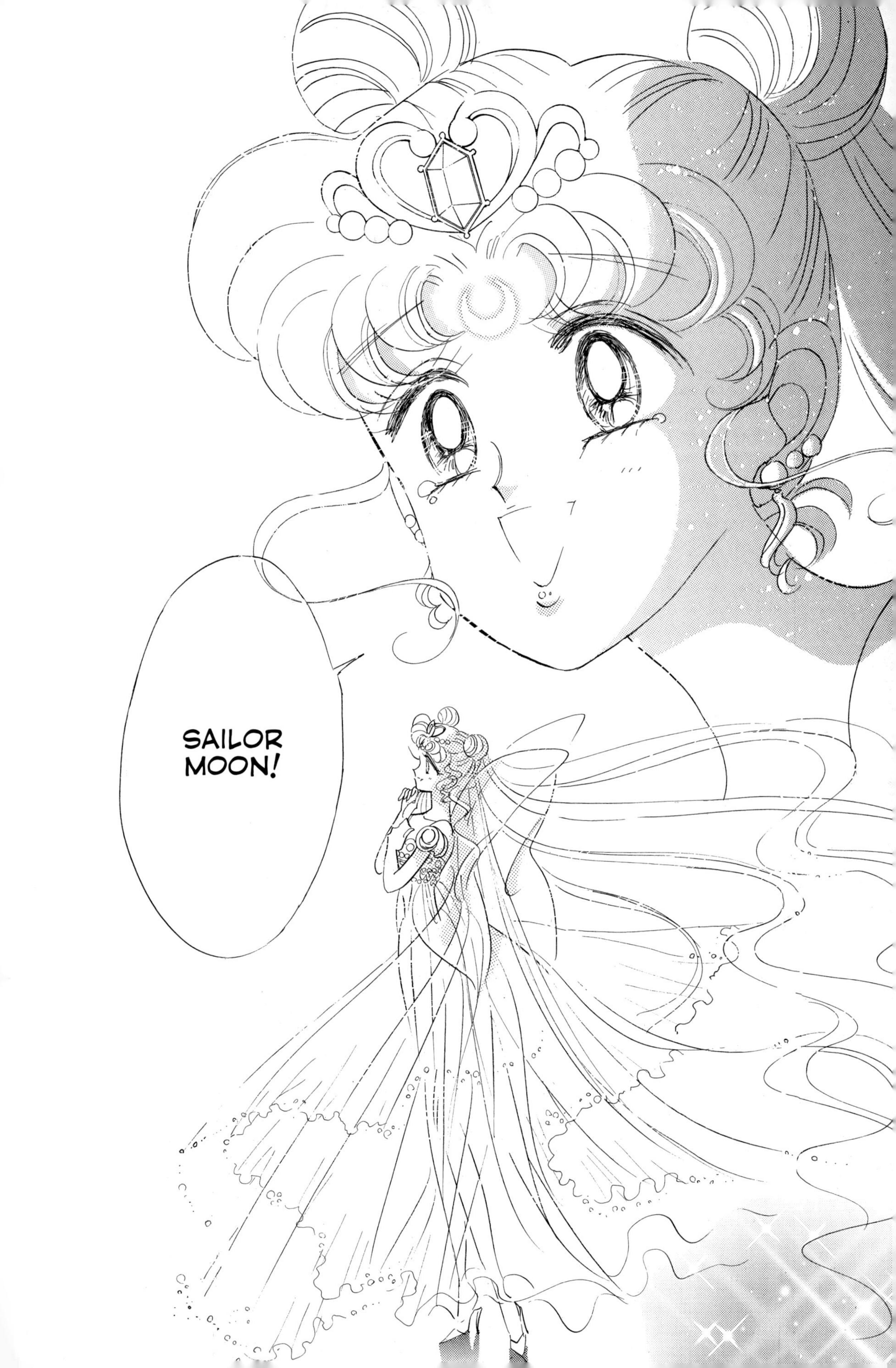
SAILOR MOON!

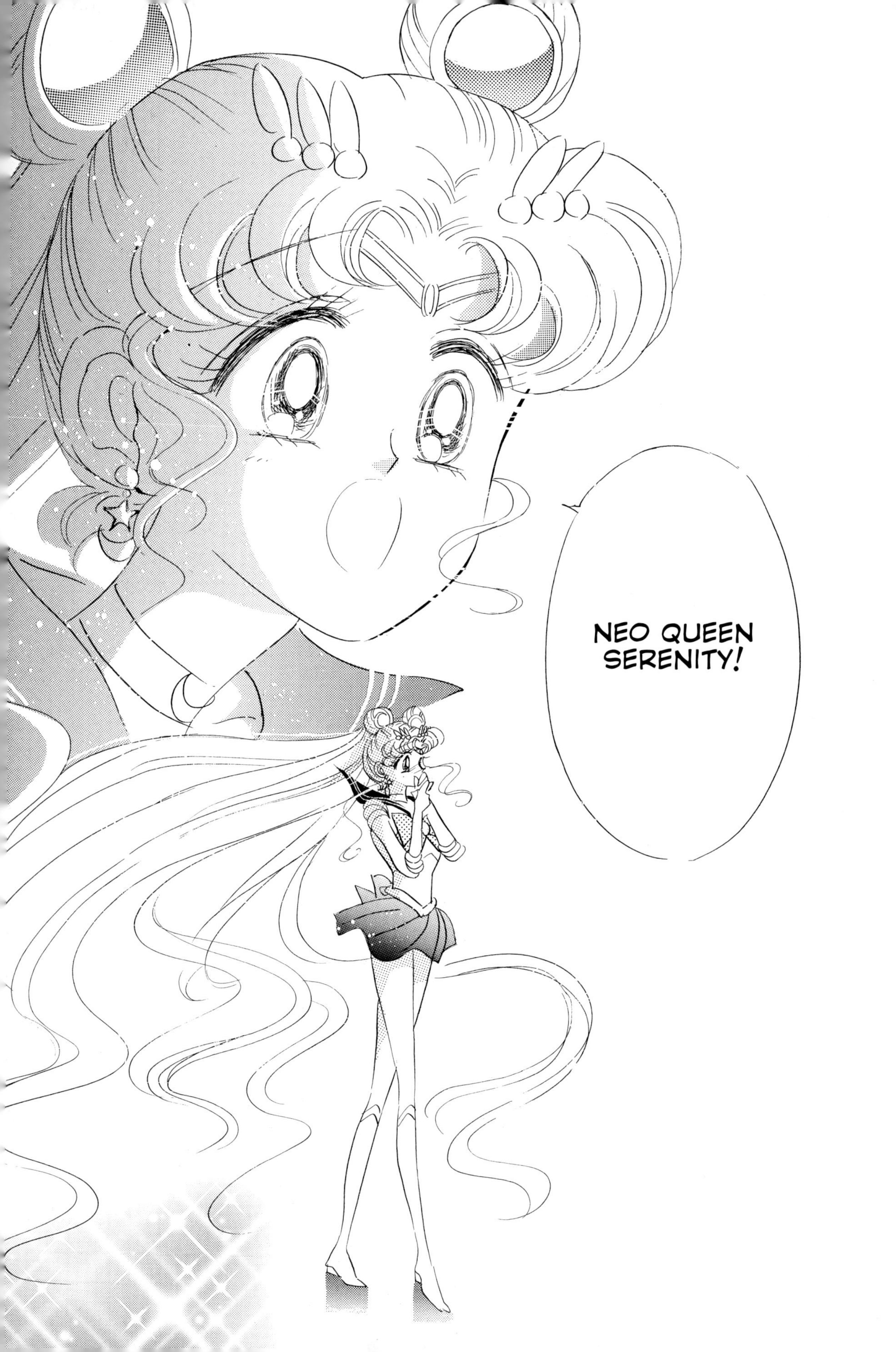
NEO QUEEN SERENITY!

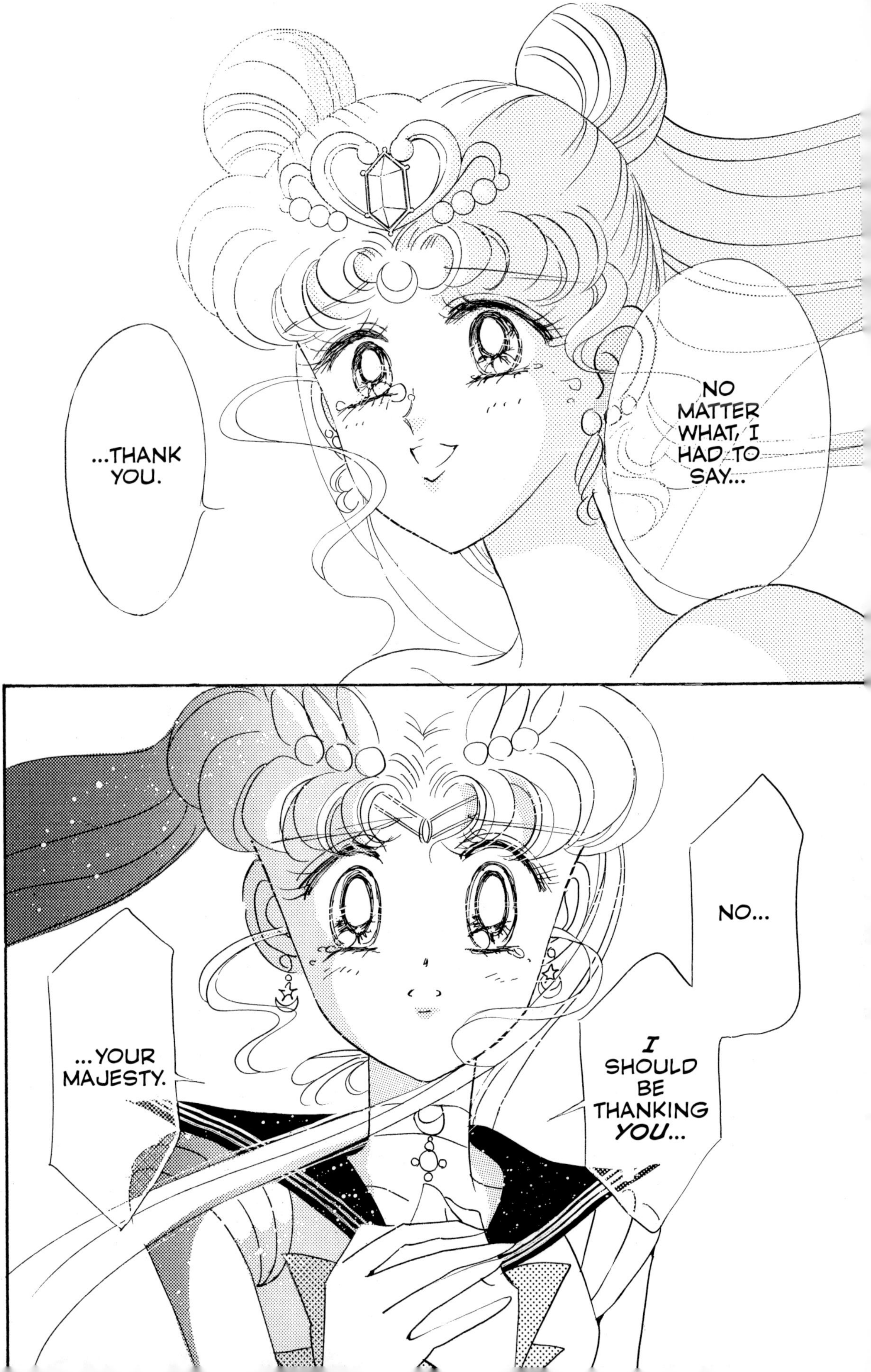
NO MATTER WHAT, I HAD TO SAY...
...THANK YOU.
NO...
I SHOULD BE THANKING *YOU*...
...YOUR MAJESTY.

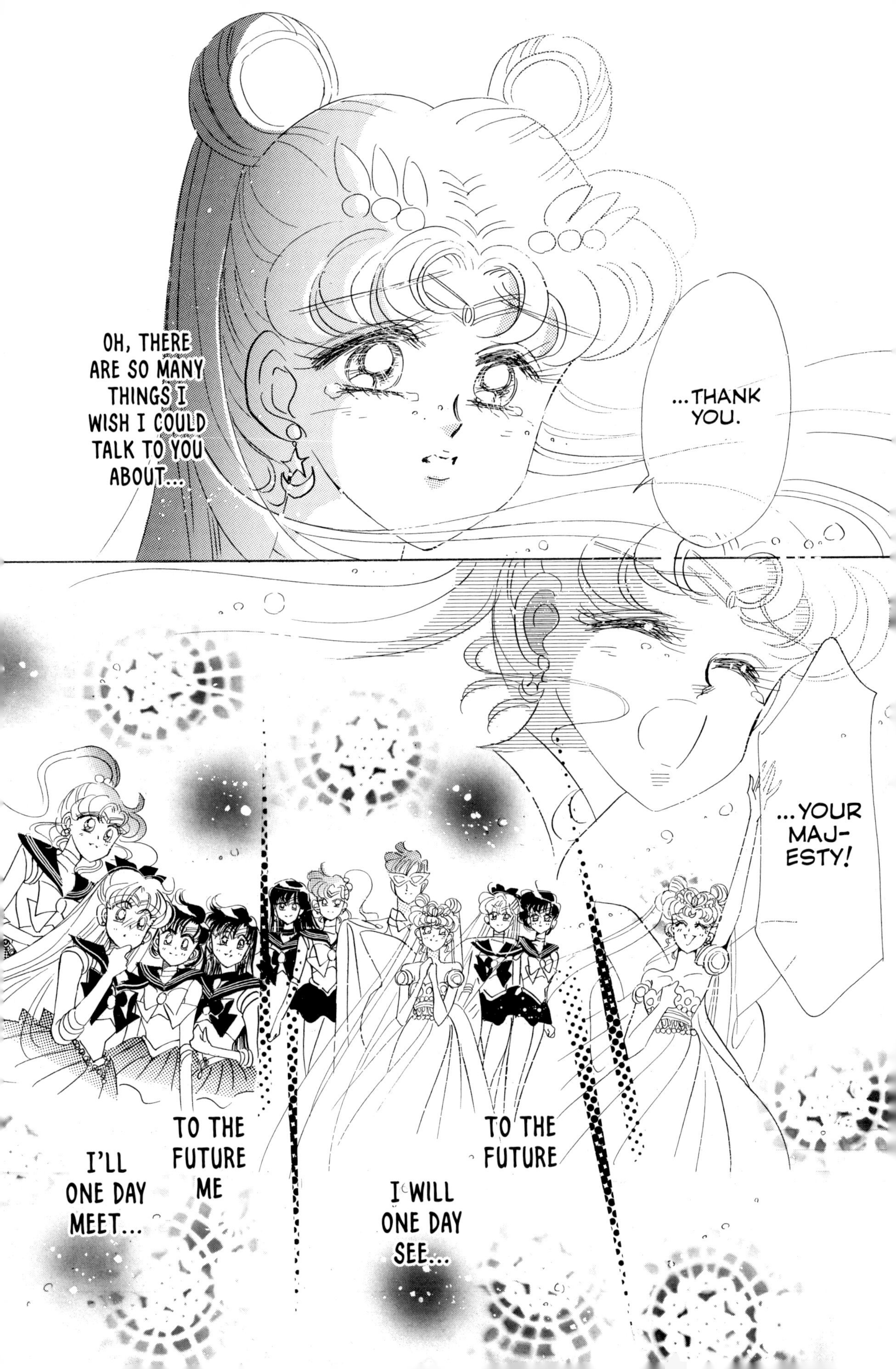
...THANK YOU.
OH, THERE ARE SO MANY THINGS I WISH I COULD TALK TO YOU ABOUT...
...YOUR MAJ-ESTY!
TO THE FUTURE
I WILL ONE DAY SEE...
TO THE FUTURE ME
I'LL ONE DAY MEET...

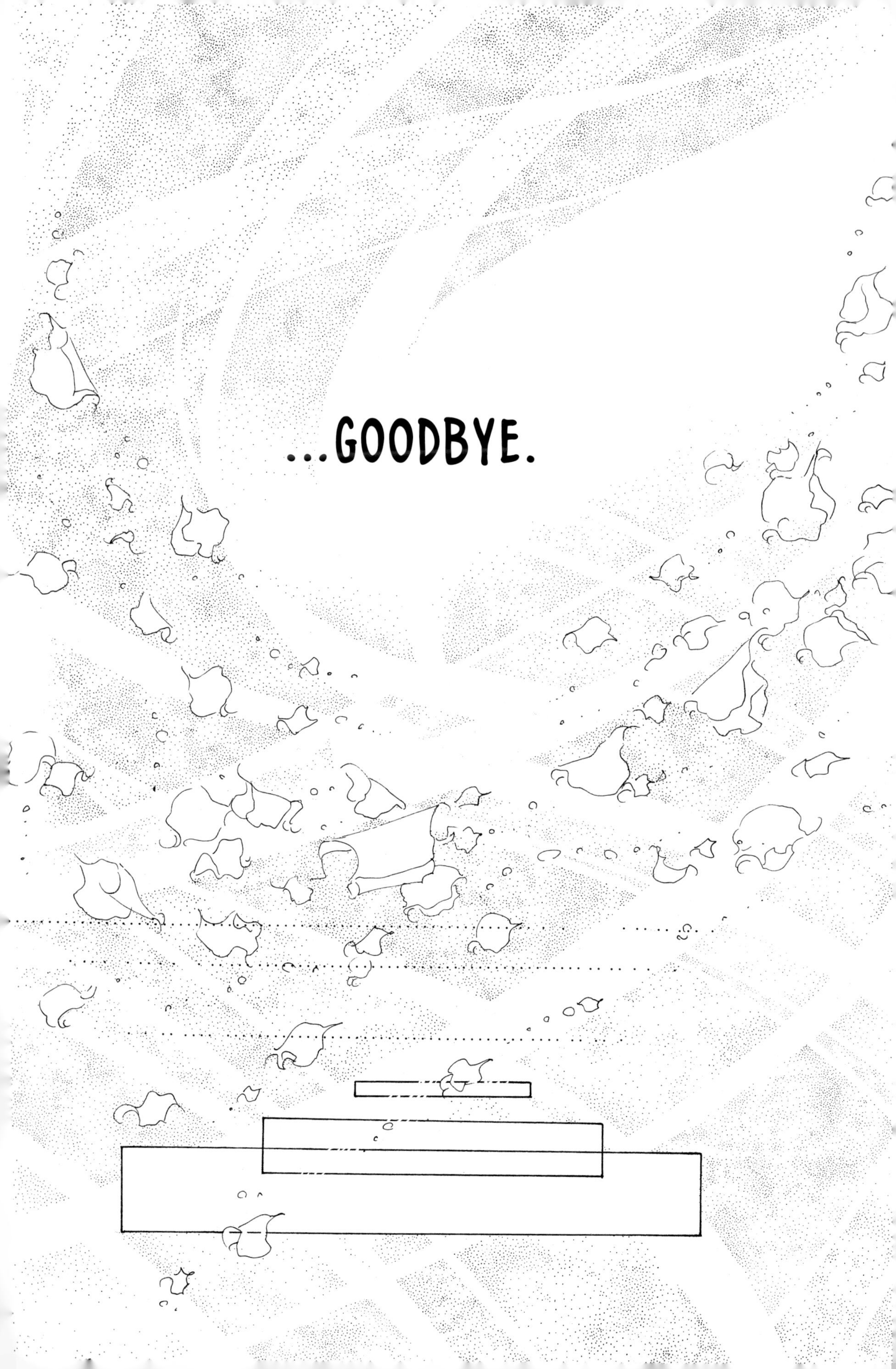
...GOODBYE.

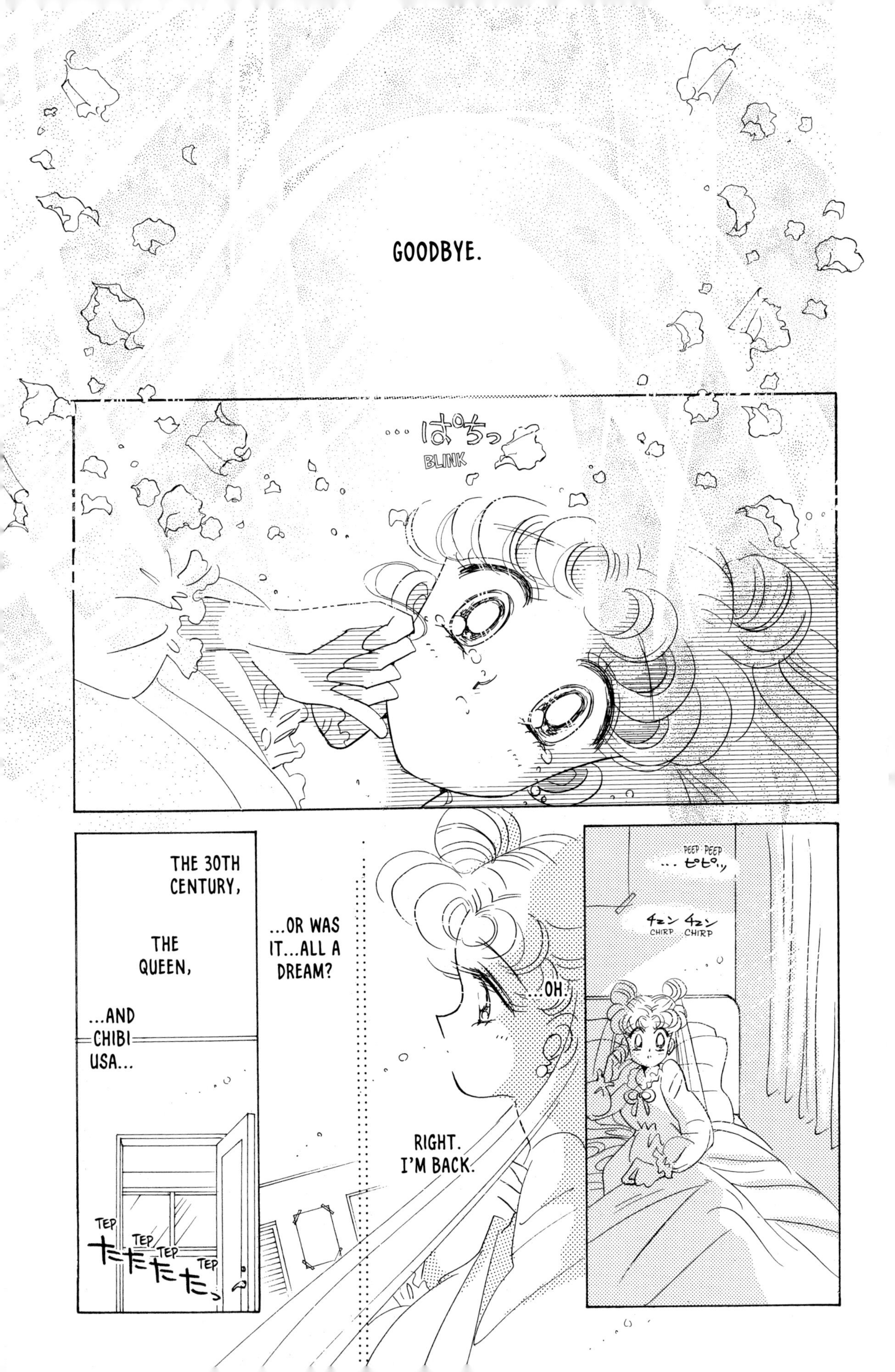
GOODBYE.
...ぱちっ
BLINK
...ピピッ
PEEP PEEP
チュン チュン
CHIRP CHIRP
...OH.
RIGHT. I'M BACK.
THE 30TH CENTURY,
THE QUEEN,
...AND CHIBI USA...
...OR WAS IT...ALL A DREAM?
たたたたっ
TEP TEP TEP TEP

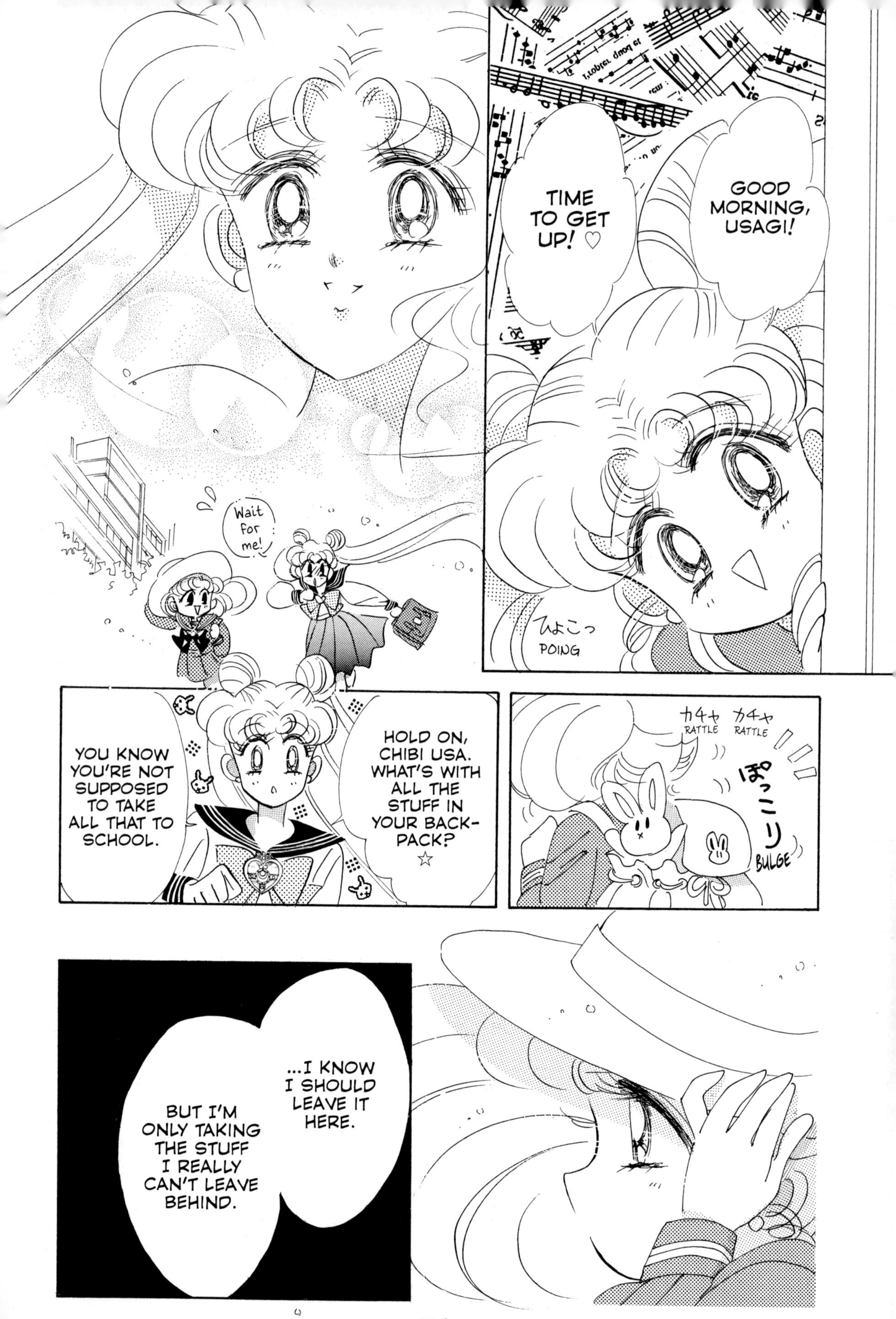
GOOD MORNING, USAGI!
TIME TO GET UP! ♡
ひよこっ
POING
Wait for me!
カチャ カチャ
RATTLE RATTLE
ぽっこり
BULGE
HOLD ON, CHIBI USA. WHAT'S WITH ALL THE STUFF IN YOUR BACK-PACK? ☆
YOU KNOW YOU'RE NOT SUPPOSED TO TAKE ALL THAT TO SCHOOL.
...I KNOW I SHOULD LEAVE IT HERE.
BUT I'M ONLY TAKING THE STUFF I REALLY CAN'T LEAVE BEHIND.

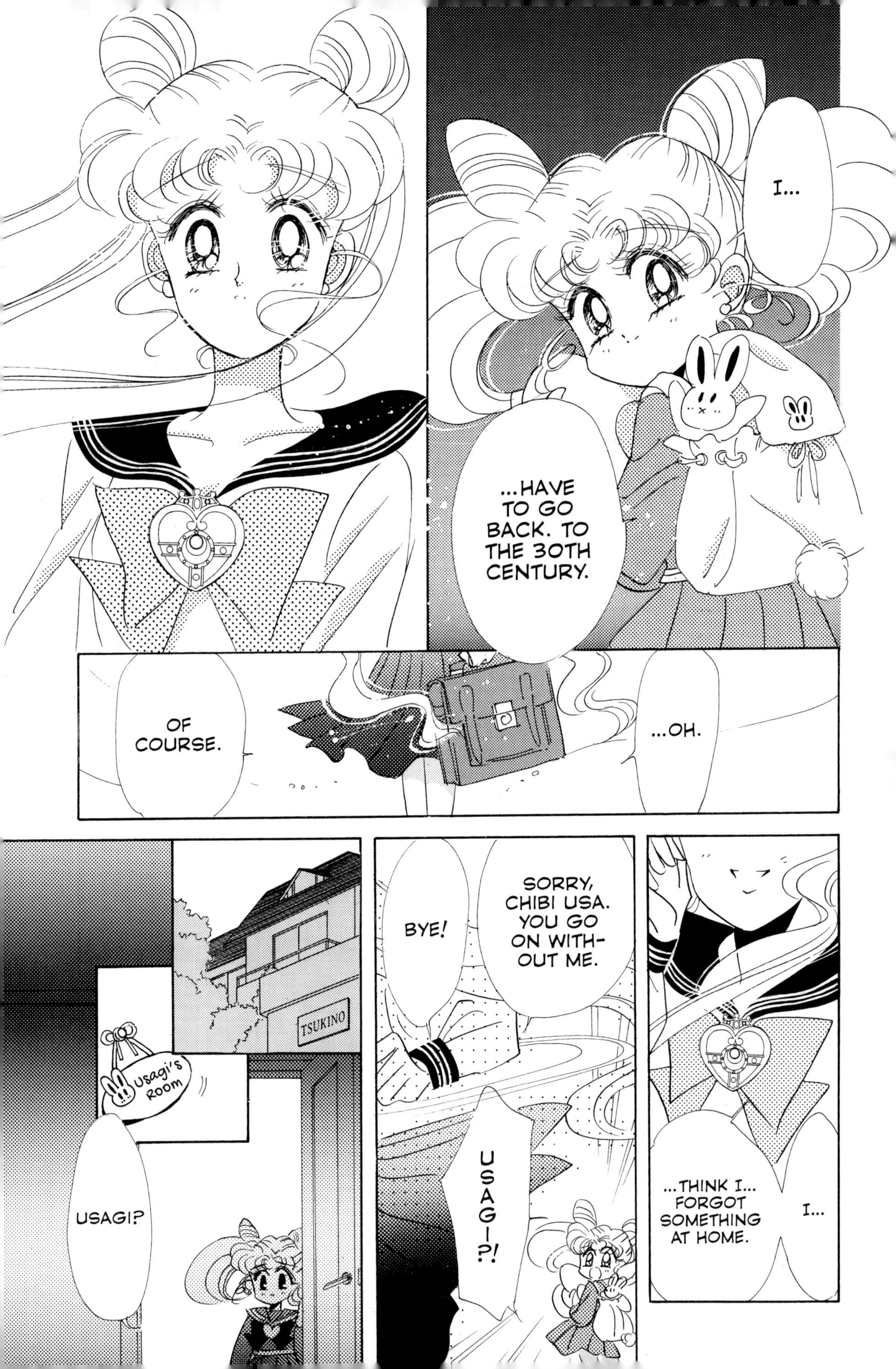
I...
...HAVE TO GO BACK. TO THE 30TH CENTURY.
...OH.
OF COURSE.
I...
...THINK I... FORGOT SOMETHING AT HOME.
SORRY, CHIBI USA. YOU GO ON WITH-OUT ME.
BYE!
USAGI?!
TSUKINO
Usagi's Room
USAGI?

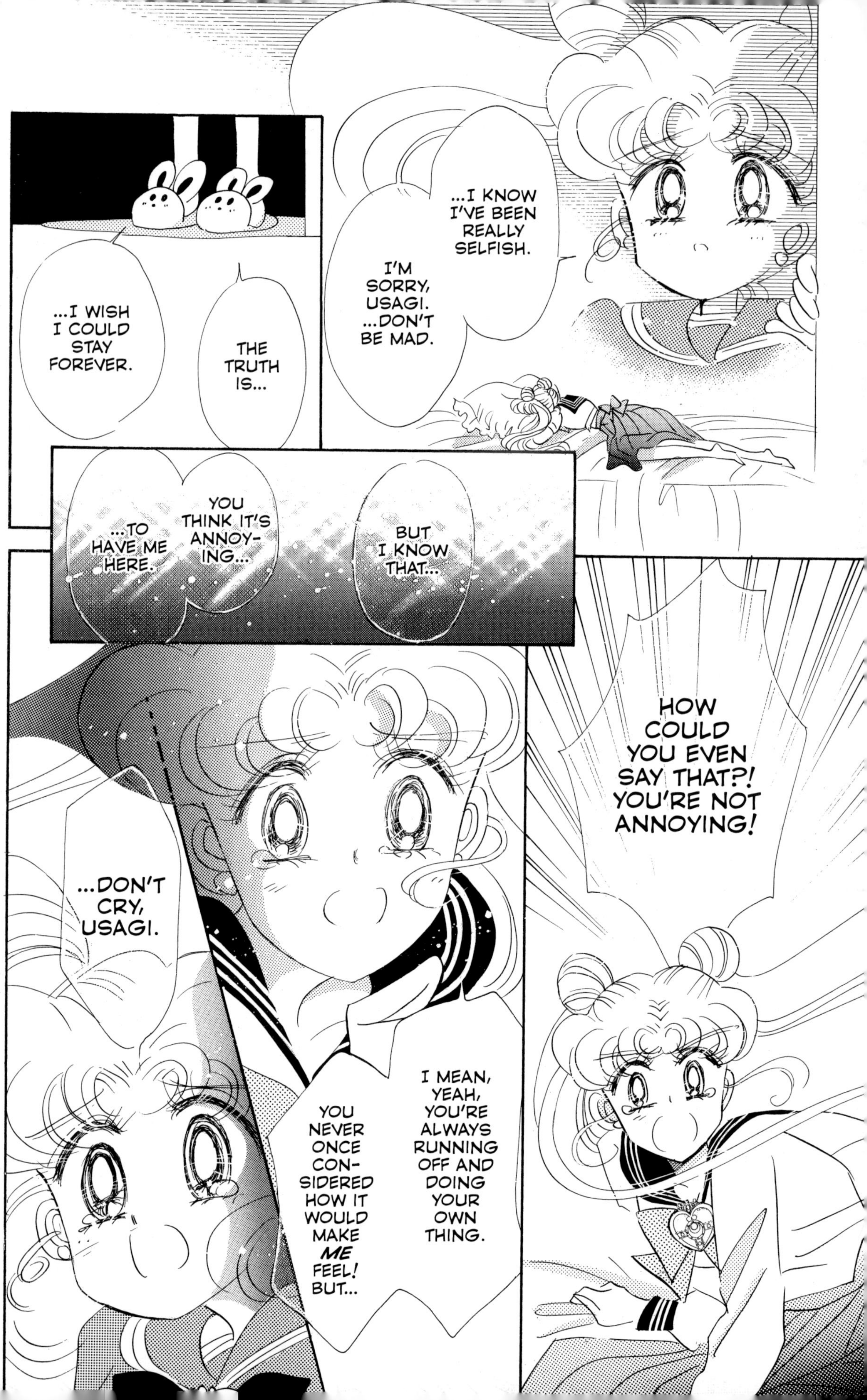
...I KNOW I'VE BEEN REALLY SELFISH.
I'M SORRY, USAGI. ...DON'T BE MAD.
THE TRUTH IS...
...I WISH I COULD STAY FOREVER.
BUT I KNOW THAT...
YOU THINK IT'S ANNOY-ING...
...TO HAVE ME HERE.
HOW COULD YOU EVEN SAY THAT?! YOU'RE NOT ANNOYING!
I MEAN, YEAH, YOU'RE ALWAYS RUNNING OFF AND DOING YOUR OWN THING.
YOU NEVER ONCE CON-SIDERED HOW IT WOULD MAKE *ME* FEEL! BUT...
...DON'T CRY, USAGI.

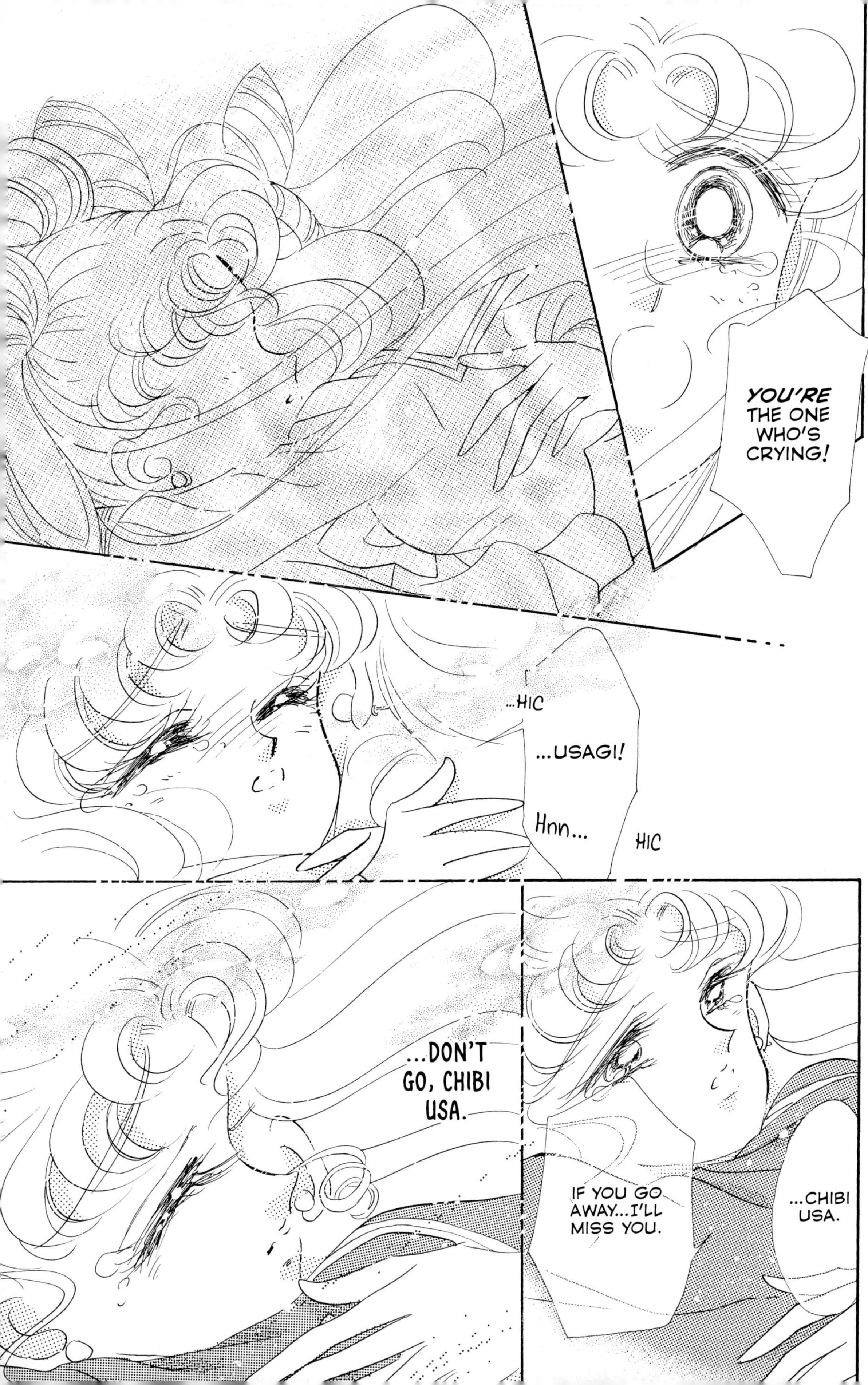
YOU'RE THE ONE WHO'S CRYING!
...HIC
...USAGI!
Hnn...
HIC
...CHIBI USA.
IF YOU GO AWAY...I'LL MISS YOU.
...DON'T GO, CHIBI USA.

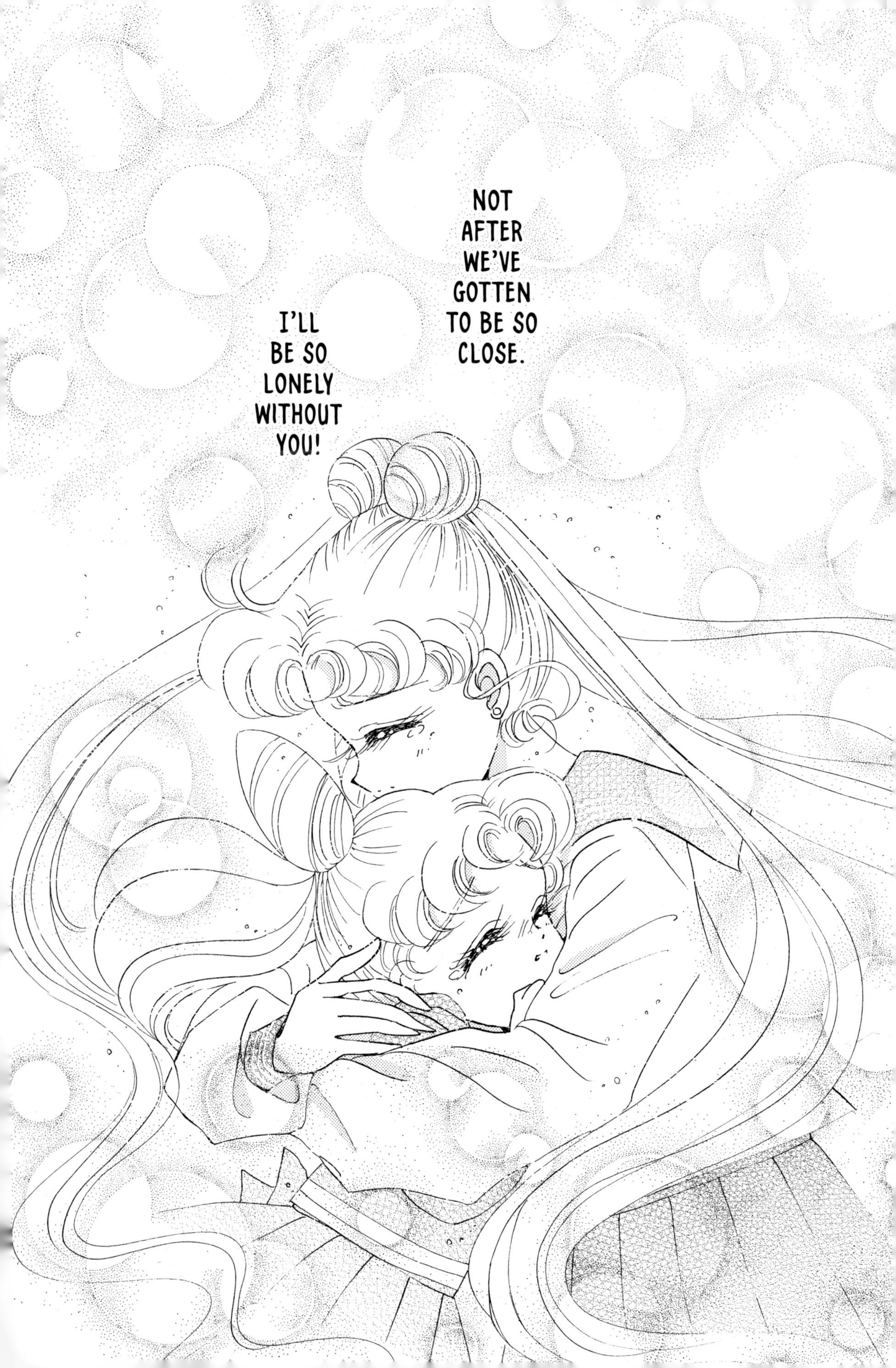
NOT AFTER WE'VE GOTTEN TO BE SO CLOSE.
I'LL BE SO LONELY WITHOUT YOU!

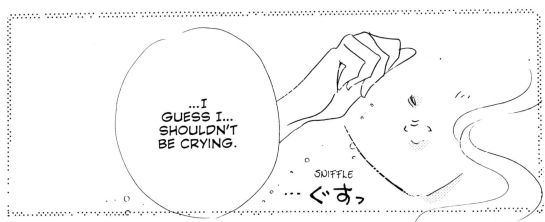

...I GUESS I... SHOULDN'T BE CRYING.

SNIFFLE ...ぐすっ

I'LL SEE YOU OFF, CHIBI USA.

THIS IS WHERE MAMO-CHAN AND I WERE KISSING WHEN CHIBI USA FELL FROM THE SKY.

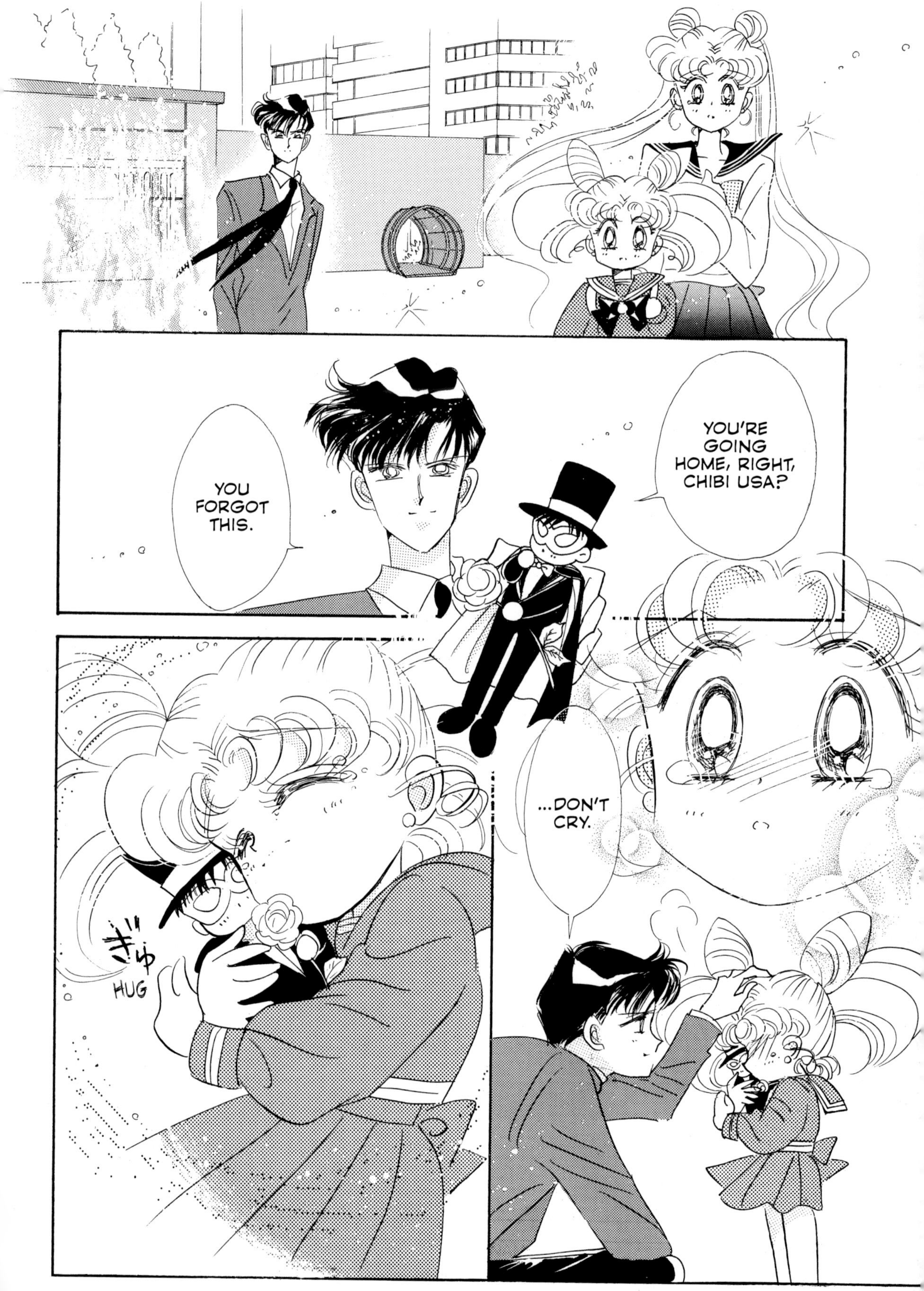
YOU'RE GOING HOME, RIGHT, CHIBI USA?
YOU FORGOT THIS.
...DON'T CRY.
ぎゅ
HUG

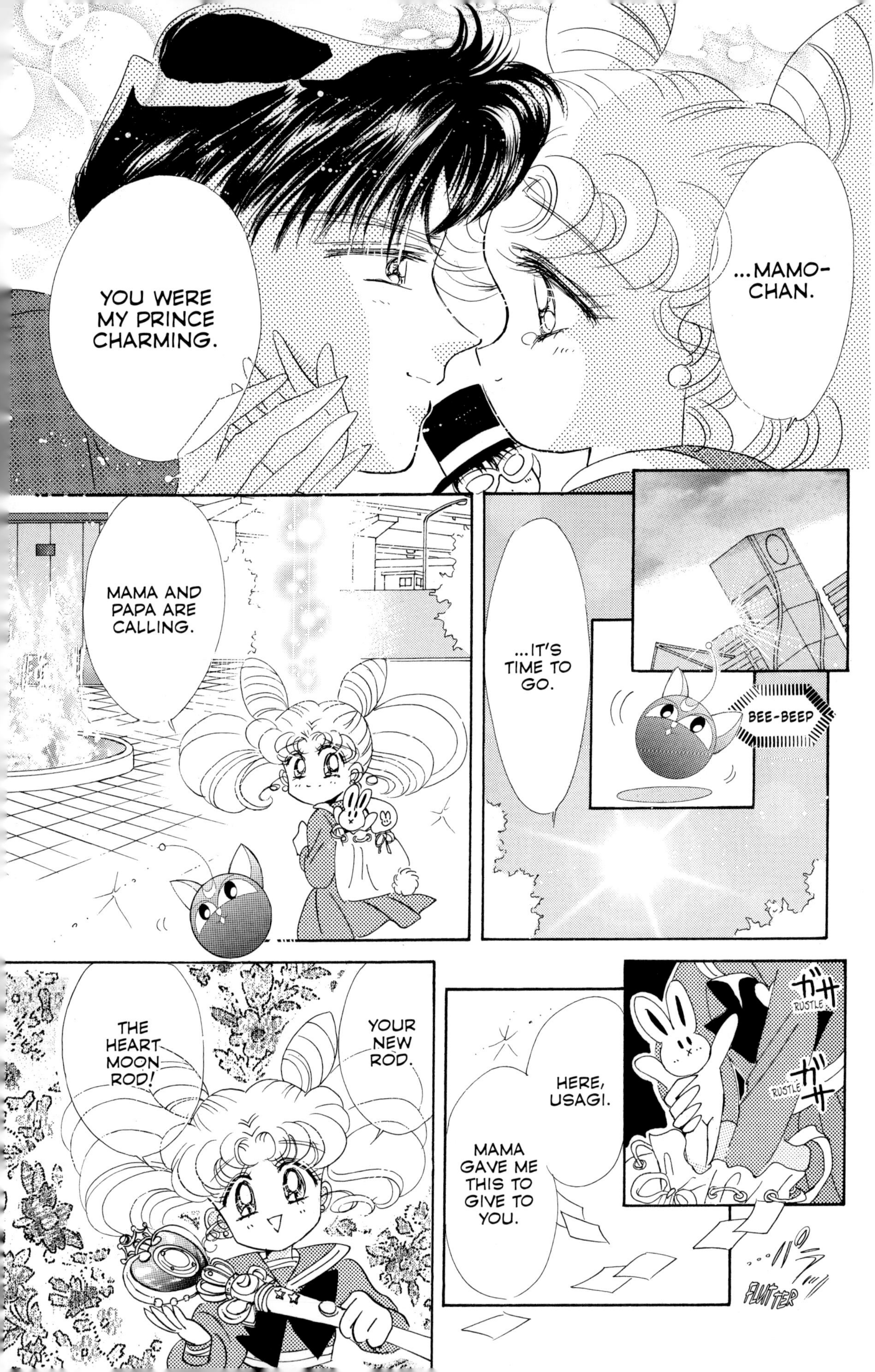
...MAMO-CHAN.
YOU WERE MY PRINCE CHARMING.
BEE-BEEP
...IT'S TIME TO GO.
MAMA AND PAPA ARE CALLING.
ガサ RUSTLE
ガサ RUSTLE
HERE, USAGI.
MAMA GAVE ME THIS TO GIVE TO YOU.
FLUTTER
YOUR NEW ROD.
THE HEART MOON ROD!

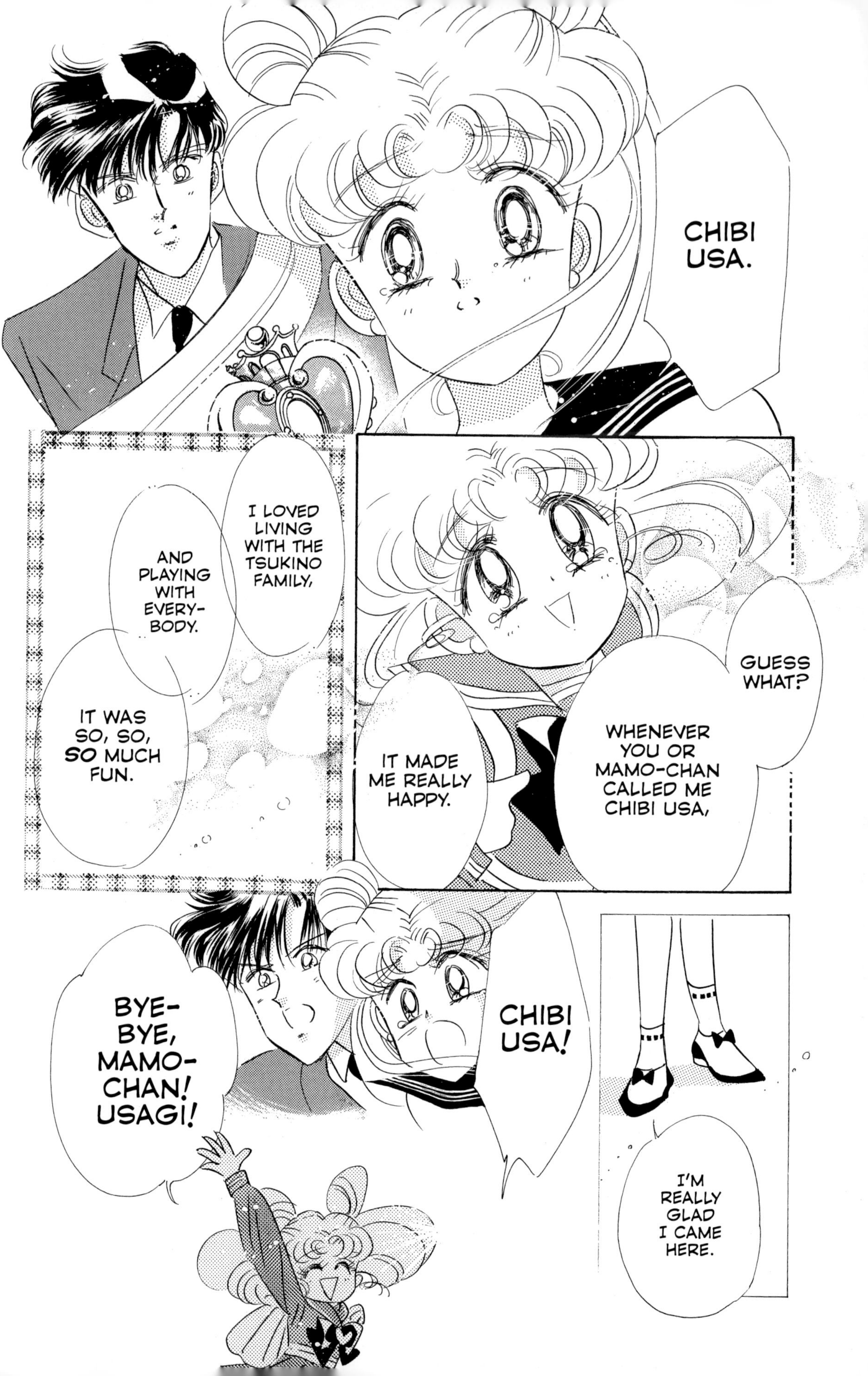
CHIBI USA.
GUESS WHAT?
WHENEVER YOU OR MAMO-CHAN CALLED ME CHIBI USA,
IT MADE ME REALLY HAPPY.
I LOVED LIVING WITH THE TSUKINO FAMILY,
AND PLAYING WITH EVERY-BODY.
IT WAS SO, SO, SO MUCH FUN.
I'M REALLY GLAD I CAME HERE.
CHIBI USA!
BYE-BYE, MAMO-CHAN! USAGI!

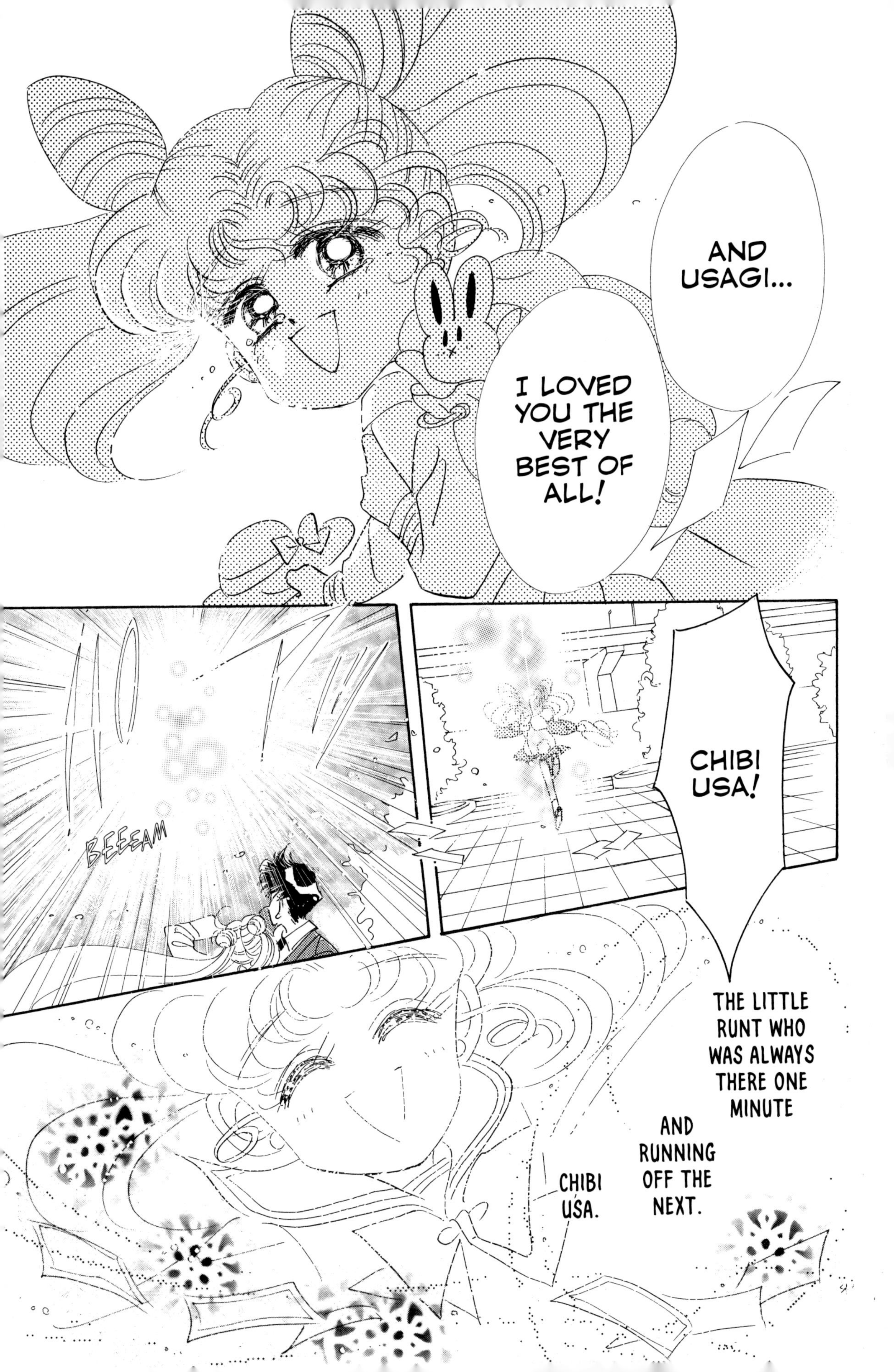
AND USAGI...
I LOVED YOU THE VERY BEST OF ALL!
CHIBI USA!
BEEEAM
THE LITTLE RUNT WHO WAS ALWAYS THERE ONE MINUTE
AND RUNNING OFF THE NEXT.
CHIBI USA.

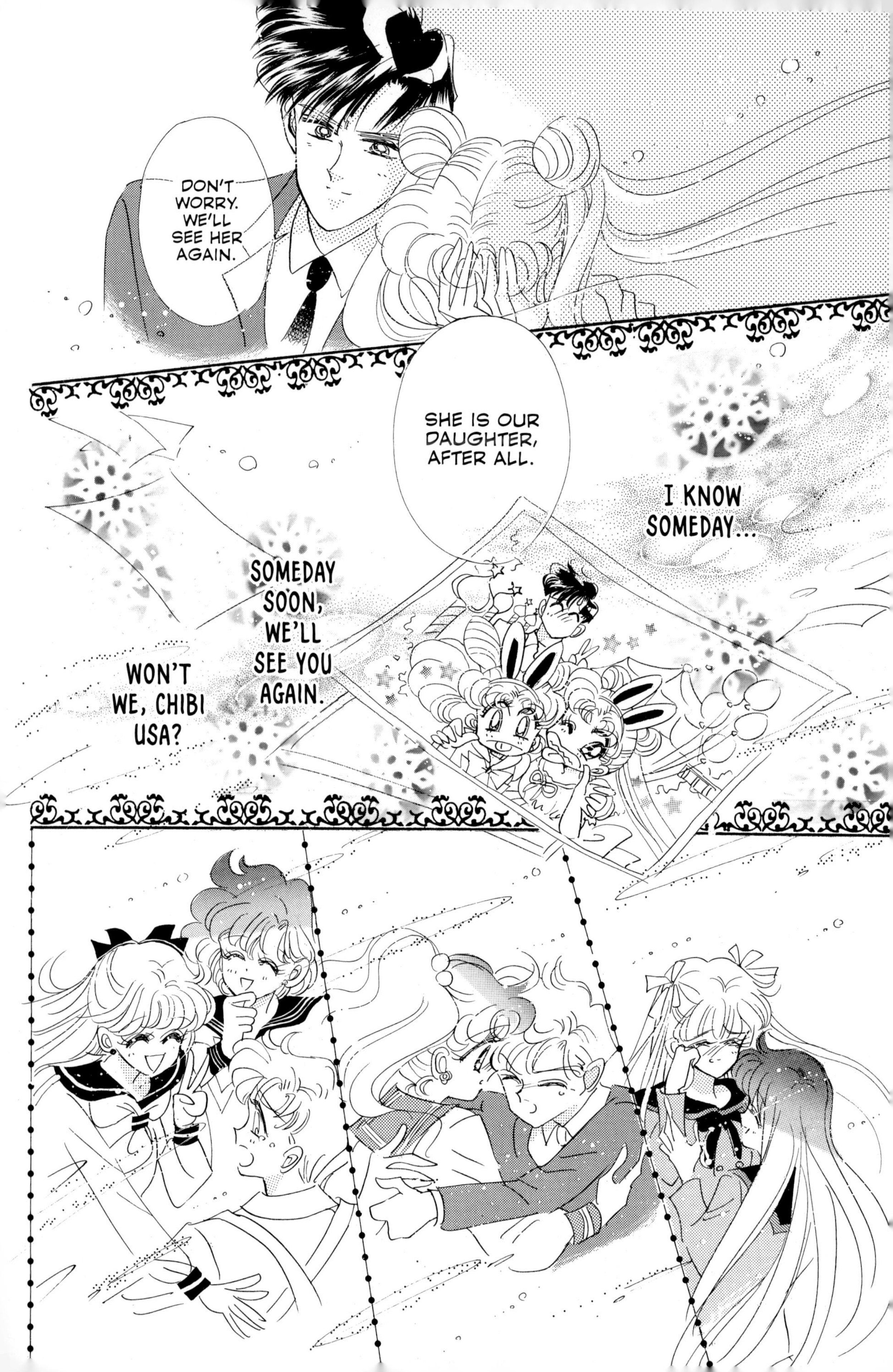
DON'T WORRY. WE'LL SEE HER AGAIN.
SHE IS OUR DAUGHTER, AFTER ALL.
I KNOW SOMEDAY...
SOMEDAY SOON, WE'LL SEE YOU AGAIN.
WON'T WE, CHIBI USA?

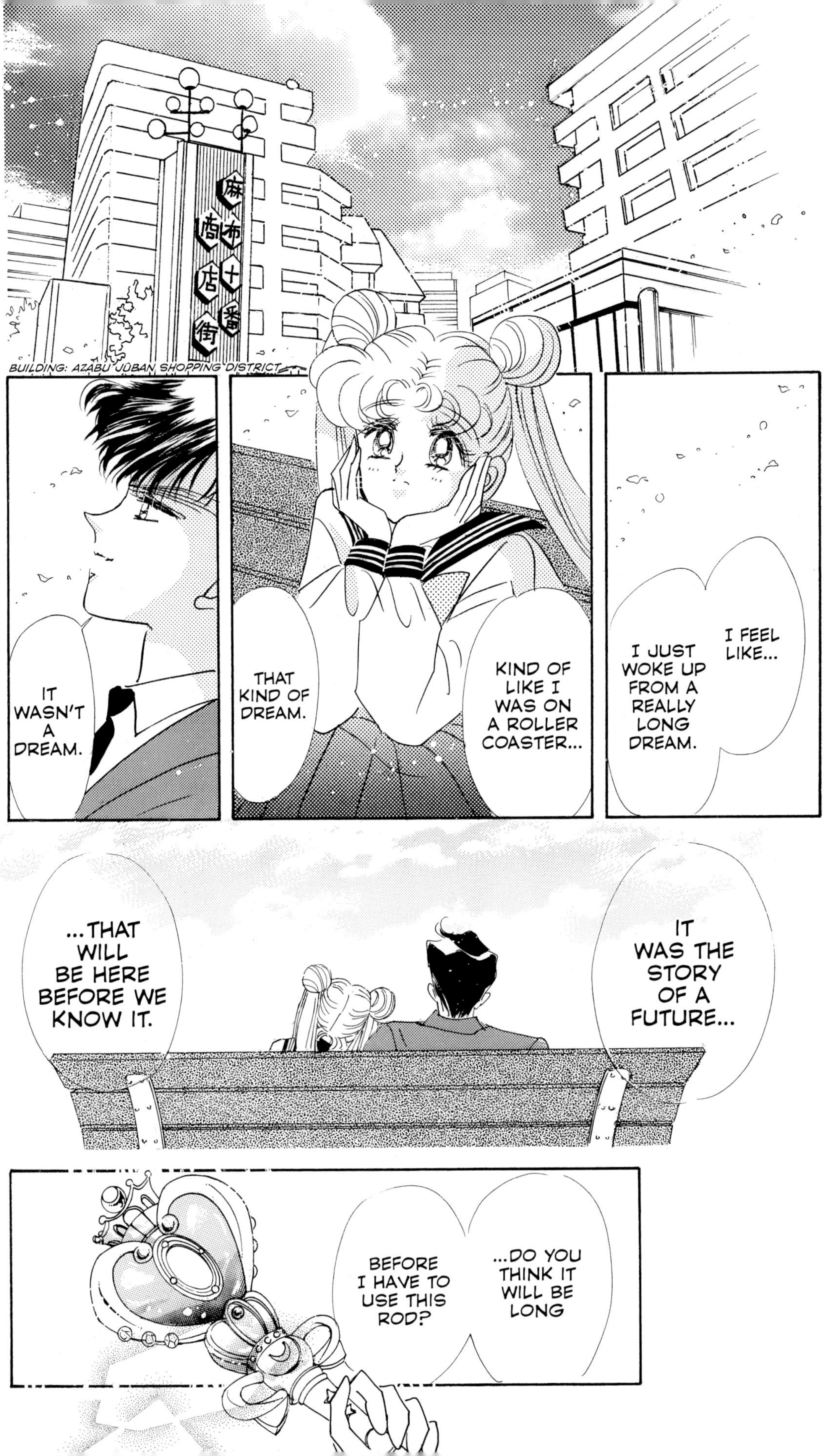
麻布十番
商店街
BUILDING: AZABU JŪBAN SHOPPING DISTRICT
I FEEL LIKE...
I JUST WOKE UP FROM A REALLY LONG DREAM.
KIND OF LIKE I WAS ON A ROLLER COASTER...
THAT KIND OF DREAM.
IT WASN'T A DREAM.
IT WAS THE STORY OF A FUTURE...
...THAT WILL BE HERE BEFORE WE KNOW IT.
...DO YOU THINK IT WILL BE LONG
BEFORE I HAVE TO USE THIS ROD?

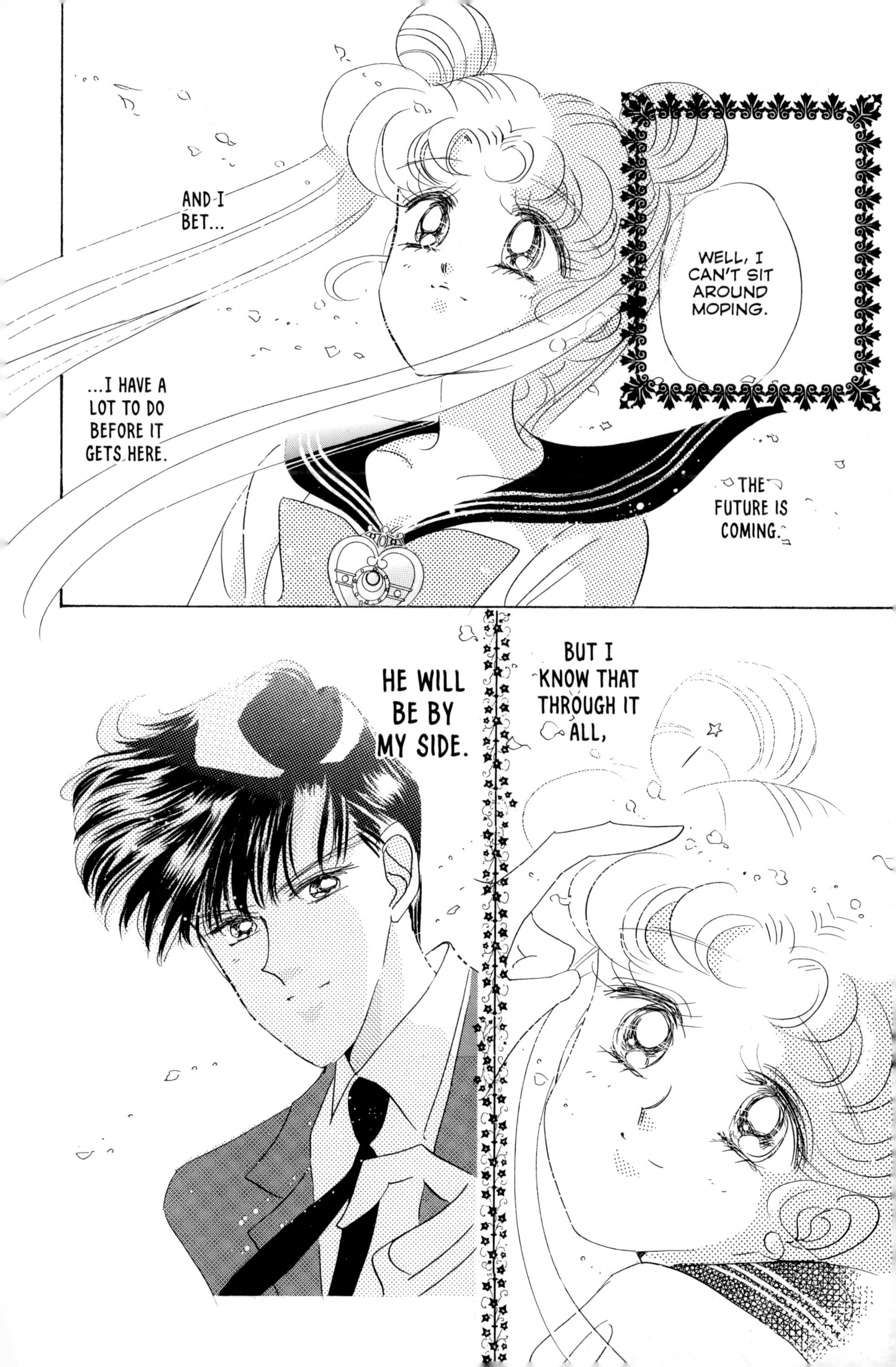
WELL, I CAN'T SIT AROUND MOPING.
THE FUTURE IS COMING.
AND I BET...
...I HAVE A LOT TO DO BEFORE IT GETS HERE.
BUT I KNOW THAT THROUGH IT ALL,
HE WILL BE BY MY SIDE.

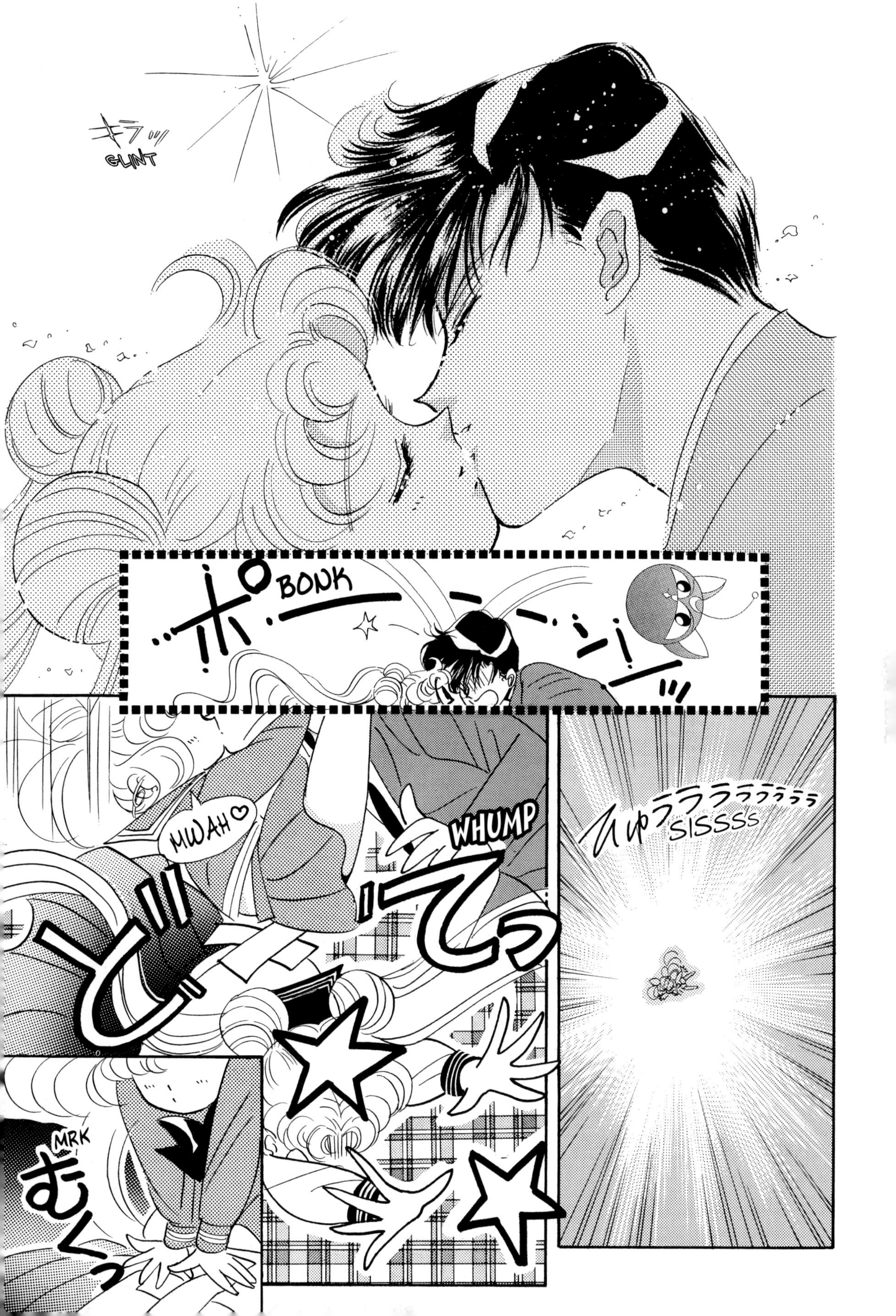
キラッ
GLINT
ポーーン
BONK
SISSSS
WHUMP
どてっ
MWAH♡
むくっ
MRK

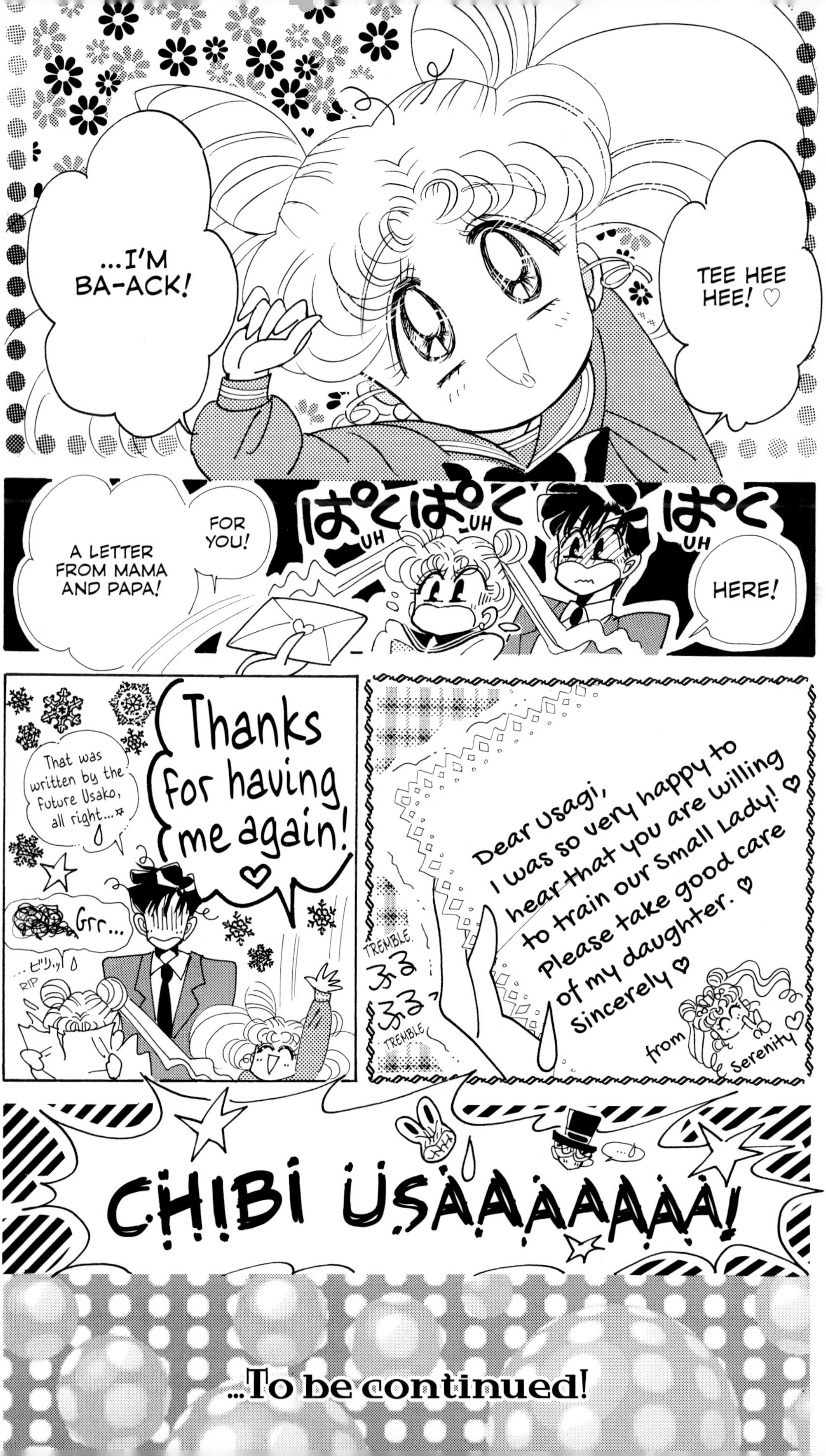
TEE HEE HEE! ♡
...I'M BA-ACK!
HERE!
ぱく UH ぱく UH ぱく UH
FOR YOU!
A LETTER FROM MAMA AND PAPA!
ふる TREMBLE ふる TREMBLE
Dear Usagi, I was so very happy to hear that you are willing to train our Small Lady! ♡ Please take good care of my daughter. ♡ Sincerely ♡
from Serenity ♡
Thanks for having me again! ♡
That was written by the future Usako, all right...
Grr...
...ビリッ RIP
CHIBI USAAAAAAA!
...To be continued!

Chibi Usa's Picture Diary Chapter 1

Beware of the Transfer Student!

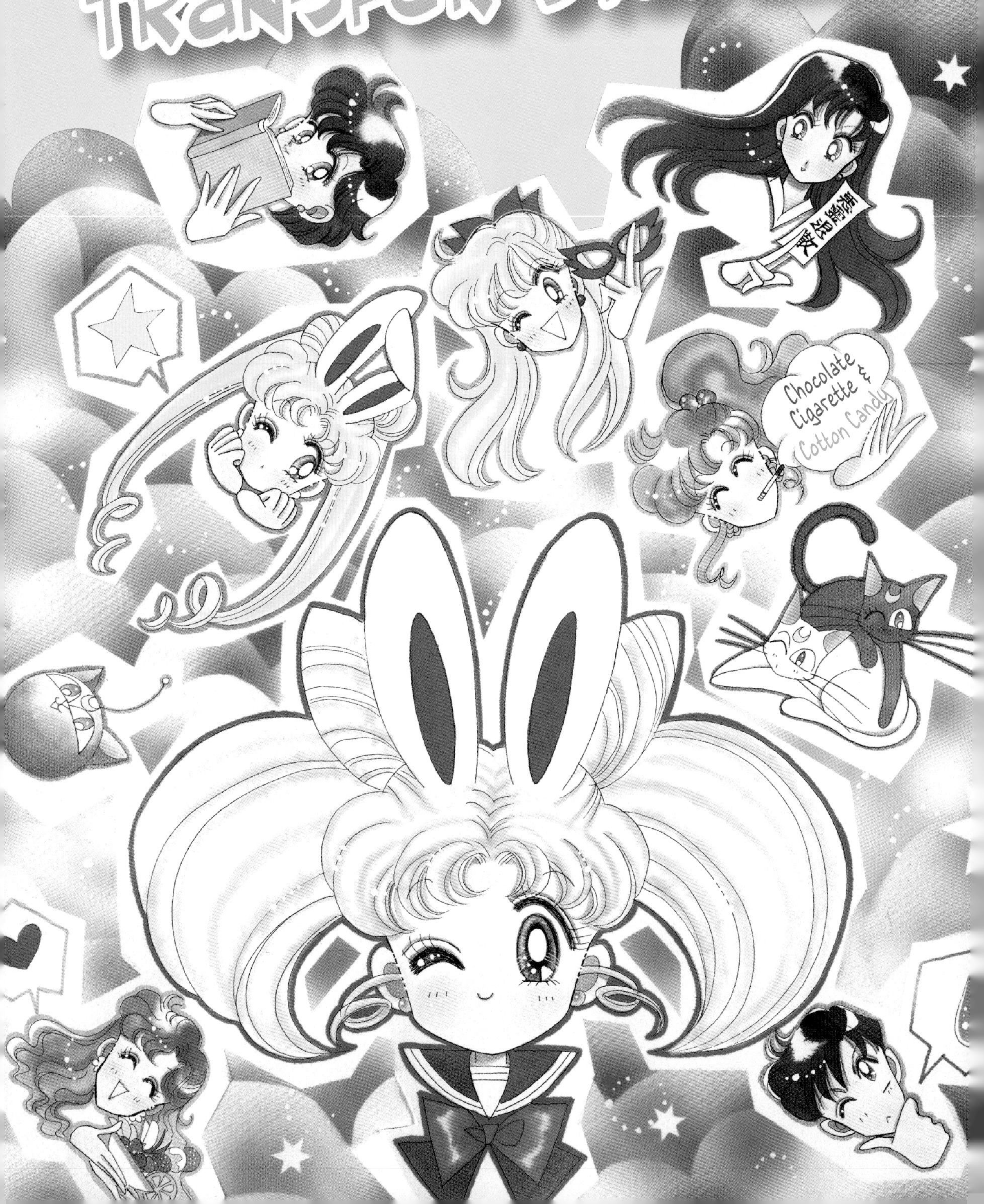
Chocolate Cigarette & Cotton Candy

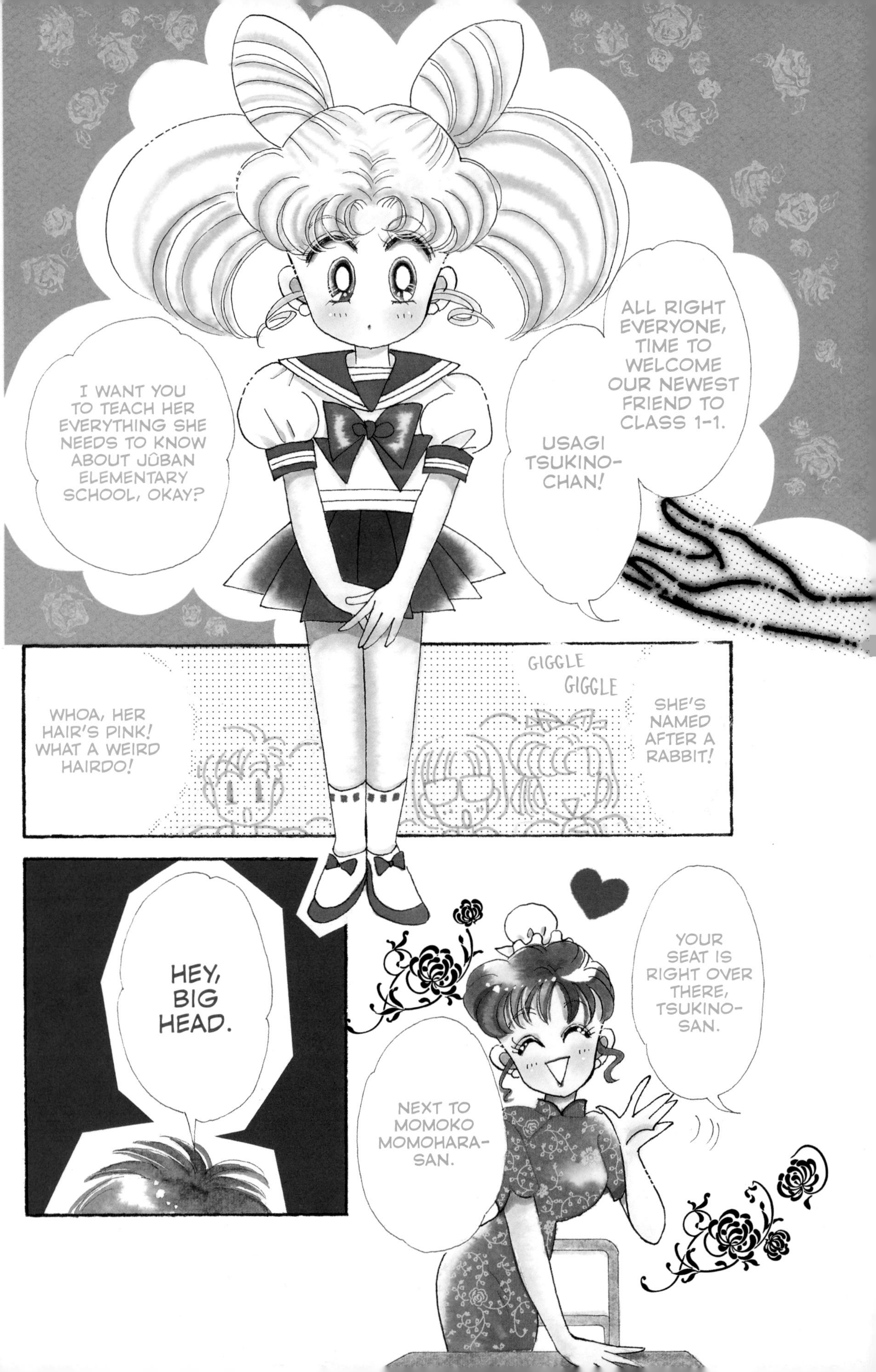
ALL RIGHT EVERYONE, TIME TO WELCOME OUR NEWEST FRIEND TO CLASS 1-1.
USAGI TSUKINO-CHAN!
I WANT YOU TO TEACH HER EVERYTHING SHE NEEDS TO KNOW ABOUT JÛBAN ELEMENTARY SCHOOL, OKAY?
SHE'S NAMED AFTER A RABBIT!
GIGGLE GIGGLE
WHOA, HER HAIR'S PINK! WHAT A WEIRD HAIRDO!
YOUR SEAT IS RIGHT OVER THERE, TSUKINO-SAN.
NEXT TO MOMOKO MOMOHARA-SAN.
HEY, BIG HEAD.

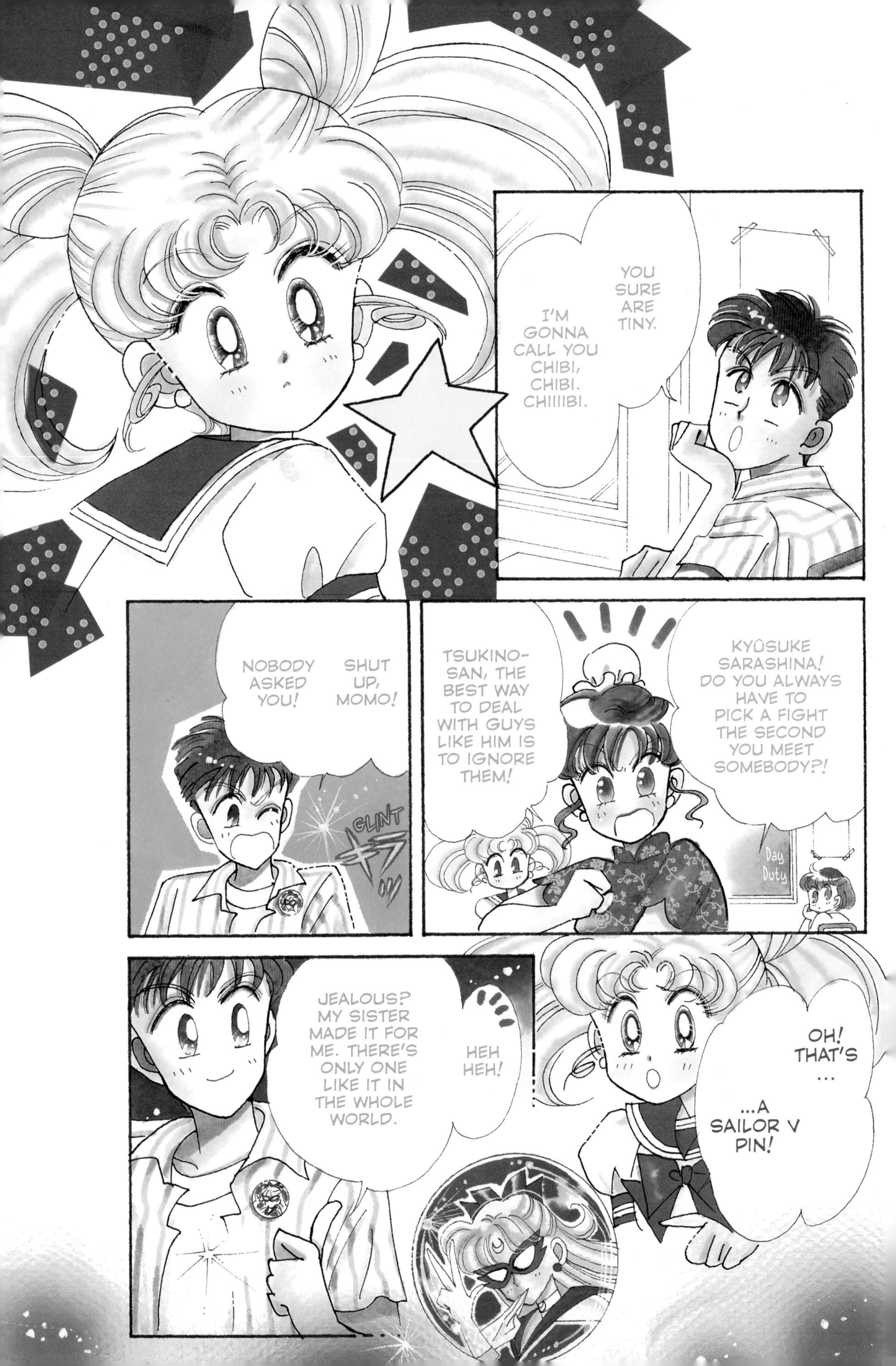
YOU SURE ARE TINY.
I'M GONNA CALL YOU CHIBI, CHIBI. CHIIIIBI.
KYÛSUKE SARASHINA! DO YOU ALWAYS HAVE TO PICK A FIGHT THE SECOND YOU MEET SOMEBODY?!
TSUKINO-SAN, THE BEST WAY TO DEAL WITH GUYS LIKE HIM IS TO IGNORE THEM!
Day Duty
SHUT UP, MOMO!
NOBODY ASKED YOU!
GLINT
OH! THAT'S ...
...A SAILOR V PIN!
HEH HEH!
JEALOUS? MY SISTER MADE IT FOR ME. THERE'S ONLY ONE LIKE IT IN THE WHOLE WORLD.

Pretty Guardian

Sailor Moon

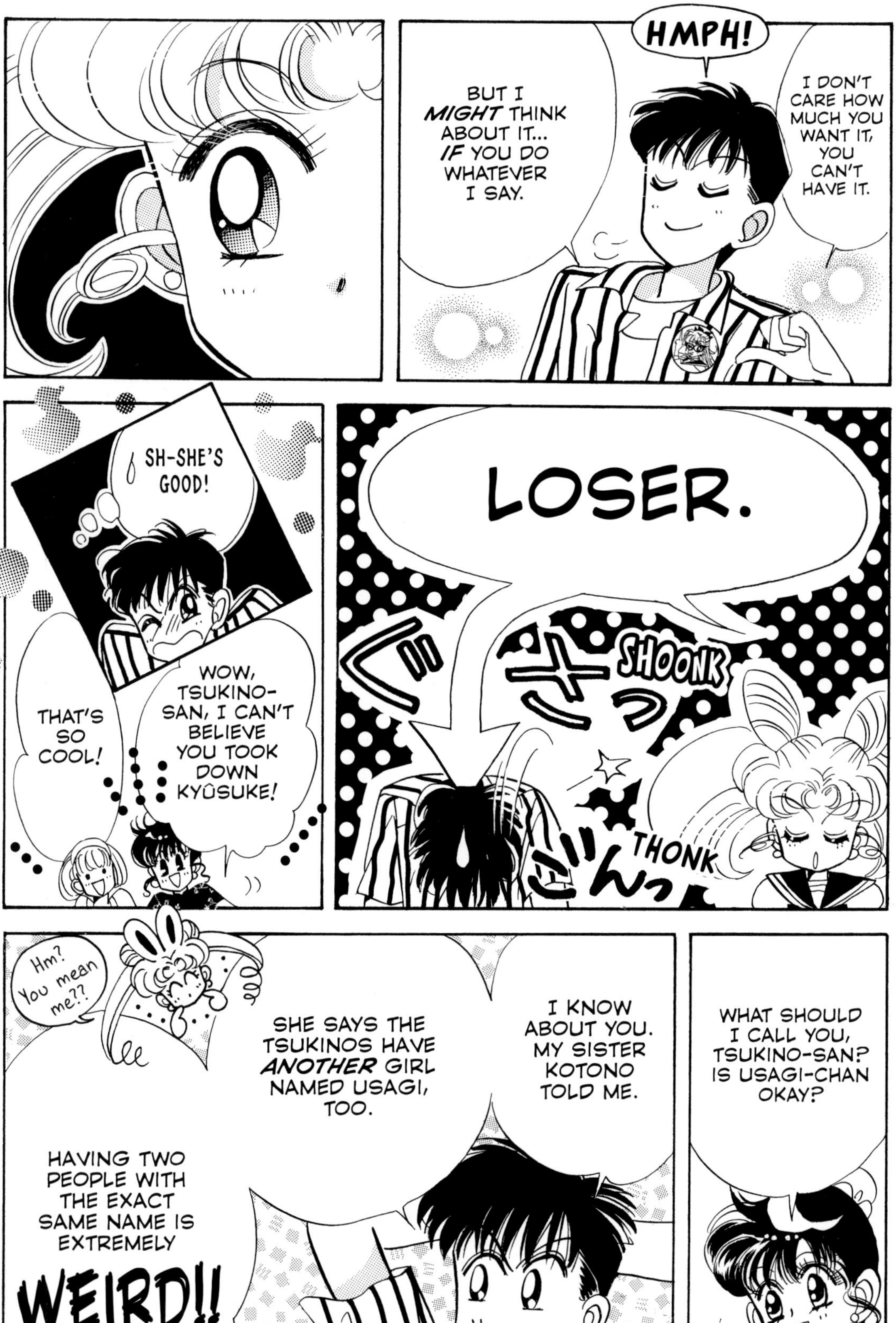
HMPH!
I DON'T CARE HOW MUCH YOU WANT IT, YOU CAN'T HAVE IT.
BUT I *MIGHT* THINK ABOUT IT... *IF* YOU DO WHATEVER I SAY.
LOSER.
ぐさっ
SHOONK
ごんっ
THONK
SH-SHE'S GOOD!
WOW, TSUKINO-SAN, I CAN'T BELIEVE YOU TOOK DOWN KYÛSUKE!
THAT'S SO COOL!
WHAT SHOULD I CALL YOU, TSUKINO-SAN? IS USAGI-CHAN OKAY?
I KNOW ABOUT YOU. MY SISTER KOTONO TOLD ME.
SHE SAYS THE TSUKINOS HAVE *ANOTHER* GIRL NAMED USAGI, TOO.
HAVING TWO PEOPLE WITH THE EXACT SAME NAME IS EXTREMELY
WEIRD!!
Hm? You mean me??

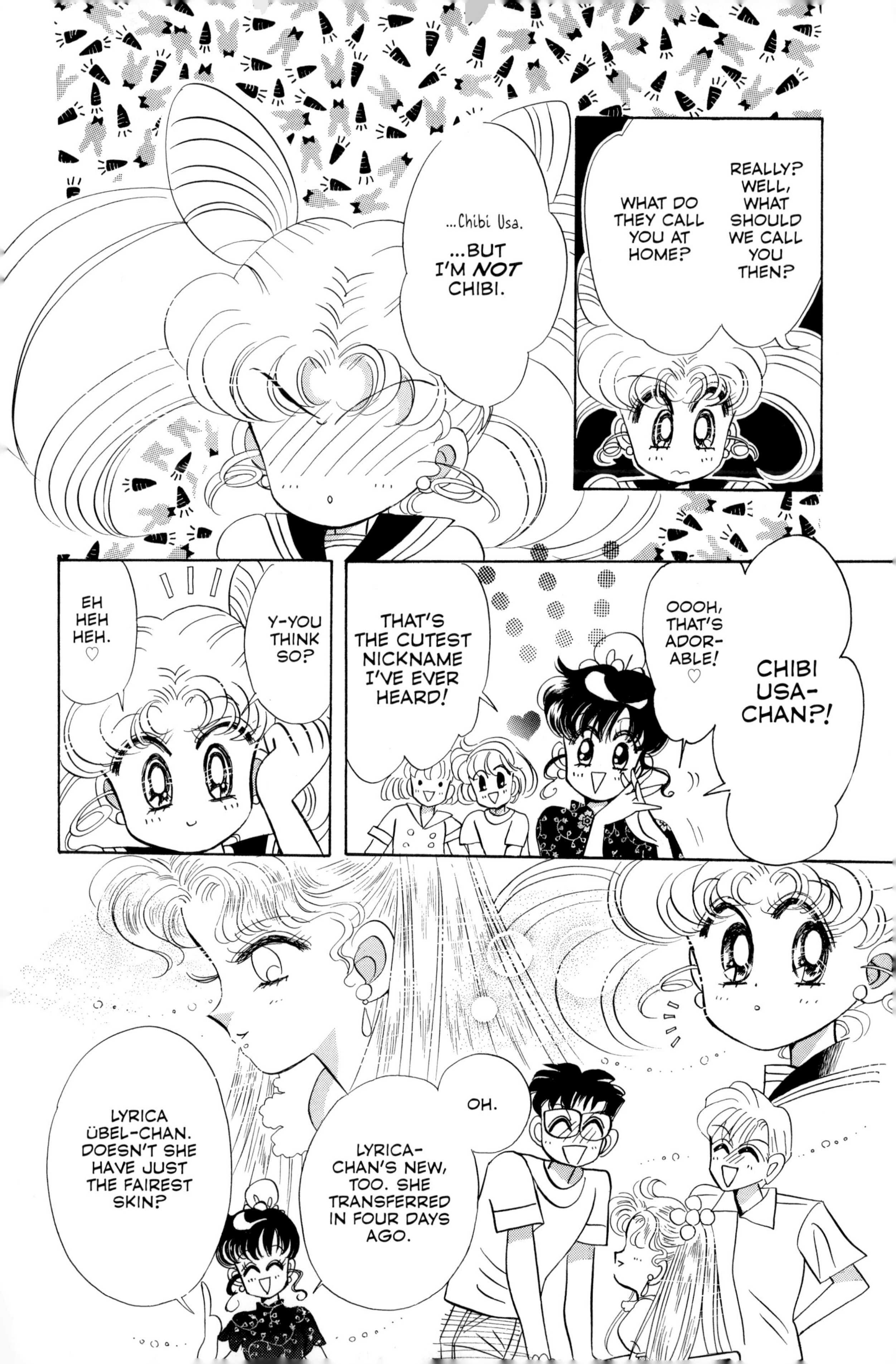
REALLY? WELL, WHAT SHOULD WE CALL YOU THEN?
WHAT DO THEY CALL YOU AT HOME?
...Chibi Usa.
...BUT I'M *NOT* CHIBI.
CHIBI USA-CHAN?!
OOOH, THAT'S ADORABLE! ♡
THAT'S THE CUTEST NICKNAME I'VE EVER HEARD!
Y-YOU THINK SO?
EH HEH HEH. ♡
OH.
LYRICA-CHAN'S NEW, TOO. SHE TRANSFERRED IN FOUR DAYS AGO.
LYRICA ÜBEL-CHAN. DOESN'T SHE HAVE JUST THE FAIREST SKIN?

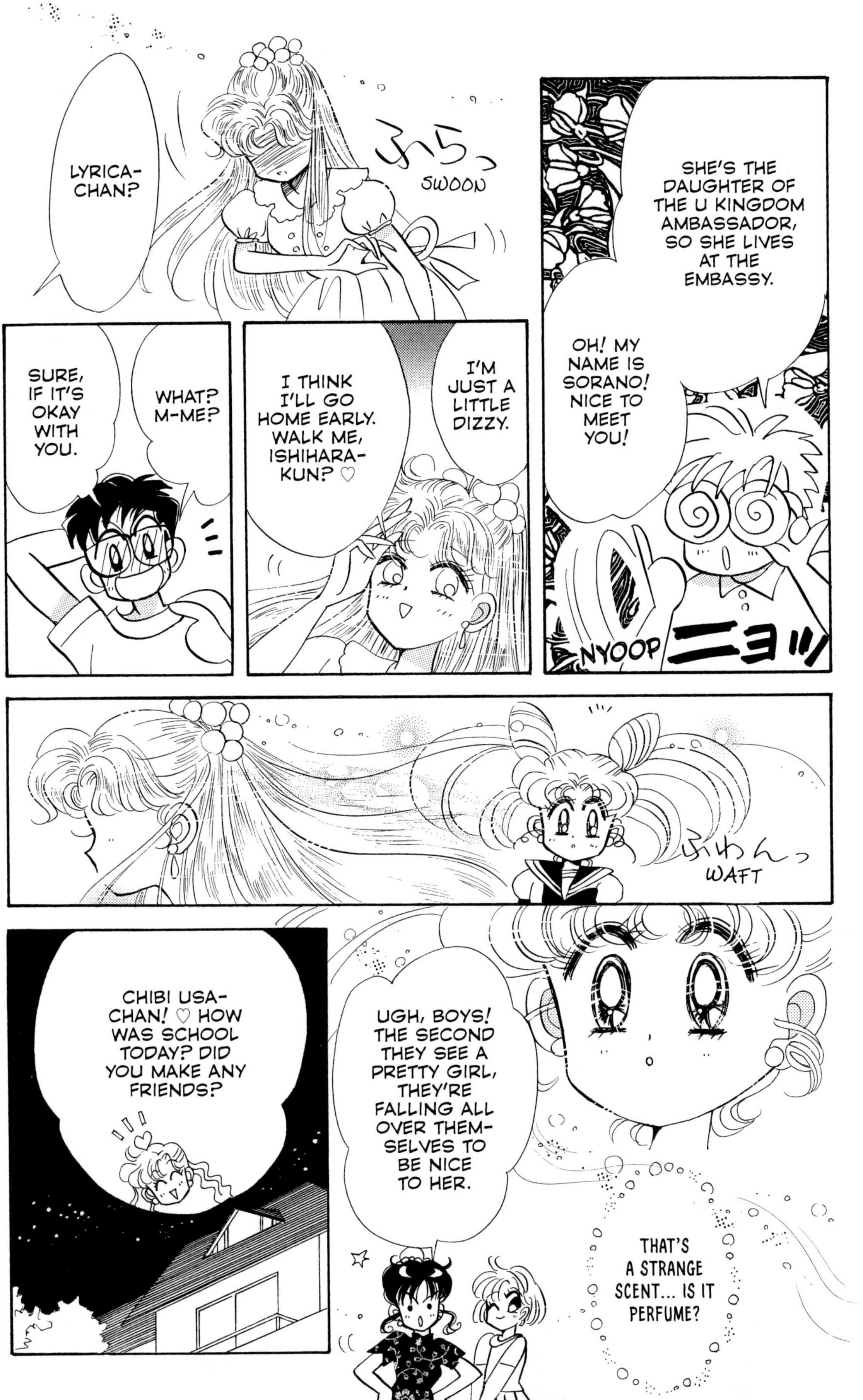

SHE'S THE DAUGHTER OF THE U KINGDOM AMBASSADOR, SO SHE LIVES AT THE EMBASSY.
OH! MY NAME IS SORANO! NICE TO MEET YOU!
ニヨッ
NYOOP
LYRICA-CHAN?
ふらっ
SWOON
I'M JUST A LITTLE DIZZY.
I THINK I'LL GO HOME EARLY. WALK ME, ISHIHARA-KUN? ♡
WHAT? M-ME?
SURE, IF IT'S OKAY WITH YOU.
ふわんっ
WAFT
UGH, BOYS! THE SECOND THEY SEE A PRETTY GIRL, THEY'RE FALLING ALL OVER THEMSELVES TO BE NICE TO HER.
THAT'S A STRANGE SCENT... IS IT PERFUME?
CHIBI USA-CHAN! ♡ HOW WAS SCHOOL TODAY? DID YOU MAKE ANY FRIENDS?

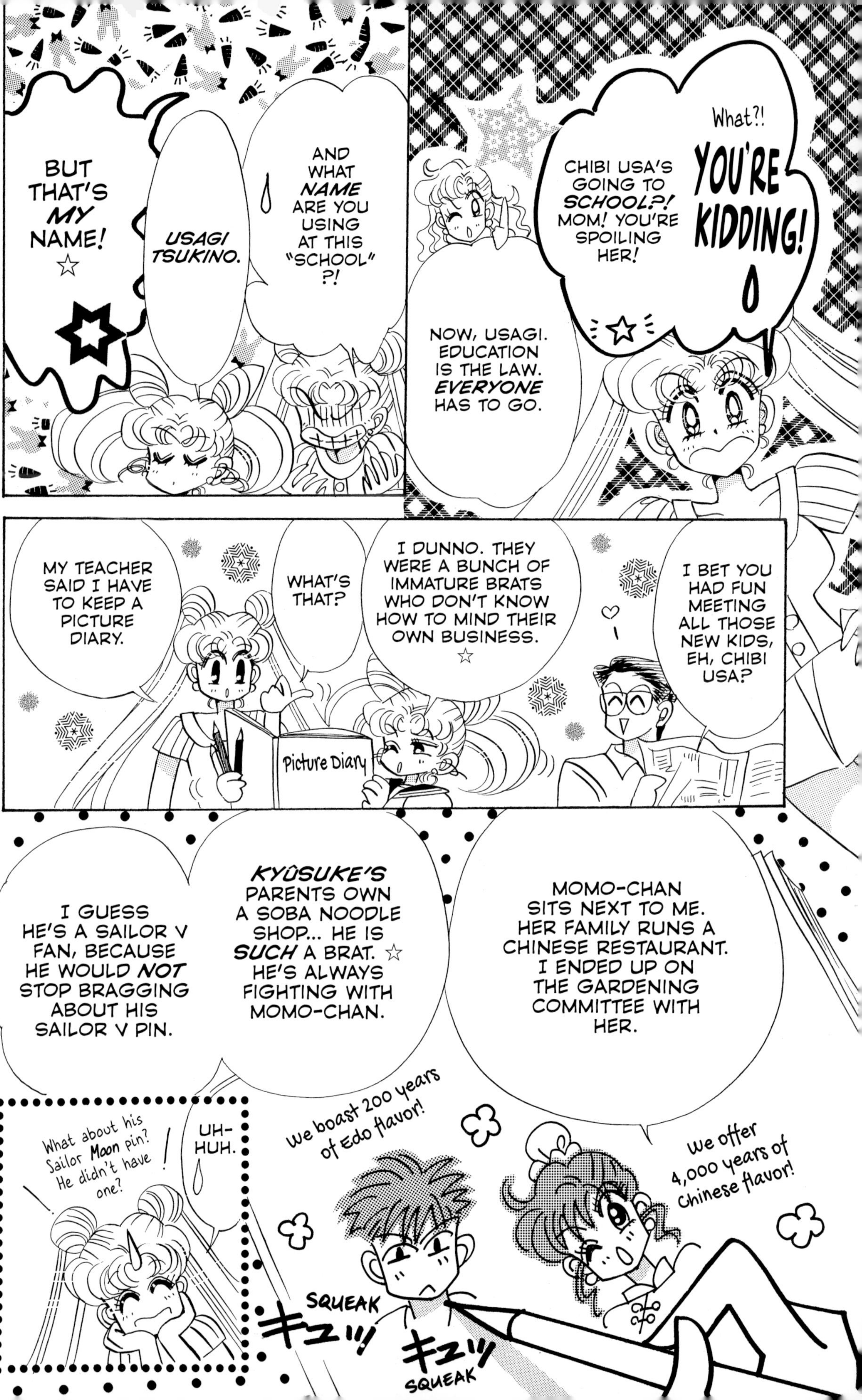

What?! YOU'RE KIDDING!
CHIBI USA'S GOING TO SCHOOL?! MOM! YOU'RE SPOILING HER!
NOW, USAGI. EDUCATION IS THE LAW. EVERYONE HAS TO GO.
AND WHAT NAME ARE YOU USING AT THIS "SCHOOL"?!
USAGI TSUKINO.
BUT THAT'S MY NAME! ☆
I BET YOU HAD FUN MEETING ALL THOSE NEW KIDS, EH, CHIBI USA?
I DUNNO. THEY WERE A BUNCH OF IMMATURE BRATS WHO DON'T KNOW HOW TO MIND THEIR OWN BUSINESS. ☆
WHAT'S THAT?
MY TEACHER SAID I HAVE TO KEEP A PICTURE DIARY.
Picture Diary
MOMO-CHAN SITS NEXT TO ME. HER FAMILY RUNS A CHINESE RESTAURANT. I ENDED UP ON THE GARDENING COMMITTEE WITH HER.
KYÛSUKE'S PARENTS OWN A SOBA NOODLE SHOP... HE IS SUCH A BRAT. ☆ HE'S ALWAYS FIGHTING WITH MOMO-CHAN.
I GUESS HE'S A SAILOR V FAN, BECAUSE HE WOULD NOT STOP BRAGGING ABOUT HIS SAILOR V PIN.
We offer 4,000 years of Chinese flavor!
We boast 200 years of Edo flavor!
SQUEAK
SQUEAK
UH-HUH.
What about his Sailor Moon pin? He didn't have one?

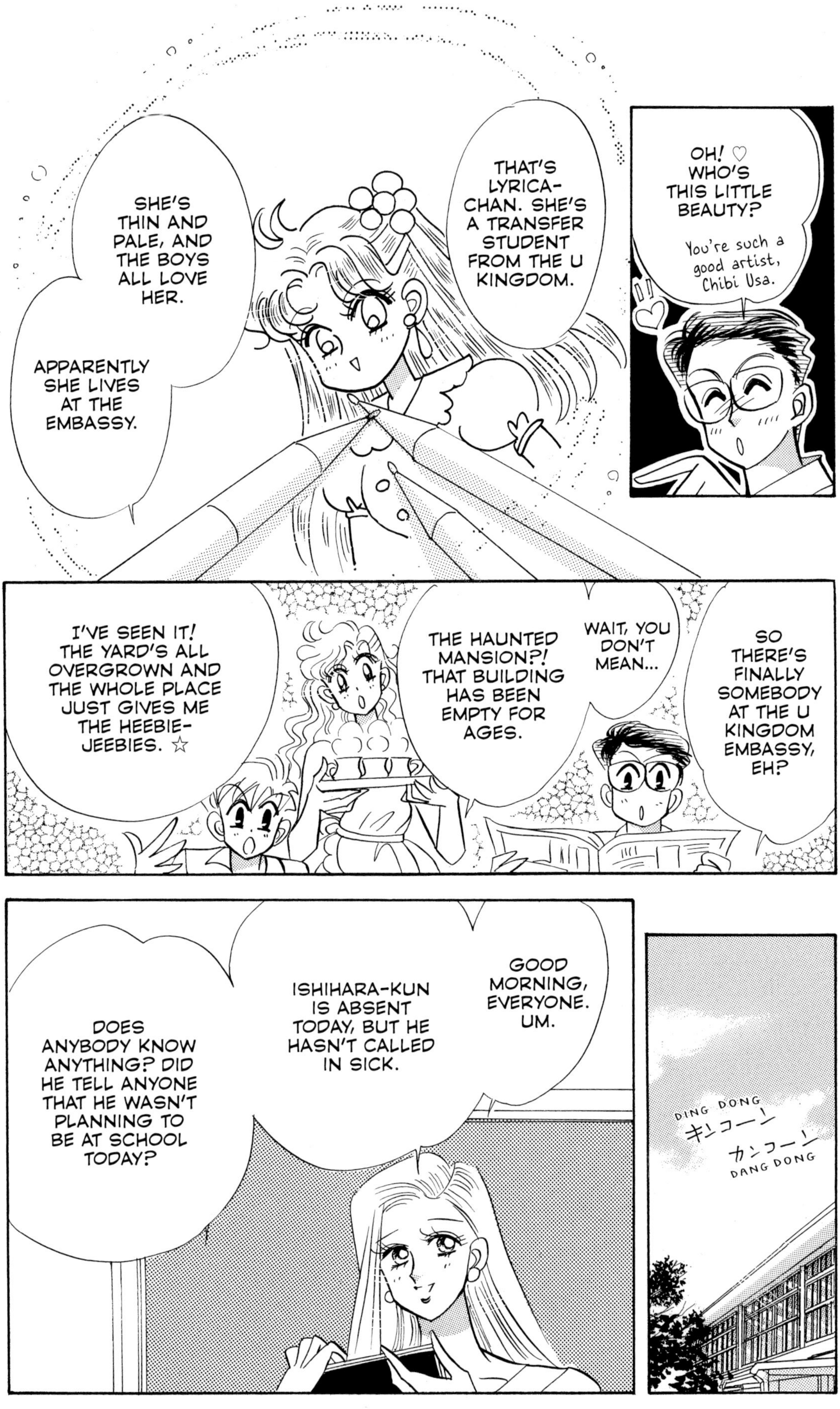
OH! ♡ WHO'S THIS LITTLE BEAUTY?
You're such a good artist, Chibi Usa.
THAT'S LYRICA-CHAN. SHE'S A TRANSFER STUDENT FROM THE U KINGDOM.
SHE'S THIN AND PALE, AND THE BOYS ALL LOVE HER.
APPARENTLY SHE LIVES AT THE EMBASSY.
SO THERE'S FINALLY SOMEBODY AT THE U KINGDOM EMBASSY, EH?
WAIT, YOU DON'T MEAN...
THE HAUNTED MANSION?! THAT BUILDING HAS BEEN EMPTY FOR AGES.
I'VE SEEN IT! THE YARD'S ALL OVERGROWN AND THE WHOLE PLACE JUST GIVES ME THE HEEBIE-JEEBIES. ☆
DING DONG
キンコーン
カンコーン
DANG DONG
GOOD MORNING, EVERYONE. UM.
ISHIHARA-KUN IS ABSENT TODAY, BUT HE HASN'T CALLED IN SICK.
DOES ANYBODY KNOW ANYTHING? DID HE TELL ANYONE THAT HE WASN'T PLANNING TO BE AT SCHOOL TODAY?

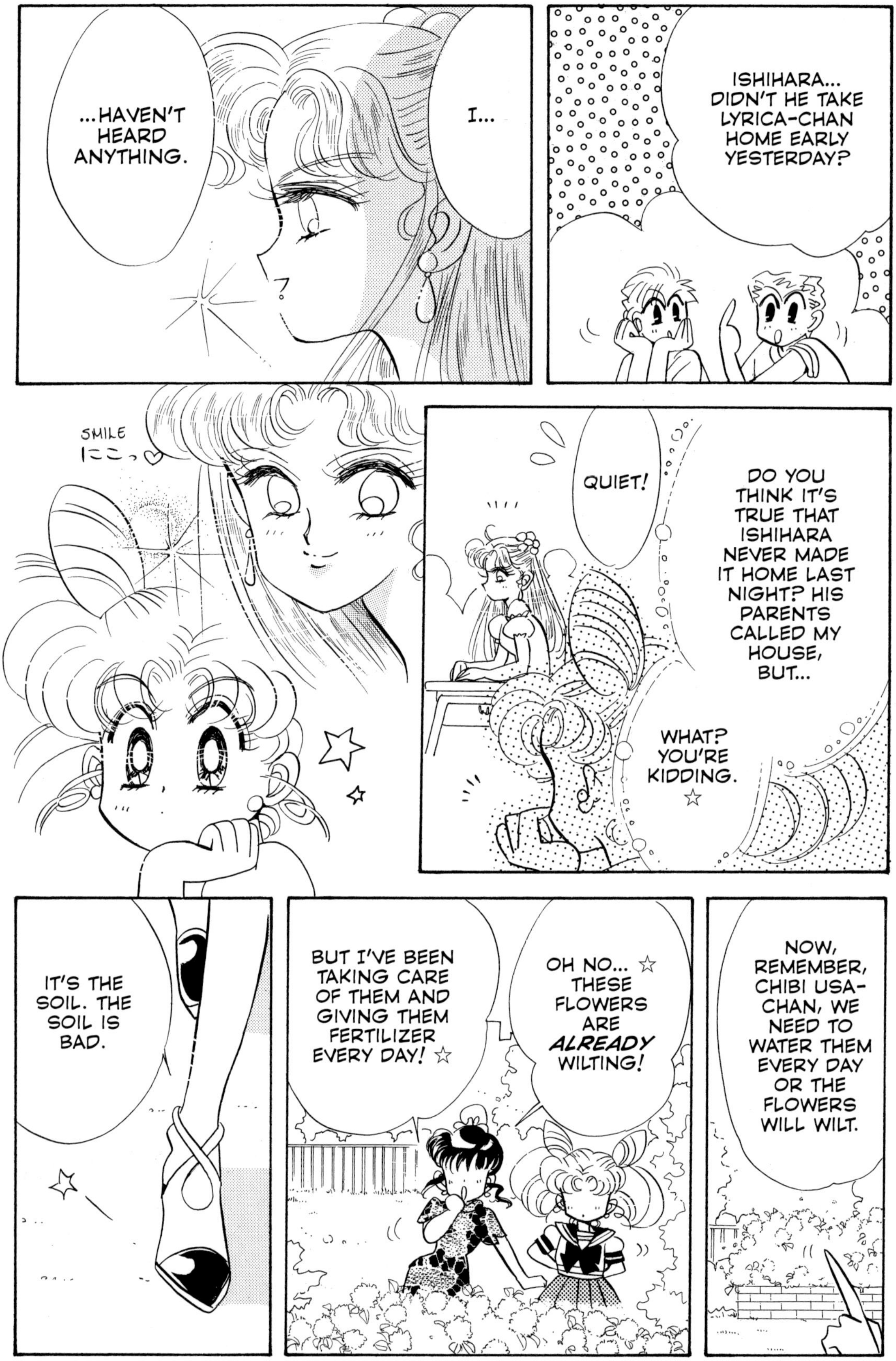
ISHIHARA... DIDN'T HE TAKE LYRICA-CHAN HOME EARLY YESTERDAY?
I...
...HAVEN'T HEARD ANYTHING.
DO YOU THINK IT'S TRUE THAT ISHIHARA NEVER MADE IT HOME LAST NIGHT? HIS PARENTS CALLED MY HOUSE, BUT...
QUIET!
WHAT? YOU'RE KIDDING. ☆
SMILE
にこっ♡
NOW, REMEMBER, CHIBI USA-CHAN, WE NEED TO WATER THEM EVERY DAY OR THE FLOWERS WILL WILT.
OH NO... ☆ THESE FLOWERS ARE *ALREADY* WILTING!
BUT I'VE BEEN TAKING CARE OF THEM AND GIVING THEM FERTILIZER EVERY DAY! ☆
IT'S THE SOIL. THE SOIL IS BAD.

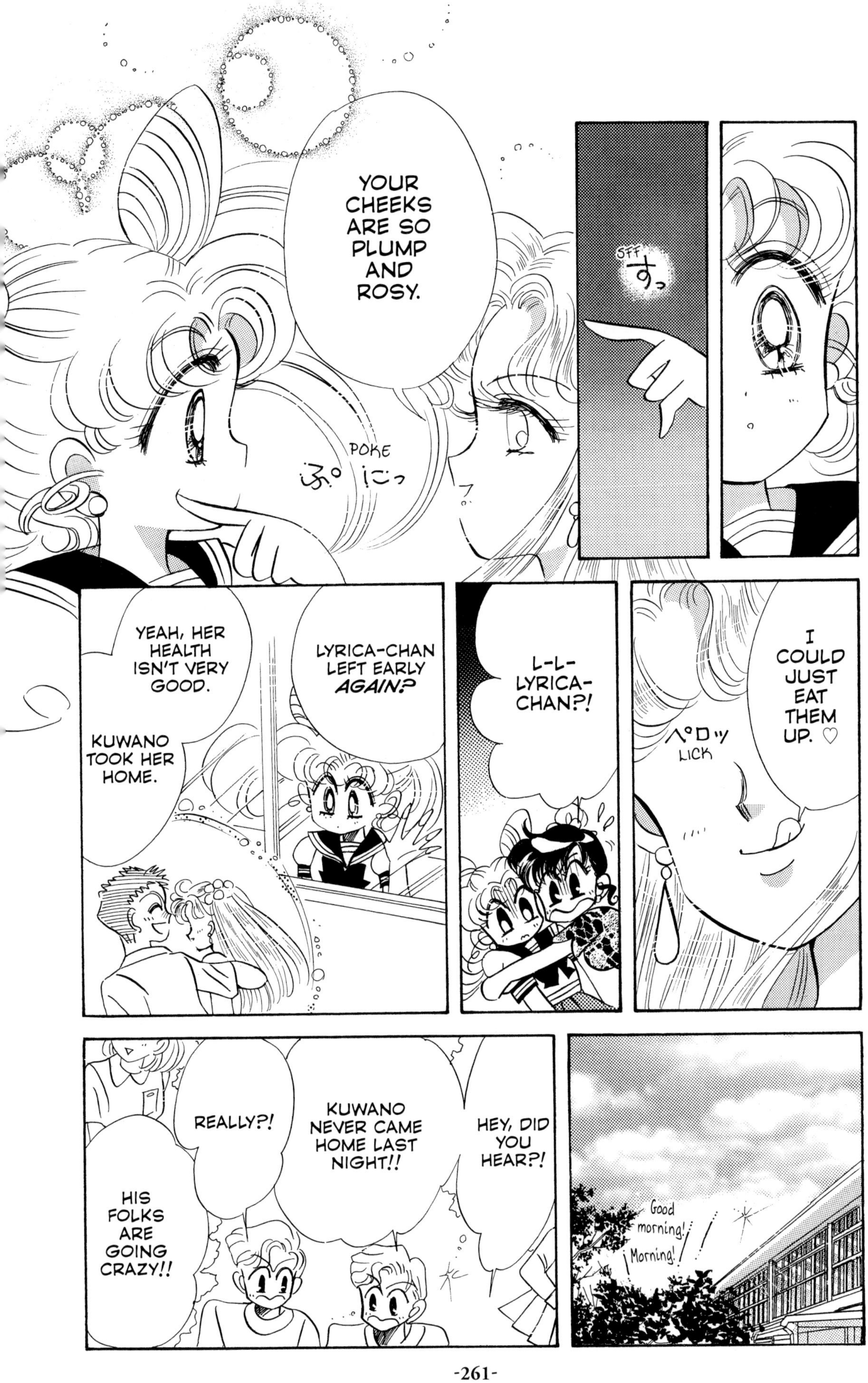
SFF
すっ
YOUR CHEEKS ARE SO PLUMP AND ROSY.
POKE
ぷにっ
I COULD JUST EAT THEM UP. ♡
ペロッ
LICK
L-L-LYRICA-CHAN?!
LYRICA-CHAN LEFT EARLY *AGAIN?*
YEAH, HER HEALTH ISN'T VERY GOOD.
KUWANO TOOK HER HOME.
Good morning!
Morning!
HEY, DID YOU HEAR?!
KUWANO NEVER CAME HOME LAST NIGHT!!
REALLY?!
HIS FOLKS ARE GOING CRAZY!!

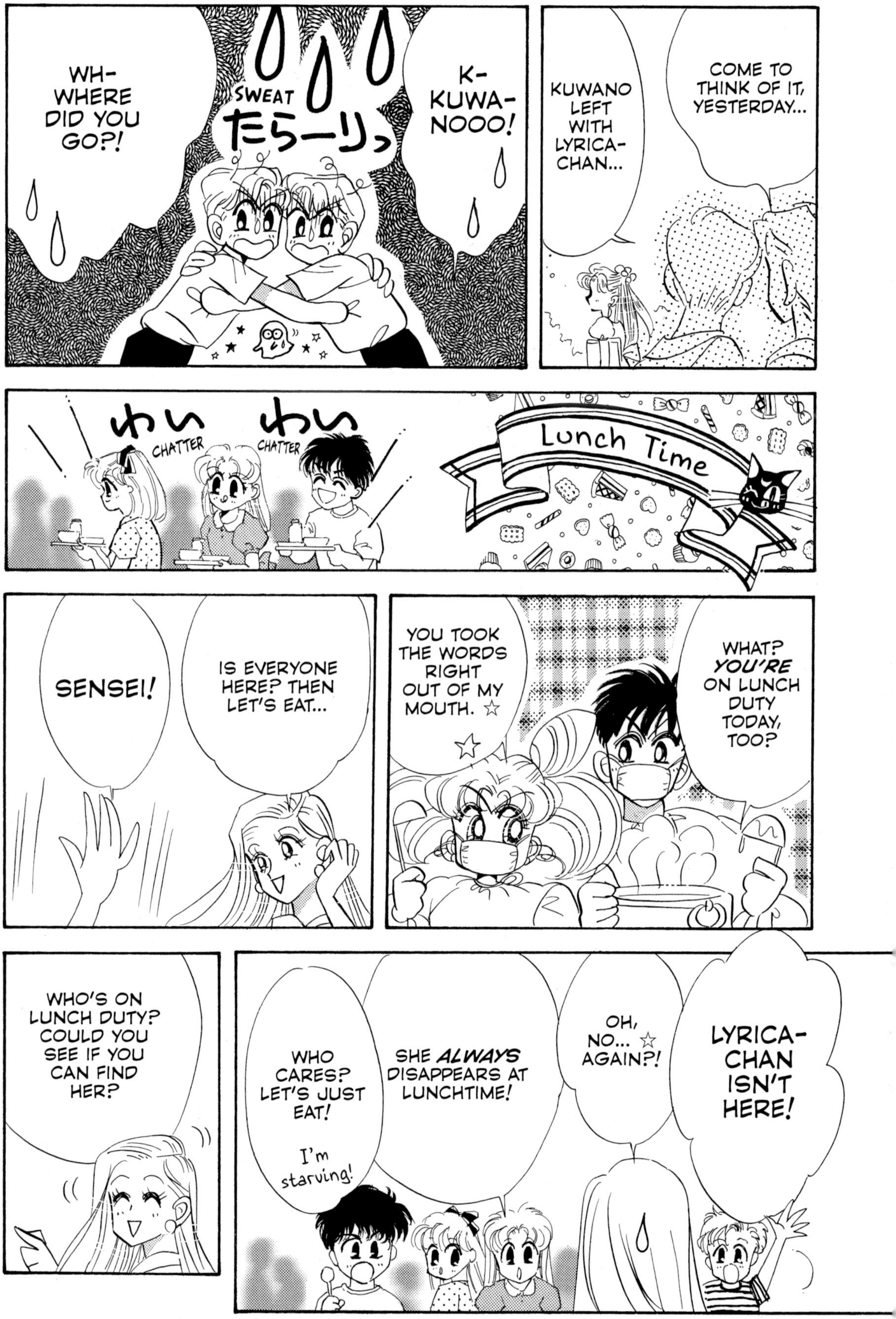
COME TO THINK OF IT, YESTERDAY...
KUWANO LEFT WITH LYRICA-CHAN...
K-KUWA-NOOO!
たらーりっ
SWEAT
WH-WHERE DID YOU GO?!
Lunch Time
わい わい
CHATTER CHATTER
WHAT? *YOU'RE* ON LUNCH DUTY TODAY, TOO?
YOU TOOK THE WORDS RIGHT OUT OF MY MOUTH. ☆
IS EVERYONE HERE? THEN LET'S EAT...
SENSEI!
LYRICA-CHAN ISN'T HERE!
OH, NO... ☆ AGAIN?!
SHE *ALWAYS* DISAPPEARS AT LUNCHTIME!
WHO CARES? LET'S JUST EAT!
I'm starving!
WHO'S ON LUNCH DUTY? COULD YOU SEE IF YOU CAN FIND HER?

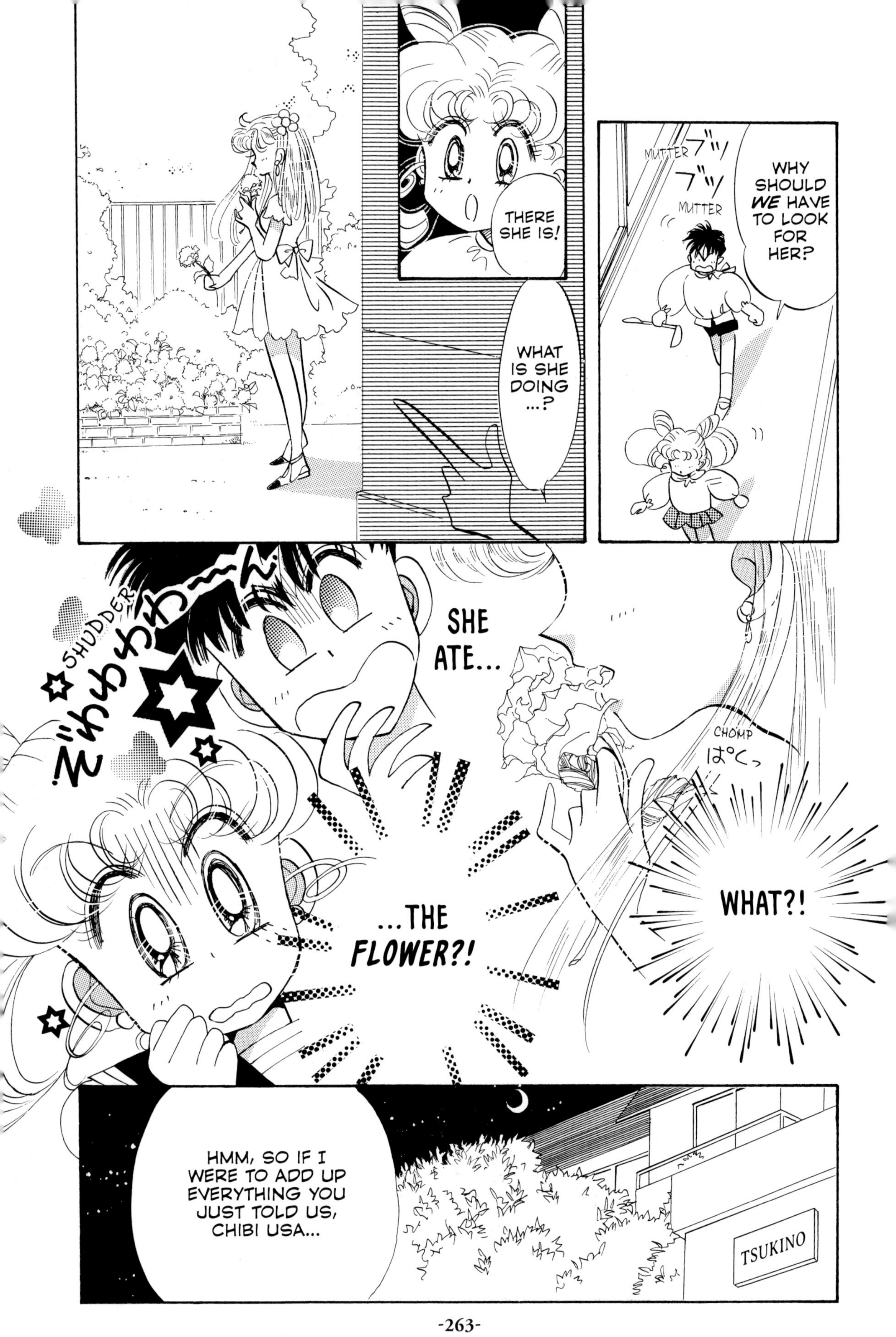
MUTTER ブツ
ブツ MUTTER
WHY SHOULD WE HAVE TO LOOK FOR HER?
THERE SHE IS!
WHAT IS SHE DOING ...?
...
CHOMP ぱくっ
WHAT?!
SHE ATE...
...THE FLOWER?!
SHUDDER ぞわわわ～ん
HMM, SO IF I WERE TO ADD UP EVERYTHING YOU JUST TOLD US, CHIBI USA...
TSUKINO

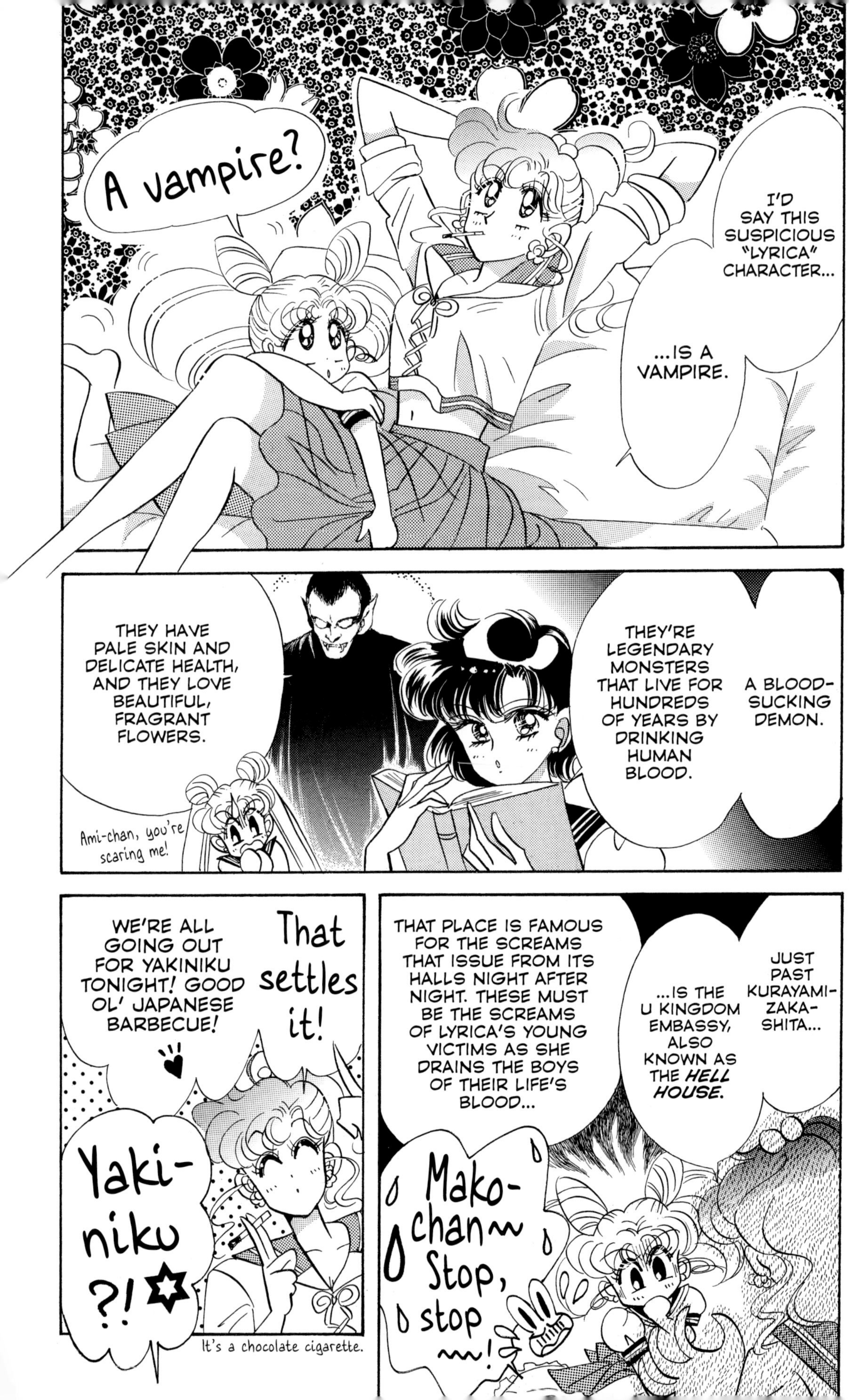
I'D SAY THIS SUSPICIOUS "LYRICA" CHARACTER...
...IS A VAMPIRE.
A vampire?
A BLOOD-SUCKING DEMON.
THEY'RE LEGENDARY MONSTERS THAT LIVE FOR HUNDREDS OF YEARS BY DRINKING HUMAN BLOOD.
THEY HAVE PALE SKIN AND DELICATE HEALTH, AND THEY LOVE BEAUTIFUL, FRAGRANT FLOWERS.
Ami-chan, you're scaring me!
JUST PAST KURAYAMI-ZAKA-SHITA...
...IS THE U KINGDOM EMBASSY, ALSO KNOWN AS THE *HELL HOUSE*.
THAT PLACE IS FAMOUS FOR THE SCREAMS THAT ISSUE FROM ITS HALLS NIGHT AFTER NIGHT. THESE MUST BE THE SCREAMS OF LYRICA'S YOUNG VICTIMS AS SHE DRAINS THE BOYS OF THEIR LIFE'S BLOOD...
Mako-chan~ Stop, stop~!
That settles it!
WE'RE ALL GOING OUT FOR YAKINIKU TONIGHT! GOOD OL' JAPANESE BARBECUE!
Yaki-niku?!
It's a chocolate cigarette.

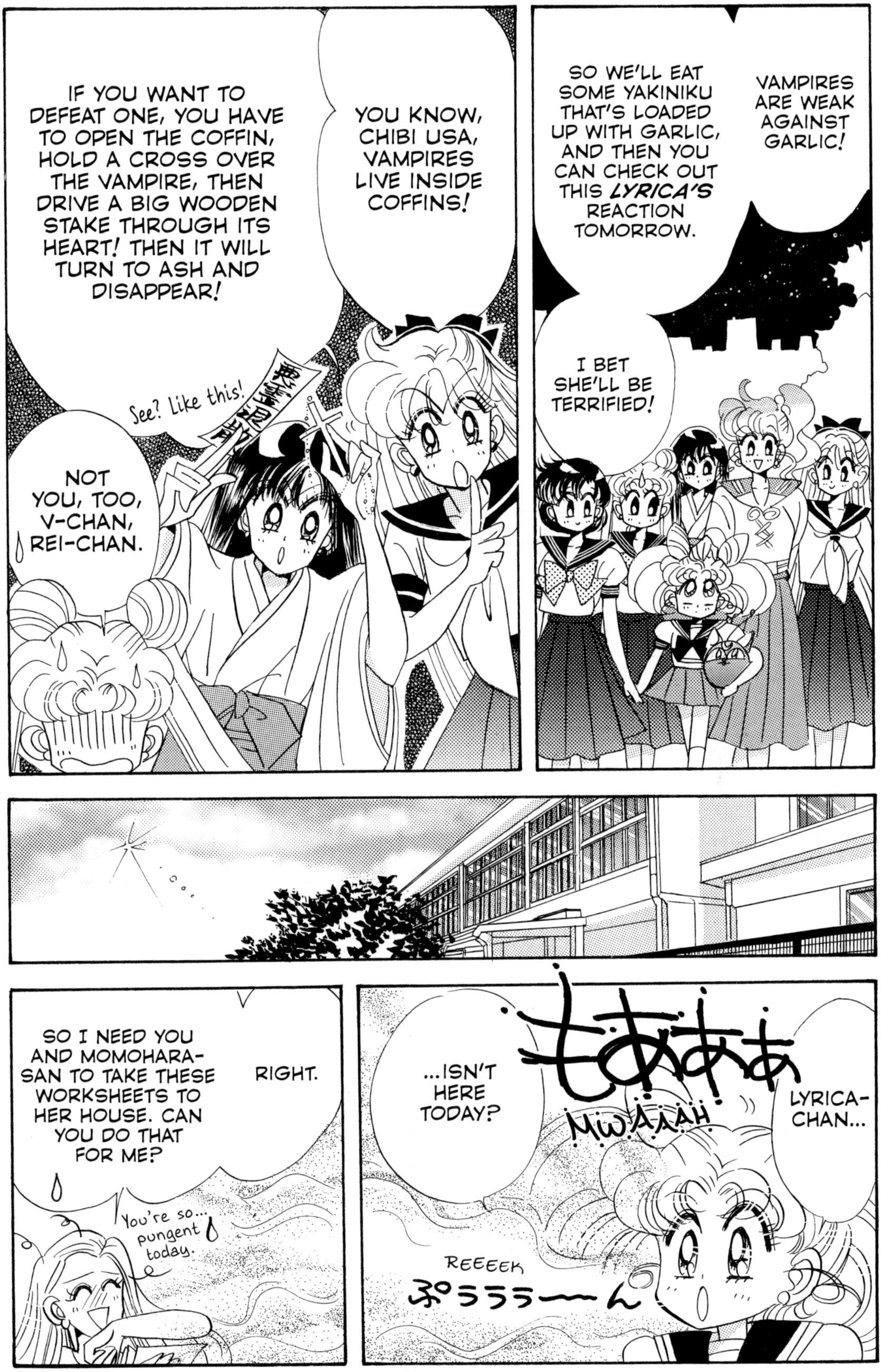
VAMPIRES ARE WEAK AGAINST GARLIC!
SO WE'LL EAT SOME YAKINIKU THAT'S LOADED UP WITH GARLIC, AND THEN YOU CAN CHECK OUT THIS *LYRICA'S* REACTION TOMORROW.
I BET SHE'LL BE TERRIFIED!
YOU KNOW, CHIBI USA, VAMPIRES LIVE INSIDE COFFINS!
IF YOU WANT TO DEFEAT ONE, YOU HAVE TO OPEN THE COFFIN, HOLD A CROSS OVER THE VAMPIRE, THEN DRIVE A BIG WOODEN STAKE THROUGH ITS HEART! THEN IT WILL TURN TO ASH AND DISAPPEAR!
See? Like this!
NOT YOU, TOO, V-CHAN, REI-CHAN.
LYRICA-CHAN...
もあああ
MWAAAH
...ISN'T HERE TODAY?
REEEEK
ぷらららーーん
RIGHT.
SO I NEED YOU AND MOMOHARA-SAN TO TAKE THESE WORKSHEETS TO HER HOUSE. CAN YOU DO THAT FOR ME?
You're so... pungent today.

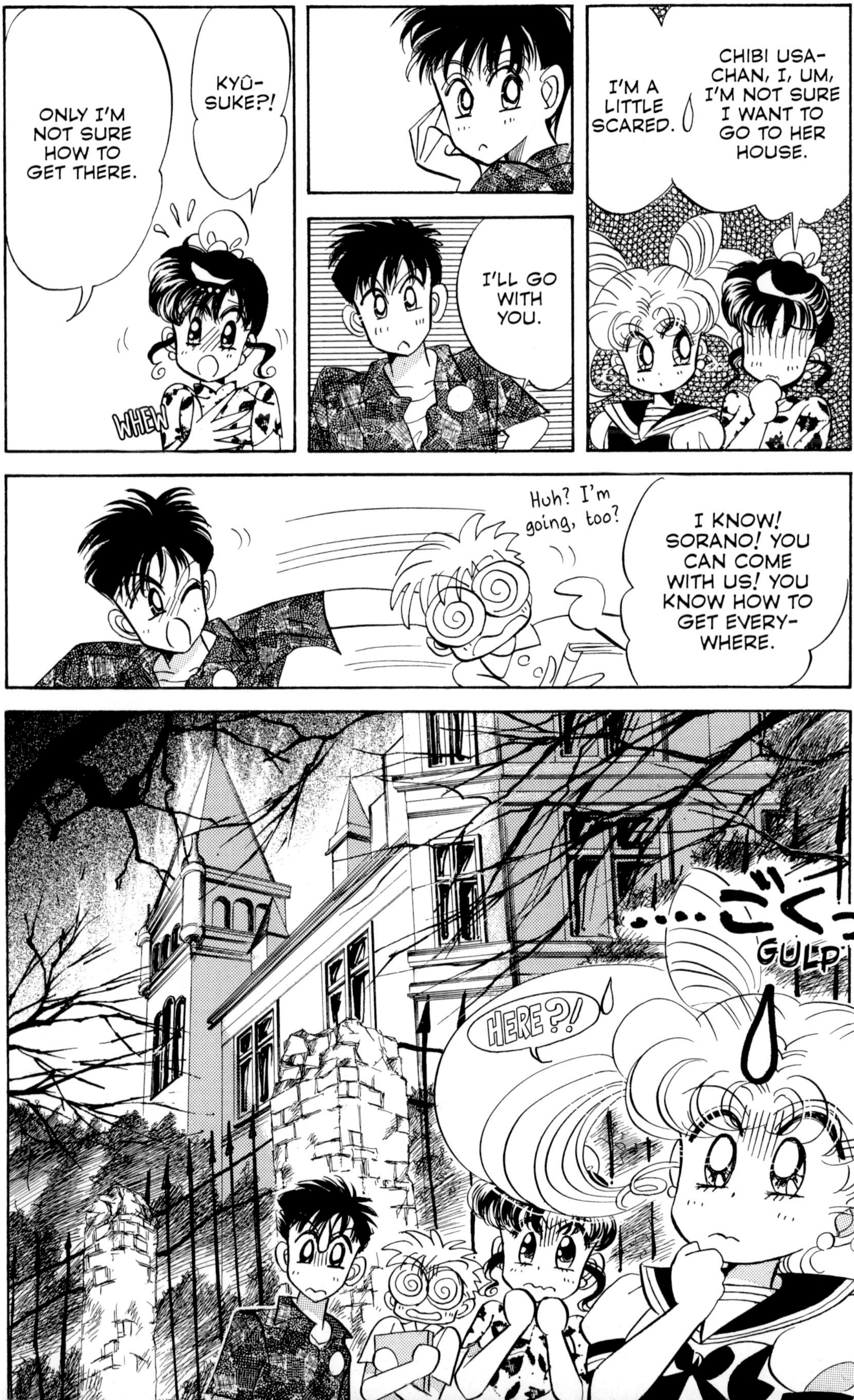
CHIBI USA-CHAN, I, UM, I'M NOT SURE I WANT TO GO TO HER HOUSE.
I'M A LITTLE SCARED.
I'LL GO WITH YOU.
KYÛ-SUKE?!
ONLY I'M NOT SURE HOW TO GET THERE.
WHEW
I KNOW! SORANO! YOU CAN COME WITH US! YOU KNOW HOW TO GET EVERY-WHERE.
Huh? I'm going, too?
……ごくっ
GULP
HERE?!

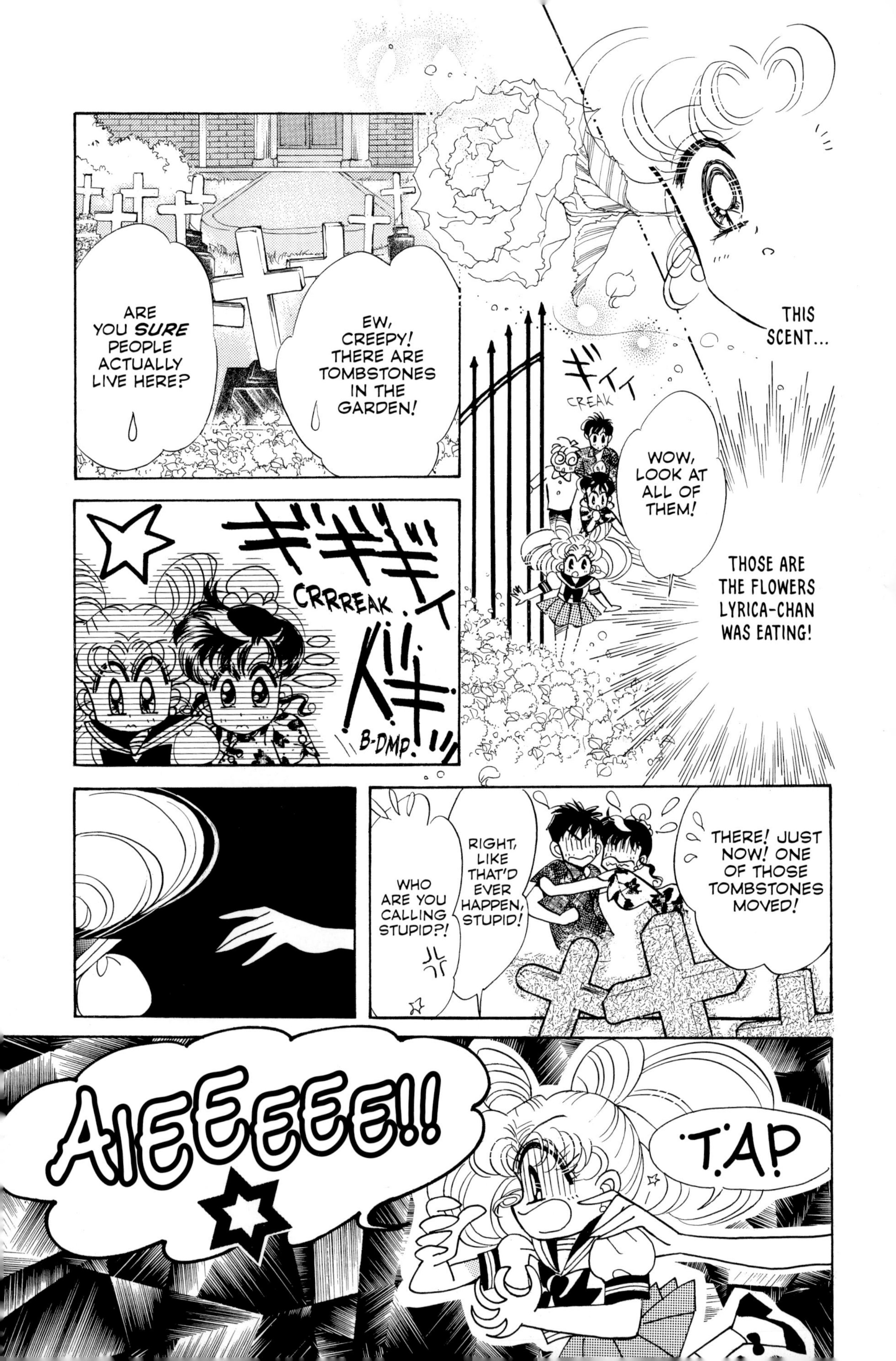
THIS SCENT...
CREAK
WOW, LOOK AT ALL OF THEM!
THOSE ARE THE FLOWERS LYRICA-CHAN WAS EATING!
EW, CREEPY! THERE ARE TOMBSTONES IN THE GARDEN!
ARE YOU SURE PEOPLE ACTUALLY LIVE HERE?
CRRREAK
B-DMP
THERE! JUST NOW! ONE OF THOSE TOMBSTONES MOVED!
RIGHT, LIKE THAT'D EVER HAPPEN, STUPID!
WHO ARE YOU CALLING STUPID?!
TAP
AIEEEEE!!

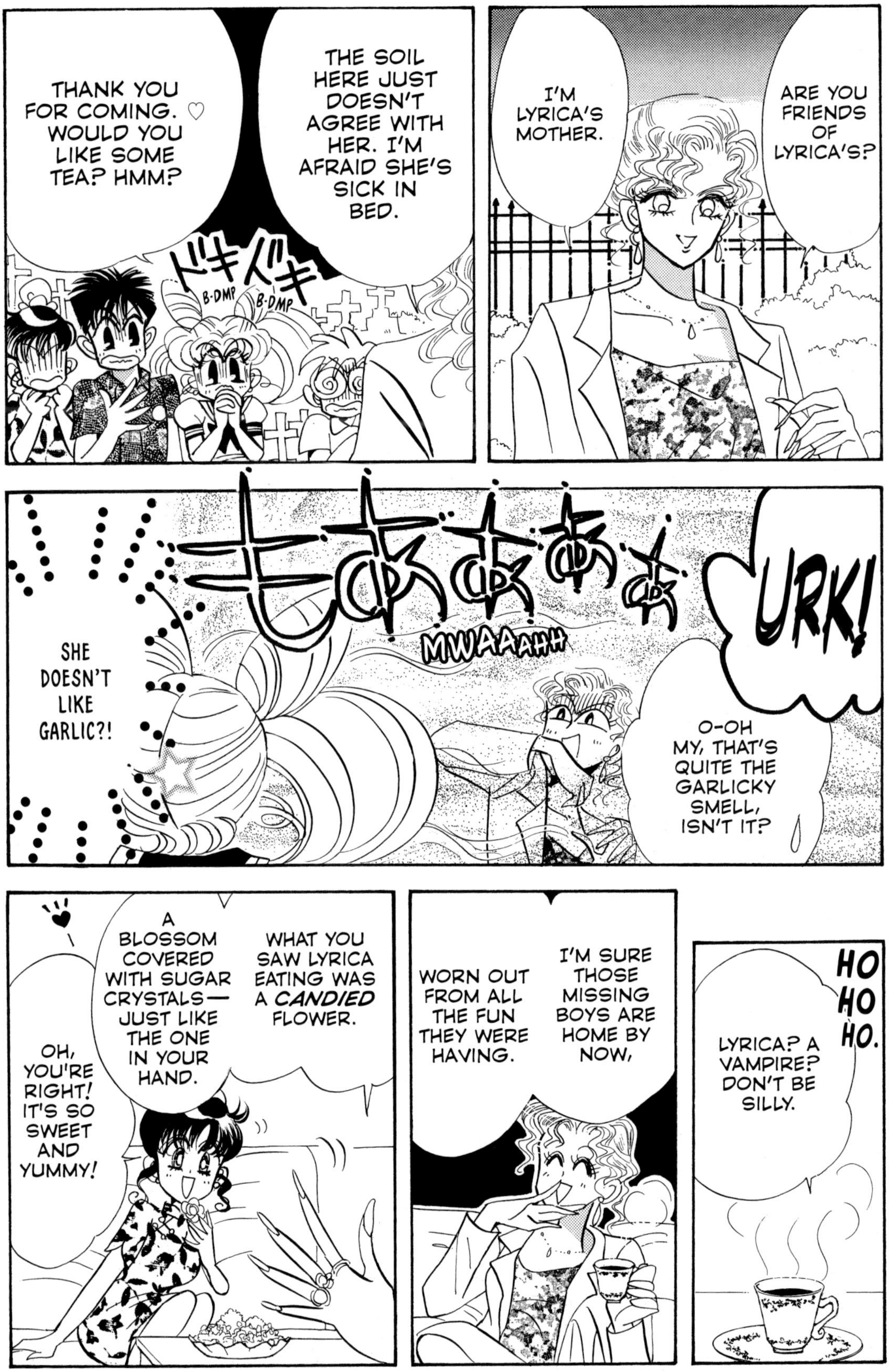
ARE YOU FRIENDS OF LYRICA'S?
I'M LYRICA'S MOTHER.
THE SOIL HERE JUST DOESN'T AGREE WITH HER. I'M AFRAID SHE'S SICK IN BED.
THANK YOU FOR COMING. ♡ WOULD YOU LIKE SOME TEA? HMM?
ドキドキ
B-DMP B-DMP
URK!
O-OH MY, THAT'S QUITE THE GARLICKY SMELL, ISN'T IT?
MWAAAHH
SHE DOESN'T LIKE GARLIC?!
HO HO HO.
LYRICA? A VAMPIRE? DON'T BE SILLY.
I'M SURE THOSE MISSING BOYS ARE HOME BY NOW,
WORN OUT FROM ALL THE FUN THEY WERE HAVING.
WHAT YOU SAW LYRICA EATING WAS A *CANDIED* FLOWER.
A BLOSSOM COVERED WITH SUGAR CRYSTALS— JUST LIKE THE ONE IN YOUR HAND.
OH, YOU'RE RIGHT! IT'S SO SWEET AND YUMMY!

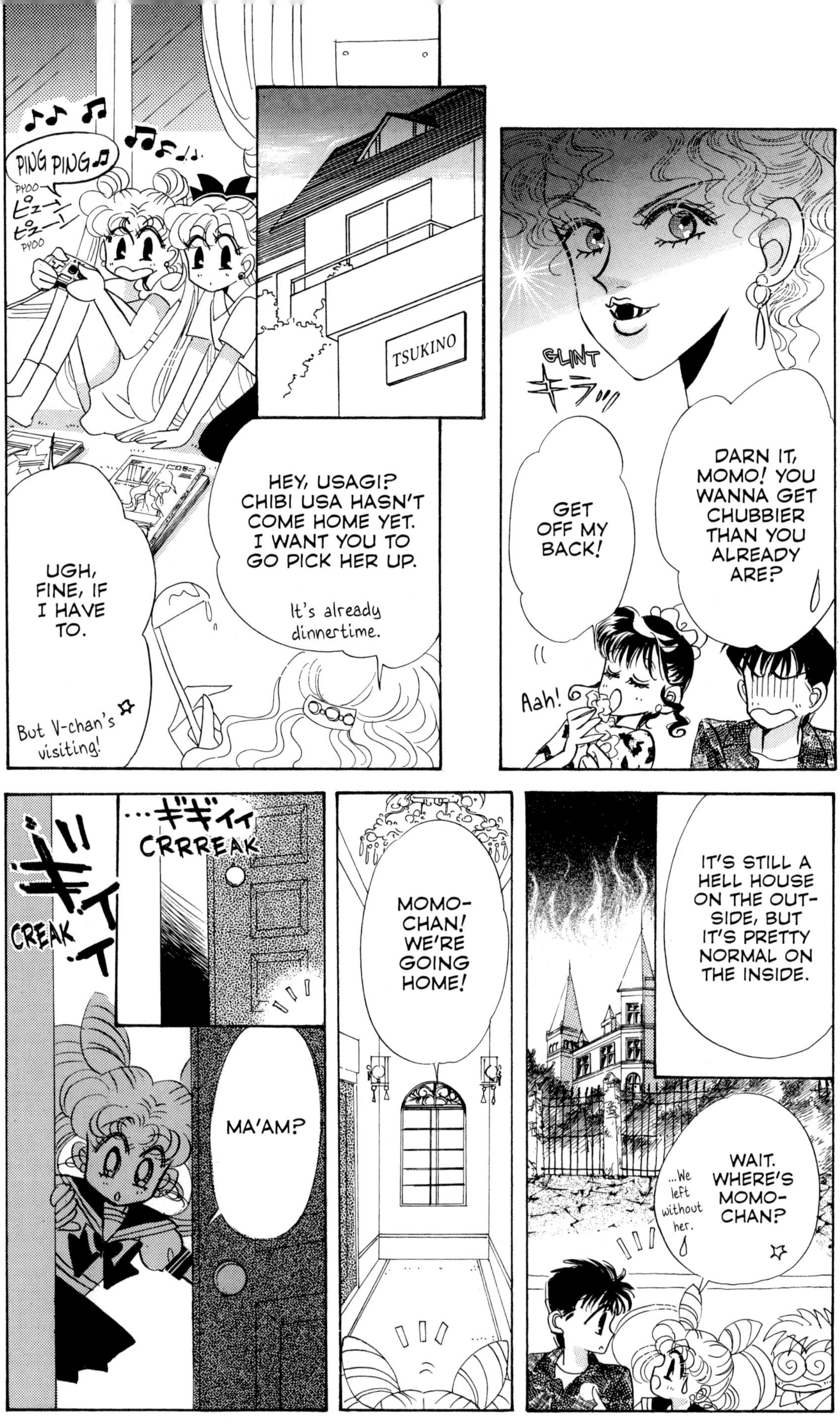
GLINT
キラッ
DARN IT, MOMO! YOU WANNA GET CHUBBIER THAN YOU ALREADY ARE?
GET OFF MY BACK!
Aah!
TSUKINO
PING PING
PYOO
PYOO
HEY, USAGI? CHIBI USA HASN'T COME HOME YET. I WANT YOU TO GO PICK HER UP.
It's already dinnertime.
UGH, FINE, IF I HAVE TO.
But V-chan's visiting!
IT'S STILL A HELL HOUSE ON THE OUT-SIDE, BUT IT'S PRETTY NORMAL ON THE INSIDE.
WAIT. WHERE'S MOMO-CHAN?
...We left without her.
MOMO-CHAN! WE'RE GOING HOME!
...ギギィィ
CRRREAK
CREAK
MA'AM?

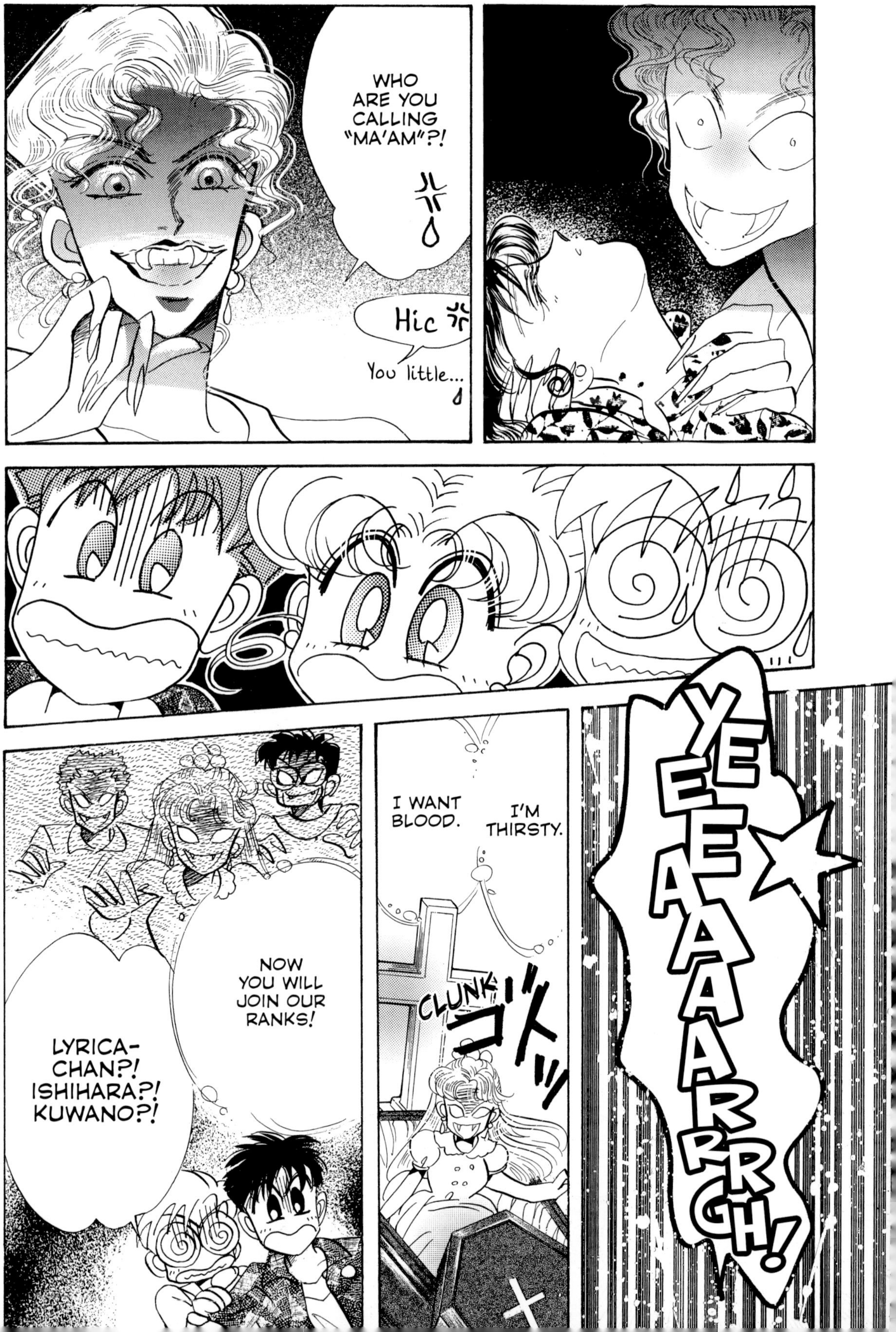
WHO ARE YOU CALLING "MA'AM"?!
Hic
You little...
YEEEAAAARRRGH!
I'M THIRSTY.
I WANT BLOOD.
CLUNK
NOW YOU WILL JOIN OUR RANKS!
LYRICA-CHAN?! ISHIHARA?! KUWANO?!

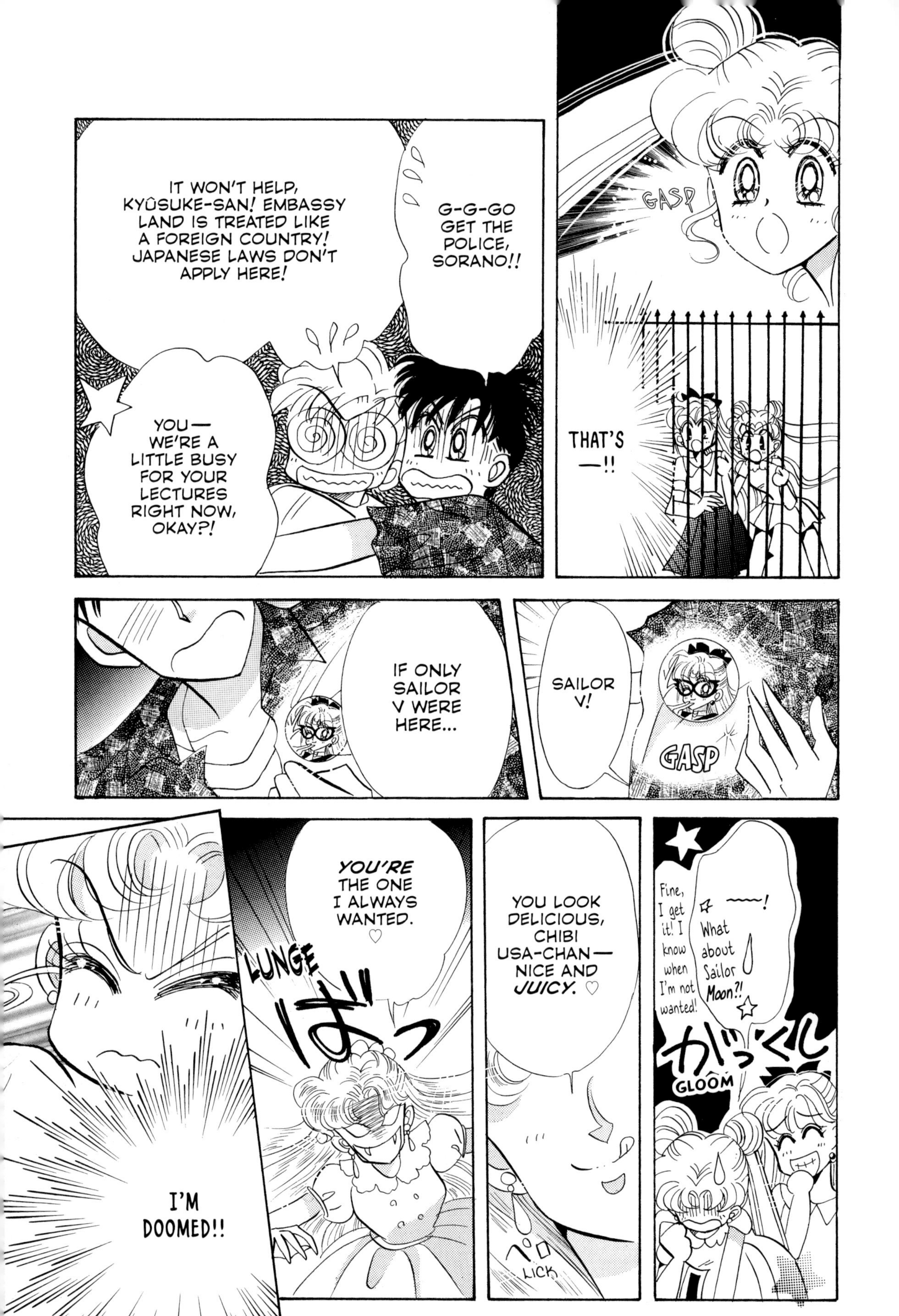
GASP
THAT'S —!!
G-G-GO GET THE POLICE, SORANO!!
IT WON'T HELP, KYÛSUKE-SAN! EMBASSY LAND IS TREATED LIKE A FOREIGN COUNTRY! JAPANESE LAWS DON'T APPLY HERE!
YOU— WE'RE A LITTLE BUSY FOR YOUR LECTURES RIGHT NOW, OKAY?!
SAILOR V!
GASP
IF ONLY SAILOR V WERE HERE...
~~~! What about Sailor Moon?!
Fine, I get it! I know when I'm not wanted!
がっくし
GLOOM
YOU LOOK DELICIOUS, CHIBI USA-CHAN— NICE AND JUICY. ♡
LICK
YOU'RE THE ONE I ALWAYS WANTED. ♡
LUNGE
ばっ
I'M DOOMED!!
~~~

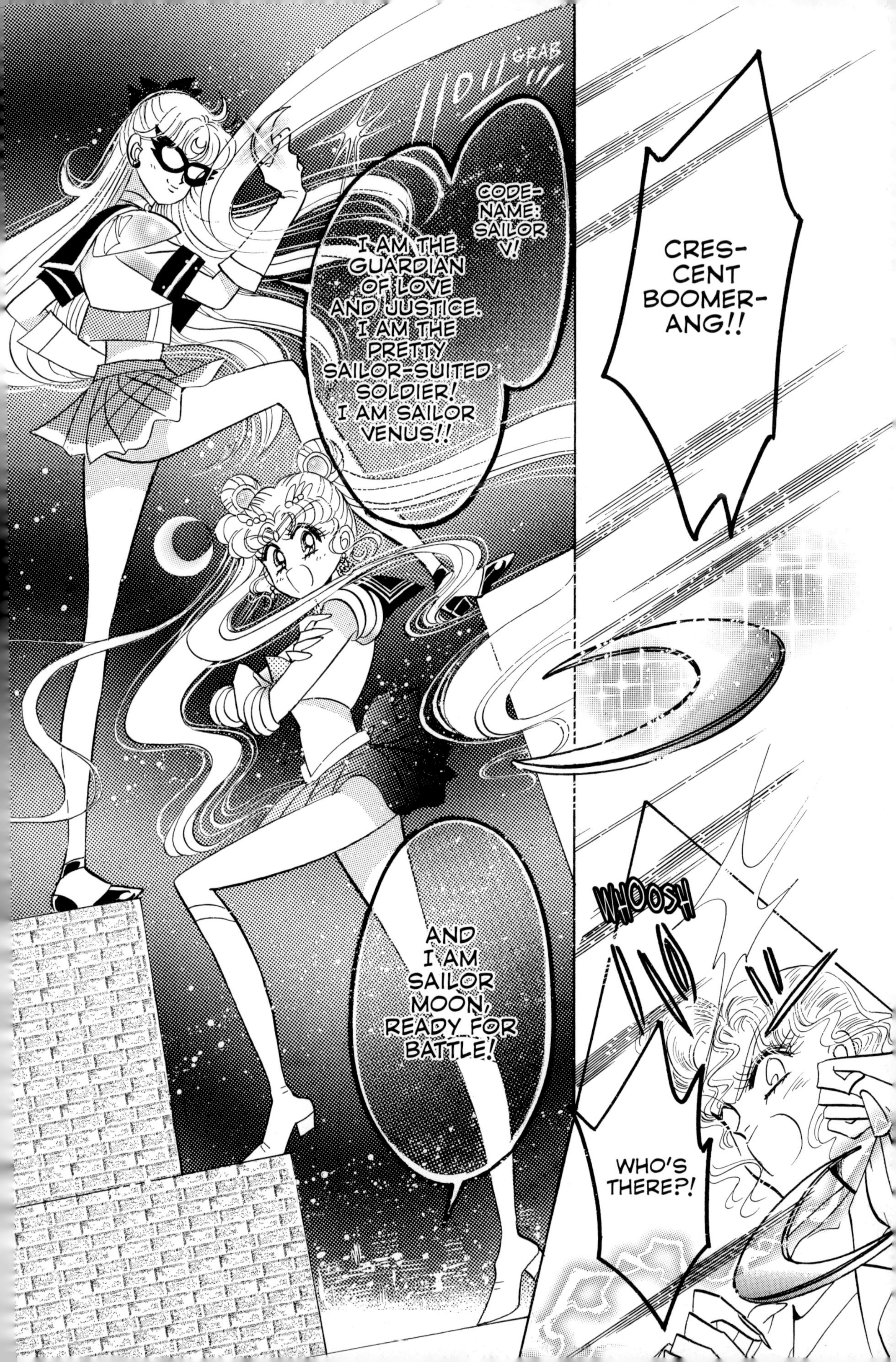
CRES-CENT BOOMER-ANG!!
WHOOSH
WHO'S THERE?!
GRAB
CODE-NAME: SAILOR V!
I AM THE GUARDIAN OF LOVE AND JUSTICE. I AM THE PRETTY SAILOR-SUITED SOLDIER! I AM SAILOR VENUS!!
AND I AM SAILOR MOON, READY FOR BATTLE!

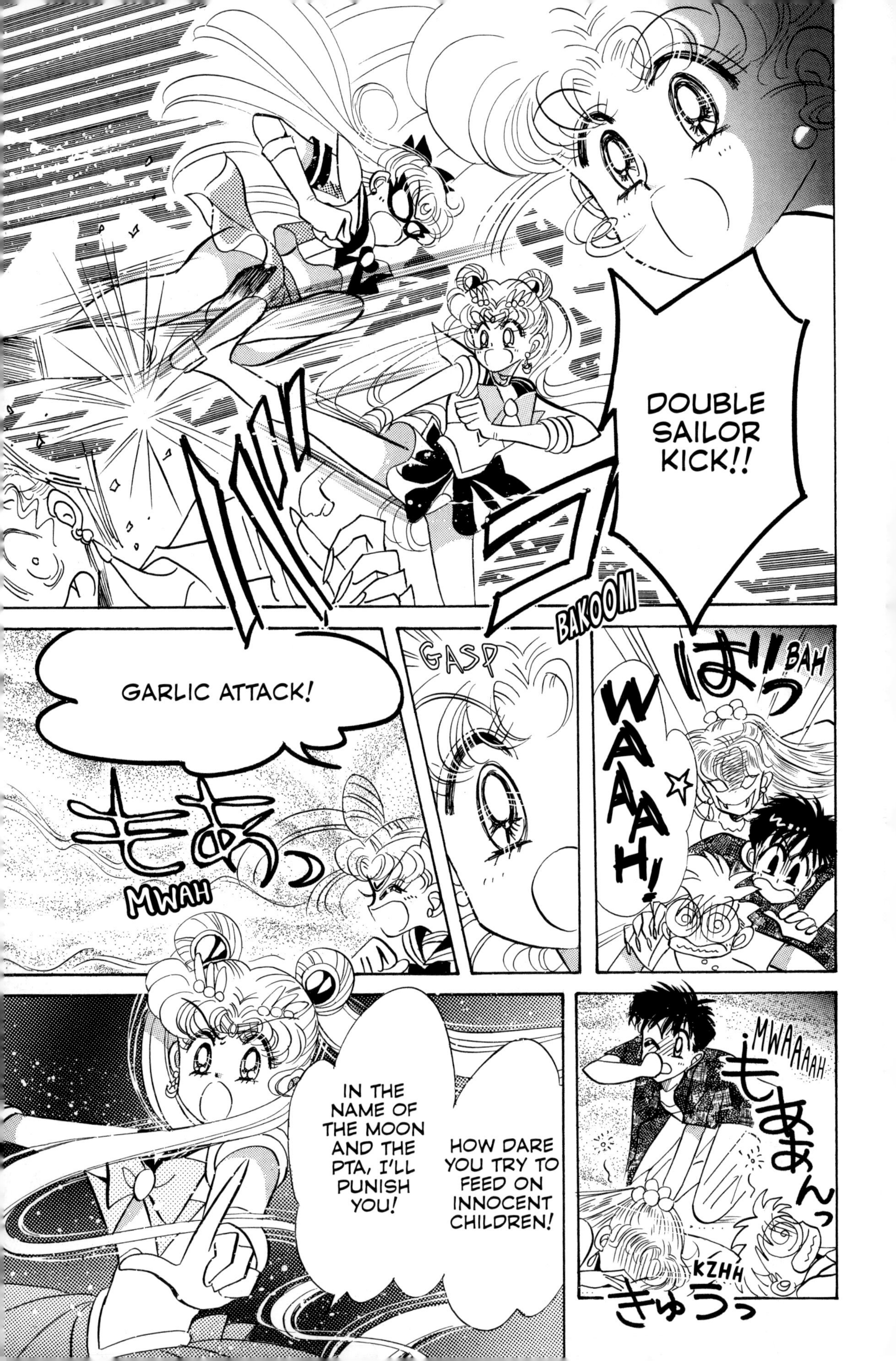
DOUBLE SAILOR KICK!!
BAKOOM
はっ
BAH
WAAAH!
GASP
GARLIC ATTACK!
MWAH
MWAAAAH
KZHH
きゅうっ
HOW DARE YOU TRY TO FEED ON INNOCENT CHILDREN!
IN THE NAME OF THE MOON AND THE PTA, I'LL PUNISH YOU!

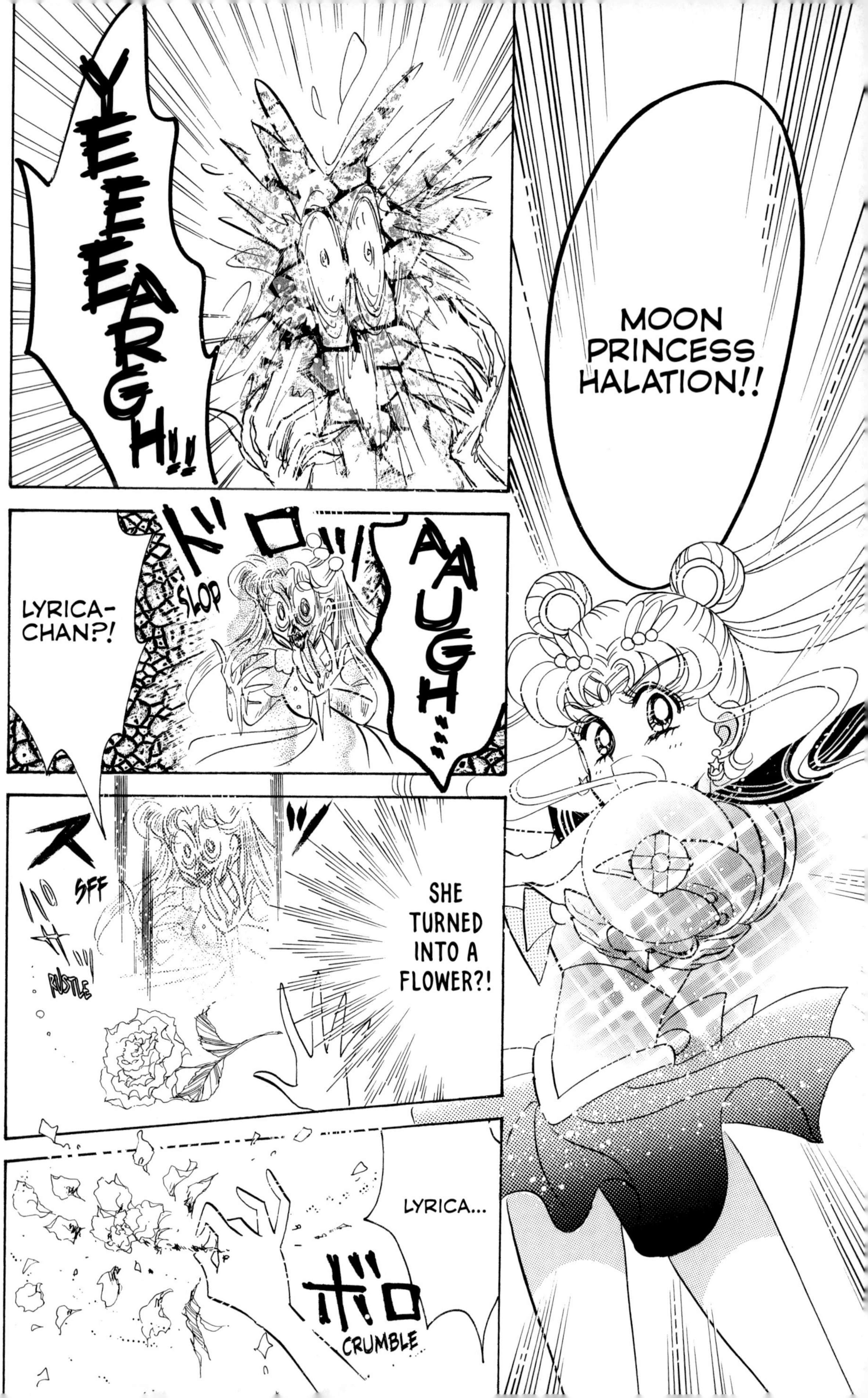
MOON PRINCESS HALATION!!
YEEEEARGH!!
AAAUGH...
ドロ
SLOP
LYRICA-CHAN?!
SHE TURNED INTO A FLOWER?!
ス
SFF
RUSTLE
LYRICA...
ボロ
CRUMBLE

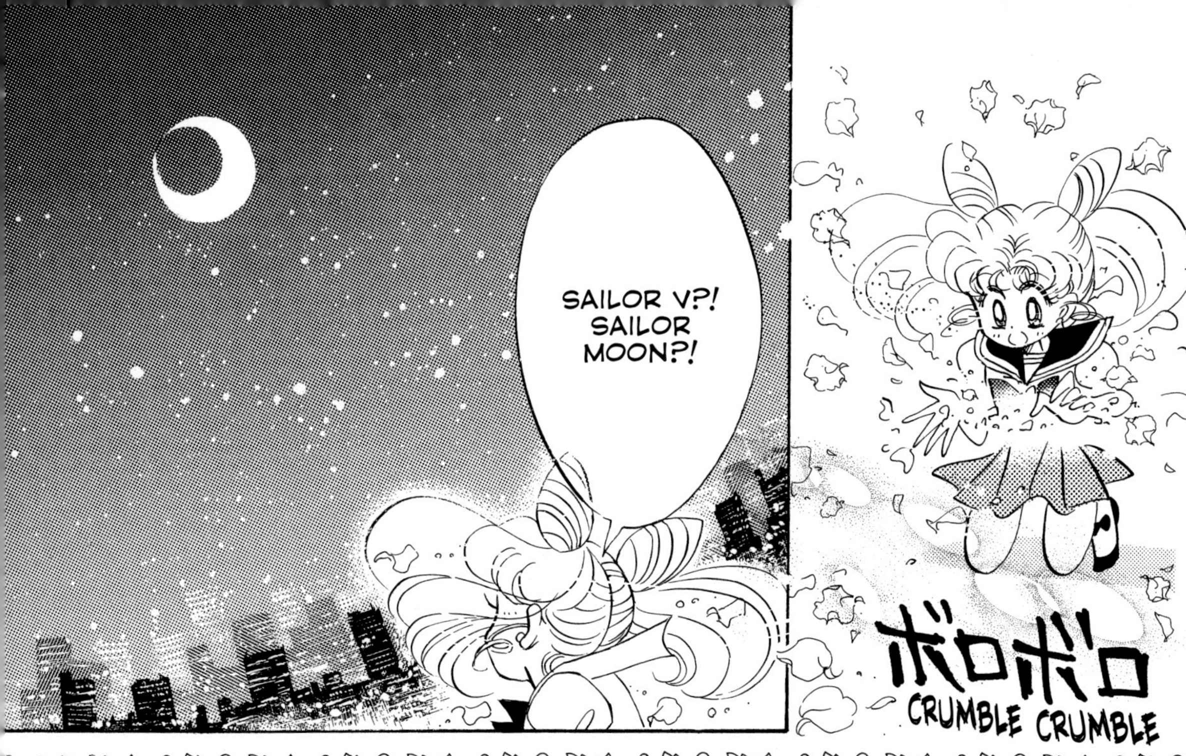
ボロボロ
CRUMBLE CRUMBLE
SAILOR V?! SAILOR MOON?!

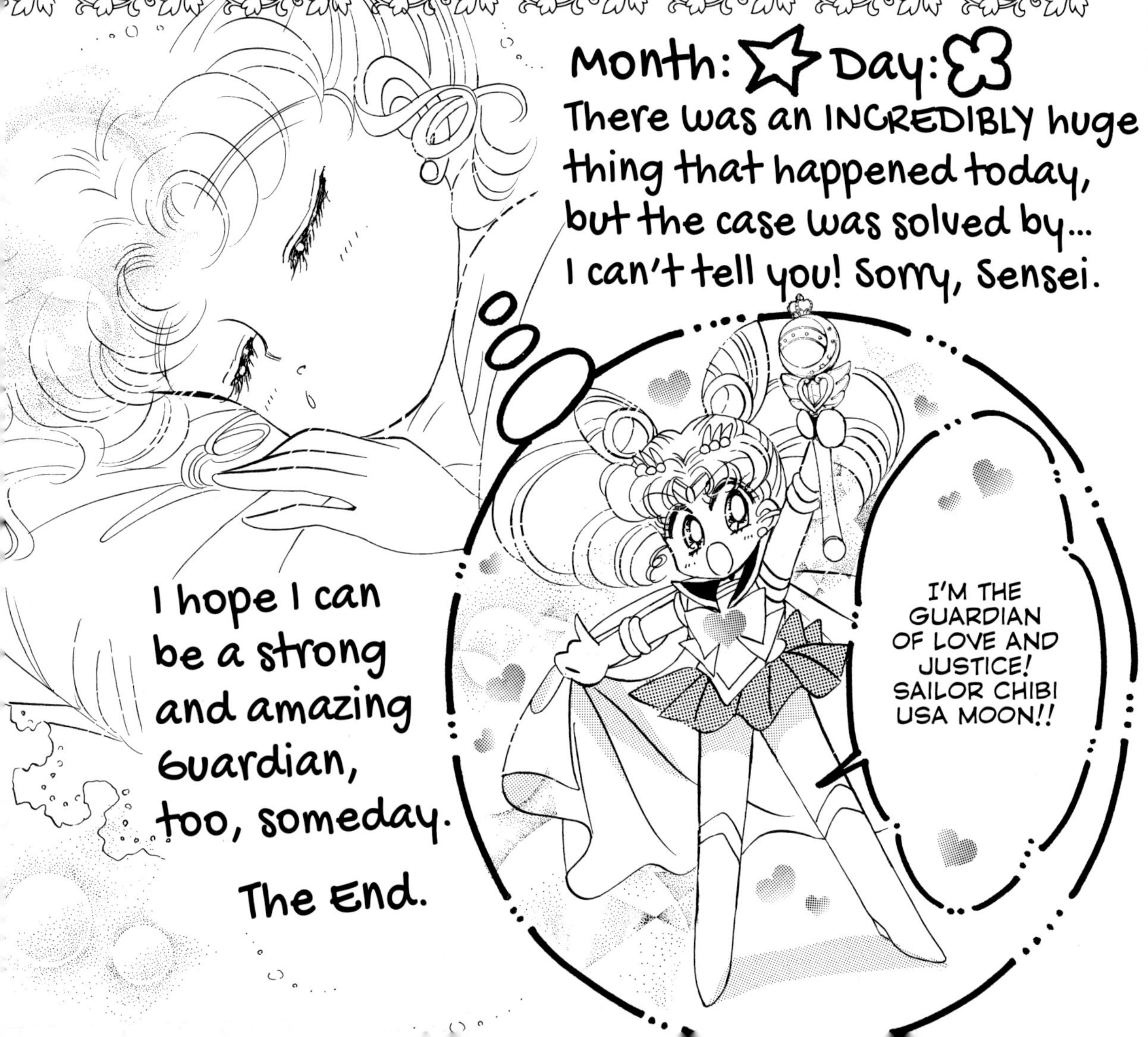
Month: ☆ Day: ✿
There was an INCREDIBLY huge thing that happened today, but the case was solved by... I can't tell you! Sorry, Sensei.
I'M THE GUARDIAN OF LOVE AND JUSTICE! SAILOR CHIBI USA MOON!!
I hope I can be a strong and amazing Guardian, too, someday.
The End.

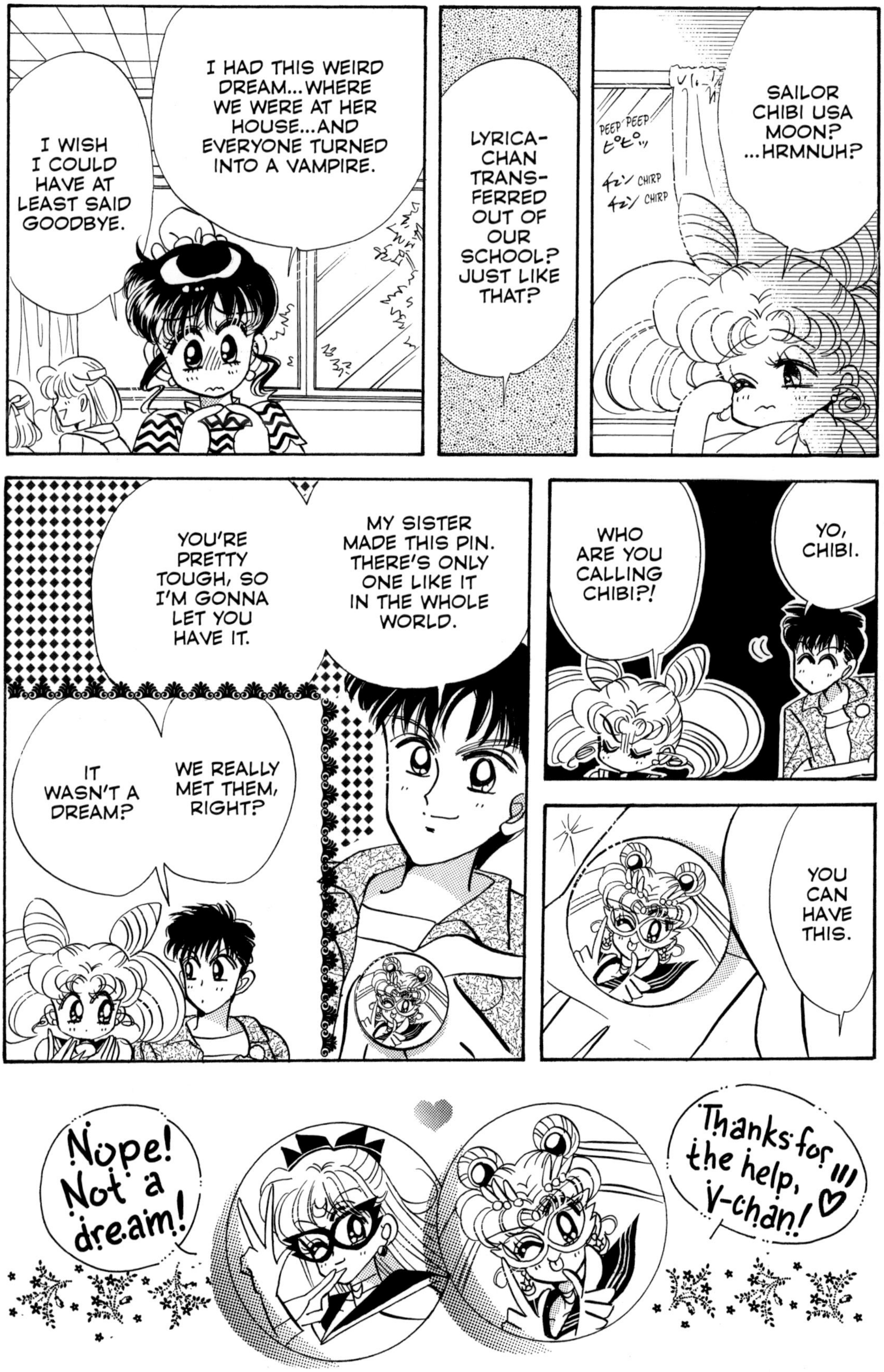
SAILOR CHIBI USA MOON? ...HRMNUH?
PEEP PEEP ピピッ
チュン CHIRP
チュン CHIRP
LYRICA-CHAN TRANSFERRED OUT OF OUR SCHOOL? JUST LIKE THAT?
I HAD THIS WEIRD DREAM...WHERE WE WERE AT HER HOUSE...AND EVERYONE TURNED INTO A VAMPIRE.
I WISH I COULD HAVE AT LEAST SAID GOODBYE.
YO, CHIBI.
WHO ARE YOU CALLING CHIBI?!
YOU CAN HAVE THIS.
MY SISTER MADE THIS PIN. THERE'S ONLY ONE LIKE IT IN THE WHOLE WORLD.
YOU'RE PRETTY TOUGH, SO I'M GONNA LET YOU HAVE IT.
WE REALLY MET THEM, RIGHT?
IT WASN'T A DREAM?
Thanks for the help, V-chan! ♥
Nope! Not a dream!

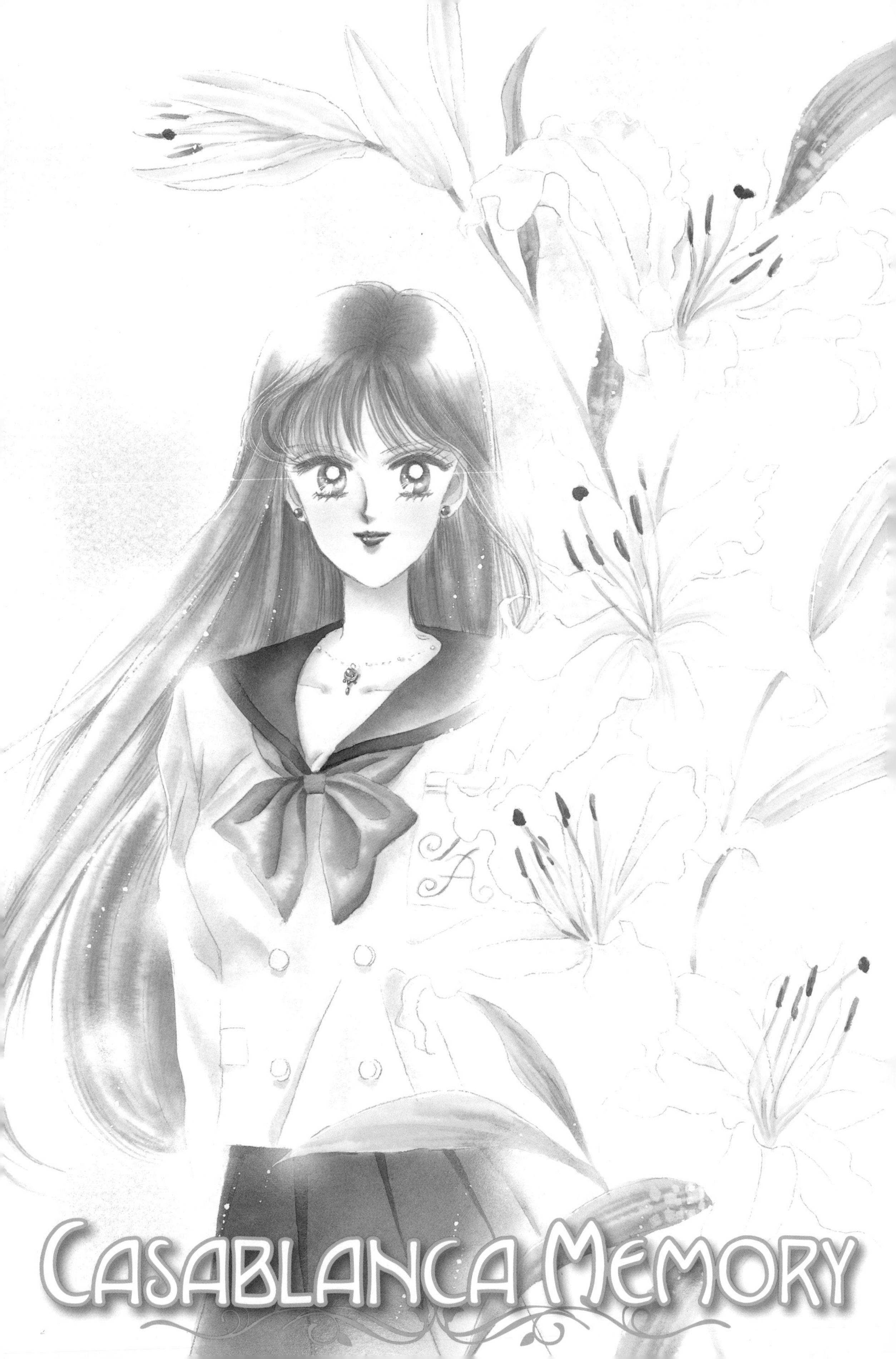

Casablanca Memory

Pretty Guardian Sailor Moon

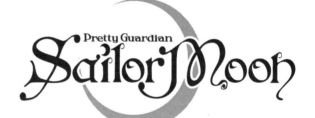

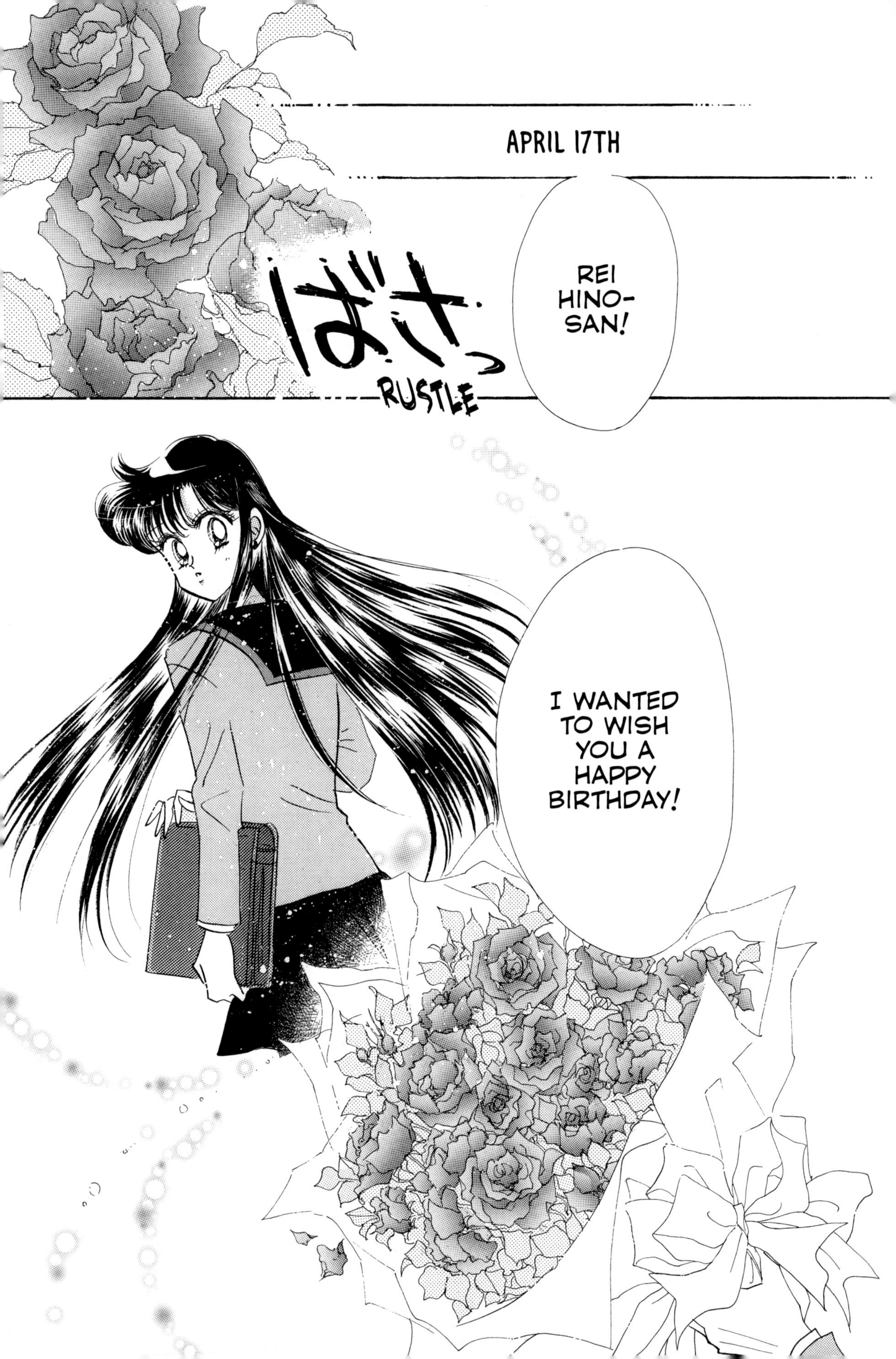
APRIL 17TH
REI HINO-SAN!
ばさっ
RUSTLE
I WANTED TO WISH YOU A HAPPY BIRTHDAY!

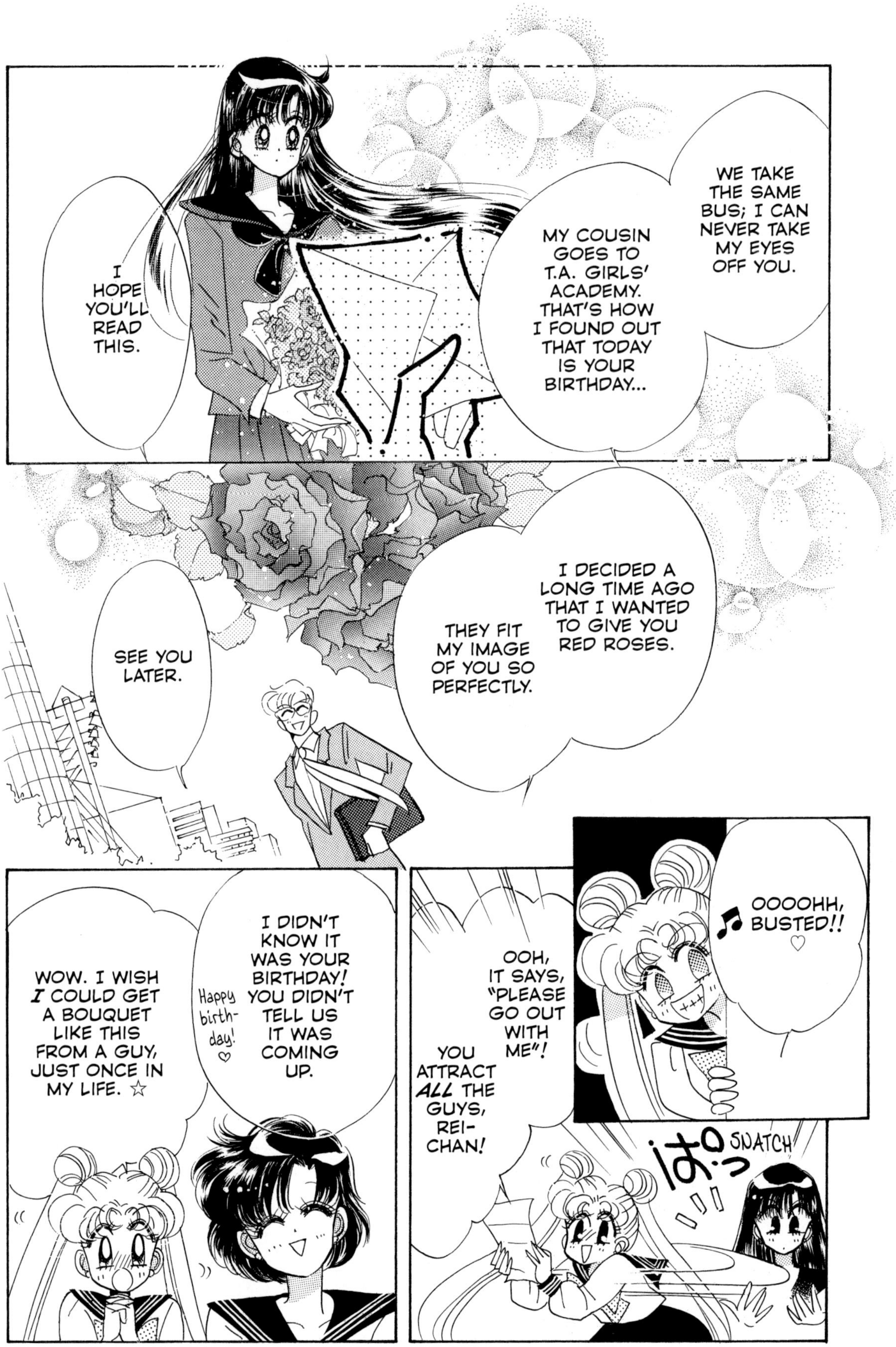
WE TAKE THE SAME BUS; I CAN NEVER TAKE MY EYES OFF YOU.
MY COUSIN GOES TO T.A. GIRLS' ACADEMY. THAT'S HOW I FOUND OUT THAT TODAY IS YOUR BIRTHDAY...
I HOPE YOU'LL READ THIS.
I DECIDED A LONG TIME AGO THAT I WANTED TO GIVE YOU RED ROSES.
THEY FIT MY IMAGE OF YOU SO PERFECTLY.
SEE YOU LATER.
♫ OOOOHH, BUSTED!! ♡
OOH, IT SAYS, "PLEASE GO OUT WITH ME"!
YOU ATTRACT *ALL* THE GUYS, REI-CHAN!
はっ SNATCH
I DIDN'T KNOW IT WAS YOUR BIRTHDAY! YOU DIDN'T TELL US IT WAS COMING UP.
Happy birthday! ♡
WOW. I WISH *I* COULD GET A BOUQUET LIKE THIS FROM A GUY, JUST ONCE IN MY LIFE. ☆

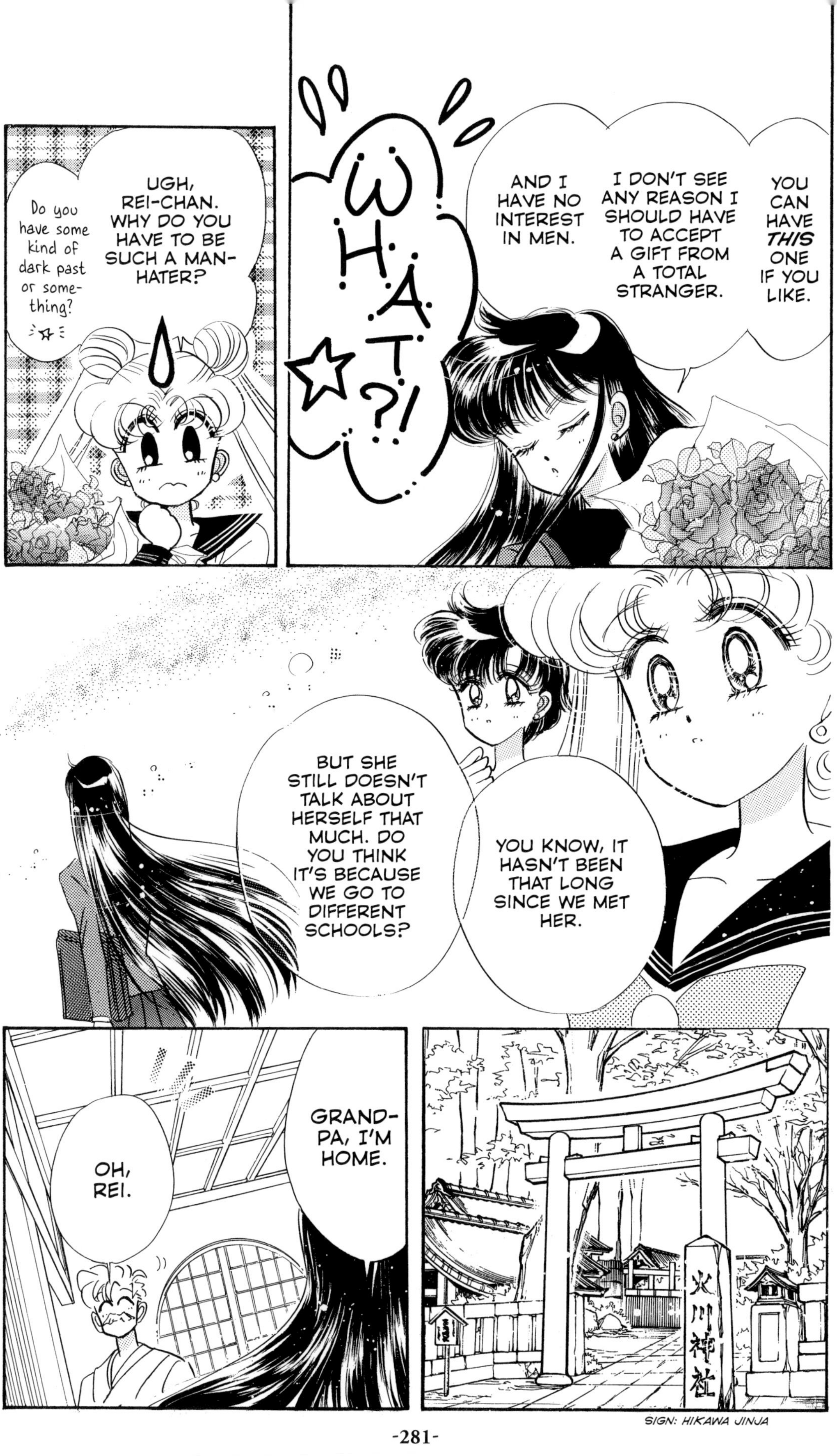
YOU CAN HAVE *THIS* ONE IF YOU LIKE.
I DON'T SEE ANY REASON I SHOULD HAVE TO ACCEPT A GIFT FROM A TOTAL STRANGER.
AND I HAVE NO INTEREST IN MEN.
WHAT?!
UGH, REI-CHAN. WHY DO YOU HAVE TO BE SUCH A MAN-HATER?
Do you have some kind of dark past or some-thing?
YOU KNOW, IT HASN'T BEEN THAT LONG SINCE WE MET HER.
BUT SHE STILL DOESN'T TALK ABOUT HERSELF THAT MUCH. DO YOU THINK IT'S BECAUSE WE GO TO DIFFERENT SCHOOLS?
火川神社
GRAND-PA, I'M HOME.
OH, REI.

SIGN: HIKAWA JINJA

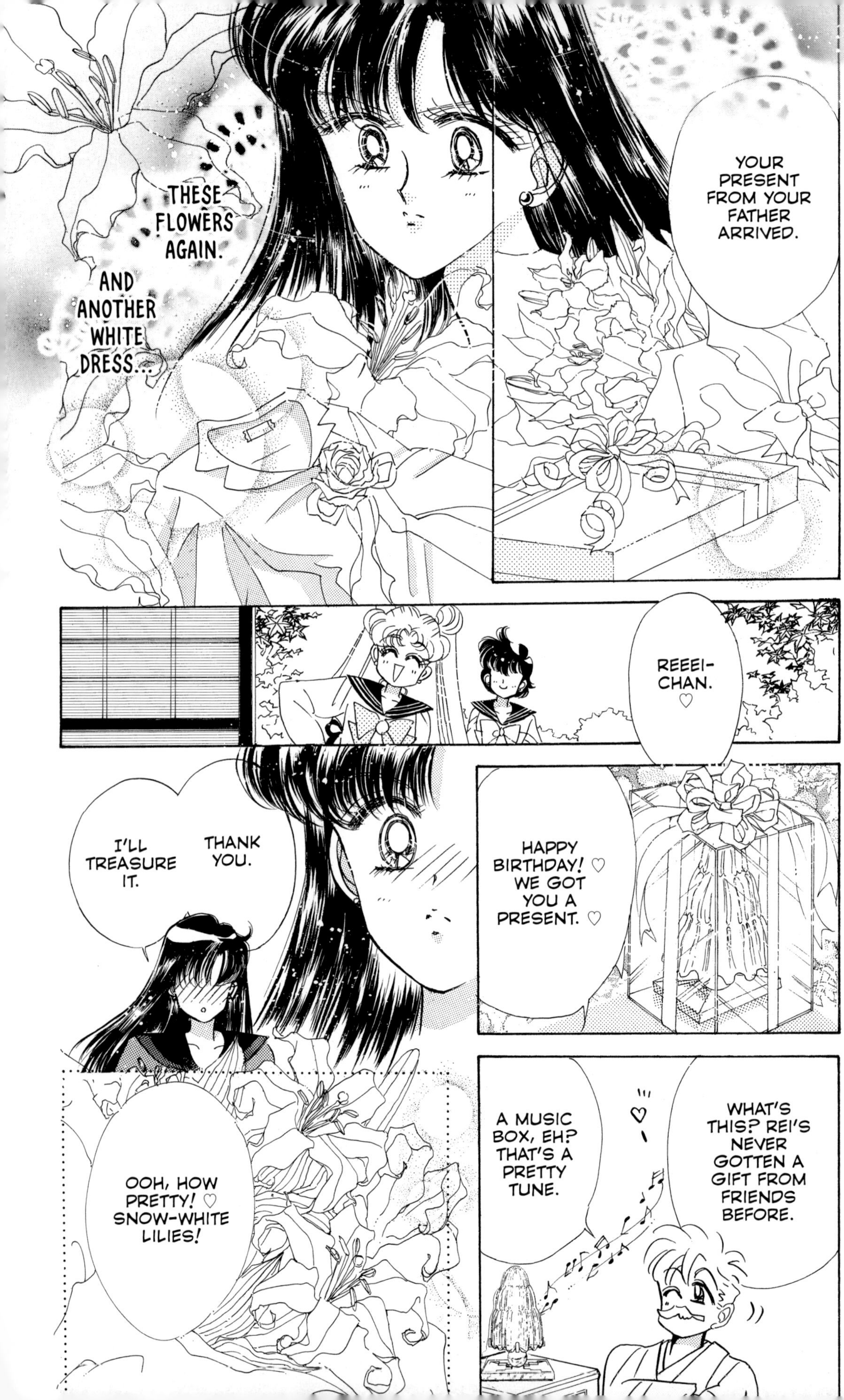
YOUR PRESENT FROM YOUR FATHER ARRIVED.
THESE FLOWERS AGAIN.
AND ANOTHER WHITE DRESS...
REEEI-CHAN. ♡
HAPPY BIRTHDAY! ♡ WE GOT YOU A PRESENT. ♡
THANK YOU.
I'LL TREASURE IT.
WHAT'S THIS? REI'S NEVER GOTTEN A GIFT FROM FRIENDS BEFORE.
A MUSIC BOX, EH? THAT'S A PRETTY TUNE.
OOH, HOW PRETTY! ♡ SNOW-WHITE LILIES!

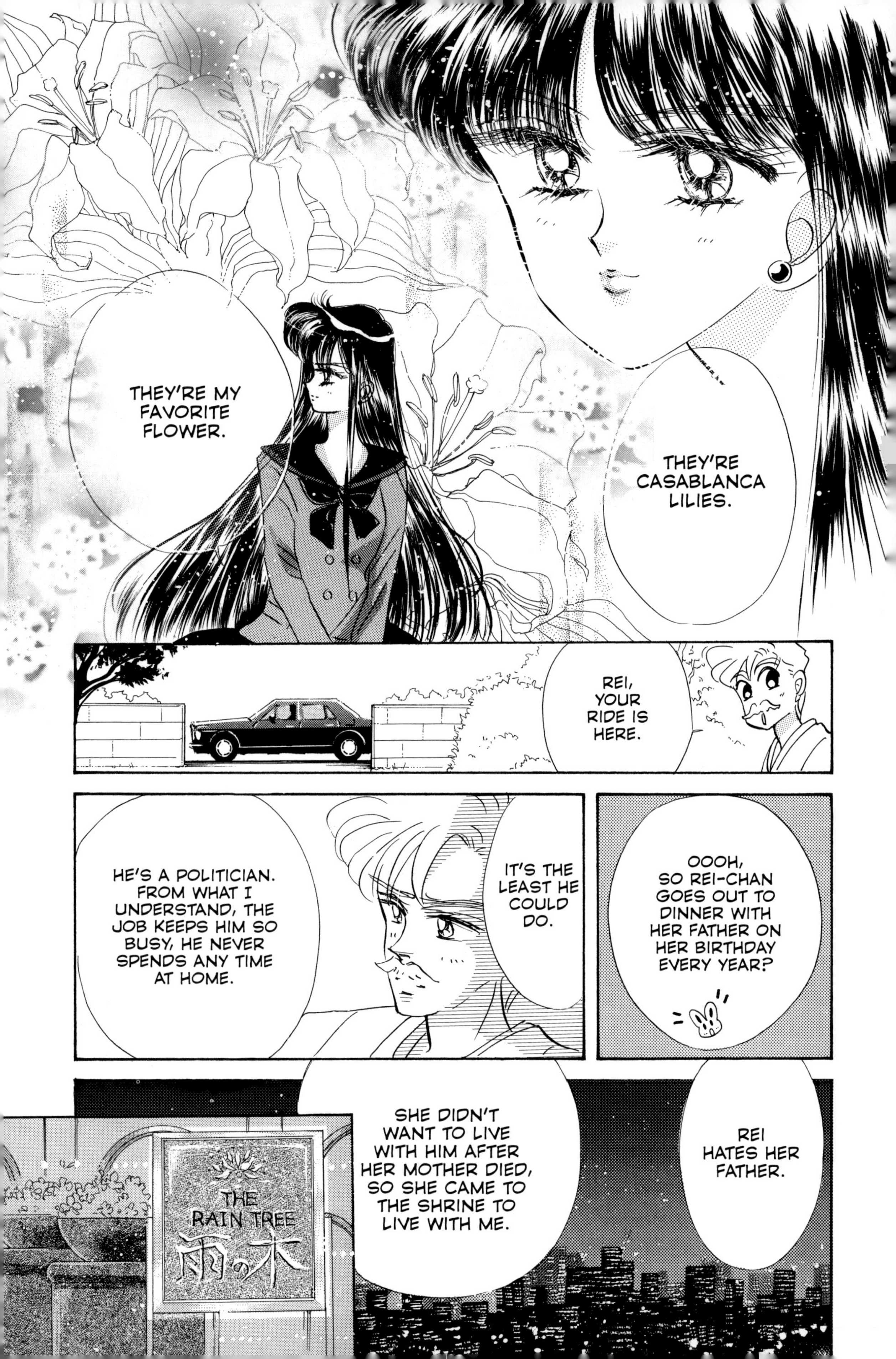
THEY'RE CASABLANCA LILIES.
THEY'RE MY FAVORITE FLOWER.
REI, YOUR RIDE IS HERE.
OOOH, SO REI-CHAN GOES OUT TO DINNER WITH HER FATHER ON HER BIRTHDAY EVERY YEAR?
IT'S THE LEAST HE COULD DO.
HE'S A POLITICIAN. FROM WHAT I UNDERSTAND, THE JOB KEEPS HIM SO BUSY, HE NEVER SPENDS ANY TIME AT HOME.
REI HATES HER FATHER.
SHE DIDN'T WANT TO LIVE WITH HIM AFTER HER MOTHER DIED, SO SHE CAME TO THE SHRINE TO LIVE WITH ME.
THE RAIN TREE
雨の木

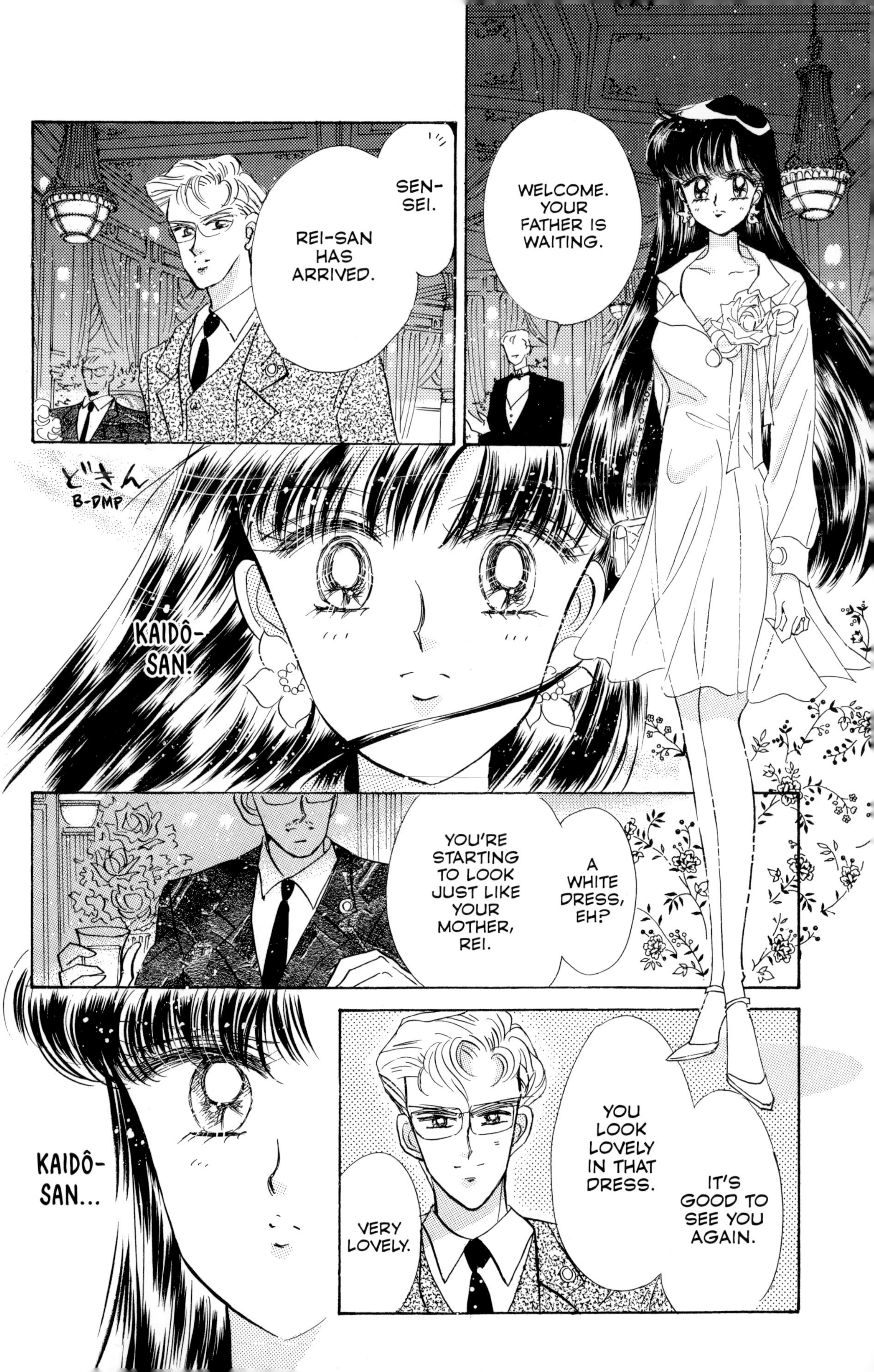
WELCOME. YOUR FATHER IS WAITING.
SEN-SEI.
REI-SAN HAS ARRIVED.
どきん
B-DMP
KAIDÔ-SAN.
A WHITE DRESS, EH?
YOU'RE STARTING TO LOOK JUST LIKE YOUR MOTHER, REI.
IT'S GOOD TO SEE YOU AGAIN.
YOU LOOK LOVELY IN THAT DRESS.
VERY LOVELY.
KAIDÔ-SAN...

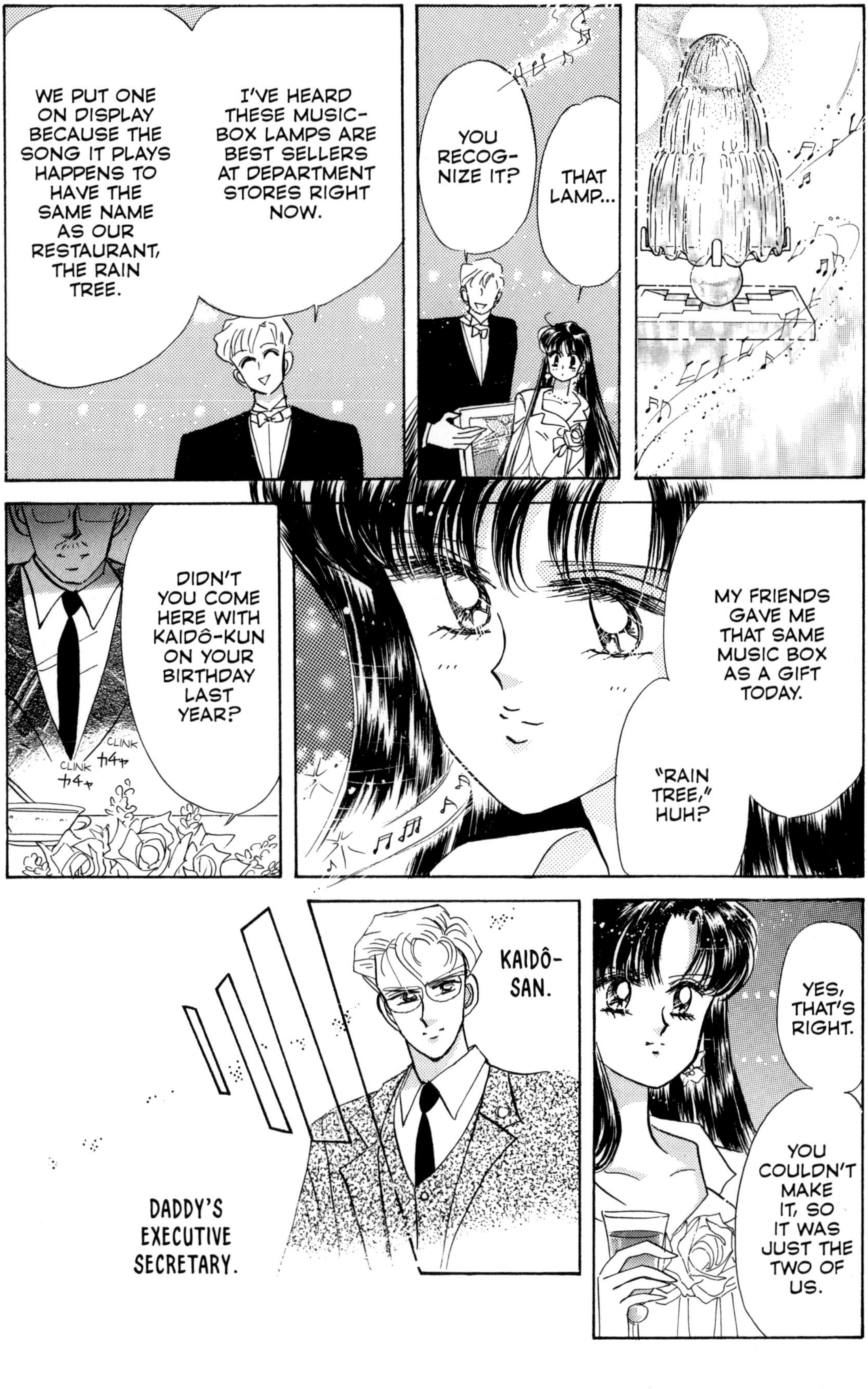
THAT LAMP...
YOU RECOGNIZE IT?
I'VE HEARD THESE MUSIC-BOX LAMPS ARE BEST SELLERS AT DEPARTMENT STORES RIGHT NOW.
WE PUT ONE ON DISPLAY BECAUSE THE SONG IT PLAYS HAPPENS TO HAVE THE SAME NAME AS OUR RESTAURANT, THE RAIN TREE.
MY FRIENDS GAVE ME THAT SAME MUSIC BOX AS A GIFT TODAY.
"RAIN TREE," HUH?
DIDN'T YOU COME HERE WITH KAIDÔ-KUN ON YOUR BIRTHDAY LAST YEAR?
CLINK
CLINK
YES, THAT'S RIGHT.
YOU COULDN'T MAKE IT, SO IT WAS JUST THE TWO OF US.
KAIDÔ-SAN.
DADDY'S EXECUTIVE SECRETARY.

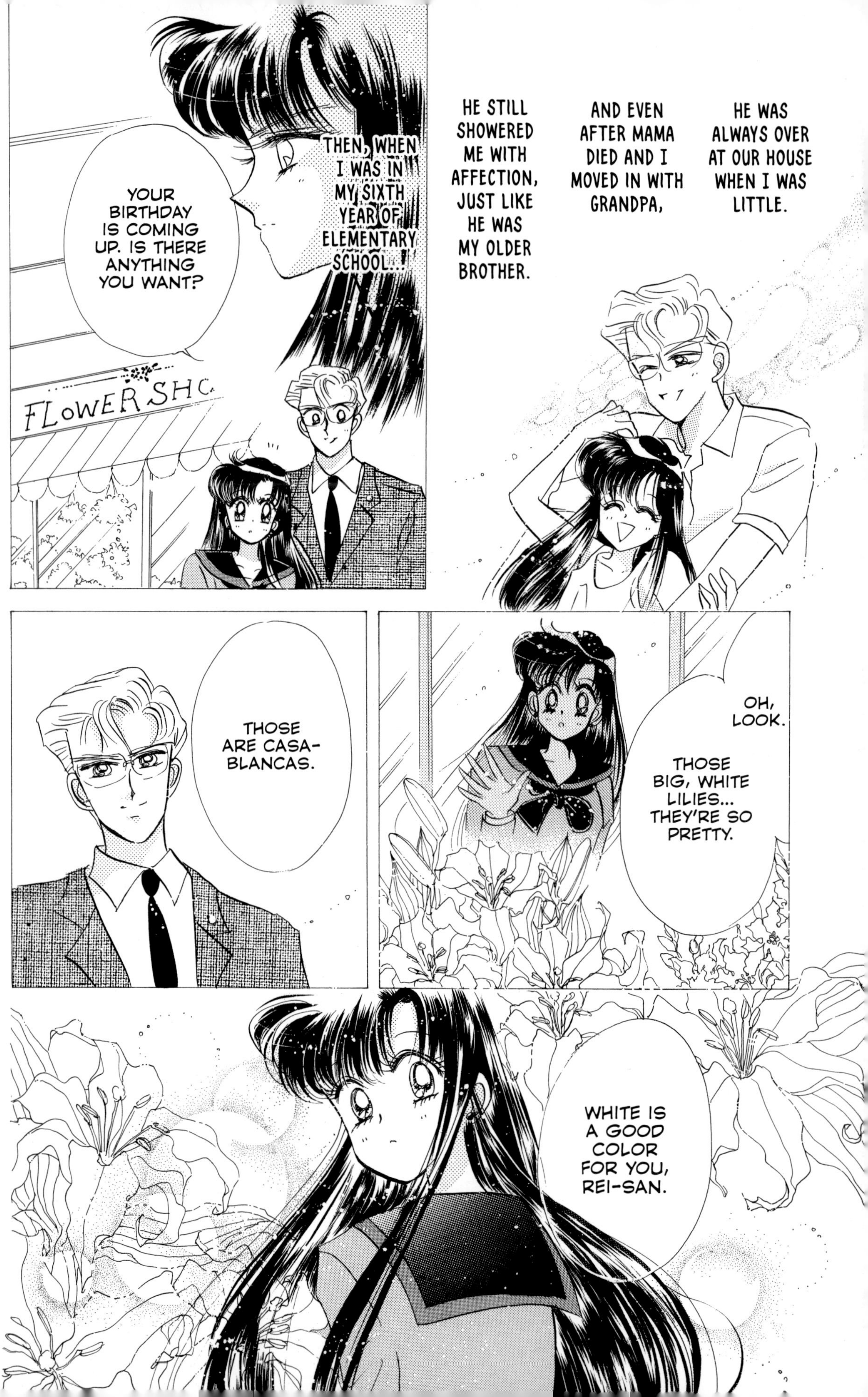
HE WAS ALWAYS OVER AT OUR HOUSE WHEN I WAS LITTLE.
AND EVEN AFTER MAMA DIED AND I MOVED IN WITH GRANDPA,
HE STILL SHOWERED ME WITH AFFECTION, JUST LIKE HE WAS MY OLDER BROTHER.
THEN, WHEN I WAS IN MY SIXTH YEAR OF ELEMENTARY SCHOOL...
YOUR BIRTHDAY IS COMING UP. IS THERE ANYTHING YOU WANT?
OH, LOOK.
THOSE BIG, WHITE LILIES... THEY'RE SO PRETTY.
THOSE ARE CASA-BLANCAS.
WHITE IS A GOOD COLOR FOR YOU, REI-SAN.

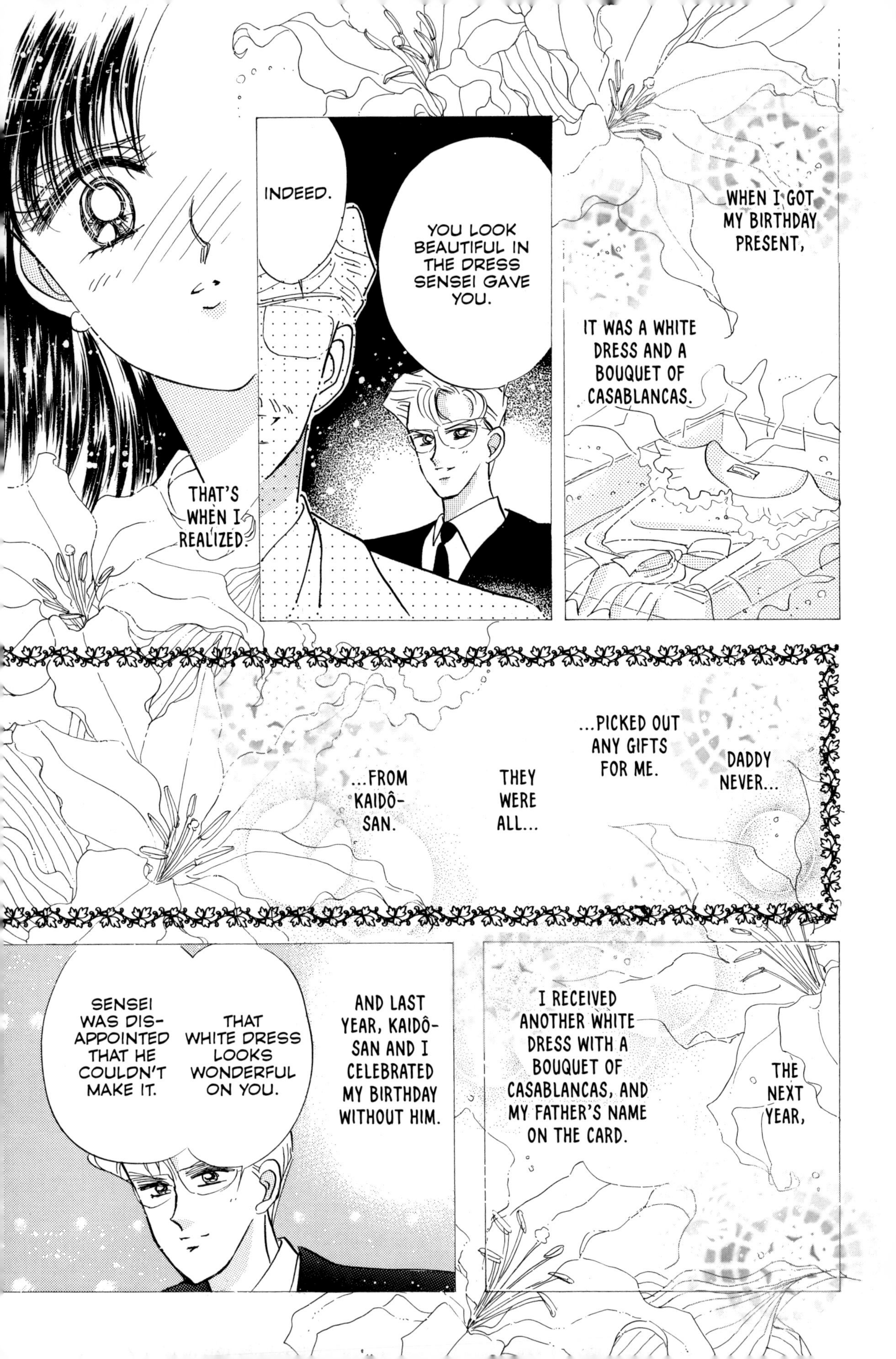
WHEN I GOT MY BIRTHDAY PRESENT,
IT WAS A WHITE DRESS AND A BOUQUET OF CASABLANCAS.
YOU LOOK BEAUTIFUL IN THE DRESS SENSEI GAVE YOU.
INDEED.
THAT'S WHEN I REALIZED.
DADDY NEVER...
...PICKED OUT ANY GIFTS FOR ME.
THEY WERE ALL...
...FROM KAIDÔ-SAN.
THE NEXT YEAR,
I RECEIVED ANOTHER WHITE DRESS WITH A BOUQUET OF CASABLANCAS, AND MY FATHER'S NAME ON THE CARD.
AND LAST YEAR, KAIDÔ-SAN AND I CELEBRATED MY BIRTHDAY WITHOUT HIM.
THAT WHITE DRESS LOOKS WONDERFUL ON YOU.
SENSEI WAS DIS-APPOINTED THAT HE COULDN'T MAKE IT.

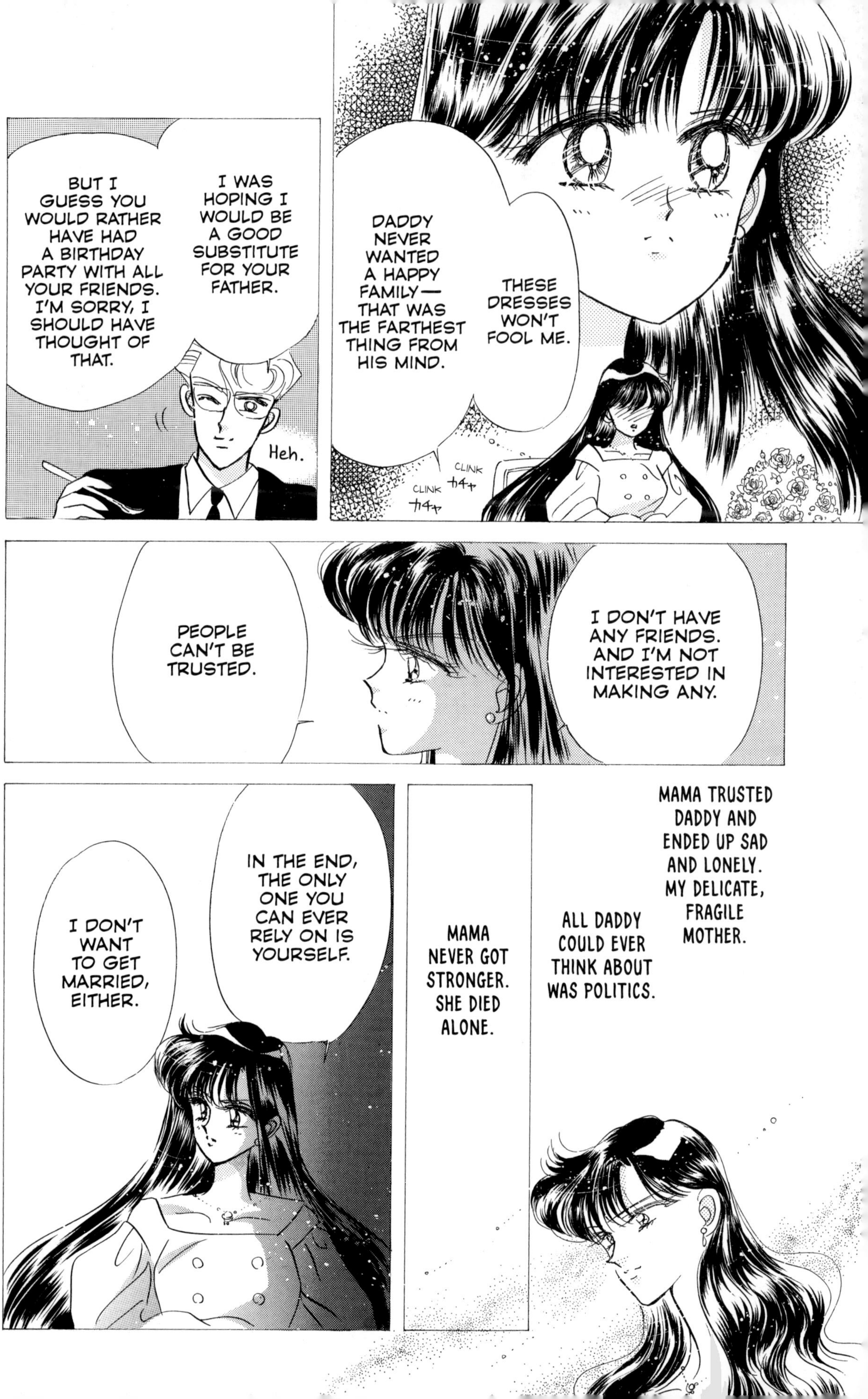
THESE DRESSES WON'T FOOL ME.
DADDY NEVER WANTED A HAPPY FAMILY—THAT WAS THE FARTHEST THING FROM HIS MIND.
CLINK カチャ
CLINK カチャ
I WAS HOPING I WOULD BE A GOOD SUBSTITUTE FOR YOUR FATHER.
BUT I GUESS YOU WOULD RATHER HAVE HAD A BIRTHDAY PARTY WITH ALL YOUR FRIENDS. I'M SORRY, I SHOULD HAVE THOUGHT OF THAT.
Heh.
I DON'T HAVE ANY FRIENDS. AND I'M NOT INTERESTED IN MAKING ANY.
PEOPLE CAN'T BE TRUSTED.
MAMA TRUSTED DADDY AND ENDED UP SAD AND LONELY. MY DELICATE, FRAGILE MOTHER.
ALL DADDY COULD EVER THINK ABOUT WAS POLITICS.
MAMA NEVER GOT STRONGER. SHE DIED ALONE.
IN THE END, THE ONLY ONE YOU CAN EVER RELY ON IS YOURSELF.
I DON'T WANT TO GET MARRIED, EITHER.

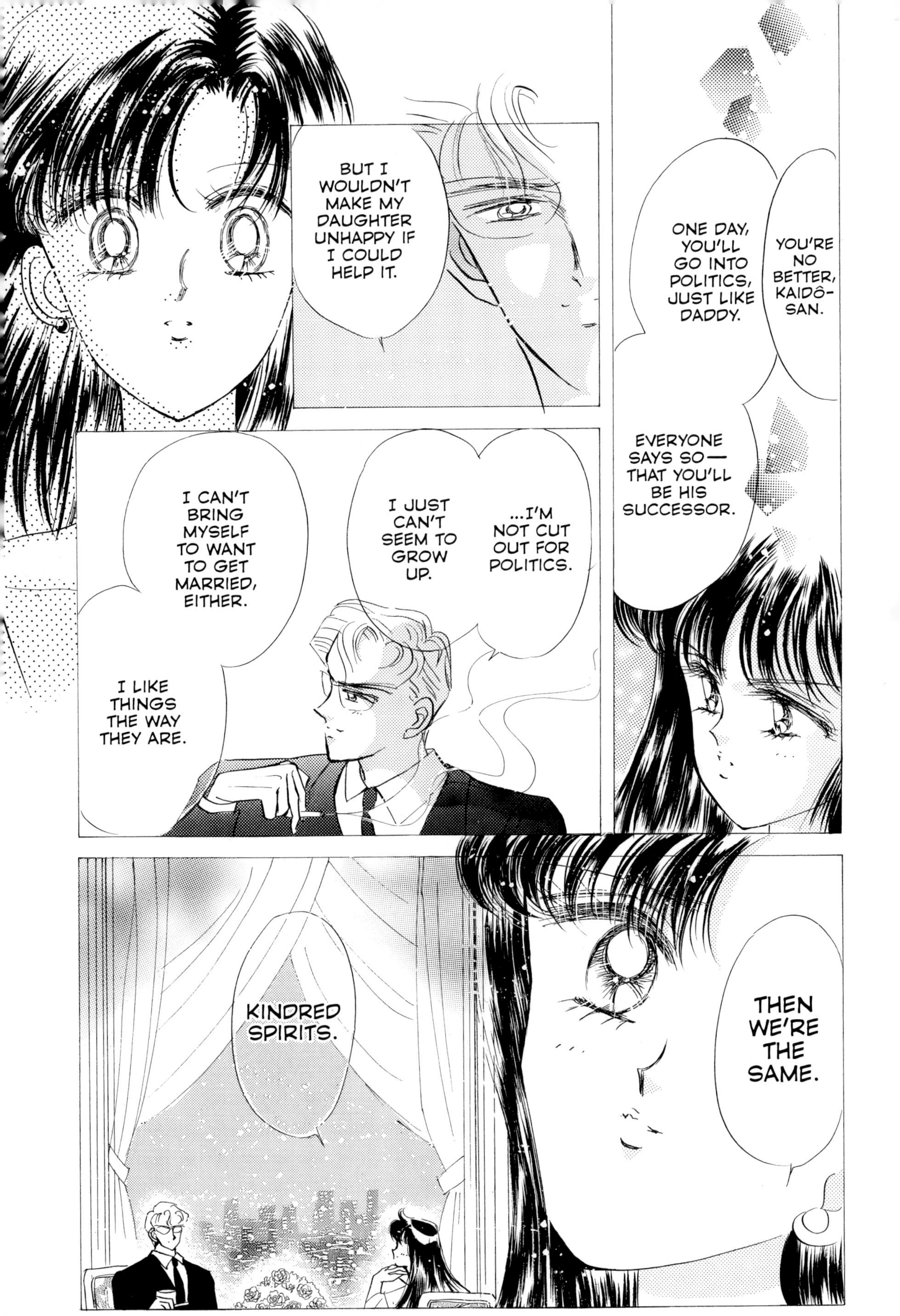
YOU'RE NO BETTER, KAIDÔ-SAN.
ONE DAY, YOU'LL GO INTO POLITICS, JUST LIKE DADDY.
EVERYONE SAYS SO— THAT YOU'LL BE HIS SUCCESSOR.
BUT I WOULDN'T MAKE MY DAUGHTER UNHAPPY IF I COULD HELP IT.
...I'M NOT CUT OUT FOR POLITICS.
I JUST CAN'T SEEM TO GROW UP.
I CAN'T BRING MYSELF TO WANT TO GET MARRIED, EITHER.
I LIKE THINGS THE WAY THEY ARE.
THEN WE'RE THE SAME.
KINDRED SPIRITS.

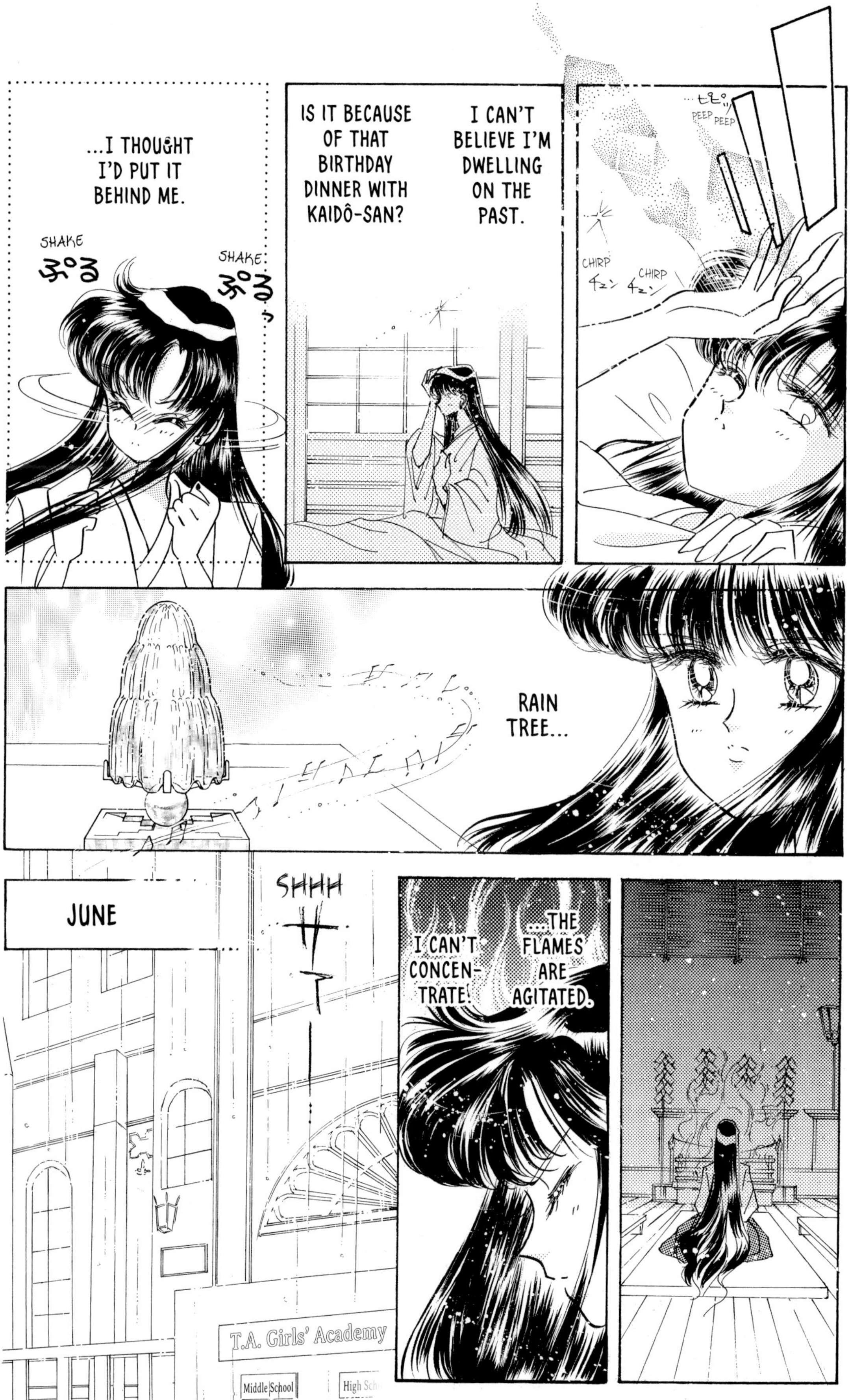
ピピッ
PEEP PEEP
CHIRP チュン
CHIRP チュン
I CAN'T BELIEVE I'M DWELLING ON THE PAST.
IS IT BECAUSE OF THAT BIRTHDAY DINNER WITH KAIDÔ-SAN?
...I THOUGHT I'D PUT IT BEHIND ME.
SHAKE ぷる
SHAKE ぷる
RAIN TREE...
...THE FLAMES ARE AGITATED.
I CAN'T CONCENTRATE.
SHHH サー
JUNE
T.A. Girls' Academy
Middle School

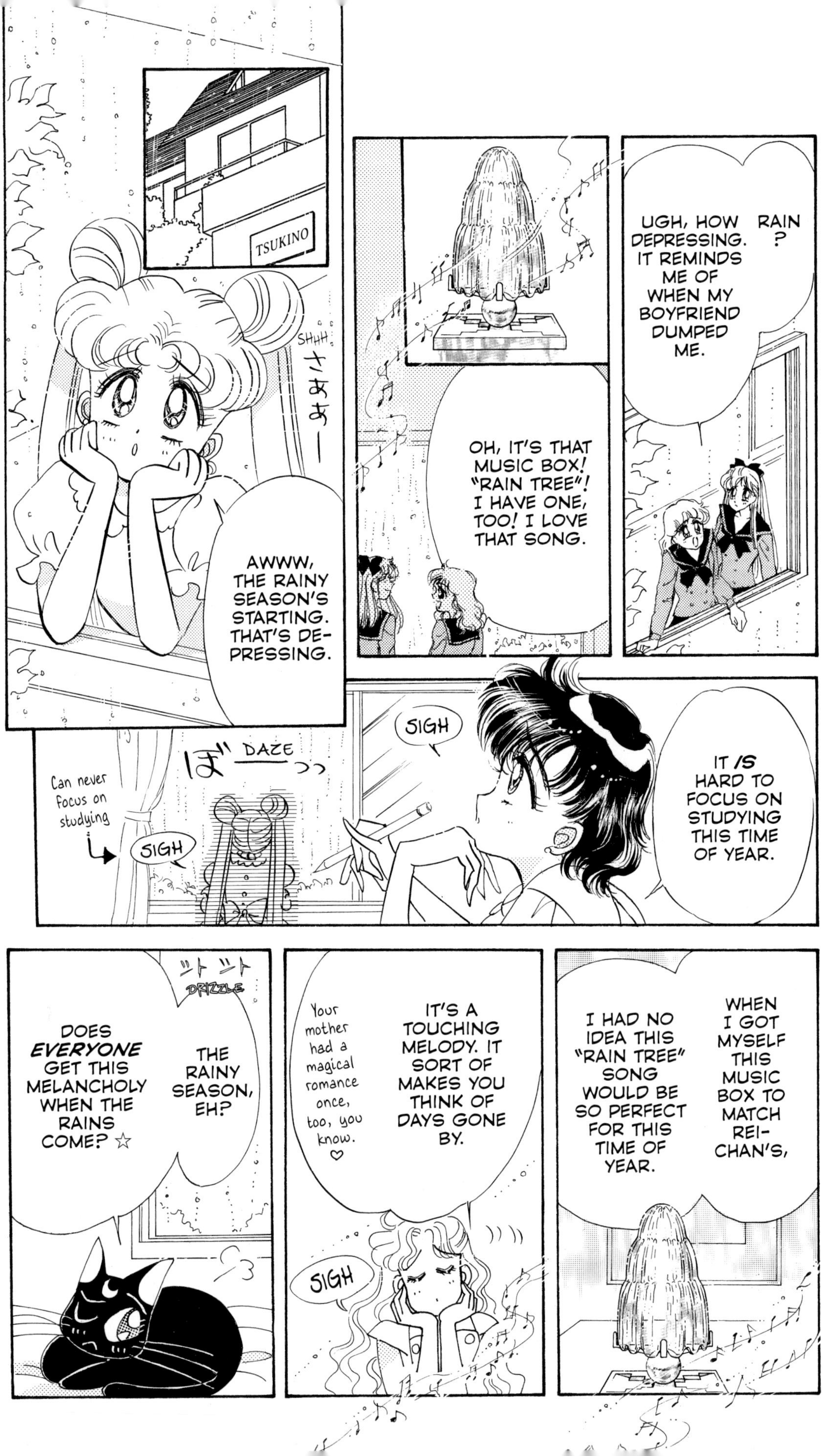
RAIN ?
UGH, HOW DEPRESSING. IT REMINDS ME OF WHEN MY BOYFRIEND DUMPED ME.
OH, IT'S THAT MUSIC BOX! "RAIN TREE"! I HAVE ONE, TOO! I LOVE THAT SONG.
TSUKINO
さあー
SHHH
AWWW, THE RAINY SEASON'S STARTING. THAT'S DE-PRESSING.
IT *IS* HARD TO FOCUS ON STUDYING THIS TIME OF YEAR.
SIGH
ぼーっっ
DAZE
Can never focus on studying
SIGH
WHEN I GOT MYSELF THIS MUSIC BOX TO MATCH REI-CHAN'S,
I HAD NO IDEA THIS "RAIN TREE" SONG WOULD BE SO PERFECT FOR THIS TIME OF YEAR.
IT'S A TOUCHING MELODY. IT SORT OF MAKES YOU THINK OF DAYS GONE BY.
Your mother had a magical romance once, too, you know. ♡
SIGH
ツトツト
DRIZZLE
THE RAINY SEASON, EH?
DOES *EVERYONE* GET THIS MELANCHOLY WHEN THE RAINS COME? ☆

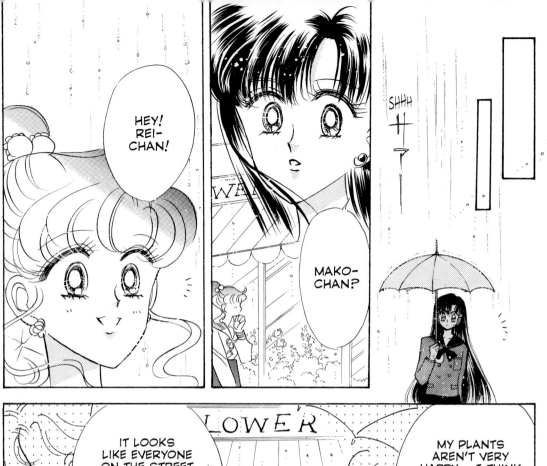

SHHH
MAKO-CHAN?
HEY! REI-CHAN!
LOWER
MY PLANTS AREN'T VERY HAPPY—I THINK ALL THIS RAIN IS GETTING TO THEM, SO I'M OUT TO BUY SOME PLANT FOOD.
IT LOOKS LIKE EVERYONE ON THE STREET IS IN A FUNK FROM THE CONSTANT RAIN.
THIS MUSIC... IT'S "RAIN TREE."
I'VE BEEN HEARING IT A LOT LATELY. IT'S KIND OF A SAD TUNE.
...MAYBE I'VE BEEN IN A FUNK, TOO.
THIS SONG HAS BEEN BRINGING UP A LOT OF OLD MEMORIES FOR ME.
ME, TOO.

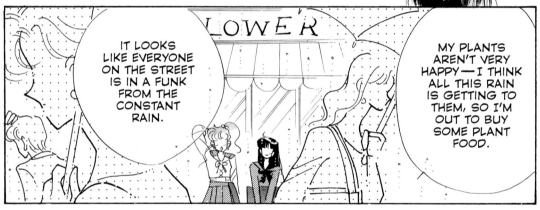

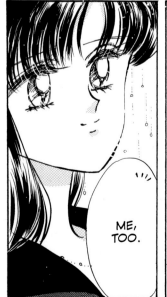

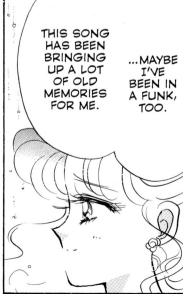

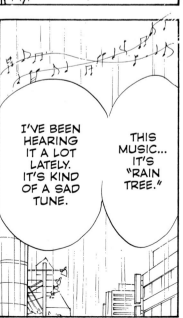

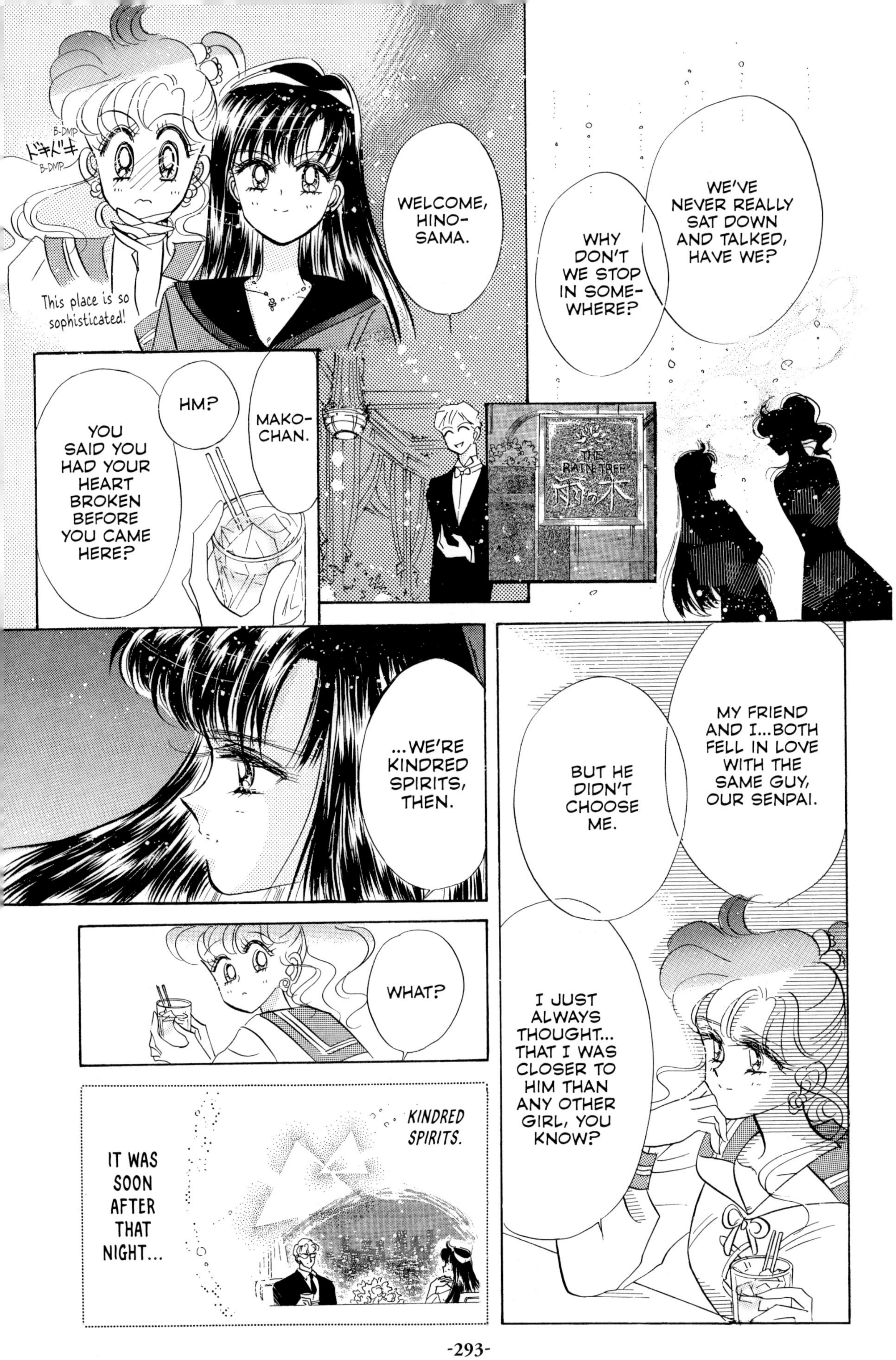
WE'VE NEVER REALLY SAT DOWN AND TALKED, HAVE WE?
WHY DON'T WE STOP IN SOMEWHERE?
THE RAIN TREE
雨の木
WELCOME, HINO-SAMA.
ドキドキ
B-DMP
B-DMP
This place is so sophisticated!
MAKO-CHAN.
HM?
YOU SAID YOU HAD YOUR HEART BROKEN BEFORE YOU CAME HERE?
MY FRIEND AND I...BOTH FELL IN LOVE WITH THE SAME GUY, OUR SENPAI.
BUT HE DIDN'T CHOOSE ME.
I JUST ALWAYS THOUGHT... THAT I WAS CLOSER TO HIM THAN ANY OTHER GIRL, YOU KNOW?
...WE'RE KINDRED SPIRITS, THEN.
WHAT?
KINDRED SPIRITS.
IT WAS SOON AFTER THAT NIGHT...

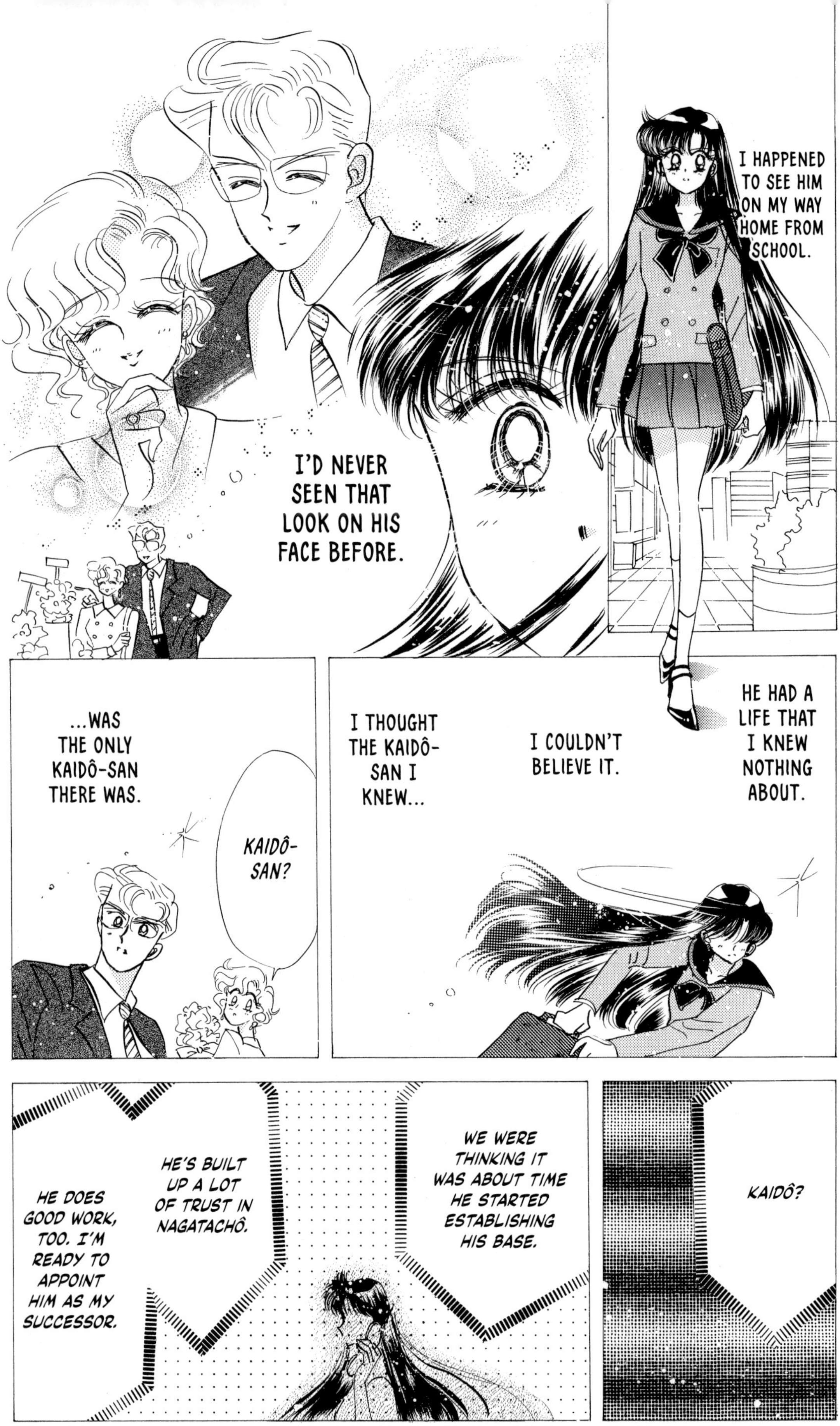
I HAPPENED TO SEE HIM ON MY WAY HOME FROM SCHOOL.
I'D NEVER SEEN THAT LOOK ON HIS FACE BEFORE.
HE HAD A LIFE THAT I KNEW NOTHING ABOUT.
I COULDN'T BELIEVE IT.
I THOUGHT THE KAIDÔ-SAN I KNEW...
...WAS THE ONLY KAIDÔ-SAN THERE WAS.
KAIDÔ-SAN?
KAIDÔ?
WE WERE THINKING IT WAS ABOUT TIME HE STARTED ESTABLISHING HIS BASE.
HE'S BUILT UP A LOT OF TRUST IN NAGATACHÔ.
HE DOES GOOD WORK, TOO. I'M READY TO APPOINT HIM AS MY SUCCESSOR.

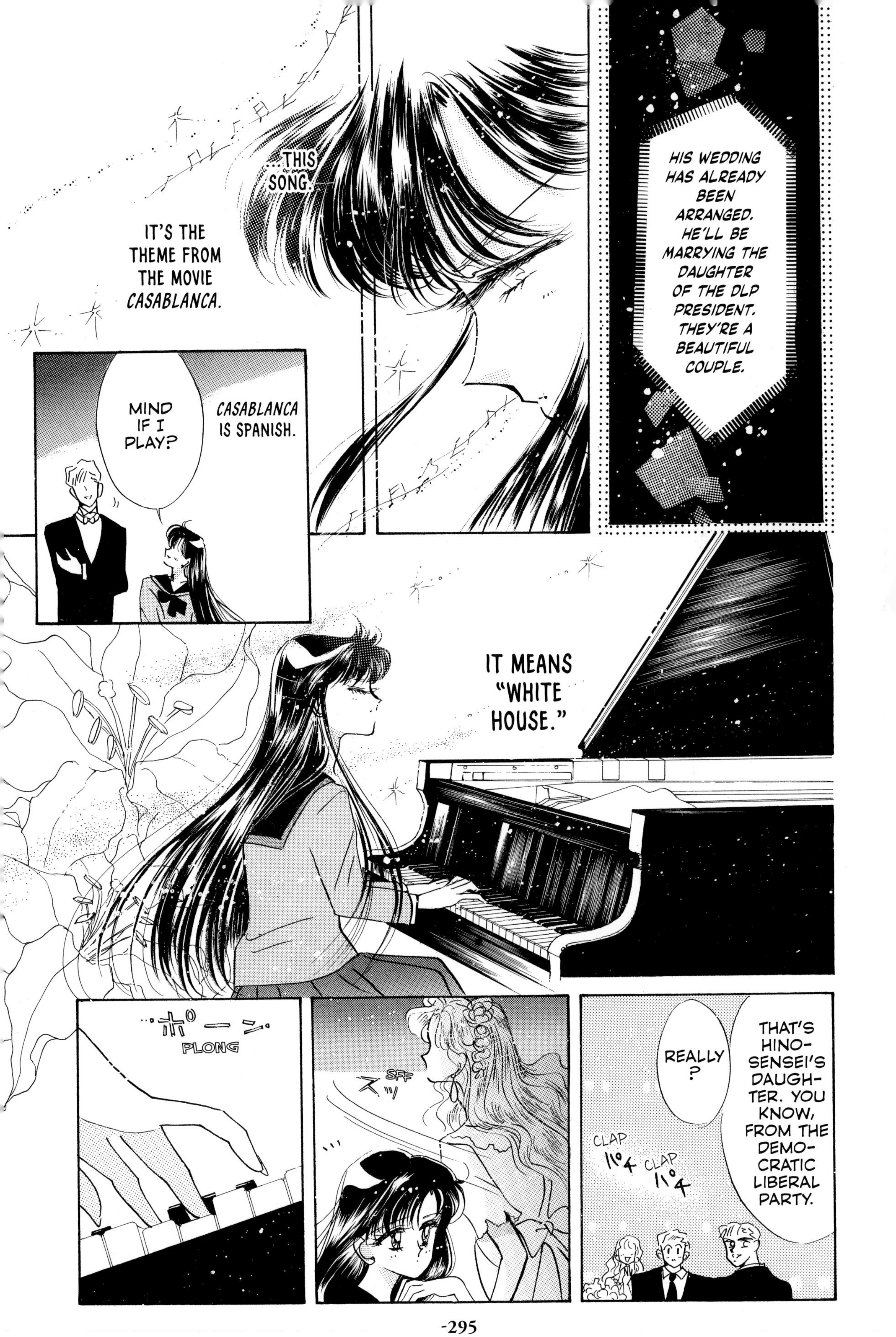
HIS WEDDING HAS ALREADY BEEN ARRANGED. HE'LL BE MARRYING THE DAUGHTER OF THE DLP PRESIDENT. THEY'RE A BEAUTIFUL COUPLE.
...THIS SONG.
IT'S THE THEME FROM THE MOVIE *CASABLANCA*.
CASABLANCA IS SPANISH.
MIND IF I PLAY?
IT MEANS "WHITE HOUSE."
THAT'S HINO-SENSEI'S DAUGHTER. YOU KNOW, FROM THE DEMOCRATIC LIBERAL PARTY.
REALLY?
CLAP パチ CLAP パチ
SFF スッ
...
ポーン
PLONG

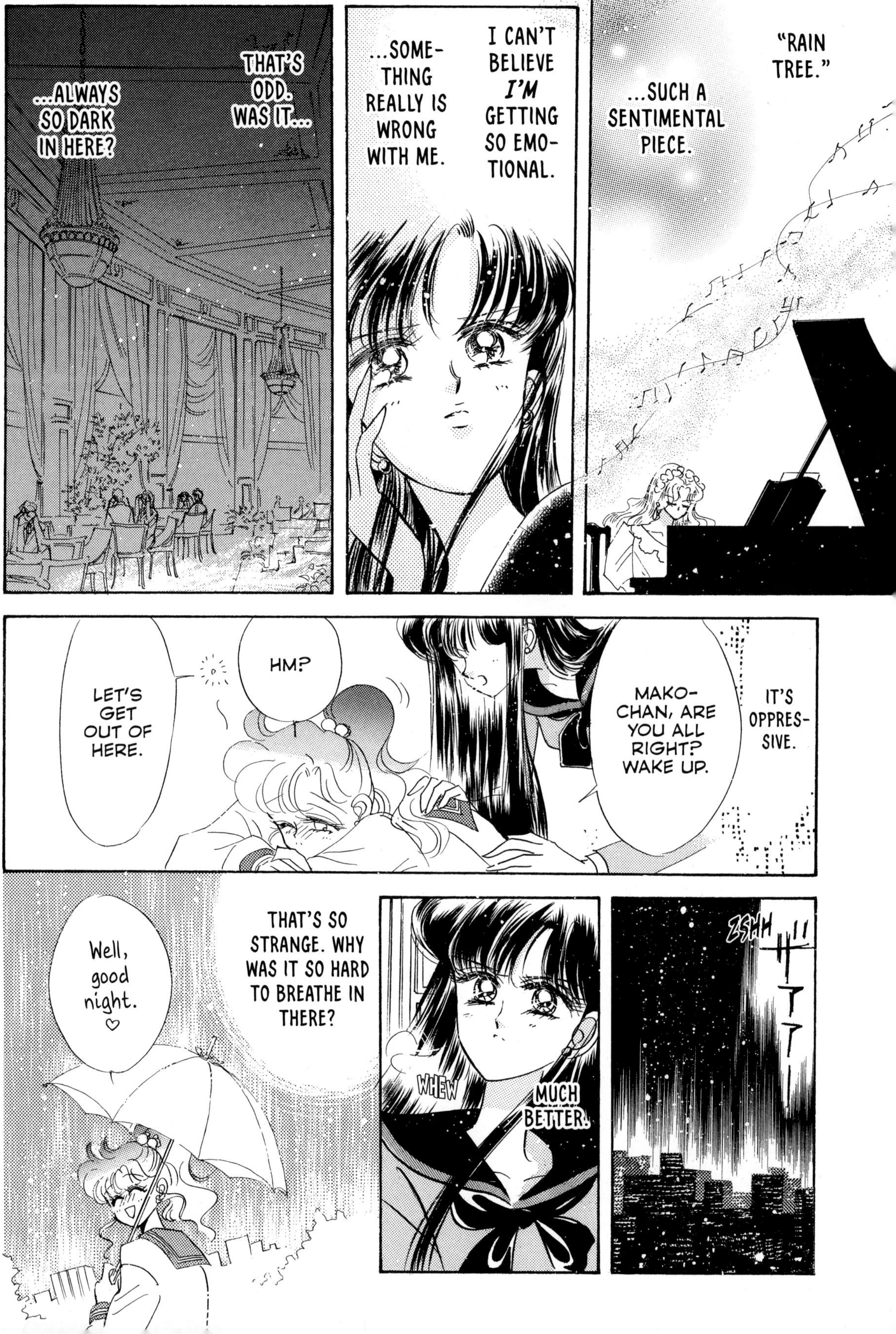
"RAIN TREE."
...SUCH A SENTIMENTAL PIECE.
I CAN'T BELIEVE *I'M* GETTING SO EMOTIONAL.
...SOMETHING REALLY IS WRONG WITH ME.
THAT'S ODD. WAS IT...
...ALWAYS SO DARK IN HERE?
IT'S OPPRESSIVE.
MAKO-CHAN, ARE YOU ALL RIGHT? WAKE UP.
HM?
LET'S GET OUT OF HERE.
ZSHH
WHEW
MUCH BETTER.
THAT'S SO STRANGE. WHY WAS IT SO HARD TO BREATHE IN THERE?
Well, good night. ♡

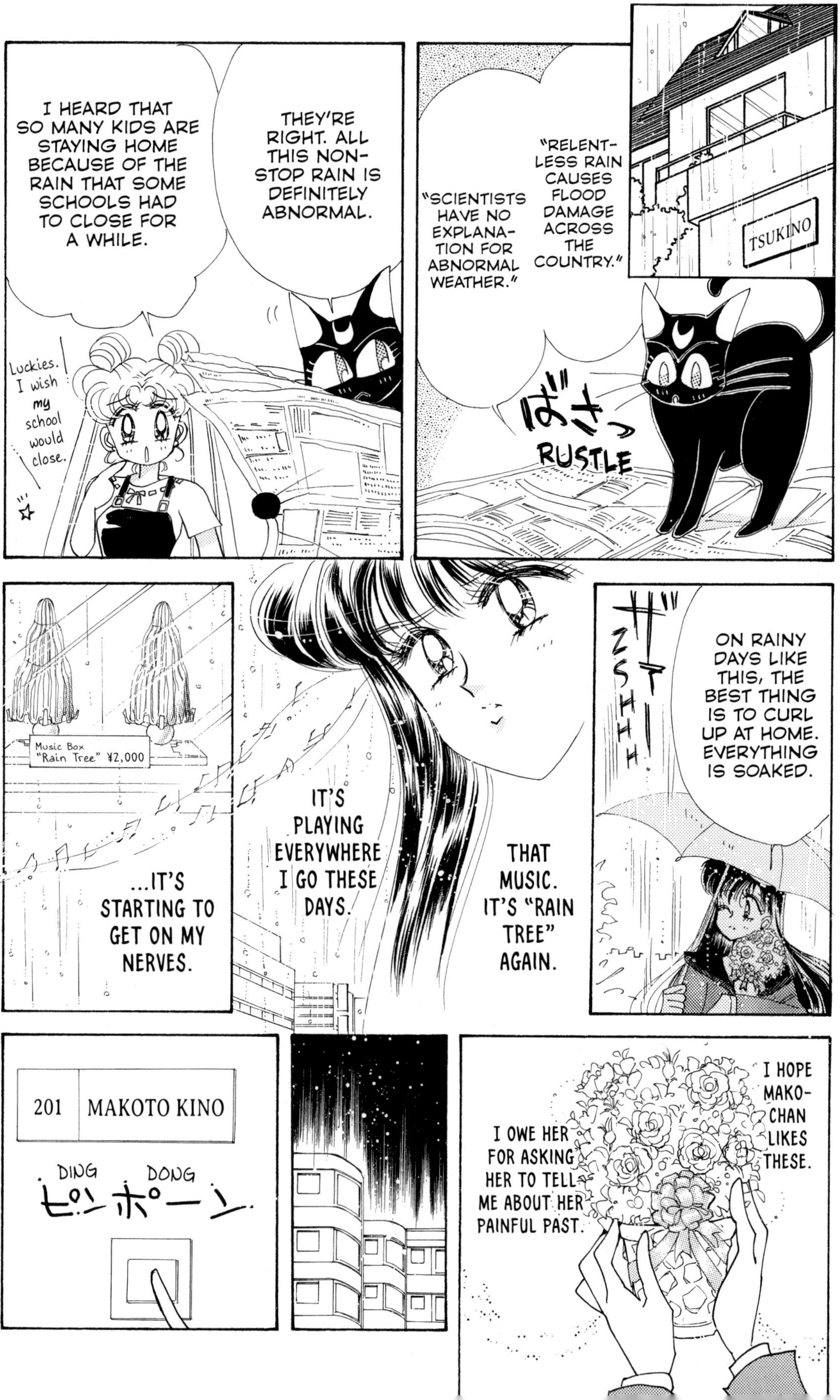
TSUKINO
"RELENTLESS RAIN CAUSES FLOOD DAMAGE ACROSS THE COUNTRY."
"SCIENTISTS HAVE NO EXPLANATION FOR ABNORMAL WEATHER."
ばさっ
RUSTLE
THEY'RE RIGHT. ALL THIS NON-STOP RAIN IS DEFINITELY ABNORMAL.
I HEARD THAT SO MANY KIDS ARE STAYING HOME BECAUSE OF THE RAIN THAT SOME SCHOOLS HAD TO CLOSE FOR A WHILE.
Luckies. I wish my school would close.
ザー
ZSHHH
ON RAINY DAYS LIKE THIS, THE BEST THING IS TO CURL UP AT HOME. EVERYTHING IS SOAKED.
THAT MUSIC. IT'S "RAIN TREE" AGAIN.
IT'S PLAYING EVERYWHERE I GO THESE DAYS.
Music Box "Rain Tree" ¥2,000
...IT'S STARTING TO GET ON MY NERVES.
I HOPE MAKO-CHAN LIKES THESE.
I OWE HER FOR ASKING HER TO TELL ME ABOUT HER PAINFUL PAST.
201 MAKOTO KINO
DING DONG
ピンポーン

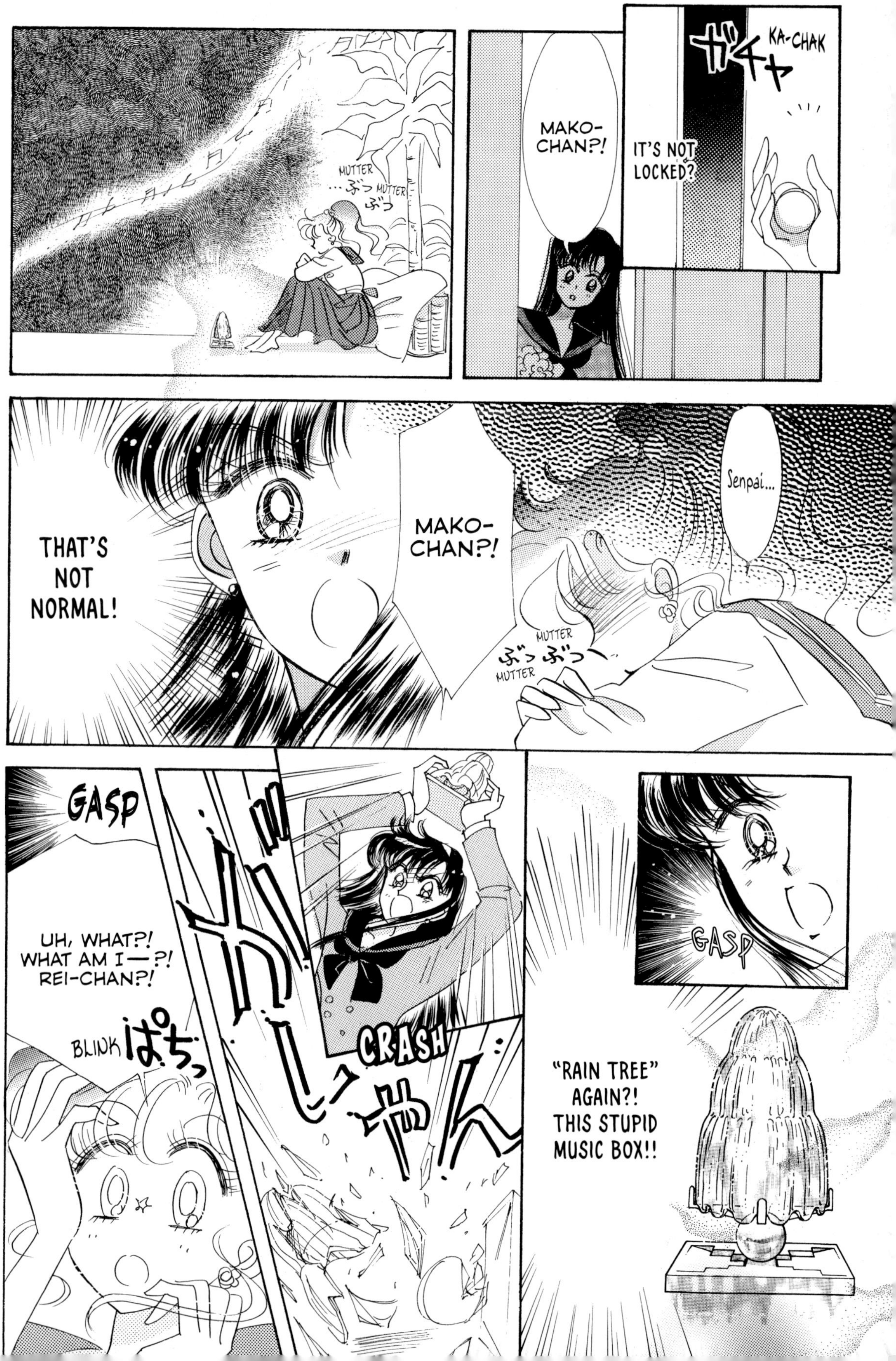
ガチャ KA-CHAK
IT'S NOT LOCKED?
MAKO-CHAN?!
MUTTER …ぶつ MUTTER ぶつ
Senpai...
MUTTER ぶつぶつ MUTTER
MAKO-CHAN?!
THAT'S NOT NORMAL!
GASP
"RAIN TREE" AGAIN?! THIS STUPID MUSIC BOX!!
ガしゃん CRASH
GASP
UH, WHAT?! WHAT AM I—?! REI-CHAN?!
BLINK ぱちっ

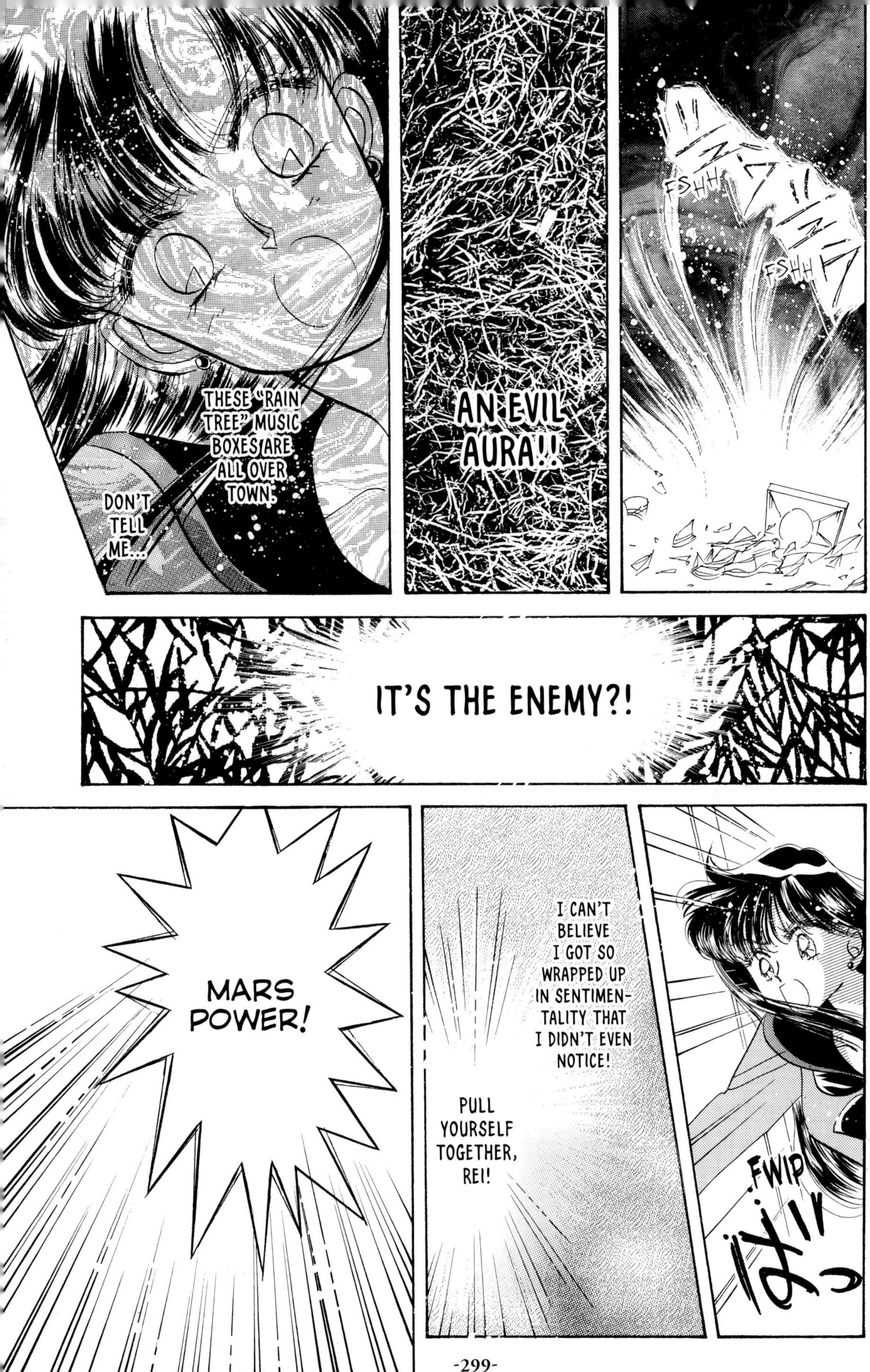
FSHH
FSHH
AN EVIL AURA!!
THESE "RAIN TREE" MUSIC BOXES ARE ALL OVER TOWN.
DON'T TELL ME...
IT'S THE ENEMY?!
FWIP
I CAN'T BELIEVE I GOT SO WRAPPED UP IN SENTIMENTALITY THAT I DIDN'T EVEN NOTICE!
PULL YOURSELF TOGETHER, REI!
MARS POWER!

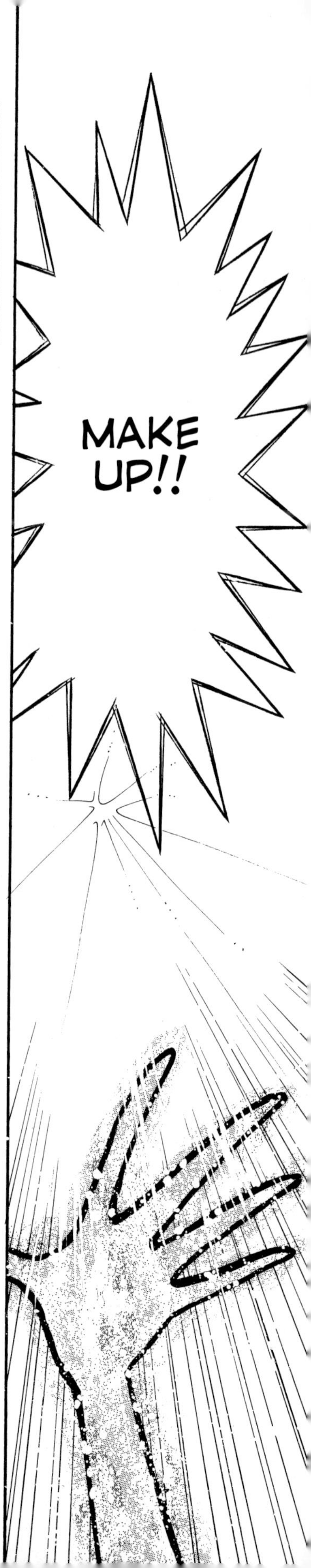
MAKE UP!!

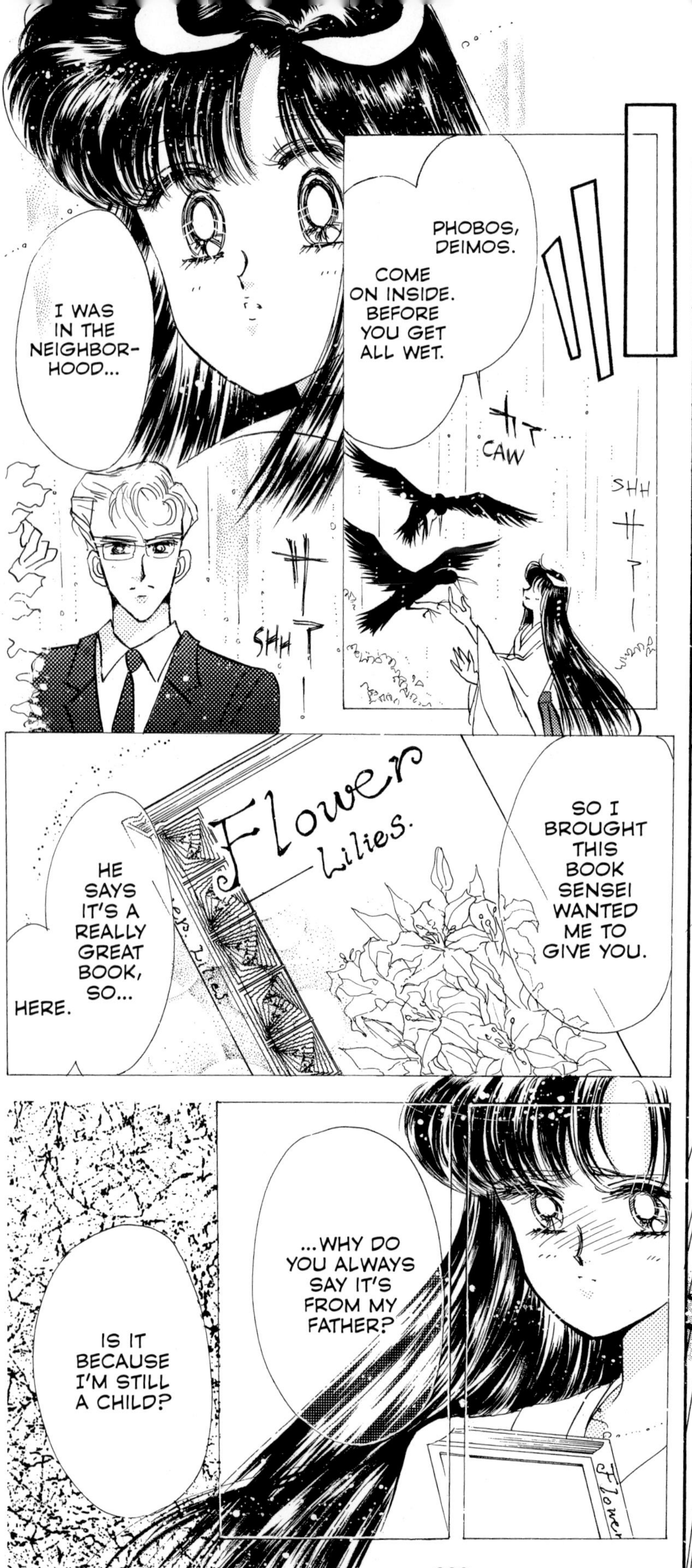
PHOBOS, DEIMOS.
COME ON INSIDE. BEFORE YOU GET ALL WET.
CAW
SHH
SHH
I WAS IN THE NEIGHBOR-HOOD...
Flower Lilies.
SO I BROUGHT THIS BOOK SENSEI WANTED ME TO GIVE YOU.
HE SAYS IT'S A REALLY GREAT BOOK, SO... HERE.
...WHY DO YOU ALWAYS SAY IT'S FROM MY FATHER?
IS IT BECAUSE I'M STILL A CHILD?

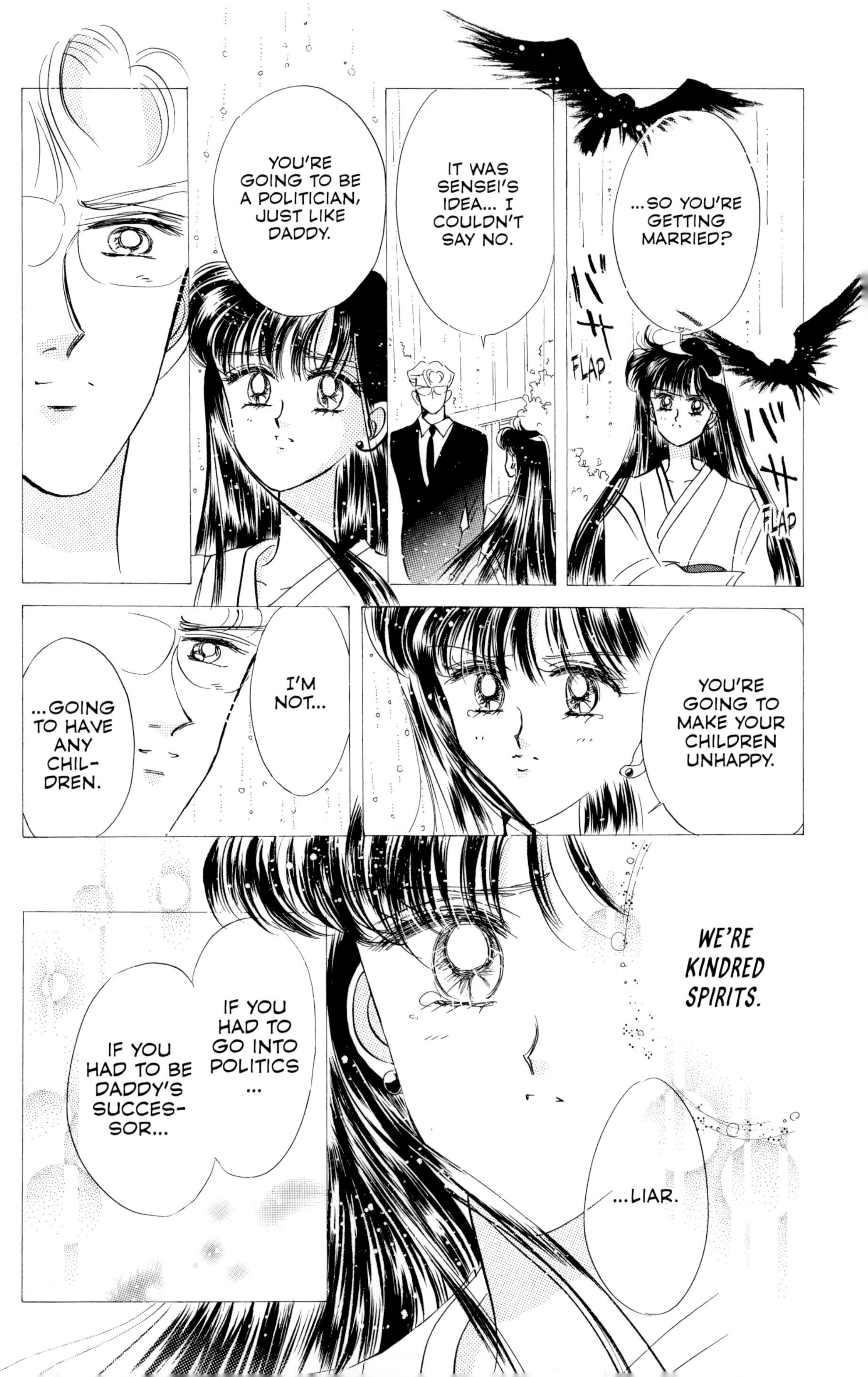

...SO YOU'RE GETTING MARRIED?
FLAP
FLAP
IT WAS SENSEI'S IDEA... I COULDN'T SAY NO.
YOU'RE GOING TO BE A POLITICIAN, JUST LIKE DADDY.
YOU'RE GOING TO MAKE YOUR CHILDREN UNHAPPY.
I'M NOT...
...GOING TO HAVE ANY CHIL-DREN.
WE'RE KINDRED SPIRITS.
...LIAR.
IF YOU HAD TO GO INTO POLITICS...
IF YOU HAD TO BE DADDY'S SUCCES-SOR...

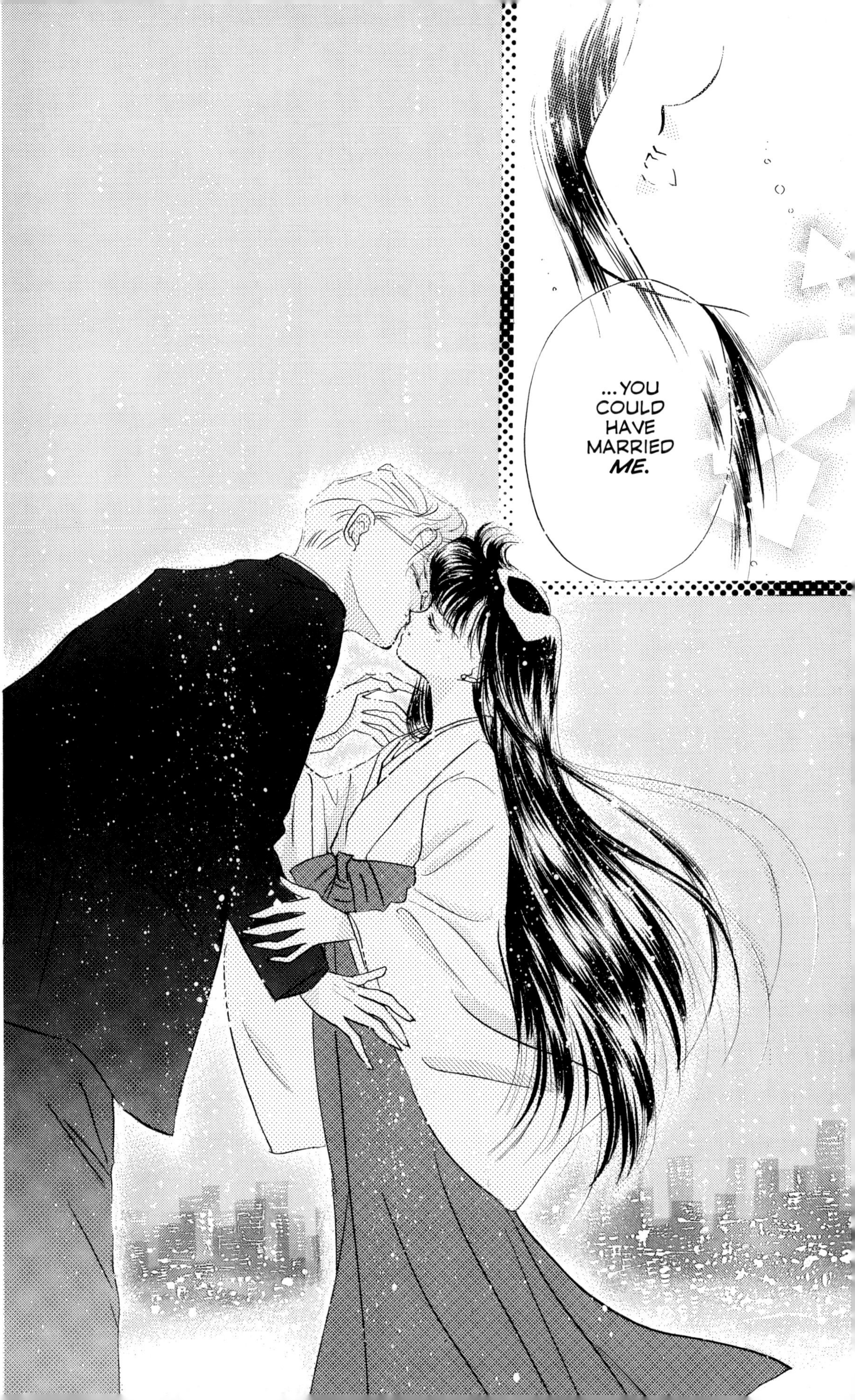
...YOU COULD HAVE MARRIED *ME.*

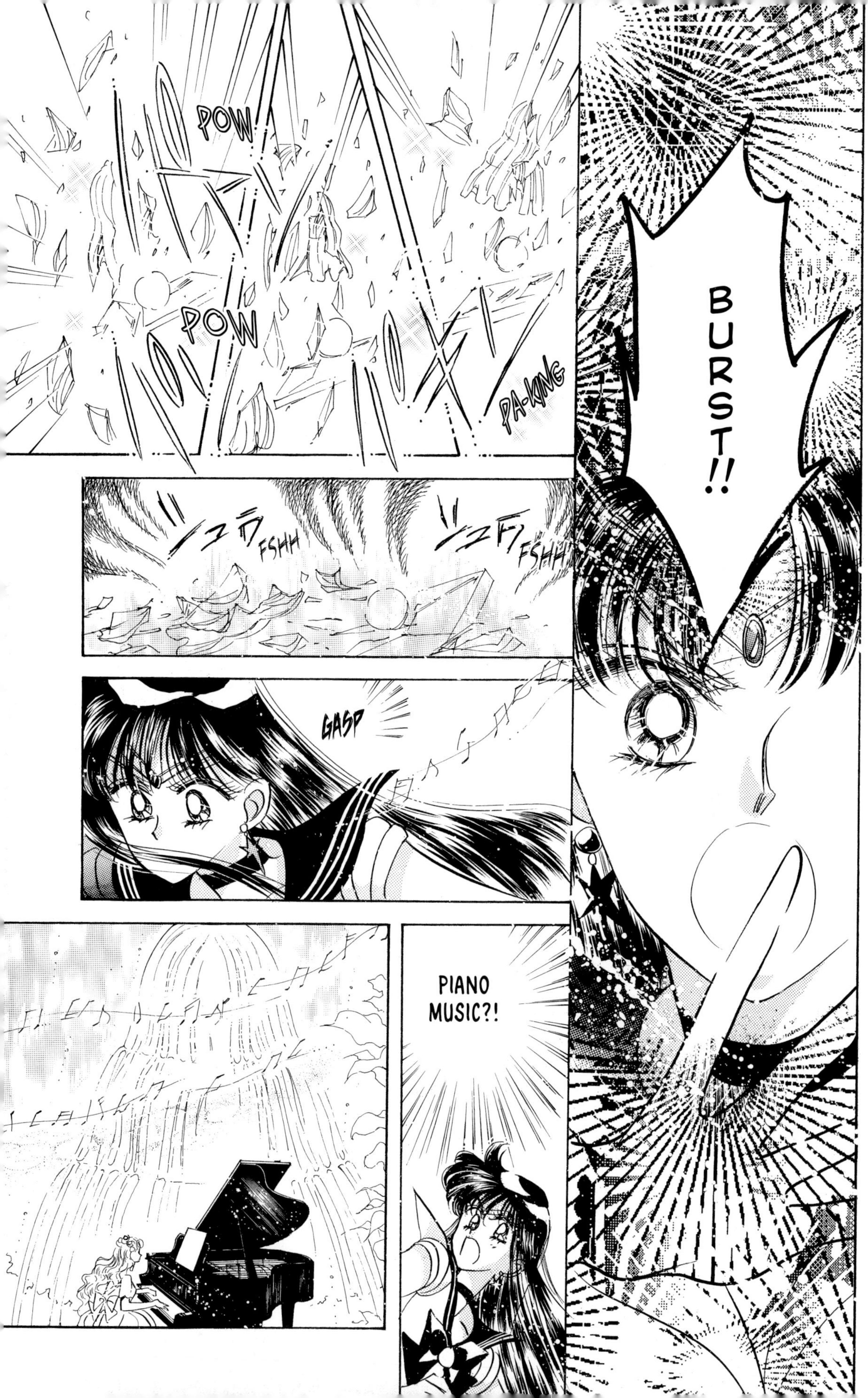
BURST!!
POW
POW
PA-KING
FSHH
FSHH
GASP
PIANO MUSIC?!

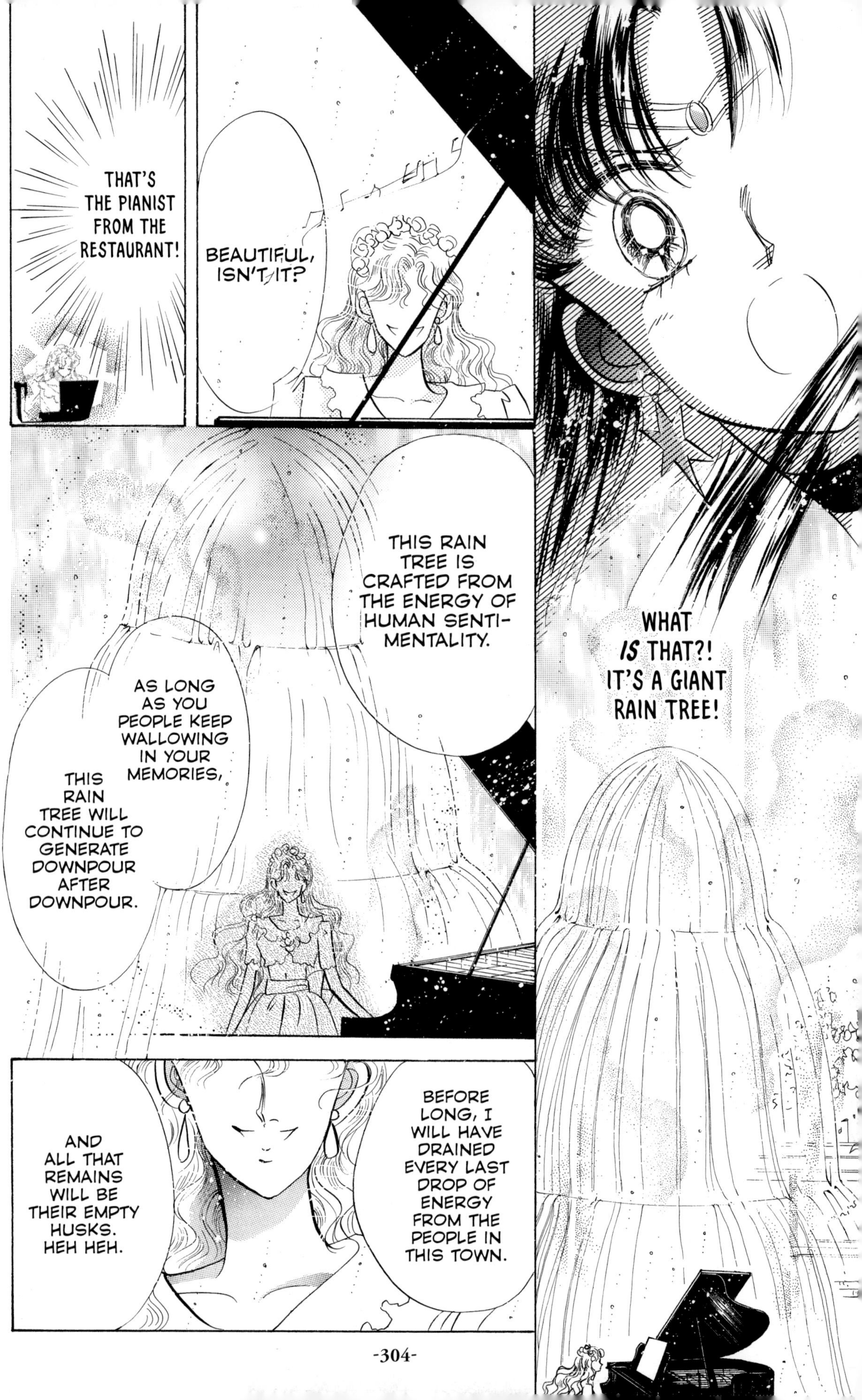
WHAT *IS* THAT?! IT'S A GIANT RAIN TREE!
BEAUTIFUL, ISN'T IT?
THAT'S THE PIANIST FROM THE RESTAURANT!
THIS RAIN TREE IS CRAFTED FROM THE ENERGY OF HUMAN SENTI-MENTALITY.
AS LONG AS YOU PEOPLE KEEP WALLOWING IN YOUR MEMORIES,
THIS RAIN TREE WILL CONTINUE TO GENERATE DOWNPOUR AFTER DOWNPOUR.
BEFORE LONG, I WILL HAVE DRAINED EVERY LAST DROP OF ENERGY FROM THE PEOPLE IN THIS TOWN.
AND ALL THAT REMAINS WILL BE THEIR EMPTY HUSKS. HEH HEH.

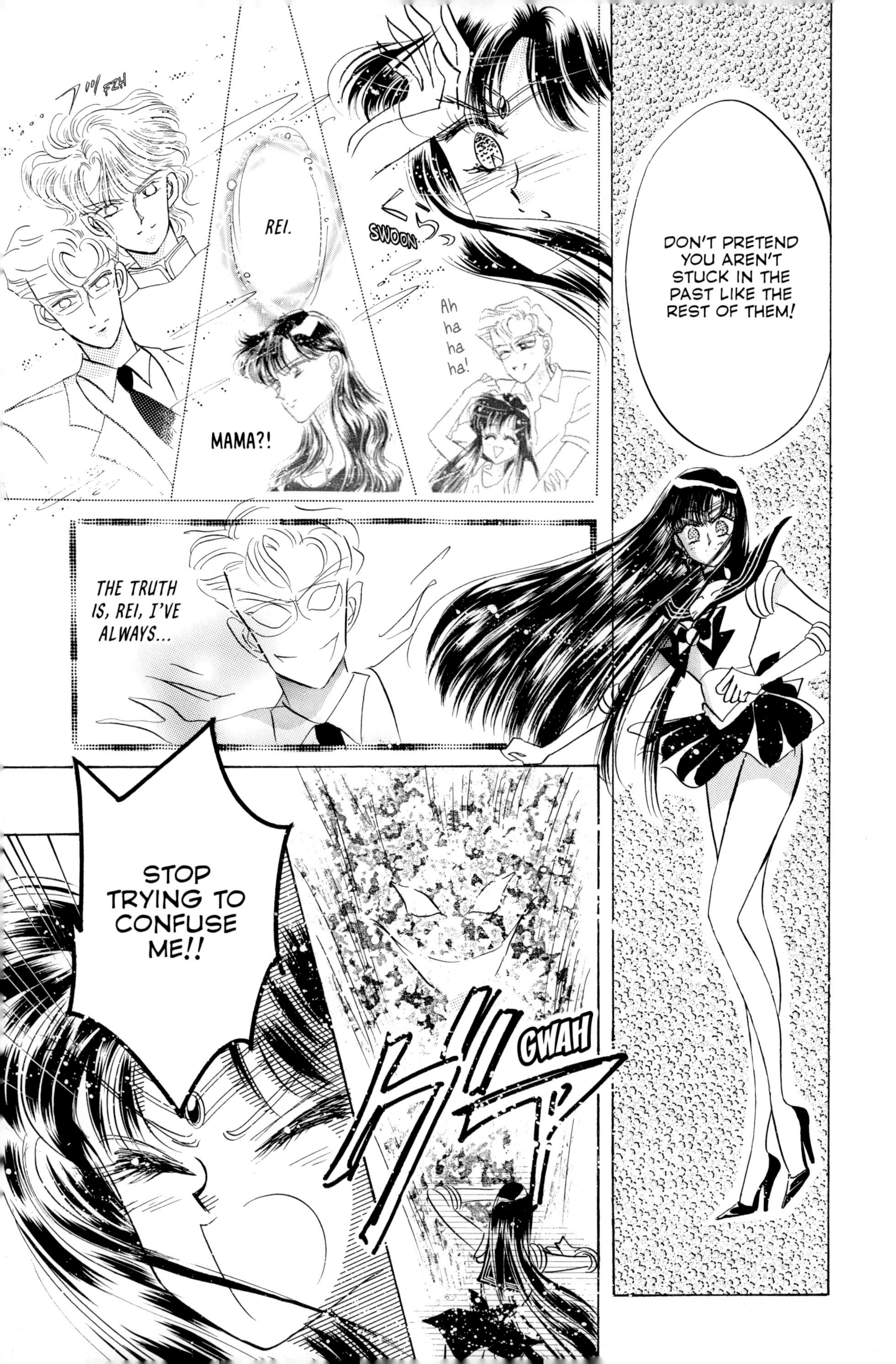

DON'T PRETEND YOU AREN'T STUCK IN THE PAST LIKE THE REST OF THEM!
SWOON
Ah ha ha ha!
REI.
MAMA?!
FZH
THE TRUTH IS, REI, I'VE ALWAYS...
GWAH
STOP TRYING TO CONFUSE ME!!

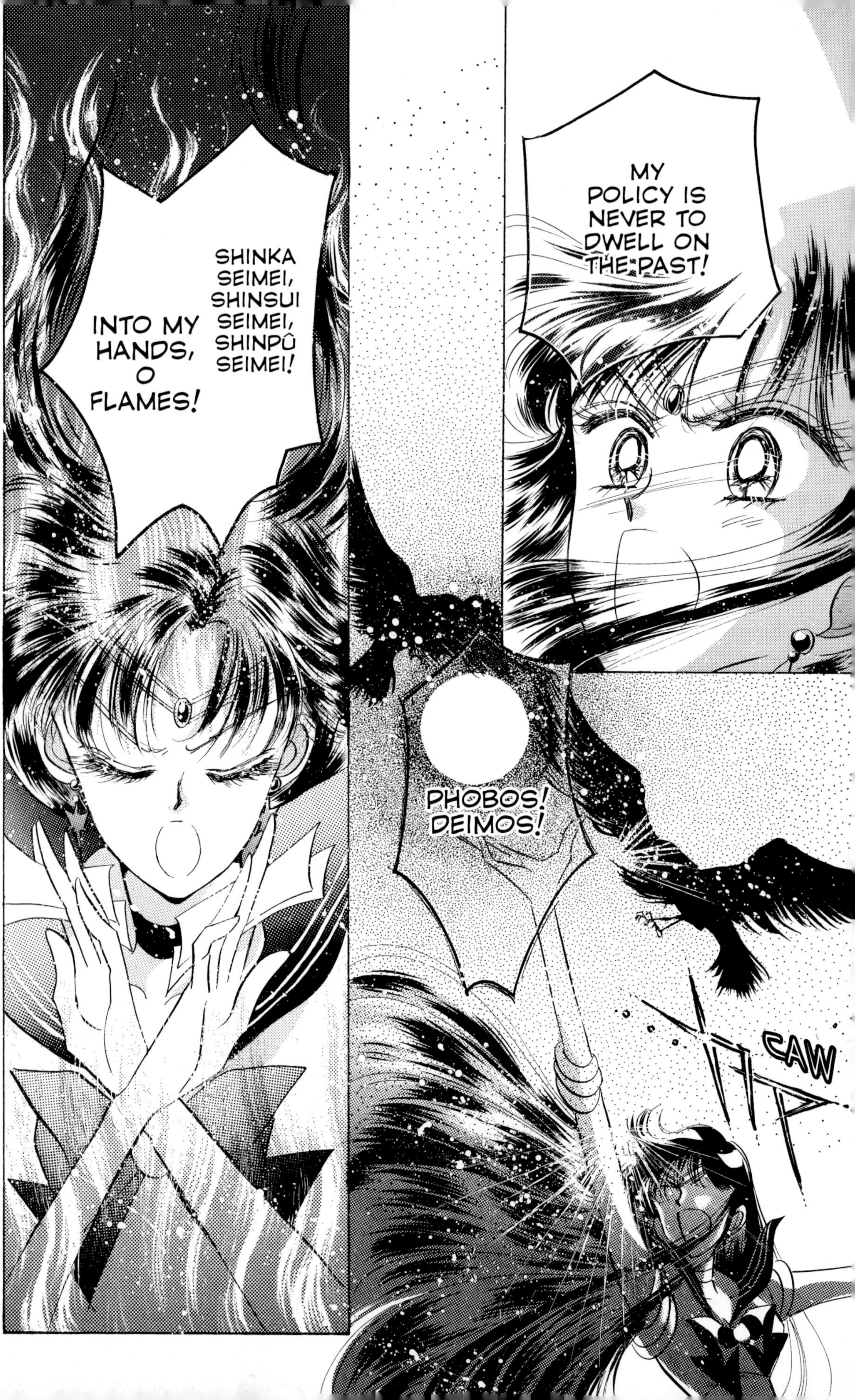
MY POLICY IS NEVER TO DWELL ON THE PAST!
PHOBOS! DEIMOS!
CAW
SHINKA SEIMEI, SHINSUI SEIMEI, SHINPÛ SEIMEI!
INTO MY HANDS, O FLAMES!

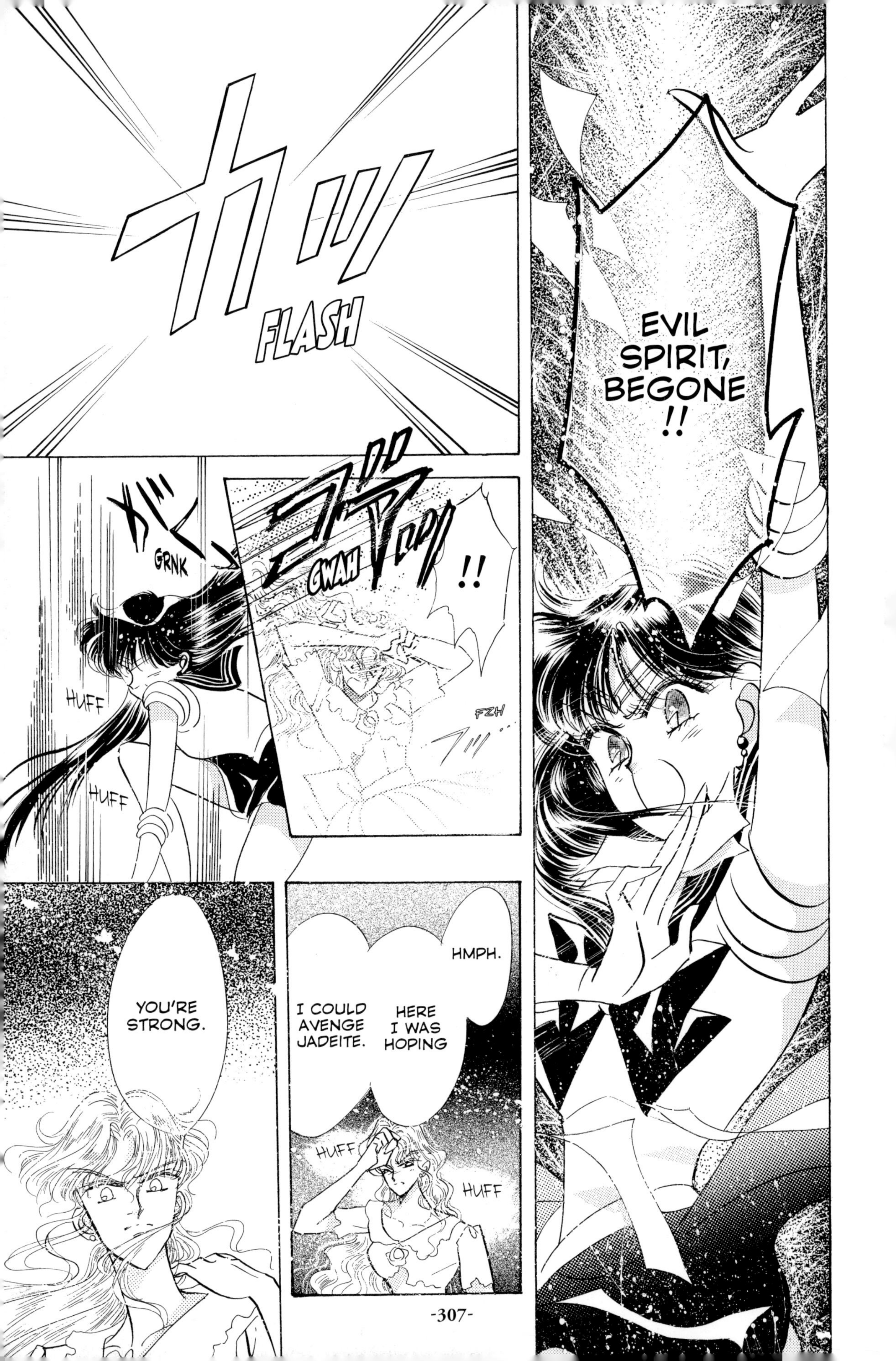
EVIL SPIRIT, BEGONE !!
カッ
FLASH
ゴァッ
GWAH
!!
FZH
フッ…
がく
GRNK
HUFF
HUFF
HMPH.
HERE I WAS HOPING
I COULD AVENGE JADEITE.
HUFF
HUFF
YOU'RE STRONG.

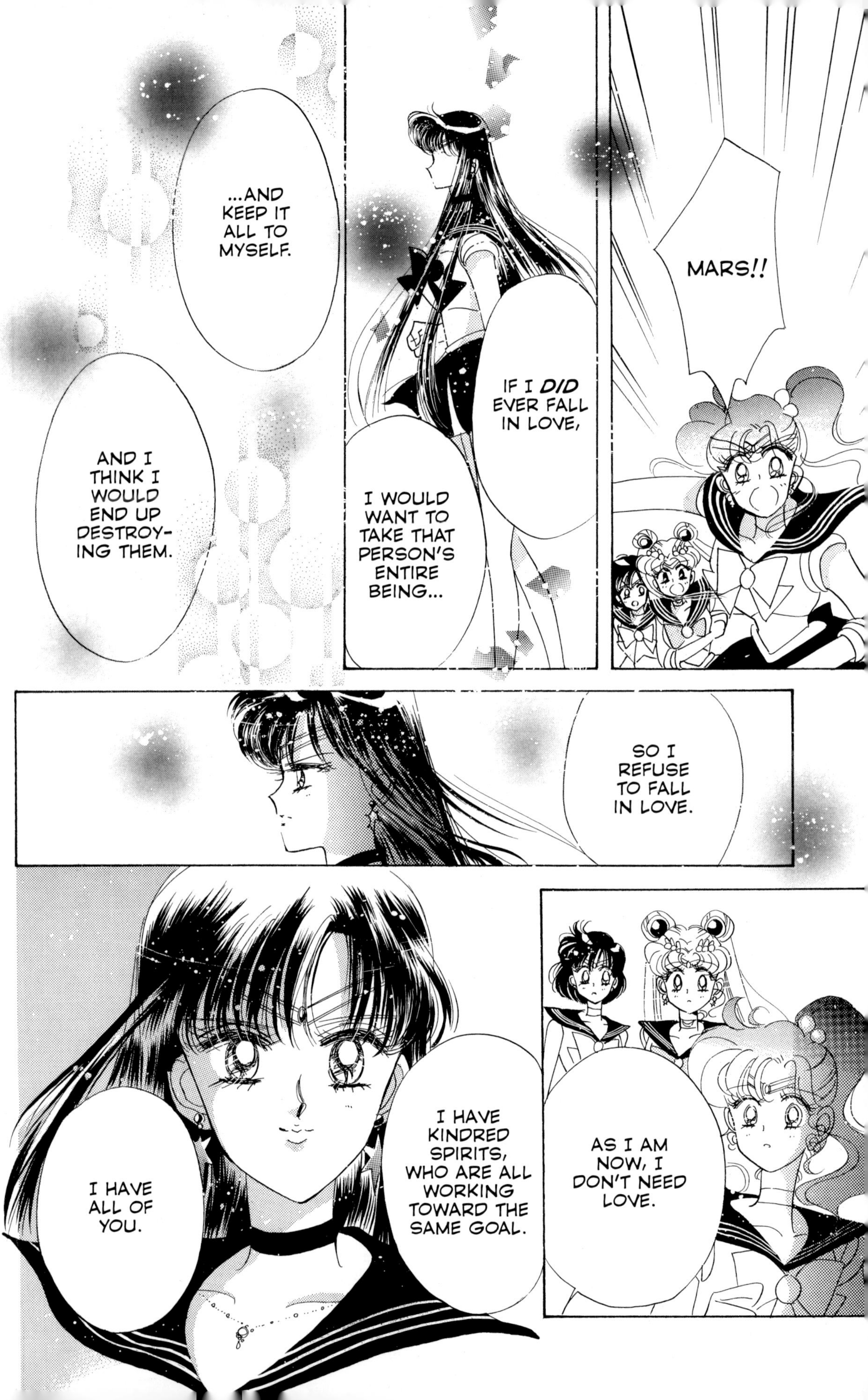
MARS!!
IF I *DID* EVER FALL IN LOVE,
I WOULD WANT TO TAKE THAT PERSON'S ENTIRE BEING...
...AND KEEP IT ALL TO MYSELF.
AND I THINK I WOULD END UP DESTROYING THEM.
SO I REFUSE TO FALL IN LOVE.
AS I AM NOW, I DON'T NEED LOVE.
I HAVE KINDRED SPIRITS, WHO ARE ALL WORKING TOWARD THE SAME GOAL.
I HAVE ALL OF YOU.

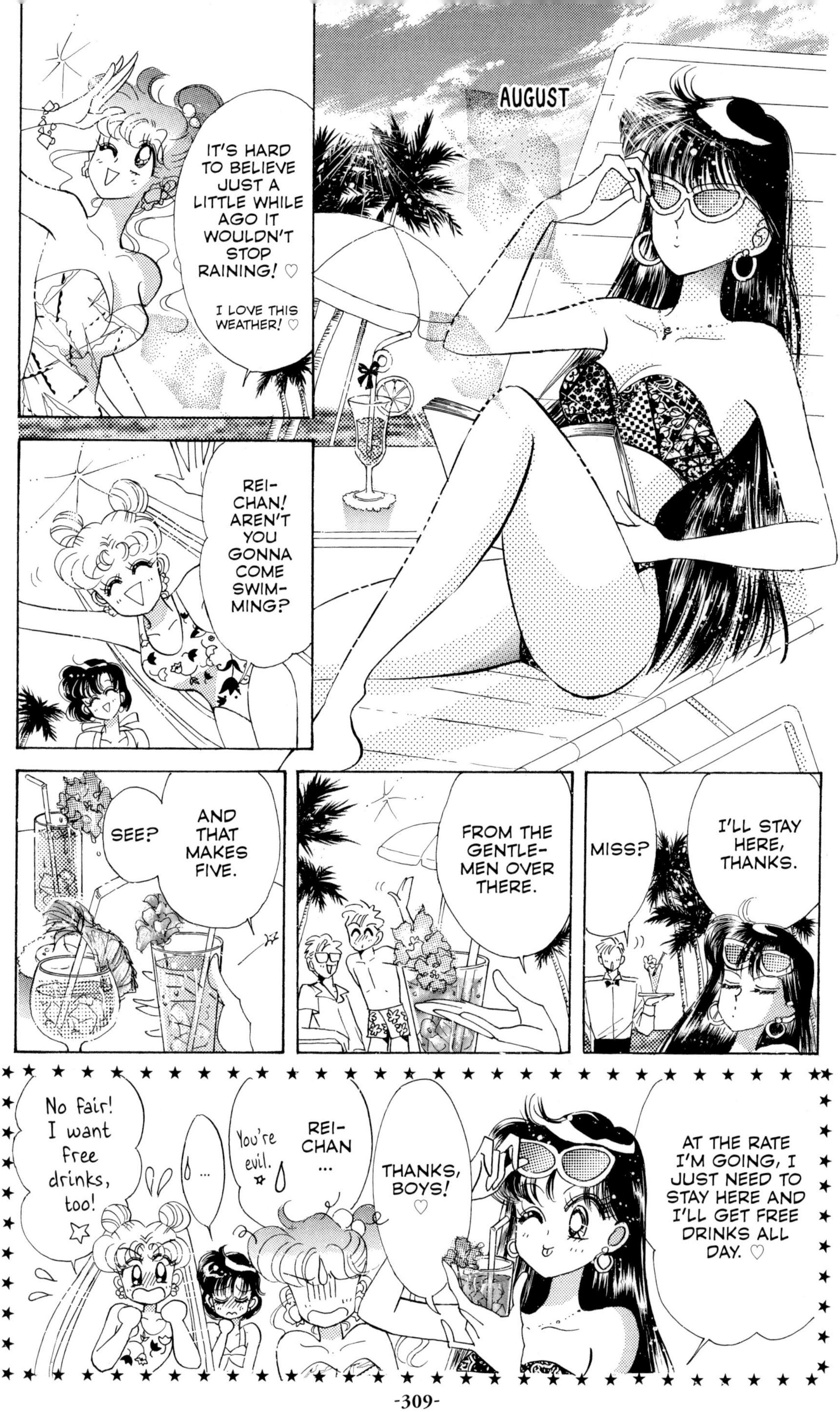
AUGUST
IT'S HARD TO BELIEVE JUST A LITTLE WHILE AGO IT WOULDN'T STOP RAINING! ♡
I LOVE THIS WEATHER! ♡
REI-CHAN! AREN'T YOU GONNA COME SWIMMING?
I'LL STAY HERE, THANKS.
MISS?
FROM THE GENTLEMEN OVER THERE.
AND THAT MAKES FIVE.
SEE?
AT THE RATE I'M GOING, I JUST NEED TO STAY HERE AND I'LL GET FREE DRINKS ALL DAY. ♡
THANKS, BOYS! ♡
REI-CHAN...
You're evil.
...
No fair! I want free drinks, too!

Translation Notes

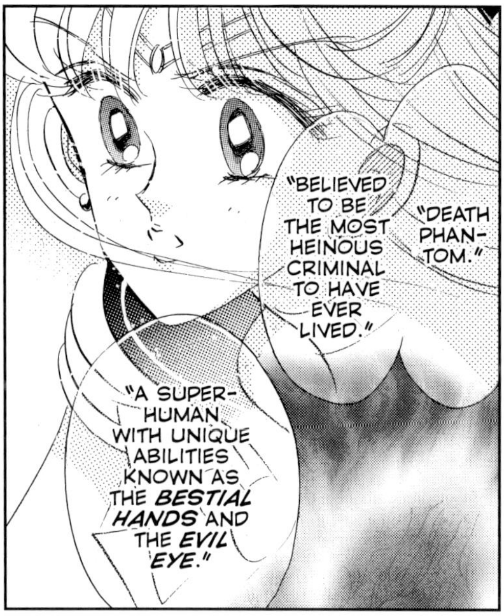
"DEATH PHANTOM."
"BELIEVED TO BE THE MOST HEINOUS CRIMINAL TO HAVE EVER LIVED."
"A SUPERHUMAN WITH UNIQUE ABILITIES KNOWN AS THE *BESTIAL HANDS* AND THE *EVIL EYE*."

Bestial Hands, page 9
The term "Bestial Hands" is translated from *yôjû no te*, which more specifically means "supernatural beast hands," but the translators felt the name of a superpower ought to be a little more succinct.

Veneti and Aquatici, page 18
These names are both Latin for different shades of blue, but the characters' names still follow the pattern of coming from minerals. According to *Antique Gems: Their Origins, Uses, and Value* by C.W. King, Veneti and Aquatici are also interchangeable terms for the sky-blue class of the jacinth, also known as the Sapphirine.

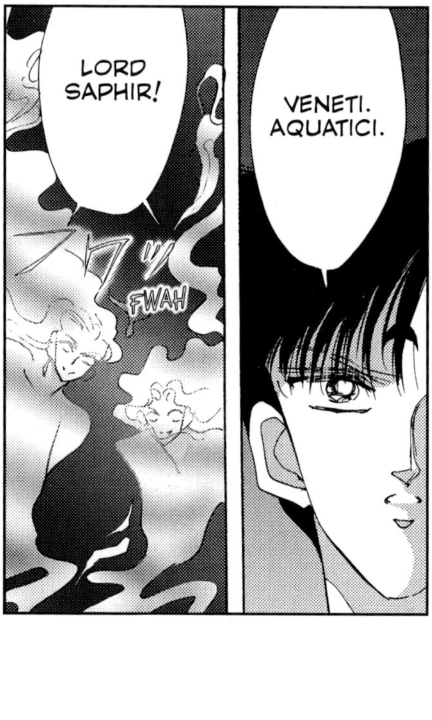
VENETI. AQUATICI.
LORD SAPHIR!
フワッ
FWAH

Neo Queen Serenity's resting place, page 79

The letters carved into Her Majesty's bed appear to be Roman numerals, specifically the number 1882. Normally, numbers on monuments such as these convey the year of the monument's significance—it wouldn't be strange to think that this was meant to represent the year Neo Queen Serenity was entombed, or perhaps the year of her birth, but 1882 is far too early for both events. One possibility is that Crystal Tokyo measures time by a new calendar, but it didn't start with Neo Queen Serenity's reign, because she hasn't been in power for that many years.

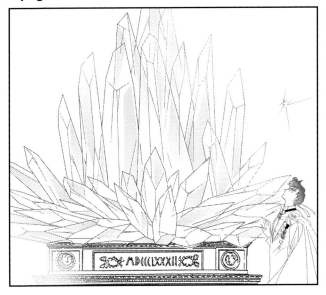

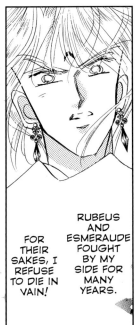

RUBEUS AND ESMERAUDE FOUGHT BY MY SIDE FOR MANY YEARS.
FOR THEIR SAKES, I REFUSE TO DIE IN VAIN!

Demande's loyal subjects, page 116

The translators felt this would be an appropriate place to point out the full names of the members of the Black Moon clan. In the previous volume, Rubeus introduced himself as Crimson Rubeus, and although it never appears in the story, official *Sailor Moon* reference material reveals the names *Midori no Esmeraude* and *Ao no Saphir,* which the translators have chosen to render as Verdant Esmeraude and Azure Saphir. Crimson, verdant, and azure are just fancy words for red, green, and blue, which are the primary colors of light. Combine them, and they create a white diamond of light. Snuff them out, and Black Lady is in charge.

Guardian of..., page 224

The reader may have noticed that these epithets for the Sailor Guardians don't all match the ones that were given them when they first awakened to their powers. The original titles were based on the element each Guardian commanded. The ones given here by Neo Queen Serenity are based on the Greek and/or Roman deity for which each planet is named. Mars is the Roman god of war, and Venus is the Roman goddess of love. Mercury, a Roman god associated with the Greek Hermes, is a cunning trickster who is a god of wisdom (of sorts), and Jupiter is the king of gods and protector of the human race. This role of the god Jupiter has some parallels with the planet Jupiter, too, as the gas giant's gravity has protected the Earth from comets that might otherwise hit us.

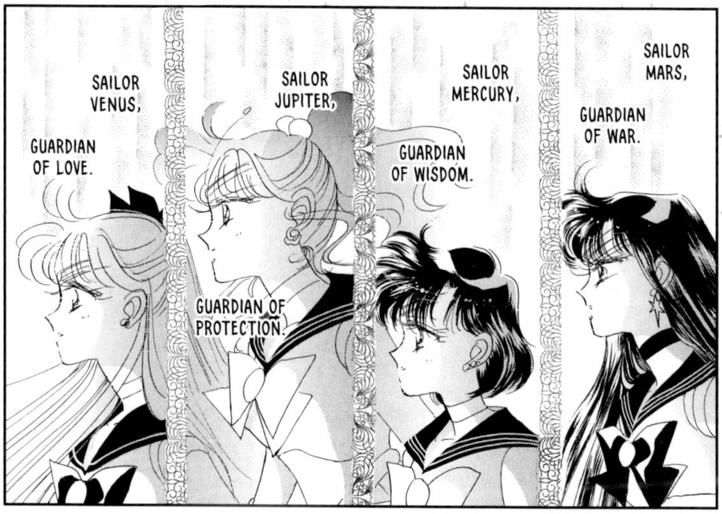
SAILOR MARS,
GUARDIAN OF WAR.
SAILOR MERCURY,
GUARDIAN OF WISDOM.
SAILOR JUPITER,
GUARDIAN OF PROTECTION.
SAILOR VENUS,
GUARDIAN OF LOVE.

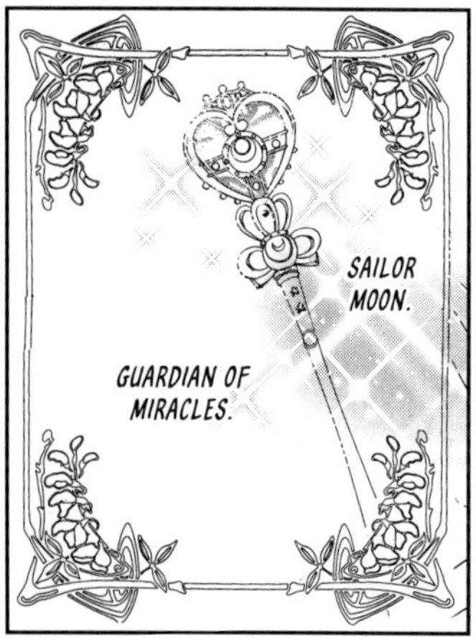
SAILOR MOON.
GUARDIAN OF MIRACLES.

Guardian of Miracles, page 225

Neo Queen Serenity calls Sailor Moon the *shinpi no senshi*, which can mean "mysterious guardian" or "guardian of mystery." Specifically, *shinpi* is defined as "(something) not explainable by, or surpassing, human knowledge," like a miracle. Literally the word means "divine secret," and is the Japanese word used to refer to sacred mysteries, which are doctrines or rites known only to the gods and those who have qualified to partake of their knowledge.

Serenity's letter, page 250

Neo Queen Serenity's letter is exactly what you might expect from the future Usagi. Letter writing in Japan is a formalized practice, with a multitude of guidebooks explaining how to write them and even providing templates. Neo Queen Serenity begins her letter with the standard *zenryaku*, which means "omitting what comes first." This is used in Japanese letters to indicate that the writer is dispensing with formalities such as, "Dear so-and-so," "How are you?", discussions of the weather, and so forth. It may be interesting to note that this is one of the few words in the letter that Her Majesty wrote in *kanji* characters, and the translators have a sneaking suspicion that she only knew the proper *kanji* because she copied them from the letter-writing instructions she was following. This suspicion is backed up by the fact that there are almost no other *kanji* in the letter, even for relatively simple words.

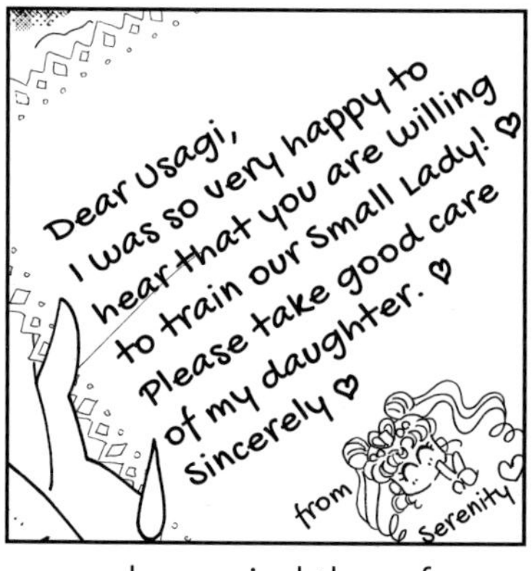
Dear Usagi,
I was so very happy to hear that you are willing to train our Small Lady!
Please take good care of my daughter.
Sincerely
from Serenity

Edo, page 258

Edo is the name that was once used for Tokyo back in the days when Japan was ruled by the shoguns of the Tokugawa clan, from 1603 to 1868. Although the Shogunate was headquartered in Edo, the official capital of Japan remained in Kyoto, meaning "capital city." When the shogunate fell in 1868, the Emperor moved his residence to Edo, and the city became the new capital of Japan and was renamed Tokyo, meaning "eastern capital."

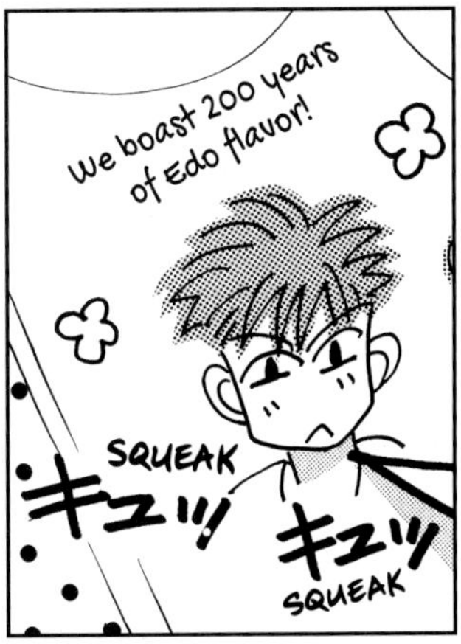
We boast 200 years of Edo flavor!
キュッ! SQUEAK
キュッ SQUEAK

Lunch duty, page 262

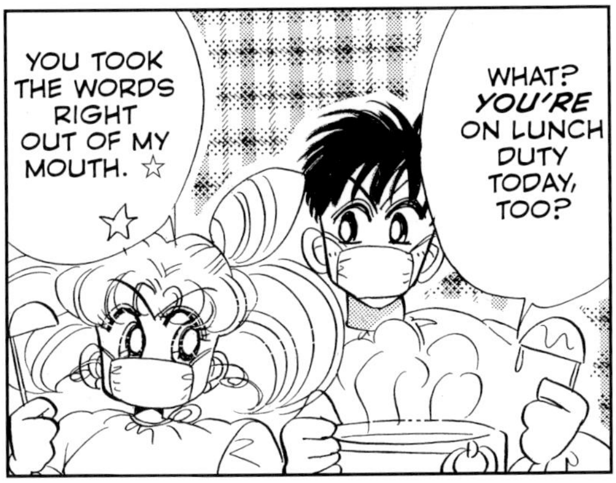
WHAT? *YOU'RE* ON LUNCH DUTY TODAY, TOO?
YOU TOOK THE WORDS RIGHT OUT OF MY MOUTH. ☆

In Japanese schools, many of the duties that one in the West might expect to be carried out by hired adults are carried out by the students themselves. Especially at elementary schools, where lunchtime is an important part of the day, children take turns being responsible for serving food to their classmates. They must dress in the special clothes provided by the school, carry the school-provided lunches (which are often good enough that the parents will ask for recipes) to their class and distribute food to everyone, and clean up when everyone is done.

Kurayamizaka, page 264

This is another slope that exists in the Azabu Jûban district. Its name translates to "darkness slope," because it was once so covered in trees and vegetation that it was dark even in the middle of the day. This darkness naturally led to various rumors of monster and ghost sightings, as well as actual incidents of highway robbery. There is a foreign embassy here in real life as well, but it is the Austrian Embassy, not that of the U Kingdom, and much of the vegetation has been removed.

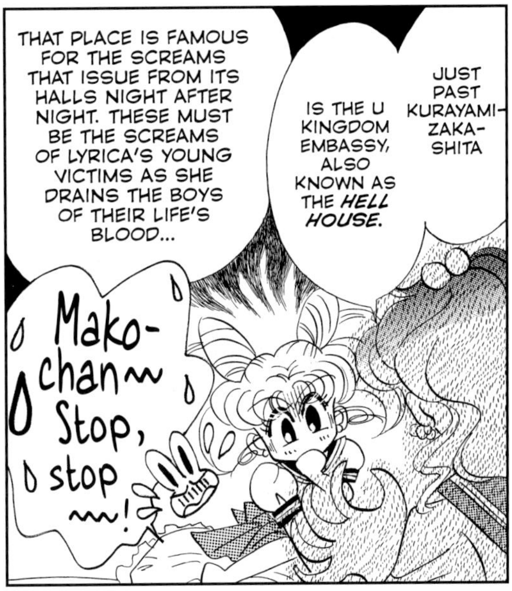
JUST PAST KURAYAMI-ZAKA-SHITA
IS THE U KINGDOM EMBASSY, ALSO KNOWN AS THE *HELL HOUSE*.
THAT PLACE IS FAMOUS FOR THE SCREAMS THAT ISSUE FROM ITS HALLS NIGHT AFTER NIGHT. THESE MUST BE THE SCREAMS OF LYRICA'S YOUNG VICTIMS AS SHE DRAINS THE BOYS OF THEIR LIFE'S BLOOD...
Mako-chan~ Stop, stop~!

I want blood, page 270

Now that Lyrica's true identity has been revealed, the translators feel it safe to discuss exactly what is in a name. The unique qualities of these particular vampires were no doubt inspired by the 1970s manga, *Poe no Ichizoku*, or *The Poe Family*, by Moto Hagio. In this manga, the vampanella subsist not only on human blood, but on roses and rose extract, explaining Lyrica's odd lunchtime behavior. This manga was in turn inspired by Shôtarô Ishinomori's short series, *Kiri to Bara to Hoshi to* (*Fog, Roses, and Stars*), which features a girl named Lily, who is turned into a vampire by Larmica. In Japanese, the names are Riri and Ramika—put them together, and the result is Ririka, or Lyrica. Her surname Übel (pronounced ooh-bell), is German for "evil."

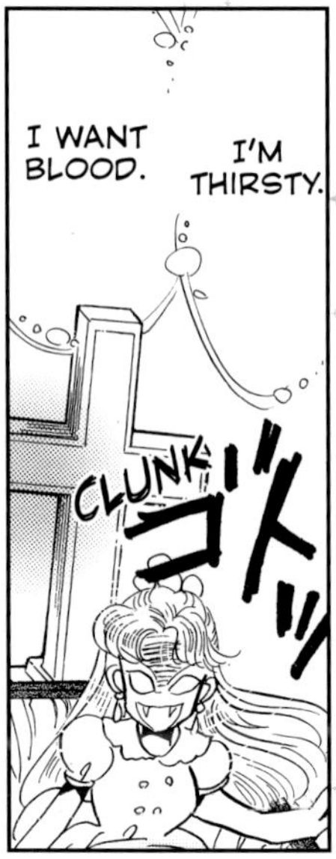
I WANT BLOOD.
I'M THIRSTY.
CLUNK
ゴトッ

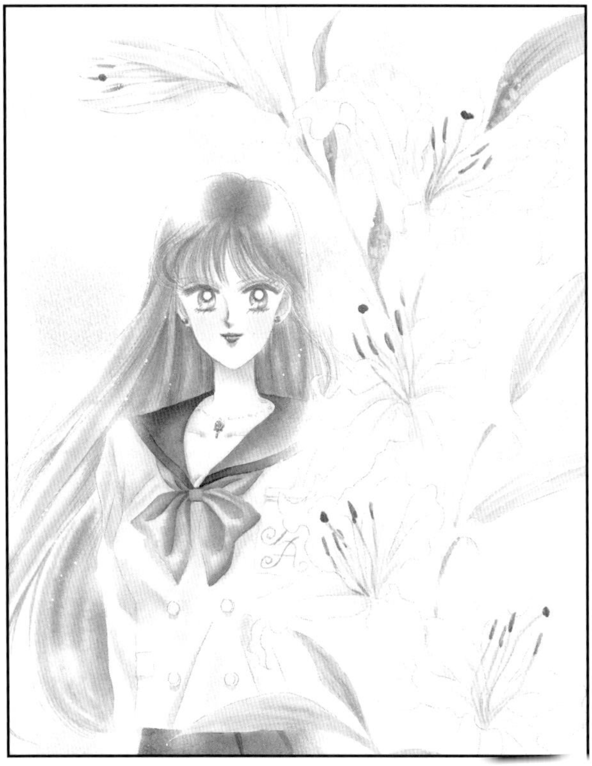

"Casablanca Memory," page 277

This story was originally published in the September 1993 edition of *RunRun*, a bimonthly *shôjo* (girls') manga magazine. That said, it features many classic motifs of the *yuri* (girls' love) genre, including lily flowers ("*yuri*" literally means "lily") and a focus on female-female relationships to the exclusion of men. *Yuri* and *shôjo* share many hallmarks, including the use of flowers and flowery language and a focus on young women, but the appearance of lilies specifically is an indicator of the closeness of young women (either platonically or romantically). The Casablanca lily that appears here also happens to be the flower that Sailor Mars's Japanese voice actress, Michie Tomizawa, identified as her own favorite while she and Takeuchi-sensei were having lunch—the event which inspired this story.

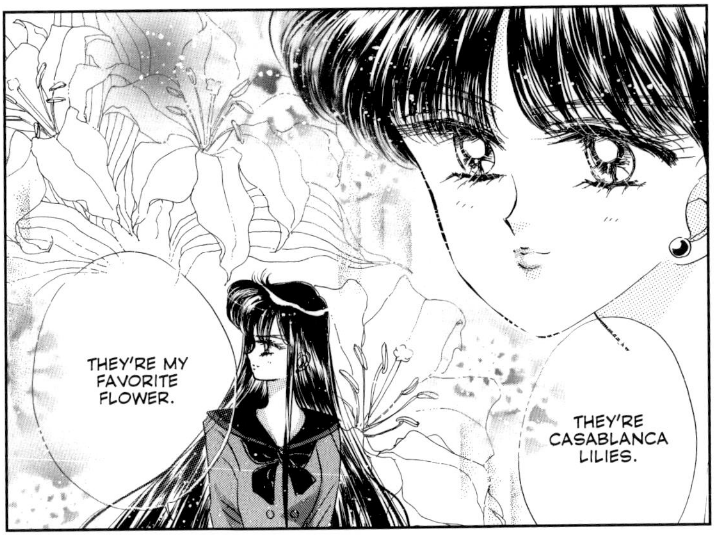
THEY'RE CASABLANCA LILIES.
THEY'RE MY FAVORITE FLOWER.

Casablanca lilies, page 283
In the language of flowers, the Casablanca lily symbolizes "nobility," "purity," "exquisite beauty," and "glorious love."

Sensei, page 284
While we've come to associate the title "sensei" with teachers and masters of the martial arts, it is used as a form of respect for mentors and experts in many disciplines, including doctors, manga artists, and politicians.

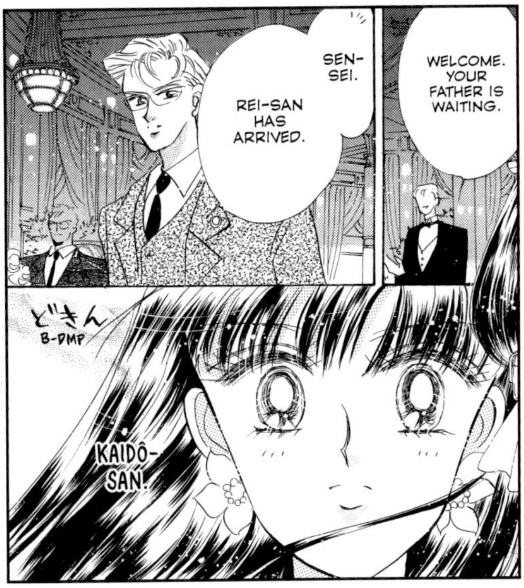
WELCOME. YOUR FATHER IS WAITING.
SEN-SEI.
REI-SAN HAS ARRIVED.
どきん
B-DMP
KAIDÔ-SAN!

Kaidô, page 284
It may be interesting to note that, while the name Kaidô literally means "ocean hall," with slightly different *kanji*, it can be the name of the midget crab apple flowers. This flower is featured along with rain in the idiom, "like a *kaidô* blossom wet with rain," which refers to something both beautiful and pitiful.

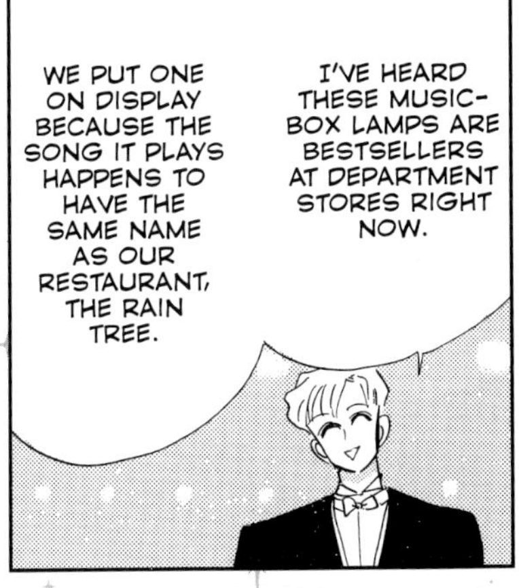
I'VE HEARD THESE MUSIC-BOX LAMPS ARE BESTSELLERS AT DEPARTMENT STORES RIGHT NOW.
WE PUT ONE ON DISPLAY BECAUSE THE SONG IT PLAYS HAPPENS TO HAVE THE SAME NAME AS OUR RESTAURANT, THE RAIN TREE.

The Rain Tree, page 285
While the name of the restaurant and the song in this story come from Naoko Takeuchi's name for her own personal antique lamp, it's possible that that name, in turn, was inspired by Kenzaburô Ôe's series of short stories collectively known as *Women Listening to the "Rain Tree."* In these stories, the Rain Tree is a tree that stores moisture in its leaves during downpours, so droplets continue to rain down long after the storm has passed. While it's likely that the only similarity between these stories and "Casablanca Memory" is that the tree is eventually burned up, the first of the stories, "The Clever Rain Tree," inspired the composer Tôru Takemitsu to write a percussion piece which he titled "Rain Tree."

Nagatachô, page 294
Nagatachô is the district of Tokyo where one can find the National Diet (Japan's legislature) and the Prime Minister's residence. That being the case, saying that Kaidô is trusted in Nagatachô would be similar to saying he is trusted in DC, if he were a politician in the United States.

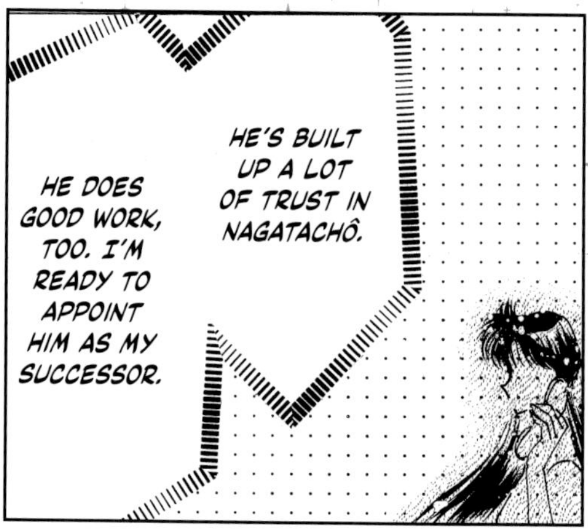
HE'S BUILT UP A LOT OF TRUST IN NAGATACHÔ.
HE DOES GOOD WORK, TOO. I'M READY TO APPOINT HIM AS MY SUCCESSOR.

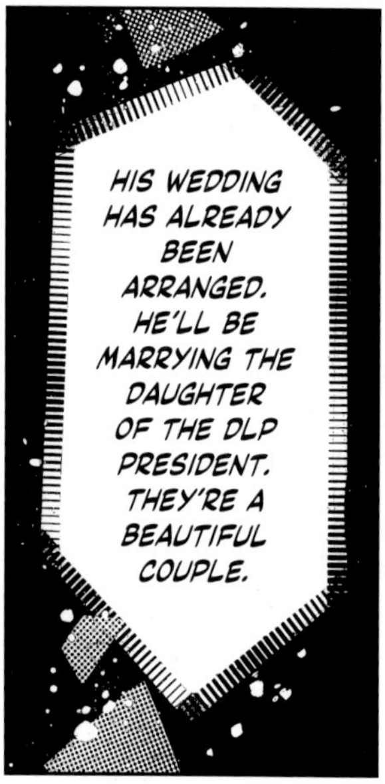
HIS WEDDING HAS ALREADY BEEN ARRANGED. HE'LL BE MARRYING THE DAUGHTER OF THE DLP PRESIDENT. THEY'RE A BEAUTIFUL COUPLE.

DLP, page 295
Short for Democratic Liberal Party, or *Minjitô*, this is the name of a real political party that existed in Japan in the past, but merged with other parties long before these events took place, to become the *Jimintô*, or Liberal Democratic Party. It is likely that this meant to be taken as the name of a fictional political party.

The theme from *Casablanca*, page 295
The theme from *Casablanca* is a song called "As Time Goes By," about the struggles of falling in love. The iconic film is about a man who fell madly in love with a woman only to find out that she was already spoken for.

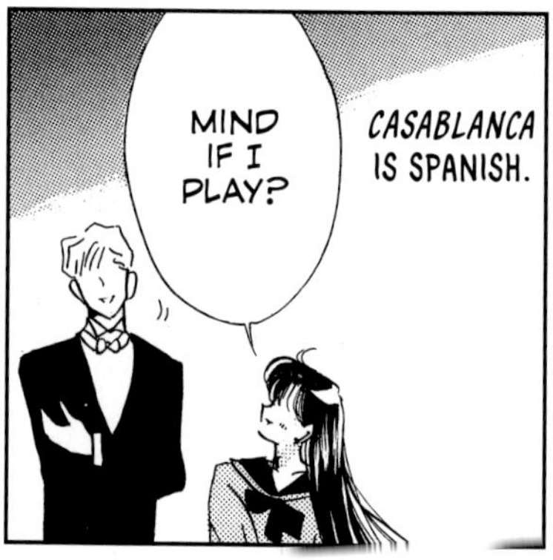
CASABLANCA IS SPANISH.
MIND IF I PLAY?

Burst, page 303
This is translated from *katsu*, which is the word for a shout used by religious leaders in certain sects to discipline their practitioners. Through this association, it has come to refer to any scolding or threatening shout. In this case, the translators have rendered it as "burst," as in an "outburst," and also as in what the music boxes do after Sailor Mars shouts at them.

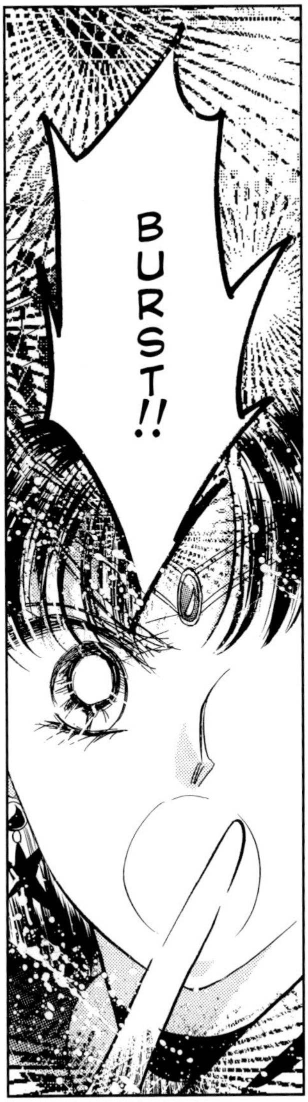
BURST!!

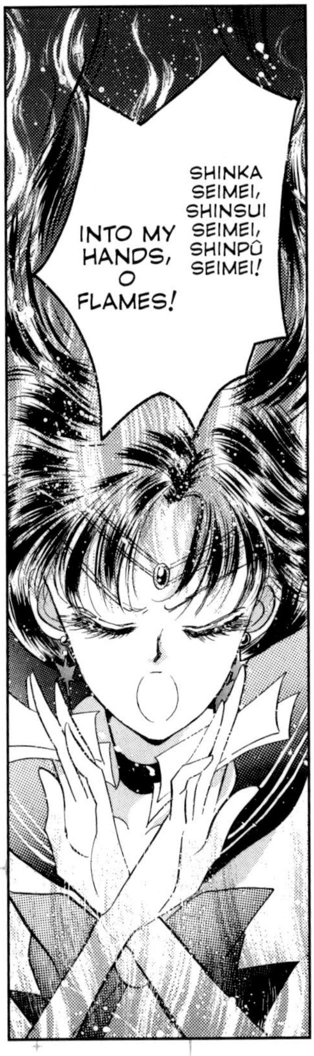
SHINKA SEIMEI, SHINSUI SEIMEI, SHINPÛ SEIMEI!
INTO MY HANDS, O FLAMES!

Shinka Seimei, Shinsui Seimei, Shinpû Seimei!, page 306
Meaning roughly, "sacred fire, purify; sacred water, purify; sacred wind, purify," this is a chant used, as the reader may safely surmise, for purification. In fact, it appears that it is used to dispel any negative energy that may have built up in an object's past, making it helpful for superstitious or very careful antique collectors. Or perhaps for Sailor Guardians dispelling evil energy from monster trees based on the author's real-life antiques.

A Kodansha Comics Trade Paperback Original
Sailor Moon Eternal Edition volume 4 copyright © 2013 Naoko Takeuchi
English translation copyright © 2019 Naoko Takeuchi
First published in Japan in 2013 by Kodansha Ltd., Tokyo.

All rights reserved.

Published in the United States by Kodansha Comics, an imprint of Kodansha USA Publishing, LLC, New York.

Publication rights for this English edition arranged through Kodansha Ltd, Tokyo.

ISBN 978-1-63236-155-4

Printed in Canada.

www.kodanshacomics.com

9 8 7 6 5 4 3 2 1

Translation: Alethea Nibley & Athena Nibley
Lettering: Lys Blakeslee
Editing: Lauren Scanlan
Kodansha Comics edition cover design by Phil Balsman